Johnson County
Tennessee

Death Record

Abstracts

1908 - 1941

Eddie M. Nikazy

HERITAGE BOOKS
2007

HERITAGE BOOKS

AN IMPRINT OF HERITAGE BOOKS, INC.

Books, CDs, and more—Worldwide

For our listing of thousands of titles see our website
at
www.HeritageBooks.com

Published 2007 by
HERITAGE BOOKS, INC.
Publishing Division
65 East Main Street
Westminster, Maryland 21157-5026

Copyright © 1992 Eddie M. Nikazy

Other books by the author:

Carter County, Tennessee Record Abstracts, Death Records, 1908-1925

Carter County, Tennessee Record Abstracts, Death Records, 1926-1934

Carter County, Tennessee Record Abstracts, Marriages, 1871-1920

*Forgotten Soldiers: History of the 2nd Tennessee Volunteer
Infantry Regiment (USA), 1861-1865*

*Forgotten Soldiers: History of the 4th Tennessee Volunteer
Infantry Regiment (USA), 1863-1865*

Greene County, Tennessee Death Record Abstracts, 1908-1918

Sullivan County, Tennessee Death Records, 1908-1918, Volume 1

Sullivan County, Tennessee Death Records, 1919-1925, Volume 2

Washington County, Tennessee Death Record Abstracts, 1908-1916

Unicoi County, Tennessee Death Record Abstracts, 1908-1936

International Standard Book Number: 978-1-55613-665-8

Foreword

This volume contains abstracts of Tennessee death records for Johnson County, Tennessee. Death records are available for rural Tennessee counties beginning in 1908. Currently records of 1908 through 1941 are available for public access in the Tennessee State Library and Archives.

The area of Johnson County was an early and important eastern Tennessee county which served as a major migration center.

In this compilation of Johnson County death records:

1.) Where the reported place of birth is different from the local county, the place of birth is stated.

2.) Name spelling variations have been preserved. When looking for a particular surname, it is may be necessary to check other possible spelling variations.

3.) Where possible, the cause of death is quoted as it appears in the record.

4.) Parenthetical entries following parents names indicate the reported place of the parents birth.

5.) Parenthetical entries following the informants name indicate place of residence.

6.) Record numbers correspond with the official death record numbers on file in the Tennessee State Archives.

Minnie MOREFIELD, age 2, place of birth: Tennessee, cause of death: "measles", death record # 143, died: 27 Feb 1912.

Annie Grace PHILIPPI, age 4 months, place of birth: Johnson County, TN, cause of death: "stomach trouble", death record # 47335, died: 22 Dec 1910.

M.J. KIESLING, female, age 49, widow, place of birth: Johnson County, TN, cause of death: "brights disease", death record #: 47336, died: 31 Jan 1911.

Ollie CUDDY, female, age 34, married, cause of death: "cancer", place of birth: Washington Co., VA, death record #: 47337, died: 30 Aug 1910.

Eliza FENNER, age 80, widow, cause of death: "breakdown", place of birth: Smythe Co., VA., death record #: 47338, died: 25 May 1911.

Okie SHUPE, female, age 28, married, cause of death: "consumption", place of birth: Johnson Co., TN,, death record #: 47339, died: 24 Feb 1911.

Betty AUSBURY, age 23, married, cause of death: "consumption", place of birth: Johnson Co., TN, death record #: 47340, died: 11 Jul 1910.

Della AUSBURY, age 1 year, cause of death: not stated, place of birth: Johnson Co., TN,, death record #: 47341, died: 11 Jun 1911.

Annie JENKINS, age 5, cause of death: "meningitis", death record #: 47342, died: 7 Apr 1911.

Bonner HASGUE, age 5, cause of death: "croup", death record #: 47343, died: 4 Dec 1910.

Parlee LEWIS, age 55, widow, place of birth: Johnson Co., TN, cause of death: "gallstones", death record #: 47344, died: 21 Oct 1910.

Willard DUVALL, age 3 months, cause of death: "croup", death record #: 47345, died: 16 Jan 1911.

Mary Jane TRIPLET, age 70, widow, place of birth: Wilkes Co., NC, cause of death: "cancer", death record #: 47346, died: 26 Jun 1910.

H.C. GENTRY, age 59, male, married, place of birth: Johnson Co., TN,, cause of death: "kidney trouble", death record #: 47347, died: 1 Aug 1910.

Florence BLACKBURN, age 24, married, place of birth Johnson Co. TN, cause of death: "consumption", death record #: 47348, died: 8 Aug 1910.

Clay JOHNSON, age 22, single, cause of death: "typhoid fever", record #: 47349, died: 8 Aug 1910.

D.M. WAGNER, age 59, male, married, place of birth: Johnson Co. TN, cause of death: "liver trouble", death record #: 47350, died: 24 Mar 1911.

E.H. MOCK, age 72, male, married, place of birth: Washington Co., VA., cause of death: not recorded, death record #: 47351, died: 26 Aug 1910.

Eliza DONNELLEY, age 74, married, place of birth: Johnson Co. TN, cause of death: "breakdown", death record #: 47352, died: 4 Jan 1911.

Ruth ASHLEY, age 11 months, cause of death: "croup", death record #: 47353, died: 7 Mar 1911.

Joseph WILSON, age 40, married, place of birth: Johnson Co. TN, cause of death: "cramps & colic", death record #: 47353, died: 7 Aug 1910.

Prescilla DOTSON, age 55, married, place of birth: Johnson Co. TN, cause of death: "consumption", death record #: 47355, died: 4 Feb 1911.

Noah ANDERSON, colored, age 63, married, place of birth: Ashe Co., NC, cause of death: "paralyzed", death record #: 47356, died: died: 12 Apr 1911.

Pearl C. WILSON, colored, age 2, cause of death: "pneumonia", death record #: 47357, died: 3 Apr 1911.

E.C. JOHNSON, male, age 52, married, place of birth: Johnson Co. TN, cause of death: "consumption", death record #: 47358, died: 14 Oct 1909.

Norma TESTAMENT, age 19, married, place of birth: Johnson Co. TN, cause of death: "heart failure", death record #: 47359, died: 7 Oct 1909.

Inez SAMMONS, age 22, married, place of birth: Johnson Co. TN, cause of death: "consumption", death record #: 47360, died: 12 Feb 1910.

Lizzie REYNOLDS, age not stated, single, place of birth: North Carolina, cause of death: "heart failure", death record #: 47361, died: 1910, (day and month not stated).

William Wallace D.. (illegible), age not stated, place of birth: Johnson Co. TN, cause of death: not stated, death record #: 47362, died: not stated, date death recorded: 11 Aug 1910.

Chelcie ROBERTSON, age 5 years, cause of death: illegible, death record #: 47363, died: 23 Oct 1909.

Henry Muncey REECE, age 4 hours, place of birth: Johnson Co. TN, cause of death: not stated, death record #: 47364, died: 18 Jan 1910.

Martha C. THOMAS, age 4 years, place of birth: Johnson Co. TN, cause of death: "burned", death record #: 47365, died: 30 Jan 1910.

Belle PHILLIPPI, age not stated, cause of death: not stated, death record #: 47366, died: 16 Jun 1910.

Alex GENTRY, age 1 day, cause of death: not recorded, death record #: 47367, died: 26 May 1910.

Barthal GENTRY, male, age 1 day, cause of death: not recorded, death record #: 47368, died: 20 May 1910.

Benjamin MOREFIELD, age 55, place of birth: Johnson Co. TN, cause of death: "consumption", death record #: 47369, died: 29 Mar 1910.

Odell FULKS, age 18 months, cause of death: "fever", death record #: 47370, died: 16 Jun 1910.

W.M. SNYDER, male, age 48 years, place of birth: Ashe County, NC, cause of death: "typhoid fever", death record #: 47371, died: 14 Sep 1909,

James W. BROWN, age 1 month, place of birth: Johnson Co. TN, cause of death: "croup", death record #: 47372, died: 15 May 1910.

J.H. WAGNER, male, age 68 years, place of birth: Johnson Co. TN, cause of death: "paralysis", death record #: 47373, died: 11 Jun 1910.

Mable SHOUN, age 8 years, place of birth: Johnson Co. TN, cause of death: "typhoid fever", death record #: 47374, died: 20 Sep 1909.

Ellen HEGPATH, age 45 years, place of birth: Johnson Co. TN, cause of death: "child birth and fever", death record #: 47375, died: 17 Jun 1910.

Baby HEGPATH, age 1 day, place of birth: Johnson Co. TN, cause of death: not recorded, death record #: 47376, died: 15 May 1910.

Nancy JENKINS, age not recorded, married, place of birth: Johnson Co. TN, cause of death: "brights disease", death record #: 47377, died: not recorded, date death registered: 13 Aug 1910.

T.J. BARRY, male, age 73 years, married, place of birth: Johnson Co. TN, cause of death: "paralysis", death record #: 47378, died: 8 Sep 1909.

Carrie L. WAYMAN, age 11 months, place of birth: Johnson Co. TN, cause of death: "indigestion", death record #: 47379, died: 4 Aug 1909.

Fannie M. WILSON, age 49 years, married, place of birth: Johnson Co. TN, cause of death: "consumption", death record #: 47380, died: 19 Apr 1910.

Esie Mae WILSON, colored, female, age 10 months, cause of death: "pneumonia", death record #: 47381, died: 18 Mar 1910.

Ruth MOCK, age 1 month, cause of death: "croup", death record #: 47382, died: 15 Oct 1909.

Malindy KING, age 48 years, female, married, place of birth: Watauga Co., NC, cause of death: "pneumonia", death record #: 47383, died: 10 Apr 1910.

F.M. CHAPEL, age 80 years, male, married, place of birth: Ashe Co., NC., cause of death: "bronchitis", death record #: 47384, died: 6 Dec 1909.

4

Annie F. (surname illegible), age 18 months, place of birth: Johnson Co. TN, cause of death: diarrhea, death record #: 47385, died: 8 Jul 1909.

Paul E. MALONE, age 2 years, place of birth: Johnson Co. TN, cause of death: "croup", death record #: 47386, died: 1 Mar 1910.

T.S. GRANT, age 69 years, male, married, cause of death: not recorded, occupation: dentist, place of birth: Washington, place of death: Knoxville, TN, death record #: 47387, died: 21 May 1910.

William WOOD, age 59 years, married, occupation: merchant, place of birth: not recorded, cause of death: "brights disease", death record #: 47388, died: 20 Jun 1910.

H.?. WAUGH, age 2 months, cause of death: not recorded, place of birth: Johnson Co. TN, death record #: 47389, died: not stated, date death recorded: 24 Aug 1910.

Nancy ARNOLD, age 33 years, married, place of birth: not recorded, cause of death: "diabetes", death record #: 47390, died: 16 May 1911.

Hugh MATHERSON, age 20 years, not married, place of birth: Johnson Co. TN, cause of death: "measles", death record #: 47391, died: 8 Dec 1911.

unnamed STOUT, male, age 6 weeks, place of birth: Johnson Co. TN, cause of death: not stated, death record #: 47392, died: 18 Nov 1911.

Daniel STOUT, age 76 years, place of birth: Johnson Co. TN, cause of death: "paralysis", death record #: 47393, died: 25 Dec 1910.

Paul MATHERSON, age 21 months, place of birth: Johnson Co. TN, cause of death: "measles", death record #: 47394, died: 2 Jun 1911.

Jemima HECK, female, age 2 years, place of birth: Johnson Co. TN, cause of death: "measles", death record #: 47395, died: 4 Jun 1911.

David V. STOUT, age 74 years, place of birth: Johnson Co. TN, married, occupation: farmer and blacksmith, cause of death: "paralysis", death record #: 47396, died: 12 Mar 1911.

unnamed STOUT, female, age 11 days, cause of death: not recorded, record #: 47397, died: 3 Dec 1911.

David L. NEATHERLY, age 7 months, cause of death: "diarrhea", death record #: 47398, died: 30 Jul 1910.

Jacob C. NEATHERLY, age 7 months, cause of death: diarrhea, death record #: 47399, died: 27 Jul 1910.

Eliza HEGAMAN, age 78 years, widow, place of birth: Johnson Co. TN, cause of death: "heart dropsy", death record #: 47400, died: 2 Feb 1911.

George FARTHING, colored, age 74 years, place of birth: Caldwell Co., NC., cause of death: "paralysis", death record #: 47401, died: 27 Aug 1910.

Cellie GILBERT, female, age 31 years, married, place of birth: Watauga Co., NC, cause of death: "consumption", record #: 47402, died: 14 Dec 1910.

Callie NEATHERLY, female, age 22 years, single, place of birth: Johnson Co. TN, cause of death: "consumption", record #: 47403, died: 14 Nov 1910.

Hugh T. SIMCOX, age 5 months and 1 day, place of birth: Johnson Co. TN, cause of death: "spinal meningitis", death record #: 47404, died: 5 Mar 1911.

William S. SIMCOX, age 17 days, place of birth: Johnson Co. TN, cause of death: "spinal meningitis", death record #: 47405, died: 10 Dec 1910.

Petibue (?) FORRESTER, male, age 55 years, place of birth: Johnson Co. TN, cause of death: "stomach trouble", death record #: 47406, died: 7 Feb 1911.

Susan TESTER, age 63 years, married, place of birth: Johnson Co. TN, cause of death: "heart trouble", death record #: 47407, died: 20 Sep 1910.

Dorra GREEN, female, age 11 years, place of birth: Johnson Co. TN, cause of death: "spasms and fits", death record #: 47408, died: 3 Mar 1911.

Cathern HAMONS, age 40 years, widow, place of birth: Johnson Co. TN, cause of death: "consumption", death record #: 47409, died: 26 May 1910.

William POTTER, age 49 years, married, place of birth: Johnson Co. TN, cause of death: "colic", death record #: 47410, died: 24 Sep 1911.

Sarah GREEN, age 18 months, place of birth: Johnson Co. TN, cause of death: not recorded, death record #: 47411, died: 10 Jan 1911.

Audie WARD, male, age 20 days, place of birth: Johnson Co. TN, cause of death: not recorded, death record #: 47412, died: 10 Aug 1910.

Caroline SLIMP, age 67 years, place of birth: Ohio, cause of death: "consumption", death record #: 47412, died: 2 Jun 1911.

Willey WOLF, age 5 days, place of birth: Johnson Co. TN, cause of death: not recorded, death record #: 47414, died: 18 May 1911.

Jacob O'NEAL, age 30 years, married, place of birth: Johnson Co. TN, cause of death: "consumption", death record #: 47415, died: 26 Apr 1911.

James SERBER, age 37 years, married, place of birth: Smith Co., VA, cause of death: "pneumonia", death record #: 47416, died: 20 Mar 1911.

Margaret E. GENTRY, age 72 years, married, place of birth: Johnson Co. TN, cause of death: "heart dropsy", death record #: 47417.

Martha HAWKINS, age 63 years, single, place of birth: Johnson Co. TN, cause of death: "complication of disease", death record #: 47418, died: 22 Jan 1911.

Sarah Jane GILLAND, age 61 years, married, place of birth: Johnson Co. TN, cause of death: "lung and liver trouble", record #: 47419, died: 27 Jun 1911.

Ira GREER, age 9 years, place of birth: Watauga Co. NC, cause of death: "diphtheria", death record #: 47420, died: 23 Sep 1910.

Albert KENSLEY (almost illegible, not sure), age 9 years, place of birth: Washington VA, cause of death: "hives", death record #: 47421, died: 30 Sep 1910.

Roscoe TILLEY, age 10 months, cause of death: dysentery, death record #: 47422, died: 2 Aug 1910.

Verna Kate TILLEY, age 7 years, place of birth: Johnson Co. TN, cause of death: "croup", death record #: 47423, died: 23 Nov 1910.

Walter Dewey SHOEMAKE, age 2 weeks, place of birth: Johnson Co. TN, cause of death: "hives", death record #: 47424, died: 15 Dec 1910.

Kerne W. LOGAN, age 9 days, place of birth: Johnson Co. TN, cause of death: "pneumonia", death record #: 47425, died: 3 Jan 1911.

Lacira DAVIS, female, age 82 years, married, place of birth: Wilkes Co. NC, cause of death: "paralysis", death record #: 47426, died: 14 Oct 1910.

J.M. ARNOLD, male, age 74 years, cause of death: "la grippe", record #: 47427, died: 21 Mar 1911.

Mrs. M.E. ROARK, age 82 years, married, place of birth: Ashe Co. NC, cause of death: complication of disease, death record #: 47428, died: 1 Jan 1911.

Pearl C. HELTON, age 10 months, cause of death: "measles", death record #: 47429, died: 26 Sep 1910.

Annie P (illegible middle name) FULLER, age 25 years, single, born: Johnson Co. TN, cause of death: "typhoid", death record #: 47430, died: 19 Oct 1910.

Julia M. MILLER, age 25 years, married, place of birth: Johnson Co. TN, cause of death: "childbirth", death record #: 34731, died: 9 Mar 1911.

Maggie MOREFIELD, age 3 years, cause of death: dysentery, death record #: 47432, died: 3 Aug 1910.

Geneva MUNDY, age 4 months, cause of death: "diarrhea", death record #: 47433, died: 14 Apr 1911.

Clifford F. DONNELLY, age 77 years, single, place of birth: Johnson Co. TN, cause of death: "dropsy", death record #: 47434, died: 6 Jun 1911.

Effie Mae ROARK, age 7 years, place of birth: Ashe Co. NC, cause of death: "measles", death record #: 47435, died: 17 Oct 1910.

Illegible first name DARNELL, female, age not stated, single, place of birth: Johnson Co. TN, death record #: 47436, died: 17 Aug 1909.

J.F. BUCE (not sure, last name illegible), male, age 85 years, married, cause of death: "bladder trouble", death record #: 47437, died: 17 Oct 1909.

David S. HAWKINS, age 1 year, 3 months, cause of death: kidney trouble, died: 30 Aug 1909.

Amanda TESTER, age 21 years, married, place of birth: Johnson Co. TN, cause of death: "pneumonia", death record #: 47439, died: 21 Mar 1910.

unnamed male, cause of death: not stated, death record #: 47440, died: 16 Mar 1910.

Samuel B. GREEN (not sure, last name illegible), age 5 years, place of birth: Johnson Co. TN, cause of death: not stated, death record #: 47441, died: 11 Jun 1910.

Rebecca SNYDER, age not stated, married, cause of death: "consumption", died: 3 Mar 1910.

Arthur HECK, age not stated, single, born: Butler, TN, cause of death: "pneumonia", death record #: 47443, died: not stated, date death registered: 14 Jul 1910.

Rebecca WARD, age 48 years, married, cause of death: not known, death record #: 47444, died: 4 Jan 1910.

Daniel PRICE, age 70 years, married, place of birth: Edgepoint NC, cause of death: "consumption", death record #: 47445, died: 9 Mar 1910.

Willie STOUT, age 6 years, place of birth: Neva TN, cause of death: not stated, death record #: 47446, died: not stated, date death registered: 18 Jul 1910.

Matilda RAINBOLT, age 13 years, place of birth: Butler TN, cause of death: "le grippe", death record #: 47447, died: 6 Dec 1909.

Unnamed male, miscarriage, place of birth: Butler TN, death record #: 47448, died: 15 Jun 1910.

Margaret Lillie Bell NAVE, age 17 months, place of birth: Doeville TN, cause of death: not recorded, death record #: 47449, died: 4 Jun 1910.

Elvy RAMBO, female, age 73 years, place of birth: Johnson Co. TN, cause of death: "run over by train", death record #: 47450, died: 26 Jun 1910.

Unnamed female, age not stated, place of birth: Butler TN, death record #: 47451, died: 28 Oct 1909.

Unnamed female, age 9 days, cause of death: not recorded, death record #: 47452, died: 10 May 1910.

Francis REESE, age 4 years, cause of death: "diphtheria", record #: 47453, died: 22 Sep 1911.

Marry J. HOLLOWAY, female, age 60 years, married, place of birth: Butler TN, cause of death: measles, death record #: 47454, died: 25 Feb 1912.

Benj. MOODY, age 10 days, cause of death: "whooping cough", death record #: 47455, died: 30 Mar 1912.

Nancy HODGE, age 92 Years, single, place of birth: Shouns TN, cause of death: "paralysis", death record #: 47456, died: 6 Oct 1911.

Fannie EDMONDS, age 19 years, single, place of birth: Shouns TN, cause of death: "consumption", death record #: 47457, died: 12 May 1912.

Daniel STOUT, age 60 years, married, place of birth: Southerland NC, cause of death: "dropsy", death record #: 47458, died: 3 Mar 1911.

Sarah POTTER, age 70 years, married, place of birth: Southerland NC, cause of death: "paralysis", death record #: 47459, died: 15 Apr 1912.

H.A. WALSH, male, age 35 years, married, place of birth: Shouns TN, cause of death: "tuberculosis", death record #: 47460, died: 28 Sep 1911.

Patty FORRESTER, age 36 years, married, place of birth: Shouns TN, cause of death: "consumption", death record #: 47461, died: 10 Sep 1911.

Harrison ROARK, age 3 months, cause of death: "bold hives", death record #: 47462, died: 8 Aug 1911.

Florence SHEPPARD, age 1 month, cause of death: "bold hives", death record #: 47463, died: 28 Aug 1911.

Clayton ARNOLD, age 2 years, cause of death: "burns", death record #: 47464, died: 5 May 1912.

Danford (illegible, Sanford?) FORRESTER, age 4 months, cause of death: "hives", death record #: 47465, died: 20 Sep 1911.

Thomas ROBERTS, age 72 years, married, place of birth: Shouns TN, cause of death: "paralysis", death record #: 47466, died: 10 Nov 1911.

David FARMER, age 6 weeks, cause of death: whooping cough, death record #: 47467, died: 15 Oct 1911.

Cute PRICE, male, age not recorded, place of birth: Shouns Tn, cause of death: "fever", death record #: 47468, died: 27 Jun 1912.

Donnie DUNN, female, age 27 years, married, place of birth: Shouns TN, cause of death: "consumption", death record #: 47469, died: 27 Jan 1912.

Nancy PRICE, age 50 years, married, place of birth: Shouns TN, cause of death: "consumption", death record #: 47470, died: 3 Dec 1911.

Virtie JOHNSON, female, age 8 years, place of birth: Shouns TN, cause of death: "whooping cough", death record #: 47471, died: 10 Oct 1911.

Carmon STOUT, age 17 years, single, place of birth: Shouns TN, cause of death: "blood poisoning", death record #: 47472, died: 4 Jan 1912.

Bettie WALSH, age 65 years, married, place of birth: Wilkes Co. NC, cause of death: "consumption", death record #: 47473, died: 4 Mar 1912.

Totie (illegible, Lotie?) PROFFITT, female, age 42 years, place of birth: Shouns TN, cause of death: "consumption", record #: 47474, died: 8 Aug 1911.

Sylvany TAYLOR, female, age 19 years, single, place of birth: Shouns TN, cause of death: "consumption", death record #: 47475, died: 10 Aug 1911.

Nancy SALMONS, age 62 years, single, place of birth: Wilkes Co. NC, cause of death: "consumption", death record #: 47476, died: 24 Apr 1912.

John BAILEY, colored, age 69 years, single, place of birth: Wilkes Co. NC, cause of death: "brights disease", death record #: 47477, died: 24 Apr 1912.

Atlantic RAMBO, age 83 years, married, place of birth: Doe Valley TN, cause of death: "brights disease", death record #: 47478, died: 6 Apr 1912.

Vina CRESS, age 70 years, widow, place of birth: Wythe Co. VA, cause of death: "le grippe", death record #: 47479, died: 8 Mar 1912.

Myrtle NELSON, age 2 months, place of birth: Johnson Co. TN, cause of death: "whooping cough", death record #: 47480, died: 13 Jan 1912.

Margaret Edna S... (illegible), age not shown, place of birth: Johnson Co. TN, cause of death: "whooping cough", death record #: 47481, died: 9 Oct 1911,

Elsie Belle GENTRY, age 2 months, place of birth: Johnson Co. TN, cause of death: "whooping cough", death record #: 47482, died: 16 Sep 1911.

Bettie FENNER, age 17 years, single, place of birth: Johnson Co. TN, cause of death: "measles", death record #: 47483, died: 10 Jan 1912.

Clyde FENNER, age 5 years, place of birth: Johnson Co. TN, cause of death: "measles", death record #: 47484, died: 8 Jan 1912.

Unnamed infant male, place of birth: Johnson Co. TN, cause of death: not stated, death record #: 47485, died: 3 Apr 1912.

Lizzie Genette WILLS, age 22 years, single, place of birth: Shouns TN, cause of death: "diabetes", death record #: 47486, died: 21 Nov 1911.

Berna FENNER, male, age 5 years, place of birth: Johnson Co. TN, cause of death: "blood poisoning", death record #: 47487, died: 14 Jan 1912.

Catherine MOREFIELD, age 64 years, place of birth: Johnson Co. TN, cause of death: "brights disease", death record #: 47488, died: 8 Jan 1912.

Mary Kate DONNELLY, age 2 months, place of birth: Johnson Co. TN, cause of death: "do not know", death record #: 47489, died: 14 Jan 1912.

Franie PARRY (PERRY?), age 58 years, married, place of birth: Johnson Co. TN, cause of death: "cancer of stomach", death record #: 47490, died: 9 Jan 1912.

Elizabeth STOUT, age 4 years, place of birth: Shouns TN, cause of death: "spinal meningitis", death record #: 47491, died: 30 May 1912.

Emaline ROARKS, age not stated, place of birth: NC, cause of death: "consumption", death record #: 47492, died: Feb (day not stated) 1912, death recorded: 24 Jul 1912.

Edna E. LEE, age 6 years, cause of death: "whooping cough", death record #: 47493, died: 5 Oct 1911.

Zon BLACKBURN, male, age 9 months, place of birth: Johnson Co. TN, cause of death: "whooping cough", death record #: 47494, died: 2 Oct 1911.

James (last name illegible), age 56 years, married, place of birth: Watauga Co. NC, cause of death: "consumption", record #: 47495, died: 27 Jan 1912.

Jane WALLACE, age 44 years, married, place of birth: Trade TN, cause of death: "fell and killed herself", death record #: 47496, died: Nov (day not stated) 1911, death recorded: 23 Jul 1912.

Willie PHILLIPS, age 22, single, born: McGuire NC, died at: Red Jacket, WVA, cause of death: "electric wire", death record #: 47497, died: 21 Feb 1912.

Simon MILLER, age 3 weeks, cause of death: "bold hives", death record #: 47498, died: 2 Feb 1912.

Unnamed female, age 7 weeks, cause of death: "le grippe", death record #: 47499, died: 2 Feb 1912.

Commelia PEARSON, age 49 years, widow, place of birth: Watauga Co NC, cause of death: "throat trouble", death record #: 47500, died: 6 Dec 1911.

John D. ELLIOTT, age 74 years, married, place of birth: Salsbury NC, cause of death: "congestion of lungs", death record #: 47501, died: 24 Oct 1911.

Landon REECE, age 63 years, married, born: Trade TN, occupation: blacksmith, cause of death: "hurt by mule", death record #: 47502, died: 4 Jan 1912.

Bonnie DAVIS, female, age 6 years, cause of death: "spinal trouble", record #: 47503, died: 20 Dec 1911.

Rosa STEWART, age 19 days, place of birth: Trade TN, cause of death: "bold hives", death record #: 47504, died: 7 Dec 1911.

11

Unnamed male, stillborn, place of birth: Doeville TN, death record #: 47505, died: date not stated, date death recorded: 1 July 1912.

John ROBINSON, age 6 months, place of birth: Doeville TN, cause of death: "whooping cough", death record #: 47506, died: Feb (day not stated) 1912.

Eliza PROFFITT, age 65 years, married, place of birth: Doeville TN, cause of death: "paralysis", death record #: 47507, died: 13 Jul 1911.

Betty ROBERTS, age 68 years, married, place of birth: Johnson Co. TN, cause of death: "brights disease", death record #: 47508, died: 5 Jan 1912.

Malissie WILSON, female, age 26 years, married, place of birth: Johnson Co. TN, cause of death: "spinal meningitis", death record #: 47509, died: 30 Sep 1911.

Nelson PIERCE, age 47 years, married, place of birth: Johnson Co. TN, cause of death: "died suddenly", death record #: 47510, died: 24 Jun 1912.

Unnamed female, "stillborn", death record #: 47511, died: 27 Apr 1912.

Ethel PLEASANT, age 10 months, place of birth: Johnson Co. TN, cause of death: whooping cough, death record #: 47512, died: 16 Feb 1912.

Marvin T. MAXWELL, age 5 months, place of birth: Johnson Co. TN, cause of death: hives, death record #: 47513, died: 8 Feb 1912.

Minnie PIERCE, age 33 years, single, place of birth: Carter Co. TN, cause of death: consumption, death record #: 47514, died: 29 Jan 1912.

Dennis WALSH, age 2 years, place of birth: Johnson Co. TN, cause of death: spinal meningitis, death record #: 47515, died: 6 Aug 1911.

Alonzo CROSSWHITE, age 56 years, married, place of birth: Washington Co. TN, cause of death: pneumonia fever, death record #: 47516, died: 28 May 1912.

Lacy BLACKBURN, male, age 2 years, place of birth: Johnson Co. TN, cause of death: whooping cough, death record #: 47517, died: 3 Nov 1911.

Unnamed male, age 3 weeks, place of birth: Johnson Co. TN, cause of death: "not known", death record #: 47518, died: 5 Sep 1912.

Hester ROBERTS, female, age 22 years, married, place of birth: Johnson Co. TN, cause of death: dropsy of heart, death record #: 47519, died: 9 Jun 1912.

Caleb SHOUN, age 75 years, married, place of birth: Johnson Co. TN, cause of death: brights disease, death record #: 47520, died: 9 Jan 1912.

Unnamed female, age 1 day, cause of death: not stated, death record #: 47521, died: 15 Feb 1912.

Eula Maud FRITTS, age 18 months, place of birth: Johnson Co. TN, cause of death: not stated, death record #: 47522, date of death: 2 Oct 1912.

Estel NORRIS, female, age 4 years, place of birth: Johnson Co. TN, cause of death: whooping cough, death record #: 47523, date of death: 13 Nov 1911.

Maud RORAKE, age 4 years, place of birth: Johnson Co. TN, cause of death: whooping cough, death record #: 47524, date of death: 13 Nov 1911.

Kinney LOWE, age 6 months, place of birth: Johnson Co. TN, cause of death: whooping cough, death record #: 47525, date of death: 7 Nov 1911.

Eula SHUPE, age 31 years, married, place of birth: Johnson Co. TN, cause of death: measles, death record #: 47526, date of death: 6 Mar 1912.

Hiram B. BLEVINS, age 2 years and 6 months, place of birth: Johnson Co. TN, cause of death: whooping cough, death record #: 47527, date of death: 3 Nov 1911.

Horton WATSON, age 64 years, married, place of birth: Wilkes Co. NC, cause of death: "rheumatism and nervous breakdown, death record #: 47528, date of death: 15 Nov 1911.

Clay H..(illegible), male, age 6 years, place of birth: Johnson Co. TN, cause of death: "spinal trouble and fever", death record #: 47529, date of death: 2 Oct 1911.

Hanna PARKER, age 67 years, married, place of birth: Washington Co. TN, death record #: 47530, date of death: 19 dec 1911.

Alex WRIGHT, age 59 years, place of birth: Johnson Co TN , cause of death: "nephritis", death record #: 47531, date of death: 5 Aug 1911.

David MCELYEA, age 16 months, place of birth: Butler TN, cause of death: meningitis, death record #: 47532, date of death: 21 Oct 1911.

Dorothy STOUT, age 5 days, place of birth: Butler TN, cause of death: unknown, death record #: 47533, date of death: 21 May 1912.

Matilda LAWS, age 16 years, place of birth: Butler TN, cause of death: measles, death record #: 47534, date of death: 25 Feb 1912.

Ada LAWS, age 3 years, place of birth: Butler TN, cause of death: brain fever, death record #: 47535, date of death: 2 Mar 1912.

Wilson HOLLOWAY, age 1 year, place of birth: Butler TN, cause of death: croup, death record #: 47536, date of death: 6 Mar 1912.

Mary M. SLIMP, age 79 years, place of birth: Johnson Co. TN (Little Doe), death cause: abscess of stomach, death record #: 47537, date of death: 21 Jul 1911.

Grace STOUT, age 1 year, place of birth: Butler TN, cause of death: unknown, death record #: 47538, date of death: 16 Aug 1911.

Cora CABLE, age 6 months, place of birth: Butler TN, cause of death: unknown, death record #: 47539, date of death: 15 Feb 1912.

Unnamed female, colored, place of birth: Butler TN, cause of death: whooping cough, death record #: 47540, date of death: 15 Feb 1912.

Ruby PLEASANT, age 3 weeks, place of birth: Johnson Co TN (Doeville), cause of death: unknown, death record #: 47541, date of death: 1 Sep 1912.

A.J.F. HYDER, male, age not stated, place of birth: Elizabethton TN, minister, cause of death: paralysis, death record #: 47542, date of death: 3 Mar 1912.

Victor V. WILSON, age 3 years, place of birth: Butler TN, cause of death: "parabys pneumonia" death record #: 47543, date of death: 25 Jan 1912.

Chas. E. WILSON, age 16 months, place of birth: Butler TN, cause of death: measles and whooping cough, death record #: 47544, date of death: 29 Mar 1912.

Everett SMITH, age 70 years, place of birth: NC, cause of death: acute indigestion, death record #: 47545, date of death: 16 Feb 1912.

Zallie ARNOLD, age 4 years, place of birth: Johnson Co TN (Doeville), date of death: measles, death record #: 47546, date of death: 8 Feb 1912.

Lafayette CLARK, age 63 years, place of birth: Johnson Co TN (Doeville), cause of death: brights disease, death record #: 45547, date of death: 25 Feb 1912.

Margaret NEELEY (not sure), age 10 months, place of birth: Johnson Co TN, cause of death: pneumonia fever, death record #: 45548, date of death: 9 Jan 1912.

M.A. DUGGER, male, age 60 years, place of birth: TN, cause of death: pneumonia fever, death record #: 45549, date of death: 1 Jun 1912.

T. (?) WHITE, male, age 6 years, place of birth: Butler TN, cause of death: unknown, death record #: 45550, date of death: 16 Jul 1911.

Eliza STANBURY, age 53 years, place of birth: NC, cause of death: heart trouble, death record #: 47551. date of death: 3 Mar 1912.

Emla BUTON, female, age 82 years, place of birth: TN, cause of death: old age, death record #: 47552, date of death: 2 Mar 1912.

Envch (Enoch ?) LUNSFORD, age 90 years, place of
birth: NC, cause of death: paralysis, death record #:
47553, date of death: 11 Apr 1912.

Ralph WALSER, age 10 months, place of birth: TN, cause
of death: whooping cough, death record #: 47554, date
of death: 17 May 1912.

Roby HODGE, age 2 months, place of birth: Neva TN.
cause of death: not known, death record #: 47555, date
of death: 23 Dec 1911.

W.F. SHELL, male, age 72 years, place of birth: Mast
NC, cause of death: heart trouble, death record #:
47556, date of death: 2 Apr 1912.

Catherine NEATHERLY, age 45 years, married, place of
birth: Neva TN, cause of death: unknown, death record
#: 47557, date of death: 13 Jul 1912.

Wm. Lester WIDNER, age 7 months and 7 days, place of
birth: Johnson Co TN, cause of death: bold hives,
death record #: 47558, date of death: 7 Jan 1912.

Unnamed male, age 6 hours, place of birth: Johnson Co
TN, cause of death: unknown, death record #: 47559,
date of death: 7 Dec 1911.

Unnamed male, age 1 day, place of birth: Johnson Co
TN, cause of death: unknown, death record #: 47560,
date of death: 20 Dec 1911.

Glen MOREFIELD, age 4 months, place of birth: TN,
cause of death: "exzema", death record #: 47561, date
of death: 25 Jan 1912.

Agnes FRITTS, age 7 month and 7 days, place of birth:
Johnson Co TN, cause of death: bold hives, death
record #: 47562, date of death: 12 Jun 1912.

Unnamed male, age 6 hours, place of birth: Johnson Co
TN, cause of death: not recorded, death record #:
47563, date of death: 12 Sep 1911.

Oscar PENNINGTON, age 9 years, place of birth: Ashe Co
NC, cause of death: blood poison, death record #:
47564, date of death: 8 Mar 1912.

Spencer DAVIDSON, age 10 months, place of birth:
Johnson Co. TN, cause of death: unknown, death record
#: 47565, date of death: 25 Nov 1911.

Anner MIKEALS, female, age 19 years, married, place of
birth: Johnson Co. TN, cause of death: unknown, death
record #: 47566, date of death: 27 Dec 1911.

James H. MIKEALS, age 88 years, place of birth: NC,
cause of death: bladder disorder, death record #:
47567, date of death: 28 Oct 1911.

Dalisa GENTRY, female, age 87 years, married, cause of
death: "by falling", death record #: 47568, date of
death: 11 Apr 1912.

Maggie DOLLAR, age 39 years, place of birth: Johnson Co. TN, cause of death: pneumonia fever, death record #: 47569, date of death: 19 Feb 1912.

Calvin POPE, age 51 years, place of birth: NC, cause of death: "catarah", death record #: 47570, date of death: 7 Aug 1909.

Mary PAYNE, age 4 months, place of birth: TN, cause of death: unknown, death record #: 47571, date of death: 17 Dec 1909.

Walter McDaniel DUNN, age 11 months, place of birth: TN, date of death: croup, death record #: 47572, date of death: 18 Oct 1909.

Verna DUNN, female, age not recorded, place of birth: TN, cause of death: croup, death record #: 47573, date of death: 22 Oct 1909.

Lonnie E. DOWELL, age 3 years, place of birth: TN, cause of death: croup, death record #: 47574, date of death: 6 Oct 1909.

Wiley Adolphus MCCOY, age 3 months, place of birth: NC, cause of death: hives, death record #: 47575, date of death: 10 Nov 1909.

Maggie PROFFIT, age 6 years, place of birth: TN, cause of death: heart failure, death record #: 47576, date of death: 28 Sep 1909.

Pollie Catherine PROFFIT, age 9 months, place of birth: TN, cause of death: not stated, death record #: 47577, date of death: 15 Jan 1909.

Annie Chelcy WALSH, age 5 months, place of birth: TN, cause of death: not stated, death record #: 47578, date of death: 26 Apr 1910.

Inez WALSH, age 2 years, place of birth: TN, cause of death: not stated, death record #: 47579, date of death: 5 Jun 1910.

Millard LEWIS, age 3 weeks, place of birth: TN, cause of death: not stated, death record #: 47580, date of death: 18 Mar 1910.

Reuben POTTER, age not stated, place of birth: TN, married, cause of death: dropsy, death record #: 47581, date of death: 22 Sep 1909.

Lydia MAY, age 60 years, place of birth: TN, cause of death: dropsy, death record #: 47582, date of death: 1 Jan 1910.

Clyde WOODARD, age 7 months, place of birth: TN, cause of death: hives, death record #: 47583, date of death: 23 Oct 1909.

Jeremiah WOODARD, age 85 years, place of birth: NC, cause of death: unknown, death record #: 47584, date of death: 28 Aug 1909.

Jacob WILLEN, age 22 years, single, cause of death: consumption, death record #: 47585, date of death: 10 Nov 1909.

Thomas WILLEN, age 77 years, married, place of birth: NC, cause of death: "white swollen", death record #: 47586, date of death: 2 Feb 1910.

Mary Elizabeth ALLEN, age 3 months and 6 days, place of birth: TN, cause of death: bold hives, death record #: 47587, date of death: 28 Jun 1910.

Donna SNIDER, age 7 years, place of birth: TN, cause of death: scarlet fever, death record #: 47588, date of death: 10 Sep 1909.

Perl ELISON, female, born dead, death record #: 47589, date of death: 5 May 1910.

Earl ELISON, male, born dead, death record #: 47590, date of death: 5 May 1910.

John SMITH, age 70 years, single, place of birth: NC, cause of death: dropsy, death record #: 47591, date of death: 31 Jul 1909.

Mary An ROARK, age 6 months, place of birth: TN, cause of death: not stated, death record #: 47592, date of death: 14 Dec 1909.

Luanie WALSH, female, age 3 months, cause of death: "abscess in side", death record #: 47612, date of death: 28 Jan 1911.

C.M. HOWARD, male, age 16 years, place of birth: Johnson Co. TN (Shouns), cause of death: heart trouble, death record #: 47613, date of death: 4 Aug 1910.

Ruth HALL, age 1 year and 9 months, place of birth: Johnson Co. TN (Shouns), cause of death: croup, death record #: 47614, date of death: 8 Jan 1911.

David DUNN, age 2 months, place of birth: Johnson Co. TN (Shouns), cause of death: bold hives, death record #: 47615, date of death: 17 Apr 1911.

Rener EASTRIDGE, female, age 33 years, place of birth: Johnson Co. TN (Shouns), cause of death: consumption, death record #: 47616, date of death: 27 Jun 1911.

Harrison ROARK, age 4 months, place of birth: Johnson Co. TN (Shouns), cause of death: bold hives, death record #: 47417, date of death: 20 Jan 1911.

Elsa PHILIPS, female, age 13 years, place of birth: Johnson Co. TN (Shouns), cause of death: diphtheria, death record #: 47618, date of death: 2 Sep 1910.

Florence EASTRIDGE, age not recorded, place of birth: Johnson Co. TN (Shouns), cause of death: meningitis, death record #: 47619, date of death: 2 Sep 1910.

Fanoie HAMMONS, female, age 19 years, single, place of birth: Johnson Co. TN (Shouns), cause of death: consumption, death record #: 47620, date of death: 20 Jun 1911.

John HOWARD, age 75 years, married, place of birth: Johnson Co. TN (Shouns), cause of death: "inflamation of bowels", death record #: 47621, date of death: 29 Jul 1910.

Maggie PAYNE, age 24 years, married, place of birth: Johnson Co. TN (Shouns), cause of death: consumption, death record #: 47622, date of death: 20 Mar 1911.

Ephran OSBORN, age 94 years, married, place of birth: Johnson Co. TN (Shouns), date of death: "old age", death record #: 47623, date of death: 30 May 1911.

Hettie Mcbell FARMER, age 16 days, place of birth: Johnson Co. TN (Laurel Bloomery), cause of death: not stated, death record #: 47624, date of death: 10 Mar 1909.

Marcus A. KEYS, age 67 years, widower, place of birth: Johnson Co. TN (Silver Lake), cause of death: not stated, death record #: 47625, date of death: 14 Oct 1908.

Ruthie Rachel VENERABLE, age 18 months, place of birth: Johnson Co. TN (Silver Lake), cause of death: not recorded, death record #: 47626, date of death: 13 Dec 1908.

Charlie MOSER, age 3 days, place of birth: Johnson Co. TN (Laurel Bloomery), cause of death: bold hives, death record #: 47627, date of death: 17 Feb 1909.

Dollie Annis GREER, age 5 months and 3 days, place of birth: Johnson Co. TN (Silver Lake), cause of death: bold hives, death record #: 47628, date of death: 26 Feb 1909.

Lizzie CAMPBELL, age 5 years, place of birth: NC, cause of death: typhoid, death record #: 47629, date of death: 11 Jun 1908.

Infant FRITTS, male, child of Bert Fritts, age 1 hour, place of birth: Johnson Co. TN (Laurel Bloomery), death record #: 47630, date of death: 3 Jun 1909.

Charlie GENTRY, age 2 years, place of birth: Johnson Co. TN (Taylors Valley), cause of death: pneumonia, death record #: 47631, date of death: 13 Jan 1909.

Emanuel REECE, age 53 years, married, blacksmith, place of birth: Johnson Co. TN (Trade), cause of death: consumption, death record #: 47632, date of death: 1 Feb 1909.

Luther Roosevelt GILBERT, age 6 weeks, place of birth: Johnson Co. TN (Taylors Valley), cause of death: cholera, death record #: 47633, died: 17 Jul 1908.

Othor O. GILBERT, age 6 weeks, place of birth: Johnson Co. TN (Taylors Valley), cause of death: cholera, death record #: 47634, date of death: 17 Jul 1908.
William DENNIS, age 53 years, place of birth: Wilkes Co. NC, married, railroader, cause of death: not recorded, death record #: 47635, died: 10 Jan 1909.
Lola BREWER, age 3 years and 3 months, place of birth: Johnson Co. TN (Sutherland), cause of death: spinal, death record #: 47636, date of death: 7 Dec 1908.
Thomas ARON, age 14 months, place of birth: Bristol TN, cause of death: bronchitis, death record #: 47637, date of death: 22 Feb 1909.
Milton MICHAELS, age 4 months, place of birth: Johnson Co. TN (Sutherland), cause of death: pneumonia fever, death record #: 47638, date of death: 15 Apr 1909.
Cora MICHAELS, age 25 years, married, place of birth: Wilkes Co. NC, cause of death: unknown, death record #: 47639, date of death: 19 Apr 1909.
Mattie MICHAELS, age 2 months, place of birth: Johnson Co. TN (Sutherland), cause of death: cholera, death record #: 47639, date of death: 1 May 1909.
Roy GILLON, age 2 months, place of birth: Johnson Co. TN (Sutherland), cause of death: cholera, death record #: 47639, date of death: 20 May 1909.
Margaret MOCK, age 76 years, married, place of birth: Damascus VA, cause of death: pneumonia, death record #: 47642, date of death: 10 Nov 1908.
Monroe DOLLAR, age 73 years, married, place of birth: Ashe Co. NC, cause of death: not stated, death record #: 47543, date of death: 14 Aug 1908.
Lydia M. RORAK, female, age 44 years, single, place of birth: Johnson Co. TN (Laurel Bloomery), cause of death: pneumonia fever, death record #: 47644, date of death: 16 Jan 1909.
John A. CABLE, age 4 years, place of birth: Johnson Co. TN, cause of death: croup, death record #: 47645, date of death: 25 Jan 1909.
Carrol CABLE, male, age 1 year and 10 months, place of birth: Johnson Co. TN (Butler), cause of death: pneumonia, death record #: 47646, died: 18 Nov 1908.
Daton DUGGER, age 1 year and 6 months, place of birth: Johnson Co. TN (Dry Run), cause of death: cholera, death record #: 47647, date of death: 7 Aug 1908.
Ruth SMITH, age 5 days, place of birth: Johnson Co. TN (Dry Run), cause of death: unknown, death record #: 47648, date of death: 13 Mar 1909.
Henry SNYDER, age 1 year and 9 months, place of birth: Johnson Co. TN (Dry Run), cause of death: "burnt", death record #: 47649, date of death: 24 Apr 1909.

Fanny A. WATSON, age 10 months, place of birth: Johnson Co. TN (Gregg Branch), cause of death: cholera, death record #: 47650, died: 24 Jun 1909.

Coy M. BURTON, age 28 days, place of birth: Johnson Co. TN (Watauga River), cause of death: hives, death record #: 47651, date of death: 23 Feb 1909.

T.F. DUGGER, male, age 58 years, place of birth: Wilkes Co. NC, cause of death: pneumonia fever, death record #: 47652, date of death: 13 Apr 1909.

James LEFLER, age 3 years, place of birth: Rt 2, Mountain City, cause of death: typhoid fever, death record #: 47653, date of death: 9 Sep 1909.

Joseph WILLIAMS, black, age 67 years, place of birth: Yadkin Co. NC, cause of death: consumption, death record #: 47654, date of death: 24 Dec 1908.

Thomas SHUPE, age 70 years, 5 months and 10 days, place of birth: Mountain City, cause of death: stomach trouble, death record #: 47655, died: 20 Mar 1909.

Unnamed female, age 5 hours, place of birth: Rt 1, Mountain City, cause of death: unknown, death record #: 47656, date of death: 5 Feb 1909.

Ranford Ethridge ROBINSON, age 1 year, 7 months and 26 days, place of birth: Rt 1, Mountain City, cause of death: not recorded, death record #: 47657, date of death: 30 May 1909.

Rebecca Jane CROSSWHITE, age 79 years, married, place of birth: Mountain City, cause of death: general breakdown, death record #: 47658, died: 12 Apr 1909.

Lee BAILEY, colored, age 47 years, married, place of birth: Mountain City, occupation: barber, cause of death: stomach trouble, death record #: 47659, date of death: 22 Jul 1908.

Augusta BALUR, female, black, age 1 year and 4 months, place of birth: Mountain City, cause of death: "catarrk", death record #: 47660, died: 29 Jan 1909.

Rebecca NICHOLS, age 40 years, place of birth: Johnson Co. TN, cause of death: typhoid fever, death record #: 47661, date of death: 5 Feb 1909.

Smith NICHOLS, male, age 13 years, place of birth: Mountain City, cause of death: typhoid fever, death record #: 47662, date of death: 20 Jan 1909.

Unnamed NICHOLS, female, stillborn, death record #: 47663, died: 4 May 1909.

Alex GRINDSTAFF, colored, age 60 years, place of birth: Johnson Co. TN, cause of death: dropsy, death record #: 47664, date of death: 1 Sep 1908.

Ray ASBURY, age 17, place of birth: Mountain City, cause of death: brights disease, death record #: 47665, date of death: 21 Nov 1909.

Laura A. BAKER, age not stated, place of birth: Johnson Co. TN, place of death: Tacoma WA, cause of death: consumption of bowels, death record #: 47667, date of death: 11 Dec 1909.

Jane PHILLIPPE, age 79 years, married, place of birth: Wythe Co. VA, cause of death: not stated, death record #: 47668, date of death: 14 Sep 1908.

Mary Elizabeth WILSON, age 51 years, married, place of birth: not recorded, cause of death: cancer, death record #: 47669, date of death: 15 Feb 1909.

John Hardy WILSON, age 15 months, place of birth: Johnson Co. TN, cause of death: flux, death record #: 47670, date of death: 30 Jun 1909.

Webster CURD, age 51 years, place of birth: Johnson Co. TN, cause of death: "shot", death record #: 47671, date of death: 27 Jun 1908.

Lona MARTIN, female, age 11 months, place of birth: Johnson Co. TN, cause of death: whooping cough, death record #: 47672, date of death: 26 Jun 1909.

W.R. DAVIS, male, age about 60 years, single, place of birth: VA, cause of death: dropsy, death record #: 47673, date of death: 9 Jan 1909.

Asie Miner JOHNSON, female, age 4 years, place of birth: Johnson Co. TN, cause of death: croup, death record #: 47674, date of death: 8 Dec 1908.

Glen GARLAND, age 2 days, place of birth: Johnson Co. TN (Sutherland), cause of death: unknown, death record #: 47676, date of death: 7 Dec 1908.

Ella M. OLIVER, age 10 months, place of birth: Johnson Co. TN, cause of death: spinal meningitis, death record #: 46677, date of death: July (day not stated) 1908, date recorded: 17 Aug 1909.

Unnamed male, age 2 days, place of birth: Johnson Co. TN (Crandwell), cause of death: unknown, death record #: 47678, date of death: 5 Oct 1908.

Nathaniel BLEVINS, age 74 years, place of birth: Johnson Co. TN (Crandwell), married, cause of death: "supposed heart attack", death record #: 47679, date of death: 16 Mar 1909.

Russell WATSON, age 1 month, place of birth: Johnson Co. TN (Crandwell), cause of death: measles, death record #: 47680, date of death: 5 Mar 1909.

Charles E. BISHOP, age 4 years and 2 months, born: Crandwell, cause of death: scarlet fever, death record #: 47681, died: 4 Nov 1908.

Martha E. RAB.... (illegible), age 18 years, married, place of birth: NC, cause of death: "pendicitis", death record #: 47682, date of death: 12 Apr 1909.

Earl BAN... (illegible), age 7 months and 22 days, place of birth: Johnson Co. TN (Crandwell), cause of death: pneumonia fever, death record #: 47683, date of death: 27 Feb 1909.

M.G. EDMISON, age 24 years, male, married, place of birth: Wilkes Co. NC, cause of death: "broken leg", death record #: 47684, date of death: 28 Mar 1909.

M.E. COLE, female, age 24 years, married, place of birth: Johnson Co. TN, cause of death: "cild bed fever", death record #: 47685, died: 10 Oct 1909.

Sarah J. WILSON, age 75 years, married, place of birth: NC, cause of death: consumption, death record #: 47686, date of death: 22 Jun 1909.

Blonde BLACKBURN, age 4 days, place of birth: Johnson Co. TN (Crandwell), cause of death: unknown, death record #: 47687, date of death: 21 Apr 1909.

Thomas B. SHOUN, age 1 month and 22 days, place of birth: Johnson Co. TN (Crandwell), cause of death: croup, death record #: 47688, died: 12 Feb 1909.

Odith MILLER, male, age 2 months and 17 days, place of birth: Crandell, cause of death: "7 month child", death record #: 47689, died: 16 Oct 1908.

Clinton LOGGINS, age 6 months, place of birth: Johnson Co. TN (Silver Lake), cause of death: cholera inflamation, death record #: 47690, died: 1 Oct 1908.

Ethel JOHNSON, age 5 years and 6 months, place of birth: Mountain City, cause of death: morphine sulfite, death record #: 47691, died: 4 Sep 1908.

Mary GENTRY, age 22 years, single, place of birth: Mountain City, cause of death: consumption, death record #: 47692, date of death: Nov (day not stated) 1908, date registered: 11 Aug 1909.

Mattie DYSON, age about 50 years, married, place of birth: Mountain City, cause of death: paralysis, death record #: 47693, date of death: June (day not stated) 1908, date registered: 11 Aug 1909.

Byron G. COMBS, age 1 year and 6 months, place of birth: NC (?), cause of death: whooping cough, death record #: 47694, date of death: 20 Aug 1908.

Thomas P. FORRESTER, age 5 months, place of birth: Johnson Co. TN (Neva), cause of death: unknown, death record #: 47695, date of death: 11 Jul 1908.

Catherine SNYDER, age 60 years, married, place of birth: Johnson Co. TN (Voughtsville), cause of death: le grippe, death record #: 47696, died: 15 Jan 1909.

Emma CHURCH, age 24 years, married, place of birth: unknown, cause of death: consumption, death record #: 47697, date of death: 25 Mar 1909.

Unnamed male, age 2 hours, place of birth: Johnson Co. TN (Neva), cause of death: unknown, death record #: 47698, date of death: 19 Dec 1908.

Fred DUNN, age 2 years and 5 months, place of birth: Johnson Co. TN (Shouns), cause of death: liver trouble, death record #: 47699, date of death: May (day not stated) 1909, death registered: 12 Aug 1909.

William C. MCELYEA, age 25 days, place of birth: Johnson Co. TN (Shouns), cause of death: unknown, death record #: 47700, date of death: 1 Feb 1909.

Edith R. MOREFIELD, age 5 months and 18 days, place of birth: Johnson Co. TN (Neva), cause of death: fever, death record #: 47701, date of death: 27 Jan 1909.

Jacob GROSS, age 65 years, married, place of birth: unknown, cause of death: stomach trouble, death record #: 47702, date of death: 12 Jan 1909.

Joseph SLIMP, age 59 years, married, place of birth: Johnson Co. TN (Neva), cause of death: consumption, death record #: 47703, date of death: 2 Jul 1908.

John F. STOUT, age 25 years and 8 months, single, occupation: teacher, cause of death: fever, death record #: 47704, date of death: 10 Jun 1909.

Eddie ARNOLD, age 6 years and 3 months, place of birth: Johnson Co. TN (Neva), cause of death: scarlet fever, death record #: 47705, died: 28 Jan 1909.

Unnamed HICKS, female, age 8 days, place of birth: Johnson Co. TN (Neva), cause of death: unknown, death record #: 47706, date of death: 29 Jan 1909.

Unnamed WORLEY, female, age 6 weeks, place of birth: Johnson Co. TN (Maymead), cause of death: unknown, death record #: 47707, date of death: 7 Feb 1909.

Nettie H. STOUT, age 2 months and 15 days, place of birth: Johnson Co. TN (Neva), cause of death: unknown, death record #: 47708, date of death: 10 Dec 1908.

Unnamed VANDIKE, male, died at birth, place of birth: Johnson Co. TN (Neva), death record #: 47709, date of death: 27 May 1909.

Eldeed DANNER, female, age 2 years and 2 months, place of birth: Johnson Co. TN (Shouns), cause of death: "spinal disease", death record #: 47710, date of death: 27 Aug 1908.

Willie STOUT, age 5 years, 8 months and 14 days, place of birth: Johnson Co. TN (Neva), death cause: scarlet fever, death record #: 47711, died: 2 Nov 1908.

William H. GREGG, age 1 year, 8 months and 9 days, place of birth: Johnson Co. TN (Shouns), death cause: croup, death record #: 47712, died: 27 Sep 1908.

23

Unnamed JENKINS, male, place of birth: Johnson Co. TN (Butler), cause of death: not stated, death record #: 47713, date of death: 6 Jun 1909.

Mrs. Hattie ALLEN, age not stated, married, place of birth: Coldwell Co. NC, cause of death: consumption, death record #: 47714, date of death: 24 Mar 1909.

(First name not given) BAKER, age 76 years, single, place of birth: Manchester NH, cause of death: heart trouble, death record #: 47715, died: 4 Apr 1909.

J.J. HOLDEN, male, age 62 years, married, place of birth: TN, cause of death: "parolisis", death record #: 47716, date of death: 14 Sep 1908.

Willis HOLDEN, age 2 months, place of birth: TN, cause of death: bold hives, death record #: 47717, date of death: 24 Jan 1909.

Margaret MCELYEA, age 33 years, married, place of birth: TN, cause of death: ? fever, death record #: 47718, date of death: 9 Dec 1908.

David STOUT, age 9 years, cause of death: "fits", death record #: 47719, date of death: 13 Aug 1908.

Lacuitia STOUT, female, age 25 years, place of birth: TN, cause of death: ? fever, death record #: 47720, date of death: 23 Jan 1909.

Salina STOUT, female, age 7 days, place of birth: TN, cause of death: premature birth, death record #: 47721, date of death: 26 Jun 1909.

Andrew FURGERSON, age 83 years, place of birth: TN, cause of death: le grippe, death record #: 47722, date of death: 18 Feb 1909.

Earl GRINDSTAFF, age 3 years, place of birth: TN, cause of death: "membranus croup", death record #: 47723, date of death: 13 Oct 1908.

Unnamed STANTON, age 30 minutes, place of birth: TN, cause of death: premature birth, death record #: 47724, date of death: 25 Apr 1909.

Mary WAGNER, age 65 years, married, place of birth: NC, cause of death: cancer of stomach, death record #: 47725, date of death: 21 Jun 1909.

Ada GUIN, female, age 14 years, place of birth: TN, cause of death: typhoid fever, death record #: 47526, date of death: 25 Dec 1908.

Dora MAXWELL, age 25 years, married, place of birth: NC, cause of death: consumption, death record #: 47527, date of death: 2 Jul 1908.

Callie VAUGHT, age 35 years, married, place of birth: NC, cause of death: heart dropsy, death record #: 47528, date of death: 1 Apr 1909.

Anlee OSBORNE, female, age 6 years, place of birth: Johnson Co. TN (Trade), death cause: "scarlet fever", death record #: 47529, date of death: 8 Oct 1910.
Ellen POTTER, age 2 years, place of birth: Johnson Co. TN (Trade), cause of death: "burned", death record #: 47230, date of death: 23 Feb 1911.
Lella REECE, female, age 4 years, place of birth: Johnson Co. TN (Trade), cause of death: "burned", death record #: 47231, date of death: 7 Nov 1910.
Henry ROBINSON, age 84 years, married, place of birth: Sarah Co. NC, cause of death: "rheumatism and heart trouble", death record #: 47232, died: 21 Jan 1911.
Elvie MADRON, age 82 years, married, place of birth: Johnson Co. TN (Trade), cause of death: "pneumonia fever", death record #: 47233, died: 28 Apr 1911.
Frank THOMAS, age 59 years, married, place of birth: Tracy NC, cause of death: "heart trouble", death record #: 47234, date of death: 2 Mar 1911.
Unnamed CRAWFORD, male, age 2 days, place of birth: Johnson Co. TN (Trade), cause of death: unknown, death record #: 47735, date of death: 13 Apr 1911.
Elizabeth ARNOLD, age 76 years, married, place of birth: Johnson Co. TN (Trade), cause of death: "dropsy", death record #: 47736, date of death: Jan (day not stated) 1911, date registered: 15 Jul 1911.
Mary MAY, age 83 years, married, place of birth: Johnson Co. TN (Trade), cause of death: "liver and kidney", death record #: 47737, died: 10 May 1911.
Hiley CORRELL, female, age 55 years, single, place of birth: Johnson Co. TN (Little Doe), cause of death: "cold and starvation", pauper, death record #: 47738, date of death: 15 Feb 1911.
Nannie CROSSWHITE, age 33 years, married, place of birth: Mountain City, cause of death: "consumption", death record #: 47739, date of death: 22 Mar 1911.
Samuel M.. (illegible) CARICO, age 8 days, place of birth: Johnson Co. TN (Shady), cause of death: "hemorage", death record #: 47740, died: 6 May 1911.
Ida Jane MILLER, age 18 months, place of birth: Johnson Co. TN (Shady), cause of death: "flux", death record #: 47741, date of death: 6 Jun 1911.
Cephas Stacy ROBERTS, age 5 months, place of birth: Alvarado VA, cause of death: "pneumonia", death record #: 47742, date of death: 18 Jun 1911.
Henry Monroe BENTLY, age not stated, married, place of birth: NC, cause of death: "pneumonia", death record #: 47743, date of death: 8 Dec 1910.

Hugh LONG, age 2 months, place of birth: Johnson Co.
TN (Shady), cause of death: "bold hives", death record
#: 47744, date of death: 10 Dec 1910.
Clay PARKER, age 7 months and 21 days, place of birth:
Shady, death cause: "spinal and stomach trouble",
death record #: 47745, date of death: 20 Jul 1910.
Civil MCQUEEN, age 17 months, place of birth: Johnson
Co. TN (Shady), cause of death: "drowned", death
record #: 47746, date of death: 24 Mar 1911.
Elbert HAWKS, age 32 years and 3 months, married,
place of birth: VA, deat cause: "pneumonia and brain
fever", death record #: 47747, died: 2 Jun 1911.
Virgie Myrtle BROOKS, age 3 years, place of birth:
Johnson Co. TN (Shady), cause of death: "burned to
death", death record #: 47748, died: 10 Jan 1911.
Myrtle CROW, age 19 years, married, place of birth:
Wilkes Co. NC, cause of death: "anemia", death record
#: 47749, date of death: Dec (day not recorded) 1910,
registered: 20 Jul 1911.
George Washington HINES, age 53 years, married, place
of birth: Grayson Co. VA, cause of death: "murdered",
death record #: 47750, date of death: 15 Mar 1911.
Ida MILLER, age 1 year and 5 days, place of birth:
Johnson Co. TN (Shady), cause of death: "diphtheria",
death record #: 47751, date of death: 17 Sep 1910.
Elbert BISHOP, age 17 years and 8 months, married,
place of birth: Watauga Co. NC, cause of death:
"drowned", death record #: 47752.
Unknown, sex not stated, age 12 days, cause of death:
not stated, death record #: 47753, died: 2 May 1911.
T.S. WATSON, male, age 63 years, married, place of
birth: NC, cause of death: "fell from a tree", death
record #: 47754, date of death: 5 Oct 1909.
Elizabeth L. HEABERLIN, age 59 years, married, place
of birth: Pulaski VA, cause of death: "consumption",
death record #: 47755, date of death: 20 Mar 1910.
S.C. WADDLE, age 14 years, male, place of birth:
Johnson Co. TN (Crandell), cause of death: "typhoid
fever", death record #: 47756, died: 31 Jul 1909.
Winford REEVES, age 4 years, place of birth: Johnson
Co. TN (Crandell), cause of death: "croup", death
record #: 47757, date of death: 19 Oct 1909.
Charlie BENTLY, age 3 years, place of birth: Sullivan
Co. TN, cause of death: "kidney disease", death record
#: 47758, date of death: 13 Jan 1910.
Dana M. WALKER, male, age 1 year, place of birth:
Johnson Co. TN (Crendell), cause of death: "spinal
meningitis", death record #: 47759, died: 14 Nov 1909.

26

A.S. GENTRY, female, age 29 years, place of birth: Sullivan Co. TN, cause of death: "fever and heart trouble", death record #: 47760, died: 31 Oct 1909.

L.C. RETHERFORD, female, age 46 years, married, place of birth: NC, cause of death: unknown, death record #: 47761, date of death: 12 Feb 1910.

Mannie ESTES, female, age 3 years, place of birth: Damascus VA, cause of death: "pneumonia", death record #: 47762, date of death: 25 Oct 1909.

Fostenia ESTES, female, age 14 months, place of birth: Johnson Co. TN (Crandell), death cause:"pneumonia", death record #: 47763, date of death: 29 Oct 1909.

Birthia TRIPLETT, age 12 years, place of birth: NC, cause of death: "spinal meningitis", death record #: 47764, date of death: 19 Nov 1909.

Bessie GARLAND, age 6 weeks, place of birth: Johnson Co. TN (Crandell), cause of death: "bold hives", death record #: 47765, date of death: 10 May 1910.

Sarah A. COLE, age 80 years, married, place of birth: Johnson Co. TN, cause of death: "old age", death record #: 47766, date of death: 12 Jul 1909.

Rebecca TIEBEL, age 28 years, married, place of birth: NC, cause of death: unknown, death record #: 47767, date of death: 15 Jan 1910.

Elan COLE, female, age 46 years, married, place of birth: Johnson Co. TN (Crandell), cause of death: "cancer", death record #: 47768, died: 20 Nov 1909.

Clinton SEVERE, age 2 years, place of birth: Johnson Co. TN (Crandell), cause of death: "scarlet fever", death record #: 47769, date of death: 20 Oct 1909.

Lester JONES, age 9 years, born: NC, cause of death: fever, death record #: 47770, died: 20 Nov 1909.

Pansie LOVELL, age 5 years, cause of death: "scarlet fever", death record #: 47771, died: 22 Nov 1909.

Bonnie LOWEL, age 3 years, born: Crandell, TN, cause of death: "tonsillitis", death record #: 47772.

Lemiel CAMPBIL, male, age 6 years, place of birth: Johnson Co. TN (Doeville), cause of death: "spinal", death record #: 47773, date of death: 30 Dec 1908.

Polly C. GENTRY, age 29 years, married, born: Johnson Co. TN (Neva), cause of death: "miscarriage of child", death record #: 47774, date of death: 13 Jan 1909.

H.R. GRINDSTAFF, male, age 49 years, married, born: Johnson Co. TN (Doeville), death cause: "stomach trouble", death record #: 47775, died: 9 Mar 1909.

Susin STOUT, age 22 years, married, place of birth: Johnson Co. TN (Doeville), death cause: "miscarriage", death record #: 47776, died: 23 Apr 1909.

Mary L. CAMPBELL, age 59 years, married, born: Johnson Co. TN (Doeville), cause of death: "new pneumonia fever", death record #: 47777, died: 11 Nov 1908.

Rachel LOYD, age 77 years, married, place of birth: Johnson Co. TN (Doeville), cause of death: le grippe, death record #: 47778, date of death: 23 Nov 1908.

Adaline GREER, age 65 years, married, place of birth: Johnson Co. TN (Trade), cause of death: unknown, death record #: 47779, date of death: 29 Oct 1908.

Elizabeth STALCUP, age 78 years, married, place of birth: Johnson Co. TN (Doeville), cause of death: le "grippe", death record #: 47780, died: 29 Nov 1908.

Lewis GARLAND, age 66 years, married, place of birth: Johnson Co. TN (Doeville), death cause: "le grippe", death record #: 47781, date of death: 21 Jan 1909.

Sarah CAMPBELL, age 61 years, married, born: Johnson Co. TN (Doeville), cause of death: "le grippe", death record #: 47782, date of death: 30 Nov 1908.

Barbie TILLEY, age 61 years, married, place of birth: Johnson Co. TN (Doeville), cause of death: "hart dropsy", death record #: 47783, diedh: 21 Feb 1909.

Joe ARNEY, age 54 years, married, place of birth: Johnson Co. TN (Doeville), cause of death: "hart dropsy", death record #: 47784, died: 3 Jan 1909.

Callie BLACKBURN, age 16 days, place of birth: Johnson Co. TN (Doeville), cause of death: "hives", death record #: 47785, date of death: 20 Jan 1909.

James MURRY, age 78 years, married, place of birth: Damascus VA, cause of death: "le grippe", death record #: 47786, date of death: 22 Jan 1909.

Birthy NYE, age 5 months, place of birth: Mountain City, cause of death: "hives", death record #: 47787, date of death: 12 Feb 1909.

Ulah HEATON, female, age 5 years, place of birth: Mountain City, cause of death: "memmerles croup", death record #: 47788, date of death: 5 Nov 1908.

Bettie JORDAN, age 40 years, married, place of birth: Johnson Co. TN (Trade), cause of death: "pneumonia fever", death record #: 47789, died: 30 Mar 1909.

Cindy ROBINSON, age 46 years, married, place of birth: Johnson Co. TN (Doeville), cause of death: "blood poison", death record #: 47790, died: 14 May 1909.

Vady GARLAND, female, age 9 months, place of birth: Johnson Co. TN (Doeville), cause of death: "le grippe", death record #: 47791, died: 21 Jan 1909.

Calvin J. CHURCH, age 75 years, married, place of birth: NC, cause of death: "lung trouble", death record #: 47792, date of death: 25 Aug 1908.

Vernia ROBERTS, female, age 11 years, place of birth: Johnson Co. TN (Little Doe), cause of death: "stomach trouble", death record #: 47793, died: 9 Feb 1909.

R.L. STOUT, age 59 years, married, place of birth: Johnson Co. TN (Pandora), cause of death: "dropsy", death record #: 47794, date of death: 14 Feb 1909.

Arthur HARPER, age 2 years, place of birth: Johnson Co. TN (Little Doe), cause of death: "scarlet fever", death record #: 47795, date of death: 23 Nov 1908.

Joel BARRY, age 1 year and 4 months, place of birth: Johnson Co. TN (Little Doe), death cause: "trouble of the head", death record #: 47796, died: 19 Nov 1908.

Willie DAVIS, age 1 month, place of birth: Johnson Co. TN (Little Doe), cause of death: "kidney trouble", death record #: 47797, date of death: 22 Jul 1908.

George CROSSWHITE, age 30 years, married, place of birth: Little Doe, death cause: "falling tree", death record #: 47798, died: 5 Jan 1909.

Willie STOUT, age 3 years and 11 months, place of birth: Johnson Co. TN (Little Doe), cause of death: "croup", death record #: 47799, died: 13 Dec 1908.

Vada ROBINSON, female, age 24 years, married, born: Johnson Co. TN (Little Doe), death cause: "kidney trouble", death record #: 47800, died: 6 Apr 1909.

Landon DUFFIELD, age 71 years, married, place of birth: Carter Co. TN, cause of death: "old age and gangrene", death record #: 47801, died: 3 Mar 1909.

Sallie STOUT, age 40 years, married, born: Johnson Co. TN (Little Doe), death cause: "consumption", death record #: 47802, died: 4 Sep 1908.

Johnie EGGESE, age 1 day, place of birth: Johnson Co. TN (Little Doe), cause of death: "strangulation", death record #: 47803, date of death: 18 Jun 1909.

Jesse ARNOLD, age 7 months, place of birth: Johnson Co. TN (Doeville), cause of death: "stomach trouble", death record #: 47804, date of death: 21 Nov 1911.

G.D. PROFFITT, male, age 76 years, married, born: Johnson Co. TN (Little Doe), death cause: "heart trouble", death record #: 47805, died: 10 May 1911.

Unnamed WILSON, male, age 2 months and 4 days, place of birth: Johnson Co. TN (Doeville), cause of death: not stated, death record #: 47806, died: 13 Nov 1910.

Unnamed ELLIOTT, female, age 3 days, place of birth: Johnson Co. TN (Doeville), cause of death: unknown, death record #: 47807, date of death: 3 Sep 1910.

J.M. ROBERTS, male, age 89 years, married, place of birth: Johnson Co. TN, cause of death: "paralysis", death record #: 47808, date of death: 14 Feb 1911.

R.A. ROBERTS, male, age 87, married, place of birth: Johnson Co. TN, cause of death: "dropsy", death record #: 47809, date of death: 10 Dec 1910.

Flo...(illegible) WATSON, female, age 22 years, married, cause of death: consumption, death record #: 47810, date of death: 12 Apr 1911.

John ROBINSON, age 37 years, married, place of birth: Johnson Co. TN, cause of death: "poison", death record #: 47811, date of death: 12 May 1911.

Millard GENTRY, age 24 years, married, place of birth: Johnson Co. TN, cause of death: "typhoid fever", death record #: 47812, date of death: 26 Aug 1910.

Pearl GENTRY, age 4 months, place of birth: Johnson Co. TN, cause of death: "typhoid fever", death record #: 47813, date of death: 6 Oct 1910.

Oni GENTRY, female, age 2 years, place of birth: Johnson Co. TN, cause of death: "typhoid fever", death record #: 47814, date of death: 21 Oct 1910.

Daniel HENSON, age 54 years, single, place of birth: Watauga Co. NC, cause of death: "dropsy", death record #: 47815, date of death: 27 Oct 1910.

William HARPER, age 42 years, married, place of birth: Johnson Co. TN, cause of death: "typhoid fever", death record #: 47816, date of death: 25 Sep 1910.

Laura A. GARLAND, age 29 years, married, place of birth: Johnson Co. TN, cause of death: "tuberculosis", death record #: 47817, date of death: 5 Jun 1911.

E. Max SHOUN, male, age 35 years, place of birth: Little Doe, death cause: "tuberculosis", death record #: 47818, died: 30 Dec 1910.

Effie LOWE, age 23 years, single, place of birth: Johnson Co. TN, cause of death: "consumption", death record #: 47819, date of death: 1 May 1911.

Polly COMER, age about 40 years, married, born: NC, cause of death: "cancer", death record #: 47820. died: Feb (day not stated), registered: 11 Jun 1911.

Nancy FRITTS, age 65 years, married, born: Johnson Co. TN, died: Sullivan Co. TN, cause of death: "apoplexy", death record #: 47821, date of death: 6 Feb 1911.

Nancy CROSSWHITE, age 70 years, married, place of birth: Johnson Co. TN, cause of death: "cancer", death record #: 47822, date of death: 26 Jan 1911.

Ellen CROSSWHITE, age 35 years, single, place of birth: Johnson Co. TN, cause of death: "consumption", death record #: 47823, date of death: 22 Apr 1911.

Rebecca FLETCHER, age 70 years, widow, born: Johnson Co. TN, cause of death: "hearth dropsy", death record #: 47824, died: Nov (day not stated) 1910, date registered: 20 Aug 1910.

Samuel GRINDSTAFF, age 38 years, married, place of birth: Carter Co. TN, cause of death: "typhoid fever", death record #: 47825, date of death: 8 sep 1909.

Ethel SLIMP, age 18 years and 1 month, single, place of birth: Johnson Co. TN, cause of death: "heart dropsy", death record #: 47826, died: 31 Dec 1909.

Unnamed female, age 15 days, place of birth: Johnson Co. TN (Butler), cause of death: "jaundice", death record #: 47827, date of death: 14 Aug 1909.

Catherine WAGNER, age 8 years, place of birth: Carter Co. TN, cause of death: "pneumonia", death record #: 47828, date of death: 8 May 1909.

A.B. GREENWELL, age 78 years, married, place of birth: Wilkes Co. NC, cause of death: "(illegible) poison", death record #: 47829, date of death: 12 Dec 1909.

Unnamed female, age 7 days, place of birth: Johnson Co. TN (Butler), cause of death: unknown, death record #: 47830, date of death: 24 Dec 1909.

Maud SLIMP, age 1 year, place of birth: Johnson Co. TN, cause of death: "stomach trouble", death record #: 47831, date of death: 23 Oct 1909.

Unnamed male, age 7 days, place of birth: Johnson Co. TN, cause of death: unknown, death record #: 47832, date of death: 29 Dec 1909.

Maud CORNETT, age 9 years, place of birth: Washington Co. TN, cause of death: "pneumonia", death record #: 47833, date of death: 15 Feb 1910.

Infant NEELY, father: Samuel NEELY, female, age 3 months, place of birth: Johnson Co. TN (Laurel Bloomery), cause of death: "fever", death record #: 47834, date of death: 5 Aug 1909.

Oscar Carl MAIN, age 18 days, place of birth: Mountain City, cause of death: "bold hives", death record #: 47835, date of death: 10 Jun 1910.

Taylor MOREFIELD, age 59 years, place of birth: Johnson Co. TN, cause of death: "paralysis", death record #: 47836, date of death: 22 Nov 1909.

Agnes EGGERS, age 14 years, place of birth: Smith Co. VA, cause of death: "bealing in head", death record #: 47837, date of death: 8 Feb 1910.

Avery WATERS, male, age 44 years, married, place of birth: Ashe Co. NC, cause of death: "paralysis", death record #: 47838, date of death: 4 Feb 1910.

Billie MOREFIELD, age 2 years, place of birth: Johnson Co. TN (Laurel Bloomery), cause of death: "scarlet fever", death record #: 47839, died: 29 Nov 1909.

William CRAMER, age 38 years, married, timber contractor, born: Ashe Co. NC, death cause: "typhoid fever", death record #: 47840, died: 20 Jan 1910.

John burton MOSURE, age 4 years, place of birth: Washington Co. VA, cause of death: "killed by falling tree", death record #: 47841, died: 23 Mar 1910.

Infant WILSON, male, age not stated, child of: Emmet WILSON, place of birth: Johnson Co. TN (Laurel Bloomery), cause of death: "still born", death record #: 47842, date of death: 20 Nov 1909.

Walter, SURBER, age 2 months, place of birth: Johnson Co. TN (Laurel Bloomery), cause of death: illegible, death record #: 47843, date of death: 26 Jan 1910.

Infant ROBINSON, male, child of: Wills ROBINSON, born: Johnson Co. TN (Laurel Bloomery), cause of death: still born, death record #: 47844, died: 4 Jan 1911.

Milborn CORNETT, age 62 years, married, born: Johnson Co. TN (Silver Lake), cause of death: cancer of stomach, death record #: 47845, died: 18 Jun 1910.

Infant CORUM, male, child of R.G. CORUM, born: Laurel Bloomery, cause of death: "still born", death record #: 47846, date of death: 29 Feb 1910.

Eliza J. GREENWELL, age 3 years, place of birth: Johnson Co. TN (Butler), cause of death: pneumonia fever, death record #: 47847, died: 15 Dec 1910.

Callie STANBURY, age 15 years, place of birth: Johnson Co. TN (Butler), cause of death: pneumonia fever, death record #: 47848, date of death: 13 Nov 1910.

Roy B. DUGGER, age 20 years, place of birth: Johnson Co. TN (Butler), cause of death: not stated, death record #: 47849, date of death: 24 May 1911.

S. (middle initial illegible) DUGGER, age 82 years, male, born: Butler, TN, death cause: brights disease, death record #: 47850, died: 12 Aug 1910.

Floy Ella MCELYEA, age 3 years, place of birth: Johnson Co. TN (Shouns), cause of death: "yellow thresh", death record #: 47851, died: 30 Aug 1911.

Bertha MCELYEA, age 4 months, place of birth: Johnson Co. TN (Neva), cause of death: bold hives, death record #: 47852, date of death: 1 Jan 1912.

Blanche FORRESTER, age 9 months, place of birth: Johnson Co. TN (Neva), cause of death: pneumonia, death record #: 47853, date of death: 2 Apr 1912.

David VAUGHT, age 17 years, single, worked at sawmill, born: Johnson Co. TN (Neva), death cause: "killed by machining", death record #: 47854, died: 27 Mar 1912.

Unnamed male, age 2 months, place of birth: Johnson Co. TN (Neva), cause of death: bold hives, death record #: 47855, date of death: 5 Apr 1912.

Annie Maud WILSON, age not stated, single, place of birth: Johnson Co. TN, (Vaughtsville), cause of death: unknown, death record #: 47856, died: 5 Apr 1911.

Unnamed male, age 20 days, place of birth: Johnson Co.
TN, (Neva), cause of death: unknown, death record #:
47857, date of death: 20 Jan 1912

J.M. VAUGHT, male, age 40 years, place of birth:
Johnson Co. TN, (Vaughtsville), cause of death: "horse
kicked", death record #: 47858, died: 16 Jun 1912.

Lelor MOREFIELD, female, age 4 years, place of birth:
Johnson Co. TN, (Butler), cause of death: croup, death
record #:, 47859, date of death: 12 Oct 1911.

Ethel MOREFIELD, age 2 years, place of birth: Johnson
Co. TN, (Butler), cause of death: measles, death
record #: 47860, date of death: 13 Feb 1913.

Ira LAW...(illegible), age 13 months, male, place of
birth: Johnson Co. TN, (Butler), cause of death:
pneumonia, death record #: 47861, died: 1 May 1912.

Unnamed female, age 9 months, place of birth: Johnson
Co. TN, (Butler), cause of death: unknown, death
record #: 47882, date of death: 4 Oct 1911.

Unnamed female, age not stated, place of birth:
(Bakers Gap), cause of death: unknown, death record #:
47863, date of death: 20 Jun 1912.

Unnamed female, age 8 months, place of birth: Cold
Creek VA, cause of death: meningitis, death record #:
47864, date of death: 2 Oct 1911.

Becka DUNN, female, age 49 years, place of birth:
Johnson Co. TN, (Shouns), single, cause of death:
pneumonia, death record #: 47865, died: 22 Dec 1911.

Unnamed male, age not stated, place of birth: Johnson
Co. TN, (Neva), cause of death: unknown, death record
#: 47866, date of death: 10 Oct 1911.

Mary Tester, age 20 months, place of birth: Johnson
Co. TN, (Neva), cause of death: "paralysie", death
record #: 47867, date of death: 3 Aug 1911.

Lillie WATKINS, age 17 years, married, born: Johnson
Co. TN, (Vaughtsville), cause of death: consumption,
death record #: 47868, date of death: 1 Apr 1912.

Ethel Mae MCELYEA, age 9 years, place of birth:
Johnson Co. TN, (Neva), cause of death: croup, death
record #: 47869, date of death: 22 Dec 1911.

Catherine HAMMONS, age 38 years, married, place of
birth: Johnson Co. TN, (Shouns), cause of death:
consumption, death record #: 47870, died: 23 Jul 1911.

Claud HAWKINS, age 19 years, single, place of birth:
Johnson Co. TN, (Neva), cause of death: consumption,
death record #: 47871, date of death: 9 Apr 1912.

Samuel FLETCHER, age 61 years, place of birth: Amantha
NC, cause of death: consumption, death record #:
47872, date of death: 8 Mar 1911.

Edward MCELYEA, age 2, born: Shouns, death cause: "thresh", death record #: 47873, died: 15 Jul 1911.

Holly WALLACE, age 24 days, place of birth: Johnson Co. TN, (Trade), cause of death: "bold hives", death record #: 47874, date of death: 25 Sep 1908.

Gracie WALLACE, age 11 days, place of birth: Johnson Co. TN, (Trade), cause of death: "fits or hives", death record #: 47875, date of death: 21 Mar 1909.

Asa WALLACE, male, age 11 days, place of birth: Johnson Co. TN, (Trade), cause of death: "bold hives", death record #: 47876, date of death: 21 Mar 1909.

Luther Blan WALLACE, age 8 weeks, place of birth: Johnson Co. TN, (Trade), cause of death: "bold hives", death record #: 47877, date of death: 14 May 1909.

Lon WALLACE, age 10 days, born Trade, TN, death cause :"bold hives", record #: 47878, died: 10 Oct 1908.

Jimmie BUMGARDNER, female, age 46 years, married, place of birth: Mountain City, death cause: "stomach trouble", death record #: 47879, died: 22 Jan 1909.

Clarence BUMGARDNER, age 5 months and 24 days, place of birth: jct (Trade), cause of death: "bold hives", death record #: 47880, date of death: 24 Jun 1909.

Mona MILLER, age 3 months, place of birth: Johnson Co. TN (Trade), cause of death: "spinal trouble", death record #: 47881, date of death: 12 Jun 1909.

Jake MAY, age 37 years, married, place of birth: Johnson Co. TN (Trade), cause of death: "dropsy", death record #: 47882, date of death: 2 June 1909.

Alice MAIN, age 23 years, married, place of birth: Johnson Co. TN (Trade), cause of death: "consumption", death record #: 47883, date of death: 9 Feb 1909.

George WALSH, age not stated, married, place of birth: Wilkes Co. NC, cause of death: "consumption", death record #: 47884, date of death: 27 Jan 1909.

Wm B. GAMBILL, age 66 years, male, place of birth: Johnson Co. TN (Neva), death cause: "kidney trouble", death record #: 47885, date of death: 21 Feb 1910.

Troy E. BURTON, age 24 years, single, place of birth: Johnson Co. TN (Butler), cause of death: "pneumonia fever", death record #: 47886, died: 3 Mar 1910.

Odnes (?) DUGGER, female, age 1 year, place of birth: Johnson Co. TN (Butler), cause of death: "croup", death record #: 47887, date of death: 6 Dec 1909.

Martha BURTON, age 54 years, married, place of birth: Johnson Co. TN (Butler), cause of death: "palsie", death record #: 47888, date of death: 20 Jun 1910.

Nancy ANDERSON, age 84 years, single, place of birth: Johnson Co. TN (Butler), cause of death: "old age palsie", death record #: 47889, died: 16 Dec 1909.

Paul STARNES, age 2 months, place of birth: Watauga Co. NC, cause of death: "back knot", death record #: 47890, date of death: 20 May 1910

(first name illegible) GREENWELL, age 2 months, place of birth: Johnson Co. TN (Butler), cause of death: "unknown", death record #: 47891, died: 3 Feb 1910.

Rolie SMITH, male, age 4 years, place of birth: Johnson Co. TN (Butler), cause of death: "croup", death record #: 47892, date of death: 23 Oct 1909.

Naley GREER, female, age 3 years and 9 months, place of birth: Johnson Co. TN (Trade), cause of death: "croup", death record #: 47893, died: 14 Dec 1909.

Sallie THOMAS, age 54 years, married, place of birth: Watauga Co. NC, cause of death: "bone consumption", death record #: 47894, date of death: 22 Dec 1909.

Maryon CARTER, male, age 3 months and 8 days, place of birth: Johnson Co. TN (Trade), cause of death: "croup", death record #: 47895, died: 20 Sep 1909.

Cecil FORD, male, age 4 months and 1 day, place of birth: Johnson Co. TN (Trade), cause of death: "croup", death record #: 47896, died: 31 Jan 1910.

Melvin ARNOLD, age 80 years, place of birth: Johnson Co. TN (Trade), married, cause of death: not stated, death record #: 47897, date of death: 18 Jul 1909.

Roby DAVIS, male, age 35 years, place of birth: Watauga Co. NC, cause of death: "tuberculosis", death record #: 47898, date of death: 11 Mar 1910.

Andy FRITTS, age 10 months, place of birth: Sullivan Co. TN, cause of death: "pneumonia", death record #: 47899, date of death: 11 Feb 1910.

R.P. WALSH, male, age 76 years, place of birth: Wilkes Co. NC, single, cause of death: "pneumonia", death record #: 47900, date of death: 27 Apr 1910.

Sybitha ROBERTS, female, age 72 years, married, place of birth: Yadkin Co. NC, cause of death: "brights disease", death record #: 47901, died: 18 Jan 1910.

H.C. ROBERTS, male, age 51 years, born: Johnson Co. TN (Little Doe), cause of death: "tuberculosis", death record #: 47902, died: 16 Nov 1908.

Herbert SHOUN, age 2 months, place of birth: Johnson Co. TN (Little Doe), cause of death: "membranus croup", death record #: 47903, died: 20 Feb 1910.

Martin FLETCHER, age 86 years, single, place of birth: Johnson Co. TN, cause of death: "old age", death record #: 47904, date of death: 3 Apr 1910.

Frank WALSH, age 38 years, married, born: Watauga Co. NC, death record #: 47905, date of death: 19 Feb 1910.

Elizabeth ROBERTS, age 76 years, single, place of birth: Johnson Co. TN, cause of death: "pneumonia", death record #: 47906, date of death: 17 May 1910.

Earl COLE, age 3 months, place of birth: Johnson Co. TN (Little Doe), cause of death: "wasting away of the body", death record #: 47907, died: 27 Jun 1910.

Emmit WALLACE, age 22 years, single, place of birth: Johnson Co. TN (Little Doe), death cause: "cholera", death record #: 47908, date of death: 26 Jun 1910.

Easter STOUT, female, age 68 years, married, place of birth: Johnson Co. TN, cause of death: "jaundice", death record #: 47909, date of death: 27 Dec 1909.

Vinnie Ruth ROBINSON, age 2 years, place of birth: Johnson Co. TN (Pandora), cause of death: "pneumonia", death record #: 47910, date of death: 27 Dec 1909.

Joe ROBINSON, age 94 years, single, place of birth: Johnson Co. TN, cause of death: "old age", death record #: 47911. date of death: 27 Dec 1909.

Andy HEATON, age 56 years, married, place of birth: Johnson Co. TN, cause of death: "dropsy", death record #: 47912, date of death: 28 May 1910.

John H. SHOUN, age 56 years, married, place of birth: Johnson Co. TN (Pandora), death cause: "consumption", death record #: 47913, date of death: 2 Mar 1910.

Cleveland GRIFFEY, age 23 years, married, place of birth: TN, cause of death: "boiler explosion", death record #: 47914, date of death: 5 Jul 1910.

Jessie R. WHITE, age 34 years, married, place of birth: Johnson Co. TN (Butler), cause of death: illegible, death record #: 47915, died: 23 May 1910.

D.C. HACKNEY, female, age 14 years, place of birth: Johnson Co. TN, cause of death: "inflammation of bowels", death record #: 47916, died: 5 Jun 1910.

Frank EGGERS, born: 15 Aug 1914, parents: Charles Eggers and Emma Norris, cause of death: "unknown", informant: Noah Pennington, burial: Valley Cemetery, died: date not stated, buried: 25 Jan 1914.

George PROFFITT, age 10 years and 9 months, parents: Monroe Proffitt and Myrtle Wagner, cause of death: "spinal meningitis", informant: R.B. Viney, death record # 12, burial: Vaughts Cem., died: 10 Jan 1914.

Ogn PHILLIPS, male, born: 20 Aug 1862 in Watauga Co. NC, parents: Wm Phillips (Watauga Co., NC) and Bettie Nichels (Ashe Co. NC), cause of death: "hemorage due to alcoholism", death record # 11, informant: W.F. Williams, date of death: 25 Jan 1914.

Judge WALKER, male, born: 3 Jan 1913, parents: John Yancy Calvin Walker and Ellen White Heaton, death cause: "pneumonia", record # 10, died: 30 Jan 1914.

Henry Clay HEATON, born: 29 Jul 1895, parents: Johnnie
Heaton (TN) and Celia Deloach (TN), cause of death:
"heart disease and lung congestion", informant: J.A.
Heaton, death record #: 9, burial: Shouns Cemetery,
date of death: 17 Jan 1914.
Carl MAIN, born 30 Sep 1913, parents: father not
stated and (first name illegible) Main, death cause:
"bold hives", death record #: 8, died: 15 Jan 1914.
Abraham Lincoln WALLACE, born: 30 March 1901, parents:
James H. Wallace and Elmira Ellison (Ashe Co. NC),
cause of death: "suicide by hanging", informant: J.M.
Wallace, death record #: 7, died: 15 Jan 1914.
Garland S. F.... (illegible), colored, born: 7 Jan
1914, parents: father's name not stated and Maggie
Fuller (? illegible), mother born: Washington Co., VA,
cause of death: "heart disease", death record #: 5,
died: 7 Jan 1914.
Mrs. Angeline PARRY, born: 27 Nov 1881, parents: John
F. Nelson (TN) and Julia Nelson (TN), death cause:
"palegra", death record #: 4, died 2 Jan 1914.
Sarah FIPPS (PHIPPS), born: 6 Oct 1881, place of
birth: Dopson NC, parents: James Edwards (NC) and
(first name not stated) Hayes (NC), cause of death:
"heart disease", informant: David S. Phipps, death
record #: 5, died: 30 Jan 1914.
Walter Glenn SNYDER, born: 20 Jan 1912 in Johnson Co.
TN (Shouns), parents: A.J. Snyder (NC) and Caroline
Wallace (Trade), cause of death: "gastritis, eating
excessive amount of beans", informant: A.J. Snyder,
death record #: 2, died: 20 Jan 1914.
Lola ROBINSON, born: 3 Jan 1889 in South Dakota,
parents: W.H. Davis and Winnie Davis, cause of death:
"tuberculosis", death record #: 1, informant: C.C.
Wilson, buried: Shouns Cemetery, died: 15 Jan 1914.
James Henry OSBORNE, born: 23 Aug 1898, parents:
St..(illegible) Osborne (Ashe Co. NC) and Inez Shupe
(TN), cause of death: "tuberculosis and meningitis",
informant: John Phillippi, death record #: 21, burial:
Phillippi Cemetery, died: 6 Feb 1914.
Stacy OSBORN, born: 17 Sep 1883 in NC, lumber
inspector, parents: W.L. Osborne (NC) and Lizzie King
(Ashe Co. NC), death cause: "tumor of brain", inform-
ant: A.C. Brooks, record #: 20, died: 12 Feb 1914.
John WATSON, age 40 years, born in Johnson Co. TN
(10th District), parents: William Watson (NC) and
Saran Bunton (NC), cause of death: "bowels locked",
died: 23 Jan 1914.

Cornelia GENTRY, age 70 years, place of birth: Johnson Co. TN, parents: General Gentry and Louisa Rambo, cause of death: "brights disease and broken hip", informant: H.C. Gentry, death record #: 18, buried: Wilson Cemetery, died: 5 Feb 1914.

Stacy STOUT, born: 29 Nov 1913, place of birth: Johnson Co. TN, parents: Stanley S. Stout and Vennie Slimp, death cause: "unknown", informant: J.E. Stout, death record #: 17, buried: Neva, died: 14 Feb 1914

William Kyle MOODY, age not stated, place of birth: Johnson Co. TN, parents: Edward Moody (Watauga Co. NC) and Zola Morefield, cause of death: "no medical aid, died suddent", informant: T.L. Moody, death record #: 16, died: 12 Feb 1914.

Liane Victoria WARD, born: 30 Sep 1913, parents: James Ward and Callie Arnold, cause of death: "fits or convulsions", informant: N.C. Tester, death record #: 15, died 20 Feb 1914.

Bro.. (illegible) ELLIOTT, age about 42, parents: Thomas Elliott (Carter Co. TN) and Frankie Pierce (?) (Carter Co. TN), cause of death: "tuberculosis", informant: B.M. Elliott, death record #: 14, buried: Howard Cemetery, died: 10 Feb 1914.

Unnamed STOUT, female, born 7 Mar 1914, parents: Samuel Stout and Ethel Garland, death cause:"unknown", buried: Heaton Cem., record #: 33, died: 9 Mar 1914.

Elizabeth Wilson, age about 70, parents: Alford Wilson and Rosa Hawkins, death cause: "appoplecty or supposed died suddent", record #: 32, died: 21 Mar 1914.

Unnamed Adams, sex not stated, parents: Wm James Adams and Martha Louise Church, cause of death: "abortion", death record #: 31, died: 30 Mar 1914.

Ernest SHUPE, born: 7 Feb 1914, parents: Troy Shupe and Nancy Fenner, cause of death: "croup", death record #: 30, died: 29 Mar 1914.

Eli Harper, male, born: 3 Jun 1832, parents: Wm Harper (NC) and Delilah Miller (NC), cause of death: "heart dropsy", informant: H.M. Miller, death record #: 29, buried: Wilson Cemetery, died: 26 Mar 1914.

Anna ARNOLD, born 20 Jun 1829, place of birth: Johnson Co. TN (Shouns), parents: Jarett Arnold and Ladise Reece (Trade), cause of death: "paralysis and le grippe", death record #: 28, died: 11 Mar 1914.

Radanill SHEPHARD, male, born: 3 Nov 1913, parents: R.M. Shephard and Biner Pope (Ashe Co. NC), cause of death: "unknown", death record #: 27, died 3 Mar 1914.

Thomas ALLEN, born: 2 Feb 1914, parents: Carter Allen
(Ashe Co. NC) and Sallie Stout (Shouns), cause of
death: "unknown", record #: 26, died: 3 Mar 1914.
John B. DAVIS, born: 26 Apr 1845, place of birth: NC,
parents: James Davis (NC) and Fannie Bryant (NC),
cause of death: "sclerosis of liver", informant: D.F.
Miller, death record #: 25, died 25 Mar 1914.
I.. (illegible) NELSON, born 16 Jun 1914, parents:
father not stated and Maggie Wagner, cause of death:
unknown, buried: Shingletown Cemetery, death record #:
24, died 20 Mar 1914.
Unnamed GREER, male, born: 18 Mar 1914, parents:
Samuel B. Greer and Rosa E. Taliner (?) (VA), cause of
death: stillborn, death record #: 22, died: 18 Mar
1914.
Unnamed male, parents: father not stated and Delilah
York, cause of death: stillborn, death record #: 23,
died: 2 Mar 1914.
Elizabeth C...(illegible), age 77 years, place of
birth: Johnson Co. TN, parents: John Proffitt and Lila
Robinson, cause of death: "pneumonia", death record #:
41, died: 10 Apr 1914.
Sarah LIPFORD, age 87 years, born 1827, parents:
Abraham Whaley (NC) and Dicey Justice (TN), cause of
death: "pneumonia", informant: A.A. Lipford, death
record #: 40, buried: Whaley Cem., died: 23 Apr 1914.
Unnamed WALKER, sex not recorded, parents: Julious
Walker (Watauga Co. NC) and Mary Harmon (Watauga Co.
NC), death cause: not stated, informant: Walter
Harmon, record #: 39, born/died: 24 Apr 1914.
Catherine MCELYEA, age 81 years, widow, parents:
Richard R. Tester and Rebecca Jackson, cause of death:
"heart disease", informant: Alex Tester, death record
#: 38, died 22 Apr 1914.
Unnamed LEWIS, male, born: 14 Apr 1914, parents: G.F.
Lewis (Ashe Co. NC) and R.L. Potter, cause of death:
"diphtheria", death record #: 37, died: 16 Apr 1914.
Martin E. BLEVINS, born: 17 Apr 1868, parents: W.W.
Blevins (NC) and Sarah E. Blevins (TN), cause of
death: "paralysis", death record #: 36, buried: Shady,
died: 22 Apr 1914.
Sarah Jane NEELY, age 84 years, born 1830, parents:
David Genrty (NC) and Sarah Buckner (NC), cause of
death: "paralysis", informant: J.O. Neely, buried:
Gentry Cemetery, death record #: 35, died: 5 Apr 1914.
James Millen TRIPLET, born: 25 Mar 1912, parents: John
Triplet (NC) and Lizzie Davis (NC), cause of death:
"pneumonia", death record #: 33, buried: Wills
Cemetery, died: 14 Apr 1914.

David V. STOUT, born: 25 Feb 1843, parents: John H.
Stout and Esther Heaton, cause of death: "chronic
....?", informant: J. B. Stout, death record #: 30,
buried: Shouns Cemetery, died: 14 May 1914.
James H. SNYDER, born: 7 Dec 1876, parents: Hamilton
Snyder (Ashe Co. NC) and Catherine Phipps (Ashe Co.
NC), cause of death: "revolver wounds, homicide,
instant death", death record #: 49, died: 30 May 1914.
Edith Mae PRICE, born: 14 May 1914, parents: Wilford
Price and Della Cornett, cause of death: unknown,
informant: Della Powell, record 48, died 25 May 1914.
Elbert J. DUNN, born: 17 Apr 1878, parents: Godfrey B.
Dunn and Rachel Wilson, death cause: "typhoid" fever",
informant: J.B. Dunn, record #: 47, died: 15 May 1914.
William Lacy OWENS, born: 28 Jul 1873, parents:
William Owens and Alice Heaton, cause of death:
"indigestion", informant: George Heaton, death record
#: 46, died 29 May 1914.
Lillie Aretta KEATON, born: date not stated, place of
birth: Sullivan Co. TN, parents: F.F. Keaton (Sullivan
Co. TN) and N.V. Cornett (Carter Co. TN), cause of
death: unknown, death record #: 45, buried: Gentry
Cemetery, died: 10 May 1914.
Samuel GILBERT, age about 19 years, parents: father
not stated and Rebecca Gilbert, cause of death:
"consumption", death record #: 44, died: 4 May 1914.
Carl B. SHORES, born: 18 Mar 1887, married, parents:
Wm Shores and Aisie Woods (NC), cause of death:
"tuberculosis", informant: Charity Shores, record #:
43, buried: Laurel Bloomery, died: 11 May 1914.
William Franklin BUSSELL, born: 31 Oct 1838, place of
birth: Wilkes Co. NC, parents: Poisley Bussell and
Polley Martin, death cause: "bronchitis", informant:
Sarah A. Bussell, record #: 42, died 28 May 1914.
Mary D. SAPP, married, born: 12 Jun 1887, parents:
Thomas Roberts and Peggy Lewis (NC), cause of death:
illegible, informant: J.C Lewis, death record #: 56,
died: 2 Jun 1914.
William Marvin BLACKBURN, born: 16 Jun 1913, parents:
R.O. Blackburn and Eva Robinson, cause of death:
"hydro...(illegible)", informant: R.O. Blackburn,
death record #: 55, buried: Howard Cem., died 28 Jun
1914.
Mary EGGERS, born: 16 Jun 1914, parents: Grant Eggers
and Retta Lunceford, cause of death: unknown, death
record #: 54, died: 2 Jul 1914.

40

Engleton WALLACE, born: 11 Oct 1912, parents: Roby Wallace and Mollie Gentry, cause of death: "died without medical attention", informant: E.L. McDulle, death record #: 53, died 30 Jun 1914.

Edgar Boyd SLIMP, born: 12 Mar 1902, parents: Frederick Slimp and Martha Stout, cause of death: "accidental drowning in Roans Creek", death record #: 52, died: 19 Jun 1914.

Daniel NEATHERLY, married, age 62 years, parents: father not stated and Betty Neatherly, cause of death: "consumption", death record #: 51, died 3 Jun 1914.

John CROSSWHITE, married, born: 28 May 1829, parents: William Crosswhite and Nancy Linzz, cause of death: "died without medical attendance – supposed to be old age", informant: G.J. Walsh, buried: old home place, death record #: 124, died: 8 Jul 1914.

Unnamed HAWKINS, female, date of birth not stated, parents: M.F. Hawkins and Nellie Main, cause of death: "unknown", death record #: 123, died: 13 Jul 1914.

S.M. GOODMAN, male, married, date of birth not stated, place of birth: VA, parents: unknown, cause of death: "died without medical attendance, died suddenly as fell dead", informant: Mollie Johnson (Shouns), death record #: 122, died: 25 Jul 1914.

Evert Hillery POTTER, born: 23 Jul 1914, parents: B.F. Hodge and Alice Potter, cause of death: stillborn, informant: Alice Potter (Shouns), death record #: 121, died: 23 Jul 1914.

Sarah E. BLEVINS, born: 14 Jul 1841, widow, place of birth: Johnson Co. TN, parents: William Blevins (Sullivan Co. TN) and Catherine M. Berry, death cause: "abdominal dropsy", informant: George S. Blevins, buried: Shady, record #: 132, died: 20 Aug 1914.

Martha HARPER, widow, born: 1 Jul 1844, place of birth: Ashe Co. NC, parents: John Miller and mother unknown, cause of death: "paralysis", informant: H.M. Miller, death record #: 131, died: 24 Aug 1914.

Rildey ROARK, female, age 41 years, parents: Landon Snyder (Ashe Co. NC) and Liley Price (Ashe Co. NC), cause of death: "pellagra", informant: T.A. Stevens, buried: Gentry Cem., record #: 130, died: 1 Aug 1914.

Infant NORRIS, male, born: 30 Aug 1914, parents: Eldridge Mack Norris (Watauga Co. NC) and Nancy Jane Bunton, cause of death: stillborn, informant: E.M. Norris (Butler), record #: 129, died 30 Aug 1914.

Walter B. VAUGHT, born: 4 Apr 1899, parents: John H. Vaught and Joda M. Lineback (Carter Co. TN), cause of death: "typhoid fever", informant: J.H. Vaught, death record #: 128, died: 30 Aug 1914.

D...(illegible) BOWMAN, black, male, born: 19 Oct 1912, parents: Thomas Bowman and Millie Monley, cause of death: "cholera", informant: informant: Thomas Bowman (Butler), record #: 127, died: 4 Jul 1914.

Joda M. VAUGHT, female, married, born: 9 Jul 1872, parents: Henry Lineback and Latta Wilson, cause of death: "typhoid fever", informant: John H. Vaught, buried: Butler, death record #: 126, died: 7 Sep 1914.

John Linville CHURCH, age about 55 years, married, parents: Jesse C. Church (NC) and Martha Wilson (NC), death cause: "heart failure", informant: J.L. Church, buried: Shouns Cem., record #: 125, died: 25 Aug 1914.

Lora Lee PLEASANT, born: 8 Jul 1914, parents: Garfield A. Pleasant and Ella Treadway (Siam, Carter Co. TN), cause of death: "cold", buried: Rambo Cem., informant: Garfield Pleasant, record #: 137, died: 27 Sep 1914.

Elih... (illegible) Alexander SHOUN, married, born: 3 Jun 1839, parents: Isaac Shoun and Mary Wills, cause of death: "paralysis", buried: "home cemetery", death record #: 136, died 6 Sep 1914.

Gayal Medford WALKER, male, born: 7 Jun 1914, parents: A.J. Walker (Wilkes Co. NC) and Rebecca Morefield, cause of death: "acute indigestion - feeding on unmodified cows milk", informant: S.A. Hodge, buried: Gentry Cem., death record #: 135 died: 20 Sep 1914.

James J. MOSTEY, born: 28 Mar 1849, widower, parents: George Mostey and Hannah Razor, cause of death: "pneumonia", informant: O.B. Haney, death record #: 134, died: 15 Sep 1914.

Mrs. Nettie MAY, born 21 Jan 1829, place of birth: NC, married, parents: J.S. Stanbery (NC) and M.A. McNiel (NC), cause of death: "tuberculosis of lungs", death record #: 133, died: 17 Sep 1914.

Infant SAYLOR, female, age 16 months and 25 days, parents: John Saylor and Sarah Saylor (Carter Co. TN), cause of death: "pulmonary tuberculosis", buried: Phillippi Cem., record #: 356, died: 12 Jul 1914.

W.D. JOHNSON, born: Dec 1857, parents: T.A. Johnson and Mary Johnson (Wilkes Co. NC), cause of death: "consumption", informant: J.W. Johnson, death record #: 357, died: 24 Apr 1914.

Alfred C. PARRY, born 3 Nov 1846, parents: G.W.D. Parry (VA) and Mary Fraker (TN), cause of death: "le grippe", death record #: 358, died: 10 Mar 1914.

James FENNER, age 82 years, 3 months and 26 days, married, parents: Jake Fenner and mother's name not stated, cause of death: "complications of lungs and heart", informant: S.L. Harbin, death record #: 355, died: 30 Apr 1914.

Bertha Arker (surname illegible), married, born: 14
Apr 1880, parents: Mitchell Cress and ? Cress (VA),
cause of death: "ulcer of stomach", informant: F.W.
Cress, death record #: 359, died: 31 May 1914.
John Harrison PROFETT, age 74 years, parents: John H.
Profett and Lyde Robinson, cause of death: "pneumonia
fever", buried: Profett Cemetery, death record #: 361,
died: 19 Aug 1914.
George W. MADRON, widower, born: 1 Nov 1825, place of
birth: Wilkes Co. NC, parents: Jack Madron (Wilkes Co.
NC) and Lida Coinstner (Wilkes Co. NC), cause of
death: "acute heart failure", informant: George W.
Madron, Jr., buried: Arrendell Cemetery, death record
#: 362, died: 11 Oct 1914.
Sallie S. CARIER, born 5 Nov 1912, parents: Alva
Carier and Salie Snyder, cause of death: "croup",
informant: M.L. Minks, cause of death: croup, death
record #: 363, died: 5 Oct 1914.
Samantha L. MANUEL, born: 1 Oct 1898 in Watauga Co.,
NC, parents: D.C. Manuel (Wilkes Co. NC) and Julia
Michalls (Wilkes Co. NC), cause of death: "gun shot
wound in face accidentally fired by small brother,
death almost instant", record #: 364, died 5 Oct 1914.
Sallie NEATHERLY, born: 20 Feb 1825, parents: William
Neatherly and Margaret Snyder, cause of death:
"general weakness, no medical aid called", informant:
D.W. Mink, death record #: 365, died: 24 Nov 1914.
Lantie V. STOUT, female, born: 28 Feb 1914, parents:
J.M. Stout and Nellie Hodge (Watauga Co. NC), cause of
death: "croup", informant: W.R. Walker, death record
#: 360, died: 11 Nov 1914.
Infant HAMMONS, born 9 Nov 1914, parents: W.M. Hammons
and Sarah Forrester, cause of death: "died without
medical attention", informant: W.M. Hammons, death
record #: illegible, died 10 Nov 1914.
Jerry LAWS, born: 19 Apr 1855, married, parents:
William Laws and mother's name illegible, death cause:
"heart disease", record #: 373, died: 27 Nov 1914.
Flora Lee JENKINS, born: 15 May 1910, parents: Ransom
L. Jenkins and Annie Corum, cause of death: "acute
membranous laryngitis", informant: R. L. Jenkins,
buried: Acre Field, record #: 359, died 9 Nov 1914.
Chelcy Mary ROBINSON, born: 22 Dec 1885, married,
parents: Thomas J. Walsh and Elvine Crosswhite, cause
of death: "tuberculosis, invalid for 5 years",
informant: Roby F. Walsh, death record #: illegible,
died: 17 Mar 1914.

Infant ROBINSON, female, born: 10 Nov 1914, parents: Daniel S.C. Robinson and Sarafina E. Smith, cause of death: stillborn, record #: 371, died: 10 Nov 1914.

Tann ? Rew ? BLACKBURN, male, born: 18 Jun 1914, parents: N.J. Blackburn (Watauga Co. NC) and E.C. Garland, cause of death: "spinal meningitis", buried: Gentry Cem., death record #: 379, died: 20 Nov 1914.

Calvin LONG, born: 17 Jun 1827, married, blacksmith, parents: Jefferson Long (NC) and Nancy Woody (NC), cause of death: "chronic ... (illegible)", buried: Stout Cemetery, informant: C.R. Long, death record #: 373, died 9 Dec 1914.

Nancy ROBINSON, age 54 years, divorced, parents: Merida Arnold and Hannah Heaton, cause of death: "tuberculosis", informant: J.W. Rambo, buried: Neva Cemetery, death record #: illegible, died 19 Dec 1914.

Ida P. JONES, born: 22 Dec 1914, parents: Roby A. Jones (NC) and Mary J. Hartschel (NC), cause of death: "died without medical attendance, found dead in bed at 5 A.M.", death record #: 12, died: 31 Dec 1914.

Mary HAYWORTH, born: 1 Oct 1914, parents: Walter Hayworth and Callie ....(illegible), cause of death: "died without medical attendance, found dead in bed", death record #: 13, died: 30 Dec 1914.

David BUMGARDNER, born: 15 Jul 1820, place of birth: Wilkes Co. NC, parents: John Bumgardner (Wilkes Co. NC) and Barbara Houck (Wilkes Co. NC), cause of death: "fall on Jan 7, 1915", buried: Snyder Cemetery, informant: G.W. Bumgardner (Trade), died: 11 Jan 1915.

Luveny SHEETS, female, age 37 years, married, parents: William Watson (Raleigh NC) and Susuan Bunton (Wilkes Co. NC), cause of death: "pneumonia fever", buried: Dugger Cem., informant: William Watson (Butler), died: 22 Jan 1915.

Mary E. SHOUN, widow, age 20 years, parents names illegible, buried: Shouns Cemetery, cause of death: "tuberculosis", died: 27 Jan 1915.

Myrtle Ruth SWIFT, age 1 year, 5 months and 29 days, parents: David Hamilton Swift and Alice Arnold, cause of death: pneumonia, buried: "near home place", informant: D.H. Nave, died: 8 Jan 1915.

Mary STANTON, widow, born: 10 Jan 1832, parents: John Dugger and Rody Cable, cause of death: dropsy, informant: Joseph Green (Butler), died: 7 Jan 1915.

Justin Greer WILSON, born: 11 May 1915, parents: Zederic Wilson and Elba Johnson (Boone NC), cause of death: "infection of stomach", buried: Stanton Cem., informant: Zederic Wilson (Butler), died: 30 Jan 1915.

Rit WATSON, age 48 years, parents: ? Watson and Susuan Bunton (Wilkes Co. NC), cause of death: "pralicies", buried: Dugger Cemetery, informant: William Watson (Butler), died: 2 Jan 1915.

Elizabeth SNYDER, widow, age about 89 years, parents: Nicholas Stout and Katy Wagner, cause of death: "no medical attendance, found dead in bed", informant: Jacob Snyder (Shouns), died: 11 Jan 1915.

Conley CURD, born: 8 Dec 1914, parents: Conley Payne and Mary Curd, death cause: "child found dead in bed", informant: Mary Curd (Shouns), died: 28 Jan 1915.

Infant PATTON, female, parents: Thomas R. Patton (Mitchell Co. NC) and Liza N. Dunn (Ashe Co. NC), cause of death: stillborn, buried: Blevins Cemetery, informant: T.R. Patton, died: 5 Jan 1915.

William M. BOMAN, born: 1 Aug 1853, married, parents: Christopher Boman (Carter Co. TN) and Sarafinal Johnson (Carter Co. TN), cause of death: heart disease, buried: Unicoi Co. TN, informant: Mrs. ? Boman, died; 26 Jan 1915.

Clyde ? VESTAL, born: 12 Jan 1915, parents: Wade Vestal (VA) and Alice McElyea, cause of death: not stated, buried: Shingletown Cem., died: 14 Jan 1915.

Mamie Ruth SMITH, born: 15 Nov 1915, parents: William H. Smith and Pearl Tester, cause of death: bold hives, informant: J.M. Wagner (Neva), died: 25 Jan 1915.

Youreethy Ively DUGGER, female, born: 2 Jun 1914, parents: William Dugger and Loura Deen (Green Co. TN), death cause: "pneumonia fever", buried: Dugger Cem., died: 1 Feb 1915.

Juanita Jane GREGG, born: 11 May 1914, parents: Joseph H. Gregg and Martha C. White, cause of death: pneumonia fever, informant: J. H. Gregg (Butler), buried: Crosswhite Cemetery, died: 7 Feb 1915.

Cathena Sizemore LONG, widow, age 76 years, parents: ? Stamper (NC) and ? Sizemore (NC), cause of death: heart disease, died: 19 Feb 1915.

Infant GILLILAND, parents: Will B. Gilliland and Lillie b. Osborn (NC), cause of death: unknown, buried: Acre Field Cemetery, informant: W.W. Widner (Laurel Bloomery), died: 7 Feb 1915.

Susan Jane HAWKINS, married, born 21 Jan 1850, parents: John Grace and Margaret Ward, cause of death: illegible, buried: Eggers Cemetery, informant: Miss Bess Hawkins (Laurel Bloomery), died: 11 Feb 1915.

Mrs. Sallie A. VAUGHT, born 10 Dec 1852, married, parents: Archibald Grant and Margaret Orr (Wash Co. VA), cause of death: "serosis of liver caused by jaundice", informant: H.T. Grant, died: 8 Feb 1915.

Clyde CROW, born 8 Mar 1915, parents: Charles Crow (Carter Co. TN) and Julia Ellen Robinson, cause of death: typhoid fever, informant: Malissa Robinson (Mountain City), died 9 Mar 1915.

Fred TOLIVER, born 6 Apr 1914, parents: M.A. Toliver (Wash Co. VA) and Dora Stanbery (Ashe Co. NC), cause of death: acute indigestion, buried: Gentry Cemetery, died: 20 Mar 1915.

Susan E. WATSON, age 72 years, widow, parents: names unknown, death cause: "paralysis on one side", buried: Blevins Cem., informant: A.F. Mays, died: 25 Mar 1915.

Clyde CROW, born 28 Jan 1914, parents: Charlie Crow (Carter Co. TN) and Julie Ellen Robinson, cause of death: pneumonia, buried: Brookshire Cem., informant: Malissa Robinson (Mountain City), died: 7 Mar 1915.

Jonathon Thomas HAMMONS, born: 6 Dec 1889, married, parents: William Hammons and Sarah Forrester, cause of death: pulmonary tuberculosis, died: 3 Mar 1915.

Darnell EASTRIDGE, born: 3 Mar 1913, parents: A.C. Eastridge and Martha Curd (NC), cause of death: unknown, buried: Laurel Spring Cem., died: 3 Mar 1915.

William BAILEY, date of birth not stated, parents: not stated, cause of death: epileptic convulsions, heart failure, informant: Ezekial Fritts, died: 21 May 1915.

Infant MATHERLY, female, parents: Edward Matherly and Georgia Mae Cress, death cause: "stillborn", informant: J.B. Matherly, buried: Matherly Cem., died 21 Mar 1915.

Thomas M. GREER, born: 30 Jun 1882, married, parents: James Greer and Julia A. Carrol (NC), cause of death: tuberculosis, informant: Joseph H. Robinson, buried: Campbell Cemetery, died; 25 Mar 1915.

Sallie TESTER, born: 10 Oct 1844, married, parents: Nathaniel Tester and Nancy McElyea, death cause: "heart dropsy", informant: N.T. Tester (Neva), died: 30 Mar 1915.

Ollie MCCULOCH, female, born: 12 Apr 1865, parents: Rhuben Fletcher and Betsy Moreland, cause of death: "tuberculosis", informant: W.M. Millhorn (Baker's Gap), died: 20 Mar 1915.

Fred MAHALA, parents: David D. Mahala (Ashe Co. NC) and Caroline Greer, cause of death: stillborn, died: 24 Mar 1915.

Vennie L. MCFADDIN, born: 2 Feb 1915, parents: John M. McFaddin and Nora Reece (Watauga Co. NC), cause of death: diphtheria, informant: John McFaddin (Trade), buried: Reece Cemetery, died: 16 Mar 1915.

Nancy L. MADRON, born: 13 Mar 1836, parents: Roland Jenkins and Anna Widby, cause of death: "le grippe", informant: John S. Main (Trade), buried: Jenkins Cemetery, died: 16 Mar 1915.

Catherine MILLER, married, born: 9 Sep 1851, place of birth: Watauga Co. NC, parents: Ephram Miller (Watauga Co. NC) and Mary Isaacs (Watauga Co. NC), death cause: "cancer of stomach", informant: Mary Isaacs (Watauga Co. NC.), buried: Arnold Cem., died 1 Mar 1915.

Amanda LUNCEFORD, born: 23 Aug 1914, parents: Z.D. Lunceford (Watauga Co. NC) and Venia Coalman (Watauga Co. NC), death cause: "grippe", informant: Z.D. Lunceford (Butler), buried: Lunceford Cem., died: 25 Mar 1915.

Rosa V. REECE, born: 11 Feb 1892, single, parents: V.B. Reece and A.M. Dugger, cause of death: "pulmonary consumption", informant: V.B. Reece (Butler), buried: Dugger Cemetery, died: 15 Mar 1915.

Thelma MOREFIELD, parents: Elmer Morefield and Bertha Abel, cause of death: stillborn, informant: Elmer Morefield (Laurel Bloomery), died: 6 Mar 1915.

Bertha MOREFIELD, age 21 years, married, parents: Robert Abel and Martha Pennington (VA), cause of death: "endo-carditis", informant: Ed. Abel (Laurel Bloomery), died: 21 Mar 1915.

Robert Martin GENTRY, born 19 Dec 1868, married, parents: Richard Gentry and Sarah Gilliland, cause of death: "facial ensyphelas", informant; Wm. Gentry (Laurel bloomery), buried: Taylor's Valley, died: 23 Mar 1915,

Elizabeth WALEN, date of birth not recorded, place of birth: NC, parents: Henry ? and ? Powers, cause of death: le grippe, informant: Wiley Rupard (Laurel Bloomery), died: 12 Apr 1915.

James W. MCELYEA, born: 5 Apr 1915, parents: Jas Davis and Ollie McElyea, cause of death: croup, informant: Pearl McElyea (Neva), died: 11 Apr 1915.

Selmer CAMPBELL, born: 16 Sep 1914, parents: Isaac Campbell and Laura S. Garland, cause of death: "unknown - died suddenly", informant: J.L. Garland (Crandell) died: 6 Apr 1915.

Infant STEVENS, parents: E.E. Stevens (Ashe Co. NC) and N.N. Bishop, cause of death: stillborn, buried: Blevins Cemetery, died: 10 Apr 1915.

John C... MILLER, born: 16 Feb 1914, parents: Luther Miller and Rebecca Fletcher, cause of death: illegible, buried: Gentry Cemetery, died 21 Apr 1915.

47

Sophia SHOEMAKER, born 1 Oct 1913, parents: C.C. Shoemaker and Rowena Proffitt, cause of death: whooping cough, informant: C.C. Shoemaker (Laurel Bloomery), died: 30 Apr 1915.
Jane WILSON, age about 56 years, single, parents: Hezakiah Wilson and ? Rhudy, cause of death: "autotoxemia, chronic gastro-intestinal indigestion", died: 16 Apr 1915.
Delilah MOREFIELD, age about 85 years, widow, parents: ? West and mother unknown, cause of death: "volvular heart disease", informant: Sam Neely (Laurel Bloomery), buried: Acre Field Cem., died 15 Apr 1915.
Muncy RAGAN, male, born 14 Feb 1915, parents: Gordon Ragan (Watauga Co. NC) and Laura Reece, cause of death: "unknown, child found dead in bed", Informant: John McFaddin (Trade), buried: Reece Cem., died 12 Apr 1915.
John H. DOWELL, born 5 Mar 1915, parents: father not stated and Callie Dowell, cause of death: diphtheria, informant: Sherman Dowell (Trade), buried: Dowell Cemetery, died: 6 Apr 1915.
Caroline MAHALA, age 38 years, married, parents: Alexander Greer (Ashe Co. NC) and Nancy Osborn (Ashe Co. NC), cause of death: "reported pneumonia", informant: David T. Mahala (Trade), died: 1 Apr 1915.
James H. WALLACE, born: 8 Apr 1855, married, parents: D... Wallace and Elizabeth Snyder, cause of death: unknown, informant: G.M. Love (Trade), buried: Wallace Cemetery, died 23 Apr 1915.
John H. SOUTH, born about 1860 in North Carolina, parents: Britain South (NC) and Annie Hamba (NC), cause of death: "epilepsy", informant: T.J. Church (Baker's Gap), buried: NC, died: 22 Apr 1915.
Ollaf Bell JOHNSON, female, born 26 Feb 1915, parents: Andrew C. Johnson (NC), and Clary M. Martin, cause of death: "died without medical attendanced", informant: A.C. Johnson (Shouns), died: 16 Apr 1915.
Susan MICHAEL, born: 4 Nov 1825, widow, parents: ? Morefield and mother unknown, cause of death: unknown, informant: R.L. Jenkins (Laurel Bloomery), buried: Michaels Cemetery, died: 7 May 1915.
Bonnie L. WINTERS, female, born 4 May 1915, parents: Wm V. Winters and Ollie Jenkins, cause of death:: not recorded, informant: John Winters (Laurel Bloomery), buried: Acre Field Cemetery, died 10 May 1915.
Della Ann OWENS, age 19 years, single, parents: John B. Owens and Francis Forrester, cause of death: not reported, informant: R.B. Forrester (Mountain City), buried: Cornett Cemetery, died: 15 May 1915.

Sarah Jane GRAYSON, age 63 years, widow, born in North Carolina, parents: John Jones (NC) and Lydia Latham (NC), death cause: not reported, buried: Oak Cem., died 26 May 1915.

Louisa FRITTS, born: 7 Jan 1840, married, parents: Louis Poarch (NC) and Susa Carby (NC), cause of death: "pneumonia", informant: A.J. Fritts (Doeville), died: 28 May 1915.

Nancy GRINDSTAFF, born: 1834, married, parents: David Robinson and mother's name unknown, cause of death: "cancer of womb", informant: Wilburn Grindstaff (Doe), died: 13 May 1915.

David Spencer MATHERLY, born 1 May 1913, parents: John Matherly and Lillie Wagner (Carter Co. TN), cause of death: "abscess", informant: Fred Matherly (Butler), buried: Matherly Cemetery, died: 30 May 1915.

Blanch HOCKADAY, born: 3 June 1892, single, parents: George Hockaday and Moriah Shoun, cause of death: tuberculosis of lungs, buried: Wilson Cem., informant: J.W. Dillon (Mountain City), died: 26 May 1915.

Sarah L. MAYS, born 1843, widow, parents: Andrew Nelson and Matilda ?, cause of death: "old age", informant: W.A. Mays (Crandell), buried: Blevins Cemetery, died: 4 May 1915.

Ora M. WALLACE, male, age 23 years, parents: Joseph Wallace and Callie St...., cause of death: "acute indigestion for one day", informant: Roby Wallace (Mountain City), buried: Trade TN, died: 30 May 1915.

Ralph E. HOCKEY, born: 19 ? 1896, parents: George Hockey (VA) and Alice Jenkins, cause of death: "tuberculosis of larynx", died: 24 Jun 1915.

Infant WARD, male, parents: James Asa Ward and Mary Ann Morefield, cause of death: not recorded, informant: N.M. Wilson (Crandell), buried: Gentry Cemetery, born/died: 21 Jun 1915.

George Washington WINTERS, parents: Wm H. Winters and Mary M. Moore, death cause: illegible, informant: Stacy McElyea (Laurel Bloomery), born/died: 14 Jun 1915.

Mary M. WINTERS, age 36 years, parents: Thomas Moore and Margaret Moore, cause of death: illegible (something to do with childbirth), informant: W.M. Winters (Laurel Bloomery), buried: Oak Cemetery, died: 29 Jun 1915.

Dane POTTER, born 2 Jun 1915, parents: Arthur Potter and Laurrie Dotson, cause of death: "died without medical attendanced", died: 11 Jun 1915.

49

Infant MCELYEA, female, parents: Millard McElyea and
Sarafina Tester, cause of death: premature birth,
born/died: 10 Jun 1915.
David S. VAUGHT, born: 6 Oct 1860, parents: J.B.
Vaught and Rachel Wagner, cause of death:
tuberculosis, died: 26 Jun 1915.
Alfred Taylor STALCUP, born: 28 Feb 1876, married,
parents: John H. Stalcup and Elizabeth Robinson, cause
of death: brights disease, informant: W.L. Gentry
(Butler), buried: Stalcup Cemetery, died: 5 Jun 1915.
William PROFFITT, born: 29 Jun 1829, married, parents:
John Proffitt and Lydia Robinson, cause of death:
cancer, informant: F.S. Proffit (Doeville), buried:
Proffitt Cemetery, died: 10 Jun 1915.
Ramin L. WILCOX, Born 25 Jun 1915, parents: Mark
Wilcox (Ashe Co. NC) and Alice Trivett (Ashe Co. NC),
informant: Mark Wilcox (Trade), cause of death:
"hypertrophy of liver", buried: Dotson Family
Cemetery, died: 17 Jul 1915.
Lucy BOWMAN, born: 7 Nov 1882, single, parents: Wm
Bowman (Unicoi Co. TN) and Elva S. Hy... (Carter Co.
TN), cause of death: tuberculosis, informant: Eva
Bowman (Butler), died: 25 Jul 1915.
Pauline OWENS, parents: Millard Owens and Bulah
Forrester, death cause: unknown, born/died: 29 Jul
1915.
Landon H. HAWKINS, born: 29 Jul 1840, married,
parents: Washington Hawkins and Elizabeth Greer, cause
of death: "? stenosis", informant: W.W. Hawkins
(Mountain City), buried: Acre Field Cemetery, died: 26
Jul 1915.
Charlie MOREFIELD, age 3 years and 9 months, born: NC,
parents: John Morefield and Martha Isaacs (NC), cause
of death: not recorded, informant: James Isaacs (Sugar
Grove, NC), died: 19 Jul 1915.
Infant PLEASANT, male, parents: Walter B. Pleasant and
Sanna Church, cause of death: stillborn, informant:
J.L. Church (Doeville), born/died: 14 Jul 1915.
Eliza L. LOWE, born: 4 Oct 1893, single, parents: U.R.
Lowe and Betty Norris (NC), cause of death: illegible,
informant: F.S. Lowe (Mountain City), died: 26 Jul
1915.
Vivian Eller BARLOW, parents: James J. Barlow and
Sarah J. Walker, cause of death: premature birth,
informant: James Barlow (Crandell), born/died: 3 Jul
1915.

Martha Ellen BLEVINS, born: 22 Feb 1849, widow, parents: Benjamin Adams (NC) and Rhoda Goodwin (Carter Co. TN), cause of death: "arthyihomia", informant: O.M. Blevins (Crandell).

Malinda LOWE, born 12 Nov 1867, married, parents: Allen Dotson (Watauga Co. NC) and Delila Pierce (Watauga Co. NC), cause of death: "dysentary", informant: J.H. Lowe (Trade), buried: Dotson Cemetery, died: 8 Jul 1915.

Elcie MOODY, parents: William Moody and Margaret Anderson, cause of death: illegible, informant: William Moody (Butler), buried: Dugger Cemetery, born/died: 11 Jul 1915.

Elmer CAMPBELL, born: Sep 1914, parents: Isaac H. Campbell and Laura Alice Garland, cause of death: cholera, informant: Lulu Garland (Doeville), buried: Campbell Cemetery, died: 3 Aug 1915.

Alice E. HOLDER, born 6 Jun 1915, parents: Isaac Thomas Holder and Alice Cole (Carter Co. TN), cause of death: cholera, informant: Isaac Thomas Holder (Doeville), buried: Campbell Cemetery, died: 16 Aug 1915.

John F. LUNCEFORD, born: 1 Aug 1842, blacksmith, parents: Enoch Lunceford (NC) and Tempa Cable, cause of death: "kidney and pneumonia", died: 24 Aug 1915.

Lillie V. PENNINGTON, born 22 Jul 1915, parents: Nick Pennington and Victoria Miller, cause of death: illegible, buried: Valley Cemetery, died: 18 Aug 1915.

Laura FRITTS, age 30 years, born: NC, parents: J. Mahaffey and mother unknown, cause of death: "pulmonary tuberculosis", informant: J. Rash (Laurel Bloomery), buried: Laurel Cemetery, died: 13 Aug 1915.

Mrs. Mattie STOUT, born: 10 Sep 1887, parents: illegible, cause of death: "pulmonary tuberculosis", buried: Shouns Cemetery, died 26 Aug 1915.

Malinda MILLER, born: Oct 1845 in Caldwell Co. NC, parents: William Cozart (Caldwell Co. NC) and Nelie Haynes (Coldwell Co. NC), cause of death: "tuberculosis of lungs", informant: Florence Reece (Trade), buried Reece Cemetery, died: 10 Aug 1915.

Eada TESTER, female, age 62 years, single, parents: Nathaniel Tester and Nancy McElyea, cause of death: dropsy, informant: S.M. Tester (Neva), died: 22 Aug 1915.

Infant SHEPARD, parents: father not stated and Bessie Shepard, cause of death: stillborn, informant: Bessie Shepard (Shouns), born/died: 11 Aug 1915.

Sarah L BROWN, born 4 Nov 1857 in North Carolina, married, parents: William R. Hodge (NC) and Nancy Triplet, cause of death: "tuberculosis of lungs", informant: M.F. Brown (Shouns), died: 9 Aug 1915.

Sabra Ann MULLINS, born: 19 Sep 1850, widow, parents: John Campbell (NC) and Docia Heaton, cause of death: illegible, informant: Alice Mullins (Doeville), died: 24 Sep 1915.

Charles MCEWEN, born: 10 Feb 1875, single, parents: E.C.R. McEwen (VA) and Manda E. Johnson (NC), cause of death: "homicidal, revolver shots", informant: L.L. Tucker (Ashland NC), died: 10 Sep 1915.

Eveline ROARK, born: 27 Nov 1909, parents: Lorence Roark (NC) and Lillie Brown (NC), cause of death: diptheria, informant: Frank Riddle (Shouns), died: 20 Sep 1915.

J.E. MOREFIELD, date of birth: illegible, parents: John Morefield and mother's name illegible, cause of death: typhoid, informant: John Morefield (Butler), died: 14 Sep 1915.

Hazie GRAYBEAL, female, born: 17 Jul 1915, parents: Oscar Graybeal (Ashe Co., NC) and Nancy Danly (Ashe Co., NC), cause of death: "acute ? ", informant: Bascomb Graybeal (Crandell), buried: Gentry Cemetery, died: 8 Sep 1915.

Sidney J. THOMAS, born: 8 Oct 1848, parents: Ezikiel Thomas (NC) and Debora Day (NC), cause of death: "rupture of ? of heart", informant: Amanda Thomas (Trade), buried: Jenkins Cemetery, died: 16 Sep 1915.

William Renfro MOREFIELD, born 1 May 1861, parents: Jas Morefield and Margaret Greer, cause of death: chronic heart disease, informant: Mrs. Emma Morefield (Laurel Bloomery), buried: Acre Field Cemetery, died: 19 Sep 1915.

Clyde ROBERTS, born: 5 May 1913, parents: Baxter Roberts and Cassie Brookshire, cause of death: pneumonia, informant: W.D. Brookshire (Doeville), buried: Wright Cemetery, died: 18 Oct 1915.

Eliza Ann SMITH, born: 9 Jan 1851 in Carter Co. TN, married, parents: David Lewis (Carter Co. TN) and ? Pierce (Carter Co. TN), cause of death: heart disease, informant: James L. Smith (Mountain City), buried: Wilson Cemetery, died: 18 Oct 1915.

Clera SNYDER, born: Jun 1865 in Ashe Co. NC, parents: Elias H. Martin (Ashe Co. NC) and Paudy Stuart, cause of death: "cancer of liver", informant: (illegible) Snyder (Trade), buried: Snyder Cemetery, died: 25 Oct 1915.

Robert Cleveland TESTER, born: 8 Jun 1885, parents: Robert D. Tester and Susanna Tester, cause of death: "general perotisos", informant: S.M. Tester (Neva), died: 7 Oct 1915.

Infant SHOUN, parents: Arthur Shoun and Grace Kite, cause of death: not stated, informant: Ora Shoun (Butler), died: 6 Oct 1915.

Infant HEABERLIN, parents: Noah Heaberlin and Ret Johnson, cause of death: stillborn, born/died: 17 Oct 1915.

Daniel Mitchell ROBERTS, born: 9 June 1901 at Wilkes Co. NC, parents: William H. Roberts (Wilkes Co. NC) and Rachel Manuel (Wilkes Co. NC), cause of death: bronchitis, buried: Blevins Cemetery, died: 10 Oct 1915.

Maggie CALAHAN, born: 25 Sep 1903 at Grayson Co. VA, parents: James Calahan (Grayson Co. VA) and Mary A. Mays (Surry Co. NC), cause of death: bronchitis, buried: Greenwood VA, died: 8 Oct 1915.

Lydia POTTER, born 13 Nov 1845, married, parents: Jacob Osborn (NC) and Margaret Curd, cause of death: heart failure, informant: T.J. Potter (Shouns), died: 15 Oct 1915.

Edward S. SHULL, born: 31 Aug 1897, parents: Nathaniel C. Shull (NC) and Laura C. Ward (TN), cause of death: "bone consumption", informant: Nathaniel C. Shull (Neva), died: 31 Nov 1915.

Betsy FORRESTER, born: 1841, single, parents: William Forrester and Nancy Greer (NC), cause of death: "ulcer of stomach", informant: Burless Shaw (Butler), died: 28 Nov 1915.

Ohalarlee (?) SIMCOX, female, born Dec 1914, parents: Thomas Simcox and Nettie Green (NC), cause of death: "acute indigestion", died: 13 Nov 1915.

Joseph Franklin ELLER, date of birth: not recorded, parents: Jesse Eller (NC) and Eliza Patrick, cause of death: not stated, informant: J.E. Sexton (Mountain City), died: 22 Nov 1915.

Hugh Rosecrans GENTRY, born 29 Sep 1915, parents: Benjamin Gentry (Carter Co. TN) and Ida S. Snyder, cause of death: "no physician, found dead in bed", buried: Gentry Cemetery, died: 19 Nov 1915.

Myrtle OSBORNE, born: 22 Apr 1897, married, parents: John Arney and Debra Davis, cause of death: illegible, informant: William Osborne (Doeville), died: 4 Nov 1915.

Rebecca SMITH, born: 26 Apr 1839, married, parents: both names illegible, cause of death: tuberculosis, informant: J.M. Smith (Doeville) died: 2 Dec 1915.

Viola OSBORNS, born: 23 Apr 1912, parents: E.G.
Osborns (NC) and Mollie Jackson, cause of death:
"accidental, got burned to death", informant: E.G.
Osborns (Shouns), died: 11 Dec 1915.

Meacy BARE, born: 30 Mar 1856 in VA, parents: James
Blevins (Ashe Co. NC) and Catherine Pennington (Ashe
Co. NC), cause of death: consumption, buried: VA,
died: 8 Dec 1915.

Hubert FARMER, born: 6 Dec 1915, parents: David Farmer
and mother's name illegible, cause of death: "found
dead in bed", died: 14 Dec 1915.

Ida Mae OWEN, born: 31 May 1906, parents: David Owen
and Mary Eastridge (NC), cause of death: tonsilitis,
informant: R.L. Jenkins (Mountain City), died: 16 Dec
1915.

Sherman Howard GENTRY, born: 14 Sep 1915, parents: Roy
W. Gentry and Flora Butler, cause of death: unknown,
informant: R.H. Gentry (Laurel Bloomery), buried: Acre
Field Cemetery, died: 9 Dec 1915.

Margaret J. ROGERS, born: 10 Nov 1838, married,
parents: father's name unknown and Kisey Gentry, cause
of death: "cerebral hemmorrhage", informant; Joseph H.
Heaton (Neva), died: 15 Dec 1915.

David Isaac BARRY, born: 4 Oct 1915, parents: Hugh
Barry and Alice Grindstaff, cause of death: croup,
informant: Alex Barry (Mountain City), died: 8 Jan
1816, record (1916) #: 1.

Nancy Jane CAUDELL, born: 4 Oct 1849, married,
parents: Thomas Johnson and Louise Green, cause of
death: "chronic intestinal nephritis", informant:
Moses Caudell (Mountain City), died: 11 Jan 1916,
record (1916) #: 2.

Calvin MAIN, born: 25 May 1844 in NC, married,
parents: John Main (NC) and Polly Potter, cause of
death: brights disease, informant: Margaret Main
(Trade), buried: Williams Cemetery, died 17 Jan 1916,
record (1916) #: 3.

Margaret MORELAND, born: 25 May 1867, married,
parents: Samuel Deloach (Carter Co. TN) and Louisa
Garrison (Carter Co. TN), cause of death:
tuberculosis, informant: M.F. Moreland (Doeville),
buried: Campbell Cemetery, died: 4 Jan 1916, record
(1916) #: 4.

John MITCHELL, age about 56 years, married, born in
NC, parents: not stated, cause of death: le grippe,
informant: J.L. Henson (Mountain City), buried:
Shingletown Cemetery, record (1916) #: 5.

Mary E. OWENS, born: 31 May 1867 in Ashe Co. NC, married, parents: Henry Eastridge (Ashe Co. NC) and Rebecca Johnson (Ashe Co. NC), cause of death: brights disease, informant: Will Graybeal (Shouns), died: 12 Jan 1916, record (1916) #: 6.

Hester CURD, born: 18 Jan 1828, married, parents: Riley West and Betsy West, cause of death: "cancer and old age", died: 28 Jan 1916, record (1916) #: 7.

Mrs. Cilia SHOUN, born: 6 Dec 1823, parents: Jessie Cole (Washington Co. VA) and Celia Brown, cause of death: "old age and le grippe", informant: A.J. Shoun, buried: Family Cemetery, died 4 Jan 1916. record (1916) #: 8.

Samuel E. SHOUN, born: 14 May 1916, parents: John S. Shoun and ? Baker, cause of death: "chronic nephritis", informant: D.B. Shoun, buried: Home Cemetery, died: 21 Jan 1916, record (1916) #: 9.

Ray Odell WALSH, born: 25 Nov 1915, parents: Roby F. Walsh and Rader Greenwell, cause of death: intestinal disorder and cold, buried: Crosswhite Cemetery, died: 24 Jan 1916, record (1916) #: 10.

Isaac Daniel BERRY, born: 4 Oct 1915, parents: D. Hugh Berry and Mary Alice Grindstaff, cause of death: diphtheria, buried: Phillippi Cemetery, died: 8 Jan 1916, record (1916) #: 11.

Ruth NEATHERLY, born: 21 May 1913, parents: Lieland Neatherly and Myrtle Greer (NC), cause of death: "accidental poisoning", informant: Lieland Neatherly (Shouns), died: 15 Jan 1916, record (1916) #: 12.

Edna Mae SLIMP, born: 23 Nov 1915, parents: George Slimp and Myrtle Hicks, cause of death: bold hives, informant: T.P. Ward (Neva), died: 20 Jan 1916, record (1916) #: 13.

Gladys A. CABLE, parents: Thomas W. Cable and Sallie M. Reece, stillborn, born/died: 12 Jan 1916, buried: Dugger Cemetery, record (1916) #: 14.

Tyler CROW, born 23 Feb 1916, parents: Jack Crow and Myrtle Luttrell, cause of death: "congenital weakness", informant: Jack Crow (Mountain City), died: 29 Feb 1916, record (1916) #: 15.

Ruby Cake FORRESTER, born: 12 Oct 1910, parents: Scott Forrester and Jossie Phillippi, cause of death: "caught fire and was burned", informant: Robert Phillippi (Mountain City), died: 12 Feb 1916, record (1916) #: 16.

Unnamed GREER, male, parents: Clarence R. Greer and Myrtle Tester, stillborn, born/died: 26 Feb 1916, record (1916) #: 17.

Unnamed SWEENEY, male, born 11 Feb 1916, parents: J.C.
Sweeney and Mary E. Estep (Carter Co. TN), cause of
death: not stated, informant: J.C. Sweeney (Doeville),
buried: Campbell Cemetery, died; 14 Feb 1916, record
(1916) #: 18.
Unnamed ESTEP, male, parents: John R. Estep (Carter
Co. TN) and Sarah E. Campbell, stillborn, informant:
Sarah E. Estep (Doeville), born/died: 12 Feb 1916,
buried: Campbell Cemetery, record (1916) #: 19.
Unnamed WINTERS, male, parents: Wm V. Winters and
Ollie C. Jenkins, stillborn, informant: Mrs. R.L.
Jenkins, buried: Acre Field Cemetery, born/died: 23
Feb 1916, record (1916) #: 20.
Samuel H. GOODWIN, born: 25 Nov 1854 in Carter Co. TN,
married, parents: Albert Goodwin (Carter Co. TN) and
Malinda Goodwin, cause of death: "hemiplegia",
informant: W.H. Stout (Crandell), buried: Gentry
Cemetery, died: 11 Feb 1916, record (1916) #: 21.
Mary Ann CHURCH, born: 21 Mar 1842 in Wilkes Co. NC,
widow, parents: Wilbur Adams (Wilkes Co. NC) and Susan
Church (Wilkes Co. NC), cause of death:pneumonia,
informant: L.A. Parsons (Crandell), buried: Blevins
Cemetery, died; 25 Feb 1916, record (1916) #: 22.
Joseph Bride BURTON, born: 6 Jan 1916, parents: Joe
Burton and Ruby White, cause of death: bold hives,
informant: Joe Burton (Butler), buried: Burton
Cemetery, died: 10 Mar 1916, record (1916) #: 23.
Beatris COWAN, born: 27 Dec 1915, parents: father not
stated and Floy Cowan, cause of death: bold hives,
informant: Floy Cowan (Butler), died: 19 Mar 1916,
record (1916) #: 24.
John Smith WALKER, born: 16 May 1915, parents: J.C.
Walker and Ellen Heaton, cause of death: pneumonia,
buried: Campbell Cemetery, died: 25 Mar 1916, record
(1916) #: 25.
Caroline JOHNSON, age 75 years, married, parents:
George Morefield and Mary Lee Frost, cause of death:
"apoplexy", informant: Adam Morefield (Mountain City),
died: 24 Mar 1916, record (1916) #: 26.
Martha D. POTTER, born: 4 Dec 1890, married, parents:
John Sheppard (NC) and Mary Owens, cause of death:
pneumonia, informant: John Sheppard (Mountain City),
died: 4 Mar 1916, record (1916) #: 27.
Clyde POTTER, born: 4 Mar 1916, parents: Daniel Boone
Potter and M.D. Sheppard, cause of death: pneumonia,
informant: John Sheppard (Mountain City), died: 24 Mar
1916, record (1916) #: 28.

Mary E. SEXTON, age 80 years, widow, parents: Andrew Pennington and Mary Pope (Ashe Co. NC), cause of death: chronic bronchitis, informant: Rev. M.H. Rambo (Mountain City), buried: Shingletown Cemetery, died: 27 Mar 1916, record (1916) #: 29.

Umbershon DUNN, age 72 years, parents: Larkin Dunn and Katie Jackson, cause of death: "septic infection", informant: Josie Dunn (Laurel Bloomery), died: 22 Mar 1916, record (1916) #: 30.

John Wesley FORD, born: 2 Jan 1853 in Wilkes Co. NC, married, parents: John R. Ford (Georgia) and Elizabeth Curry (Wilkes Co. NC), cause of death: heart disease, informant: J.M. Phillips (Shouns), died: 17 Mar 1916, record (1916) #: 31.

John JOHNSON, born: 5 Aug 1875, single, parents: Andrew Johnson (NC) and Titia Martin, cause of death: "Potts disease or disease of the spine", died: 24 Mar 1916, record (1916) #: 32.

Myrtle Pauline BLEVINS, born: 7 Nov 1915, parents: J.W. Blevins and Millie Ritchie, cause of death: le grippe, informant: J.W. Blevins (Crandell), buried: Blevins Cemetery, died: 15 Mar 1916, record (1916) #: 33.

Albert FORRESTER, born 20 Apr 1915, parents: Floyd Forrester and Vanie Proffitt, cause of death: pneumonia, died: 18 Mar 1926, record (1916) #: 34.

Soloman CROSSWHITE, born: 26 Mar 1830, widower, parents: John Crosswhite and Betsie Loyd, cause of death: "old age and le grippe", informant: D.N. Cole (Mountain City), buried: Laws Cemetery, died: 22 Mar 1916, record (1916) #: 35.

Cora WALKER, age 34 years, divorced, parents: William H. Walker (Watauga Co. NC) and Matitie Snyder, cause of death: consumption, informant: L.V. Walker (Neva), died: 23 Apr 1916, record (1916) #: 36.

Unnamed WARD, male, parents: James Ward and Maggie Wilson, stillborn, born/died: 27 Apr 1916, record (1916) #: 37.

William NELSON, born: 1 Jan 1863 in Sullivan Co. TN, parents: John Nelson (NC) and Nancy Phipps (Sullivan Co. TN), cause of death: "liesion of heart", informant: M.J. Nelson (Crandell), buried: Gentry Cemetery, died: 7 Apr 1916, record (1916) #: 38.

John WRIGHT, born: 4 Feb 1852, single, parents: Andrew Wright and Susan Wright, cause of death: pneumonia, informant: David Wright (Crandell), buried: Gentry Cemetery, died: 10 Apr 1916, record (1916) #: 39.

Myrtle Beatrice HEATON, born: 7 Aug 1912, parents: father not stated and Nora Etta Heaton, cause of death: "abscess of lungs", informant: N.E. Heaton (Crandell), buried: Gentry Cemetery, died: 19 Apr 1916, record (1916) #: 40.

Eugene Wyatt ANDERSON, born: 25 Dec 1912 in Coldwell Co. NC, parents: William H. Anderson (Wilkes Co. NC) and Lana R. Minton (Watauga Co. NC) cause of death: "pneumonia of both lungs", informant: James Cruse (Crandell), buried: Gentry Cemetery, died: 20 Apr 1916, record (1916) #: 41.

John D. WILCOX, born: 1 Apr 1916, parents: W.M. Wilcox (Watauga Co. NC) and Ida Vanoy (Wilkes Co. NC), death cause: "consumption of lungs", informant: W.M. Wilcox (Crandell), died: 24 Apr 1916, record (1916) #: 42.

Hobart GUFFEY, born 20 Jun 1898, single, parents: George Guffey (NC) and Catherine Guffey, cause of death: "killed in sawmill by main wheel", informant: Catherine Guffey (Butler), died: 21 Apr 1916, record (1916) #: 43.

Mrs. Martha SHUPE, born 28 June 1889, married, parents: William Roberts and Julia Dillon (NC), cause of death: tuberculosis and brights, buried: Wright Cemetery, died: 20 Apr 1916, record (1916) #: 44.

Unnamed HODGE, male, parents: Samuel Hodge (Watauga Co. NC) and Annie Pierce (Watauga Co. NC), stillborn, born/died: 26 Apr 1916, informant: Samuel Hodge (Trade) buried: Reece Cemetery, record (1916) #: 45.

Unnamed MCELYEA, female, parents: Mack M. McElyea and Callie Dunn, stillborn, born/died: 10 Apr 1916, record (1916) #: 46.

Unnamed WOODARD, male, parents: Alexander Woodard and Lillie Fulks, stillborn, buried: Phillippi Cemetery, born/died: 3 May 1916, record (1916) #: 47.

Ray DAY, born: 10 Dec 1915, parents: David Day and Mae Dugger, cause of death: "meningitis", informant: David Day (Butler), buried: Mount View Cemetery, died: 12 May 1916, record (1916) #: 48.

J.N.O. WALSH, born 19 Mar 1826 in SC, parents: Andrew Walsh and Mary Blanches, cause of death: "died suddenly with old age", informant: F.M. Walsh (Shouns), died: 7 May 1916, record (1916) #: 49.

James H. ROBINSON, born: 27 Aug 1846, widower, parents: Nicholas Robinson and Mary Howard, cause of death: illegible, informant: J.G. Robinson (Doeville), buried: Rambo Cemetery, died: 29 May 1916, record (1916) #: 50.

Infant DUNN, male, parents: J.M. Dunn and Rebecca
Main, cause of death: stillborn, born/died: 14 May
1916, informant: Dr. W.W. Vaught, record (1916) #: 51.
Harve E. BROWN, born: 18 Dec 1864 in NC, married,
parents: William Brown (NC) and Jane Nelson (NC),
cause of death: "intestinal neflesitis", informant:
Emory Brown (Mountain City), buried: Ashe Co. NC,
died: 6 May 1916, record (1916) #: 52.
Jasper TRIPLETT, parents: father not stated and Eva
Triplett, cause of death: stillborn, informant:
Rebecca Mahe (Mountain City, buried: Shingletown
Cemetery, born/died: 7 May 1916, record (1916) #: 53.
Oscar TRIPLETT, parents: father not stated and Eva
Triplett, cause of death: stillborn, informant:
Rebecca Mahe (Mountain City, buried: Shingletown
Cemetery, born/died: 7 May 1916, record (1916) #: 53.
Isabel RAY, born 17 Jul 1851 in VA, married, parents:
J. Oliver Gentry (VA) and Dorcas Debush (VA), cause of
death: "heart disease", informant: L.L. Ray (Laurel
Bloomery), buried: Valley Cemetery, died: 8 May 1916,
record (1916) #: 55.
Infant WINTERS, male, parents: Edward M. Winters and
Bessie Corum, cause of death: stillborn, born/died: 29
May 1916, informant: L.L. Jenkins (Mountain City),
buried: Michaels Cemetery, record (1916) #: 56.
Hobart Henry MINTON, born: 28 Jan 1913 at Watauga Co.
NC, parents: Allen Minton (Watauga Co. NC) and Mary A.
Watson (Wilkes Co. NC), cause of death: "gun shot
wound in right shoulder and neck severing the spinal
column, shot accidental by female child about 6 years
old, death instantaneous", informant: Allen Minton
(Crandell), died: 9 May 1916, record (1916) #: 57.
Robert Worley GENTRY, born: 17 Apr 1916, parents: W.
Oliver Gentry (VA) and Fronia Fritz, cause of death:
"bronchial pneumonia", informant: W.O. Gentry (Laurel
Bloomery), burial: Taylors Valley, died: 4 Jun 1916,
record (1916) #: 58.
Christopher Columbus SHOEMAKER, age 55 years, married,
parents: Frank Shoemaker (NC) and mother not stated,
cause of death: "chronic perenchymatous nephritis",
buried: Shingletown Cemetery, died: 10 Jun 1916,
record (1916) #: 59.
Infant CAMPBELL, male, parents: Samuel Campbell and
Cora Heaton, cause of death: stillborn, informant:
J.J. Campbell (Doeville), buried: Campbell Cemetery,
born/died: 26 Jun 1916, record (1916) #: 60.

Infant PROFFITT, female, father not stated and Elamay Proffitt, cause of death: stillborn, informant: Stacy Proffitt, buried: Proffitt Cemetery, born/died: 9 Jun 1916, record (1916) #: 61.

Charles H. HEATON, born: 24 Aug 1897, single, parents: John W. Heaton and Martha A. Rambo, cause of death: "accidental death caused by a falling tree fracturing skull and spine", informant: John W. Heaton (Crandell), buried: Gentry Cemetery, died: 6 Jun 1916, record (1916) #: 62.

Betty HALL, born: 4 Jun 1841 in NC, married, parents: father not stated and Mary Arnold, cause of death: "heart disease", informant: C.H. Hall (Shouns), died: 6 Jun 1916, record (1916) #: 63.

Mary A. CROUSE, born: 12 Jul 1841, married, parents: Britain Stwart (NC) and Abigail Taylor (NC), cause of death: "blood poisoning", informant: R.S. Stewart (Shouns), died 18 Jun 1916, record (1916) #: 64.

Oskar A. WILSON, born: 1 Jan 1847, married, parents: William Wilson and Roda Adams, cause of death: "chronic diarrhea", informant: Sarah Wilson (Shouns), died: 19 Jun 1916, record (1916) #: 65.

Rebecca DUNN, born: 20 Dec 1873, married, parents: Houston Main and Lisey Fletcher, death cause: "heart disease - fatty heart", informant: Tennessee Tester (Shouns), died: 23 Jun 1916, record (1916) #: 66.

Elizabeth Is....., date of birth not recorded, born: Watauga Co. NC, married, parents: John Moretz (NC) and Nancy Jane Miller (NC), cause of death: "heart dropsy", informant: K.S. Moretz (Shouns), died: 21 Jun 1916, record (1916) #: 67.

Margaret STOUT, born: 27 Mar 1845, widow, parents: J.K. Bradley and ? Smith, cause of death: "brights disease", informant: James R. Butler (Butler), died: 27 Jul 1916, record (1916) #: 68.

Sarah CAMPBELL, age 80 years, parents: Daniel Robinson and Katie Stout, cause of death: "heart disease", informant: John Estep (Doeville), buried: Campbell Cemetery, died: 14 Jul 1916, record (1916) #: 69.

Grant ROBINSON, born: 17 Jun 1913, parents: Daniel Robinson and Elizabeth Hodge, death cause: "cholera", informant: D.R. Robinson (Doeville), buried: Nave Cem., died: 3 Jul 1916, record (1916) #: 70.

Infant DUGGER, born: 22 Jul 1916, parents: illegible Dugger and Liddie Guy (NC), cause of death: "typhoid fever", buried: Dugger Cemetery, died: 22 Jul 1916, record (1916) #: 71.

Enlo Grace MILLER, born: 12 Jun 1915, parents: Luther
Miller and Beckie Fletcher (Carter Co. TN), cause of
death: "supposed to be cholera infection", informant:
Coy Phillips (Crandell), buried: Gentry Cemetery,
died: 20 Jul 1916, record (1916) #: 72.

John S. FARTHING, born: 7 Aug 1841 at Watauga Co. NC,
married, parents: William Young Farthing (NC) and
Annie Farthing (NC), cause of death: "old age",
informant: R.G. Vannoy (Neva), died: 31 Jul 1916,
record (1916) #: 73.

May MOREFIELD, age 11 years, parents: Landon Morefield
and Mollie Slimp, cause of death: "intestinal
obstruction", died 29 Jul 1916, record (1916) #: 74.

Worley Connelly GARLAND, born: 1 Sep 1915, parents:
Allan G. Garland and Vinnie E. Blevins, cause of
death: "congestion of the lungs and brain", informant:
Allan Garland (Crandell), buried: Blevins Cemetery,
died: 2 Jul 1916, record (1916) #: 75.

William WILSON, born: 15 Mar 1840, parents: father not
stated and Rebecca Wilson (Wilkes Co. NC), cause of
death: "cancer of the face", informant: W.W. Stout
(Crandell), buried: Gentry Cemetery, died: 4 Jul 1916,
record (1916) #: 76.

Infant SLUDER, female, parents: E.E. Sluder (NC) and
N.N. Bishop, cause of death: "premature birth",
informant: E.E. Sluder (Crandell), born/died: 5 Jul
1916, record (1916) #: 77.

Nora N. SLUDER, born: 30 Aug 1896, parents: Robert L.
Bishop (NC) and Margaret Nichols (NC), cause of death:
"childbirth", informant: R;L. Sluder (Crandell),
buried: Blevins Cemetery, died: 7 Jul 1916, record
(1916) #: 78.

Glen Butler MAY, born 19 Jul 1914, parents: Riley May
and Pearlie Snyder, cause of death: "illio-calitis",
informant: Hyram Snyder (Crandell), buried: Gentry
Cemetery, died: 8 Jul 1916, record (1916) #: 79.

Nancy BLEVINS, born: 6 Aug 1832 in Ashe Co. NC, widow,
parents: John Graybeal (Ashe Co. NC) and ..... King
(Ashe Co. NC), informant: J.F. Graybeal (Crandell),
buried: Blevins Cemetery, died: 8 Jul 1916, record
(1916) #: 80.

Malinda GARLAND, born: 23 Dec 1842 in Wilkes Co. NC,
parents: Alfred Shepherd (NC) and Sarah Jones (NC),
cause of death: " (illegible) of bile duct",
informant: J.C. Garland (Crandell), died: 15 Jul 1916,
record (1916) #: 81.

Everett Lee SHORES, born: 30 May 1915, parents: Enoch Shores and Alice Taylor (NC), cause of death: "entero-calitis", informant: Enoch Shores (Mountain City), died: 25 Jul 1916, record (1916) #: 82.

Mary SIMMONS, age 84 years, born in NC, widow, parents: unknown, death cause: not stated, informant: Jack Morefield (Mountain City), buried: Shingletown Cem., died: 24 Jul 1916, record (1916) #: 83.

Nancy Jane COWAN, born: 18 May 1836, parents: father not stated and Charlotte Dugger, cause of death: "paralysis", buried: Cowan Cemetery, died: 6 Jul 1916, record (1916) #: 84.

Kemp MURPHEY, born: 20 Jul 1841, parents: Abraham Murphey and Mary Walker, cause of death: "congestion of lungs", informant: H.E. Murphey (Mountain City), buried: Mountain View Cemetery, died: 18 Jul 1916, record (1916) #: 85.

Dayton Hunter ARNOLD, born: 26 Dec 1916, parents: Kinnie Arnold and Hattie Campbell, cause of death: "diahorrea". informant: Dayton Campbell (Doeville), buried: Stout Cemetery, died: 17 Aug 1916, record (1916) #: 86.

Elizabeth DUVALL, born 1 Jun 1915 in VA, parents: Haggy Duvall and Laura Burgess, cause of death: "acute gastritis", informant: Lizzie Duvall (Mountain City), buried: Cornett Cemetery, died: 19 Aug 1916, record (1916) #: 87.

Addie TRIPLETT, age 32 years, single, parents: Tol Triplett and mother not stated, cause of death: "cancer of face", informant: J.W. Keys (Mountain City), buried: Wills Cemetery, died: 29 Aug 1916, record (1916) #: 88.

John ROBERTS, age about 40 years, parents: Thomas Roberts and ? Morley, cause of death: "obstruction of bowels", informant: Ben Pleasant (Mountain City), buried: Roberts Cemetery, died: 29 Aug 1916, record (1916) #: 89.

Infant JONES, male, parents: James Jones (NC) and Ann Owens, stillborn, informant: James Jones (Laurel Bloomery), buried: Acre Field Cemetery, died: 25 Aug 1916, record (1916) #: 90.

Jasper OWENS, born 12 Sep 1916, parents: William Owens and Martha A. Heaton, cause of death: "influenza", informant: J.L. Garland (Crandell), buried: Gentry Cemetery, died: 27 Sep 1916, record (1916) #: 91.

Ray FURCHESS, born: 17 Apr 1916, parents: Millard Furchess and Neva Farmer, cause of death: "cattarrah of bowels", informant: Roy Stanton (Vaughtsville), died: 11 Sep 1916, record (1916) #: 92.

Carl H. POTTER, born: 8 May 1915, parents: James Potter (Watauga Co. NC) and Martilda Greer (Watauga Co. NC), cause of death: "the child was weekly from birth, almost a dwarf", informant: James Potter (Trade), died: 16 Sep 1916, record (1916) #: 93.

Amanda GREER, born: 23 Apr 1873, married, parents: Richard Vanover (NC) and Betsy Ann Snyder (NC), cause of death: "unemia following nephritis, sick about 30 hours", informant: James Greer (Trade), buried: Greer Cemetery, died: 23 Sep 1916, record (1916) #: 94.

Blanche Ethelmae HOWARD, born: 12 May 1912, parents: George W. Howard and Lizzie Snyder, cause of death: "bronchopneumonia", informant: G.W. Howard (Shouns), died: 27 Sep 1916.

Aubre Donia STOUT, male, born: 15 Jul 1915, parents: J. Brown Stout and Nancy E. Snyder, cause of death: not stated, informant: J.B. Stout (Doeville), buried: Shoun Cem., died: 11 Sep 1916, record (1916) #: 96.

Laura HARPER, born: 6 Jan 1873, married, parents: Alexander A. Berry and Rachel Reece, cause of death: "cancer of uterus", informant: John Dyer (Mountain City), buried: Wilson Cemetery, died 24 Sep 1916, record (1916) #: 97.

Landon HENDERSON, age about 24 years, parents: William Henderson (NC) and mother unknown, cause of death: "typhoid fever", informant: Fred Southerland (Mountain City), buried: Shingletown Cemetery, died: 2 Sep 1916, record (1916) #: 98.

Ula ROBINSON, born: 1916 (date illegible), parents: James D. Robinson and Nannie McQueen, death cause: unknown, died: 12 Sep 1916, record (1916) #: 99.

Rebecca JOHNSON, age 63 years, widow, parents: Calloway Elrod (NC) and Fannie Jones (NC), cause of death: "cancer", buried: Phillippi Cemetery, died: 28 Sep 1916, record (1916) #: 100.

Mrs. Nora FORRESTER, age 41 years, married, parents not stated, death cause: "pellagra", buried: Phillippi Cem., died: 27 Sep 1916, record (1916) #: 101.

Robert MCELYEA, born 17 Sep 1916, parents: Jacob McElyea and Mary Dunn, cause of death: "congenital underformation, harelip", informant: Jacob McElyea (Mountain City), buried: Phillippi Cemetery, died: 22 Sep 1916, record (1916) #: 102.

N.... Gladys WALSH, born: 16 Sep 1916, parents: James K. Walsh and Mary Wills, cause of death: "congenital atelictosis", informant: James Walsh (Mountain City), buried: Donnelly Cemetery, died: 16 Sep 1916, record (1916) #: 103.

Gilbert MOCK, negro, born: 30 Nov 1854, married, parents: Alvin Mock (VA) and Nannie Moorr (VA), cause of death: illegible, buried: Mountain View Cemetery, died: 10 Sep 1916, record (1916) #: 104.

Minerva ADAMS, born: 19 Apr 1843, widow, parents: Eligah Arnold and ? Venable (VA), death cause: "chronic ?)", informant: Mrs. J.A. Sammons (Mountain City), died: 21 Sep 1916, record (1916) #: 105.

Stella MCQUEEN, born 20 Nov 1905, parents: Jim McQueen and Betty Lock, death cause: "epalipsy", informant: Jim McQueen (Mountain City), buried: Mountain View Cem., died: 23 Sep 1916, record (1916) #: 106.

Jeanette O. CROSS, age 53 years, widow, parents: John G. Johnson (NC) and Martha Wagner, cause of death: "cancer of the stomach and breast", buried: Cross Cemetery, died: 9 Sep 1916, record (1916) #: 107.

Vernia Rebecca GENTRY, born 13 Sep 1916, parents: Melvin Gentry and Maggie Gentry, cause of death: not stated, informant: Eliga Gentry (Laurel Bloomery), died: 13 Sep 1916, record (1916) #: 108.

Noah Nathaniel POTTER, age 59 years, parents: James Potter and ? Shuffield, cause of death: "cancer of rectum", buried: Potter Cemetery, died: 2 Oct 1916.

Virgie SHEPARD, born: 3 Jul 1916, parents: Sam Forrester and Biner Shepard, cause of death: "cramp colic in stomach", informant: J.M. Mast (Shouns), died: 4 Oct 1916, record (1916) #: 110.

Mrs. Rebecca WILSON, age 81 years, widow, parents: Joseph Wilson and Polly Wills, cause of death: "(illegible) congestion", buried: Phillippi Cemetery, died: 20 Oct 1916, record (1916) #: 111.

Oliver CRISSINGER, age about 75 years, born in Ohio, parents unknown, cause of death: "chronic intestinal nephritis", informant: John Treadway (Shouns), died: 4 Oct 1916, record (1916) #: 112.

Pattie HOLDER, age about 74 years, married, parents: Marion Arnold and Hannah Heaton, cause of death: "organic heart disease", informant: David Holder (Doeville) died: 1 Oct 1916. record (1916) #: 113.

Minirve LOWE, age about 48 years, parents: David Holder and Pollie Arnold, cause of death: "tuberculosis", informant: Will Lowe (Doeville), buried: Campbell Cemetery, died: 5 Oct 1916, record (1916) #: 114.

Hiram EGGERS, born: 25 Mar 1853, married, parents: Brazill Eggers (NC) and Sallie Isaacs (NC), death cause: "pulmonary tuberculosis", informant: Roy Eggers (Trade), buried in NC, died: 26 Oct 1916, record (1916) #: 115.

George W. MCFADDIN, born: 22 Sep 1916, parents: John McFaddin and Nora Reece, cause of death: "diptheria", informant: John McFaddin (Trade), buried: Reece Cemetery, died: 7 Oct 1916, record (1916) #: 116.

Rebecca JENNINGS, born: 28 Dec 1824 in North Carolina, parents: unknown, death cause: "pulmonary ?", informant: T.J. Jennings (Trade), buried: Greer Cem., died: 4 Oct 1916.

William A. STOUT, born: 17 Apr 1858, parents: Thomas J. Stout and ? Grindstaff, cause of death: "brights disease", died: 16 Oct 1916, record (1916) #: 118.

Murl RITCHIE, female, born: 22 Oct 1911, parents: Robert Ritchie (Sullivan Co. TN) and Lula Smith, cause of death: "pneumonia", informant: Wiley Smith (Butler), died: 17 Oct 1916, record (1916) #: 119.

Alexander CHURCH, born: 22 Nov 1916, parents: Jeff Church and (illegible) Arnold, cause of death: "not known, died suddent", informant: Wheeler Garland (Neva), died 24 Nov 1916, record (1916) #: 120.

Joseph D. TESTER, born: 9 Oct 1916, parents: Elbert Tester and Nora Dunn, cause of death: "supposed to be croup", informant: Elbert Tester (Neva), died: 16 Nov 1916, record (1916) #: 121.

Dora STOUT, born 1 Aug 1916, parents: Wain Stout and Norah May, cause of death: "unknown, found dead in bed", informant: Wain Stout (Neva), died: 3 Nov 1916, record (1916) #: 122.

Infant KING, male, parents: James S. King and Lassie South (NC), stillborn, informant: C.W. King (Trade), born/died: 13 Noc 1916.

Aeron STALCUP, born: 27 Aug 1853, married, parents: John H. Stalcup and Elizabeth Robinson, cause of death: "dilitation of heart", informant: W.H. Stalcup (Doeville), buried: Stalcup Cemetery, died: 13 Nov 1916, record (1916) #: 124.

Nettie ARNOLD, born: 16 Nov 1894, single, parents: John Arnold and Elizabeth Robinson, death cause: "typhoid fever", informant: J.H. Arnold (Butler), buried: Nave Cem., died: 4 Nov 1916, record (1916) #: 125.

Ira G. PHILLIPS, born: 20 Aug 1916, parents: S.F. Phillips and Ethel Howard, cause of death: "croupes pneumonia", informant: S.F. Phillips (Shouns), died: 2 Nov 1916, record (1916) #: 126.

Geeter WILLIN, born: 2 Oct 1916, parents: W.A. Willin and Edna Perkins (NC), cause of death: "croupes pneumonia", informant: W.A. Willin (Shouns), died: 11 Nov 1916, record (1916) #: 127.

Sallie DUGGER, age 81 years, single, parents: John Dugger and Rodie Cable, cause of death: "le grippe – information from her brother, James K. Dugger", informant: John E. Dugger (Butler), buried: Dugger Cemetery, died: 25 Nov 1916, record (1916) #: 128.

Everett Hughes OWENS, born: 1 Nov 1916, parents: Millard Owens and Bulah Forrester, cause of death: "congenital sypilis", informant: Dan Owens (Laurel Bloomery), buried: Cornett Cemetery, died: 11 Nov 1916, record (1916) #: 129.

Lavinia DUNN, born: 1866, widow, parents: not stated, cause of death: "intestinal nephritis", informant: James Reece (Mountain City), buried: Noah Wagner Cemetery, died: 10 Nov 1916, record (1916) #: 130.

Garrett SWENEY, born: 25 Sep 1916, parents: Thomas Baty Sweney and Minnie June Estep (Carter Co. TN), cause of death: not stated, died: 10 Nov 1916, record (1916) #: 131.

Infant SHOUN, parents: J.H. Shoun and Bessie Robinson, stillborn, born/died: 10 Nov 1916, record (1916) #: 132.

Infant DUNN, male, parents: Huston Dunn and Mary Tester, stillborn, informant: J.O. Minks (Neva), born/died: 5 Nov 1916.

Franklin PERKINS, age about 50 years, born in Ashe Co. NC, parents: unknown, cause of death: "cerebral hemorage", died: 25 Nov 1916, record (1916) #: 134.

James C. PAYNE, born: 24 Apr 1858, married, parents: George Payne and Elizabeth J. Greg, cause of death: "abscess of lungs", informant: Mrs. Tom White (Butler), died: 24 Nov 1916, record (1916) #: 135.

Robert E. GLOVER, born: 24 Apr 1879, single, parents: John Glover (Carter Co. TN) and Mary McKinney (Carter Co. TN), death cause: "tuberculosis", informant: G.S. Morley (Butler), died: 20 Dec 1916, record (1916) #: 136.

Gus JOHNSON, born: 25 Dec 1900, parents: Smith Johnson and Martha Cress, cause of death: "gunshot wound (accidental)", buried: Cress Cemetery, died: 1 Dec 1916, record (1916) #: 137

Katherine JENKINS, born: 7 Dec 1846, parents: James Nave and Celia Shull, cause of death: "cancer of liver", informant: Olliv Jenkins (Mountain City), buried: Phillippi Cemetery, died: 31 Dec 1916, record (1916) #: 138.

Robert Swain MCDADE, born: 28 Mar 1851 in NC, parents: Robert McDade (NC) and Mary Moore (NC), cause of death: " ? tumor", informant: E.L. McDade (Mountain City), buried: Mountain View Cemetery, died: 26 Dec 1916, record (1916) #: 139.

Mary Alice SHUPE, born: 27 Sep 1916, parents: James Shupe and Martha Phillippi, cause of death: "pneumonia", informant; Edward Phillippi (Mountain City) buried: Phillippi Cemetery, died: 24 Dec 1916, record (1916) #: 140.

Edward Taylor PHILLIPPI, Jr., born: 26 Oct 1915, parents; Edward Taylor Phillippi and Virginia Shupe, cause of death: "pneumonia", buried: Phillippi Cemetery, died: 12 Dec 1916, record (1916) #: 141.

Mattie Stone Molle OWENS, born: 2 Feb 1866 in VA, parents: William Stone (VA) and Martha Stone (VA), cause of death: " ? of stomach", buried: Phillippi Cemetery, died: 2 Dec 1916, record (1916) #: 142.

Audie DUGGER, born: 27 Nov 1916, parents: Audie Dugger and Callie Spars (Greene Co. TN), cause of death: "croup", informant: Callie Spars (Butler), buried: Dugger Cem., died: 2 Dec 1916, record (1916) #: 143.

Nancy E. ELLIOTT, born: 10 Oct 1848, widow, parents: father not stated and Rebecca Morefield, cause of death: "intestinal nephritis", informant: Walter Elliott (Trade), buried in Burnsville NC, died: 20 Dec 1916, record (1916) #: 144.

Holla POTTER, female, born: 16 Nov 1916, parents: W.A. Potter and Lonnie Dotson, cause of death: "found dead in bed", informant: Otha Potter (Shouns), died: 23 Dec 1916, record (1916) #: 145.

Biner SHEPARD, born: 17 Apr 1874, single, parents: Martin Shepard (NC) and Anna Forrester, cause of death: "disease of the heart", informant: N.J. Mast (Shouns), died 10 Dec 1916, record (1916) #: 146.

Susan FLETCHER, age about 90 years, parents: Silas Fletcher (NC) and Betsy Lunsford (NC), cause of death: not stated, informant: Stacy Fletcher (Mountain City), buried: Morley Cemetery, died: 28 Dec 1916, record (1916) #: 147.

Infant SWINEY, parents: Jessie Swiney and Mary Estep (Carter Co. TN), stillborn, informant: Jessie Swiney (Doeville), buried: Campbell Cemetery, died: 15 Dec 1916, record (1916) #: 148.

Henry Shelton SHUPE, date of birth left blank, parents: Jim Shupe and Martha Phillippi, cause of death: "heart disease", informant: Stephen Phillippi, buried: Phillippi Cemetery, record (1916) #: 149.

J.B. TOWNSEND, age 61 years, born in Ashe Co. NC, married, parents: Alison Townsend (NC) and Pattie Johnson (VA), cause of death: "cirrhosis of liver, alcoholism", informant: W.H. Stout (Crandell), died: 2 Dec 1916, record (1916) #: 150.

Vicie CAMPBELL, born: 17 Jan 1838, parents: Zacharia Campbell and Annie Marston, cause of death: "consumption", informant: Sarah Campbell (Butler), died: 28 Jan 1917, record (1917) #: 1.

Winey BREWER, born 19 Jun 1882, married, parents: Bloom Patrick (NC) and Catherine Ashley (NC), cause of death: "paralysis", informant: J.E. Sexton (Mountain City), buried: Mock Cemetery, died: 28 Jan 1917, record (1917) #: 2.

Honey L. ARNEY, born: 1 Apr 1882 in Watauga Co. NC, married, parents: S.W. Coffee (Watauga Co. NC) and Mrs. R.L. Danner (Watauga Co. NC), cause of death: "pneumonia fever", buried: Brown Cemetery, died: 28 Jan 1917, record (1917) #: 3.

Infant DUGGER, female, parents: Frank Dugger and (illegible) Isaacs, stillborn, born/died: 29 Jan 1917, record (1917) #: 4.

F... Love HODGE, female, age about 90 years, born on June 10, parents: Joseph Mullens and Sarah Warren, cause of death: "tuberculosis ? - no psysician in attendance", informant: William Perdue (Shouns), buried: Lewis Cemetery, died: 12 Jan 1917, record (1917) #: 5.

Honey Danner ARNEY, age 32 years, born at Watauga Co. NC, married, parents: Thomas Coffee (Watauga Co. NC) and ? Danner (Watauga Co. NC), cause of death: "pneumonia fever", informant: J.A. Arney (Bakers Gap), buried: Brown Cemetery, died: 28 Jan 1917, record (1917) #: 6.

Samuel P. WILLS, born: 15 Jan 1842, parents: John Wills and Polly Neal (VA), cause of death: "heart disease", informant: J.M. Davis (Vaughtsville), buried: Wills Cemetery, died: 13 Jan 1917, record (1917) #: 7.

J. Oliver NEELY, born: 25 Apr 1874, parents: William Neely and Sarah Jane Gentry, cause of death: "unknown, sudden death", informant: J.S. Neely (Laurel Bloomery), buried: Acre Field Cemetery, died: 9 Jan 1917, record (1917) #: 8.

William J. GREER, born: Jun 1842, widower, parents: not stated, cause of death: "tuberculosis of lungs", informant: W.M. Wilson (Laurel Bloomery), buried: Taylors Valley Cemetery, died: 26 Jan 1917, record (1917) #: 9.

John A. WILSON, born: 2 May 1849 in Washington Co. VA, parents: Isacarah Wilson (Wash. Co. VA) and Jane Rudy (Wash. Co. VA), cause of death: "chronic heart disease", informant: J.S. Wilson (Laurel Bloomery), buried: Valley Cemetery, died: 31 Jan 1917, record (1917) #: 10.

Mrs. T.B. MORLEY, born: 4 May 1863, married, parents: John E. Lowe and Anna Cole (Carter Co. TN), cause of death: "cancer of face", informant: Thomas Morley (Mountain City), buried: Home Cemetery, died: 4 Jan 1917, record (1917) #: 11.

Infant AGERS, parents: W.D. Agers and C.L. Shoun, stillborn, informant: W.D. Agers (Mountain City), born/died: 2 Jan 1917, record (1917) #:: 12.

Hattie Millon ARNOLD, born: 11 Jan 1917, parents: James B. Arnold and Mary Elizabeth SWIFT, cause of death: "croup", informant: J.B. Arnold (Mountain City), died: 30 Jan 1917, record (1917) #: 13.

William E. LOWE, born: 20 Apr 1844, married, parents: Abram Lowe and ? Crosswhite, cause of death: "le grippe", informant: Joseph Lowe (Mountain City), buried: Lowe Cemetery, died: 30 Jan 1917, record (1917) #: 14.

James D. BARLOW, born: 31 Jan 1917, parents: James J. Barlow and Sarah J. Walker, cause of death: "premature birth", informant: James J. Barlow (Crandell), buried: Gentry Cem., died: 31 Jan 1917, record (1917) #: 15.

Infant BERRY, male, born: 15 Dec 1916, parents: E.W. Berry and Minnie C. Stout, cause of death: "unknown", informant: E.W. Berry (Crandell), buried: Gentry Cemetery, died: 2 Jan 1917, record (1917) #: 16.

Alvin WILCOX, born: 19 Jul 1841 at Ashe Co. NC, married, minister, parents: William Wilcox (Ashe Co. NC) and Vina Haddon (Watauga Co. NC), cause of death: "grippe", buried: Blevins Cemetery, died 17 Jan 1917, record (1917) #: 17.

Clifford Lester CHESTER, born: 12 Jun 1910, parents: ? Chester and Rebeca Manial, cause of death: "pneumonia and typhoid fever", informant: Rebeca Manial (Crandell), buried: Blevins Cemetery, died: 17 Jan 1917, record (1917) #: 18.

Infant MULLINS, female, born: 15 Jan 1917, parents: L.M. Mullins (VA) and Carrie Brooks (NC), cause of death: "congestion lungs", informant: L.M. Mullins (Crandell), buried: Blevins Cemetry, died: 20 Jan 1917, record (1917) #: 19.

Elmine CABLE, age 41 years, born in NC, married, parents: Tin Reece (NC) and Retta Proffitt (NC), cause of death: "pneumonia fever", buried: Guin Cemetery, died: 14 Jan 1917, record (1917) #: 20.

Nora CARDWELL, age 20 years, born at Wilkes Co. NC, single, parents: J.G. Cardwell (Wilkes Co. NC) and Mary Eller (Iowa), cause of death: "pneumonia fever", buried: Dugger Cemetery, died: 30 Jan 1917, record (1917) #: 21.

Jane FENNER, age 74 years, born in Virginia, widow, parents: Joseph Davis (VA) and mother's name illegible (VA), cause of death: "influenza", informant: R.G. Johnson (Mountain City), buried: Phillippi Cemetery, died: 6 Jan 1917, record (1917) #: 22.

James Richard FENNER, born: 30 Dec 1916, parents: Alexander Fenner and Margaret Luttrell, cause of death: "influenza ?", informant: Lem Fenner (Mountain City), buried: Phillippi Cemetery, died: 7 Jan 1917, record (1917) #: 23.

Infant NOLEN, male, parents: A.W. Nolen and Renette Brookshire, stillborn, buried: Phillippi Cemetery, born/died: 17 Jan 1917, record (1917) #: 24.

Mary NORRIS, born: 16 Jan 1917, parents: Walter Norris and Rildia Parsons, cause of death: "congenital syphilis ?", informant: Landon Parsons (Mountain City), buried: Donnelly Cemetery, died: 22 Jan 1917, record (1917) #: 25.

Infant ISAACS, parents: Carl Isaacs and Ida Belle Hodge, death cause: "stillborn", died: 27 Jan 1917, record (1917) #: 26.

Adam MOREFIELD, born: 6 Aug 1836 in NC, widower, parents: Gabrial Morefield (NC) and Sallie Robinson (NC), cause of death: "chronic intestinal nephritis", informant: T.A. Wills (Mountain City), buried: Donnelly Cem., died: 26 Jan 1917, record (1917) #: 27.

Mary WILCOX, born: 22 Jul 1884, single, parents: James Wilcox and Rebecca Wilcox, cause of death: "died sudden, no psysician in attendance", informant: W.D. Wilcox (Shouns), buried: Potter Cemetery, died: 30 Jan 1917, record (1917) #: 28.

Caroline LOCK, Black, born: 9 Oct 1858, single, parents: Jack Lock and Amy Moore, cause of death: "cancer of womb", informant: Walter Lock (Mountain City), buried: Mountain View Cemetery, died: 18 Jan 1917, record (1917) #: 29.

Bill Hill MOREFIELD, born: 8 Nov 1849, widower, parents: father's name not stated and Lee Cindy Morefield, death cause: "intestinal nephritis", informant: Joe Morefield (Mountain City), buried: Cornett Cem., died: 19 Jan 1917, record (1917) #: 30.

Luttitia LOWE, age 62 years, born: 1855, married, parents: Jackson Stalcup and Betsy Robinson, cause of death: "le grippe", informant: Joseph Lowe (Mountain City), buried: Lowe Cemetery, died: 2 Feb 1817, record (1917) #: 31.

Bill Hill MOREFIELD, born: 8 Nov 1849, widower, parents: father's name not stated and Lee Cindy Morefield, cause of death: "chronic intestinal nephritis", informant: Joe Morefield (Mountain City), buried: Cornett Cemetery, died: 19 Jan 1917, record (1917) #: 30.

Luttitia LOWE, age 62 years, born: 1855, married, parents: Jackson Stalcup and Betsy Robinson, cause of death: "le grippe", informant: Joseph Lowe (Mountain City), buried: Lowe Cemetery, died: 2 Feb 1817, record (1917) #: 31.

James Burlin SAMMONS, born: 15 Dec 1916, parents: Jess Sammons and Alice Sammons, cause of death: "unknown, found dead in bed", informant: Jess Sammons (Mountain City), buried: Taylor Johnson Cemetery, died: 4 Feb 1917, record (1917) #: 32.

Carter Stanley ALLEN, born: 20 Dec 1915, parents: Carter Allen (NC) and Sallie Stout, cause of death: "pneumonia", informant: Thomas Stout (Shouns), died: 6 Feb 1917, record (1917) #: 33.

Marion J. JOHNSON, male, born: 9 Jun 1897, single, parents: Andrew C. Johnson (NC) and Clara M. Martin, cause of death: "paralysis general", informant: Andrew C. Johnson (Shouns), died: 8 Feb 1917, record (1917) #: 34.

Eliza B. MAST, born: 21 Nov 1835, widow, parents: John S. Vaught and Mary Shoun, cause of death: "tuberculosis pulmonary", informant: C.R. Potter (Shouns), died 9 Feb 1917, record (1917) #: 35.

Lan R. RAGAN, born: 30 Jan 1917, parents: Gordon E. Ragen (NC) and Lavina J. Reece, cause of death: "supposed to be diphtheria", informant: John M. McFaddin (Trade), buried: Reece Cemetery, died: 9 Feb 1917, record (1917) #: 36.

Nancy WARD, born: 4 Mar 1841, widow, parents: Nicholas Stout and Catherine Wagner, cause of death: "le grippe", died: 9 Feb 1917, record (1917) #: 37.

James Denver ROBERTS, born: 2 Jul 1912, parents: E.D. Roberts and Mary Jane Stout, cause of death: "puppeisa hemorrhagia", informant: L.F. Roberts (Mountain City), buried: Wright Cemetery, died: 13 Feb 1917, record (1917) #: 38.

Eadeth P. CROWDER, born: 18 Mar 1916, parents: Manley M. Crowder (NC) and Cora Starns, cause of death: "tuberculosis", informant: Manley Crowder (Shouns), died: 13 Feb 1917, record (1917) #: 39.

Infant JENKINS, parents: Hugh Jenkins and Mary L. Morefield, cause of death: unknown, born/died: 18 Feb 1917, buried: Robinson Cemetery, record (1917) #: 40.

Thelma Pauline ARNOLD, born: 15 Feb 1917, parents: Robert M. Arnold and Mattie Lee McGuire (Russell Co. VA), cause of death: "premature birth", buried: Blevins Cemetery, died: 26 Feb 1917, record (1917) #: 41.

Marry CHURCH, born: 28 Feb 1917, parents: Charley Church and Cassie Dowell, cause of death: "lack of rasperation ateleatosis", informant: Charley Church (Vaughtsville), died: 1 Mar 1917, record (1917) #: 42.

Eli BISHOP, date of birth not stated, born at Wilkes Co. NC, parents: Elbert Bishop (Wilkes Co. NC) and Martha J. Madron (Wilkes Co. NC), cause of death: "measles", informant: R.L. Bishop (Crandul), buried: Blevins Cemetery, died: 4 Mar 1917, record (1917) #: 43.

Mary Lee STURGILL, born: 19 Jan 1917, parents: father not stated and Biner Sturgill, cause of death: "unknown, found dead in bed", informant: Jim Arnold (Mountain City), buried: Wills Cemetery, died: 6 Mar 1917, record (1917) #: 44.

Infant STOUT, born: 20 Nov 1915, parents: Allen Stout and Sarah Absher, cause of death: "pulmonary tuberculosis", died: 8 Mar 1917, record (1917) #: 45.

Hugh M. CHURCH, born: 12 Jul 1832 in Wilkes Co. NC, married, parents: Amos Church (NC) and Alice Billings (NC), cause of death: "blood clot on brain", informant: R. H. Snyder (Crandul), buried: Blevins Cemetery, died: 13 Mar 1917, record (1917) #: 46.

Jacob ROBERTS, born: 16 Oct 1837 in VA, parents: Jacob Roberts (VA) and ? (first name not stated) Robinson, cause of death: "chronic brights", informant: Callie Roberts (Mountain City), buried: home cemetery, died: 18 Mar 1917, record (1917) #: 47.

Mary Sophrinia GENTRY, born: 16 Jan 1883, married, parents: James Fritz and Sarah Pierce, death cause: "measles", informant: W.O. Gentry (Laurel), buried: Valley Cem., died: 19 Mar 1917, record (1917) #: 48.

Ida Melissa GENTRY, born: 14 Mar 1917, parents: William Oliver Gentry (VA) and Mary Saphronia Fritz, cause of death: "measles", informant: John Gentry (Taylor's Valley, VA), buried: Valley Cemetery, died: 21 Mar 1917, record (1917) #: 49.

Martha E. HEATON, born: 6 Jan 1872, married, parents: Ham Rambo and Lucinda Robinson, cause of death: "cancer of uteris and rapid childbirth", buried: Gentry Cem., died: 22 Mar 1917, record (1917) #: 50.

Charles EASTRIDGE, born: 23 Jun 1916, parents: W.W. Eastridge and S.L. Prather (NC), death cause: "disease of liver and stomach" informant: W.W. Eastridge (Shouns), died: 24 Mar 1917, record (1917) #: 51.

Amanda R. THOMAS, born: 5 Nov 1848, widow, parents: Roland Jenkins and Annie Widby, cause of death: "acute ? (illegible)", informant: A.A. Thomas (Trade), died: 24 Mar 1917, record (1917) #: 52.

Roy TESTER, born 18 Mar 1917, parents: Stephen M. Tester and Julia Proffitt, cause of death: "supposed to be croup", informant: Stephen M. Tester (Neva), died: 30 Mar 1917, record (1917) #: 53.

David HOLDER, born: 1844 in NC, age: 73 years, widower, parents: Thomas Holder (NC) and Mary Clark (NC), death cause: "paralysis", informant: W.H. Lowe (Doeville), died: 31 Mar 1917, record (1917) #: 54.

Infant CLAIMANS, parents: Worley Claimans and Ida Ham (VA), stillborn, informant: Worley Claimans (Doeville), died: 28 Mar 1917, record (1917) #: 55.

Henry W. TESTER, born 3 Aug 1840, parents: Nathaniel Tester and Nancy McElyea, cause of death: "died suddent, heart failure", informant: John M. Tester (Neva), died: 2 Apr 1917, record (1917) #: 56.

Earl WALKER, born: 15 Nov 1916, parents: William R. Walker (Watauga Co. NC) and Sallie Stout, cause of death: "croup suposed to be the cause", died: 8 Apr 1917, record (1917) #: 57.

Thomas Howard SNYDER, born: 13 Feb 1917, parents: Ham Hockaday and Kate Snyder, cause of death: "whooping cough supposed to be the cause", informant: E.A. Blevins (Crandul), buried: Gentry Cemetery, died: 11 Apr 1917, record (1917) #: 58.

Elbert Glenn SHORES, born: 16 Jan 1913, parents: Carl Shores and Charity Kilby (NC), cause of death: "chronic endo carditis", informant: Emerson Rupard (Laurel Bloomery), buried: Shingletown Cemetery, died: 11 Apr 1917, record (1917) #: 59.

Stacy FLETCHER, born: 18 Jan 1866, married, parents:
Martin Fletcher and Caroline Adams, cause of death:
"nephritis", informant: D.L. Slimp (Mountain City),
buried: Mountain City, died: 13 Apr 1917, record
(1917) #: 60.
Thomas SWEINLY, born: 23 May 1850, married, parents:
Thomas Sweinly and Sally Campbell, cause of death:
"tuberculosis", informant: J.C. Sweinly, buried:
Campbell Cem., died: 14 Apr 1917, record (1917) #: 61.
Rebecca STANSBERRY, age 41 years, single, born at
Wilkes Co. NC., parents: Center Stansberry (NC) and
Mary Stansberry, cause of death: "heart dropsy",
informant: Mary Stansberry (Butler), buried: Burton
Cemetery, died: 15 Apr 1917, record (1917) #: 62.
Elbert BISHOP, born: 9 Dec 1833 in Wilkes Co. NC,
widower, parents: John Bishop (Wilkes Co. NC) and
Bettie Smith (Wilkes Co. NC), cause of death:
"gangrene in right thigh caused by a fall in February
1917", informant: J.C. Bishop (Crandul), buried:
Blevins Cem., died: 15 Apr 1917, record (1917) #: 63.
Infant MCNEILL, parents: W.A. McNeill (NC) and S.P.
Eller (NC), cause of death: "premature birth, 6
months", informant: W.A. McNeill (Crandul), buried:
Blevins Cemetery, born/died: 20 Apr 1917, record
(1917) #: 64.
Eva Maud DYSON, born: 13 Sep 1916, parents: Rum Dyson
and Tildy Morefield, cause of death: "bronchol
pnumia", informant: Rum Dyson (Mountain City), buried:
Donnelly Cem., died: 24 Apr 1917, record (1917) #: 65.
Sallie R. COLE, born: 15 Jul 1882, single, parents:
Isaac E. Cole and Martha Walker, cause of death:
"organic heart disease", buried: Coles Cemetery, died:
30 Apr 1917, record (1917) #: 66.
Andrew J. Stuffel STREET, born: 8 Jan 1836, widower
parents: Criston Stuffel Street and Pollie Grindstaff
(Carter Co. TN), cause of death: illegible, informant:
Matilda Stuffel Street (Doeville), died: 7 May 1917,
record (1917) #: 67.
Henry Evert WINTERS, born: 24 Apr 1917, parents: John
Winters and Susie Arnold, cause of death: "premature
delivery", informant: John Winters (Laurel Bloomery),
buried: Cornett Cemetery, died: 8 May 1917, record
(1917) #: 68.
Matilda SMITH, born 20 Aug 1833 in Johnson Co. TN,
widow, parents: Jerry Laws (Wilkes Co. NC) and
mother's name not stated, believed to be born in
Johnson Co. TN, cause of death: "auterio seterosis and
paralysis", buried: Greenwell Cemetery, died: 9 May
1917, record (1917) #: 69.

Catherine GOODWIN, born: 3 Jun 1845, widow, parents: Isaac Shoun and Mary Wills, cause of death: "cancer of uterus", informant: S.A. Goodwin (Mountain City), buried: cemetery at home, died: 10 May 1917, record (1917) #: 70.

William Howard FARMER, born: 15 Apr 1895, single, parents: father not stated and mother's first name illegible Farmer (Grayson Co. VA), cause of death: "accidental lick on the head by a wire stretcher breaking while working on a fence", informant: C.G. Shoun (Mountain City), buried: Shoun Cemetery, died: 12 May 1917, record (1917) #: 71.

Infant TOLIVER, male, parents: Martin A. Toliver, (Washington Co. VA) and Dora Stansberry (Ashe Co. NC), cause of death: "premature birth", informant: M.A. Toliver (Crandul), buried: Gentry Cemetery, born/died: 21 May 1917, record (1917) #: 72.

Pearl LEWIS, parents: Carlis Lewis (NC) and Bethel Roark (NC), cause of death: "thought to be due to not being born at full term", informant: Carlis Lewis (Shouns), born/died: 23 May 1917, record (1917) #: 73.

Mary Elizabeth MATTON, born: 20 Apr 1917, parents: Arthor Matton and Faye Gentry, cause of death: "influenza ?", informant: Isaac Gentry (Mountain City), buried: Phillippi Cemetery, died: 28 Feb 1917, record (1917) #: 74.

William BLANKENBECKLOR, age about 48 years, widower, parents: not stated, cause of death: tuberculosis, informant: Oscar Blankenbecklor, buried: Phillippi Cemetery, died: 25 May 1917, record (1917) #: 75.

Glenn Hobart FENNER, born: 14 Nov 1915, parents: Joseph Fenner and Susie Swift, cause of death: "pneumonia", informant: Charles Fenner (Mountain City), buried: Wilson Cemetery, died: 25 May 1917, record (1917) #: 76.

Bruce JOHNSON, born: 18 Apr 1917, parents: Lemon Johnson (VA) and Pearl Hess (VA), cause of death: "unknown, found dead in bed", informant: Lemon Johnson (Trade), buried: Potter Cemetery, died: 27 May 1917, record (1917) #: 77.

John Henry ROBBINS, born: 29 Apr 1917, parents: R.D. Robbins (Wilkes Co. NC) and Cora Crosswhite, cause of death: "not known, found dead in bed", informant: R.L. Bishop (Crandul) buried: Blevins Cemetery, died: 29 May 1917, record (1917) #: 78.

Infant MCELYEA, female, parents: Clyde McElyea and Connie Tester, cause of death: "premature birth", informant: Tennessee Tester (Shouns), born/died: 29 May 1917, record (1917) #: 79.

Infant LEWIS, female, parents: Roby Lewis (Ashe Co. NC) and Callie Dowell, stillborn, born/died: 11 May 1917, record (1917) #: 80.

Wesley MOSER, parents: Isaac N. Moser (VA) and Phache Owens (NC), stillborn, informant: I.N. Moser (Laurel Bloomery), buried: Acre Field Cemetery, born/died: 28 May 1917, record (1917) #: 81.

Bettie GREER, age about 67 years, single, parents: David Greer and Barbara Speer, cause of death: "hypostatic pneumonia", informant: J.A. Cole (Laurel Bloomery), buried: Valley Cemetery, died: 3 Jun 1917, record (1917) #: 82.

Lenna Kate SIMCOX, born: 10 Nov 1910, parents: Joseph G. Simcox and Blanche May (Watauga Co. NC), cause of death: "autoinfection", died: 4 Jun 1917, record (1917) #: 83.

John MAIN, age about 80 years, born in NC, married, parents: Charles Main (NC) and Nancy Walters (NC), cause of death: "brights disease", informant: J.A. Denny (Trade), buried: Crawford Cemetery, died: 12 Jun 1917, record (1917) #: 84.

Susan M. PAYNE, born: Jan 1844, parents: Parker Stout and Martha Pearce, cause of death: "heart disease", informant: Oma Johnson (Shouns), died: 18 Jun 1917, record (1917) #: 85.

Alexander MCQUEEN, born: 17 May 1865, married, parents: Isaac Finley McQueen and Mary Jane Bradley, cause of death: "tuberculosis", Informant: Roe McQueen (Butler), buried: McQueen Cemetery, died: 18 Jun 1917, record (1917) #: 86.

Sarah POWELL, age about 40 years, widow, parents: Ben White and Martha Crosswhite, cause of death: "tuberculosis of lungs", informant: Martilda Powell (Shouns), died: 19 Jun 1917, record (1917) #: 87.

Lou GREGG, female, born: 12 Jul 1842 in Carter Co. Tn, widow, parents: George Pierce (NC) and mother's first name not stated Campbell, mother born in Carter Co. TN., cause of death: "paralysis", informant: D.P. Pierce (Butler), buried: Dugger Cemetery, died: 25 Jun 1917, record (1917) #: 89.

Craton GREGG, born: 14 Apr 1917, parents: Clyde Gregg and Ethel Lewis (NC), cause of death: "bold hives", informant: Clyde Gregg (Butler), buried: Dugger Cemetery, died: 27 Jun 1917, record (1917) #: 90.

Infant PENNINGTON, parents: M.F. Pennington (NC) and Ada Farmer (NC), cause of death: "unknown", informant: R.W. Scott (Crandul), buried: Gentry Cemetery, born/died: 28 Jun 1917, record (1917) #: 91.

William JENKINS, age 78 years, 6 months and 26 days,
married, parents: B. (illegible) Jenkins and Josephine
Hyder, death cause: "heart disease", informant: Thomas
Jenkins (Mountain City), buried: Phillippi Cem., died:
26 Jun 1917, record (1917) #: 92.

Russell E. MAIN, born: 22 Feb 1917, parents: Hiram E.
Main (NC) and Hattie L. Bumgardner (Trade), cause of
death: "cause not known, found dead in bed",
informant: M.F. Bumgardner (Trade), buried: Dotson
Cemetery, died: 29 Jun 1917, record (1917) #: 93.

Infant JONES, male, parents: James Jones (NC) and Ann
Owens, cause of death: "premature delivery,
stillborn", informant: Susan Owens (Laurel Bloomery),
buried: Cornett Cemetery, died: 2 Jun 1917, record
(1917) #: 94.

Nathaniel MORGAN, parents: William Morgan (NC) and
Josie Evans, stillborn, informant: William Morgan
(Butler), buried: Potter Cemetery, died: 4 Jun 1917,
record (1917) #: 95.

Jacob WILSON, born: 18 May 1832, widower, parents:
Lemuel Wilson (NC) and Rebecca Reece (NC), death
cause: "unemic poisoning", informant: William Wilson
(Trade), buried in NC, died: 8 Jul 1917, record (1917)
#: 96.

Olley PROFFITT, born: 23 Jun 1878, married, parents:
Thomas Stanton and Cleary McElyea, cause of death:
"cancer of womb", informant: J.N. McElyea
(Elizabethton), buried: Johnson Cemetery, died: 23 Jul
1917, record (1917) #: 88.

Lizzie Mildred TRIPLETT, age 2 years, 9 months and 10
days, parents: John Triplett and Lizzie Davis (NC),
cause of death: "broncho pneumonia", informant: John
Triplett (Mountain City), buried: Wills Cemetery,
died: 21 Jul 1917, record (1917) #: 97.

Infant PROFFITT, male, parents: David Proffitt and
Deborah Davis, stillborn, informant: John Arnold
(Doeville), buried: Proffitt Cemetery, born/died: 18
Jul 1917, record (1917) #: 98.

David Edmond STOUT, born: 2 Sep 1916, parents: Gre
Stout and Bertha Roreak (NC), cause of death: "spinal
miningitis", informant: Gre Stout (Butler), buried:
Butler Cem., died: 7 Aug 1917, record (1917) #: 99.

Minnie B. STOUT, born: 14 Jun 1917, parents: P. Glenn
Stout and Mellie M. Morley, cause of death:
"dysentery", informant: E.H. Stout (Mountain City),
buried: P.R. Shoun Cemetery, died: 13 Aug 1917, record
(1917) #: 100.

Sarah Jane UNDERWOOD, born: 6 Nov 1902, parents: Thomas Underwood and Olie Bor... (illegible), cause of death: "tuberculosis", informant: Jane B.. (illegible)(Mountain City), buried: Mountain View Cemetery, died: 14 Aug 1917, record (1917) #: 101.

Isaac PIERCE, born: 25 Feb 1858 in Carter Co. TN, married, parents: Isaac Pierce (Carter Co. TN) and ? Crow (Carter Co. TN), cause of death: "heart disease", informant: D.C. Pierce (Mountain City), buried: Home Cemetery, died: 16 Aug 1917, record (1917) #: 102.

Catherine M. PATRICK, born: 21 Apr 1846 at Ashe Co. NC, widow, parents: W.M. Ashley (NC) and Polly Roten (NC), cause of death: "flux", informant: Jess Eller (Damascus VA), buried: Mock Cemetery, died: 21 Aug 1917, record (1917) #: 103.

Robert D. WILSON, age 66 years, married, parents: Richard L. Wilson and mother not listed, cause of death: "3 tumors on different parts of body", informant: E.L. McDade (Mountain City), buried: Wilson Cemetery, died: 28 Aug 1917, record (1917) #: 104.

Bonnie PAYNE, born: 11 Sep 1916, parents: Charley Payne (NC) and Della Johnson, cause of death: "whooping cough and pneumonia", informant: J.S. Johnson, buried: Phillippi Cemetery, died: 13 Sep 1917, record (1917) #: 105.

Nancy WRIGHT, born: 25 Oct 1837, widow, parents: E.J. Buckles and Susana Shoun, cause of death: "old age and heart lesion", informant: David Wright, buried: Gentry Cemetery, died: 14 Sep 1917, record (1917) #: 106.

Edward DICKENS, born 31 Aug 1916, parents: John Dickens (Watauga Co. NC) and Linda Dugger (Butler), cause of death: "intermenton fever", informant: John Dickens (Butler), buried: Dugger Cemetery, died: 15 Sep 1917, record (1917) #: 107.

Bertha Ganaway WILLS, born: 14 Aug 1861, parents: Peter W. Wills and Sarah Orr (Washington Co. VA), cause of death: "cerrosis of liver", informant: S.A. Fuller (Mountain City), buried: Wills Cemetery, died: 28 Sep 1917, record (1917) #: 108.

Infant MCCULLOCH, male, parents: J. Ray McCulloch and Maggie Wagner, cause of death: "cranistory due to deformed pelvis of mother", informant: Ray McCulloch (Maymead), died: 3 Sep 1917, record (1917) #: 109.

Polly Catherine SHOUN, born: 16 Jun 1839, married, parents: Daniel Robinson and Katy Stout, cause of death: "dropsy", informant: Thomas Grindstaff (Butler), buried: Doeville, died: 1 Oct 1917, record (1917) #: 110.

Mary Elizabeth BRADLEY, born: 4 Sep 1864, married, parents: John Snyder and Rachel Vaught, death cause: "dropsy", informant: Peter Kyle Bradley, buried: Butler, died: 2 Oct 1917, record (1917) #: 111.

James Edward WARD, born: 3 Sep 1917, parents: Roby Ward and Bessie Jones, cause of death: "congenital syphilis", informant: Roby Ward (Mountain City), buried: Mountain View Cemetery, died: 3 Oct 1917, record (1917) #: 112.

Tennessee TESTER, born: 7 Aug 1853, married, parents: William Tester and Malinda Jackson, cause of death: "diarrhea", informant: Stacy Tester (Shouns), died: 7 Oct 1917, record (1917) #: 113.

Martha A. DAVIS, age 84 years, born: 1833 in NC, parents: unknown, cause of death: "old age", informant: James F. Davis (Mountain City), buried: Doeville, died: 13 Oct 1917, record (1917) #: 114.

Walter ESTEP, born: 22 Jan 1917, parents: John Estep and Cordelia Campbell, death cause: "whooping cough", informant: John Estep (Doeville), buried: Campbell Cem., died: 16 Oct 1917, record (1917) #: 115.

Raleigh R. FARTHING, born: 2 Nov 1911, parents: Walter H. Farthing and Tiney Slimp, cause of death: "concussion of brain caused by falling from a horse", informant: L.L. Stout (Bakers Gap), died: 18 Oct 1917, record (1917) #: 116.

John Phillip WATERS, born: 6 May 1843 in NC, parents: William Waters and Zilpha Thompson, cause of death: "pellagra", informant: Wiley Rupard (Laurel Bloomery), buried: Dark Hollow Cemetery, died: 19 Oct 1917, record (1917) # 117.

Joseph MAIN, born: 2 Nov 1856, married, parents: Sidney Main (NC) and Pollie Dunn, cause of death: "carcinoma of stomach", informant: B... Hammons (Shouns), died: 26 Oct 1917, record (1917) #: 118.

Infant MAIN, parents: John Main and Lillie Wallace, stillborn, informant: John Main (Trade), buried: Reece Cemetery, died: 12 Oct 1917, record (1917) #: 119.

Melvina PERDUE, born: 15 May 1846, married, parents: John Shuffield (NC) and mother's name unknown, cause of death: "tuberlicer abscess", died: 1 Nov 1917, record (1917) #: 120.

Thomas W. JOHNSON, age 81 years, born: 1836 in NC, parents: unknown, cause of death: "chronic diarrhea, old age", informant: Will Canter (Mountain City), buried: Wilson Cemetery, died: 2 Nov 1917, record (1917) #: 121.

Andrew SHAW, colored, born: 7 Nov 1899, parents: Melvin Shaw (Wake Co. NC) and Lillie Williams, cause of death: "consumption", informant: S.W. Widley (Mountain City), buried: Mountain View Cemetery, died: 5 Nov 1917, record (1917) #: 122.

John HENDERSON, born: 24 Aug 1834 in NC, parents: unknown, married, cause of death: "hypo-static pneumonia", informant: Boone Owens (Mountain City), buried: Cornett Cemetery, died: 10 Nov 1917, record (1917) #: 123.

David Kitsmiller ROBINSON, born: 22 Sep 1884, married, parents: James Robinson (VA) and Mary Reece, cause of death: "typhoid fever", informant; W.J. Robinson (Mountain City), buried: Walter Shoun Cemetery, died: 15 Nov 1917, record (1917) #: 124.

Sarah E. STANTON, born: 5 Mar 1858, single, parents: Franklin Stanton (Coldwell NC) and Polly Dugger (TN), cause of death: "le grippe and tuberculosis", informant: Alex McElyea (Neva), died: 18 Nov 1917, record (1917) #: 125.

Myrtle Grace PARKS, born: 20 Sep 1917 in VA, parents: Robert W. Parks and (first name illegible) M. Denney, cause of death: "measles", informant: B.M. Denney (Trade), buried: Parks Cemetery, died: 18 Nov 1917, record (1917) #: 126.

John L. TRIPLETT, born: 13 Feb 1894 at Wilkes Co. NC, married, parents: John Triplett (Wilkes Co. NC) and first name not stated Simmons (Coldwell Co. NC), cause of death: "typhoid fever", informant: A.W. Shoun (Doeville), buried: Shoun Cemetery, died: 19 Nov 1917, record (1917) #: 127.

Empire MAIN, female, born: 29 Dec 1837 in NC, widow, parents: Ezekiel Thomas (NC) and Delia Day (NC), cause of death: "paralysis", informant: J.E. Denney (Trade), buried: Crawford Cemetery, died: 24 Nov 1917, record (1917) #: 128.

Robert Galen CORUM, born: 1 Jul 1842 in NC, married, parents: father not stated and Martha Corum (NC), cause of death: "no psysician in attendance, sudden death", buried: Cornett Cemetery, died: 24 Nov 1917, record (1917) #: 129.

Pharibe R. MATHERLY, born: 8 Oct 1827, widow, parents: John McCall and Nancy Haynes, cause of death: "cold and old age", informant: D.G. Matherly (Butler), buried: Matherly Cemetery, died: 25 Nov 1917, record (1917) #: 130.

Bessie BUCHANAN, born: 27 Aug 1917 in West VA, parents: J.B. Buchanan (NC) and Venie Brookshire, cause of death: "croup", informant: J.M. Buchanan (Mountain City), buried: Buchanan Cemetery, died: 27 Nov 1917, record (1917) #: 131.

Richard W. BLACKBURN, born: 18 Jan 1841, married, parents: Noah Blackburn (NC) and Nancy Wilson, cause of death: "heart trouble, dropped dead", informant: R.O. Blackburn (Doeville), buried: Rambo Cemetery, died: 13 Dec 1917, record (1917) #: 132.

Mary E. CROSSWHITE, born: 9 Jul 1832, married, parents: Andrew Shoun and Elizabeth Powel (NC), cause of death: "bulbar paralysis", informant: T.J. Walsh (Mountain City), buried: home cemetery, died: 24 Dec 1917, record (1917) #: 133.

Blanch GREER, born 1 Dec 1917, parents: Ben Greer (NC) and Adelade Greer (NC), cause of death: "congenital syphilis", informant: Ben Greer (Mountain City), buried: Donnelly Cemetery, died: 4 Dec 1917, record (1917) #: 134.

Nathaniel Cole DAVIS, born: 22 Nov 1917, parents: Monroe Davis (NC) and Calie Hagan (NC), cause of death: "lumbellical hemorage", informant: L.L. Stout (Neva), died: 7 Dec 1917, record (1917) #: 135.

Mollie BEAR, born 15 Oct 1893, married, parents: Millard F. Forrester and Amanda McElyea, cause of death: "tuberculosis of spine", informant: Isaac Bear (Homer, Ill.), died: 9 Dec 1917, record (1917) #: 136.

Joseph P. ARNOLD, born: 20 Jul 1853, married, parents: M.... Arnold and mother not stated, cause of death: "labor pneumonia", informant: James Arnold (Mountain City), buried: Nave Cemetery, Doeville, died: 11 Dec 1917, record (1917) #: 137.

Samuel GARLAND, born 18 Nov 1833 in Carter Co. TN, widower, parents: Lewis Garland (Carter Co. TN) and Susie Cole, cause of death: "valvular lieson of heart", informant; W.H. Stout (Crandul), buried: J.C. Garland Cem., died: 12 Dec 1917, record (1917) #: 138.

L.G. EGGERS, born: 31 Jul 1915, parents: Alexander Clayton Eggers and Julia M. Stout, cause of death: "whooping cough", informant: A.C. Eggers (Mountain City), buried: Roberts Cemetery, died: 12 Dec 1917, record (1917) #: 139.

Bessie ABEL, born 10 Dec 1917, parents: Henry Clayton Abel and Kate Gentry, cause of death: "unknown, found dead in bed", informant: Curt Abel (Laurel Bloomery), buried: Valley Cemetery, died: 14 Dec 1917, record (1917) #: 140.

Rebeckah BROOKS, age 76 years, widow, parents: Eliga Arnold and Nancy Arnold, cause of death: "shock, falling fracture of hip and shoulder", informant: R.R. Brooks (Mountain City), buried: Mountain View Cemetery, died: 23 Dec 1917, record (1917) #: 141.

George W. WALLACE, age 85 years, married, parents: Drewry Wallace (NC) and Elizabeth Snyder, cause of death: "paralysis", informant: W.M. Wallace (Trade), buried: Wallace Cemetery, died: 22 Dec 1917, record (1917) #: 142.

Delmar GARLAND, born 9 Sep 1917, parents: Jessie H. Garland and Eliza J. Jenkins, cause of death: "compound pneumonia", informant: J.H. Garland (Crandul), buried: Blevins Cemetery, died: 28 Dec 1917, record (1917) #: 143.

Earnestine NEATHERLY, parents: Walter Neatherly and Ellen Tester, stillborn, born/died: 11 Dec 1917, record (1917) #: 144.

Earnest NEATHERLY, parents: Walter Neatherly and Ellen Tester, stillborn, born/died: 11 Dec 1917, record (1917) #: 145.

James ROBINSON, born: 8 Aug 1834, widow, parents: Mo... Robinson (VA) and Catherine Robinson (VA), cause of death: "la grippe", informant: W,J. Robinson (Mountain City), buried: Walter Shoun Cemetery, died: 3 Jan 1918, record (1918) #: 1.

Ellen Stout WILEY, born: 25 Dec 1917, parents: Stanel Wiley and Eller Clock (Watauga Co. NC), cause of death: "well at bedtime, found dead at 2 a.m.", informant: M.M. Dunn (Shouns), died: 4 Jan 1918, record (1918) #: 2.

Spencer OSBORNE, born: 17 Oct 1911, parents: Roby Osborne (NC) and Pedia Johnson (NC), cause of death: "unknown", informant: W.H. Stout (Crandull), buried: Gentry Cemetery, Died: 4 Jan 1918, record (1918) #: 3.

James MINTON, born: 6 Jan 1918, parents: father not known and Cynthie E. Minton (NC), cause of death: "unknown", informant: Allen Minton (Crandull), buried: Blevins Cem., died: 7 Jan 1918, record (1918) #: 4.

William A. GREEN, born: 26 Jan 1854, married, parents: Thomas Green (NC) and Nancy Council (NC), cause of death: "thought to be organic heart disease and brights disease", informant: James A. Green (Shouns), buried: Woods Cemetery, died: 12 Jan 1918, record (1918) #: 5.

Franklin J. HOPPERS, born: 16 Jan 1833, parents: unknown, cause of death: "found dead, jury inquest held, verdict freezing", informant: W.H. Stout (Crandull), buried: Sparta, NC, died: 15 Jan 1918, record (1918) #: 6.

Infant LOWE, born: 13 Jan 1918, parents: Jacob M. Lowe and Sallie Norris, cause of death: "unknown", informant: Jacob M. Lowe (Mountain City), buried: Robinson Cem., died: 15 Jan 1918, record (1918) #: 7.

James W. JORDAN, born: 20 Sep 1867 in Carter Co. TN, widower, parents: E.S. Jordan (Carter Co. TN) and Elizabeth Stout, cause of death: "pneumonia fever", informant: T.H. Jordan (Doeville), buried: Shouns Cemetery, died: 20 Jan 1918, record (1918) #: 8.

Ogden ALLEN, born: March 1897, parents: A.L. Allen and Hattie Farthing (NC), cause of death: "pulmonary tuberculosis", informant: D.J. Farthing (Butler), died: 23 Jan 1918, record (1918) #: 9.

Fred Albert DUVALL, infant, date of birth not stated, parents: Henry Duvall (NC) and Sally Burgess, cause of death: "unknown", informant: J.E. Sexton (Mountain City), buried: Shingletown Cemetery, died: 23 Jan 1918, record (1918) #: 10.

George BUNTON, born: June 8, age 25 years, parents: Taylor Bunton and Janis White, cause of death: "measles and pneumonia", informant: Taylor Bunton (Butler), buried: Bunton Cemetery, died: 29 Jan 1918, record (1918) #: 11.

Earnest Clayton DUGGER, born: 7 Jan 1918, parents: Raleigh Dugger and Lula Norris, cause of death: "measles", informant: Raleigh Dugger (Butler), buried: Bunton Cem., died: 30 Jan 1918, record (1918) #: 12.

Infant WARD, parents: Asa Ward and Mary Morefield, cause of death: "premature birth", informant: Asa Ward (Crandull), buried: Gentry Cemetery, born/died: 12 Jan 1918, record (1918) #: 13.

Wiley DOWELL, born: 22 Oct 1889, parents: Noah Dowell and Sabra McElyea, cause of death: "hodkins disease", informant: Roby Lewis (Vaughtsville), died: 3 Feb 1918, record (1918) #: 14.

Luther MCQUEEN, born: 4 Aug 1903, parents: Sherman McQueen and Mollie Stout, cause of death: "pneumonia fever and measles", informant: Sherman McQueen (Butler), buried: Rainbolt Cemetery, died: 5 Feb 1918, record (1918) #: 15.

William C. TILLEY, born: 10 Oct 1842, widower, parents: Hamilton Tilley (NC) and Lucinda More, cause of death: "pneumonia fever", informant: J.C. Tilley (Jonesboro, TN), buried: Rambo Cemetery, died: 6 Feb 1918, record (1918) #: 16.

Melvin E. WOLF, born: 20 October, age 75 years, parents: T. Wolf (NC) and Elizabeth Smith, cause of death: "chronic bulbar paralysis", died: 11 Feb 1918, record (1918) #: 17.

Celia Jane JONES, age about 79 years, widow, parents: Jerry Osborn (NC) and Martha Graybeal (NC), cause of death: "thought to be organic heart disease", informant: R.S. Payne (Shouns), died: 12 Feb 1918, record (1918) #: 18.

Mary Essa BUCHANAN, born: 27 Aug 1917, parents: J.B. Blackburn (Mitchell Co. NC) and Venie Brookshire, cause of death: "gastritis", informant: J.M. Buchanan (Mountain City), buried: Buchanan Cemetery, died: 12 Feb 1918, record (1918) #: 19.

George W. CAMPBELL, age 46 years, married, parents: Powell Campbell and R. Becky Pierce, cause of death: "measles and pneumonia", informant: Powell Campbell (Butler), buried: Elk River Cemetery, died: 13 Feb 1918, record (1918) #: 20.

Callie GARLAND, born: 10 Feb 1918, parents: Wheeler Garland and Bessie Church, cause of death: "unknown", informant: Garfield Arnold (Doeville), died: 13 Feb 1918, record (1918) #: 21.

Mary Adaline MARHIAS, born: 14 Jan 1838, widow, parents: Hiram Hicks (NC) and first name not known Tester (NC), cause of death: "rheumatism of heart", died: 14 Feb 1918, record (1918) #: 22.

Annie BREWER, born: February 1849, age 68 years, married, Parents: Samuel Dugger and Hannah Potter (Carter Co. TN), cause of death: "tuberculosis complicated pneumonia", informant: A.G. Brewer (Butler), buried: Grindstaff Cem., died: 17 Feb 1918.

Victoria PENNINGTON, born: 20 Mar 1882, married, parents: A.J. Miller (NC) and Rena Perry (NC), cause of death: "peritonitis", informant: Vec Miller (Laurel Bloomery), buried: Valley Cemetery, died: 20 Feb 1918, record (1918) #: 24.

Donley GARLAND, born: 10 Feb 1918, parents: Wheeler Garland and Bessie Church, cause of death: "unknown", informant: Garfield Arnold (Doeville), buried: Shouns Cemetery, died: 23 Feb 1918, record (1918) #: 25.

Miles F. BREWER, born: July 1840, age 67 years, widower, parents: Joseph Brewer (NC) and Polly Lusk (NC), death cause: "dicilation of heart complicated pneumonia", informant: A.J. Brewer (Butler), buried: Grindstaff Cem., died: 23 Feb 1918, rec. (1918) #: 26.
Mabel ARNOLD, parents: Clarence Arnold and Alice Snyder, cause of death: "premature birth", born/died: 9 Mar 1918, informant: M.G. Snyder (Crandull), buried: Gentry Cemetery, record (1918) #: 27.
Hirbert Wade BROWN, born: 17 Jan 1918, parents: E.L. Brown and Ethel Brown, cause of death: "broncho pneumonia", informant: E.L. Brown (Shouns), died: 11 Mar 1918, record (1918) #: 28.
John Paul WINTERS, born: 4 Mar 1918, parents: John R. Winters and Susan Elizabeth Arnold, cause of death: "icterus neonatourne", informant: N.D. Owens (Mountain City), died: 12 Mar 1918, record (1918) #: 29.
David Jessie FARTHING, born: 28 Jul 1846 in Watauga Co. NC, married, parents: Brown Farthing (Wake Co. NC) and Annie Kindrel (Wilkes Co. NC), cause of death: "unknown", inforamant: Mrs. D.J. Farthing (Butler), died: 14 Mar 1918, record (1918) #: 30.
Mollie Virginia ARNOLD, born: 27 Mar 1918, parents: Alfred Arnold and Mamie Bess Jordan, cause of death: "premature birth", informant: Alfred Arnold (Crandull), died: 30 Mar 1918, record (1918) #: 31.
Infant SIMCOX, female, parents: John T. Simcox and Nettie Green (Watauga Co. NC), stillborn, informant: John T. Simcox (Neva), born/died: 12 Mar 1918, record (1918) #: 32.
Flora HASH, age 23 years, parents: James Greer and Victoria Vanover (NC), cause of death: "pneumonia", informant: James Greer (Trade), buried: Green Cemetery, died: 4 Apr 1918, record (1918) #: 33.
Elmer GRAYSON, born: 2 Jan 1912, parents: Ben Grayson and Mary Moore (NC), cause of death: "clothing caught fire at fireplace, accidental burns on extensive surface of body", informant: Ben Grayson (Welsh West VA), buried: Oak Cemetery, died: 5 Apr 1918, record (1918) #: 34 and 38 (duplicate).
Mary J. LEWIS, born: 20 Sep 1851, married, parents: William H. Howard and Mary Sanders (VA), cause of death: "valvular disease of heart", informant: G.F. Lewis (Shouns), buried: Forrester Cemetery, died: 6 Apr 1918, record (1918) #: 35.
Flora HASH, age 23 years, parents: James Greer and Victoria Vanover (NC), cause of death: "pneumonia", informant: James Greer (Trade), buried: Green Cemetery, died: 4 Apr 1918, record (1918) #: 33.

Elmer GRAYSON, born: 2 Jan 1912, parents: Ben Grayson and Mary Moore (NC), cause of death: "clothing caught fire at fireplace, accidental burns on extensive surface of body", informant: Ben Grayson (Welsh West VA), buried: Oak Cemetery, died: 5 Apr 1918, record (1918) #: 34 and 38 (duplicate).

Mary J. LEWIS, born: 20 Sep 1851, married, parents: William H. Howard and Mary Sanders (VA), cause of death: "valvular disease of heart", informant: G.F. Lewis (Shouns), buried: Forrester Cemetery, died: 6 Apr 1918, record (1918) #: 35.

Isaac Leander LEWIS, age about 82 years, married, parents: Gidden Lewis (NC) and Nancy Osborn (VA), cause of death: "auterosclerosis", informant: G.F. Lewis (Shouns), buried: Forrester Cemetery, died: 6 Apr 1918, record (1918) #: 36.

Cora Elizabeth DOLLAR, age 33 years, born in Ashe Co. NC, parents: Isaac Roark (NC) and first name not stated Cornett (NC), cause of death: "tuberculosis of lungs", informant: J.C. Dollar (Mountain City), buried: Wilson Cemetery, died: 11 Apr 1918, record (1918) #: 37.

Roy Denson DOLLAR, born: 17 Jul 1910 in Ashe Co. NC, parents: J.C. Dollar and Cora Roark (NC), cause of death: "accident, falling tree", informant: J.C. Dollar (Mountain City), buried: Wilson Cemetery, died: 15 Apr 1918, record (1918) #: 38.

Vada M. MCFADDIN, female, born: 6 Apr 1918, parents: John McFaddin and Nora Reece, cause of death: "unknown", informant: John McFaddin (Trade), buried: Reece Cem., died: 15 Apr 1918, record (1918) #: 39.

John H. DOUGHERTY, age 77 years, born in Ashe Co. NC, parents: Allen Daugherty (Ashe Co. NC) and Drucy Lewis (Ashe Co. NC), cause of death: "old age and brights disease", informant: Cilia Dunn (Shouns), died: 15 Apr 1918, record (1918) #: 40.

Caroline POWELL, age about 84 years, parents: James Powell (NC) and Nancy Lenderman (NC), cause of death: "organic heart disease", informant: J.G. Powell (Shouns), buried: Powell Cemetery, died: 16 Apr 1918, record (1918) #: 41.

Infant WILSON, male, parents: Daniel Wilson and Nettie Jenkins, cause of death: "7 month birth", died: 16 Apr 1918, record (1918) #: 42.

Infant WILSON, female, born 16 Apr 1918, parents: Daniel Wilson and Nettie Jenkins, cause of death: "7 month birth", died: 17 Apr 1918, record (1918) #: 43.

Floid T. WARD, born: 25 Dec 1884, single, parents: Noah Ward and Bettie Forrester, cause of death: "tuberculosis", informant: N.G. Ward (Bakers Gap), died: 21 Apr 1918, record (1918) #: 44.

Glen A. PRICE, born: 20 Oct 1912 in Oregon, parents: J.M. Price and J.P. Dungan, cause of death: "inflammation of bowels", informant: J.M. Price (Crandull), died: 25 Apr 1918, record (1918) #: 45.

Homer SHORES, born: 19 Mar 1918, parents: father not stated and Callie Shores (Green Co. TN), cause of death: "bold hives", informant: Callie Shores (Butler), buried: Dugger Cemetery, died: 28 Apr 1918, record (1918) #: 46.

Infant ELLIOTT, male, parents: Bishop M. Elliott (Carter Co. TNO and M.C. Nave, stillborn, informant: B.M. Elliott (Doeville), died: 22 Apr 1918, record (1918) #: 47.

Winnie F. FRITTS, born: 26 Aug 1883, married, parents: J.H. Jordan and Martha Shoun, cause of death: "tuberculosis of lungs", informant: J.H. Jordan (Mountain City), buried: Walker Cemetery, died: 1 May 1918, record (1918) #: 48.

Benjamin D. CABLE, born: 6 Aug 1835, parents: Benjamin Cable and mother unknown, cause of death: "apoplexy", informant: William Cable (Butler), buried: Dugger Cemetery, died: 2 May 1918, record (1918) #: 49.

Ella Lee CURD, born: 30 Apr 1918, parents: T.J. Curd and Hattie Parkins (NC), cause of death: "measles, it's mama had the measles", informant: T.J. Curd (Shouns), died: 12 May 1918, record (1918) #: 50.

Walter Retze ROARK, born: 14 May 1918, parents: Daniel Roark (NC) and Deffealsa Dollar (NC), cod "premature birth", informant: N.Y. Furchess (Crandull), buried: Gentry Cem., died: 14 May 1918, record (1918) #: 51.

Willie Gray GREGG, female, born: 25 Mar 1918, parents: J.C. Gregg and Ethel Lewis (Boone, NC), cod "bold hives", informant: J.C. Gregg (Butler), buried: Dugger Cemetery, died: 15 May 1918, record (1918) #: 52.

Dock HINES, age 32 years, born in NC, parents: George W. Hines (Grayson Co. VA) and Malisa E. Pennington (Ashe Co. NC), cod "fit and just fell dead", informant: M.E. Sluder (Crandull), buried: Blevins Cemetery, died: 18 May 1918, record (1918) #: 53.

Alvin CURD, born: 1 Jul 1874, married, parents: Ezekiel Curd and Maryon Hammons, cod "sephritis", informant: Susan Curd (Shouns), buried: Curd Cemetery, died: 17 May 1818, record (1918) #: 54.

Odell PRICE, born: 21 Jul 1907 in Boone, NC, parents:
Thomas C. Price (NC) and C.E. Sluder (NC), cause of
death: "rheumatism acute asticular and muscular weak
heart", informant: Evert Sluder (Crandull), buried:
Price Cem., died: 19 May 1918, record (1918) #: 55.
Walter WAGNER, black, date of birth or age not stated,
married, parents: Noah Wagner (NC) and Lyndia Baker
(NC), cause of death: "gun shot wound by unknown
party", informant: John Deal (Mountain City), buried:
Mountain View Cemetery, died: 22 May 1918, record
(1918) #: 56.
Infant DUNN, female, born: 24 May 1918, parents: W.M.
Dunn and Maud Roark (NC), cause of death: "measles",
informant: W.M. Dunn (Shouns), buried: Howard
Cemetery, died: 25 May 1918, record (1918) #: 57.
Mary E. GLENN, born: 15 Aug 1906 in NC, parents: W.D.
Glenn (NC) and Mattie McColoch, cause of death:
"tuberculosis", informant: J.W. Vannoy (Bakers Gap),
died: 29 May 1918, record (1918) #: 58.
Adam P. ISAACS, born 12 Apr 1918, parents: father's
first name illegible, Isaacs (NC) and Laura Green
(NC), cause of death: "bronchitis and indigestion",
died: 12 Jun 1918, record (1918) #: 59.
Nancy EASTRIDGE, born: 30 Jul 1880, married, parents:
George W. Noland and Fannie Davidson (VA), cause of
death: "pelegra", informant: J.E. Sexton (Mountain
City), buried: Shingletown Cemetery, died: 14 Jun
1918, record (1918) #: 60.
Ella C. PLEASANT, born: 1882 in Carter Co. TN, age
about 36, parents: Robert Treadway and Eva Crumley,
cause of death: "measles and pneumonia fever",
informant; G.A. Pleasant (Doeville), buried: Hinter
(Hunter ?) TN, died: 21 Jun 1918, record (1918) #: 61.
Infant MORLEY, male, born 20 May 1918, parents: father
not stated and Winnie E. Morley, cause of death:
"cough and cold", informant: W.D. Morley (Doeville),
buried: Morley Cemetery, died: 21 Jun 1918.
Ivan LEWIS, born: 2 Jun 1918, parents: James Lewis and
Clara Cardue (?) (Carter Co. TN), cause of death:
illegible, died: 25 Jun 1918, record (1918) #: 63.
Carbin D. DAVIS, born: 26 Feb 1917, parents: E.J.
Davis and Josie Hicks, cause of death: "measles and
pneumonia fever", informant: E.J. Davis (Butler),
Wright Cem, died: 25 Jun 1918, record (1918) #: 64.
Roby ROBBINS, born: 11 Jun 1918, parents: R.D. Robbins
(NC) and C.M. Crosswhite, cause of death: "found dead
in bed", informant: R.D. Robbins (Crandull), buried:
Blevins Cem., died: 28 Jun 1918, record (1918) #: 65.

Richard L. HEATON, age 60 years, married, parents: Godfrey Heaton and Mary Moreland, cause of death: "valvular lesion of heart", informant: Wile Brinkley (Crandull), buried: Gentry Cemetery, died: 29 Jun 1918, record (1918) #: 66.

Jannie BUNTON, age 97 years, widow, parents: Thomas Whitehead (Carter Co. TN) and Catherine Stout, cause of death: "epoplexy", informant: Tom Baker (Butler), buried: Baker Cemetery, died: 2 Jul 1918, record (1918) #: 67.

Baxter Grant ARNOLD, born: 29 May 1898, single, parents: John Henry Arnold and Telilah O. Michaels, cause of death: "heart failure", informant: N.D. Owens (Mountain City), buried: Michaels Cemetery, died: 4 Jul 1918, record (1918) #: 68.

Jess BAILEY, born 21 Jul 1877, widower, parents: Frank Bailey (NC) and Jane Bass (NC), cause of death: "chronic chloral poisoning, not suicidal", informant: James Bailey (Mountain City), buried: Mountain View Cemetery, died: 8 Jul 1918, record (1918) #: 68.

Martha Florence POWELL, born: 25 Sep 1849, widow, parents: Joseph Adams and Mary Kizer (NC), cause of death: "chronic intestinal nephritis", informant: Marion Powell (Mountain City), buried: Mountain View Cemetery, died: 16 Jul 1918, record (1918) #: 70.

Martha HANKINS, born: 27 Jul 1916, parents: Earl Hankins and Ada Jenkins, cause of death: "taxeax poison", died: 18 Jul 1918, record (1918) #: 71.

Ruby PLUMMER, born: 29 Dec 1917, parents: Landon Plummer (VA) and Laura Berry, cause of death: "spina bifida", informant: R.A. Cole (Crandull), buried: Gentry Cem., died: 19 Jul 1918, record (1918) #: 72.

Clyde F. MCQUEEN, born: 29 Aug 1917, parents: Civ McQueen and Annie J. Montgomery, cause of death: "acute indigestion", informant: Civ McQueen (Crandull), buried: McQueen Cemetery, died: 21 Jul 1918, record (1918) #: 73.

Wade WALLACE, born: 5 Mar 1918, parents: James Wallace and Ellen Wilson (NC), cause of death: "chronic diarrhea", informant: James I. Wallace (Trade), buried: Wallace Cemetery, died: 24 Jul 1918, record (1918) #: 74.

Mary RAY, age 79 years, parents: W.M. Foster (NC) and Nancy (last name not stated)(NC), cause of death: "ovarian cyst", informant: J.R. Ray (Crandull), buried: Gentry Cemetery, died: 24 Jul 1918, record (1918) #: 75.

Stelina GREEN, age 80 years, born in NC, married, parents: John Keller (NC) and Phoebe Keller (NC), cause of death: "old age", informant: William Green (Crandull), buried: Gentry Cemetery, died: 26 Jul 1918, record (1918) #: 76.

Luke SIMPSON, age 1 year, parents: not stated, cause of death: "diarrhea", died: 28 Jul 1918, record (1918) #: 77.

Enola HAMPTON, born: 2 Nov 1883 in Ashland, NC, married, parents: Filmore Price (Ashland, NC) and Nancy Price (Ashland, NC), cause of death: "pulmonary tuberculosis", informant: Lilard Hampton (Shouns), buried: Arnold Cemetery, died: 3 Aug 1918, record (1918) #: 78.

Millard SLIMP, born: 8 May 1854, single, parents: David Slimp and Evaline Matheson, cause of death: "paralysis of throat", informant: Thomas Davis (Neva), died: 8 Aug 1918, record (1918) #: 79.

Martha Lucy BEELER, born: 6 Dec 1845, single, parents: A.B. Beeler and Lucy Acre (NC), cause of death: "dysentery", informant: Lucy Colton (Bristol, TN), died: 13 Aug 1918, record (1918) #: 80.

Josiah JONES, born: 10 Mar 1854, married, parents: John Jones (NC) and Patsey Ashley (NC), cause of death: "cancer on face", buried: Gentry Cemetery, died: 16 Aug 1918, record (1918) #: 81.

Jake GRINDSTAFF, born: 24 Aug 1867, married, parents: George Grindstaff and Elizabeth Smith, cause of death: illegible, died: 17 Aug 1918, record (1918) #: 82.

Floy L. MCELYEA, born: 29 Mar 1918, parents: Millard F. McElyea and Sarah F. Tester, cause of death: "acute indigestion", informant: M.F. McElyea (Shouns), died: 29 Aug 1918, record (1918) #: 83.

Mildridge Ugean ROBINSON, born: 23 Apr 1918, parents: W.J. Robinson and Grace Kirby (NC), cause of death: "entero collitis", informant: W. J. Robinson (Mountain City), buried: Walter Shoun Cemetery, died: 1 Sep 1918, record (1918) #: 84.

Gladys Lucil FRITZ, born: 1 Sep 1918, parents: Allen Fritz and Mary Maxwell, cause of death: "unknown", informant: Will S. Robinson (Laurel Bloomery), died: 2 Sep 1918, record (1918) #: 85.

Herald Lane SHOUN, born: 25 Jul 1918, parents: Carl R. Shoun and Winnie M. Fritts, cause of death: "cholera", informant: Carl R. Shoun (Mountain City), buried: Shoun Cemetery, died: 3 Sep 1918, record (1918) #: 86.

Grace CROW, born: 14 Jun 1918, parents: Charlie Crow and Julia Hunt, cause of death: "influenza", informant: Charlie Crow (Mountain City), died: 10 Sep 1918, record (1918) #: 87.

Dany WILSON, born: July 1853, age 65 years, parents: Hezekiah Wilson and Jane Rhudy, cause of death: "unknown", buried: Valley Cemetery, died: 20 Sep 1918, record (1918) #: 88.

Infant HENSON, female, parents: David Ray Henson and Sallie Gentry, cause of death: not stated, informant: David Henson (Mountain City), died: 23 Sep 1918, record (1918) #: 89.

Mrs. Parnaissie GENTRY, born: 24 Sep 1851, married, parents: General Gentry and Liza Gentry, death cause: "broncho pneumonia", informant: Ed Gentry (Mountain City), died: 24 Sep 1918, record (1918) #: 90.

John D. HEATON, born: 15 May 1900, single, parents: Sam Heaton (NC) and Mathie Tester (NC), cause of death: "flux", informant: Sam Heaton (Butler), buried: Dugger Cem., died: 25 Sep 1918, record (1918) #: 91.

Infant VAUGHT, male, parents: Rosco Vaught and Mary Absher, stillborn, born/died: 10 Sep 1918, record (1918) #: 92.

Julia DOLLAR, born: 17 Oct 1857 in NC, widow, parents: William Forrester and Nancy Greer, cause of death: illegible, informant: C.C. Dollar (Shouns), buried: Forrester Cem., died: 2 Oct 1918, record (1918) #: 93.

Edward Jr. ROBERTS, born: 1 Oct 1918, parents: Ed Roberts and Mary J. Roberts, cause of death: "unknown", informant: Ed Roberts (Mountain City), buried: Wright Cemetery, died: 9 Oct 1918, record (1918) #: 94.

Lawson E. STOUT, born: 28 Sep 1841, parents: Godfrey D. Stout and Mary Vaught (VA), cause of death: "pneumonia", informant: L.L. Stout (Bakers Gap), died: 9 Oct 1918, record (1918) #: 95.

Emaly JOHNSON, born: 3 Dec 1838, widow, parents: William Shupe (VA) and Nancy Hawkins, cause of death: "arterio sclerosis paralysis", informant: Robert J. Johnson (Mountain City), buried: Phillippi Cemetery, died: 13 Oct 1918, record (1918) #: 96.

Joe R. SMITH, born: 26 Mar 1903, parents: S.J. Smith (NC) and Martha E. Main, cause of death: "influenza", informant: S.J. Smith (Damascus, VA), buried: Martin Cemetery, died: 15 Oct 1918, record (1918) #: 97.

James E. HINES, born: Jan 1884 in Ashe Co. NC, married, parents: G.W. Hines (NC) and M.E. Pennington (VA), cause of death: "broncho pneumonia", buried: Crandull TN, died: 15 Oct 1918, record (1918) #: 98.

Mrs. Martha CRESS, age 54 years, widow, parents: C.M. Arnold and Sarah Phillippi (Wythe Co. VA), cause of death: "influenza", informant: J.S. Arnold (Mountain City), buried: Phillippi Cemetery, died: 20 Oct 1918, record (1918) #: 99.

John Thomas PLEASANT, born: 12 Jun 1916, parents: James Pleasant (NC) and Bessie Lee (NC), cause of death: "influenza", informant: Bessie Pleasant (Mountain City), buried: Wright Cemetery, died: 23 Oct 1918, record (1918) #: 100.

James W. ALLEN, born: 24 Jul 1918, parents: Carter Allen (NC) and Sallie Stout, cause of death: "Spanish influenza", informant: Carter Allen (Shouns), buried: Arnold Cem., died: 24 Oct 1918, record (1918) #: 101.

Eva Virginia STURGILL, born: 1 Apr 1918, parents: Benjamin Sturgill and Cora Dollar, cause of death: "pneumonia following influenza", informant: M.E. Wills (Mountain City), buried: Shingletown Cemetery, died: 26 Oct 1918, record (1918) #: 102.

Bertha May NEELY, born: 6 May 1892, single, parents: William Smith Neely and Mattie Butler, cause of death: "influenza and heart failure", informant: Will S. Robinson (Laurel Bloomery), buried: Acre Field Cemetery, died: 27 Oct 1918, record (1918) #: 103.

Ettie ARNIE, born: 3 Mar 1891, married, parents: R.F. Garland and Sallie Morefield (NC), cause of death: "heart dropsy", informant: R.F. Garland (Doeville), buried: Rambo Cemetery, died: 27 Oct 1918, record (1918) #: 104.

Mary Ann STOUT, age 73 years, widow, parents: Andrew Stout (VA) and mother's name not stated, cause of death: "heart dropsy", informant: A.J. Stout (Butler), buried: Rainbolt Cemetery, died: 27 Oct 1918, record (1918) #: 105.

Nannie Fay ROBINSON, born: 1 Feb 1916, parents: Garda F. Robinson and Sallie Stout, cause of death: "tuberculosis", informant: G.F. Robinson (Butler), buried: Rambo Cemetery, died: 28 Oct 1918, record (1918) #: 106.

John P. DAVIS, born 22 Oct 1918, parents: Jack Davis and Josie Hicks, cause of death: "Spanish influenza", informant: John P. Davis (Mountain City), buried: Wright Cem., died: 28 Oct 1918, record (1918) #: 107.

Alvon Ray CRESS, born: 10 Jul 1900, single, parents: A.M. Cress and Nellie Johnson, cause of death: "influenza followed by pneumonia", informant W.A. Cress (Mountain City), buried: Cress cemetery, died: 30 Oct 1918, record (1918) #: 108.

Elbert W. WATSON, born: 22 Apr 1883, parents: Pink Watson (NC) and Sarah Michaels (NC), cause of death: "influenza", informant: N.V. Watson (Crandull), buried: Blevins Cemetery, died: 30 Oct 1918, record (1918) #: 109.

Mildred Dorothy GENTRY, born: June 1918, parents: W. Scott Gentry and mother's name not stated, cause of death: "unknown", informant: John Reuben Triplett (Mountain City), died: 30 Oct 1918, record (1918) #: 110.

Sallie CROW, age 3 years, parents: Arvil C. Crow and Bessie Smith, cause of death: illegible, died: 30 Oct 1918, record (1918) #: 111.

Hugh Alexander JENKINS, born: 5 Aug 1845, parents: Hughie Jenkins (Indiana) and Susan Grindstaff (TN), cause of death: "chronic intestinal nephritis", informant: Hattie Jenkins (Mountain City), buried: Mountain View Cemetery, died: 31 Oct 1918, record (1918) #: 112.

Infant LOWE, parents: R.S. Lowe and Cassie South, stillborn, informant: R.S. Lowe (Mountain City), buried: Shoun Cemetery, born/died: 20 Oct 1918, record (1918) #: 113.

Reuette BROOKSHIRE, age 23 years, divorced, parents: Joel Brookshire and Lizzie Shepard (NC), cause of death: "typhoid fever", died: 2 Nov 1918, record (1918) #: 114.

Edgar Dave BROOKS, born: 27 Oct 1900, parents: Kemp Brooks and Callie Snyder, cause of death: "broncho pneumonia", informant: R.K. Brooks (Mountain City), died: 3 Nov 1918, record (1918) #: 115.

Ruby Selvia JONES, born: 21 Jul 1914 in Wise Co. VA, parents: R.E. Jones and Mary E. Isaacs, cause of death: "influenza", buried: Donelly Cemetery, died: 6 Nov 1918, record (1918) #: 116.

James L. MAIN, born: 28 Sep 1917, parents: father not stated and Lela Main, cause of death: "influenza", buried: Reece Cemetery, died: 7 Nov 1918, record (1918) #: 117.

Zelda Pearl CAMPBELL, born: 13 Jan 1914, parents: Richard L. Campbell and Sabra Walker, cause of death: "influenza", informant: Richard L. Campbell (Doeville), buried: Shoun Cemetery, died: 8 Nov 1918, record (1918) #: 118.

Infant MCQUEEN, born: 7 Nov 1918, parents: Jim McQueen and Bettie Lock, cause of death: unknown, informant: Pete Landers (Mountain City), buried: Mountain View Cemetery, died: 10 Nov 1918, record (1918) #: 119.

John D. MCQUEEN, born: 10 June 1914, parents: Jim McQueen and Bettie Lock, cause of death: "influenza", informant: Jim McQueen (Mountain City), buried: Mountain View Cemetery, died: 11 Nov 1918, record (1918) #: 120.

Tyler G. SWIFT, born: 1 Feb 1913, parents: father not stated and Lennie Swift, cause of death: "tubercular meniges", informant: Ham Swift (Mountain City), buried: Wilson Cemetery, died: 14 Nov 1918, record (1918) #: 121.

Robert SWIFT, born: 4 Dec 1917, parents: Dewey Swift (NC) and Arola Harmon (NC), cause of death: "pneumonia following influenza", died: 15 Nov 1918, record (1918) #: 122.

Camel T. GUIN, born: 25 Oct 1899, single, parents: Monroe Guin and Martha Atwood, informant: John Vannoy (Bakers Gap), died: 15 Nov 1918, record (1918) #: 123.

Lora May WALKER, born: 26 Apr 1917, parents: John C. Walker and Ellen Heaton, cause of death: "cold and influenza", informant: John C. Walker (Doeville), buried: Campbell Cemetery, died: 21 Nov 1918, record (1918) #: 124.

Otis LEWIS, born: 31 Jan 1910, parents: John C. Lewis and Callie Hampton, cause of death: "Spanish influenza", informant: John C. Lewis (Shouns), buried: Forrester Cemetery, died: 23 Nov 1918, record (1918) #: 125.

Lizzie MCFADDIN, born: 24 Nov 1887, married, parents: E.N. Miller (NC) and Nancy Woodring (NC), cause of death: "said to be pulmonary consumption", informant: E.N. Miller (Trade), buried in North Carolina, died: 24 Nov 1918, record (1918) #: 126.

Susannah STOUT, born: 13 Aug 1872, married, parents: not stated, cause of death: "influenza", buried in Doeville, died: 26 Nov 1918, record (1918) #: 127.

Willard STANSBERRY, born: 13 Mar 1915, parents: John Stansberry (NC), and Ellie Bunton, cause of death: "influenza", informant: John Stansberry, buried: Bunton Cem., died: 27 Nov 1918, record (1918) #: 128.

Mary MANUEL, born: 16 Oct 1842 in North Carolina, parents: Charlie Hamby and Rebecca Minton (NC), cause of death: "cancer of breast", informant: Coy Manuel (Crandull), buried: Belvins Cemetery, died: 27 Nov 1918, record (1918) #: 129.

Loretta MELVIN, born: 18 May 1917 in Washington Co. VA, parents: George W. Melvin (VA) and Tabitha Leonard (VA), cause of death: "whooping cough and acute indigestion", buried in Bristol, died: 28 Nov 1918, record (1918) #: 130.

Infant MCELYEA, parents: Jim McElyea and P.. (illegible) Dunn, cause of death: "born dead", informant: J.S. Butler (Shouns), buried: Noah Wagner Cemetery, born/died: 5 Nov 1918, record (1918) #: 131.

Roscoe VAUGHT, born: 19 May 1879, married, parents: David H. Vaught and Evaline Snyder, cause of death: "Spanish influenza followed by pneumonia", died: 1 Dec 1918, record (1918) #: 132.

Mary SHOUN, born: May 1873, married, parents: Noah Stout and Amanda Baly (Bailey ?), cause of death: "influenza", informant: J.M. Stout (Neva), died: 3 Dec 1918, record (1918) #: 133.

David HORN, born: 19 Apr 1910, parents: Edward Horn and Martha Wills, cause of death: "Spanish influenza", informant: W.J. Tester (Neva), died: 5 Dec 1918, record (1918) #: 134.

William O.... (illegible), age 23 years, born in Illinois, parents: not stated, cause of death: "accidental gunshot wound", buried in Illinois, died: 7 Dec 1918, record (1918) #: 135.

Delie HEATON, born: Aug 1878, married, parents: Andrew Combs and Mary Madron, death cause: "pneumonia following influenza", informant: C.F Heaton (Vaughtsville), died: 8 Dec 1918, record (1918) #: 136.

Vera CHRISTIE, born: 1 Aug 1886, parents: N.C. Tester and Dealie (Cordelia) Ward, cause of death: "influenza followed by pneumonia", died: 12 Dec 1918, record (1918) #: 137.

Ora ROARK, born: 24 Jul 1898, parents: Joseph Dowell and Dicy Taylor, death cause: "childbirth", informant: J.S. Dowell (Mountain City), buried: Shingletown Cem., died: 13 Dec 1918, record (1918) #: 138.

Lonnie H. ROBERTS, born: 27 Sep 1899, parents: E.G. Roberts and Mary Jane Stout, cause of death: "influenza", buried: Wright Cemetery, died: 13 Dec 1918, record (1918) #: 139.

Blain Evert WILSON, born: 16 Aug 1918, parents: William Wilson (VA) and Callie Dowell, cause of death: "hooping cough followed by influenza", informant: Dewey Dowell (Shouns), died: 14 Dec 1918, record (1918) #: 140.

Hubert HORN, born: 1 Dec 1914 in Virginia, parents: Edron Horn and Martha (surname not stated), cause of death: "pneumonia following influenza", informant: Dewey Dowell (Shouns), died: 14 Dec 1918, record (1918) #: 141.

Okie Ann NORRIS, age 15 years, parents: Mack Norris (NC) and Nannie Bunton, cause of death: "pneumonia fever", informant: Mack Norris (Butler) buried: Bunton Cemetery, died: 14 Dec 1918, record (1918) #: 142.

Charles PATRICK, born: 11 Apr 1899, parents: Willis Patrick and Sallie Phillippi, cause of death: "pneumonia following influenza", informant: A.J. Forrester (Mountain City), buried: Phillippi Cemetery, died: 15 Dec 1918, record (1918) #: 143.

Jellada DUNN, born: 19 Sep 1918, parents: J.H. Dunn and Lucy Bailey, cause of death: "thought to be influenza", informant: J.H. Dunn (Shouns), died: 16 Dec 1918, record (1918) #: 144.

Infant SWIFT, parents: Richard Swift and Ethel Roberts, cause of death: "premature delivery", informant: Richard Swift (Mountain City), born/died: 18 Dec 1918.

Roescrans, Jr. SHAW, date of birth not recorded, parents: Rosecrans Shaw and (first name illegible) Walten, cause of death: "influenza", buried: Mountain View Cem., died: 19 Dec 1918, record (1918) #: 146.

Ethel Roberts SWIFT, born: May 1894, married, parents: Ed Roberts and Mary Jane Stout, cause of death: "pulmonary edema, influenza", informant: Gray Roberts (Mountain City), buried: Wilson Cemetery, died: 19 Dec 1918, record (1918) #: 147.

Mandie TESTER, born: 17 Dec 1918, parents: Martin Tester (Watauga Co. NC) and Arizona Payne, cause of death: not stated, informant: Martin Tester (Butler), buried: Payne Cemetery, died: 21 Dec 1918, record (1918) #: 148.

Mary E. ARNOLD, born: 20 Dec 1918, parents: Andrew J. Arnold and Elizy Stout, cause of death: unknown, informant: A.J. Arnold (Vaughtsville), died: 25 Dec 1918, record (1918) #: 149.

John ROARK, born: 14 Jul 1918, parents: Avery Roark (Ashe Co. NC) and Ainer Church (Wilkes Co. NC), cause of death: "influenza", buried: Wilson Cemetery, died: 29 Dec 1918, record (1918) #: 150.

Donald RANKINS, age 1 year and 1 month, parents: Ed Rankins and Lake Cuddy (NC), cause of death: "pneumonia followed by influenza", died: 29 Dec 1918, record (1918) #: 151.

Felist Stout ROBERTS, male, born: 16 Sep 1916, parents: David A. Roberts and Etta Stout, cause of death: "influenza", informant; David A. Roberts (Mountain City), buried: Walter Shoun Cemetery, died: 31 Dec 1918, record (1918) #: 152.

Infant PIERCE, sex not stated, parents: James Pierce and Laura Lawson, stillborn, informant: Bettie Pope (Mountain City), buried: Shingletown Cemetery, died: 31 Dec 1918, record (1918) #: 153.

Infant SHOUN, female, parents: L.P. Shoun and Laura E. Roberts, stillborn, informant: L.P. Shoun (Mountain City), buried: Wright Cemetery, born/died: 6 Dec 1918, record (1918) #: 154.

Infant SHOUN, female, parents: L.P. Shoun and Laura E. Roberts, stillborn, informant: L.P. Shoun (Mountain City), buried: Wright Cemetery, born/died: 6 Dec 1918, record (1918) #: 155.

Blanche Delina LEWIS, born: 18 Dec 1918, parents: David C. Lewis and Chelsie Lee Lewis, cause of death: "born dead", informant: G.W. Lewis (Crandull), buried: Blevins Cem., died: 18 Dec 1918, record (1918) #: 156.

Infant SWIFT, sex not recorded, parents: Richard Swift and Ethel Roberts, cause of death: "premature delivery, mother had influenza" born/died: 18 Dec 1918, record (1918) #: 157.

Ramon MOREFIELD, born: 2 Jan 1915, parents: Wiley Morefield and Lynda Byers, cause of death: "pneumonia", informant: Wiley Morefield (Vaughtsville), died: 2 Jan 1919, record (1919) #: 1.

Blaine HEATON, born: 5 Jan 1917, parents: Sam Heaton (NC) and Marthie Tester (NC), cause of death: "flue", informant: Sam Heaton (Butler), buried: Dugger Cemetery, died: 3 Jan 1919, record (1919) #: 2.

Ellen ARNOLD, born: 5 Jan 1915, parents: John Arnold and Martha Church, cause of death: "influenza", informant: John Arnold (Doeville), buried: Rambo Cemetery, died: 5 Jan 1919, record (1919) #: 3.

Doran Donally ROBERTS, born: Nov 1917, parents: Ed Roberts and Mary Jane Stout, cause of death: "influenza and broncho pneumonia", informant: M.E. Wilson (Mountain City), buried: Wright Cemetery, died: 5 Jan 1919, record (1919) #: 4.

Eller STOUT, female, born: 22 Apr 1916 in Montana, parents: John H. Stout and Sue Hammons, cause of death: "caught on fire and burned to death in house", informant: John H. Stout (Shouns), buried: Stout Cemetery, died: 6 Jan 1919, record (1919) #: 5.

Virgia Othie Shupe PHILLIPPI, born: 23 May 1888, married, parents: W.T. Shupe and Margaret Blevins, cause of death: "pneumonia", informant: John Phillippi (Mountain City), buried: Phillippi Cemetery, died: 7 Jan 1919, record (1919) #: 6.

Lucie STOUT, born: 12 Aug 1917, parents: Ascy Shupe and Annie Price, cause of death: "supposed to be croup", informant: J.M. Stout (Neva), died: 11 Jan 1919, record (1919) #: 7.

Mrs. Mollie CHURCH, age 20 years, parents: Albert Hicks and Eliza Rankins, cause of death: "influenza followed by pneumonia", buried: Phillippi Cemetery, died: 12 Jan 1919, record (1919) #: 8.

Hytie Bell WILSON, born: 17 Mar 1892, single, parents: Robert Wilson and Lutitia Fritts, cause of death: "influenza followed by pneumonia", informant: S.L. Harbins (Mountain City), died: 14 Jan 1919, record (1919) #: 9.

Sally HACKNEY, born: 12 Jul 1840, widow, parents: Akly Beard (NC) and Louisa Cammel, cause of death: "diarrhea following weakness", informant: Tom Hackney (Neva), died: 16 Jan 1919, record (1919) #: 10.

Millie Ida BOWERS, born: 28 Jul 1891, married, parents: D.L. Reece and D.C. Ward, cause of death: "broncho pneumonia, premature delivery and influenza", informant: D.L. Reece, died: 16 Jan 1919, record (1919) #: 11.

Memphis M GENTRY, female, age 33 years, 2 months and 12 days, parents: Jas Wills and Rachael Greer, cause of death: "influenza", informant: A.J. Forrester (Mountain City), buried: Phillippi Cemetery, died: 17 Jan 1919, record (1919) #: 12.

Mrs. Elizie POWELL, age 75 years, parents: James Powell (NC) and mother not stated, cause of death: "influenza", informant: A.M. Stout (Mountain City), buried: Powell Cemetery, died: 18 Jan 1919, record (1919) #: 13.

Ethel BROWN, age about 24 years, married, parents: J.H. Brown (NC) and Elizabeth Potts, cause of death: "Spanish influenza", informant: T.F. Brown (Shouns), died: 19 Jan 1919, record (1919) #: 14.

Mrs. Myra Bowers DUGGER, black, age about 57 years, born in NC, parents: not stated, cause of death: "influenza", informant: R.E. Donally (Mountain City), died: 20 Jan 1919, record (1919) #: 15.

Lillie Loretta HEABERLIN, born: 19 May 1916, parents: James W. Heaberlin and Liza L. Phillipps, death cause: "whooping cough and broncho pneumonia", informant: J.W. Heaberlin (Crandull), buried: Heaberlin Cem., died: 22 Jan 1919, record (1919) #: 16.

Jasper Parked WILSON, born: 2 Dec 1918, parents: Zederic Wilson and Ella Johnson, cause of death: "flue", informant: Zederic Wilson (Butler), buried: Snider Cem., died: 22 Jan 1919, record (1919) #: 17.

Myrtle FLETCHER, born: 11 Dec 1918, parents: Ora Fletcher and Bertha Rvans (NC), cause of death: "measles", informant: David Roark (Crandull), died: 23 Jan 1919, record (1919) #: 18.

Robert Logan MAYS, born: 12 Mar 1918, parents: Tom Mays (NC) and Julia Fletcher, cause of death: "influenza", informant: Tom Mays (Crandull), buried: Tom Mays Cem., died: 23 Jan 1919, record (1919) #: 19.

Garfield CHURCH, age about 1 year, parents: Irvin Church and Mollie Hicks, death cause: "influenza", informant: Reba Asbury (Mountain City), buried: Phillippi Cem., died: 23 Jan 1919, rec. (1919) #: 20.

Norma Rebecca FARTHING, born: 3 May 1898, single, parents: Abner Farthing (NC) and Millie Oliver (NC), cause of death: "influenza and broncho pneumonia", buried: Mountain View Cemetery, died: 25 Jan 1919, record (1919) #: 21.

Baxter R. GENTRY, age about 40 years, married, parents: Lafayette Gentry and mother's name illegible (Fenner ?), cause of death: "pneumonia and influenza", Phillippi Cem, died: 26 Jan 1919, record (1919) #: 22.

Leta Hazel FLETCHER, born: 3 Mar 1914, parents: James Fletcher (VA) and Sara Cole, cause of death: "measles", informant: Mrs. J.M. Shoun (Crandull), died: 27 Jan 1919, record (1919) #: 23.

Sallie B. GARFIELD, born: 24 Mar 1864, married, parents: James Morefield and Margaret Greer, cause of death: "influenza and pneumonia", informant: R.T. Garfield (Doeville), buried: Rambo Cemetery, died: 29 Jan 1919, record (1919) #: 24.

Mrs. Sarah MOCK, colored, age about 53 years, born in NC, parents: Charles Davenport (NC) and mother's name not stated, cause of death: "chronic brights", informant: Will Mock (Mountain City), buried: Mountain View Cemetery, died: 29 Jan 1919, record (1919) #: 25.

Malinda Caroline DOWELL, age 76 years, parents: Larkin Dunn and Katy Jackson, death cause: "old age", informant: W.L. Roark (Mountain City), buried: Shingletown, died: 30 Jan 1919, record (1919) #: 26.

Andrew Dewey ISAACS, born: 22 Sep 1918, parents: Carl Isaacs and Rosa Belle (Surname illegible), cause of death: "supposed to be influenza", informant: Carl Isaacs (Doeville), buried: Shoun Cemetery, died: 30 Jan 1919, record (1919) #: 27.

Norma Rebecca FARTHING, born: 3 May 1898, single, parents: Abner Farthing (NC) and Millie Oliver (NC), cause of death: "influenza and broncho pneumonia", buried: Mountain View Cemetery, died: 25 Jan 1919, record (1919) #: 21.

Baxter R. GENTRY, age about 40 years, married, parents: Lafayette Gentry and mother's name illegible (Fenner ?), cause of death: "pneumonia and influenza", buried: Phillippi Cemetery, died: 26 Jan 1919, record (1919) #: 22.

Leta Hazel FLETCHER, born: 3 Mar 1914, parents: James Fletcher (VA) and Sara Cole, cause of death: "measles", informant: Mrs. J.M. Shoun (Crandull), died: 27 Jan 1919, record (1919) #: 23.

Sallie B. GARFIELD, born: 24 Mar 1864, married, parents: James Morefield and Margaret Greer, cause of death: "influenza and pneumonia", informant: R.T. Garfield (Doeville), buried: Rambo Cemetery, died: 29 Jan 1919, record (1919) #: 24.

Mrs. Sarah MOCK, colored, age about 53 years, born in NC, parents: Charles Davenport (NC) and mother's name not stated, cause of death: "chronic brights", informant: Will Mock (Mountain City), buried: Mountain View Cemetery, died: 29 Jan 1919, record (1919) #: 25.

Malinda Caroline DOWELL, age 76 years, parents: Larkin Dunn and Katy Jackson, cause of death: "old age", informant: W.L. Roark (Mountain City), buried: Shingletown Cemetery, died: 30 Jan 1919, record (1919) #: 26.

Andrew Dewey ISAACS, born: 22 Sep 1918, parents: Carl Isaacs and Rosa Belle (Surname illegible), cause of death: "supposed to be influenza", informant: Carl Isaacs (Doeville), buried: Shoun Cemetery, died: 30 Jan 1919, record (1919) #: 27.

Bertha FLETCHER, born: 1 Jun 1895, married, parents: David Roark (NC) and Matilda Snyder (NC), cause of death: measles, informant: Mrs. Ethel Shoun (Crandull), buried: Gentry Cemetery, died: 30 Jan 1919, record (1919) #: 28.

Benie Mae BROOKS, female, age 5 months, parents: Walter Brooks and Billie (surname, illegible), cause of death: "pneumonia following influenza", died: 31 Jan 1919, record (1919) #: 29.

Infant WAGNER, female, parents: M.R. Wagner and Augusta Brown, cause of death: "stillborn, mother ill with influenza 5 days", buried: Mountain View Cemetery, died: 16 Jan 1919, record (1919) #: 30.

Infant BROWN, female, parents: E.L. Brown and Ethel Brown, stillborn, informant: T.F. Brown (Shouns), buried: Dowell Cemetery, born/died: 18 Jan 1919, record (1919) #: 31.

Infant MCQUEEN, black, parents: Arthur McQueen and Susia Anderson, stillborn, informant: Arthur Anderson, died: 26 Jan 1919, record (1919) #: 32.

Infant CORUM, female, parents: Roy Corum and N...
Jenkins, cause of death: "premature birth", informant:
R.L. Jenkins (Mountain City), buried: Cornett
Cemetery, born/died: 1 Jan 1919, record (1919) #: 33.

Martha PLEASANT, born: 5 Oct 1860, parents: David
Howard and Eva Shoun, cause of death: "heart dropsy,
informant: W.H. Pleasant (Doeville), buried: Rambo
Cemetery, died: 1 Feb 1919, record (1919) #: 34.

Mrs. Rebecca Pennington ELLIS, age about 38 years,
born at Ashe Co. NC, parents: I.... Pennington (NC),
and Rebecca Pope (NC), cause of death: "pulmonary
tuberculosis", informant: Robert Ellis (Mountain
City), died: 3 Feb 1919, record (1919) #: 35.

Sanford GARLAND, born: 2 Nov 1899, parents: R.T.
Garland and Sallie Morefield, cause of death:
"influenza and pneumonia fever", informant: R.T.
Garland (Doeville), buried: Rambo Cemetery, died: 4
Feb 1919, record (1919) #: 36.

Nettie Belle ARNOLD, age about 3 years, parents: Ed
Arnold and Christine Sheppard (Ashe Co. NC), cause of
death: "influenza", informant: D.P. Phillippi
(Mountain City), buried: Phillippi Cemetery, died: 7
Feb 1919, record (1919) #: 37.

Birtha BENTLY, born: 13 Jan 1912, parents: George
Bently and Alice Bowling, cause of death: "influenza
and whooping cough", informant: S.H. Bowling
(Crandull), buried: Gentry Cemetery, died: 10 Feb
1919, record (1919) #: 38.

Ruby Jane ELDRITH, born: 9 Mar 1916, parents: J.R.
Eldrith (NC) and Flossie Willen, cause of death:
"Spanish influenza", informant: J.R. Eldrith (Shouns),
buried: Willen Cemetery, died: 15 Feb 1919, record
(1919) #: 39.

Margaret TAYLOR, age about 80 years, born in Virginia,
widow, parents: Riley West (VA) and mother unknown,
cause of death: "disease of heart and kidneys",
informant: N.J. Taylor (Shouns), buried: Dunn
Cemetery, died: 16 Feb 1919, record (1919) #: 40.

Arlena HEATON, born: 8 Jan 1916, parents: Ben Heaton
(Carter Co. TN) and Verdie Blackburn, cause of death:
"influenza and pneumonia fever", informant: Ben Heaton
(Doeville), buried: Rambo Cemetery, died: 20 Feb 1919,
record (1919) #: 41.

Myrtle Elizabeth LEWIS, black, age about 4 years, born
in Virginia, parents: Carl Lewis (Alabama) and Francis
Lewis (NC), cause of death: illegible, informant:
Hezakiah Wilson (Mountain City), buried: Mountain View
Cemetery, died: 21 Feb 1919, record (1919) #: 42.

Beatrice JOHNSON, age about 6 years, born in Montana, parents: Glenn Johnson and Oma Payne, cause of death: "spinal meningitis following influenza", informant: J.S. Potter (Mountain City), buried: Phillippi Cemetery, died: 23 Feb 1919, record (1919) #: 43.

S.D. PHILLIPPI, age about 1 year, parents: Samuel Phillippi and Pearl Gentry, cause of death: "bronchial pneumonia following influenza", buried: Phillippi Cemetery, died: 23 Feb 1919, record (1919) #: 44.

Jasper Newton MCELYEA, born: 13 Dec 1884, single, parents: John Joseph McElyea and Victoria M. Vaughan (Ashe Co. NC), cause of death: illegible, informant: John J. McElyea (Mountain City), buried: Shingletown Cemetery, died: 27 Feb 1919, record (1919) #: 45.

Infant FORRESTER, female, parents: Scott Forrester and Jossie Phillippi, cause of death: "born dead", informant: C.L. Gentry (Mountain City), buried: Phillippi Cemetery, born/died: 12 Feb 1919, record (1919) #: 46.

Infant FORRESTER, female, parents: Scott Forrester and Jossie Phillippi, cause of death: "born dead", informant: C.L. Gentry (Mountain City), buried: Phillippi Cemetery, born/died: 12 Feb 1919, record (1919) #: 47.

Elbert JORDAN, born: 14 Feb 1844 IN Carter Co., TN, widower, parents: John Jordan and mother's first name not stated Hilton, cause of death: "labor pneumonia", informant: Callie Jordan (Doeville), buried: Shouns Cemetery, died: 1 Mar 1919, record (1919) #: 48.

Melvin R. SHAW, black, born: 22 Nov 1845 in North Carolina, parents: John Morgan (NC) and Isabelle Shaw (NC), cause of death: "cerebral hemorege", informant: Lizzie Shaw (Mountain City), buried: Mountain View Cemetery, died: 2 Nov 1919, record (1919) #: 49.

Mary POTTER, born: 16 Nov 1910 in North Carolina, parents: E.F. Potter (NC) and Susy Potter (NC), cause of death: "typhoid fever followed by pneumonia", informant: Frank Main (Butler), died: 5 Mar 1919, record (1919) #: 50.

Frederick GENTRY, born: 5 Mar 1919, parents: John A. Gentry and Martha Maxwell, cause of death: "undetermined", informant: Walter Gentry (Laurel Bloomery), died: 8 Mar 1919, record (1919) #: 51.

Elvy Grace WILSON, born: 28 Jan 1918, parents: Marvin S. Wilson and Fredie M. Parks, cause of death: "supposed to be influenza", informant: Robert Parks (Trade), buried: Parks Cemetery, died: 11 Mar 1919, record (1919) #: 52.

Malinda HODGE, age about 68 years, widow, parents: Samuel Hodge and Margie Wilson, cause of death: "influenza", informant: J.H. Hodge (Doeville), buried: Loyd Cemetery, died: 17 Mar 1919, record (1919) #: 53.

Hannah DOUGHORTY, born: 26 Feb 1826 in North Carolina, parents: Andrew McBride (NC) and Rachel Dancy (NC), cause of death: "old age", informant: T.N. Tester (Bakers Gap), died: 20 Mar 1919, record (1919) #: 54.

Andrew Nameyard GENTRY, born: 17 Dec 1848, married, parents: General Gentry and Eliza Rambo, cause of death: illegible, informant: John F. Filler (Mountain City), buried: Gentry Cemetery, died: 23 Mar 1919, record (1919) #: 55.

Herald Wallace BENTLEY, born: 9 Feb 1916, parents: John Bentley and Minnie B. Hawkins, cause of death: "whooping cough and bronco pneumonia", informant: Fred Gentry (Crandull), buried: Gentry Cemetery, died: 26 Mar 1919, record (1919) #: 56.

Vivian Rose HORN, born 28 Sep 1918, parents: Thomas D. Horn and Selva Grewville, cause of death: "acidosis", informant: R.B. Brown (Mountain City), buried: Brown Cemetery, died 30 Mar 1919, record (1919) #: 57.

Joseph W. MAIN, parents: John Main and Lillie Wallace, cause of death:"stillborn, not known", informant: John Main (Trade), buried: Reece Cemetery, born/died: 15 Mar 1919, record (1919) #: 58.

Infant ARNOLD, male, parents: Milton Arnold and Selvie Fritts, stillborn, born/died: 16 Mar 1919, record (1919) #: 59.

Wiley Elbert PRESTON, black, age about 69 years, born in North Carolina, parents: not stated, cause of death: "fell from wagon, head struck rock, fractured skull", informant: C.H. Preston (Mountain City), buried: Mountain View Cemetery, died: 9 Apr 1919, record (1919) #: 60.

Almira MILLER, born: 26 Aug 1834 in North Carolina, parents: William Moffatt (NC) and Eliza Byrd (NC), cause of death: "not known", informant: W.R. Miller (Trade), buried: Arnold Cemetery, died: 12 Apr 1919, record (1919) #: 61.

James Donnelly GENTRY, born: 8 Dec 1853, parents: John J. Gentry and Dicie Greer, death cause: "pulmonary odema", informant: Mary E. Gentry (Laurel Bloomery), Gentry Cem., died: 16 Apr 1919, record (1919) #: 62.

Alfred E. MILLER, born: 20 Jun 1858, widower, Minister of Gospel, parents: Wayne Miller (NC) and Lucrecia Marlow (NC), cause of death: "brights disease", informant: J.R. Miller (Trade), buried: Reece Cemetery, died: 17 Apr 1919, record (1919) #: 63.

Martha S. TRIPLETT, age 67 years, 5 months and 18 days, married, parents: Wilson Hendrix (NC) and Peggy West (NC), cause of death: "paralysis", informant: Jas D. Robinson (Butler), died: 18 Apr 1919, record (1919) #: 64.

George Hamilton ROBINSON, born: 9 Dec 1844, married, merchant, parents: James J. Robinson and Susan Jackson, death cause: "chronic gastritis", informant: Sarah Robinson (Laurel Bloomery), buried: Acre Field Cem., died: 18 Apr 1919, record (1919) #: 65.

Infant FARMER, male, parents: Robert Farmer and Glennie Potter, cause of death: "born at 7 months, lived 2 hours", informant: J. B. Davis (Vaughtsville), born/died: 20 Apr 1919, record (1919) #: 66.

Bernice WIDENER, born: 23 Aug 1918, parents: Silas T. Widener and Mae Greer, cause of death: "gastro-enteritis", informant: Silas Widener (Laurel Bloomery), buried: Taylor's Valley Cemetery, died: 20 Apr 1919, record (1919) #: 67.

Tildy MOREFIELD, born: 1852, age 67 years, married, parents: Colonel Estep and Rebecca Laws, cause of death: "paralysis" informant: J.G. Stout (Neva), died: 21 Apr 1919, record (1919) #: 68.

James Edgar THOMAS, born: 14 Jun 1914, parents: Frank Thomas (NC) and Lizzie Ellis (NC), cause of death: "influenza, broncho pneumonia", informant: Frank Thomas (Mountain City), buried: Mountain View Cemetery, died: 30 Apr 1919, record (1919) #: 69.

Zena HAMBY, born: 10 Apr 1919, parents: Charles Hamby (West VA) and Cora Reece, cause of death: "not known", informant: Albert Reece (Trade), buried in Watauga Co. NC, died: 3 May 1919, record (1919) #: 70.

Ernest SHORS, born: 24 Apr 1919, parents: father's name not given and Callie Shors, cause of death: "bold hives", informant: Callie Shors (Butler), buried: Dugger Cem., died: 5 May 1919, record (1919) #: 71.

Gertie Wanda MCQUEEN, born: 22 Apr 1919, parents: C.W. McQueen and Annie S. Montgomery, cause of death: "acute gastritis due to milk becoming poisonous", informant: Willis McQueen (Crandull), buried: McQueen Cemetery, died: 7 May 1919, record (1919) #: 72.

Mary Ann PENNINGTON, born: 2 Nov 1839 in Ashe Co. NC, parents: Joseph Graybeal (Ashe Co. NC) and Linda Testerman (Ashe Co. NC), cause of death: "heart disease", informant: Roby Pennington (Mountain City), buried: Shingletown Cemetery, died: 20 Mat 1919, record (1919) #: 73.

Sarah Emaline VENABLE, born 12 Nov 1972, married, parents: Richard Gentry and Sarah Gilland, cause of death: "pulmonary tuberculosis", buried: Taylor's Valley, died: 26 May 1919, record (1919) #: 74.

Mae Bell REECE, born: 27 May 1919, parents: James Reece (NC) and Cora Pen..... (NC), cause of death: "congental weak", buried: Wilson Cemetery, died: 29 May 1919, record (1919) #: 75.

Berthie Lee MORGAN, born: 21 Jan 1901, married, parents: John Morefield and Ellen Ashley (NC), cause of death: "acute endo carditis", informant: Ellen Morefield (Laurel Bloomery), died: 30 May 1919, record (1919) #: 76.

William Brady NETHERLY, parents: Jacob Netherly and Maggie McElyea, stillborn, born/died: 1 May 1919, record (1919) #: 77.

Infant OSBORN, male, parents: Jno Osborn and Susan Elliott, stillborn, informant: Jno Osborn (Doeville), buried: Rambo Cemetery, born/died: 6 May 1919, record (1919) #: 78.

Martha Osborn BOWMAN, born: 12 Apr 1836 in North Carolina, parents: Abner Osborn and mother's name unknown, cause of death: "cirsosis of liver", informant: R.L. Bowman (Doeville), died: 2 Jun 1919, record (1919) #: 79.

Lura E.C. HAYWORTH, age about 48 years, single, parents: Nathan J. Hayworth (NC) and Kizzie Walsh (NC), cause of death: "paralysis", informant: J.G. Hayworth (Silver Lake), buried: Dunn Cemetery, died: 2 Jun 1919, record (1919) #: 80.

W.B. BOWMAN, age 87 years, parents: father's name not stated and Sallie Bowman, cause of death: "general break down", informant: Aberham Guin (Butler), buried: Dugger Cem., died: 3 Jun 1919, record (1919) #: 81.

Mrs. Sarah Arnold CHURCH, age 39 years, married, parents: Joseph Arnold and Lucey Arney, cause of death: "cancer of uterous", informant: James Church, buried: Wilson Cemetery, died: 6 Jun 1919, record (1919) #: 82.

Earnest MOODY, date of birth not stated, parents: William Moody and Margaret Anderson, cause of death: "bold hives", informant: William Moody (Butler), buried: Dugger Cemetery, died: 7 Jun 1919, record (1919) #: 83.

Nora ROARK, born: 13 Dec 1918, parents: Donnelley Roark (NC) and Nora Dowell, death cause: "cholera inflamation", informant: Donnelley Roark (Shouns), Davis Cem, died: 12 Jun 1919, record (1919) #: 84.

105

Renora ROARK, born: 13 Dec 1918, parents: Donnelley
Roark and Nora Dowell, cause of death: "cholera",
died: 15 Jun 1919, record (1919) #: 85.
Thomas James PROFFITT, born: 3 Oct 1899 in North
Carolina, parents: Alex Proffitt and Malinda Spi....
(NC), cause of death: "appendicitis", informant: Alex
Proffitt (Doeville), buried: Proffitt Cemetery, died:
20 Jun 1919, record (1919) #: 86.
Benjamin J. GENTRY, age 84 years, parents: William
Gentry and Polly Greer, cause of death: "apoplexy",
Phillippi Cem, died: 23 Jun 1919, record (1919) #: 87.
Worley CAMPBELL, born: 7 Jul 1917, parents: Samuel
Campbell and Cora Heaton, cause of death: "pneumonia
fever", informant: Samuel Campbell (Doeville), buried:
Garland Cem., died: 23 Jun 1919, record (1919) #: 88.
Alexander GREER, born: 1836 in North Carolina, age 82
years, parents: Alexander Greer (NC) and Lida Curd,
cause of death: "supposed paralysis", informant: James
Greer (Trade), buried: Greer Cemetery, died: 23 Jun
1919, record (1919) #: 89.
Maud Lilian REECE, born: 27 Jun 1916, parents: Harve
Reece and Salva Potter, cause of death: "measles",
informant; Harve Reece (Butler), died: 27 Jun 1919,
record (1919) #: 90.
Mollie Emmett JONES, born: 1861 in Sullivan Co. TN,
age 58 years, parents: Felty Emmett and Tilda (surname
unknown), cause of death: "had rheumatism and heart
trouble", informant: R.A. Cole (Crandull), buried:
Gentry Cem., died: 3 Jul 1919, record (1919) #: 91.
Rhoda HOWARD, born: 2 Nov 1841, widow, parents: Mahlon
Doughdorty (NC), and Abbie Roark (NC), cause of death:
"old age and ascending paralysis", informant: Callie
Johnson (Shouns), buried: McEwen Cemetery, died: 7 Jul
1919, record (1919) #: 92.
Andrew TAYLOR, born: 18 Mar 1863, married, parents:
Eli Taylor and Margaret West (NC), cause of death:
"abscess sinus and para typhoid", informant: Bruce
Taylor (Mountain City), buried: Cornett Cemetery,
died: 11 Jul 1919, record (1919) #: 93.
Frank BAKER, black, age 69 years, born in North
Carolina, parents: Richard Thomas and Eliza Baker
(NC), cause of death:"carcinoma liver", informant: Bud
Baker (Mountain City), buried in North Carolina, died:
13 Jul 1919, record (1919) #: 94.
Nealey CRESS, female, age about 53 years, married,
parents: William Johnson and mother's name not stated,
cause of death:"apoplexy, informant: Smith Fenner
(Mountain City), buried: Cress Cemetery, died: 13 Jul
1919, record (1919) #: 95.

Peter Kyle BRADLEY, born: 15 May 1860, parents: Erven Bradley and Jane Smith, cause of death:"gastric ulcer", informant: Eva Bradley (Butler), died: 14 Jul 1919, record (1919) #: 96.

Joseph H. DUGGER, born: 13 Feb 1845, married, parents: William Dugger and Lizzie Holclaw (Watauga Co. NC), cause of death: "heart dropsy", buried: Dugger Cemetery, died: 14 Jul 1919, record (1919) #: 97.

Infant WOODLEY, female, born: 19 Jul 1919, parents: Sam Woodley and Olie Maxwell, cause of death: "congenital weak", informant: Sam Woodley (Mountain City), buried: Mountain View Cemetery, died: 20 Jul 1919, record (1919) #: 98.

Safronia GALLAINE, age 56 years, married, parents: Eli Harper and Eveline Langston, cause of death: "pulmonary tuberculosis", died: 21 Jul 1919, record (1919) #: 99.

William George PLEASANT, born: 4 Jul 1919, parents: Benjamin Pleasant and Minnie Lowe, cause of death: "unknown", informant: Benj Pleasant (Mountain City), buried: Eggers Cemetery, died: 21 Jul 1919, record (1919) #: 100.

Albertte STOUT, born: 20 Jul 1919, parents: R.W. Stout and Nora Wilson, cause of death: not stated, informant: R. W. Stout (Mountain City), buried: Shoun Cemetery, died: 22 Jul 1919, record (1919) #: 101.

James Newton WILLS, born: 3 Nov 1853, married, parents: Peter Dick Wills and Sophie S. Wills (Washington Co. VA), cause of death: "pulmonary edema", buried: Wills Cemetery, died: 25 Jul 1919, record (1919) #: 102.

Infant HORN, male, parents: Robert Horn and Airo Davis, stillborn, informant: Robert Horn (Mountain City), buried: Brown Cemetery, died: 18 Jul 1919, record (1919) #: 103.

Jesse H. GARLAND, Sr., born: 1 Apr 1838, parents: Lewis Garland and Susan Cole, cause of death: "heart and old age", buried: Blevins Cemetery, died: 5 Aug 1919, record (1919) #: 104.

Charles Robert VENEY, born: 6 Jan 1918, parents: Robert Veney and Caris Valie Abshire, cause of death: "broncho pneumonia", informant: Robert Veney (Shouns), died: 19 Aug 1919, record (1919) #: 105.

William Russell JENNINGS, born: 2 Aug 1918, parents: Thomas Jennings and Archie Dishman, cause of death: "dysentary", informant: Thomas Jennings (Shouns), died: 13 Aug 1919, record (1919) #: 106.

Charles Washington NEELY, born: 13 Feb 1916, parents: Clinton W. Neely and Francis E. Waters, cause of death: "food poison", died: 22 Aug 1919, record (1919) #: 107.

Ray WRIGHT, born: 7 Feb 1917, parents: father not stated and Liley Wright, cause of death: "flux", buried: Gentry Cemetery, died: 23 Aug 1919, record (1919) #: 108.

Rebecca ORNEAL, age about 67 years, born at Sullivan Co. TN, parents: Daniel Rhymer (Sullivan Co. TN) and Eliza Shaver, cause of death: "flucks" informant: Joseph Orneal (Doeville), buried: Grindstaff Cemetery, died 23 Aug 1919, record (1919) #: 109.

Lena Kate ADAMS, born: 3 Apr 1919, parents: B.M. Adams and Mae Wills Adams, cause of death: "due to chronic indigestion from artificial feeding", informant: R.B. Brown (Mountain City), buried: Phillippi Cemetery, died: 5 Sep 1919, record (1919) #: 110.

Maggie Emaline GARLAND, born: 19 Jul 1919, parents: M.G. Garland and Virgie Blevins, cause of death: "condition of stomach due to milk not digesting", informant: M.G. Garland (Crandull), buried: Blevins Cemetery, record (1919) #: 111.

Russmann Washington STOUT, born: 5 Apr 1919, parents: George W. Stout and Manda Harris (Marion, VA), cause of death: "entero collitis", informant: Joe Blaine Stout (Doeville), buried: Marion, VA, died: 26 Sep 1919, record (1919) #: 112.

Auston Windom GARLAND, born: 12 Mar 1919, parents: Charlie D. Garland and Sabra Alice Howell (NC), cause of death: "illio colilis", informant: Charlie D. Garland (Crandull), buried: Gentry Cemetery, died: 29 Sep 1919, record (1919) #: 113.

Argus Gaines MATNEY, 18 Jun 1884, single, teacher, parents: W.W. Matney (NC) and Sallie Donnely, cause of death: "pulmonary tuberculosis", informant: W.W. Matney (Mountain City), buried: Mountain View Cemetery, died: 30 Sep 1919, record (1919) #: 114.

Essie JOHNSON, age 9 years, parents: Hugh Johnson and Ida Payne, cause of death: "typhoid fever", died: 30 Sep 1919, record (1919) #: 115.

Nancy Lorettie DUNN, born: 15 Apr 1837, parents: Mathias Wagner and Mary Vaught Wagner, cause of death: "apoplexy", informant: John I. Ward (Shouns), buried: Wagner Cem., died: 5 Oct 1919, record (1919) #: 116.

Betie Ann FORRESTER, parents: Monroe Forrester and Vesta Guy (NC), stillborn, born/died: 26 Oct 1919, record (1919) #: 117.

Christian FRITTS, Jr., born: 9 Mar 1843, married, parents: Christian Fritts and Polly Grindstaff, cause of death: "general paralysis", informant: J. A. Dugger (Butler), buried: Mountain View Cemetery, died: 5 Nov 1919, record (1919) #: 118.

Robert E. LEE, born: 7 Jul 1918 at Portland, Maine, parents: Robert H. Lee (NC) and Mary Pomaway (Canada), cause of death: "diarrhoea", informant: Sarah Lee (Mountain City), died: 11 Nov 1919, record (1919) #: 119.

Lessie Frances GRAYSON, born: 8 Jun 1918, parents: Gilliam B. Grayson (Ashe Co. NC) and Rhoda Frances Mahaffey (Washington Co. VA), cause of death: not stated, informant: G.B. Grayson (Laurel Bloomery), buried: Gentry Cemetery, died: 12 Nov 1919, record (1919) #: 120.

Oma J, FORRESTER, born: 17 Apr 1918, parents: J.M.R. Forrester and Vestie Guy, cause of death: "supposed to be croup", informant: J.M.R. Forrester (Shouns), died: 25 Nov 1919, record (1919) #: 121.

Infant KILBY, male, parents: William L. Kilby and mother's name illegible, stillborn, born/died: 12 Nov 1919, record (1919) #: 122.

Infant MAIN, male, parents: Assa Main and Mary Reece (NC), cause of death "stillborn", died: 14 Nov 1919, record (1919) #: 123.

Mrs. Elizabeth WILSON, born: 22 Jul 1843, widow, parents: Daniel M. Stout and Sallie Shoun, cause of death: "brights", informant: Roy D. Wilson (Mountain City), buried: Wilson Cemetery, died: 5 Dec 1919, record (1919) #: 124.

Crumley H. WAGNER, age 32 years, married, parents: father's first name not stated Wagner and Naoma Wagner, cause of death: "died suddenly, cause unknown, buried: Baker Cemetery, died: 10 Dec 1919, record (1919) #: 125.

Gill Truman MOREFIELD, born: 6 Feb 1902, parents: James Morefield and Elizabeth Morefield, cause of death: "gun shot wound", informant: J.H. Morefield (Laurel Bloomery), buried: Eggers Cemetery, died: 11 Dec 1919, record (1919) #: 126.

Clyde VALENTINE, Negro, born: 5 Mar 1919, parents: Frank Valentine (Ashe Co. NC) and Gregin Goins, cause of death: "labor pneumonia", buried: Shouns, died: 14 Dec 1919, record (1919) #: 127.

David BYARS, age 80 years, born in North Carolina, parents: "don't know", cause of death: "acute nephritis", informant: Alenzo Byars (Mountain City), buried: Neva, died: 15 Dec 1919, record (1919) #: 128.

America LOMAX, age 89 years, born in North Carolina, parents: "don't know", cause of death: "suppose age", informant: John Sales (Shouns), buried: Mountain View Cemetery, died: 16 Dec 1919, record (1919) #: 129.

Stacy MCELYEA, age 24 years, single, parents: Bug McElyea and Dealia Allen, death cause: "burn over entire body due to boiler explosion", informant: John Keys (Mountain City), died: 16 Dec 1919, record (1919) #: 130.

Hubert STOUT, born: 5 Oct 1904, parents: John L. Stout and Alic Wilson, cause of death: "pulmonary tuberculosis", buried: Wilson Cemetery, died: 18 Dec 1919, record (1919) #: 131.

Herbert William JENKINS, born: 5 Mar 1856 in New York, married, parents: Isaac H. Jenkins (NY) and Rebecca Congden (NY), death cause: "thought to be organic heart disease", informant: Mary C. Jenkins (South Williamsport, PA), died: 19 Dec 1919, record (1919) #: 132.

Opal HARPER, born: 20 Dec 1919, parents: Nelson Harper and Lottie Price, cause of death: "supposed to be hyves or croup", informant: Nelson Harper (Mountain City), buried: Wilson Cemetery, died: 20 Dec 1919, record (1919) #: 133.

William MCQUEEN, born 18 Nov 1918, parents: J.W. McQueen and Ida Lowe, cause of death: "broncho pneumonia fever, both lungs", informant: J.W. McQueen (Doeville), buried: Lowe Cemetery, died: 26 Dec 1919, record (1919) #: 134.

Jacob Willace DUNN, born: 1 Jun 1835, married, parents: Booker Dunn and Becky Wagner, cause of death: "thought to be old age", informant: J.D. Wagner (Shouns), buried: Shouns, died: 26 Dec 1919, record (1919) #: 135.

Infant ROARK, parents: Timothy Roark and Vancy Allen (NC), cause of death: "born at 8 months, informant: Timothy Roark (Shouns), buried: Arnold Cemetery, died: 29 Dec 1919, record (1919) #: 136.

Infant RED, female, color/race: illegible, parents: Thomas Red (NC) and Lorette Bailey, stillborn, informant: Will Mock (Mountain City), died: 22 Dec 1919, record (1919) #: 137.

Infant JENKINS, parents: M.B. Jenkins and Etta Snyder, cause of death: "died one-half hour after birth", informant: M.B. Jenkins (Mountain City), buried: Phillippi Cem., died: 2 Jan 1920, record (1920) #: 1.

John STANSBERRY, born: 12 Mar 1878 in North Carolina, married: parents: Center Stansberry (NC) and Mary Stansberry (NC), death cause: "heart dropsy due to kidney disease", informant: Taylor Burton (Butler), buried: Burton Cemetery, died: 6 Jan 1920, record (1920) #: 2.

Thomas Stewart ROBERTS, born 21 Jan 1902, parents: J.J. Roberts and Victoria Jenkins. cause of death: "accident caused by saw mill", informant: J.J. Roberts (Mountain City), buried: Morley Cemetery, died: 7 Jan 1920, record (1920) #: 3.

Rebecca WILCOX, age 80 years, married, parents: William Wilson and Rebecca Wilson, cause of death: "supposed age", informant: William Wilcox (Shouns), died: 4 Jan 1920, record (1920) #: 4.

Joolian STOUT, female, born: 6 Jan 1920, parents: W.H. Stout and Eliza Proffitt, cause of death: "not known", informant: Ada Stout (Vaughtsville), died: 9 Jan 1920, record (1920) #: 5.

Jane HUTCHINSON, born: 17 Oct 1841 in North Carolina, widow, parents: David Sparks (NC) and Kisiah Holloway (NC), informant: J.C. Hutchinson (Crandull), buried: Hutchinson Cem, died: 18 Jan 1920, record (1920) #: 6.

Horton Filmore HARPER, born 2 Sep 1905 (must have been 1895), age 24 years, 4 months and 11 days, married, parents: William Harper and Dicie Barry, cause of death: "shock due to gun shot wound of right leg, not accident", buried: Wilson Cemetery, died: 14 Jan 1920, record (1920) #: 7.

Latitia CAMPBELL, born: 8 Oct 1892, married, parents: Waulfaurn (?) Grindstaff and Louisie Arnold, cause of death: "pulmonary tuberculosis", died: 20 Jan 1920, record (1920) #: 8.

Orval Gray BLEVINS, born: 9 Aug 1916, parents: Jessie W. Blevins and Millie B. Ritchie, cause of death: "pneumonia of both lungs", informant: Jessie Blevins (Crandull), buried: Blevins Cem., died: 21 Jan 1920.

Joe MCELYEA, born: 4 Dec 1918, parents: Mack McElyea and Callie Dunn, cause of death: "was tuberculosis", informant: Jim Reece (Mountain City), buried: Wilson Cem., died: 25 Jan 1920, record (1920) #: 10.

J.C. BROOKS, born: 28 May 1843, parents: Rubin Brooks and Betsy Carriger, cause of death: "pneumonia", informant: R.M. McKinney (Shouns), died: 26 Jan 1920, record (1920) #: 11.

Julia HEATON, born: 10 Apr 1905, parents: John Heaton and Martha Rambo, cause of death: illegible, informant: John Heaton (Mountain City), buried: Shoun Cem., died: 28 Jan 1920, record (1920) #: 12.

Bernie PAYNE, age 6 years, parents: Charles Payne and Dellie Johnson, cause of death: "broncho pneumonia", buried: Cress Cemetery, died: 30 Jan 1920, record (1920) #: 13.

Rankins ALLEN, born: 11 Dec 1919, parents: Carter Allen (NC) and Sallie Stout, cause of death: "Spanish influenza", informant: Carter Allen (Shouns), buried: Arnold Cem., died: 3 Feb 1920, record (1920) #: 14.

Delilah Olivene ARNOLD, born: 14 Feb 1871, married, parents: James Michael (NC) and Susan Morefield, cause of death: "tuberculosis of liver", informant: John Arnold (Mountain City), buried: Michaels Cemetery, died: 9 Feb 1920, record (1920) #: 15.

Cora Lee DUNN, born: 19 Jan 1920, parents: Danny Dunn and Elvie Dunn Reece, cause of death: "found dead in bed", informant: Thadins Reece (Shouns), died: 12 Feb 1920, record (1920) #: 16.

Abraham WILSON, age 78 years, married, parents: William Wilson and Patsy Nave, cause of death: illegible, buried: Wilson Cemetery, died: 12 Feb 1920, record (1920) #: 17.

Nancy WAGNER, born: 6 Jan 1893, single, parents: A.B. Wagner and Winnie Dunn, cause of death: "influenza and tuberculosis", informant: John M. Potter (Shouns), died: 16 Feb 1920, record (1920) #: 18.

William Lee MINTON, born: 15 Aug 1865 in North Carolina, married, parents: Isaac Minton and Milly Mallen (NC), cause of death: "labor pneumonia of right lung", buried: Blevins Cemetery, died: 21 Feb 1920, record (1920) #: 19.

Lottie TESTER, born: 22 Jun 1893, widow, parents: William Proffitt and Atha Forrester, cause of death: "tuberculosis", informant: Effie Proffitt (Neva), died: 22 Feb 1920, record (1920) #: 20.

Susanna CABLE, born: 30 Jan 1836 in Carter Co. TN, widow, parents: Jacob Simerly (Carter Co. TN) and Mary Marton (Carter Co. TN), cause of death: "chronic brights disease", informant: William Cable (Butler), Cable Cem, died: 22 Feb 1920, record (1920) #: 21.

Bessie Catherine GENTRY, born: 22 Feb 1920, parents: Noah Gentry and Martha Elizabeth Gentry, cause of death: "unknown", informant: Ferd Gentry (Laurel Bloomery), buried: Valley Cemetery, died: 25 Feb 1920, record (1920) #: 22.

Massie O. BALDWIN, female, born: 18 Sep 1910, parents: William W. Baldwin (NC) and Minnie O. Sanders (NC), cause of death: "gun shot wound in the neck accidentally discharged by little sister", buried: Gentry Cem., died: 29 Feb 1920, record (1920) #: 23.

Infant JONES, parents: James M. Jones (NC) and Annie Owens (NC), cause of death: "premature delivery caused by influenza", informant Susan Owens (Laurel Bloomery), buried: Cornett Cemetery, born/died: 29 Feb 1920, record (1920) #: 24.

Sallie E. LAWRENCE, parents: James B. Lawrence (NC) and Margie Thomas, stillborn, informant: James B. Lawrence (Trade), born/died: 12 Feb 1920, record (1920) #: 25.

Infant OWENS, parents: Roby Owens (NC) and Hattie Henderson, cause of death: "premature delivery caused by influenza", informant: Roby Owens (Mountain City), buried: Cornett Cemetery, died: 23 Feb 1920, record (1920) #: 26.

Enoch OSBORN, born: 12 Jan 1857, married, parents: Ephron Osborn and Nancy Potter (NC), cause of death: "pneumonia and influenza", informant: Lydia Osborn (Shouns), buried: Osborn Cemetery, died: 2 Mar 1920, record (1920) #: 27.

Missouri WARD, female, age 75 years, single, parents: John Ward (NC) and Nancy Wilson, cause of death: "not known", informant: Joseph Lunsford (Butler), died: 6 Mar 1920, record (1920) #: 28.

Margaret L. BISHOP, born: 29 Jan 1869 in North Carolina, married, parents: Andrew Nichols (NC) and Nancy E. Bishop (NC), death cause: illegible, informant: R.L. Bishop (Crandull), buried: Blevins Cemetery.

Infant OWENS, parents: Roby Owens (NC) and Hattie Henderson, cause of death: "premature delivery caused by influenza", informant: Roby Owens (Mountain City), buried: Cornett Cemetery, died: 23 Feb 1920, record (1920) #: 26.

Enoch OSBORN, born: 12 Jan 1857, married, parents: Ephron Osborn and Nancy Potter (NC), cause of death: "pneumonia and influenza", informant: Lydia Osborn (Shouns), buried: Osborn Cemetery, died: 2 Mar 1920, record (1920) #: 27.

Missouri WARD, female, age 75 years, single, parents: John Ward (NC) and Nancy Wilson, cause of death: "not known", informant: Joseph Lunsford (Butler), died: 6 Mar 1920, record (1920) #: 28.

Margaret L. BISHOP, born: 29 Jan 1869 in North Carolina, married, parents: Andrew Nichols (NC) and Nancy E. Bishop (NC), cause of death: illegible, informant: R.L. Bishop (Crandull), buried: Blevins Cemetery, died: 7 Mar 1920, record (1920) #: 29.

Mrs. Stella SIMPSON, age 24 years, married, parents:
Bartholemew Gentry and first name illigible Owens,
cause of death: "pulmonary tuberculosis" informant:
Scott Fritts (Mountain City), buried: Phillippi
Cemetery, died: 7 Mar 1920, record (1920) #: 30.

Molvinie Elizabeth ABEL, age 57 years, married,
parents: Abraham Pennington (VA) and first name not
stated Blevins (VA), cause of death: "influenza",
informant: Robert Abel (Laurel Bloomery), buried:
Valley Cem., died: 7 Mar 1920, record (1920) #: 31.

Lillie Victoria ABEL, born: 2 Oct 1899, married,
parents: Melvin Gentry and Margaret Gentry, cause of
death: "influenza", informant: Melvin Gentry (Laurel
Bloomery), buried: Valley Cemetery, died: 9 Mar 1920,
record (1920) #: 32.

Eliza SHOUN, born: 18 May 1834, married, parents: John
Loyd (VA) and Anna Loyd (VA), cause of death:
"pneumonia", informant: J.H. Jordan (Mountain City),
buried: Walker Cemetery, died: 10 Mar 1020, record
(1920) #: 33.

Eliza DUGGER, born: 13 Jul 1889, parents: Roby Dugger
and Mary Bunton, cause of death: "influenza and
broncho pneumonia fever", informant: Jas D. Robinson
(Butler), buried: Dugger Cemetery, died: 12 Mar 1920,
record (1920) #: 34.

Carl G. HEATON, born: 14 Feb 1920, parents: Glen
Heaton and Eddie Mcaron, cause of death: "unknown
cause", informant: E.S. Heaton (Doeville), buried:
Rambo Cem., died: 12 Mar 1920, record (1920) #: 35.

Curtis ABEL, born: 16 Sep 1892, married, parents:
Robert Abel and Malninie Pennington (VA), cause of
death: "influenza", informant: Robert Abel (Laurel
Bloomery), buried: Valley Cemetery, died: 14 Mar 1920,
record (1920) #: 36.

Elizabeth J. CHURCH, born: 24 Mar 1842 in North
Carolina, widow, parents: Wilburn Adams (Wilkes Co.
NC) and Susan Church (Wilkes Co. NC) cause of death:
"labor pneumonia and old age", informant: Clate
Parsons (Crandull), buried: Blevins Cemetery, died: 14
Mar 1920, record (1920) #: 37.

Alma Theala SLUDER, born: 17 Aug 1919, parents: Ray
Sluder and Nancy J. May, cause of death: "pneumonia",
informant: Ray Sluder (Crandull), buried: Blevins
Cemetery, died: 15 Mar 1920, record (1920) #: 38.

Mary F. GREGG, born: 2 Jul 1859 in North Carolina,
widow, parents: Elysa Greenwell (NC) and mother's name
not known, cause of death: "exact cause is not known",
informant: Clarence Gregg (Butler), buried: Crosswhite
Cemetry, died: 15 Mar 1920, record (1920) #: 39.

S.C. DELOACH, born: 1 Apr 1844, married, parents:
Nathan Deloach and Margaret Atkins, cause of death:
"dementia paralytica", informant: J.H. Deloach
(Doeville), buried: Deloach Cemetery, died: 15 Mar
1920, record (1920) #: 40.
Infant MAY, parents: Carl May and Lura Robinson, cause
of death: "premature birth", informant: Carl May
(Trade), born/died: 15 Mar 1920, record (1920) #: 41.
J.M. LOVE, Jr., born: 18 Feb 1919, parents: J.M. Love
and Alice Mullins, cause of death: "pneumonia",
buried: Brookshire Cemetery, died: 16 Mar 1920, record
(1920) #: 42.
Pearl PRESNELL, born: 24 Feb 1900 at Beech Creek NC,
single, parents: Ben Presnell (NC) and Sarah E.
Trivett (NC), cause of death: "influenza and bronchial
pneumonia", informant: D.H. Reece (Beech Creek, NC),
buried in NC, died: 18 Mar 1920, record (1920) #: 43.
Ettie DUGGER, age 39 years, divorced, parents: Dow
Dugger and Nancy Greenwell, death cause: "influenza,
broncho-pneumonia", informant: R.J. Dugger (Butler),
Dugger Cem, died: 18 Mar 1920, record (1920) #: 44.
Ida May CROWDER, born: 18 Mar 1893, married, parents:
Henry Johnson (KY) and Mary Haney (PA), cause of
death: "influenza", informant: Wiley Crowder (Shouns),
died: 19 Mar 1920, record (1920) #: 45.
Rosa REECE, born: 7 Sep 1891 in North Carolina,
married, parents: James M. South (NC) and Lida Hammons
(NC), cause of death: "influenza", informant: James M.
South (Tamarack, NJ), buried: Thomas Cemetery Watauga
Co. NC, died: 19 Mar 1920, record (1920) #: 46.
Enoch CANTER, born: 1 Apr 1844 in North Carolina,
married, parents: father's name not known and Nancy
Canter (NC), cause of death: "not known", informant:
Wiley Miller (Trade), buried: Arnold Cemetery, died:
20 Mar 1920, record (1920) #: 47.
James W. PRESNELL, infant, parents: William H.
Presnell (NC) and Ida Keaton (NC), cause of death:
"not known", informant: Mrs. Jane Cable (Butler),
Midwife, buried: Dugger Cemetery, born/died: 21 Mar
1920, record (1920) #: 48.
Elizabeth TRIVETT, born: 17 Aug 1842 in North
Carolina, parents: Soloman Trivett (NC) and Elizabeth
Trivett (NC), cause of death: "bronchial pneumonia
fever", informant: Mary Trivett (Butler), buried:
Cobbs Creek, died: 23 Mar 1920, record (1920) #: 49.
Clarence CROWDER, born: 8 Mar 1920, parents: Manley
Crowder (NC) and Ella Warnn, cause of death: "found
dead in bed", informant: E.C. Crowder (Shouns), died:
24 Mar 1920, record (1920) #: 50.

Alfred Taylor BURTON, born: 6 Jan 1890, parents: John L. Burton and Celia Cable, cause of death: "appendicitis", informant: J.C. Anderson (Butler), buried: Burton Cemetery, died: 25 Mar 1920, record (1920) #: 51.

George GREENE, born: 5 Mar 1882, parents: Lee Greene and Mary Bumgardner, cause of death: "influenza", informant: A.A. Thomas (Trade), buried: Zionville NC, died: 25 Mar 1920, record (1920) #: 52.

John H. WILLS, born: 17 Aug 1880, married, parents: David W. Wills and Nancy Robinson (VA), cause of death: "influenza", informant: J.P. Wills (Mountain City), buried: Phillippi Cemetery, died: 25 Mar 1920, record (1920) #: 53.

Lillie Fay STOUT, born: 19 Sep 1895, single, parents: Joseph Stout and Rettie Matherson, cause of death: "tsilosis", informant: J.N. Stout (Butler), buried: Morley Cem., died: 29 Mar 1920, record (1920) #: 54.

Jennie REECE, age 44 years, parents: Toliver Triplett (NC) and Mary Widby, cause of death: "influenza", informant: William Triplett (Trade), buried: Reece Cemetery, died: 30 Mar 1920, record (1920) #: 55.

Infant FRITZ, male, parents: Isaac Allen Fritz and Mary Ellen Maxwell, cause of death: "premature birth" informant: Allen Fritz (Laurel Bloomery), buried: Valley Cem., died: 7 Mar 1920, record (1920) #: 56.

Infant ABEL, male, parents: Curtis Abel and Lillie Victoria Gentry, cause of death: "premature delivery caused by influenza", informant: Melvin Gentry (Laurel Bloomery), buried: Valley Cemetery, born/died: 8 Mar 1920, record (1920) #: 57.

Infant OSBORN, male, parents: Jno Osborn and Susan Elliott, stillborn, informant: Jno Osborn (Doeville), buried: Rambo Cemetery, born/died: 25 Mar 1920, record (1920) #: 58.

Robert E. STOUT, parents: Thomas Stout and Polly Smith, stillborn, informant: Thomas Stout (Shouns), buried: Arnold Cemetery, born/died: 28 Mar 1920, record (1920) #: 59.

Amos POTTER, parents: Jacob Potter and Rosa Head, cause of death: "died at birth", informant: Rosa Potter (Shouns), buried: McEwen Cemetery, born/died: 2 Apr 1920, record (1920) #: 60.

L.C. DUGGER, age 62 years, married: parents: James C. Dugger and first name unknown Vines, cause of death: "broncho pneumonia", informant: R.J. Dugger (Butler), buried: private cemetery, died: 3 Apr 1920, record (1920) #: 61.

Joseph Alexander COLE, born: 6 Jun 1853, married, parents: Bishop J. Cole (VA) and Sarah Ann Abel, cause of death: "pulmonary tuberculosis", informant: Callie Cole (Laurel Bloomery), buried: Valley Cemetery, died: 4 Apr 1920, record (1920) #: 62.

Ellis N. MARTIN, age 85 years, married, parents: W.M. Martin (NC) and Anna Snider, cause of death: "uremic poison from retention of urine", informant: Allen M. Stout (Mountain City), buried: Heaberlin Cemetery, died: 6 Apr 1920, record (1920) #: 63.

Sarah C. NAVE, age 81 years and 18 days, widow, parents: Jackson Bailey and Polly Slimp, cause of death: "tuberculosis and influenza", informant: W.C. Matherson (Neva), died: 6 Apr 1920, record (1920) #: 64.

Charles REECE, born: 2 May 1919, parents: Thad Reece and Danford Musgrave, cause of death: "broncho pneumonia", informant: R.L. Nave (Shouns), died: 9 Apr 1920, record (1920) #: 65.

Alfred H. STOUT, age 75 years, married, parents: Parkey Stout and Martha Pierce, cause of death: "enlargement of prostrate gland", informant: S.A. Stout (Mountain City), buried: Morley Cemetery, died: 18 Apr 1920, record (1920) #: 66.

Earl HEAD, parents: Samuel Greer (NC) and Alice Head, cause of death: "died at birth", informant: Alice Head (Shouns), born/died: 18 Apr 1920, buried: Curd Cemetery, record (1920) #: 67.

Pearl HEAD, parents: Samuel Greer (NC) and Alice Head, cause of death: "died at birth", informant: Alice Head (Shouns), born/died: 18 Apr 1920, buried: Curd Cemetery, record (1920) #: 67.

Rosevelt FORRESTER, born: 7 Sep 1901, parents: J.R. Forrester and Pollie Sluder, cause of death: "pulmonary tuberculosis", informant: J.R. Forrester (Shouns), buried: Forrester Cemetery, died: 18 Apr 1920, record (1920) #: 69.

Mrs. Nanie BLANKENBECKLER, age 56 years, married, parents: Richard Lutrell and Mary Treadway, cause of death: "paralysis due to cerebral hemorage", informant: Oscar Blakenbeckler (Mountain City), buried: Robinson Cemetery, died: 26 Apr 1920, record (1920) #: 70.

Maud SHELL..., born: 20 Jan 1897 in North Carolina, married, parents: George Triplett (NC) and Mary Triplett, cause of death: "pneumonia and influenza", buried: Phillippi Cemetery, died: 26 Apr 1920, record (1920) #: 71.

Kizzie BROWN, born: 10 Apr 1880, single, parents: father's first name illegible, Hayworth (NC) and Nancy Osborn, cause of death: "pulmonary tuberculosis", informant: J.M. Brown (Shouns), buried: Dunn Cemetery, died: 28 Apr 1920, record (1920) #: 72.

Infant DANNER, female, parents: father's name not known and Runa Danner (NC), stillborn, born/died: 3 Apr 1920, record (1920) #: 73.

Infant ARNOLD, male, parents: father's name not given and Mollie Arnold, stillborn, buried: Phillippi Cemetery, born/died: 4 Apr 1920, record (1920) #: 74.

Raymond H. ELLIOTT, born: 25 Mar 1920, parents: Walter Elliott and Elamay Proffitt, cause of death: "found dead in bed", informant: Walter Elliott (Doeville), buried: Rambo Cemetery, died: 14 Mat 1920, record (1920) #: 75.

Alma L. BURTON, born: 6 May 1920, parents: Riley Burton and Stella Reece (NC), cause of death: illegible, buried: Cable Cemetery, died: 7 May 1920, record (1920) #: 76.

Mrs. Mary NAVE, born: 3 Jul 1841, married, parents: Samuel Dugger and Hannah Potter, cause of death: "pneumonia followed by paralysis of right side", informant: D.K. Nave (Mountain City), buried: Wilson Cemetery, died: 25 May 1920, record (1920) #: 77.

Infant PENNELL, parents: Dillard Pennell (NC) and Katie Eisenhour (NC), cause of death: illegible, informant: Dillard Pennell (Shouns) born/died: 26 May 1920, record (1920) #: 78.

Hannah EGGERS, age 73 years, married, parents: Hugh Reece (NC) and Mary Reece (NC), cause of death: "cause not known", informant: Landrine Eggers (Trade), buried: Reece Cemetery, died: 28 May 1920, record (1920) #: 79.

Infant JORDAN, female, parents: Hedrick Jordan and Bunnie (?) Smith, stillborn, buried: Wilson Cemetery, born/died: 14 May 1920, record (1920) #: 80.

Infant MOREFIELD, male, parents: E.C. Morefield and Lottie Forrester, stillborn, informant: A.C. Reece (Neva), born/died: 16 May 1920, record (1920) #: 81.

Mrs. Temperance BAIRD, born: 26 Jul 1832, parents: Phillip Shull and mother's name not stated, cause of death: "chronic brights", buried: Wesley Chapel Cemetery, died: 21 Jun 1920, record (1920) #: 82.

Casey PHIPPS, born: 10 Jun 1920, parents: David Phipps (Carter Co. TN) and Latitia Stalcup, cause of death: "not known", informant: David Phipps (Doeville), buried: Rambo Cemetery, died: 22 Jun 1920, record (1920) #: 83.

Mrs. Fina MORRELL, born: 16 Nov 1893, parents: W.H. Davis and Winnie Shoun, cause of death: "tuberculosis of lungs and stomach and bowels", informant: C.C. Wilson (Mountain City), buried: Fairview Cemetery, died: 4 Jul 1920, record (1920) #: 84.

Joseph D. ARNEY, born: 7 apr 1920, parents: Isaac Arney and Bessie Edwards, cause of death: "billious fever and stomach trouble", informant: D.J. Arney (Doeville), buried: Garland Cemetery, died: 7 Jul 1920, record (1920) #: 85.

Thomas Russ JACKSON, age 63 years, divorced, parents: James Wiley Jackson and Nanie Margaret Ross, cause of death: "apoplexy", informant; R.W. Jackson (Mountain City), buried in Virginia, died: 8 Jul 1920, record (1920) #: 86.

Eula PROFFITT, age 35 years, single, parents: John Proffitt (NC) and Blanch Crawford (NC), cause of death: "chronic brights", died: 8 Jul 1920, record (1920) #: 87.

Maud May LUNCEFORD, born: 12 May 1920, parents: Z.C. Lunceford (NC) and Mary Coleman (NC), cause of death: "cause not known", informant: Coy Coleman (Butler), buried: Lunceford Cemetery, died: 14 Jul 1920, record (1920) #: 88.

Elizabeth TESTER, born: 12 Sep 1852, parents: Richard Tester and Rebecca Jackson, cause of death: "bone serofflons", informant: J.M. Tester (Neva), died: 27 Jul 1920, record (1920) #: 89.

Sarah SWEINEY, born: 30 May 1852, widow, parents: Jessie C. Church (NC) and Marth Watson, cause of death: "heart dropsy", informant: G.H. Sweiney (Doeville), buried: Campbell Cemetery, died: 23 Jul 1920, record (1920) #: 90.

Edna May WILCOX, born: 30 Apr 1920, parents: C.C. Wilcox and Mayr Hodge, cause of death: "croup and pneumonia", informant: J.C. Miller (Shouns), died: 29 Jul 1920, record (1920) #: 91.

Infant DAVIS, female, parents: Clay Davis and Ella Robinson, stillborn, informant: S.C. Davis (Doeville), Rambo Cem, born/died: 6 Jul 1920, record (1920) #: 92.

Louisa MAIN, born: 1 Mar 1856, parents: Martin Fletcher (VA) and Adline Adams, cause of death: "pneumonia and valvular leison heart", informant: M.R. Wills (Shouns), died: 7 Aug 1920, record (1920) #: 93.

David F. MILLER, born: 15 Mar 1868, parents: Ephraim Miller (NC) and Mary Isaacs (NC), cause of death: "wound of stomach and liver received by kick of a horse", informant: Mattie Miller (Trade), buried: Dotson Cem., died: 11 Aug 1920, record (1920) #: 94.

Pauline MOREFIELD, born: 9 Dec 1821, widow, parents: Alexander Wilson and (first name not stated) Neal, cause of death: "cancer of face", informant: J.R. Wills (Mountain City), buried: Donnelly Cemetery, died: 13 Aug 1920, record (1920) #: 95.

Girtie SHELTON, born: 22 Mar 1920, parents: Frank Shelton and Maud Triplett, cause of death: "acute indigestion", buried: Phillippi Cemetery, died: 18 Aug 1920, record (1920) #: 96.

Loura Blanche CAMPBELL, born: 27 Feb 1914, parents: N.D. Campbell and Callie Rambo, cause of death: "diarrhea", informant: N.D. Campbell (Doeville), buried: Campbell Cemetery, died: 25 Aug 1920, record (1920) #: 97.

Colonel T. WALKER, born: 28 Oct 1919, parents: Jno C. Walker and Ellen Heaton, cause of death: "diarrhea", informant: Jno C. Walker, (Doeville), buried: Campbell Cemetery, died: 4 Sep 1920, record (1920) #: 98.

Elizabeth CABLE, age about 86 years, born in North Carolina, parents: Jacob Cook (NC) and Elizabeth Cook (NC), cause of death: "sudden cold and acute gastritis", buried: Cable Cemetery, died: 6 Sep 1920, record (1920) #: 99.

Oma WELLS, born: 15 Jan 1903 in Wilkes Co. NC, parents: J.L. Triplett (Wilkes Co. NC) and Elizabeth (illegible) (Wilkes Co. NC), cause of death: "dysentary", informant: John L. Triplett (Doeville), buried: Shouns Cemetery, died: 9 Sep 1920, record (1920) #: 100.

Buck SHOEMAKER, born: 14 Apr 1915, parents: Christopher Shoemaker and Rowie Proffitt, cause of death: not stated, informant: Mrs. C.C. Shoemaker (Laurel Bloomery), buried: Gentry Cemetery, died: 12 Sep 1920, record (1920) #: 101,

Ardia Blanche SLUDER, born: 15 Sep 1912, parents: Roby Sluder (NC) and Magnatia Sturgill (NC), death cause: "dysentary", informant: Mrs. Magnatia Sluder (Mountain City), died: 14 Sep 1920, record (1920) #: 102.

Daniel Turley DONNELLY, born: 26 Jul 1910, parents: R. Ross Donnelly and Mattie Peck Turley, cause of death: "infection of foot", informant: R. Ross Donnelly (Shouns), died: 16 Sep 1920, record (1920) #: 103.

Mary Ann PARSONS, age 53 years, single, born in North Carolina, parents: George Parsons (NC) and Eve Parsons (NC), cause of death: "cancer of stomach", informant: Land Parsons (Mountain City), buried: Mountain View Cemetery, died: 16 Sep 1920, record (1920) #: 104.

Tamalchus Elmer ANDERSON, born: 27 Nov 1916, parents: John S. Anderson and Alice Moody, cause of death: "dirrhea and inflamation of bowels", informant: J.R. Anderson (Butler), buried: Dugger Cemetery, died: 18 Sep 1920, record (1920) #: 105.

John P. PAYNE, born: 12 Feb 1881, single, parents: Franses M. Payne and Lydia C. Farmer (NC), cause of death: "chronic intestinal nephritis", informant: Jessie Arnold (Shouns), buried: Farmer Cemetery, died: 20 Sep 1920, record (1920) #: 106.

Liddia GENTRY, age 50 years, married, parents: Reland Jenkins and Eva Davis, cause of death: "cancer of stomach", informant: Huston Jenkins (Mountain City), buried: Phillippi Cemetery, died: 25 Sep 1920, record (1920) #: 107.

John ARNEY, born: 28 Apr 1915, parents: Godfrey Arney and Ellen Walker, cause of death: "diarrhea", informant: Godfrey Arney (Doeville), buried: Campbell Cemetery, died: 24 Sep 1920, record (1920) #: 108.

Susie Bernice ANDERSON, born: 4 Jul 1918, parents: John S. Anderson and Alice Anderson, cause of death: "diarrhea and inflamation of bowels", informant: J.R. Anderson (Butler), buried: Dugger Cemetery, died: 25 Sep 1920, record (1920) #: 109.

Willis Roscoe LOWE, born: 25 Aug 1920, parents: Jacob Lowe and Bell Lowe, cause of death: "natural death", informant: Roy Lowe (Mountain City), buried: Roberts Cemetery, died: 27 Sep 1920, record (1920) #: 110.

Infant DYSON, female, parents: R.F. Dyson and Matildia (surname illegible), cause of death: "congenital weakness", buried: Donnelly Cemetery, born/died: 27 Sep 1920, record (1920) #: 111.

James Roby DICKSON, age 4 months, parents: Roy Dickson and Ellen Ward, cause of death: "labor pneumonia", informant Roy Dickson (Mountain City), died: 29 Sep 1920, record (1920) #: 112.

Bessie ARNEY, born: 26 Apr 1895 in North Carolina, married, parents: Harrison Lee (NC) and Sarah Lee (NC), cause of death: "caught fire and burned", informant: Isaac Arney (Doeville), buried: Rambo Cemetery, died: 30 Sep 1920, record (1920) #: 113.

Martha PRICE, born: 23 Dec 1844, married, parents: John Asham (NC) and Nancy Graybeal (NC), cause of death: "cancer of stomach", informant: James Price (Shouns), buried: Price Cemetery, died: 4 Oct 1920, record (1920) #: 114.

Carl Forrest WALLACE, born: 13 Nov 1919, parents: Stacy Wallace and Alice Stout, cause of death: "diarrhea", informant: Stacy Wallace (Doeville), buried: Shouns Cemetery, died: 6 Oct 1920, record (1920) #: 115.

Mabel SNYDER, born: 9 Apr 1917, parents: Stanley Snyder and Cora Dickens, cause of death: "acute gastro....", informant: Stanley Snyder (Mountain City), buried: Donnelly Cemetery, died: 8 Oct 1920, record (1920) #: 116.

Charlie BROWN, black, age 82 years, born in North Carolina, parents: Jackson Brown (NC) and Patsey Brown (NC), cause of death: "acute cyotitis", informant: Wilson Wall (Mountain City), buried: Mountain View Cemetery, died: 8 Oct 1920, record (1920) #: 117.

Infant GENTRY, female, parents: Harve Gentry and Ada Horn, cause of death: "premature birth", Phillippi Cem., born/died: 9 Oct 1920, record (1920) #: 118.

Susie DOUGHERTY, age about 45 years, single, teacher, parents: Thomas Dougherty (NC) and Polly McBride (NC), cause of death: "infective diarrhea", informant: F.C. Dougherty (Butler), buried: Dougherty Cemetery, died: 10 Oct 1920, record (1920) #: 119.

Isabelle WELLS, born: 30 Nov 1919, parents: Robert Wells and Oma Triplett, cause of death: "diarrhea", informant: Jno Triplett (Doeville), died: 10 Oct 1920, record (1920) #: 120.

John F. REEVES, born: 13 Sep 1842 in North Carolina, widower, parents: "don't know", cause of death: "heart failure", informant: H.S. Reeves (Crandull), buried: Blevins Cem., died: 12 Oct 1920, record (1920) #: 121.

Silvester CORNETT, Jr., age 3 years, parents: Silvester Cornett and Maud McElyea, cause of death: "labor pneumonia", informant: W.F. Williams (Shouns), died: 13 Oct 1920, record (1920) #: 122.

Infant BURGIS, male, born: 6 Sep 1920, parents: McKinley Burgis and Mary Eggers, cause of death: "influenza and broncho pneumonia", informant: Wiley Burgis (Mountain City), buried: Donnelly Cemetery, died: 16 Oct 1920, record (1920) #: 123.

Infant GENTRY, male, parents: Leach Gentry and Laura Barry, cause of death: "influenza and broncho pneumonia", informant: J.W. Gentry (Mountain City), buried: Wilson Cemetery, died: 17 Oct 1920, record (1920) #: 124.

Infant WILSON, male, born: 18 Sep 1920, parents: Tyler Wilson and Anna Wilson, cause of death: "influenza and broncho pneumonia", buried: Wilson Cemetery, died: 17 Oct 1920, record (1920) #: 125.

Samuel Carter SLIMP, born: 6 Feb 1860, single, parents: not stated, cause of death: "cancer of nose", died: 20 Oct 1920, record (1920) #: 126.

Russell MINKS, age 60 years, married, parents: William Mink (NC) and Sally Neatherly, cause of death: "heart dropsy", informant: R.D. Vannoy (Neva), died: 21 Oct 1920, record (1920) #: 127.

Nancy MARTIN, born: June 1837 in North Carolina, widow, parents: Thomas Stout and Lizzie Potter, cause of death: "heart disease", informant: G.W. Martin (Shouns), buried: Martin Cemetery, died: 23 Oct 1920, record (1920) #: 128.

Elizabeth BUNTING, age about 80 years, married, parents: Thomas Cable and Jane Whitehead, cause of death: "infective diarrhea", informant: Duffie Tester (Butler), buried: Dugger Cemetery, died: 25 Oct 1920, record (1920) #: 129.

Mattison L. HAMMONS, born: 14 May 1855, married, parents: Henry W. Hammons and Sarah A. Willen (NC), cause of death: "heart failure", informant: U.B. Payne (Shouns), died: 27 Oct 1920, record (1920) #: 130.

John Clarence BARRY, born: 6 Jun 1920, parents: Hugh Barry and Alice Grindstaff, cause of death: "bronchal pneumonia", informant: Hugh Barry (Mountain City), buried: Wilson Cemetery, died: 28 Oct 1920, record (1920) #: 131.

Lucy Anna GREER, age 4 years, 9 months and 5 days, parents: Isaac Greer (NC) and June Greer, cause of death: "labor pneumonia", buried: Wilson Cemetery, died: 29 Oct 1920, record (1920) #: 132

Nanie HAMBY, born: 20 May 1859, married, parents: Smith Neely and Hannah Hand, cause of death: "appoplexy and brights disease", informant: Clint Waters (Damascus, VA), buried: Sutherland, TN, died: 29 Oct 1920, record (1920) #: 133.

Vilva Ruth WATSON, bonr: 7 Mar 1917, parents: Thomas Watson and (illegible) Gregg (Avery Co. NC), cause of death: "croup", buried: Dugger Cemetery, died: 30 Oct 1920, record (1920) #: 134.

Mable EGGERS, born: 3 Apr 1914, parents: Wm. D. Eggers and Callie Shoun, cause of death: "diptheria", buried: Wilson Cem., died: 30 Oct 1920, record (1920) #: 135.

William OSBORN, born: 11 Sep 1854, widower, parents: Elijah Osborn (Wilkes Co. NC) and mother's name unknown, cause of death: "heart dropsy", informant: John Osborn (Doeville), buried: Wagener Cemetery, died: 12 Nov 1920, record (1920) #: 136.

Verna May SHOUN, born: 22 Jun 1912 in Oregon, parents: Marcellis Shoun and Bessie Robinson, cause of death: "pneumonia", informant: J.M. Shoun (Mountain City), died: 15 Nov 1920, record (1920) #: 137.

Mary Isabella LOYD, born: 7 Jan 1847, married, parents: Washington Blevins (VA) and Susannah Blevens, cause of death: "cancer around eye and eyeball", informant: L,C. Loyd, buried: Loyd Cemetery, died: 17 Nov 1920, record (1920) #: 138.

Hannah PROFFITT, age about 65 years, married, parents: John Campbell (NC) and Delia Heaton (NC), cause of death: "heart dropsy", informant: John Proffitt (Doeville), buried: Campbell Cemetery, died: 18 Nov 1920, record (1920) #: 139.

John William HODGES, born: 24 Sep 1920, parents: James Hodges (NC) and Bessie Norris, cause of death: "broncho pneumonia", informant: Bessie Hodges (Mountain City), buried: Shingletown Cemetery, died: 18 Nov 1920, record (1920) #: 140.

Devona MOODY, born: 14 Nov 1918, parents: Jim Moody and Cora Anderson, cause of death: "infective diarrea", informant: Jim Moody (Butler), buried: Dugger Cem., died: 21 Nov 1920, record (1920) #: 141.

John A. DUGGER, Sr., age about 75 years, parents: John A. Dugger, Sr. and mother's name not known, cause of death: "muscular rhumatism and nephritis", informant: J.D. Arney (Butler), buried: Dugger Cemetery, died: 25 Nov 1920, record (1920) #: 142.

Minnie ISAACS, parents: Jack Isaacs (NC) and Mary Swift (NC), death cause: "labor pneumonia", informant: Jack Isaacs (Mountain City), buried: Donnelly Cem., died: 27 Nov 1920, record (1920) #: 143.

Geneva LEWIS, born: 10 Dec 1919, parents: Carley Lewis (NC) and Bethel Roark (NC), cause of death: "thought to be cholera", informant: Carley Lewis (Shouns), buried: Hampton Cemetery, died: 30 Nov 1920, record (1920) #: 144.

Infant WILSON, male, parents: Will Wilson and Bessie Myers (VA), stillborn, born/died: 27 Nov 1920, record (1920) #: 145.

Nelle RAGAN, born: 10 Sep 1920, parents: Gordon H. Ragan (NC) and Lula Reece, cause of death: "unknown", informant: Gordon Ragan (Trade), buried: Reece Cem., died: 1 Dec 1920, record (1920) #: 146.

Ulysis Grant RASH, born: 4 Apr 1920, parents: Arthur D. Rash (NC) and Annie May Ray (NC), cause of death: "pneumonia", buried: Rash Cemetery, died: 4 Dec 1920, record (1920) #: 147.

Arthur Ray BROWN, born: 19 Jan 1897 in North Carolina,
single, parents: William A. Brown (NC) and Juliatte
Fletcher (NC), death cause: "pulmonary tuberculosis",
informant: W.A. Brown (Crandull), buried: Blevins
Cem., died: 9 Dec 1920, record (1920) #: 148.

Infant DYSON, male, born: 24 Nov 1920, parents: Worley
Dyson and Rebecca Bryant, cause of death: "broncho
pneumonia", informant: Andy Dyson (Mountain City),
buried: Donnelly Cemetery, died: 12 Dec 1920, record
(1920) #: 149.

Matilda PHILLIPS, age about 60 years, born in North
Carolina, parents: father's name not stated and Mary
Smith (Watauga Co. NC), death cause: "typhoid fever",
informant: Wesley Phillips (Butler), buried in North
Carolina, died: 13 Dec 1920, record (1920) #: 150.

Laura RUSTIN, black, married, age about 60 years, born
in North Carolina, parents: father not stated and
Lanners Thomas (NC), death cause: illegible,
informant: Calvin Rustin (Mountain City), Mountain
View Cem., died: 15 Dec 1920, record (1920) #: 151.

Emerson Ethridge RUPARD, born: 14 May 1889, parents:
Wiley R. Rupard (NC) and Amanda Waters, cause of
death: "killed suddenly by being caught in machinery
while operatin saw mill", informant: W.R. Rupard
(Laurel Bloomery), buried: Waters Cemetery, died: 17
Dec 1920, record (1920) #: 152.

Mattie L...(illegible)..., age 56 years, married,
parents: A.J. Brooks and first name illegible Rankins,
cause of death: "pulmonary tuberculosis", died: 22 Dec
1920, record (1920) #: 153.

Mattie L...(illegible)..., age 56 years, married,
parents: A.J. Brooks and first name illegible Rankins,
cause of death: "pulmonary tuberculosis", died: 22 Dec
1920, record (1920) #: 153.

Eugene MOREFIELD, age 42 years, married, parents:
father's name not stated and Margaret Morefield, cause
of death: "tuberculor asthema", buried: Donnelly
Cemetery, died: 23 Dec 1920, record (1920) #: 154.

Landen LOYD, born: 8 Jan 1841, widower, parents: John
Loyd (VA) and Anna Crosswhite, cause of death:
"locomotor ataria", informant: W.W. Loyd (Mountain
City), died: 22 Dec 1920, record (1920) #: 155.

Baker SWEENEY, age 76 years, widower, parents: David
Seeeney and mother's name unknown, cause of death:
"labor pneumonia", informant: H.A. Seeeney (Mountain
City), buried: Wilson Cemetery, died: 30 Dec 1920,
record (1920) #: 156.

Dora FARMER, born: 13 Mar 1890 in Illinois, married, parents: J.D. Estes (VA) and Lydia Blevins (VA), cause of death: "pulmonary tuberculosis", informant: Fielder Farmer, (Crandull), buried: Gentry Cemetery, died: 31 Dec 1920, record (1920) #: 157.

Infant HAMMONS, male, parents: S.T. Hammons and O.E. Curd, stillborn, informant: S.T. Hammons (Shouns), buried: Hammons Cemetery, born/died: 3 Dec 1920, record (1920) #: 158.

Infant FRITZ, parents: Allen Fritz and Mary Maxwell, cause of death: "premature delivery", informant: Mary Maxwell (Laurel Bloomery), buried: Taylor Valley Cem., born/died: 20 Dec 1920, record (1920) #: 159.

Alex Stanley PIERCE, born: 12 Mar 1855, married, parents: Isaac Pierce and Martha Stout, cause of death: illegible, informant: D.C. Pierce (Mountain City), died: 3 Jan 1921, record (1921) #: 177.

Mrs. Sarah DYER, age 73 years, married, born in Watauga Co. NC, parents: John Walker (Davie Co. NC) and Rebecca Ward (Watauga Co. NC), death cause: "labor pneumonia", informant: Jno W. Dyer, buried: Wilson Cem., died: 3 Jan 1921, record (1921) #: 178.

Shelton Graham ROBERTS, born: 5 Jan 1920, parents: Graham Roberts and Venie C. Stout, cause of death: "pneumonia", informant: Gray Roberts (Mountain City), buried: Roberts Cemetery, died: 5 Jan 1921, record (1921) #: 179.

John Q. BURTON, born: 2 Jul 1821, married, parents: Hiram Burton (NC) and Louise Dugger, cause of death: "organic heart disease", informant: Vicy Anderson (Butler), buried: Cable Cemetery, died: 8 Jan 1921, record (1921) #: 180.

Everett STANSBERRY, age 61 years, parents: "unknown", cause of death: "heart dropsy", informant: J.L. Ward (Butler), died: 10 Jan 1921, record (1921) #: 181.

Miss Hattie VAUGHT, born: 24 Mar 1895, single, parents: David S. Vaught and Sarah Coffee (NC), cause of death: "pulmonary tuberculosis", informant: W.W. Vaught (Shouns), buried: family cemetery, died: 13 Jan 1921, record (1921) #: 182.

Elizabeth N..(illegible).., age 85 years, born in Ashe Co. NC, parents: Thomas Stout and Elizabeth Potter, cause of death: "descase of natural values", died: 14 Jan 1921, record (1921) #: 183.

Epsy ARNEY, female, born: 21 Jan 1862, married, parents: not stated, cause of death: "heart dropsy", informant: Charlie Slimp (Neva), died: 20 Jan 1921, record (1921) #: 184.

Maxwell D. WILLIAMS, born: 29 Nov 1860 in Lynchburg, VA, parents: James Williams and mother's first name unknown, Mays, cause of death: "chronic brights", informant: Mrs. M.D. Williams, buried: Bristol, VA, died; 26 Jan 1921, record (1921) #: 185.

Ruby Ruth DOWELL, born: 14 Dec 1919, parents: William Dowell and Josie South, cause of death: "intestinal infection", informant: J.M. Dowell (Shouns), buried: Powell Cem., died: 30 Jan 1921, record (1921) #: 186.

Enoch Finley MINTON, age 40 years, born in North Carolina, parents: Enoch Minton (NC) and Cynthia Watson (NC), cause of death: "gun shot wound in left shoulder severing artery", informant: Allen Minton (Crandull), buried: Blevins Cemetery, died: 4 Feb 1921, record (1921) #: 187.

Emmer DUNN, female, born: 1 May 1888 in North Carolina, married: parents: H.L. Roark (NC) and Martha C. Main (NC), cause of death: "pulmonary tuberculosis", informant: H.L. Roark (Shouns), buried: McEwen Cem., died: 6 Feb 1921, record (1921) #: 188.

Bessie M. WOODARD, born: 12 Apr 1903 in North Carolina, single, parents: R.S. Osborn (KY) and Mary R. Ray (NC) cause of death: "shot in back with gun by Deliar Woodard, ... killed dead", informant: Mary R. Ray (Shouns), buried: Osborn Cemetery, died: 12 Feb 1921, record (1921) #: 189.

James Irwin SAMMONS, born: 7 Oct 1917, parents: S.S. Sammons and E..(illegible).. Snodgrass, cause of death: "la grippe and severe diarrea", informant: S.S. Sammons (Mountain City), buried: Donnelly Cemetery, died: 22 Feb 1921, record (1921) #: 190.

Edna May REECE, born: 21 Jul 1920, parents: Dave Reece and Birdie Phillippi, death cause: "an abnormal child", informant: M.E. Wills (Mountain City), buried: Phillippi Cem., died: 23 Feb 1921, record (1921) #: 191.

L.D. ROARK, born: 1899 in North Carolina, married, parents: N.L. Roark (NC) and Martha C. Main (NC), cause of death: "he was shot in the back, died suddenly from pistol wound by one R.G. Lipfird", informant: H.L. Roark (Shouns), buried: McEwen Cemetery, died: 24 Feb 1921, record (1921) #: 192.

Millard Filmore ROBERTS, born: 4 Apr 1850, married, parents: J.M. Roberts and Lucinda Arnold, cause of death: "labor pneumonia", informant: Tyler Roberts, buried: Wright Cemetery, died: 26 Feb 1921, record (1921) #: 193.

Docia ARNEY, age 75 years, parents: Abraham Nave and Sarah Nave, cause of death: "cold followed by absess of lungs", informant: C.F. Arney (Neva), died: 26 Feb 1921, record (1921) #: 194.

Vira JONES, born: 2 Feb 1921, parents: Walter F. Jones (NC) and Locke J. Roark (NC) cause of death: "premature birth", informant: Frank Jones (Crandull), died: 2 Feb 1921, record (1921) #: 195.

Willie JONES, born: 2 Feb 1921, parents: Walter F. Jones (NC) and Locke J. Roark (NC) cause of death: "premature birth", informant: Frank Jones (Crandull), died: 2 Feb 1921, record (1921) #: 196.

Infant LEE, female, parents: R.A. Lee and Mary Pleasant, stillborn, informant: R.A. Lee (Mountain City), born/died: 16 Feb 1921, record (1921) #: 197.

Delia DUGGER, born: 2 Mar 1908, parents: Benjamin Dyer (NC) and mother's name not stated, cause of death: "pneumonia", informant: Mack Arnold (Neva), died: 1 Mar 1921, record (1921) #: 198.

Roby E. HOLDEN, born: 22 Feb 1881, married, parents: James, J. Holden and Mary Norris, cause of death: "chronic brights disease", informant: Mary Holden (Butler), died: 5 Mar 1921, record (1921) #: 199.

Mrs. T ...(illegible).. SIMMONS, born: 5 Feb 1843 in Surry Co. NC, married, parents: Joel Harris and Sallie Norman, cause of death: illegible, informant: Joel Simmons (Mountain CitY), buried: Shingletown Cemetery, died: 8 Mar 1921, record (1921) #: 200.

Connelly OWENS, born: April 1892, married: parents: Daniel B. Owens and Mary Eastridge, cause of death: "dementia of the me... (illegible).., informant: R.L. Jenkins (Mountain City), buried: Ashe Co. NC, died: 10 Mar 1921, record (1921) #: 201.

Bettie A. DUNN, born: 20 Oct 1855, parents: Vincen Morefield and Deliah West, cause of death: "chronic brights", informant: H.C. Dunn, buried: Dunn Cemetery, died: 12 Mar 1921, record (1921) #: 202.

Infant CHURCH, female, parents: J.C. Church and S.W. Smith, cause of death: "a natural death, cause not known", born/died: 12 Mar 1921, record (1921) #: 203.

Infant PAYNE, male, born: 12 Mar 1921, parents: Joe Payne and Mary Hicks (NC), cause of death: "cause not known", informant: Joe Ward (Butler), buried: Payne Cem, died: 13 Mar 1921, record (1921) #: 204.

Sarah Margaret WIDNER, born: 1840 in Virginia, parents: James Bashel (VA) and Susie Sexton (VA), cause of death: "labor pneumonia", informant: W.L. Roark (Mountain City), buried: Shingletown Cemetery, died: 19 Mar 1921, record (1921) #: 205.

Kitte Lee MICHAELS, age 4 years, parents: M.F. Michaels and Esther Sturgill, cause of death: "broncho pneumonia", buried: Donnelly Cemetery, died: 19 Mar 1921, record (1921) #: 206.

Clyde Franklin SNYDER, born: 17 Apr 1901, parents: William R. Snyder and C.L. Wallace (NC), death cause: "broncho pneumonia", informant: William R. Snyder (Trade), died: 12 Mar 1921, record (1921) #: 207.

Rosa BLACKBURN, born: 31 Jan 1921, parents: W.B. Blackburn and Ethel Greer, cause of death: "not known", informant: W.B. Blackburn (Butler), buried: Rambo Cem, died: 21 Mar 1921, record (1921) #: 208.

Mrs. Louisa FARTHING, born: 10 Jan 1899 in Watauga Co. NC, parents: Calvin Farthing (Watauga Co. NC) and Bessie Farthing (Watauga Co. NC) death cause: "acute nephritis", informant: J.C. Farthing, buried: Watauga Co. NC, died: 22 Mar 1921, record (1921) #: 209.

Earl WILSON, born: 27 Feb 1921 in Carter Co. TN, parents: Edgar Wilson and Erma Laws, cause of death: "not known", informant: Edgar Wilson (Doeville), died: 25 Mar 1921, record (1921) #: 210.

Ruby G. BROWN, born: 6 Mar 1921, parents: E.S. Brown and Flossie Dunn, cause of death: "unknown, natural cause", buried: Brown Cemetery, died: 30 Mar 1921, record (1921) #: 211.

Infant RUSSELL, female, parents: Geo Russell (Ashe Co. NC) and Mary Bailey, stillborn, born/died: 31 Apr 1921, record (1921) #: 212.

Mrs. Melviania ELLER, born: 20 Dec 1829 in North Carolina, widow, parents: Larkin Maxwell (NC) and Elizabeth J. Maxwell (NC), cause of death: "influenza", buried: Cornett Cemetery, died: 2 Apr 1921, record (1921) #: 213.

Nora WALLACE, born: 3 Apr 1921, parents: Jordan Wallace and Alice Snyder, cause of death: "cause not known", informant: Jordan Wallace (Trade), buried: Snyder Cem, died: 3 Apr 1921, record (1921) #: 214.

William H. PLEASANT, born: 3 Aug 1834 in Washington Co. TN, parents: Isaac Pleasant and mother's name not known, cause of death: "nephritis and hardening of arteries", informant: R.B. Pleasant (Doeville), buried: Rambo Cemetery, died: 4 Apr 1921, record (1921) #: 215.

Moses CAUDILL, male, born: 19 Sep 1848, widower, parents: Stephen Caudill (NC) and Sudie Adams (NC), death cause: "chronic intestinal nephritis", informant: Willard Caudill, buried: Donnelly Cem., died: 12 Apr 1921, record (1921) #: 216.

Earl WILSON, born: 27 Feb 1921 in Carter Co. TN, parents: Edgar Wilson and Erma Laws, cause of death: "not known", informant: Edgar Wilson (Doeville), died: 25 Mar 1921, record (1921) #: 210.

Ruby G. BROWN, born: 6 Mar 1921, parents: E.S. Brown and Flossie Dunn, cause of death: "unknown, natural cause", buried: Brown Cemetery, died: 30 Mar 1921, record (1921) #: 211.

Infant RUSSELL, female, parents: Geo Russell (Ashe Co. NC) and Mary Bailey, stillborn, born/died: 31 Apr 1921, record (1921) #: 212.

Mrs. Melviania ELLER, born: 20 Dec 1829 in North Carolina, widow, parents: Larkin Maxwell (NC) and Elizabeth J. Maxwell (NC), cause of death: "influenza", buried: Cornett Cemetery, died: 2 Apr 1921, record (1921) #: 213.

Nora WALLACE, born: 3 Apr 1921, parents: Jordan Wallace and Alice Snyder, cause of death: "cause not known", informant: Jordan Wallace (Trade), buried: Snyder Cem, died: 3 Apr 1921, record (1921) #: 214.

William H. PLEASANT, born: 3 Aug 1834 in Washington Co. TN, parents: Isaac Pleasant and mother's name not known, cause of death: "nephritis and hardening of arteries", informant: R.B. Pleasant (Doeville), buried: Rambo Cemetery, died: 4 Apr 1921, record (1921) #: 215.

Moses CAUDILL, male, born: 19 Sep 1848, widower, parents: Stephen Caudill (NC) and Sudie Adams (NC), death cause: "chronic intestinal nephritis", informant: Willard Caudill, buried: Donnelly Cem., died: 12 Apr 1921, record (1921) #: 216.

Rachel FENNER, age 50 years, single, parents: Jas Fenner and Nancy Elliott, cause of death: "brights", buried: McCown Cemetery, died: 15 Apr 1921, record (1921) #: 217.

James Franklin SMITH, born: May 1848, parents: Abner Smith and Sudie Hurley (NC), cause of death: "pulmonary tuberculosis", informant: J.G. Smith (Butler), buried: Grindstaff Cemetery, died: 15 Apr 1921, record (1921) #: 218.

Ardria A. ROARK, born: 13 Mar 1919 in North Carolina, parents: A.L. Roark (NC) and A.A. Lewis (NC), cause of death: "broncho pneumonia", informant: A.L. Roark (Shouns), buried: Roark Cemetery, died: 15 Apr 1921, record (1921) #: 219.

Nancy FORRESTER, born: 16 Feb 1863, parents: Nathaniel Tester and Nancy Tester, cause of death: "broncho pneumonia", informant: J.L. Tester (Butler), died: 16 Apr 1921, record (1921) #: 220.

Andrew Jackson MILLER, born: 22 Nov 1848 in North Carolina, married, parents: Abraham Miller (NC) and Elizabeth Poe (NC), cause of death: "chronic nephritis", informant: Mrs. R.J. Miller (Laurel Bloomery), buried: Acre Field Cemetery, died: 27 Apr 1921, record (1921) #: 222.

Ellen ARNEY, age about 40 years, married, parents: Jno Walker and Mary Campbell, cause of death: "puepurel septicimia", informant: Jno Walker (Doeville), buried: Campbell Cem., died: 29 Apr 1921, record (1921) #: 223.

Dora WALLACE, parents: Jordan Wallace and Alice Snyder, stillborn, born/died: 3 Apr 1921, informant: Jordan Wallace (Trade), buried: Snyder Cemetery, record (1921) #: 224.

Sarah J, MCNEILL, born: 10 Jan 1876 in North Carolina, married, parents: Hallison H. Eller (NC) and Martha Brown (NC), cause of death: "childbirth", informant: W.A. McNeill (Crandull), buried: Blevins Cemetery, died: 8 May 1921, record (1921) #: 225.

Silvy FRITTS, born: 8 Apr 1921, parents: McKinley Fritts and Mary Dickens (NC), cause of death: "bool hives", informant: McKinley Fritts (Neva), died: 10 May 1921, record (1921) #: 226.

Ray POTTER, born: 2 Apr 1921, parents: Jacob H. Potter and Rosa Head, cause of death: "whooping cought", informant: Clarence Potter (Shouns), buried: Dunn Cem., died: 12 May 1921, record (1921) #: 227.

Margrate Luthena PROFFITT, born: 9 Mar 1845, widow, parents: Daniel R. Stout and mother's name illegible, cause of death: "brights disease", informant: J.L. Proffitt (Doeville), buried: Proffitt Cemetery, died: 14 May 1921, record (1921) #: 228.

Orevil Edward MCQUEEN, born: 22 Apr 1921, parents: Guy E. McQueen and Lydia E. Osborn (Big Creek, TN), cause of death: "found dead in bed", informant: Guy E. McQueen (Butler), died: 19 May 1921, record (1921) #: 229.

Mahalia JACKSON, born: Oct 1848, single, parents: Archibald Jackson and Polly May, cause of death: "burnt to death in house that burnt down", informant: Mollie Osborn (Shouns), buried: McEwen Cemetery, died: 19 May 1921, record (1921) #: 230.

Cleo SHOUN, born: 22 Apr 1920, parents: L.P. Shoun and Laura Roberts, cause of death: "acute gastro euteritis", informant: L.P. Shoun (Mountain City), buried: Shoun Cemetery, died: 28 May 1921, record (1921) #: 231.

131

Venia Elizabeth EGGERS, born 25 Feb 1881, divorced, parents: Robert D. Wilson and Lutitia Fritts, cause of death: "tuberculosis of intestines", informant: Shelton Wilson (Mountain City), buried: Wilson Cemetery, died: 28 May 1921, record (1921) #: 232.

Thurman LEWIS, born: 26 Mar 1906, parents: N.M. Lewis and Lilla Prather (NC), cause of death: "accident, revolver wound of bowels", informant: W.M. Lewis (Shouns), buried: family cemetery, died: 28 May 1921, record (1921) #: 233.

Virda C.T. DUNN, born: 11 Mar 1907, parents: W.M. Dunn and Caldonia Howard, cause of death: "pulmonary tuberculosis", informant: W.M. Dunn (Shouns), buried: McEwen Cem., died: 1 Jun 1921, record (1921) #: 234.

Sallie REECE, born: 1 Jul 1838 in North Carolina, widow, parents: William Willian (England) and Sarah Hudgin (England), cause of death: "general paralysis", informant: William Hammons (Shouns), buried: Hammons Cemetery, died: 1 Jun 1921, record (1921) #: 235.

James Danie PLEASANT, born: 1 Feb 1921, parents: B.W. Pleasant and Nina Lowe, cause of death: "cholera", informant: B.W. Pleasant (Mountain City), buried: Roberts Cem., died: 6 Jun 1921, record (1921) #: 236.

Nellie DUNN, born: 2 Jan 1921 in Virginia, parents: J.L. Dunn (VA) and Ward B. Reece (VA), cause of death: "colary inflantion", died: 2 Jun 1921, record (1921) #: 237.

Glen E. ROARK, born: 15 Nov 1918, parents: W.F. Roark and Nancy J. Martin, cause of death: "whooping cough", informant: W.F. Roark (Shouns), buried: Martin Cemetery, died: 11 Jun 1921, record (1921) #: 238.

Martha ROBINSON, age about 42 years, married, parents: James Mullins and Sabra Campbell, cause of death: "cancer of uterus", informant: J.R. Robinson (Doeville), buried: Rambo Cemetery, died: 12 Jun 1921, record (1921) #: 239.

Jasper S. LONG, born: 4 Sep 1920, parents: H.R. Long and Mary Arney, cause of death: "acute colitis", died: 14 Jun 1921, record (1921) #: 240.

Elizabeth BERRY, born: 5 Feb 1839, married, parents: Geo W. Scott (VA) and Annie Cole, cause of death: "chronic bronchitis and ententis", informant: Chester C. Blevins (Crandull), buried: Gentry Cemetery, died: 18 Jun 1921, record (1921) #: 241.

Agness L. ROARK, born: 14 Sep 1920, parents: W.L. Roark and Nancy J. Martin, cause of death: "whooping cough", informant: W.F. Roark (Shouns), buried: Martin Cemetery, died: 20 Jun 1921, record (1921) #: 242.

Mollie CROSSWHITE, born: 5 Jan 1845, widow, parents: "not known", cause of death: "hemipleyia", informant: John Bentley (Crandull), buried: Gentry Cementery, died: 20 Jun 1921, record (1921) #: 243.

Sarah J. TESTER, age about 64 years, married, parents: Thomas Forrester and Polly Tester, cause of death: "infective dirrhea", informant: J.C. Proffitt (Butler), buried: Sugar Grove Cemetery, died: 23 Jun 1921, record (1921) #: 244.

Mary C. SHUPE, born: Apr 1843 in Carter Co. TN, parents: Henderson Smith and E.. (illigible) Wilson, cause of death: "acute colitis", informant: C.E. Shupe (Mountain City), buried: Wilson Cemetery, died: 24 Jun 1921, record (1921) #: 245.

Lula Belle GILBERT, born: 17 Jul 1897 in Ashland, NC, married, parents: W.H. Graybeal (NC) and Adella Roark (NC), cause of death: "flux with acute delelobar of heart", buried: Ashland, NC. died: 28 Jun 1921, record (1921) #: 246.

Mary PHILLIPS, (widow of Eli Phillips), age 62 years, 2 months and 3 days, parents: Shade Potter (NC) and Bettie Forrester, cause of death: "brights disease", informant: Polly Swift (Mountain City), buried: Forrester Cemetery, died: 28 Jun 1921, record (1921) #: 247.

Mary MINKS, born: 17 Nov 1833, widow, parents: John H. Vaught (VA) and Sarah Vaught, cause of death: "dysentery, informant: E.J. Minks (Shouns), died: 29 Jun 1921, record (1921) #: 248.

Ray WALLACE, born 13 Apr 1919, parents: Roby A. Wallace and Sarah Rash, cause of death: "supposed to be diarhea", informant: Polly Wallace (Trade), buried: Wallace Cem., died: 30 Jun 1921, record (1921) #: 249.

Infant CURD, female, parents: Will Curd and Lelia Dunn, stillborn, informant: Will Curd (Mountain City), buried: Wilson Cemetery, born/died: 13 Jun 1921, record (1921) #: 250.

Fern HOLLOWAY, age about 9 years, parents: R.A. Holloway and Louies Tester, cause of death: "infective dirrhea", informant: J.C. Proffitt (Butler), buried: Sugar Grove, died: 1 Jul 1921, record (1921) #: 251.

Lillie May CAMPBELL, born: 29 Dec 1920, parents: R.L. Campbell and Sabra Walker, cause of death: "dysentary", informant: R.L. Campbell (Mountain City) died: 1 Jul 1921, record (1921) #: 252.

Maggie WALKER, born: 2 Jun 1921, parents: John Walker and Ellen Heaton, cause of death: "not known", informant: John Walker (Doeville), buried: Campbell Cemetery, died: 2 Jul 1921, record (1921) #: 253.

James LEWIS, born: 1 Mar 1902 in North Carolina, single, parents: John C. Lewis (NC) and Callie Hampton, cause of death: "typhoid fever and labor pneumonia", informant: G.E. Lewis (Shouns), buried: Forrester Cem, died: 4 Jul 1921, record (1921) #: 254.

Infant MARTIN, male, born: 3 Jul 1921, parents: J.W. Martin and Josie Main, cause of death: "unknown", informant: J.W. Martin (Shouns), buried: Forrester Cemetery, died: 6 Jul 1921, record (1921) #: 255.

Mina Grace BLEVINS, born: 23 Apr 1919, parents: Wesley Blevins and Della Cole, cause of death: "flux", informant: Mrs. J.A. Cole (Laurel Bloomery), buried: Valley Cem., died: 6 Jul 1921, record (1921) #: 256.

Grace WALLACE, born: 28 Mar 1917, parents: William H. Wallace and Jane Arnold, cause of death: illegible, informant: Jane Wallace (Trade), buried: Wallace Cem, died: 6 Jul 1921, record (1921) #: 257.

Blanch BLEVINS, born: 16 Feb 1917, parents: Wesley Blevins and Della Cole, cause of death: "flux", informant: Mrs. J.A. Cole (Laurel Bloomery), buried: Valley Cem., died: 9 Jul 1921, record (1921) #: 258.

William Kendrick DONNELLY, born: 14 Jan 1827, parents: William Donnelly (VA) and Sallie McQueen (VA), cause of death: "chronic infective mechitis", informant: H.A. Donnelly (Mountain City), buried: Mountain View Cem, died: 6 Jul 1921, record (1921) #: 259.

Claude GENTRY, age 1 year, parents: Ed Gentry and Corela Potter, cause of death: "acute gastro en.. (illegible), buried: Phillippi Cemetery, informant: Wesley Gentry, died: 9 Jul 1921, record (1921) #: 260.

Thomas J. JENNINGS, born: 30 Sep 1868 in North Carolina, parents: Wiley Jennings (NC) and Rebecca Foltz (NC), cause of death: "pulmonary tuberculosis", buried: Greer Cemetery, died: 21 Apr 1921, record (1921) #: 221.

Thelma WALLACE, born: 19 Aug 1920, parents: Walter Wallace and Maggie Wilson (NC), cause of death: "acute colitis", buried: Wallace Cemetery, died: 10 Jul 1921, record (1921) #: 261.

Herman BLEVINS, born: 15 Oct 1914, parents: Wesley Blevins and Della Cole, cause of death: "flux", informant: Mrs. J.A. Cole (Laurel Bloomery), buried: Valley Cem., died: 12 Jul 1921, record (1921) #: 262.

Carie GILBERT, born: 12 Feb 1907, parents: Dudley Gilbert and Celia Vanoy (NC) cause of death: "tuberculosis", informant: Ot Bunton (Neva), buried in North Carolina, died: 16 Jul 1921, record (1921) #: 263.

Martha SMITH, born: 12 Jun 1869, widow, parents: A.J. Fritts and Louise Porch (NC), cause of death: "cancer of liver", informant: Brown Fritts (Doeville), buried: Fritts Cem., died: 12 Jul 1921, record (1921) #: 264.

Hazel POTTER, born: 30 Jun 1921, parents: Frank Potter and Bessie Main, cause of death: "found dead in bed", informant: David Green (Trade), buried: Reece Cemetery, died: 17 Jul 1921, record (1921) #: 265.

Rouena BLEVINS, born: 23 May 1917, parents: Wesley Blevins and Della Cole, cause of death: "suppose flux", informant: Mrs. J.A. Cole (Laurel Bloomery), buried: Valley Cemetery, died: 19 Jul 1921, record (1921) #: 266.

Thomas STOUT, age about 61 years, born in North Carolina, married, parents: Thomas Stout and Elizabeth Potter, cause of death: "brights disease", informant: John H. Stout (Shouns), buried: Stout Cemetery, died: 21 Jul 1921, record (1921) #: 267.

Stacy Orville MOREFIELD, age 3 years, parents: Elmer Morefield and Lucy Ellen Able, cause of death: "colitis", informant: J.C. Miller (Laurel Bloomery), buried: Valley Cemetery, died: 22 Jul 1921, record (1921) #: 268.

Verna M. WALLACE, born: 16 Apr 1917, parents: Roby A. Wallace and Sarah Rash, cause of death: "colitis", informant: Roby A. Wallace (Trade), buried: Wallace Cemetery, died: 24 Jul 1921, record (1921) #: 269.

Fred HEATON, born: 10 Apr 1920, parents: C.F. Heaton and Vernia Lewis (NC), cause of death: "acute gastro enterites", informant C.F. Heaton (Mountain City), buried: Mountain View Cemetery, died: 25 Jul 1921, record (1921) #: 270.

Infant MCELYEA, male, parents: James McElyea and Vertie Tester, cause of death: illegible, born/died: 25 Jul 1921, record (1921) #: 271.

Fred HEATON, age 1 year, 3 months and 15 days, parents: Columbus Heaton and Venie J. Roues (NC), cause of death: "gastro enteritis", informant: Columbus Heaton (Mountain City), died: 26 Jul 1921, record (1921) #: 272.

Andrew POTTER, born: 6 Nov 1907, parents: James Potter (NC) and Martitia Greer (NC), death cause: "ilio colitis, acute", informant: Martitia Potter (Trade), Potter Cem, died: 26 Jul 1921, record (1921) #: 273.

Elizabeth Victoria WAGNER, born: 6 Jun 1861, widow, parents: William E. Johnson and .... Wilson, cause of death: "acute entro-colitis", informant: D.E. Wagner (Mountain City), buried: Wagner Cemetery, died: 28 Jul 1921, record (1921) #: 274.

Roby TESTER, age about 32 years, married, parents: Robert Tester and Sarah Forrester, cause of death: "infective dirrhea", informant: Duffie Tester (Butler), buried: Sugar Grove Cemetery, died: 30 Jul 1921, record (1921) #: 275.

Sara Jinnith MCNEILL, born: 3 May 1921, parents: W.A. McNeill (NC) and S.J. Eller (NC), cause of death: "cholera", informant W.A. McNeill (Crandull), buried: Blevins Cem., died: 31 Jul 1921, record (1921) #: 276.

Alphns E. ELISON, (married to Abbie Elison), age about 65 years, born in Ashe Co. NC, parents: Jerry Elison and Betsy (Illegible), cause of death: "pulmonary tuberculosis, informant: Abie Elison (Shouns), buried: Osborn Cemetery, died: 31 Jul 1921, record (1921) #: 277.

Fred MCEWEN, born: 8 Dec 1919, parents: Samuel McEwen and Lillie Howard, cause of death: "flux", informant: Samuel McEwen (Doeville), buried: Shouns Cemetery, died: 5 Aug 1921, record (1921) #: 278.

Nannie WARD, age 38 years, married, parents: Roof May and Annie Norris (NC), cause of death: "tuberculosis", informant: L.L. Stout (Neva), died: 8 Aug 1921, record (1921) #: 279.

Della MINKS, age 54 years, 4 months and 28 days, married, parents: Housford Eller (NC) and Polly Reynolds (NC), death cause: "carcinoma of (illegible), died: 10 Aug 1921, record (1921) #: 280.

John DOTSON, age about 25 years, married, parents: Bill Dotson and Janie Reece, cause of death: illegible, informant: Charles King (Mountain City), buried: Wilson Cemetery, died: 13 Aug 1921, record (1921) #: 281.

Nat Romulus BURTON, born: 11 Aug 1921, parents R.(illegible) Dotson and Stella Reece (NC), cause of death: "atelictasis", informant: Jas D. Robinson (Butler), buried: Cable Cemetery, died: 16 Aug 1921, record (1921) #: 282.

Donnie WALTYER, female, born: 26 May 1904, single, cause of death: "typhoid fever", buried: Rainbolt Cemetery, died: 16 Aug 1921, record (1921) #: 283.

John Shelton PHILLIPPI, age 1 year, parents: Fred Phillippi and Bula Stout, cause of death: not recorded, informant: J.H. Stout (Mountain City), buried: Phillippi Cemetery, died: 22 Aug 1921, record (1921) #: 284.

Milton P. WARD, born: 22 Aug 1871, married, parents: Alex Ward and Caroline Shull (NC), cause of death: "acute nephritis", informant: C.M. Nave (Neva), died: 29 Aug 1921, record (1921) #: 285.

Roy Dewey PAYNE, born: 19 Sep 1912, parents: U.B.
Payne and Pearl Hammons, cause of death: "collitis",
informant: U.B. Payne (Shouns), buried: Hammons
Cemetery, died: 31 Aug 1921, record (1921) #: 286.

Infant OSBORN, male, parents: John Osborn and Susie
Elliott, stillborn, informant: Jno Osborn (Doeville),
buried: Rambo Cemetery, died: 16 Aug 1921, record
(1921) #: 287.

Jorden HECK, Jr., born: 28 Sep 1849, married, parents:
Jorden Heck (PA) and Lisia Snyder, cause of death:
"paralysis of long duration", died: 6 Sep 1921, record
(1921) #: 288.

Mary EGGERS, age about 67, widow, parents: Alexander
Roberts and Mary Roberts, cause of death: "nephritis",
informant: Rettie Eggers (Mountain City), buried:
Roberts Cem., died: 1 Sep 1921, record (1921) #: 289.

Leva ARNOLD, male, born: 14 Dec 1902, parents: Emanuel
Arnold and Rachel Snyder, cause of death: "thrown from
a horse, injury to spinal cord and spine", informant:
G.W. Howard (Shouns), buried: Arnold Cemetery, died: 5
Sep 1921, record (1921) #: 290.

Revinnie Pearl PAYNE, born: 22 Sep 1890, married,
parents: John R. Hammons and Maggie B ..(illegible),
cause of death: "dysentary", informant: U.B. Payne
(Shouns), buried: Hammons Cemetery, died: 7 Sep 1921,
record (1921) #: 291.

Lydia REECE, born: 24 Feb 1874, married, parents:
Enoch Potter and Nancy Osborn, cause of death:
"typhoid pneumonia fever", informant: Emanuel Dunn
(Shouns), buried: Dunn Cemetery, died: 7 Sep 1921,
record (1921) #: 292.

Ellis GREER, born: 18 Aug 1917, parents: Edd Greer and
Ollie Wilson, cause of death: "colitis, informant: Edd
Greer (Laurel Bloomery), buried: Valley Cemetery,
died: 7 Sep 1921, record (1921) #: 293.

Infant DUGGER, female, parents: James L. Dugger and
Ordie Arney, cause of death: "premature delivery",
informant: J.C. Dugger (Butler), buried: Sugar Grove
Cemetery, born/died: 8 sep 1921, record (1921) #: 294.

Lula REEVES, born: 9 Sep 1892, married, parents: Henry
Thomas (Watauga Co. NC) and Katie Stout, cause of
death: "apoplexy", informant: Geo Reeves (Mountain
City), died: 9 Sep 1921, record (1921) #: 295.

Mary ANDERSON, born: 3 Mar 1857, widow, parents: W.A.
Goins (Sarah [sic] Co. NC) and Francis Teals
(Allegania [sic] Co. NC), cause of death: "intestinal
nephritis", informant; Milton Anderson (Shouns), died:
10 Sep 1921, record (1921) #: 296.

Mrs. America WILSON, age 53 years, widow, parents: Frank Bailey (NC) and mother's name not stated, cause of death: "apoplexy", buried: Mountain View Cemetery, died: 11 Sep 1921, record (1921) #: 297.

Hazle CABLE, age about 13 years, parents: U.G. Cable and Mina Reece (NC), cause of death: "drowned in bathing, got in deep water and drowned, accidental", informant: U.G. Cable (Butler), buried: Cable Cemetery, died: 16 Sep 1921, record (1921) #: 298.

Lear ISENHOUR, female, age 3 years, parents: John Isenhour (NC) and Jane Proffitt, cause of death: "dropsy", died: 19 Sep 1921, record (1921) #: 299.

Mrs. Martha ARNOLD, born: 12 Sep 1859, married, parents: Eli Phillips (Wilkes Co. NC) and Bettie Lewis, cause of death: "chronic intestinal nephritis", informant: H.A. Campbell (Mountain City), buried: Shingletown Cemetery, died: 24 Sep 1921, record (1921) #: 300.

Pauline FULKES, parents: J.C. Fulkes and Ada Phillips (NC), cause of death: "asphyxia due to prolonged premature labor", born/died: 26 Sep 1921, record (1921) #: 301.

Infant NORRIS, female, parents: Abrsy Norris (Watauga Co. NC) and Julia C. Mullins (Watauga Co. NC), stillborn, informant: Abrsy Norris (Butler), died: 19 Sep 1921, record (1921) #: 302. (also see record 304 below)

Infant DYSON, male, parents: W.C. Dyson and Celva Walsh, cause of death: stillborn, informant: D.F. Proffitt (Shouns), buried: Price Cemetery, born/died: 13 Sep 1921, record (1921) #: 303.

Infant NORRIS, female, parents: Abrsy Norris (Watauga Co. NC) and Julia C. Mullins (Watauga Co. NC), stillborn, informant: Abrsy Norris (Butler), died: 19 Sep 1921, record (1921) #: 304.

Rachel Matilda DUNN, age about 72 years, married, parents: William Wilson and Susie Tester, cause of death: "chronic heart disease", informant: J.G. Dunn (Shouns), died: 3 Oct 1921, record (1921) #: 305.

William VENERABLE, age 84 years, parents: father's name unknown and Polly Venerable, cause of death: "chronic intestinal nephritis", informant: Sara Venerable (Mountain City), buried: Wills Cemetery, died: 6 Oct 1921, record (1921) #: 306.

Sarah PAYNE, born: 3 Oct 1921, parents: Dana Payne and Sarah Stansberry, cause of death: "not known, died in bed", informant: Dana Payne (Butler), buried: Payne Cemetery, died: 7 Oct 1921, record (1921) #: 307.

Elizabeth ROBINSON, born: 29 Mar 1845 in North Carolina, parents: J.M. Robinson (NC) and Caroline Gray (NC), cause of death: "osteosouresurs left superior maxilla", informant: Mrs. Mollie Ashley (Shouns), buried: Shouns, TN., died: 9 Oct 1921, record (1921) #: 308.

Infant V. LONG, female, born: 27 Sep 1921, parents: Lawrence J. Long and Edney Blevins, cause of death: "premature birth", buried: Blevins Cemetery, died: 4 Oct 1921, record (1921) #: 309.

Launia M. ABLE, age 62 years, married, parents: James Able and Jane Gentry, cause of death: "cancer of womb", informant: Luther M. Able (Mountain City), buried: Shingletown Cemetery, died: 9 Oct 1921, record (1921) #: 310.

Annie Mae GRINDSTAFF, born: 16 Aug 1919, parents: Jessie Grindstaff and Ora Benton, cause of death: "indigestion of stomach", informant: Jessie Grindstaff (Doeville), buried: Holden Cemetery, died: 10 Oct 1921, record (1921) #: 311.

Infant PROFFITT, male, parents: Wm Clyde Proffitt and Cory May Morefield, cause of death: "acute pulmonary edema", died: 11 Oct 1921, record (1921) #: 312.

Infant MCGINNIS, male, parents: James McGinnis and Sallie S. Eastridge (NC), cause of death: "premature birth", informant: James McGinnis (Crandull), died: 13 Oct 1921, record (1921) #: 313.

Lena Pearl ROUSE, born: 28 May 1818, parents: C.B. Rouse and M.A. Ford, cause of death: "deptheria", informant: C.B. Rouse (Crandull), buried: Gentry Cemetery, died: 16 Oct 1921, record (1921) #: 314.

Edith DUNN, born: 25 Feb 1913, parents: Henry Dunn and Elizabeth Wilson, cause of death: "acute ..(illegible) nephritis", informant: Conley Powell (Shouns), buried: Dunn Cem., died: 16 Oct 1921, record (1921) #: 315.

Thomas PRICE, born: 7 May 1850 in North Carolina, married, parents: "not known", cause of death: "diabetes", informant: E.E. Sluder (Crandull), buried: Price Cem., died: 17 Oct 1921, record (1921) #: 316.

Easter CAMPBELL, born: 23 Dec 1862, single, parents: Wilborn Campbell and Sarah Robinson, cause of death: "heart dropsy", informant: James Campbell (Doeville), buried: Campbell Cemetery, died: 17 Oct 1921, record (1921) #: 317.

Mary E. DUNN, born: 18 Sep 1921, parents: George Dunn and Stella Riddles, cause of death: "unknown cause", informant: Conley Powell (Shouns), buried: Dunn Cemetery, died: 20 Oct 1921, record (1921) #: 318.

Alexander Andrew RASH, born: 4 Apr 1920, parents: Arthur Donnelly Rash (NC) and Annie Mae Ray (NC), cause of death: "broncho pneumonia", informant: J.A. Dowell (Mountain City), buried: Rash Cemetery, died: 23 Oct 1921, record (1921) #: 319.

Lila Mae BROOKSHIRE, born: 9 Dec 1910, parents: W.D. Brookshire and Julia Heaton, death cause: "scarlet fever", informant: W.D. Brookshire (Doeville), died: 29 Oct 1921, record (1921) #: 320.

Louisa ROBERTS, age 84 years, divorced, parents: Jacob Roberts and mother's first name not stated, Robinson, cause of death: "a natural death from unknown causes", informant: W.A. Walsh (Mountain City), buried: Roberts Cemetery, died: 28 Oct 1921, record (1921) #: 321.

Infant BUTLER, female, parents: James D. Butler and Ana May Hazlewood, stillborn, informant J.D. Butler (Butler), buried: Hazlewood Cemetery, died: 2 Oct 1921, record (1921) #: 322.

Infant HODGE, male, parents: Sam Hodge and Annie Pierce, stillborn, informant: John M. Potter (Shouns), died: 9 Oct 1921, record (1921) #: 323.

Sarah Mabel DISH..(illegible), born: 4 Apr 1905, married, parents: Baxter Parsons and Minnie Price, cause of death: "(illegible)..infection", died: 3 Nov 1921, record (1921) #: 324.

T.S. POTTER, born: 17 Jul 1844, widower, parents: Abraham Potter and Elvie Hynes (NC), cause of death: "brights disease", informant: G.F. Lewis (Shouns), Dunn Cemetery, died: 7 Nov 1921, record (1921) #: 325.

George FARMER, age 12 years, parents: Wm Farmer and Pollie Williams, cause of death: "flux", died: 8 Nov 1921, record (1921) #: 326.

Willie Lee SHORT, born: 4 Dec 1918, parents: B.D. Short (NC) and Martha Shores (NC), cause of death: "whooping cough and broncho pneumonia", informant: J.K. Wilson (Mountain City), buried: Phillippi Cemetery, died: 9 Nov 1921, record (1921) #: 327.

Mrs. Nellie King WAGNER, born: 25 Aug 1842 in McMinn Co. TN, married, parents: Charles L. King (Henrico Co. VA) and Julie McElyea (Loudon Co. TN), death cause: "chronic brights", informant: Charles M. Wagner, Mtn View, died: 10 Nov 1921, record (1921) #: 328.

Infant HODGE, male, parents: Sam Hodge and Annie Pierce, stillborn, informant: John M. Potter (Shouns), died: 9 Oct 1921, record (1921) #: 323.

Sarah Mabel DISH..(illegible), born: 4 Apr 1905, married, parents: Baxter Parsons and Minnie Price, cause of death: ".....(illegible) infection", died: 3 Nov 1921, record (1921) #: 324.

T.S. POTTER, born: 17 Jul 1844, widower, parents: Abraham Potter and Elvie Hynes (NC), cause of death: "brights disease", informant: G.F. Lewis (Shouns), Dunn Cemetery, died: 7 Nov 1921, record (1921) #: 325.

George FARMER, age 12 years, parents: Wm Farmer and Pollie Williams, cause of death: "flux", died: 8 Nov 1921, record (1921) #: 326.

Willie Lee SHORT, born: 4 Dec 1918, parents: B.D. Short (NC) and Martha Shores (NC), cause of death: "whooping cough and broncho pneumonia", informant: J.K. Wilson (Mountain City), buried: Phillippi Cemetery, died: 9 Nov 1921, record (1921) #: 327.

Mrs. Nellie King WAGNER, born: 25 Aug 1842 in McMinn Co. TN, married, parents: Charles L. King (Henrico Co. VA) and Julie McElyea (Loudon Co. TN), cause of death: "chronic brights", informant: Charles M. Wagner, buried: Mountain View Cemetery, died: 10 Nov 1921, record (1921) #: 328.

Hershell C.V. DYER, born: 12 Sep 1919, parents: Calvin V. Dyer (Watauga Co. NC) and Bettie A. Wilson, cause of death: "poison by swallowing carbolic acid, accidental", informant: C.V. Dyer (Butler), buried: Rainbolt Cem, died: 11 Nov 1921, record (1921) #: 329.

Brison EVANS, born: 7 Jul 1849 in North Carolina, married, parents: "unknown", cause of death: "brights disease", informant: J.F. Morgan (Butler), buried: Bunton Cem, died: 15 Nov 1921, record (1921) #: 330.

Francis Elizabeth REECE, born: 28 Jun 1921, parents: James Reece (NC) and Cora Dunn, cause of death: "acute colitis", informant: James Reece (Mountain City), buried: Wilson Cemetery, died: 16 Nov 1921, record (1921) #: 331.

Florence HALL, born: 16 May 1848, widow, parents: William Stout and Nancy Stout, cause of death: "heart dropsy", informant: Rufus Cress (Butler), buried: Morley Cem, died: 17 Nov 1921, record (1921) #: 332.

Wiley DIXON, age 4 years, parents: W.M. Dixon and Ellen Ward (NC), death cause: "whooping cough and pneumonia", died; 18 Nov 1921, record (1921) #: 333.

James G. BUTLER, born: 4 Apr 1849, doctor, widower, parents: R.R. Butler (VA) and Mary Donnelly, cause of death: "died suddenly, general paralysis", informant: Jessie Snyder (Shouns), buried: Donnelly Cemetery, died: 2 Dec 1921, record (1921) #: 334.

Due Virgil BLANKENBECKLER, born: 15 Mar 1921, parents: C.T. Blankenbeckler and Pearl Fenner, cause of death: "whooping cough and broncho pneumonia", informant: C.T. Blankenbeckler (Doeville), buried: Wilson Cemetery, died: 12 Dec 1921, record (1921) #: 335.

Roby LOWE, Jr., born: 12 Jan 1921, parents: Roby Lowe, Sr. and Mary Guinn, cause of death: "acute pneumonia, died: 23 Dec 1921, record (1921) #: 336.

James E. DOWELL, age 82 years, 11 months and 6 days, born in Wilkes Co. NC, parents: John Dowell (NC) and Nancy Jarvis (NC), cause of death: "carcinoma of stomach", informant: R. Ross Donnelly (Shouns), died: 21 Dec 1921, record (1921) #: 337.

Thomas J. WALSH, born: 12 Jun 1859, married, parents: Robert Walsh (NC) and Polly Roberts, cause of death: "chronic intestinal nephritis and (contributory) fall from a wagon", informant: Roderick Walsh (Mountain City), buried: Walsh Cemetery, died: 24 Dec 1921, record (1921) #: 338.

Marion WALLACE, male, born: 5 Jan 1917, parents: John I. Wallace and Ellen Wilson (NC), cause of death: "supposed to be membranous croup", informant: John Wallace (Trade), buried: Wallace Cemetery, died: 25 Dec 1921, record (1921) #: 339.

G.G. GENTRY, Jr., born: 7 Nov 1920, parents: G.G. Gentry and Laura Shupe, cause of death: "whooping cough and pneumonia", buried: Johnson Cemetery, died: 28 Dec 1921, record (1921) #: 340.

Minnie Belle STOUT, born: Sep 1879, married, parents: J.F. Davis (NC) and Ellen Wilson, cause of death: illegible, informant: T.G. Stout (Mountain City), died: 28 Dec 1921, record (1921) #: 341.

Maggie BRYAND, age 19 years, born in North Carolina, parents: Sam Wood (NC) and Dealice Holman (NC), cause of death: "pulmonary tubrculosis", informant: Sam Bryand (Mountain City), died: 30 Dec 1921, record (1921) #: 342.

Peggie HODGE, born: 10 Sep 1876 in North Carolina, single, parents: "don't know", cause of death: "apoplexy and chronic intestinal nephritis" informant: Mrs. R.H. Butler (Mountain City), died: 30 dec 1921, record (1921) #: 343.

Infant BRADLEY, parents: father's name not stated and Neta Bradley, stillborn, informant: J.D. Robinson (Butler), died: 6 Dec 1921, record (1921) #: 344.

Thomas Everett JONS, born: 29 Aug 1921, parents: Robert Jons and Bell Smith, cause of death: "whooping cough", buried: Donnelly Cemetery, died: 4 Jan 1922, record (1922) # 181.

Lorene Grace BRYANT, born: 4 Apr 1921, parents: Samuel Bryant and Maggie Ward (NC), cause of death: "tuberculosis", buried: Donnelly Cemetery, died: 7 Jan 1922, record (1922) # 182.

142

Cary Lee STOUT, born: 22 Apr 1913, parents: Wm Stout and Luna Morefield, cause of death: "diptheria", informant: Wm Stout (Doeville), died: 8 Jan 1922, record (1922) # 183.

Simon P. POTTER, age about 70, married, born at Elk Park, NC, parents: "not known", cause of death: "the exact cause not known", informant: Thomas Dellinger (Butler), buried: Sugar Grove Cemetery, died: 22 Jan 1922, record (1922) # 184.

Creed F. DAVIDSON, born: 28 Jan 1852 at Smythe Co. VA, parents: Wm A. Davidson (Smythe Co. VA) and Millie Moore (Smythe Co. VA), cause of death: "apoplexy", informant: Ruby Fritz (Mountain City), buried: Shingletown Cemetery, died: 13 Jan 1922, record (1922) # 185.

James Elic WILKERSON, born: 11 Jan 1850 in North Carolina, parents: Mark Wilkerson (NC) and Ellen Baker (NC), cause of death: "sarcoma in right region that spread to intestines and liver', buried: Smith Cemetery, died: 16 Jan 1922, record (1922) # 186.

Joseph Landon LOYD, born: 19 Jan 1863, married, parents: Hendreson Loyd and Rachel Howard, cause of death: "cancer of prostrate gland", died: 19 Jan 1922, record (1922) # 187.

Verna Golden LOWE, born: 24 Mar 1895, single, parents: John A. Lowe and S. Roretta Wills, cause of death: "appendicitis", informant: John A. Lowe (Mountain City), buried: Phillippi Cemetery, died: 21 Jan 1922, record (1922) # 188.

William Dana WALLACE, born: 7 Oct 1911, parents: Stacy Wallace and Alice Stout, cause of death: "scarletina", informant: Stacy Wallace (Doeville), buried: Stout Cemetery, died: 21 Jan 1922, record (1922) # 189.

William H. ROBERTS, born: 8 May 1856 in North Carolina, married, parents: Rufus Roberts (NC) and Lena Church (NC), cause of death: "paralysis". informant: Bob Roberts (Crandull), buried: Blevins Cemetery, died: 25 Jan 1922, record (1922) #: 190.

Roy Fred MARLOW, born: 5 Dec 1921, parents: W.N. Marlow (NC) and Nancy Moore (NC), death cause: not stated, informant: W.N. Marlow (Damascus, VA), buried: Southerland Cem, died: 28 Jan 1922, record (1922) #: 191.

Infant PENNINGTON, female, born: 30 Jan 1922, parents: Joseph C. Pennington and Anne Greer, cause of death: not stated, informant: Joseph C. Pennington (Laurel Bloomery), buried: Acre Field Cemetery, died: 31 Jan 1922, record (1922) #: 192.

Infant GRINDSTAFF, female, parents: Roby Grindstaff
and Hanah Stout, stillborn, informant: Roby Grindstaff
(Doeville), buried: Grindstaff Cemetery, born/died: 8
Jan 1922, record (1922) #: 193.
Eveline BENTLEY, parents: George D. Bentley and Mary
Alice Bowling, stillborn, informant: George D. Bentley
(Crandull), buried: Bentley Cemetery, born/died: 26
Jan 1922, record (1922) #: 194.
Ida May WILSON, born: 7 Nov 1921, parents: Ed. C.
Wilson (NC) and Betty Carroll (NC), cause of death:
"unknown", informant: Ed. C. Wilson (Shouns), died: 1
Feb 1922, record (1922) #: 195.
Sarah Affie DOWELL, born: 31 Jan 1922, parents:
McKinley Dunn and Lula Dowell, cause of death:
"unknown", informant: Ed Wilson (Shouns), died: 2 Feb
1922, record (1922) #: 196.
John B. VAUGHT, born: 24 Aug 1841, widower, parents:
John S. Vaught (VA) and Rebecca Shoun, cause of death:
"chronic brights", informant: W.W. Vaught, buried:
family cem, died: 2 Feb 1922, record (1922) #: 197.
James G. WILSON, born: 24 May 1842, married, parents:
Richard L. Wilson and Elizabeth Fenner, cause of
death: "influenzy", informant: Joe Wilson (Neva),
died: 7 Feb 1922, record (1922) #: 198.
Martha Ellen RAINBOLT, born: 10 Feb 1860, widow,
parents: Dugger Rainbolt and Lucinda Venable, cause of
death: "broncho pneumnoia", informant: Mary Rainbolt
(Butler), buried: Rainbolt Cemetery, died: 7 Feb 1922,
record (1922) #: 199.
Pauline DIXON, born: 10 Oct 1921, parents: W.M. Dixon
and Ellen Ward, cause of death: "broncho pneumonia
following flue", informant: M.F. Ward, died: 9 Feb
1922, record (1922) #: 200.
George F. MCGLAMERY, age 83 years, born 1839 in North
Carolina, parents: father not known and Snooky
McGlamery (NC), cause of death: "died sudden, cause
not known", informant: W.F. McGlamery (Trade), buried:
Reece Cem, died: 8 Feb 1922, record (1922) #: 201.
Tilda FLANNERY, born: 30 Jan 1922, parents: Joe
Flannery (NC) and Tilda Moody, cause of death: "cause
not known", informant: R.A. Flannery (Reece, NC),
buried: Dugger Cemetery, died: 8 Feb 1922, record
(1922) #: 202.
Arthor Glen JONES, born: 24 Nov 1921, parents: Walter
S. Jones (Ashe Co. NC) and Donsie Farmer (Ashe Co.
NC), cause of death: "unknown", informant: M.E. Jones
(Shouns), died: 10 Feb 1022, record (1922) #: 203.

Nancy HOLDER, age about 75 years, widow, parents:
George Moody and Elizabeth Day, cause of death: "died
a natural death", informant: W.M. Garland (Doeville),
buried: Campbell Cemetery, died: 12 Feb 1922, record
(1922) #: 204.
Jackson STOUT, age about 75 years, married, parents:
Nicholas Stout and Catherine Wagner, cause of death:
"heart dropsy", informant: Mack Arnold (Neva), died:
12 Feb 1922, record (1922) #: 205.
Infant MCQUEEN, female, parents: Guy McQueen and Lydia
Osborn (Sullivan Co. TN), cause of death: "premature,
between 6 and 7 months", buried: Rainbolt Cemetery,
born/died: 19 Feb 1922, record (1922) #: 206.
Minnie WILLEN, born: 19 Mar 1897, married: parents:
James Eller (NC) and Lilie Forrester, cause of death:
"tuberculosis of lungs", informant: T.H. Willen
(Shouns), buried: Dunn Cemetery, died: 20 Feb 1922,
record (1922) #: 207.
Silva STREET, born: 11 Dec 1921, parents: Alfonzo
Street and Estell Maxwell, cause of death: "whooping
cough and bronchial pneumonia", informant: Geo W.
Maxwell (Laurel Bloomery), buried: Gentry Cemetery,
died: 24 Feb 1922, record (1922) #: 208.
Asa GENTRY, born: 2 Aug 1878, mail carrier, parents:
Mahlon Gentry and Mary Stout, cause of death: "gun
shot wound in left side of neck, homicidal, informant:
Mary Gentry (Crandull), buried: Gentry Cemetery, died:
27 Feb 1922, record (1922) #: 209.
Viola Lee May WIDBY, colored, born: 2 Oct 1905,
parents: Samuel Widby (Ashe Co. NC) and Ollie Maxwell
(Washington Co. TN), cause of death: "tuberculosis",
died: 28 Feb 1922, record (1922) #: 210.
Eula ARNOLD, age 10 years, parents: Jas. S. Arnold and
Belle W. Pearce (West VA), cause of death: "broncho
pneumonia", buried: Phillippi Cemetery, died: 28 Feb
1922, record (1922) #: 211.
Retha Jane JONES, born: 18 Nov 1921, parents: Sam
Jones (Ashe Co. NC) and Inez Graybeal (Ashe Co. NC),
cause of death: "unknown", inform-ant: Jane Jones
(Shouns), died: 28 Feb 1922, record (1922) #: 212.
Infant GARLAND, male, parents: W.M. Garland and Clara
Holder, stillborn, informant: W.M. Garland (Doeville),
buried: Garland Cemetery, born/died: 19 Feb 1922,
record (1922) #: 213.
Zollie LUNCEFORD, age about 44 years, born in Watauga
Co. NC, married, parents: Z.D. Lunceford (Watauga Co.
NC) and Mary Lunceford (NC), cause of death: "broncho
pneumonia", informant: J.C. Dugger (Butler), died: 4
Mar 1922, record (1922) #: 214.

Lucinda RAINBOLT, born: 22 Oct 1826 in Virginia, parents: Joseph Venable (VA) and Matilda Merlott (VA), cause of death: "organic heart disease", informant: Mary Rainbolt (Butler), buried: Rainbolt Cemetery, died: 14 Mar 1922, record (1922) #: 215.

Blair B. DELLINGER, born: 6 Mar 1922, parents: Thomas Dellinger (NC) and Dollie Potter, cause of death: "died almost sudden, not a mature child", informant: W.J. Potter (Butler), buried: Sugar Grove Cemetery, died: 18 Mar 1922, record (1922) #: 216.

Rebecca DUGGER, born: 12 Jul 1865, married, parents: B.D. Cable and Susan Simerly (Carter Co. TN), cause of death: "tuberculosis of lungs", informant: H.H. Norris (Butler), buried: Cable Cemetery, died: 21 Mar 1922, record (1922) #: 217.

Emaline LUNSFORD, age 80 years, single, parents: Elias Lunsford and Laney Ward, cause of death: "unknown, died suddent", informant: D.A. Ward (Neva), died: 22 Mar 1922, record (1922) #: 218.

Polly WALLACE, born: 7 Feb 1849 in North Carolina, widow, parents: Alfred Thomas (NC) and Malinda Wilson (NC), cause of death: "chronic bronchitis", informant: Roby Wallace, buried: Wallace Cemetery, died: 24 Mar 1922, record (1922) #: 220.

Alonzo P. GLENN, born: 27 Jul 1878 in North Carolina, parents: Newell Glenn (NC) and Mary Nading (NC), cause of death: "influnezy", inform-ant: C.E. Tester (Neva), died: 22 Mar 1922, record (1922) #: 219.

Samuel WIDBY, colored, born: 28 Dec 1921, parents: Samuel Widby (Ashe Co. NC) and Ollie Maxwell (Washington Co. TN), cause of death: "labor pneumonia", died: 24 Mar 1922, record (1922) #: 221.

Infant EGGERS, female, parents: Waller Eggers and Lillie Stal... (illegible), cause of death: "premature birth", buried: Valley Cemetery, born/died: 25 Mar 1922, record (1922) #: 222.

Joe PAYNE, Jr., parents: Joe Payne and Mary Hicks (NC), cause of death: "dead born", informant: Mrs. R. Tester (Butler), buried: Payne Cemetery, born/died: 1 Mar 1922, record (1922) #: 223.

John E. SHUPE, born: May 1885, married, parents: W.T. Shupe and Margaret Blevins, cause of death: "acute dillilaler heart", informant: Jas W. Shupe (Mountain City), buried: Phillippi Cemetery, died: 1 Apr 1922, record (1922) #: 224.

Alexander WARD, born: 11 Apr 1847, parents: Thomas Ward (NC) and Lila Bradley, cause of death: "tuberculosis", informant: Dolf Ward (Neva), died: 11 Apr 1922, record (1922) #: 225.

Hazel Fay DUNN, born: 4 Apr 1922, parents: J.M. May and Vada Dunn, cause of death: "unknown", informant: J.W. Dunn (Shouns), buried: Osborn Cemetery, died: 14 Apr 1922, record (1922) #: 226.

Ruth SMITH, born: 9 Mar 1922, parents: Walter Smith and Lettie Ellis, cause of death: not stated, informant: J.W. Dinkins (Mountain City), buried: Lefler Cem, died: 16 Apr 1922, record (1922) #: 227.

Joseph J.D. HODGE, born: 29 Mar 1922, parents: Dallas Hodge (Mable, NC) and Elizabeth Stout, cause of death: "whooping cough", informant: J.F. Grindstaff (Doeville), died: 18 Apr 1922, record (1922) #: 228.

Boyd Rilell CARDWELL, born: 28 Mar 1922, parents: J.R. Cardwell (Wilkes Co. NC) and Myrtle Fletcher, cause of death: "cholera", informant: J.R. Cardwell (Butler), buried: Sugar Grove Cemetery, died: 17 Apr 1922, record (1922) #: 229.

Mandy Rebecca MAIN, born: 21 Oct 1855, married, parents: John L. Dunn and Sabra Wagner, cause of death: "meningitis", informant: Daniel M. Main (Shouns), died: 18 Apr 1922, record (1922) #: 230.

Enoch H. YORK, born: 12 Jul 1841 in North Carolina, married, parents: Adam York (NC) and Mary Woodruff (NC), cause of death: "died suddenly", informant: Ida Tribett (Johnson City, TN), died: 23 Apr 1922, record (1922) #: 231.

Hellen Joyce DONELLEY, born: 18 Oct 1920, parents: J.C. Donelley and Valoma Lynville, cause of death: "acute colitis", buried: Johnson City, TN, died: 24 Apr 1922, record (1922) #: 232.

Samuel E. Payton MCQUEEN, born: 24 Dec 1839, married, parents: John B. McQueen and Abigail Nave, cause of death: "labor pneumonia", informant: E.C. McQueen (Mountain City), buried: Wills Cemetery, died: 25 Apr 1922, record (1922) #: 233.

Lizzie Pearl JONES, born: 27 Feb 1922, parents: Walter F. Jones (NC) and Lottie Otto Roark (NC), cause of death: "found dead in bed", informant: T.D. Roark (Crandull), died: 25 Apr 1922, record (1922) #: 234.

Inez Dora B. FORRESTER, born: 22 Sep 1905, parents: J.R. Forrester and Polly Sluder (Ashe Co. NC), cause of death: "tuberculosis of breast and lungs", informant: J.R. Forrester (Shouns), buried: Forrester Cemetery, died: 4 May 1922, record (1922) #: 235.

Ray BURTON, born: 4 May 1922, parents: Raliegh Burton and Stella Reece (NC), cause of death: "cause not known", informant: W.F. Cable (Butler), buried: Cable Cem., died: 4 May 1922, record (1922) #: 236.

Elizabeth Ann PATTON, born: 25 Jan 1886 in North
Carolina, married, parents: Joseph N. Dunn (NC) and
Janie Rose (NC), cause of death: "childbirth",
informant: J.R. Patton (Crandull), buried: Blevins
Cemetery, died: 6 May 1922, record (1922) #: 237.

Diskey Hagn CRAWFORD, born: 9 Nov 1870 in Virginia,
married, parents: William Crawford (VA) and Catherine
A. Shout..(illegible), cause of death: "intestinal
nephritis", died: 14 May 1922, record (1922) #: 238.

Sarah Jane HAYWORTH, born: 12 Apr 1851 in Ashe Co. NC,
married, parents: Daniel Head (Surrey Co. NC) and Mary
Willen (Ashe Co. NC), cause of death: "apoplexy",
informant: R.H. Taylor (Mountain City), buried:
Cornett Cem, died: 16 May 1922, record (1922) #: 239.

Irine May WILLEN, born: 7 Jan 1918, parents: W.A.
Willen and Edna Perkins (NC), cause of death:
"meningitis", informant: W.A. Willen (Shouns), buried:
Dunn Cem., died: 20 May 1922, record (1922) #: 241.

Ellen CAMPBELL, born: 5 Dec 1869, married, parents:
Albert Walker and Mary Brooks, cause of death: "heart
dropsy", informant: W.D. Campbell (Doeville), buried:
Campbell Cem, died: 20 May 1922, record (1922) #: 240.

Mary PATTON, born: 6 May 1922, parents: Thomas R.
Patton (NC) and Elizabeth A. Dunn (NC), cause of
death: "diarrhoea due to bottle feeding causing
indigestion", informant: Thomas R. Patton (Crandull),
buried: Blevins Cemetery, died: 22 May 1922, record
(1922) #: 242.

Joe SMITH, black, age 56 years, born in North
Carolina, parents "don't know", cause of death:
"apoplexy", died: 29 May 1922, record (1922) #: 243.

Nellie Elizabeth JONES, parents: James M. Jones (Ashe
Co. NC) and Annie Owens, stillborn, informant: James
M. Jones (Mountain City), buried: Cornett Cem.,
born/died: 28 May 1922, record (1922) #: 244.

Infant DUGGER, female, parents: Sandy B. Dugger and
Janie Rainbolt (Carter Co. TN), stillborn, informant:
S.B. Dugger (Butler), buried: Rainbolt Cemetery,
born/died: 28 May 1922, record (1922) #: 245.

Hany HILLIARD, age 83 years, born in North Carolina,
parents: Alfred Hilliard (NC) and Rachel Willis (NC),
cause of death: "paralysis", informant: Roby Shull
(Neva), died: 6 Jun 1922, record (1922) #: 246.

Infant SMITH, female, parents: James C. Smith and Mary
Rector, death cause: "premature", informant: A.B.
English (Butler), died: 6 Jun 1922, record (1922) #:
247.

148

John PROFFITT, age about 63 years, widower, parents: William Proffitt and Polly South, cause of death: "pulmonary tuberculosis", informant: David Proffitt (Doeville), buried: Campbell Cemetery, died: 7 Jun 1922, record (1922) #: 248.

Ray Blaine CORNETT, born: 13 Nov 1890, married, parents: Reuben Cornett and Mary D. Eller (NC), cause of death: "abscess of liver", informant: E.C. McQueen (Mountain City), buried: Cornett Cemetery, died: 10 Jun 1922, record (1922) #: 249.

Mrs. Ma.... WILSON, born: 31 May 1862, parents: John M. Cress and Melvice Fenis (Wythe Co. VA), cause of death: "inflamation of stomach", informant: W.A. Brown (Mountain City), buried: Wilson Cemetery, died: 15 Jun 1922, record (1922) #: 250.

Thomas ISAACS, born: 24 Mar 1853 in North Carolina, married, parents: Elias Isaacs (NC) and Eliza Reece (NC), cause of death: "ulcer of stomach", informant: Ray Isaacs (Butler), buried: Sugar Grove Cemetery, died: 21 Jun 1922, record (1922) #: 251.

Sydid Jane JONES, born: 14 Feb 1866, widow, parents: Harrison Proffitt and Margaret Stout, cause of death: "colitis", informant: David Stout (Shouns), buried: Stout Cem, died: 29 Jun 1922, record (1922) #: 252.

Infant WILSON, male, parents: Edgar Wilson and Erma Laws, stillborn, informant: Edgar Wilson (Doeville), buried: Rambo Cemetery, born/died: 17 Jun 1922, record (1922) #: 253.

Ivory Hugh WARD, born: 18 Jun 1916, parents: Tapley Ward and Ollie J. Proffitt, cause of death: "acute dysentary", informant: Tapley Ward (Butler), buried: Neva TN, died: 6 Jul 1922, record (1922) #: 254.

Lucil WOODARD, born: 20 Jul 1921, parents: McKinley Woodard and Attry Forrester, cause of death: "diarrhea", informant: McKinley Woodard (Shouns), Curd Cem., died: 7 Jul 1922, record (1922) #: 255.

Mamie F. MCFADDIN, born: 26 Jun 1921, parents: Wiley McFaddin and Mary Richardson, cause of death: "not known", informant: Wiley McFaddin (Trade), buried: Arnold Cem, died: 8 Jul 1922, record (1922) #: 256.

Wm Henry SMALL, born: 10 Jun 1921 in Carter Co. TN, parents: Wm E. Small (Canada) and Jula N. Campbell (Carter Co. TN), cause of death: "cholera", informant: Wm E. Small (Butler), buried: Wilbur, TN, died: 10 Jul 1922, record (1922) #: 257,

Gaston HORTON, black, age 76 years, born in North Carolina, parents: "unknown", cause of death: "pellagra", informant: Baxter Horton (Mountain City), died: 10 Jul 1922, record (1922) #: 258.

William E. BRUER, born: 30 Jun 1921 in West Virginia, parents: Will Bruer and Bova Potter, cause of death: "colitis", informant: Will Bruer (Shouns), died: 11 Jul 1922, record (1922) #: 259.

Burket HOWARD, born: 15 Jan 1917, parents: James H. Howard and Melda M. Martin, cause of death: "diarrhea", informant: James H. Howard (Shouns), buried: Martin Cemetery, died: 13 Jul 1922, record (1922) #: 260.

Mary DUNN, age 36 years, born: 1886, married, parents: T.T. Tester and .... Forrester, cause of death: "colitis, contributory: abortion", died: 20 Jul 1922, record (1922) #: 261.

Edward S. HAWKS, born: 1 NOv 1920, parents: R.C. Hawks and Villas Phipps (NC), cause of death: "scarlet fever", informant: R.C. Hawks (Crandull), buried: Hawks Cem, died: 21 Jul 1922, record (1922) #: 262.

Crawford WILSON, born 28 Dec 1918 in Carter Co. TN, parents: Ray S. Wilson (Carter Co. TN) and May Pierce (Carter Co. TN), cause of death: "colitis", informant: R.S. Wilson (Voughtsville), died: 22 Jul 1922, record (1922) #: 263.

Charlie C. ELLISON, born: 19 Jul 1922, parents: Jacob Ellison (NC) and Vina Snider (NC), cause of death: "cause not known", informant: D.H. Ellison (Trade), buried: Watauga Co. NC, died: 24 Jul 1922, record (1922) #: 264.

Richard DUNN: born: 28 Apr 1921, parents: Denny Dunn and Effie Reece, cause of death: "acute ilio colitis", informant: Thadius Reece (Shouns), died: 25 JUl 1922, record (1922) #: 265.

Nancy ARNOLD, age 78 years, married, parents: Daniel Stout and Polly Vaught (VA), cause of death: "brights disease", informant: J.M. Stout (Neva), died: 27 Jul 1922, record (1922) #: 266.

Edward Smith PAYNE, born: 20 Jun 1922, parents: David M. Payne and Dona Jones (Ashe Co. NC), cause of death: "broncho pneumonia", informant: David M. Payne (Shouns), buried: Payne Cemetery, died: 28 Jul 1922, record (1922) #: 267.

Jacob MCELYEA, parents: James M. McElyea and Virtie Tester, cause of death: "not known, died suddent", informant: Jane McElyea (Neva), born/died: 31 Jul 1922, record (1922) #: 268.

Millard L. HORN, born: 22 Jul 1921, parents: Worley Horn and Bill Isenhour (NC), cause of death: "flux", informant: Worley Horn (Vaughtsville), died: 31 Jul 1922, record (1922) #: 269.

Infant WOODARD, male, parents: David Woodard and Danford E. Powell, stillborn, informant: David Woodard (Shouns), buried: Osborn Cemetery, born/died: 16 Jul 1922, record (1922) #: 270.

Infant LAWS, male, parents: Joe Laws and .(first name not stated). Pardue, stillborn, born/died: 26 Jul 1922, record (1922) #: 271.

Margaret L. MCELYEA, born: 9 Dec 1888, parents: Daniel Stout and Jane Greenwell, cause of death: "post partum hemorrhage due to adherent planenta", buried: Dry Hill, died: 2 Aug 1922, record (1922) #: 272.

Addie DUGGER, born: 25 Apr 1922, parents: father not stated and Addie Dugger, cause of death: "broncho pneumonia", informant: H.A. Guy (Butler), buried: Dugger Cem. died: 5 Aug 1922, record (1922) #: 273.

Dora BURTON, born: 4 Oct 1867 in Sullivan Co. TN, married, parents: G.W. Brace and Amanda Lambert (Franklin Co, VA), cause of death: "chronic heart disease", informant: J.W. Brace (Bristol, TN), buried: Worley Cem, died: 10 Aug 1922, record (1922) #: 274.

Bruce C. WALLACE, born: 27 Feb 1921, parents: Roby A. Wallace and Sarah Rash, cause of death: "cholera", informant: Roby A. Wallace (Trade), buried: Wallace Cemetery, died: 15 Aug 1922, record (1922) #: 275.

Nancy BLACKBURN, age about 59 years, widow, parents: N.D. Robinson and Mary Howard, cause of death: "pulmonary tuberculosis", informant: D.R. Robinson (Butler), buried: Rambo Cemetery, died: 22 Aug 1922, record (1922) #: 276.

Finley P. CURTIS, born: 21 May 1841 in Caldwell Co. NC, married, parents: Hezakiah Curtis (Caldwell Co. NC) and Celia Coffee (Coldwell Co. NC), cause of death: "paralysis", informant: W.B. Curtis (Butler), died: 26 Aug 1922, record (1922) #: 277.

James K. MAY, age 64 years, born: 1858, married, parents: Jefferson May and Polly Arrendell, cause of death: "accident, by falling from an over turning sled", informant: M.A. Rash (Trade), buried: Greer Cemetery, died: 30 Aug 1922, record (1922) #: 278.

Nancie Nye PERKINS, colored, born, 21 Jul 1838 at Jefferson, Ashe Co. NC, parents: Joe Calloway (NC) and Annie Carpenter (NC), cause of death: "acute colitis", informant: Smiley Perkins (Shouns), died: 21 Aug 1922, record (1922) #: 279.

Infant MCELYEA, male, parents: John McElyea and Margaret L. Stout, cause of death: "premature", informant: Jno A. Duncan (Butler), born/died: 2 Aug 1922, record (1922) #: 280.

Louise DELOACH, born: 9 Apr 1844 in North Carolina, widow, parents: John Garrison (NC) and Disey Loving (NC), cause of death: "pulmonary tuberculosis", informant: J.A. Deloach (Doeville), buried: Campbell Cemetery, died: 1 Sep 1922, record (1922) #: 281.

Wiley Ross HECK, born: 27 Jul 1922, parents: Gar Heck and Cora Benfield (NC), cause of death: "not known, died suddent", informant: David Nave (Neva), died: 3 Sep 1922, record (1922) #: 282.

Samuel WILSON, black, age 79 years, parents: Louis Wilson (NC) and mother's name unknown. cause of death: "chronic intestinal nephritis", informant: James Wilson (Mountain City), buried: Mountain View Cemetery, died: 3 Sep 1922, record (1922) #: 283.

Von E. HOWARD, born: 14 Mar 1921, parents: James H. Howard and Meda M. Martin, cause of death: "diarrhea", informant: James H. Howard (Shouns), buried: Martin Cem, died: 4 Sep 1922, record (1922) #: 284.

Margaret MCFADDIN, born: 3 Oct 1840, widow, parents: Richman Roberts (NC) and Lucy Adkins, cause of death: "general paralysis", informant: J.C. Fulkes (Shouns), buried: Forrester Cemetery, died: 8 Sep 1922, record (1922) #: 285.

Myrtle M. MCELYEA, age 56 years, widow, parents: Larkin McElyea and Catherine Tester, cause of death: "acute ...(illegible).", informant: Rachel McElyea, buried: Wilson Cemetery, died: 10 Sep 1922, record (1922) #: 286.

David C. DAVIS, born: 24 May 1836 in North Carolina, married, parents: James Davis (NC) and Nancy Fullbright (NC), cause of death: "paralysis", informant: Mack Davis (Trade), buried: Zionville, NC, died: 11 Sep 1922, record (1922) #: 287.

Billie STOUT, born: 8 Aug 1921, parents: Roby Stout and Maud Smith, cause of death: "colitis", died: 20 Sep 1922, record (1922) #: 288.

Harrison JONES, born: 18 Feb 1855, married, parents: "unknown", cause of death: "lymphatic lukemia", buried: Roberts Cemetery, died: 20 Sep 1922, record (1922) #: 289.

Rody DUGGER, female, born: 18 Mar 1921, parents: Crawford Dugger and Ceily Hatley (Carter Co. TN), cause of death: "diptheria", informant: D.B. Dugger (Butler), died: 26 Sep 1922, record (1922) #: 290.

Fred Lee SLUDER, born: 27 Jan 1921, parents: Roy Sluder and Nancy Jane May, cause of death: "colitis", informant: Roy Sluder (Shouns), buried: Martin Cemetery, died: 26 Sep 1922, record (1922) #: 291.

Caroline MCELYEA, age 64 years, widow, parents: John
Perdue (NC) and Sarah Adams (NC), cause of death:
"colitis", informant: Minnie Minks (Shouns), died: 28
Sep 1922, record (1922) #: 292.
Zella May BLACKBURN, born: 5 Jul 1922, parents:
father's name not stated and Pearl Blackburn, cause of
death: "not known", informant: Sam Campbell
(Doeville), buried: Campbell Cemetery, died: 30 Sep
1922, record (1922) #: 293.
Belva SCOTT, born: 30 Jul 1915, parents: R.W. Scott
and Jennie Woods (VA), cause of death: "diptheria",
informant: Roy P. Plevins (Crandull), buried: Woods
Cemetery, died: 12 Oct 1922, record (1922) #: 294.
Virginia Belle THOMAS, born: 10 Nov 1921, parents:
Robert Thomas (NC) and Anna Eggers (NC), cause of
death: "scarlet fever", informant: A.B. Thomas
(Trade), buried: Union Cemetery, NC, died: 13 Oct
1922, record (1922) #: 295.
Callie CAMPBELL, born: 3 Feb 1881, married, parents:
William Rambo and Melvania Blackburn, cause of death:
"tuberculosis", informant: N.D. Campbell (Doeville),
buried: Campbell Cemetery, died: 14 Oct 1922, record
(1922) #: 296.
Daniel H. CRESS, born: 16 Jun 1842, widower, parents:
Nicholas Cress and Susie Colbaugh (Carter Co. TN),
cause of death: "chronic intestinal nephritis",
informant: John Wilson (Butler), buried: Mountain View
Cemetery, died: 16 Oct 1922, record (1922) #: 297.
Nancy Caroline BRADLEY, born: 6 Feb 1847, parents:
Richard Bradley and Nancy Jane Smith, cause of death:
"abscess of lungs", informant: Charles Morley
(Butler), died: 18 Oct 1922, record (1922) #: 298.
Susanah ADAMS, born: 12 Oct 1834, widow, parents:
Jessie Crosswhite and mother's name unknown, cause of
death: "supposed to be old age", informant: W.J. Adams
(Doeville), buried: Stout Cemetery, died: 20 Oct 1922,
record (1922) #: 299.
Mary A. PIERCE, born: 5 Jul 1843, widow, parents:
Joseph Wagner and Nancy Wagner, cause of death: "acute
indigestion", informant: W.J. Pierce (Butler), died:
20 Oct 1922, record (1922) #: 300.
Ray HARBIN, born: 17 Apr 1905, parents: John Harbin
(NC) and Ellen Stout, cause of death: "perforated
ulcer", informant: Geo Pierce (Mountain City), buried:
Shoun Cem, died: 30 Oct 1922, record (1922) #: 301.
Delcenia FRITTS, born: 14 Sep 1853 in North Carolina,
parents: "not known", cause of death: "parlaysis",
informant: R.D. Campbell (Butler), buried: Holden Cem,
died: 4 Nov 1922, record (1922) #: 302.

David R. STOUT, doctor, born: 30 Sep 1860, married, parents: Thomas J. Stout and (first name illegible) Grindstaff, cause of death: "pneumonia", informant: C.E. Stout (Butler), buried: Rainbolt Cemetery, died: 7 Nov 1922, record (1922) #: 303.

Benie Bernice MINTON, born: 3 Apr 1922, parents: father's name not stated and Cynthia E. Minton (NC), cause of death: illegible, informant: Mary Minton (Crandull), buried: Blevins Cemetery, died: 7 Nov 1922, record (1922) #: 304.

Ople PRICE, born: 8 Sep 1922, parents: Wilford Price and Ada Denney, cause of death: "found dead in bed", informant: Lillard Hampton (Shouns), buried: Arnold Cem, died: 8 Nov 1922, record (1922) #: 305.

Minnie Malinda HODGE, born: 25 Jun 1920, parents: John H, Hodge and Suzania Roark (NC), cause of death: "burn from falling in hot ashes", informant: J.H. Hodge (Crandull), died: 1 Dec 1922, record (1922) #: 306.

Ople PRICE, born: 8 Sep 1922, parents: Wilford Price and Ada Denney, cause of death: "found dead in bed", informant: Lillard Hampton (Shouns), buried: Arnold Cem, died: 8 Nov 1922, record (1922) #: 305.

Minnie Malinda HODGE, born: 25 Jun 1920, parents: John H, Hodge and Suzania Roark (NC), cause of death: "burn from falling in hot ashes", informant: J.H. Hodge (Crandull), died: 1 Dec 1922, record (1922) #: 306.

Caroline Frances FARTHING, born: 7 Jun 1845 in Coldwell Co. NC, widow, parents: McCaleb Coffee (Coldwell Co. NC) and Betsy Colbert (Caldwell Co. NC), cause of death: "organic heart dropsy", informant: Jerrie Coffee (Boone, NC), buried: Pierce Cem, died: 2 Dec 1922, record (1922) #: 307.

Delmer Ray SHUPE, born: 8 Nov 1921, parents: Sherman Shupe and E... Lewis (NC), cause of death: "labor pneumonia", informant: D.G. Shupe (Mountain City), buried: Wilson Cemetery, died: 5 Dec 1922, record (1922) #: 308.

Harrison BUNTING, age about 84 years, widower, parents: "not known", cause of death: "broncho pneumonia", informant: Duff Tester (Butler), Sugar Grove Cem, died: 10 Dec 1922, record (1922) #: 309.

Clyde MILLER, age about 13 years, parents: John M. Miller and mother's name not known, cause of death: "deptheria", buried: Gentry Cemetery, died: 13 Dec 1922, record (1922) #: 310.

James Charles DICKENS, born: 28 May 1920, parents: Thomas Dickens and Cassie O'Neal, cause of death: "diptheria or membranous croup", informant: Thomas Dickens, died: 16 Dec 1922, record (1922) #: 311.

Elizabeth PENNINGTON, age 84 years, widow, parents: Alex Osborn and mother's name unknown, cause of death: "supposed to be a blood clot in brow", informant: William Pennington (Crandull), died: 18 Dec 1922, record (1922) #: 312.

Mollie CRESS, age about 66 years, born in Carter Co. TN, married, parents: John Glover (Carter Co. TN) and Margaret Kite (Carter Co. TN), cause of death: "acute gastritis", informant: Josie Wilson (Butler), buried: Pierce Cem, died: 20 Dec 1922, record (1922) #: 313.

Andrew HAYWORTH, born: 21 Apr 1883, married, parents: J.O. Hayworth (NC) and Nancy Osborn, cause of death: "acute cardiac dilatation", buried: Hammons Cemetery, died: 20 Dec 1922, record (1922) #: 314.

Sarah STANSBERRY, age about 64 years, born in North Carolina, single, parents: "not known", cause of death: "apoplexy", informant: J.L. Ward (Butler), died 24 Dec 1922, record (1922) #: 315.

Mary Jane HOBWAY, born: 22 Feb 1865, widow, parents: James Dugger and Rebecca V... (illegible)(NC), cause of death: "pulmonary tuberculosis", informant: J.G. Hobway (Butler), buried: Sugar Grove Cemetery, died: 26 Dec 1922, record (1922) #: 316.

Infant BLEVINS, female, born: 25 Dec 1922, parents: Ira Blevins and Nealie Pleasant, cause of death: not stated, informant: Ira Blevins (Doeville), buried: Campbell Cem, died: 26 Dec 1922, record (1922) #: 317.

John TRIPLETT, Jr., born: 2 May 1922, parents: John T. Triplett (NC) and Sallie Hicks (NC), cause of death: not stated, informant: John Triplett (Butler), died: 27 Dec 1922, record (1922) #: 318.

Edith Blanche BLEVINS, born: 11 Nov 1912, parents: Jessie W. Blevins and Millie Ritchie, cause of death: "labor pneumonia", informant: Jesse Blevins (Crandull), buried: Blevins Cemetery, died: 31 Dec 1922, record (1922) #: 319.

Edward SLIMP, age 23 years, married, parents: Joseph Slimp and Emma Jackson (VA), cause of death: "tuberculosis of lungs", informant: J.M. Stout (Neva), died: 1 Jan 1923, record (1923) #: 167.

Alza Ellen REECE, born: 25 Mar 1841, widow, parents: Peter Dugger and Elizabeth Cable (Carter Co. TN), cause of death: "broncho pneumonia", informant: Arther Reece (Butler), buried: Sugar Grove Cemetery, died: 2 Jan 1923, record (1923) #: 168.

Mary Jane MAIN, born: 10 Oct 1922, parents: John Main and Lillie Wallace, cause of death: "cause not known", informant: John Main (Trade), buried; Reece Cem, died: 3 Jan 1923, record (1923) #: 169.

155

Gladys Mildred MCELYEA, born: 21 May 1920, parents: Wm McCrary McElyea and Laura M. Winters, cause of death: "diptheria", buried: Shingletown Cemetery, died: 5 Jan 1923, record (1923) #: 170.
Rachel MAIN, age 82 years, widow, parents: Larkin Dunn and Katy Jackson, cause of death: "influenza", informant: D.M. Main (Shouns), died: 6 Jan 1923, record (1923) #: 171.
Worley ADAMS, born: 2 Aug 1920, parents: W.J. Adams and Martha Church, cause of death: "broncho pneumonia", informant: W.J. Adams (Doeville), buried: Stout Cem, died: 8 Jan 1923, record (1923) #: 172.
Hamilton RAMBO, age 74 years, married, parents: Aaron Rambo (VA) and mother not stated, death cause: "obstruction of bowels", informant: S.A. Stout, died: 13 Jan 1923, record (1923) #: 173.
Margaret Caroline POTTER, born: 13 May 1846, married, parents: M.B. Dunn (VA) and Rebecca Wagner, cause of death: "influenza", informant: John M. Potter (Shouns), died: 16 Jan 1923, record (1923) #: 174.
Grover Delmar BLEVINS, born: 23 Aug 1921 in Virginia, parents: Wesley J. Blevins and Della C... (illegible)(VA), cause of death: "labor pneumonia", informant W.J. Blevins (Crandull), buried: Blevins Cemetery, died: 17 Jan 1923, record (1923) #: 175.
Celia BURTON, age about 64 years, widow, parents: Ben Cable and Susie Simerly (Carter Co. TN), cause of death: "broncho pneumonia", informant: J.R. Anderson (Butler), buried: Cable Cemetery, died: 19 Jan 1923, record (1923) #: 176.
Jody C. REED, born: 11 Jan 1923, parents: Joseph Reed and Blanche Holloway, cause of death: "child was deformed at birth", informant: Lillie Holloway (Butler), born: 20 Jan 1923, record (1923) #: 177.
Finnie CAMPBELL, born: 20 Sep 1905, parents: N.D. Campbell and Callie Rambo, cause of death: "diptheria", informant: N.D. Campbell (Doeville), buried: Campbell Cemetery, record (1923) #: 21 Jan 1923, record (1923) #: 178.
William ARNETTE, age about 74 years, born in North Carolina, married, parents: "not known", cause of death: "influenza", informant: W.M. Reed (Butler), buried: Holden Cemetery, died: 25 Jan 1923, record (1923) #: 179.
Bettie ANDERSON, age about 70 years, born in North Carolina, widow, parents: "not known", cause of death: "influenza and broncho pneumonia", informant: Will Moody (Butler), buried: Dugger Cemetery, died: 27 Jan 1923, record (1923) #: 180.

Rachall SNYDER, age about 77 years, born in North
Carolina, widow, parents: not known, informant: Lem
Snyder (Butler), cause of death: "influenza and
broncho pneumonia", buried: Snyder Cemetery, died: 28
Jan 1923, record (1923) #: 181.

Roby EGGERS, born: 19 Nov 1876, single, parents: Hiram
Eggers and Martha Jones, cause of death: "supposed to
be tuberculosis", informant: Roy Eggers (Trade),
buried: Zionville, NC, died: 30 Jan 1923, record
(1923) #: 182.

Infant BURNETTE, male, parents: Franklin Burnette and
Elva L. Wright, stillborn, buried: Gentry Cemetery,
born/died: 1 Jan 1923, record (1923) #: 183, (see
record 185, below for twin).

Jane DELLINGER, parents: T.B. Dellinger (NC) and
Dollie Potter, cause of death: "dead born", informant:
T.B. Dellinger (Butler), buried: Sugar Grove Cemetery,
born/died: 1 Jan 1923, record (1923) #: 184.

Infant BURNETTE, male, parents: Franklin Burnette and
Elva L. Wright, stillborn at 5 pm, informant: David
Wright (Crandull), buried: Gentry Cemetery, born/died:
1 Jan 1923, record (1923) #: 185.

Alexander MOREFIELD, age 82 years, widower, parents:
Daniel Morefield and Anna Neatherly, cause of death:
"supposed to be paralysis of bowales", informant:
Floid Morefield (Neva), died: 2 Feb 1923, record
(1923) #: 186.

Lola WOLF, born: 31 Jul 1867 in North Carolina,
married, parents: Newel Glenn (NC) and Mary Nading
(NC), cause of death: illegible, informant: C.E.
Tester (Neva), died: 3 Feb 1923, record (1923) #: 187.

Arthur Blain MAIN, born: 12 Jul 1884, married:
parents: N.H. Main and Lizy Fletcher, cause of death:
"pulmonary tuberculosis", informant: N.H. Main
(Shouns), died: 5 Feb 1923, record (1923) #: 188.

Hannah GREGG, born: 6 Aug 1835 in Carter Co. TN,
widow, parents: James Whitehead (NC) and Kate Stout,
cause of death: "influenza and broncho pneumonia",
informant: J.H. Gregg (Butler), buried: Crosswhite
Cemetery, died: 6 Feb 1923, record (1923) #: 189.

Dorcus Bessie BLEVINS, born: 3 Jul 1885, single,
parents: Alfred H. Blevins and Malinda Scott, cause of
death: "ovarian carcinonia", informant: A.H. Blevins
(Crandull), buried: Blevins Cemetery, died: 10 Feb
1923, record (1923) #: 190.

Caroline HARISON, born: 18 Jan 1859 at Watauga Co. NC,
widow, parents: Larane Wolf (NC) and Sarah E. Smith,
death cause: "broncho pneumonia" informant: Sarah
Potter, died: 12 Feb 1923, record (1923) #: 191.

.... Belle THOMAS, colored, age 47 years, born in North Carolina, married, parents: Alfred Thompson (NC) and Jane Moore (NC), cause of death: "tuberculosis", informant: George Thomas (Mountain City), Mountain City Cem, died: 13 Feb 1923, record (1923) #: 192.

Martin WINTERS, age 72 years, married, parents: William Winters and mother's name unknown, cause of death: "influenza", informant: Richard Wood (Mountain City), buried: Donnelly Cemetery, died: 19 Feb 1923, record (1923) #: 193.

Anie DIXON, age 65 years, widow, parents: "don't know father's name" and Annie Ausborn (NC), cause of death: "chronic brights disease", informant: Wiley Dixon, died: 20 Feb 1923, record (1923) #: 194.

Quince DUGGER, age about 75 years, married, parents: Quince Dugger, Sr. and Rhoda May (NC), cause of death: "influenza and broncho pneumonia", informant: John Dickens (Butler), buried: Dugger Cemetery, died: 23 Feb 1923, record (1923) #: 195.

Walter SMITH, born: 28 Jun 1898, married: parents: father not stated and Florence Smith, cause of death: "suicide, hanged self", informant: H.B. Wills (Mountain City), buried: Leffler Cemetery, died: 26 Feb 1923, record (1923) #: 196.

Hiley MULLINS, born: 2 May 1844, single, parents: Joseph Mullins (NC) and Sarah Walker (NC), cause of death: not stated, informant: Catherine Mullins (Doeville), buried: Campbell Cemetery, died: 27 Feb 1923, record (1923) #: 197.

Infant WILSON, female, black, parents: Sam Wilson and Mannie Forrester (NC), cause of death: "congenital weakness", informant: James Wilson (Mountain City), born/died: 27 Feb 1923, record (1923) #: 198.

Louisa SMITH, born: 18 Nov 1833, widow, parents: Michael Smithpeter and Mary .... (illegible)(NC), cause of death: "broncho pneumonia", informant: S.N. Smith, died: 8 Mar 1923, record (1923) #: 199.

Claud C. PHILLIPS, born: 13 Sep 1897 in North Carolina, married, parents: John W. Phillips (NC) and Nelle Eggers, cause of death: "pulmonary tuberculosis", informant: John W. Phillips (Trade), buried: Snyder Cemetery, died: 9 Mar 1923, record (1923) #: 200.

Mary Belle JENKINS, born: 8 Mar 1923, parents: Nat T. Jenkins and Mollie Michaels, cause of death: not stated, informant: Ray Corum (Mountain City), buried: Michaels Cem, died: 10 Mar 1923, record (1923) #: 201.

Ross D. DEAN, born: 2 Feb 1923, parents: Hobart Dean (Greeneville, TN) and Flossie Cowans, cause of death: "whooping cough", informant: Hobart Dean (Butler), buried: Dugger Cemetery, died: 10 Mar 1923, record (1923) #: 202.

Mattie ASHLEY, born: 30 Apr 1848 in North Carolina, parents: J.M. Robinson (NC) and Caroline Gray (NC), cause of death: "broncho pneumonia and influenza", informant: Enoch Ashley (Shouns), died: 12 Mar 1923, record (1923) #: 203.

William M. SCOTT, born: 22 Jun 1836, married, parents: George W. Scott (VA) and Annie Cole, cause of death: "influenza", informant: Mrs. W.F. Blevins (Crandull), buried: Gentry Cemetery, died: 16 Mar 1923, record (1923) #: 204.

Cleo STANTON, age 1 year and 4 months, parents: Grayson Stanton and Martha Arney, cause of death: "callery inflamation", informant: Ruth McQueen (Neva), died: 17 Mar 1923, record (1923) #: 205.

Mrs. Eunice Louise HAWKINS, born: 2 Nov 1844, widow, parents: William Keys and Susan Wills, cause of death: "chronic myacordites dermaid cyst", informant: W.W. Hawkins (Mountain City), buried: Acre Field Cemetery, died: 19 Mar 1923, record (1923) #: 206.

Aileen POTTER, born: 10 Jun 1922, parents: David C. Potter and Hattie McElyea, cause of death: "whooping cough and broncho pneumonia", informant: T.B. Dellinger (Butler), buried: Sugar Grove Cemetery, died: 20 Mar 1923, record (1923) #: 207.

Nancy A. STOUT, age about 97 years, widow, parents: David Stout (Carter Co. TN) and Nancy Carrtner (Carter Co. TN), cause of death: "broncho pneumonia", informant: J.P. Stout (Butler), died: 20 Mar 1923, record (1923) #: 208.

Grady O. GREER, born: 26 Feb 1923, parents: father not stated and Ora Greer, cause of death: "not known", informant: James Greer (Trade), buried: Greer Cemetery, died: 22 Mar 1923, record (1923) #: 209.

John Joseph FLANERY, born: 12 Jan 1923, parents: Joe Flanery (NC) and Tilda Moody, cause of death: "whooping cough and broncho pneumonia", informant: W.R. Moody (Butler), buried: Dugger Cemetery, died: 25 Mar 1923, record (1923) #: 210.

Joseph W. DUNN, age about 84 years, born 1839, parents: Godfrey Dunn and Hilda Wilson, cause of death: "chronic intestinal nephritis", informant: Sherman Dunn (Shouns), buried: Dunn Cemetery, died: 30 Mar 1923, record (1923) #: 211.

Infant WIDBY, female, colored, parents: Samuel Widby and Ollie Maxwell, stillborn, born/died: 6 Mar 1923, record (1923) #: 212.

Infant WINTERS, female, parents: Martin Edd. Winters and Bernic C. Corum, stillborn, informant: John Winters (Mountain City), buried: Michaels Cemetery, born/died: 8 Mar 1923, record (1923) #: 213.

Infant CAMPBELL, male, parents: D.A. Campbell and Jella Price, stillborn, informant: D.A. Campbell (Doeville), buried: Shoun Cemetery, born/died: 10 Mar 1923, record (1923) #: 214.

Nancy Lacira FARMER, born: 26 Jul 1860 in Wilkes Co. NC, widow, parents: Elija Davis (Wilkes Co. NC) and Lacira Millsaps (Wilkes Co. NC), cause of death: "influenza", informant: J.P. Farmer (Shouns), buried: Farmer Cemtery, died: 1 Apr 1923, record (1923) #: 215

Thomas Butler MORLEY, born: 28 Mar 1860, widower, parents: George Morley and .... Razar, cause of death: "dementia paralytica", informant: C.H. Lowe (Mountain City), buried: Morley Cemetery, died: 1 Apr 1923, record (1923) #: 216.

Lyda ROBINSON, age about 73 years, single, parents: Daniel Robinson and Katie Stout, cause of death: "diarrhoea", informant: Rebecka Stout (Doeville), buried: Norris Cemetery, died: 2 Apr 1923, record (1923) #: 217.

Sarah M. MCQUEEN, black, age 84 years, widow, parents: father's name illegible and mother's name unknown, cause of death: "influenza", informant: Thomas McQueen, died: 5 Apr 1923, record (1923) #: 218.

Polly Ann PALMER, age 83 years, widow, born at Surry Co. NC, parents: James Johnson (Surry Co. NC) and Dorthy Johnson (Surry Co. NC), cause of death: "chronic brights disease", informant: Lizzie Warren (Mountain City), buried: Shingletown Cemetery, died: 6 Apr 1923, record (1923) #: 219.

Roby J. DUGGER, age about 61 years, married, parents: Quince Dugger and McNary Dugger, cause of death: "pneumonia fever", informant: Cefford Dugger (Butler), buried: Dugger Cemetery, died: 12 Apr 1923, record (1923) #: 220.

Caroline REECE, born: 15 Dec 1849 in North Carolina, widow, parents: Joseph Thomas (NC) and Peggy Wilson (NC), cause of death: "died suddenly, cause not known", informant: Asa Reece (Trade), buried: Reece Cemetery, died: 18 Apr 1923, record (1923) #: 221.

Elizabeth BLEVINS, born: 30 Mar 1856 in Virginia, parents: Robert Smith (VA) and Sarah Taylor (NC), cause of death: "cerebral hemorrhage", informant: D.H. Blevins (Crandull), buried: Blevins Cemetery, died: 20 Apr 1923, record (1923) #: 222.

Salina GREEN, born: 5 Mar 1864 at Watauga Co. NC, married, parents: Elias Isaacs (Watauga Co. NC) and Eliza Reece (Watauga Co. NC), cause of death: "broncho pneumonia", informant: Babe Isaacs, buried: Watauga Co. NC, died: 20 Apr 1923, record (1923) #: 223.

John CARDWELL, born: 30 Mar 1923, parents: Rosco Cardwell (NC) and Myrtle Fletcher, cause of death: "unknown", buried: Sugar Grove Cemetery, died: 21 Apr 1923, record (1923) #: 224.

Infant DINKENS, female, born: 21 Apr 1923, parents: John Dinkens and Millie Dinkens (NC), cause of death: not stated, died: 23 Apr 1923, record (1923) #: 225. (Twin's record below).

Charles JOHNSON, age 26 years, married, parents: A.S. Johnson and Myrtle Cress, death cause: "acute brights disease", informant: Hugh Johnson, buried: Phillippi Cemetery, died: 22 Apr 1923, record (1923) #: 226.

Infant CORNETT, male, parents: Newt Cornett and Fay Harbin, stillborn, informant: Oscar Cornett, buried: Cornett Cemetery, born/died: 19 Apr 1923, record (1923) #: 227.

Infant DINKENS, female, parents: John Dinkens and Milly Johnson, stillborn: born/died: 21 Apr 1923, record (1923) #: 228, (Twin's record above).

Infant SIMCOX, male, parents: James Simcox and Mattie Mathison, stillborn, born/died: 30 Apr 1923, record (1923) #: 229.

A.M. CRESS, age 62 years, widower, parents: W.L. Cress and Clara Wilson, cause of death: "brights disease", informant: Jas W. Johnson (Mountain City), died: 3 May 1923, record (1923) #: 230.

Emmett Augustus LATHAM, born: 18 Nov 1879 at Ashe Co. NC, married, parents: David Latham (Ashe Co. NC) and Elizabeth Graybeal (Ashe Co. NC), cause of death: "indo carditis", informant: Annie Latham (Laurel Bloomery), died: 5 May 1923, record (1923) #: 231.

William M. SLIMP, born: 2 May 1878, single, parents: Martin A. Slimp and Mary A. Ward, cause of death: "inflamatory rhumatism", informant: R.G. Vannoy (Neva), died: 6 May 1923, record (1923) #: 232.

Dortha Ree FORRESTER, born: 14 Jun 1922, parents: Luther Forrester and Claudie Morefield, cause of death: "cause not known", informant: Roy Moody (Shouns), died: 14 May 1923, record (1923) #: 233.

Bruce NEATHERLY, born: 28 May 1922, parents: Jacob Neatherly and Maggie McElyea, cause of death: "collary mobis, supposed", informant: J.I. Neatherly (Neva), died: 28 May 1923, record (1923) #: 234.

Ruth Glades HORN, born: 30 May 1923, parents: Worley Horn and Bell Isenhour (NC), cause of death: "bold hives", informant: Charlie Church (Voughtsville), died: 3 May 1923, record (1923) #: 235.

Luther Swanner BUNTON, born: 12 Aug 1918, parents: Samuel Bunton and Ettie Gregg, cause of death: "typhoid fever and spinal menengitis", informant: Samuel Bunton (Butler), buried: Bunton Cemetery, died: 31 May 1923, record (1923) #: 236.

Victoria Jenkins ROBERTS, born: 6 Jun 1876, married, parents: Wm Jenkins and Fina Owens, cause of death: "cancer of uterus", informant: D.E. Slimp (Mountain City), died: 5 Jun 1923, record (1923) #: 237.

W.D. CAMPBELL, born: 2 Oct 1866, widower, parents: Samuel Campbell and Emley Hardin, cause of death: "mitral regen.. (illegible) of heart", informant: W.K. Arnold (Doeville), buried: Campbell Cemetery, died: 8 Jun 1923, record (1923) #: 238.

Infant EGGERS, female, age 3 months, parents: father's name not stated and Myrtle Eggers, cause of death: "broncho pneumonia", informant: Onnie Guy, died: 9 Jun 1923, record (1923) #: 239.

Virginia Ruth BARRY, age 2 years, parents: Stacy Barry and Con... (illegible) Gentry, cause of death: "acute colitis", informant: D.K. Barry (Mountain City), Wilson Cem, died: 19 Jun 1923, record (1923) #: 240.

Everett Smith HAMMONS, born: 25 Apr 1922, parents: Wise Hammons and Lillie Gambill, cause of death: "colitis", informant: Lillie Hammons (Shouns), died: 21 Jun 1923, record (1923) #: 241.

Dual BLEVINS, born: 21 Oct 1919, parents: T.E. Blevins and A.D. Mays, cause of death: "dysentary", informant: T.E. Blevins (Crandull), buried: Blevins Cemetery, died: 22 Jun 1923, record (1923) #: 242.

Annie D.A. STOUT, born: 4 Sep 1922, parents: John H. Stout and Sue Hammons, cause of death: "colitis", informant: J.D. Stout (Shouns), buried: Stout Cemetery, died: 23 Jun 1923, record (1923) #: 243.

Mary A. REEVES, black, age 14 years, parents: Lee Reeves and Mary Rustin, death cause: "tuberculosis", died: 28 Jun 1923, record (1923) #: 244.

Spencer FARMER, born: 29 Jun 1923, parents: William Farmer and Myrtle Taylor, cause of death: "unknown", informant: Cassie Arnold (Shouns), buried: Farmer Cemetery, died: 29 Jun 1923, record (1923) #: 245.

Isaac Stacy RAMBO, born: 24 Jul 1871, banker, married, parents: James T. Rambo and Elva Shoun, cause of death: "saracoina intestines", informant: J.C. Rambo, died: 29 Jun 1923, record (1923) #: 246.

Edgar HAMMONS, born: 3 Jan 1920, parents: Roy B. Hammons and Emes O. Willin, cause of death: "colitis", informant: Emes O. Hammons (Shouns), died: 1 Jul 1923, record (1923) #: 247.

Mandie Blanche HAMMONS, born: 15 Jan 1922, parents: Roy B. Hammons and Ennes Willin, cause of death: "colitis", died: 1 Jul 1923, record (1923) #: 248.

Thomas R. PATTON, born: 16 Jul 1873, widower, parents: "unknown", cause of death: "dropsy", informant: R.A. Cole (Crandull), buried: Blevins Cemetery, died: 8 Jul 1923, record (1923) #: 249.

Joseph WARREN, born: 23 Apr 1896, single, parents: Landon Warren (NC) and Laura Lomax (NC), cause of death: "pulmonary tuberculosis", died: 9 Jul 1923, record (1923) #: 250.

Crissie Luttrena PROFFITT, born: 4 Jun 1912, parents: Jody C. Proffitt and Mollie Robinson, cause of death: "..... (illegible) of face and throat", died: 12 Jul 1923, record (1923) #: 251.

Stella Inez HAMMONS, born: 27 Jul 1904, single, parents: J.T. Hammons and Nancy Hampton, cause of death: "colitis", informant: J.T. Hammons (Shouns), died: 13 Jul 1923, record (1923) #: 252.

Rody SMITH, born: 14 Nov 1922, parents: A.L. Smith and Corda Killans (NC), cause of death: "cause not known, died suddenly", informant: Corda May (Shouns), buried: Arnold Cem, died: 15 Jul 1923, record (1923) #: 253.

W.H. WILLIAMS, born: 7 Feb 1857 in North Carolina, married, parents: Stephen Williams and Mary Grimsley (NC), cause of death: "acute paralysis", informant: Susan Williams (Shouns), buried: Main Cemetery, died: 16 Jul 1923, record (1923) #: 254.

Joseph R. HAMPTON, born: 19 Feb 1923, parents: Lillard Hampton and Nettie Wallace, cause of death: "unknown, died suddently", informant: Lillard Hampton (Shouns), Arnold Cem, died: 22 Jul 1923, record (1923) #: 255.

Emanuel DUNN, age about 84 years, parents: Godfrey B. Dunn and H.C. Wilson, cause of death: "old age", informant: Betty Dunn (Shouns), buried: Dunn Cemetery, died: 23 Jul 1923, record (1923) #: 256.

Elizabeth RIDDLE, age 63 years, born in North Carolina, married, parents: Calvin Howell (NC) and Rachel Roten (NC), cause of death: "acute colitis", informant: Hobart Gentry (Laurel Bloomery), Acre Field Cemetery, died: 28 Jul 1923, record (1923) #: 257.

Frederick STORNS, age about 68 years, born in Washington Co. TN, parents: H. Stornes and Elizabeth Kid, cause of death: "pulmonary tuberculosis", informant: Alice Stornes (Butler), buried: Neva, TN, died: 29 Jul 1923, record (1923) #: 258.

Andy JONES, black, age 29 years, single, parents: father's name unknown and Amanda Jones, cause of death: "tuberculosis", died: 31 Jul 1923, record (1923) #: 259.

Russell Haydin BLEVINS, parents: Dennis O. Blevins and Ethel R. McNeill, stillborn, informant; Dennis O. Blevins (Crandull), born/died: 5 Jul 1923, record (1923) #: 260.

Infant MATHERLY, male, parents: Garfield Matherly and Panford Grindstaff, "stillborn, prolapse cord", informant: I.A. Grindstaff (Butler), died: 30 Jul 1923, record (1923) #: 261.

Eliza POTTER, born: 4 Sep 1851, married, parents: Drewry Wallace (NC) and Elizabeth Snyder, cause of death: "broncho pneumonia", informant: Reuben Potter (Trade), buried: Potter Cemetery, died: 3 Aug 1923, record (1923) #: 262.

Vinta LUNSFORD, born: 7 Nov 1921, parents: C.A. Lunsford and Lillie Ward, cause of death: "infantile paralysis", informant: Braidy Fritts (Neva), died: 5 Aug 1923, record (1923) #: 263.

Olie WIDBY, black, age 35 years, married, parents: David Maxwell (NC) and mother's name not stated, cause of death: "acute mileans tuberculosis", informant: Sam Widby (Mountain City), buried: Shouns, died: 7 Aug 1923, record (1923) #: 264.

Walsey COOK, born: 1 May 1923, parents: Elbert Cook and Laura Garland, cause of death: "acute indigestion", informant: Elbert Cook (Doeville), Rambo Cem, died: 9 Aug 1923, record (1923) #: 265.

Cornelia MCELYEA, age 14 years, parents: James McElyea and Rachael Potter, cause of death: "acute colitis", informant: James Reece (Mountain City), died: 10 Aug 1923, record (1923) #: 266.

Tenie MOODY, female, born: 6 Mar 1918, parents: Will R. Moody and Margaret Anderson, cause of death: "scarlet fever and indigestion", informant: J.S. Anderson (Butler), buried: Dugger Cemetery, died: 22 Aug 1923, record (1923) #: 268.

James Edgar DICKENS, born: 26 Mar 1923, parents: Dowel Dickens and Mattie Pearl Burgess, cause of death: "unknown, found dead in bed", informant: Dowell Dickens (Mountain City), buried: Wills Cemetery, died: 12 Aug 1923, record (1923) #: 267.

Bertha Elvira DUNN, born: 29 Mar 1922, parents: father's name not stated and Bell Dunn, cause of death: "acute colitis", informant: Denly Gilbert (Laurel Bloomery), buried: Valley Cemetery, died: 22 Aug 1923, record (1923) #: 269.

Saddie O. MINTON, born: 26 Dec 1918, parents: father's name not stated and Lizzie Minton (NC), cause of death: "deptheria", informant: Allen Minton (Crandull), buried: Blevins Cemetery, died: 28 Aug 1923, record (1923) #: 270.

Margarette M. SCOTT, born: 22 May 1846, married, parents: Rice McQueen and Elizabeth Blevins, cause of death: "carcinoma of bowels and stomach", informant: Z.A. Scott (Crandull), buried: Woods Cemetery, died: 30 Aug 1923, record (1923) #: 271.

Salina Edith STOUT, born: 21 Oct 1922, parents: Roy Stout and Alice Green (Carter Co. TN), cause of death: "pneumonia and cholera infection", informant: J.P. Robinson (Butler), buried: Walnut Mountain, died: 31 Aug 1923, record (1923) #: 272.

Martha Ellen FLETCHER, age 58 years, married, parents: Patton Biar and Zena Whitehead, cause of death: "paralysis, blood clot in brain", informant: Daniel Fletcher (Crandull), buried: Gentry Cemetery, died: 31 Aug 1923, record (1923) #: 273.

Infant (last name illegible), black, parent's names: illegible, stillborn, born/died: 19 Aug 1923, record (1923) #: 274.

Callie Francis HAMMONS, born: 16 Nov 1918, parents: W.E. Hammons and I.L. Payne, cause of death: "menengitis", informant: W.E. Hammons (Shouns), died: 1 Sep 1923, record (1923) #: 275.

Josephine SNYDER, born: 9 Mar 1856, married, parents: Daniel Cress and Sarah Rose, cause of death: "cancer on the face", informant: Fred Snyder (Neva), died: 7 Sep 1923, record (1923) #: 276.

James R. ALLEN, age 75 years, married, parents: W.L. Allen (NC) and Caroline Donnelley, cause of death: "mysearditis", informant: W.L Allen, Jr. (Mountain City), died: 10 Sep 1923, record (1923) #: 277.

Joseph Stoffer MAIN, born: 14 Dec 1910, parents: David S. Main and Maggie Hodge, cause of death: "don't know", informant: David S. Main (Shouns), died: 12 Sep 1923, record (1923) #: 278.

Jessey M. GAMBILL, born: 14 Mar 1834, parents: Billie Gambill (NC) and Betsy Razor (VA), cause of death: "labor pneumonia", informant: W.L. Arnold (Neva), died: 12 Sep 1923, record (1923) #: 279.

Claud FARMER, parents: J.P. Farmer and Maggie Jones (Ashe Co. NC), cause of death: "measles causing premature birth", buried: Payne Cemetery, died: 12 Sep 1923, record (1923) #: 280.

Martha E. SNYDER, born: 9 Jul 1851, parents: James Culbert and Martha Hawkins, cause of death: "ulcer of stomach", informant: J.W. Snyder (Butler), buried: Maymead, died: 18 Sep 1923, record (1923) #: 281.

Daniel D. SHUPE, born: 2 Sep 1899, married, parents: William Shupe and Estellie Barry, cause of death: "para-typhoid, broncho pneumonia", died: 21 Sep 1923, record (1923) #: 282.

Ora N. SHOUN, born: 13 Apr 1893, single, parents: Thomas J. Shoun and Elen Wilson, cause of death: "tuberculosis caused by removing tonsels", informant; T.J. Shoun (butler), buried: Pierce Cemetery, died: 22 Sep 1923, record (1923) #: 283.

Wiley Glen RASH, born: 1 Jul 1922, parents: A.P. Rash (Ashe Co. NC) and Etta Nichols (Ashe Co. NC), cause of death: "spinal menengitis", informant: Etta Rash (Shouns), buried: Payne Cemetery, died: 22 Sep 1923, record (1923) #: 284.

Nauel CROW, born: 8 Aug 1922, parents: Charlie Crow (Carter Co. TN) and Julia Robinson, cause of death: "stomach euta", informant: Charlie Crow (Butler), buried: Brookshire Cemetery, died: 23 Sep 1923, record (1923) #: 285.

Howard THOMAS, black, age 17 years, single, parents: George Thomas (NC), and Laura Thompson (NC), cause of death: "para-typhoid", informant: Geo Thomas (Mountain City), buried: Mountain View Cemetery, died: 24 Sep 1923, record (1923) #: 286.

Lillian Ruth CAWOOD, age 25 years, born in North Carolina, married, parents: Enoch Miller and Fannie Woodsay (NC), cause of death: illegible, informant: W.P. Cawood (Crandull), buried: Gentry Cemetery, died: 28 Sep 1923, record (1923) #: 1923.

Mrs. Richard MCELYEA, age 51 years, parents: Thomas Potter and Lewany Dowell, death cause: "para-typhoid", informant: James Reece (Mountain City), buried: Shouns, TN, died: 29 Sep 1923, record (1923) #: 288.

Emmet OLIVER, jr., parents: Emmt Oliver (Watauga Co. NC) and Martha Lunceford (Watauga Co. NC), stillborn, informant: Mrs. Amanda Cable (Butler), Sugar Grove Cemetery, born/died: 4 Sep 1923, record (1923) #: 289.

Frank DICKENS, parents: John Dickens (Watauga Co. NC) and Linda Dugger, cause of death: stillborn, informant: John Dickens (Butler), buried: Dugger Cemetery, born/died: 7 Sep 1923, record (1923) #: 290.

Cecil Carl CAWOOD, parents: W.J. Cawood and Lilian R. Miller (NC), stillborn, informant: W.J. Cawood (Crandull), buried: Gentry Cemetery, born/died: 26 Sep 1923, record (1923) #: 291.

Yarborough DUNN, age 60 years, widower, parents: Will Dunn and Malary Dunn, cause of death: "pellagra", informant: Hugh Dunn (Shouns), died: 2 Oct 1923, record (1923) #: 292.

Charlotte WALKER, born: 10 Jan 1841 in North Carolina, married, parents: Thornton Proffitt (NC) and Elizabeth Proffitt (NC), cause of death: "abdominal ... illegible ... causing valvular liesion of heart", informant: Calvin Walker, buried: Woods Cemetery, died: 2 Oct 1923, record (1923) #: 293.

Walter BUNTING, age 48 years, married, parents: W.H. Bunting (Avery Co. NC) and Elizabeth Cable, cause of death: "cerebral hemorrhage", informant: Dewey Bunting, buried: Sugar Grove Cemetery, died: 4 Oct 1923, record (1923) #: 294.

Joseph Henry DUNN, born: 24 Oct 1922, parents: Chas C. Dunn and Bessie Main, cause of death: "broncho pneumonia", informant: C.C. Dunn (Shouns), died: 4 Oct 1923, record (1923) #: 295.

John WALKER, born: 12 Jun 1844, married, parents: Yonce Walker and Polly Fritts, cause of death: "paralysis", informant: J.C. Walker (Doeville), buried: Campbell Cemetery, died: 9 Oct 1923, record (1923) #: 296.

Martha E. SMITH, age about 67 years, married, parents: John Main (Wilkes Co. NC) and Polly Potter, cause of death: "carcinoma of liver", informant: Susan Williams (Shouns), buried: Martin Cemetery, died: 9 Oct 1923, record (1923) #: 297.

John J. ROBINSON, born: 25 Sep 1879, married, parents: Geo H. Robinson and Mariah Grace, cause of death: "chronis intestinal nephritis", informant: D.E. Gentry (Laurel Bloomery), buried: Acre Field Cemetery, died: 10 Oct 1923, record (1923) #: 298.

Walter BUNTING, age 48 years, married, parents: W.H. Bunting (Avery Co. NC) and Elizabeth Cable, cause of death: "cerebral hemorrhage", informant: Dewey Bunting, buried: Sugar Grove Cemetery, died: 4 Oct 1923, record (1923) #: 294.

Joseph Henry DUNN, born: 24 Oct 1922, parents: Chas C. Dunn and Bessie Main, cause of death: "broncho pneumonia", informant: C.C. Dunn (Shouns), died: 4 Oct 1923, record (1923) #: 295.

John WALKER, born: 12 Jun 1844, married, parents: Yonce Walker and Polly Fritts, cause of death: "paralysis", informant: J.C. Walker (Doeville), buried: Campbell Cemetery, died: 9 Oct 1923, record (1923) #: 296.

Martha E. SMITH, age about 67 years, married, parents: John Main (Wilkes Co. NC) and Polly Potter, cause of death: "carcinoma of liver", informant: Susan Williams (Shouns), buried: Martin Cemetery, died: 9 Oct 1923, record (1923) #: 297.

John J. ROBINSON, born: 25 Sep 1879, married, parents: Geo H. Robinson and Mariah Grace, cause of death: "chronis intestinal nephritis", informant: D.E. Gentry (Laurel Bloomery), buried: Acre Field Cemetery, died: 10 Oct 1923, record (1923) #: 298.

George YOUNCE, born: 19 Mar 1830 in North Carolina, parents: Soloman Younce (NC) and Sallie Roten (NC), cause of death: "cause not known", informant: S. S. Younce (Zionville, NC), buried: Zionville, NC, died: 10 Oct 1923, record (1923) #: 299.

Rosie LIPFORD, born: 14 May 1914, parents: Arch Lipford and Lutitia Sluder (NC), cause of death: "dyptheria", informant: Arch Lipford (Butler), died: 10 Oct 1923, record (1923) #: 300.

Mary Ruth PARDUE, age 62 years, married, parents: Sam Hodge and Trulove Mullins, cause of death: "labor pneumonia", informant: Wm Pardue (Shouns), died: 14 Oct 1923, record (1923) #: 301.

Wiley MCELYEA, age 17 years, single, parents: James McElyea and Rachael Potter, cause of death: "paratyphoid", informant: James Reece, died: 16 Oct 1823, record (1923) #: 302.

Dana Linell BUNTON, parents: Scott Bunton and Rebecca Bunton, cause of death: "born dead", informant: Scott Bunton (Butler), buried: Sugar Grove Cemetery, born/died: 7 Oct 1923, record (1923) #: 303.

Infant JORDAN, male, parents: R.C. Jordan and Bertha Allen, stillborn, informant: R.C. Jordan (Doeville), buried: Rambo Cemetery, born/died: 9 Oct 1923, record (1923) #: 304.

Infant SWIFT, male, parents: Wiley Swift and Venia Harmon, stillborn, born/died: 22 Oct 1923, record (1923) #: 305.

Infant RAINBOLT, female, parents: McKinley Rainbolt and Mytrtl Hinkel, stillborn, buried: Rainbolt Cem, born/died: 30 Oct 1923, record (1923) #: 306.

Nancy Jane FORRESTER, born: 22 Nov 1853, single, parents: William Forrester and Nancy Greer, cause of death: "tuberculosis of lungs", informant: Charles Forrester (Shouns), buried: Forrester Cemetery, died: 2 Nov 1923, record (1923) #: 307.

Jacob WILSON, born: 1 Aug 1923, parents: James Wilson (NC) and Bettie Snyder, cause of death: "diptheria", informant: James Wilson (Shouns), buried: Arnold Cem, died: 4 Nov 1923, record (1923) #: 308.

Amos BRYANT, age 87 years, born in North Carolina, married, parents: George Bryant and mother's name not known, cause of death: "accidental fracture of skull from falling on a rock", informant: G.W. Snyder (Trade), buried: Snyder Cemetery, died: 5 Nov 1923, record (1923) #: 309.

James Shelton BLEVINS, born: 21 Nov 1922, parents: Geo Blevins and Maggie Hamby (NC), cause of death: "whooping cough", buried: Blevins Cemetery, died: 22 Nov 1923, record (1923) #: 310.

Ellen PROFFITT, age about 65 years, married, parents: John Campbell (NC) and Doshie Heaton, cause of death: "heart dropsy and influenza", informant: Daniel Proffitt (Doeville), buried: Campbell Cemetery, died: 22 Nov 1923, record (1923) #: 311.

Edith Merly LINCASTER, born: 17 Nov 1923, parents: Claude Lincaster (NC) and Edith Bryant, cause of death: "premature birth, 7 months", died: 24 Nov 1923, record (1923) #: 312.

Ambros GARLAND, born: 4 Aug 1844, widower, parents: James Garland and Susie Cole, cause of death: "influenza and cerebral hemorrhage", buried: Gentry Cemetery, died: 29 Nov 1923, record (1923) #: 313.

Infant FARTHING, female, parents: G. Clapton Farthing (NC) and Rachel Farthing (NC), stillborn, born/died: 15 Nov 1923, record (1923) #: 314.

Eva PLEASANT, born: 12 Jan 1921, parents: Robert Pleasant and Onnie Arnold, cause of death: "spasmodic croup", informant: Robert Pleasant (Doeville), buried: Rambo Cem, died: 1 Dec 1923, record (1923) #: 315.

Lillie HOWARD, born: 12 Jul 1887, married, parents: H.B. Howard and Eliza Blevins, cause of death: "permicorious anemia", informant: S.R. McEwen (Doeville), buried: Shouns Cemetery, died: 3 Dec 1923, record (1923) #: 316.

Jane WOODARD, born: 26 Feb 1846, widow, parents: William Willin (England) and Sarah Willin (Englane), cause of death: "old age", informant: J.M.W. Hammons (Shouns), buried: Dunn Cem, died: 3 Dec 1923, record (1923) #: 317.

J.V. DAVIS, born: 4 Jul 1923, parents: Clay Davis and
Ode Estep, cause of death: "not known, found dead in
bed", informant: W.B. Arnold (Doeville), buried:
Shouns Cem, died: 9 Dec 1923, record (1923) #: 318.
Celia A. MADRON, born: 29 Jan 1852, widow, parents:
Caswell T. Reece and Joannah Reece (note, her record
below)(Watauga Co. NC), cause of death: "lobar
pneumonia", informant: H.E. Madron (Trade), buried:
Reece Cem, died: 12 Dec 1923, record (1923) #: 319.
Joannah REECE, born: 27 Mar 1828 at Watauga Co. NC,
widow, parents: Hugh Reece (Watauga Co. NC) and Annie
Ford (Watauga Co. NC), cause of death: "lobar
pneumonia", informant: H.E. Madron (Trade), buried:
Reece Cem, died: 12 Dec 1923, record (1923) #: 320.
Juanita M. GRINDSTAFF, born: 28 Oct 1917, parents:
Joseph D. Grindstaff and Catherine Holden, cause of
death: "typhoid fever", informant: J.D. Grindstaff
(Doeville), died: 14 Dec 1923, record (1923) #: 321.
Thomas Hawkins GREER, born: 30 Jul 1900, single,
parents: R.W. Greer and May Hawkins, cause of death:
"pulmonary tuberculosis", informant: R.W. Greer, died:
25 Dec 1923, record (1923) #: 322.
Infant GARLAND, male, parents: Edgar Garland and Maud
Luttrell, stillborn, informant: Edgar Garland
(Mountain City), buried: Phillippi Cemetery, died: 1
Dec 1923, record (1923) #: 323.
Ida Wills WILSON, parents: Wheeler Wilson and Connie
McQueen, stillborn, informant: Wheeler Wilson
(Butler), buried: Rainbolt Cemetery, born/died: 12 Dec
1923, record (1923) #: 324.
Catherine ROBINSON, born: 16 Nov 1837, widow, parents:
Peter Elliott and Catherine Grindstaff, cause of
death: "paralysis", informant: Roby Norris (Doeville),
buried: Norris Cemetery, died: 4 Jan 1924, record
(1924) #: 178.
Carl DYSON, born: 23 Dec 1919, parents: Andy Dyson and
Cora Forrester, cause of death: "bronchial pneumonia",
informant: Karl Wills (Mountain City), buried: Wagner
Cemetery, died: 12 Jan 1924, record (1924) #: 179.
Elizabeth R. LAWS, born: 26 Aug 1863, parents: Clate
White and Elizabeth White, cause of death: "sudden
cold and nephritis", informant: Jas D. Robinson
(Butler), buried: Stallings Cemetery, died: 15 Jan
1924, record (1924) #: 180.
Polly E. YORK, age about 37 years, born at Watauga Co.
NC, parents: James (surname illegible) and Elizabeth
McCloud, cause of death: "broncho pneumonia", died: 15
Jan 1924, record (1924) #: 181.

Infant DYSON, male, born: 25 Dec 1923, parents: Andy Dyson and Coni Forrester, cause of death: "broncho pneumonia", informant: Karl Wills (Mountain City), buried: Wagner Cemetery, died: 15 Jan 1924, record (1924) #: 182.

Peter PHIPPS, age about 80 years, parents: Abram Phipps (VA) and mother's name unknown, cause of death: "le grippe and heart trouble", informant: John Phipps (Doeville), buried: Proffitt Cemetery, died: 20 Jan 1924, record (1924) #: 183.

Dewey LiTtleton DOWELL. born: 7 Jan 1894, married, parents: Thomas Dowell and Mary Hodge, cause of death: "tuberculosis", informant: Mrs. Minnie Dowell (Shouns), died: 22 Jan 1924, record (1924) #: 184.

Mrs. Litha Estes GREENE, born: 4 Sep 1897 at Watauga Co. NC, parents: G. Wiseman Greene (NC) and Caroline Adams, cause of death: "pulmonary tuberculosis", informant: M.H. Greene (Butler), buried: Bluff City, TN, died: 22 Jan 1924, record (1924) #: 185.

John Henry JONES, born: 10 Jan 1924, parents: James Jones (NC) and Annie Owens, cause of death: "found dead in bed", informant: Roy Corum (Mountain City), Cornett Cem, died: 23 Jan 1924, record (1924) #: 186.

Valter Francis TESTER, born: 25 Aug 1923, parents: Fonzo Tester and Dottie Proffitt, cause of death: "bold hives", informant: N.C. Tester (Neva), died: 25 Jan 1924, record (1924) #: 187.

David W. MOCK, born: 28 Jun 1831 in North Carolina, parents: Lewis Mock (NC) and Miss Dewey (NC), cause of death: "cerebral sof...(illegible)", informant: A.F. Mock (Mountain City), buried: Wills Cemetery, died: 21 Jan 1924, record (1924) #: 188.

David Harson TESTER, born: 29 Feb 1843 in North Carolina, parents: Robin Tester and mother's name not stated, cause of death: "pneumonia, informant: Sam Heaton (Butler), buried: Sugar Grove Cemetery, died: 29 Jan 1924, record (1924) #: 189.

Jacob F. GRINDSTAFF, born: 12 May 1836, parents: Nicholas Grindstaff and Martha Wagner, cause of death: "organic heart disease due to old age", informant: James T. Grindstaff (Doeville), died: 29 Jan 1924, record (1924) #: 190.

Infant MCCOY, female, parents: Millard McCoy and Belle Corum (NC), stillborn, informant: Millard McCoy (Neva), born/died: 5 Jan 1924, record (1924) #: 191.

Robert Scott FORRESTER, parents: Bud Forrester and Dora Gentry, stillborn, buried: Forrester Cemetery, born/died: 16 Jan 1924, record (1924) #: 192.

Infant FORRESTER, male, parents: Luther Forrester and Dora Gentry, stillborn, buried: Wills Cemetery, born/died: 31 Jan 1924, record (1924) #: 193.

Infant MCELYEA, male (twins see record below), parents: Mac McElyea and Callie Dunn, stillborn, buried: Phillippi Cemetery, born/died: 31 Jan 1924, record (1924) #: 194.

Infant STANTON, female, parents: James L. Stanton and Martha Arney, cause of death: "born dead", informant: Martha Arney (Butler), born/died: 31 Jan 1931, record (1924) #: 195.

Infant MCELYEA, male, parents: Mac McElyea and Callie Dunn, stillborn, informant: Hayes Smith (Mountain City), buried: Phillippi Cemetery, born/died: 31 Jan 1924, record (1924) #: 196.

William MOORE, born: 3 Sep 1846 at Wilkes Co. NC, married, parents: W.M. Moore (Wilkes Co. NC) and Emiline Nance (Wilkes Co. NC), cause of death: "cancer of face", informant: Matilda Moore (Doeville), buried: Sutherland, died: 3 Feb 1924, record (1924) #: 197.

Louisa GENTRY, born: 4 Dec 1923, parents: F.C. Gentry and Bertha Lewis, cause of death: "broncho pneumonia", buried: Wilson Cemetery, died: 15 Feb 1924, record (1924) #: 198.

Ralph Eugene BLEVINS, born: 31 Jan 1924, parents: E.G. Blevins and Eliza Manuel (NC), cause of death: not stated, informant: E.G. Blevins (Crandull), buried: Blevins Cem, died: 7 Feb 1924, record (1924) #: 199.

Vina POTTER, born: 30 Sep 1843 in Carter Co. TN, married, parents: William Andrews (Carter Co. TN) and Lilla Younce (Carter Co. TN), cause of death: "broncho pneumonia", died: 7 Feb 1924, record (1924) #: 200.

Dana Daniel HEAD, born: 26 Jul 1906, parents: W.S. Head and Oma Forrester, cause of death: "pulmonary tuberculosis", informant: W.S. Head (Shouns), buried: Dunn Cem, died: 12 Feb 1924, record (1924) #: 201.

Ruby Fay ARNOLD, born: 25 Mar 1923, parents: Clyde Arnold and Pearl Roark (NC), cause of death: "broncho pneumonia", informant; Clyde Arnold (Shouns), buried: Arnold Cem, died: 15 Feb 1924, record (1924) #: 202.

Alice SIMPSON, age 58 years, single, parents: Henry Simpson and Celia Simpson, cause of death: "nephritis", buried: Phillippi Cemetery, Died: 17 Feb 1924, record (1924) #: 203.

Mary HOLDEN, born: 1 Oct 1850, widow, parents: Franklin Norris (NC) and Lottie Green (nC), cause of death: "pulmonary tuberculosis", informant: P.B. Elliott (Butler), buried: Home cemetery, died: 17 Feb 1924, record (1924) #: 205.

Josephine DUNN, born: 3 Mar 1853, widow, parents: William Wilson and Susan Tester, cause of death: "nephritis", informant: Della Dunn (Laurel Bloomery), buried: Valley Cemetery, died: 17 Feb 1924, record (1924) #: 204.

Hubert Lincoln WHITEHEAD, born: 7 Jan 1906 in Carter Co. TN, parents: Carson Whitehead (Carter Co. TN) and Ada Campbell (Carter Co. TN), cause of death: "broncho pneumonia", informant: Carson Whitehead (Butler), buried: Goodwin Cemetery, died: 19 Feb 1924, record (1924) #: 206.

Robert Stephen STEWART, born: 17 Apr 1851, married, parents: Britain Stewart (NC) and Abbie Taylor (NC), cause of death: "lobar pneumonia", informant: S.A. Stewart (Shouns), buried: Arnold Cemetery, died: 24 Feb 1924, record (1924) #: 207.

Edward Garfield WILSON, born: 16 Feb 1924, parents: Alexander Wilson (NC) and Lottie Stanton, cause of death: "unknown, mother had measles", died: 27 Feb 1924, record (1924) #: 208.

Earl GALAHAR, born: 1 Jan 1912 in North Carolina, parents: "unknown", cause of death: "accidental shot gun wound in head", informant: H. Pennington (Crandull), buried: Wood Cemetery, died: 28 Feb 1924, record (1924)#: 209.

John Clarence MCQUEEN, Negro, born: 30 Jun 1914, parents: Mack McQueen and Emma Mock, cause of death: "menengitis", informant: Mack McQueen (Shouns), died: 4 Mar 1924, record (1924) #: 210.

John MOODY, born: 15 Jan 1862 in North Carolina, married, parents: "unknown", cause of death: "chronic intestinal nephritis", informant: W.S. Crowder (Mountain City), buried: Snyder Cem, died: 5 Mar 1924, record (1924): 211.

Robert Dale LOWE, born: 10 May 1910, parents: R.S. Lowe and Cassie Shoun, cause of death: "accident caused by run away horse", buried: Shoun Cemetery, died: 6 Mar 1924, record (1924) #: 212.

Henry LINEBACK, age 75 years and 5 months, widower, parents: Joseph Lineback and Sarah Bunton, cause of death: "cancer of face and neck", informant: W.W. Lineback (Elk Park, NC), buried: Lineback Cemetery, died: 8 Mar 1924, record (1924) #: 217.

Walter Andrew LONG, born: 22 Jan 1919, parents: Jefferson L. Long (NC) and Bessie B. Blevins, cause of death: "influenza", buried: Blevins Cemetery, died: 11 Mar 1924, record (1924) #: 214.

Martha C. BROWN, born: 23 Sep 1842, married, parents:
John Wagner and Celia Perkins (NC), cause of death:
"chronic intestinal nephritis", informant: R.R. Brown
(Shouns), buried: Brown Cemetery, died: 13 Mar 1924,
record (1924) #: 215.

Rilda POTTER, age about 68 years, widow, born in North
Carolina, parents: "unknown", cause of death:
"pulmonary tuberculosis", informant: D.C. Potter
(Butler), buried: Sugar Grove Cem, died: 16 Mar 1924,
record (1924) #: 216.

William D. MOODY, born: 1 Mar 1924, parents: W.R.
Moody and Margaret Anderson, cause of death:
"enteritis", informant: Loni Moody (Butler), buried:
Dugger Cem, died: 17 Mar 1924, record (1924) #: 217.

Mamie Lagurta ANDERSON, Negro, born: 11 Jul 1894,
parents: L.K. Anderson (NC) and Nancy Wagner, cause of
death: "lobar pneumonia", informant: L.K. Anderson
(Shouns), died: 18 Mar 1924, record (1924) #: 218.

Willie Lucile CRESS, female, born: 26 Jan 1924,
parents: H.F. Hardin and Anna Cress, cause of death:
"broncho pneumonia", informant: R.L. Cress (Neva),
died: 18 Mar 1924, record (1924) #: 219.

Franklin ARNEY, born: 20 Aug 1849, widower, parents:
John Arney and Christina Vaught, cause of death: "died
suddent, cause unknown", informant: Curtis Glenn
(Bakers Gap), died: 20 Mar 1924, record (1924) #: 220.

Louisa E. CANTER, born: 9 Mar 1847 in North Carolina,
widow, parents: Wayne Miller (NC) and Elizabeth Canter
(NC), cause of death: "cause not known", informant:
J.H. Canter (Trade), buried: Arnold Cemetery, died: 23
Mar 1924, record (1924) #: 221.

Phineous Horton BLACKBURN, born: 14 Feb 1852, widower,
parents: Soloman Blackburn (NC) and Polly Elrod (NC),
cause of death: "apoplexy", informant: Andrew
Blackburn (Pulaski, VA), buried: Shingletown Cemetery,
died: 23 Mar 1924, record (1924) #: 222.

Gerry DUGGER, born: 5 Aug 1923, parents: Peter Dugger
and Mina Guy (NC), cause of death: "broncho
pneumonia", informant: A.M. Baker (Butler), buried:
Baker Cem, died: 24 Mar 1924, record (1924) #: 223.

Lilley HAYWORTH, born: 21 Jun 1877, widow, parents:
O.A. Simcox and Luzina Brown, cause of death:
"pulmonary tuberculosis", informant: S.B. Gambill,
Dunn Cem, died: 26 Mar 1924, record (1924) #: 224.

Raleigh HARMON, age about 67 years, born in North
Carolina, married, parents: W.R. Harmon (NC) and Betty
Harmon (NC), cause of death: "cancer of stomach",
informant: M.L. Harmon (Butler), buried: Mt Gilead
Cemetery, died: 26 Mar 1924, record (1924) #: 225.

Viola Grace MULLINS, born: 29 Jan 1924, parents: S.C. Mullins and Jina B. Lee, cause of death: illegible, informant: Walter Lee (Mountain City), Brookshire Cemetery, died: 27 Mar 1924, record (1924) #: 226.

Lanie Bruce WINTERS, born: 23 Dec 1923, parents: John Winters and Susie Arnold, cause of death: "lobar pneumonia", informant: Ed Corum (Mountain City), Michaels Cem, died: 28 Mar 1924, record (1924) #: 227.

Retta BRUON, colored, born: 12 Mar 1888, married, parents: Rufus Smith and Celia Wagner, cause of death: "pulmonary tuberculosis", informant: Hays Smith, died: 28 Mar 1924, record (1924) #: 228.

Maggie RASH, born: 13 Apr 1885, single, parents: Arnie Rash and Betty Ann Jennings (NC), cause of death: "lobar pneumonia", informant: Cau McElyea (Shouns), died: 29 Mar 1924, record (1924) #: 239.

Atlas HEDGEPATH, colored, age 88 years, widower, parents: Richard Hedgepath (NC) and mother's name unknown, cause of death: "chronic intestinal nephritis", informant: Hezekiah Wilson (Mountain City), died: 29 Mar 1924, record (1924) #: 230.

Joe PAYNE, parents: Joe Payne and Nancy Anderson, stillborn, informant: L.B. Dellinger (Butler), Payne Cem, born/died: 13 Mar 1924, record (1924) #: 231.

Infant WINTERS, female, parents: Edd Winters and Bessie Corum, stillborn, buried: Michaels Cemetery, born/died: 15 Mar 1924, record (1924) #: 232.

Augusta A. MCQUEEN, female, born: 22 Feb 1849, widow, parents: John Rainbolt and mother's name unknown, cause of death: "broncho pneumonia", informant: A.M. Rainbolt (Butler), buried: Rainbolt Cemetery, died: 1 Apr 1924, record (1924) #: 233.

Minnie CRESS, age 35 years, 2 months and 10 days, married, parents: J.W. Wilson and Amanda Snyder, cause of death: "pulmonary tuberculosis", informant: R.L. Cress (Neva), died: 7 Apr 1924, record (1924) #: 234.

John S. MAIN, born: 21 Mar 1870, married, parents: Calvin Main and Margaret May, cause of death: "lobar pneumonia", informant: Argus S. Main (Trade) died: 8 Apr 1924, record (1924) #: 235.

John Beltz HOOVER, born: 7 Jan 1841 in Pennsylvania, parents: "not known", cause of death: "chronic intestinal nephritis", informant: Mrs. John Beltz Hoover (Mountain City), died: 8 Apr 1924, record (1924) #: 236.

Basa L. CAMPBELL, born: 3 Oct 1878, married, parents: Joseph D. Matherly and Lanthena Smithpeters, cause of death: "lobar pneumonia", informant: Robert Campbell (Butler), died: 10 Apr 1924, record (1924) #: 237.

Stacy E. BARRY, age 29 years, married, parents: Alex Barry and Omah Harper, cause of death: "pulmonary tuberculosis", informant: Hugh Barry (Mountain City), buried: Wilson Cemetery, died: 12 Apr 1924, record (1924) #: 238.

Fred FRITTS, age about 77 years, widower, parents: Christian Fritts and Polly Grindstaff, cause of death: "influenza", informant: R.D. Campbell (Butler), buried: Holden Cemetery, died: 17 Apr 1924, record (1924) #: 239.

Jennia Crockett BERRY, born: 12 Mar 1862, parents: R.A.J. Crockett and Rodg Williams, cause of death: "olio colitis acute", informant: J. Muse (Mountain City), died: 18 Apr 1924, record (1924) #: 240.

Jennie ROARK, age 72 years, single, parents: "not known", cause of death: "pulmonary tuberculosis", informant: S.S. Pennington (Crandull), buried: Prices Cemetery, died: 21 Apr 1924, record (1924) #: 241.

Mary SAUNDERS, age 35 years, married, parents: Reeves Cress and Alice Simpson, cause of death: illegible, informant: David Saunders (Mountain City), buried: Johnson Cem, died: 25 Apr 1924, record (1924) #: 242.

Mary Ivalee ISAACS, born: 4 Oct 1923, parents: Carrol Isaacs and Rosabell Barlow, cause of death: "supposed to be T.B.", died: 26 Apr 1924, record (1924) #: 243..

Sarah CAMPBELL, age about 50 years, born in Carter Co. TN, married, parents: Nat K. Hyder (Carter Co. TN) and Ollie McKinney (Carter Co. TN), cause of death: "pulmonary tuberculosis", informant: B.L. Hyder (Hampton, TN), buried: Stallings Cemetery, died: 27 Apr 1924, record (1924) #: 244.

Charles F. WARD, born: 17 Dec 1923 in North Carolina, parents: Selmar Ward and Cora Eller (NC), cause of death: "pneumonia", informant: Curtis Glenn (Neva), died: 28 Apr 1924, record (1924) #: 245.

Lyda Ann WILLIN, born: 31 Jul 1850, parents: Abraham Potter (Ashe Co. NC) and Elva Hynes (Ashe Co. NC), cause of death: "organic heart disease", informant: C.O. Willin (Shouns), buried: Dunn Cemetery, died: 28 Apr 1924, record (1924) #: 246.

Infant CURD, male, parents: father not stated and Fronice Curd, stillborn, informant: R.S. Nichols (Mountain City), buried: Wilson Cemetery, died: 2 Apr 1924, record (1924) #: 247.

Johnson GRINDSTAFF, born: 19 Feb 1872, married, parents: William Grindstaff and Eliza Oliver, cause of death: "was shot by unknown party", informant: W.H. Grindstaff (Carter, TN), buried: Rambo Cemetery, died: 10 May 1924, record (1924) #: 248.

Earl HENDERSON, born: 28 Mar 1924, parents: father not stated and Pearl Henderson, cause of death: "no known cause", buried: Cornett Cemetery, died: 15 May 1924, record (1924) #: 249.

Edward ROARK, born: 21 Mar 1923, parents: Aaron Roark (NC) and Attria Lewis (NC), cause of death: "broncopneumonia", informant: Aaron Roark (Shouns), buried in North Carolina, died: 16 May 1924, record (1924) #: 250.

Mary E. DONNELLY, born: 21 Nov 1869, parents: Robert C. Rhea (West VA) and Caroline McQueen, cause of death: "influenza", informant: E. Bruce Rhea (Shouns), died: 12 May 1924, record (1924) #: 251.

Francis Irene PAYNE, born: 24 Feb 1924, parents: Mac Payne (NC) and Betie Johnson, cause of death: "whooping cough and broncho pneumonia", buried: Cress Cemetery, died: 21 Aug 1924, record (1924) #: 252.

Wm McKendrick BLEVINS, born: 14 Sep 1852, parents: Mathus Blevins and Eliza J. Berry, cause of death: "chronic intestinal nephritis", informant: Clyde Mays (Crandull), buried: Blevins Cemetery, died: 25 May 1924, record (1924) #: 253.

Naoma L. STOUT, born: 3 May 1923, parents: Donald G. Stout and Stella Smith, cause of death: "broncho pneumonia", informant: J.K. Stout (Butler), buried: D.B. Wagner Cemetery, died: 26 May 1924, record (1924) #: 254.

Claude C. HARMON, born: 11 May 1924, parents: Garnet M. Harmon (NC) and Maud Mast (NC), cause of death: "not known", informant: T.W. Ward (Neva), died: 26 May 1924, record (1924) #: 255.

Infant CAMPBELL, male, parents: D.A. Campbell and (mother's first name not stated) Price (NC), stillborn, informant: D.A. Campbell (Doeville), born/died: 11 May 1924, record (1924) #: 256.

Robert Stephen FARMER, parents: Willie Farmer and Myrtle Taylor, stillborn, informant: M.J. Hammons (Shouns), buried: Farmer Cemetery, born/died: 16 May 1924, record (1924) #: 257.

Jennie McGuin WILLS, born: 9 Dec 1847, married, parents: Archibold Grant (VA) and Margaret Orr (VA), cause of death: "multiple sclerosis", informant: H.J.D. Wills (Shouns), died: 1 Jun 1924, record (1924) #: 258.

Ruby SMITH, born: 26 May 1924, parents: Wiley Smith and Ora Cornett (NC), cause of death: "fits", informant: Wiley Smith (Vaughtsville), died: 5 Jun 1924, record (1924) #: 259.

Ronda Clyde LUNSFORD, male, born: 1 MaY 1924, parents: Joe Lunsford and Eliza Morefield, cause of death: "not known", informant: R.B. Slimp (Butler), died: 9 Jun 1924, record (1924) #: 260.

Isaac ARNEY, born: 22 Mar 1877, married, parents: Joseph Arney and (first name not stated) Grindstaff, cause of death: "cancer of stomach", informant: Mrs, Isaac Arney (Doeville), buried: Rambo Cemetery, died: 11 Jun 1924, record (1924) #: 261.

Rebecca MABE, (not sure of surname spelling) born: 6 Oct 1889, parents: Lewis Mains (NC) and (first name not stated) Greer, cause of death: "embolism of brain", informant: Roby Owens (Mountain City), buried: Shingletown Cem, died: 13 Jun 1924, record (1924) #: 262.

Thomas BAILEY, colored, age about 40 years, parents: Frank Bailey and Jule Anderson, cause of death: "infective diarrohea", informant: Hayes Smith, died: 23 Jun 1924, record (1924) #: 263.

Infant ELLISON, male, parents: Emmett Ellison (NC) and Betty Williams, stillborn, buried: Potter Cemetery, born/died: 5 Jun 1924, record (1924) #: 264.

Infant LOWE, male, parents: Duey Lowe and Annie Crosswhite, stillborn, born/died: 20 Jun 1924, record (1924) #: 265 (twin below).

Infant LOWE, male, parents: Duey Lowe and Annie Crosswhite, stillborn, born/died: 20 Jun 1924, record (1924) #: 266.

Infant ELLER, female, parents: Charles Eller and Francis M.. (last name illegible), stillborn, informant: Charles Eller (Butler), buried: Rainbolt Cem, born/died: 24 Jun 1924, record (1924) #: 267.

Mannie Louise BOWMAN, parents: David Bowman and Raina Potter, stillborn, buried: Dugger Cemetery, born/died: 24 Jun 1924, record (1924) #: 268.

William BROWN, born: 30 Feb 1924, parents: Roby Brown and Rebecca Morefield, cause of death: "consumption of bowels", died: 1 Jul 1924, record (1924) #: 269.

Caroline RUSSEAN, black, age 81 years, widow, parents: "not known", cause of death: "chronic intestinal nephritis", informant: Hesekiah Wilson (Mountain City), died: 6 Jul 1924, record (1924) #: 270.

Jane M. HAWKS, born: 13 Jul 1854 in Virginia, married, parents: father not stated and Jane Lyons (VA), cause of death: "hypertorphy of heart", informant: Thomas Hawks (Crandull), buried: Hawks Cemetery, died: 12 Jul 1924, record (1924) #: 271.

Peter PHIPPS, born: 12 Jun 1921, parents: J.H. Phipps (Carter Co. TN) and Amanda Wilkins, cause of death: "diarrhea", informant: J.H. Phipps (Doeville), buried: Rambo Cem, died: 14 Jul 1924, record (1924) #: 272.

L.R. JENNINGS, born: 1 Feb 1840 in North Carolina, married, parents: Wiley Jennings (NC) and Rebecca Felts (NC), cause of death: "chronic intestinal nephritis", informant: Wm Jennings (Trade), died: 15 Jul 1924, record (1924) #: 273.

John W. KEYS, born: 29 Apr 1870, married, parents: Marcus Keys and Mary E. Smith, cause of death: "angina pectorus", buried: Wills Cemetery, died: 23 Jul 1924, record (1924) #: 274.

Fonia May Belle CURD, born: 17 Jun 1897, single, parents: father's name unknown and Jennie Arnold, cause of death: "she was an epeliptic", buried: Wilson Cemetery, died: 23 Jul 1924, record (1924) #: 275.

Samuel GARLAND, born: 16 May 1902, single, parents: Robert M. Garland and Luta M. Blevins, cause of death: "acute delitation of the heart caused by violent exercise", buried: Blevins Cemetery, died: 24 Jun 1924, record (1924) #: 276.

John C. SPEER, born: 14 Oct 1843 in Washington Co. VA, parents: John Speer (Washington Co. VA) and Sidury Catron (Washington Co. VA), cause of death: "organic liver and kidney disease", informant: E.G. Speer (Carter, TN), buried at Little Doe, died: 27 Jul 1924, record (1924) #: 277.

Infant GARLAND, male, parents: W.M. Garland and C.E. Holder, stillborn, buried: Rambo Cemetery, born/died: 14 Jul 1924, record (1924) #: 278.

David L. CAMPBELL, age 66 years, born in Iredell Co. NC, widower, parents: "unknown", cause of death: "cancer liver", buried: Lewis Cemetery in North Carolina, died: 6 Aug 1924, record (1924) #: 279.

R.N. GOODURN, Jr., born: 28 Nov 1923, parents: Ronder H. Goodurn and Beulah E. Rambo, cause of death: "cholera", died: 9 Aug 1924, record (1924) #: 280.

Jessee OSBORN, age 58 years, married, parents: Harison Osborn (NC) and Diteltha Price (NC), cause of death: "said to be dropsy", buried: on home farm, died: 10 Aug 1924, record (1924) #: 281.

Mary Alice WINTERS, born: 7 Jan 1861, widow, parents: Vincent G. Morefield and Dililah West (NC0, cause of death: "carcinoma of uterus", informant: Geo F. Creed (Mountain City), buried: Michaels Cemetery, died: 12 Aug 1924, record (1924) #: 282.

Randal E. VINES, born: 25 Mar 1923 in Carter Co. TN, parents: Grover C. Vines (Carter Co. TN) and Bessie Sims (Carter Co. TN), cause of death: "cholera", buried: Fish Springs, TN, died: 13 Aug 1924, record (1924) #: 283.

Gertrude EVANS, born: 17 Nov 1894, parents: Mack Norris and N. Bunting, cause of death: "tuberculosis", died: 15 Aug 1924, record (1924) #: 284.

Alice CAMPBELL, born: 4 Jun 1901, married, parents: David Fletcher and Ellen Bear, cause of death: "pulmonary tuberculosis", informant: David Fletcher (Crandull), buried: Gentry Cemetery, died: 18 Aug 1924, record (1924) #: 285.

Nancy CLAWSON, age 94 years, widow, parents: not stated, cause of death: "acute colitis", informant: M.C. Phillippi (Mountain City), died: 22 Aug 1924, record (1924) #: 286.

Henry Lee MARLOW, born: 20 Aug 1923, parents: W. Newt Marlow (Wilkes Co. NC) and Mary Jane Moore (NC), cause of death: "allio colitis", informant: W.N. Marlow (Damascus, VA), buried: Southerland, TN, died: 23 Aug 1924, record (1924) #: 287.

Eva SHULL, born: 24 Apr 1869 in Carter Co. TN, married, parents: Phillip Finey and Catherine Greenwell, cause of death: "cancer of stomach", died: 5 Sep 1924, record (1924) #: 288.

Mrs. Sallie ARNOLD, born: 6 Oct 1855 in Virginia, parents: Allen G.. (illegible) and (first name not stated) Wilson (VA), cause of death: "acute colitis", informant: M.M. Arnold, buried: Phillippi Cemetery, died: 5 Sep 1924, record (1924) #: 289.

Martha E. GENTRY, born: 7 Jun 1884, married, parents: John A. Wilson and Loviza Mink (VA), cause of death: "diabetes", informant: O.R. Gentry (Laurel Bloomery), buried: Valley Cemetery, died: 7 Sep 1924, record (1924) #: 290.

Martha E. GENTRY, born: 7 Jun 1884, married, parents: John A. Wilson and Loviza Mink (VA), cause of death: "diabetes", informant: O.R. Gentry (Laurel Bloomery), buried: Valley Cemetery, died: 7 Sep 1924, record (1924) #: 290.

Mac MCELYEA, age about 40 years, parents: not stated, cause of death: "chronic brights disease", buried: Wilson Cem, died: 7 Sep 1924, record (1924) #: 291.

Thomas HUSKINS, born: Aug 1924, parents: Emory Huskins and Monise Gentry, cause of death: not stated, informant: J.L. Gentry (Mountain City), buried: Phillippi Cem, died: 7 Sep 1924, record (1924) #: 292.

J.W. SNYDER, born: 25 Oct 1846, parents: Daniel Snyder and Polly Forrester, cause of death: "acute nephritis", informant: O.A. Simcox (Butler), died: 9 Sep 1924, record (1924) #: 293.

Millard Filmore TESTER, born: 26 Apr 1856, married, parents: Wm Mansfield Tester and Rebecca Forrester, cause of death: "fracture skull, fractured right four ribs with ruptured lung", informant: C.E. Tester, died: 12 Sep 1924, record (1924) #: 294.

Infant GOINS, female, black, parents: Robert Goins and Asbell Andrexon, stillborn, informant: Robert Goins (Shouns), died: 22 Sep 1924, record (1924) #: 295.

Infant GREER, female, parents: father's name not stated and Lelar Greer, stillborn, informant: Tom Greer (Laurel Bloomery), born/died: 24 Sep 1924, record (1924) #: 296.

Wm H. NAVE, born: 17 Jun 1843 in Carter Co. TN, widower, parents: Leonard Nave (Carter Co. TN) and Celia Colbolt (Carter Co. TN), cause of death: "acute colitis", informant: D.H. Nave (Mountain City), buried: Wilson Cemetery, died: 7 Oct 1924, record (1924) #: 297.

Alexander Lafayette GENTRY, age 78 years, widower, parents: Dick Gentry and Sarah Gilliland, cause of death: "cerebral hemorhage", informant: Onie Gentry (Laurel Bloomery), buried: Valley Cemetery, died: 8 Oct 1924, record (1924) #: 298.

Elizabeth ARNOLD, born: 23 Aug 1924, parents: Clyde Arnold and Pearl Roark (NC), cause of death: "broncho pneumonia fever", informant: Clyde Arnold (Shouns), buried: Arnold Cemetery, died: 9 Oct 1924, record (1924) #: 299.

Henry Lee JONES, born: 16 Aug 1861 in North Carolina, married, parents: Samuel Jones (NC) and Katy Lewis (Ashe Co. NC), cause of death: "typhoid fever", informant: Will Jones (Mountain City), buried: Ashe Co. NC, died: 9 Oct 1924, record (1924) #: 300.

Trillie CORNETT, age 3 years, parents: Filmore Cornett (NC) and Manel McElyea, cause of death: "whooping cough, acute colitis", informant: R.F. Icenhour, Wilson Cem, died: 10 Oct 1924, record (1924) #: 301.

Infant KITE, male, born: 15 Oct 1924, parents: W.M. Kite and Maggie Stalcup, cause of death: not stated, informant: W.M. Kite (Butler), buried: Stalcup Cemetery, died: 16 Oct 1924, record (1924) #: 302.

Snoull Lee BROWN, female, born: 6 Sep 1924, parents: E.S. Brown and F.A. Dunn, cause of death: "broncho pneumonia", informant: E.L. Brown (Shouns), buried: Dwell Cem, died: 18 Oct 1924, record (1924) #: 303.

181

Infant STEWARD, male, parents: Henry Steward and
Hattie Wilson, cause of death: "congenital heart
disease", informant: Jas J. Wilson (Mountain City),
born/died: 27 Oct 1924, record (1924) #: 304.
Lula NICHOLS, born: Mar 1882 at Ashe Co. NC, married,
parents: Ruben Sutherland (Ashe Co. NC) and Clara
Winebarger (Ashe Co. NC), cause of death: "thought to
be acute paralysis", informant: W.A. Nichols (Shouns),
buried: Payne Cemetery, died: 29 Oct 1924, record
(1924) #: 305.
Clytie HAMMONS, female, parents: Wise Hammons and
Lillie Gambill (Ashe Co. NC), stillborn, informant:
Wise Hammons (Shouns), buried: Hammons Cemetery, died:
22 Oct 1924, record (1924) #: 306.
Mamie PHIPPS, born: 29 Oct 1903, married, parents:
Richard Norris and Polly Campbell, cause of death:
"teverperal septisemia", informant: Garret Phipps
(Doeville), buried: Stalcup Cemetery, died: 7 Nov
1924, record (1924) #: 307.
Satitia PERKINS, female, born: 23 Sep 1904, parents:
E.D. Wagner and Alice Grindstaff, cause of death:
"acute nephritis", informant: Tedia Wagner (Butler),
buried: Wagner Cemetery, died: 13 Nov 1924, record
(1924) #: 308.
Infant ELDRITH, female, born: 8 Nov 1924, parents:
Bruce Taylor and Lettie Eldrith, cause of death:
"unknown", informant: Roby Eldrith (Shouns), buried:
Dunn Cem, died: 15 Nov 1924, record (1924) #: 309.
Infant CORUM, male, parents: father's name not stated
and Belle Corum, cause of death: "atelectosis",
informant: E.C. McQueen (Mountain City), buried:
Cornett Cemetery, born/died: 21 Nov 1924, record
(1924) #: 310.
David H. BLEVINS, born: 28 Jan 1847, widower, parents:
William Blevins and Catherine Berry, cause of death:
"endo corditis", informant: G.S. Blevins (Crandull),
buried: Blevins Cemetery, died: 27 Nov 1924, record
(1924) #: 311.
George H. STURGILL, born: 4 Dec 1858 in North
Carolina, married, parents: William Sturgill (Ashe Co.
NC) and mother's name not stated (NC), cause of death:
"softening of brain", died: 23 Nov 1924, record
(1924) #: 312.
Joseph H. NEELY, born: 3 Nov 1841, parents: Hugh Smith
Neely (NC) and Jane Bridges (Old Virginia), cause of
death: "cancer on face", informant: C.W. Neeley
(Damascus, VA), buried: Wright's Chapel, VA), died: 23
Nov 1924, record (1924) #: 313.

Dora Marie BARRY, age 1 year and 4 months, parents: Stacey Barry and Nelie Gentry, cause of death: "lobar pneumonia and pulmonary tuberculosis", informant: A.J. Forrester (Mountain City), buried: Phillippi Cemetery, died: 24 Nov 1924, record (1924) #: 314.

Jason P. PERKINS, born: 6 Nov 1924, parents: Clinton Perkins (NC) and Lutitia Wagner, cause of death: "unknown", informant: Robert Perkins (Doeville), buried: Wagner Cemetery, died: 27 Nov 1924, record (1924) #: 315.

William F. FUGGETTA, born: 27 Jul 1924, parents: Calvin Fuggetta (NC) and Adalade Dugger, cause of death: "broncho pneumonia", informant: Calvin Fuggetta (Butler), buried: Sugar Grove Cemetery, died: 29 Nov 1924, record (1924) #: 316.

Bessie WATSON, parents: Vanley Watson (NC) and Mamie A. Walker, stillborn, informant: W.T. Walker (Crandull), buried: Gentry Cemetery, died: 3 Nov 1924, record (1924) #: 317.

Garnet G. PARSONS, born: 27 Oct 1924, parents: H.W. Parsons and Jany Hampton, cause of death: "broncho pneumonia", informant: H.W. Parsons (Shouns), buried: Arnold Cem, died: 1 Dec 1924, record (1924) #: 318.

Mrs. S.K. FARNSWORTH, born: 18 Jul 1851 in Virginia, widow, parents: J.B. Kent (VA) and Martha Ann Campbell (VA), cause of death: "pneumonia", informant: C. Kent (Mountain City), buried: Glade Springs, VA, died: 2 Dec 1924, record (1924) #: 319.

A.L. BURTON, Jr., born: 23 May 1923, parents: A.L. Burton and Lucinda Isaacs, cause of death: "acute brights following broncho pneumonia", buried: Sugar Grove Cem, died: 5 Dec 1924, record (1924) #: 320.

Rebecca LUNSFORD, born: 13 Nov 1841, widow, parents: Smith Ford (NC) and Easter Adams (NC) cause of death: "arterosclerosis", informant: B.O. Fritts (Neva), died: 15 Dec 1924, record (1924) #: 321.

Lilian M. ARNOLD, born: 4 Mar 1924, parents: W.B. Arnold and Myrtle Pleasant, cause of death: "spasmodic croup", informant: W.B. Arnold (Doeville), buried: Rambo Cem, died: 15 Dec 1924, record (1924) #: 322.

Anna Francis BUNTON, born: 23 Apr 1924 in Warren Co. KY, parents: Wm G. Bunton (Carter Co. TN) and Eliza A. Smith, cause of death: "broncho pneumonia", informant: Wm G. Bunton (Butler), buried: Rainbolt Cemetery, died: 21 Dec 1924, record (1924) #: 323.

Stilly JENNINGS, born: 12 Nov 1905, single, parents: Thomas J, Jennings (NC) and Emma Main, cause of death: "died sudden, cause not known", buried: Arnold Cem, died: 22 Dec 1924, record (1924) #: 324.

Dilra PROFFITT, age 48 years, married, parents: Thomas Davis and Hannah Davis, cause of death: "cancer of uterus", informant: David Proffitt (Doeville), died: 24 Dec 1924, record (1924) #: 325.

Joseph W. HODGE, born: 15 Sep 1923, parents: Boone F. Hodge and Annie Wilson (NC), cause of death: "cause not known", informant: Boon Hodge (Trade), buried: Reece Cemetery, died: 24 Dec 1924.

Nancy Calvina MCELYEA, born: 2 Feb 1880, single, parents: Thomas J. McElyea and Margaret Nolan (VA), cause of death: "broncho pneumonia and influenza", buried: Shingletown Cemetery, died: 28 Dec 1924, record (1924) #: 327.

Infant MACHAMER, female, parents: Roy Machamer and Pauline Donnelly, cause of death: "premature birth", born/died: 29 Dec 1924, record (1924) #: 328.

General Wilburn GRINDSTAFF, age about 79 years, parents: Nicholas Grindstaff and Pollie Wagner, cause of death: "paralysis", informant: D.B. Grindstaff (Doeville), died: 30 Dec 1924, record (1924) #: 329.

Helen BISHOP, parents: Reece Bishop (VA) and Stella Blevins (VA), stillborn, informant: S.J. Bishop (Laurel Bloomery), buried: Taylor Valley Cemetery, born/died: 28 Dec 1924, record (1924) #: 330.

Relee CORNETT, born: 16 Jun 1921, parents: Filmore Cornett and Maud McElyea, cause of death: "scarlet fever and acute brights disease", buried: Cornett Cemetery, died: 2 Jan 1925, record (1925) #: 208.

Heskiah WILSON, Negro, born: 6 Oct 1878, parents: Rhubin Wilson (NC) and Annis Walker (NC), cause of death: "influenza and acute brights disease", informant: James Bailey (Mountain City), died: 8 Jan 1925, record (1925) #: 209.

David FLETCHER, age 65 years, parents: "not known", cause of death: "pulmonary tuberculosis", informant: Luther Miller (Crandull), buried: Gentry Cemetery, died: 8 Jan 1925, record (1925) #: 210.

Infant SNYDER, male, born: 31 Dec 1924, parents: father not known and M.. (illegible) Snyder, cause of death: "congenital syphilis", informant: Samantha Snyder (Mountain City), died: 12 Jan 1925, record (1925) #: 211.

Rachel SHOUN, born: 23 Apr 1835 in North Carolina, widow, parents: Joseph Sutherland (NC) and Elizabeth Wagner, cause of death: "cancer of stomach", informant: C.G. Shoun (Mountain City), buried: Shoun Cemetery, died: 16 Jan 1925, record (1925) #: 212.

Maggie Anna Lee TRIVETT, born: 11 Oct 1924, parents: John Trivett (NC) and Inez Martin, cause of death: "broncho pneumonia", informant: John Trivett (Shouns), buried: Martin Cemetery, died: 18 Jan 1925, record (1925) #: 213.

Joel BROOKSHIRE, born: 26 Jul 1839 in "Elexandr" Co. NC, parents: Joel Brookshire (NC) and mother's name not stated, cause of death: "bronchitis", informant: W.D. Brookshire (Doeville), buried: Brookshire Cemetery, died: 19 Jan 1925, record (1925) #: 214.

Bell ELDRIDGE, born: 18 Nov 1901, married, parents: M.F. Brown (NC) and Sarah Hodge, cause of death: "pulmonary tuberculosis", informant: M.L. Mast (Shouns), buried: Dowell Cemetery, died: 21 Jan 1925, record (1925) #: 215.

Mariah HARDIN, colored, age about 80 years, born in North Carolina, widow, parents: father's name not known and Hannah Dobbins (NC), cause of death: "brights disease", informant: Arthur Anderson, died: 25 Jan 1925, record (1925) #: 216.

Infant COMBS, female, born: 20 Jan 1925, parents: Manley Combs (NC) and Flora Parsons (NC), cause of death: "premature delivery", informant: Landon Parsons, died: 28 Jan 1925, record (1925) #: 217.

Infant WILSON, female, parents: Kelly Wilson and Cora Smith, cause of death: "premature delivery", born/died: 2 Feb 1925, record (1925) #: 218.

Infant FORRESTER, male, parents: father's name not stated and Oda Forrester, cause of death: "8 month child", informant: Oda Forrester (Shouns), buried: Forrester Cemetery, born/died: 5 Feb 1925, record (1925) #: 219.

Delila J. LEWIS, born: 25 Sep 1865, married, parents: Isaac Laws and Jennia Greenwell, cause of death: "chronic colitis or diarrhea", buried: Church Hill cemetery, died: 8 Feb 1925, record (1925) #: 220.

Reta DAVIS, born: 13 Jul 1922, parents: S.C. Davis and Ella Robinson, cause of death: "spasmodic croup", informant: S.C. Davis (Doeville), buried: Rambo Cemetery, died: 8 Feb 1925, record (1925) #: 221.

Floyd PHIPPS, age 63 years, married, parents: Eli Phipps and Polly Phipps, cause of death: "valvulor heart liseon", informant: Charlie Huffman (Green Cove, VA), buried in North Carolina, died: 14 Feb 1925, record (1925) #: 222.

Earl Bruce LEWIS, born: 1 Feb 1925, parents: Earl B. Lewis (NC) and Alma R. Barlow (NC), cause of death: "broncho pneumonia", Mountain View Cemetery, died: 15 Feb 1925, record (1925) #: 223.

Baxter, MCEWEN, born: 14 Dec 1862, single, parents: Sam McEwen and Matilda Smithpeters, cause of death: "cancer of bowels", informant: J.D. McEwen (Doeville), buried: McEwen Cemetery, died: 15 Feb 1925, record (1925) #: 224.

Bruce TRIVETT, born: 26 Apr 1924, parents: Charles Trivett and Myrtle Eggers, cause of death: "meningitis sporatic", buried: Zionville, NC, died: 22 Feb 1925. record (1925) #: 225.

Noah WAGNER, born: 6 Mar 1844, married, parents: Tice Wagner and Mary Vaught, cause of death: "broncho pneumonia, influenza", informant: J.M. Potter (Shouns), buried: Shouns, TN, died: 24 Feb 1925, record (1925) #: 226.

James W. SHUPE, age 50 years, married, parents: Thompson Shupe and Margaret Blevins, cause of death: "gun shot wound in head, instant death", Phillippi Cem, died: 25 Feb 1925, record (1925) #: 227.

Infant WINTERS, male, parents: John R. Winters and Susan Arnold, cause of death: "premature delivery", buried: Michaels Cemetery, born/died: 28 Feb 1925, record (1925) #: 228.

Infant WINTERS, female, born: 28 Feb 1925, parents: John R. Winters and Susan Arnold, cause of death: "premature delivery", buried: Michaels Cemetery, died: 1 Mar 1925, record (1925) #: 229.

Garfield PLEASANT, born: 15 Aug 1881, married, parents: W.H. Pleasant and Martha Howard, cause of death: "dropped dead", informant: R.B. Pleasant (Doeville), buried: Rambo Cemetery, died: 2 Mar 1925, record (1925) #: 230.

William F. BUCKLES. born: 20 Jan 1858 in Virginia, parents: William Buckles (VA) and Mary Davidson (VA), cause of death: "pyarrhoea (and something to do with teeth)", informant: Laura Buckles (Crandull), buried: Gentry Cem, died: 4 Mar 1925, record (1925) #: 231.

Lydea DUGGER, age about 80 years, born in North Carolina, widow, parents: "unknown", cause of death: "heart dropsy", informant: John Dickens (Butler), buried: Dugger Cemetery, died: 6 Mar 1925, record (1925) #: 232.

Margaret SALES, Negro, born: 8 Jan 1858 in North Carolina, married, parents: Peter Lomax (NC) and America Wade (NC), cause of death: carcinoma of bowel", informant: S.W. Widly, buried: Shouns, TN, died: 9 Mar 1925, record (1925) #: 233.

S. Florence GARLAND, age 43 years, born in Virginia, parents: William Forrester (VA) and Margaret Neal (VA), cause of death: "tuberculosis, meningitis", informant: Rushia Garland (Crandull), buried: Blevins Cemetery, died: 10 Mar 1925, record (1925) #: 234.

Mary Jane GREER, born: 16 Dec 1837, widow, parents: Alford Smith and Mary Vincel (VA), cause of death: "found dead in bed", informant: J.S. Greer (Lodi, VA), buried: Valley Cemetery, died: 11 Mar 1925, record (1925) #: 235.

James FLETCHER, born: 26 Nov 1857, married, parents: John Fletcher and Rebecca Riner (NC), cause of death: "organic heart disease", informant: Daniel Fletcher (Butler), buried: Fletcher Cemetery, died: 11 Mar 1925, record (1925) #: 236.

Sarah E. DAVIS, born: 19 Sep 1845, widow, parents: Allen Dotson (NC) and Deliah Pierce (NC), cause of death: "broncho pneumonia", informant: D.S. Dotson (Damascus, VA), buried: Dotson Cemetery, died: 12 Mar 1925, record (1925) #: 237.

Arthur Cecil CURD, born: 2 Jan 1925, parents: Wm Curd and Lelah Dunn, cause of death: "acute menengitis", informant: Wm Curd (Shouns) died: 15 Mar 1925, record (1925) #: 238.

Susan Elmas OSBORN, born: 17 Mar 1925, parents: David Osborn and Lizzie May, cause of death: "unknown", informant: David Osborn (Shouns), buried: Arnold Cemetery, died: 18 Mar 1925, record (1925) #: 239.

Gladys BLACKBURN, born: 8 Jul 1921, parents: "father not known" and Pearl Blackburn, cause of death: "spinal meningitis and broncho pneumonia", informant: Pearl Blackburn (Butler), buried: Campbell Cemetery, died: 22 Mar 1925, record (1925) #: 240.

Mary CORNETT, age 6 years, parents: Roy Cornett and Onie Morefield, cause of death: "influenza, intestinal type", informant: M.C. Cornett (Mountain City), buried: Cornett Cemetery, died: 26 Mar 1925, record (1925) #: 241.

Mahlon GENTRY, born: 14 Feb 1841, married, parents: General Gentry and Lizzie Rambo, cause of death: "paraplegia, blood clot in brain", informant: Mrs. W.F. Walker (Crandull), buried: Gentry Cemetery, died: 28 Mar 1925, record (1925) #: 242.

Robt Alfred HAWKINS, born: 13 Oct 1846, widower, parents: Washington Hawkins (NC) and Betsy Greer (NC), cause of death: "chronic colitis", informant: E.C. Hawkins (Laurel Bloomery), buried: Eggers Cemetery, died: 30 Mar 1925, record (1925) #: 243.

Pauline DUNN, born: 20 Jan 1925, parents: George Dunn and Stella Riddle, cause of death: not stated, informant: W.M. Riddle (Shouns), died: 30 Mar 1925, record (1925) #: 244.

Sallie Liona GENTRY, born: 22 May 1924, parents: James Gentry and Rosa Cornett (NC), cause of death: "illio colitis (flux)", informant: A.J. Forrester (Mountain City), buried: Phillippi Cemetery, died: 31 Mar 1925, record (1925) #: 245.

Agnes Bessie DUNN, born: 24 Mar 1925, parents: W.G. Dunn and Verda Mae Proffitt, cause of death: "broncho pneumonia", died: 31 Mar 1925, record (1925) #: 246.

Joseph Arthur WAGNER, parents: Arthur Wagner and Ella Gregg, stillborn, informant: A.B. Wagner (Butler), buried: Sugar Grove Cemetery, born/died: 7 Mar 1925, record (1925) #: 247.

Infant MCQUEEN, female, black, parents: Arther McQueen and Susie Anderson, stillborn, born/died: 17 Mar 1925, record (1925) #: 248.

Ida Thelmar OSBORN, born: 17 Mar 1925, parents: David Osborn and Lizzie May, cause of death: "unknown", died: 1 Apr 1925, record (1925) #: 249.

Julia Ann CAURTHUR, born: 12 Sep 1865, parents: John Arnold and Rachel Morefield, cause of death: "paralysis", informant: Lessie Grindstaff (Doeville), died: 3 Apr 1925, record (1925) #: 250.

Wade ROBINSON, born: 20 Apr 1923, parents: David Robinson and Vada Osborn (NC), cause of death: "acute colitis", informant: Moore Robinson (Mountain City), buried: Robinson Cemetery, died: 6 Apr 1925, record (1925) #: 251.

Joseph M. FRITZ, born: 6 Oct 1861, married, parents: John Fritz and Isabella Speer, cause of death: "chronic nephritis", informant: J.A. Fritz (Laurel Bloomery), buried: Valley Cemetery, died: 19 Apr 1925, record (1925) #: 252.

Caroline ANDERSON, age about 71, married, parents: "unknown", cause of death: "cancer", informant: W.L. Rece (Butler), buried: Sugar Grove Cemetery, died: 23 Apr 1925, record (1925) #: 253.

R.A. LIPFORD, born: 13 May 1839 in North Carolina, parents: Anthony Lipford and (mother's first name not stated) Atkins (NC), cause of death: "mitral regurgitation", informant: B.A. Lipford (Butler), buried: Rainbolt Cemetery, died: 23 Apr 1925, record (1925) #: 254.

Robert L. LAMBERSON, born: 21 Oct 1863 in Virginia, parents: John Lamberson (VA) and Sallie Speer (VA), cause of death: "chronic brights disease", informant: Robert Lamberson, Jr. (Kingsport, TN), buried: Jenkins Cemetery, died: 26 Apr 1925, record (1925) #: 255.

William Melvin BERRY, born: 16 May 1836, widower, parents: Charles Berry (VA) and Abbie Razor, cause of death: "influenza", informant: D.H. Berry (Crandull), Gentry Cem, died: 26 Apr 1925, record (1925) #: 256.

Thomas MOODY, parents: Will Moody and Margaret Anderson, stillborn, buried: Dugger Cemetery, born/died: 25 Apr 1925, record (1925) #: 257.

Infant COURTNER, male, parents: R. Allen Courtner and May Neatherly, stillborn, informant: R. Allen Courtner (Butler), buried: Rainbolt Cemetery, born/died: 27 Apr 1925, record (1925) #: 258.

Clyde ELLISON, born: 25 Jan 1903 at Tomarack, North Carolina, single, parents: C.C. Ellison (NC) and Sarrah Ellison (NC), cause of death: "tuberculosis meningitis", buried in North Carolina, died: 10 May 1925, record (1925) #: 259.

Carmon PHIPPS, born: 29 Oct 1924, parents: Garret Phipps and Mammie Norris, cause of death: "cholera", informant: David Phipps (Doeville), buried: Stalcup Cemetery, died: 22 May 1925, record (1925) #: 260.

Mertell Caroline VAUGHT, born: 22 Jan 1879 in North Carolina, married, parents: Marshall Pennington (NC) and Mary Graybeal (NC), death cause: illegible, informant: J.A. Vaught, died: 31 May 1925, record (1925) #: 261.

Infant MCQUEEN, female, black, parents: Arther McQueen and Susie Anderson, stillborn, born/died: 17 May 1925, record (1925) #: 262.

Caleb R. REID, born: 5 Jan 1862, married, parents: Andrew Reid and Jane Denkins, cause of death: "cancer involving face and neck", informant: Mrs. C.R. Reid (Mountain City), buried: Shingletown Cemetery, died: 1 Jun 1925, record (1925) #: 263.

Alafair ICENHOUR, female, born: 25 Feb 1876 in North Carolina, parents: Calvin Shores (NC) and Sarah Perdue (NC), cause of death: "cancer womb", informant: Russell Icenhour (Mountain City), buried: Phillippi Cemetery, died; 4 Jun 1925, record (1925) #: 264.

John Wesley ELDRETH, age about 70 years, born in North Carolina, parents: Levi Eldreth (NC) and Nancy Ward (NC), cause of death: "apoplexy", informant: W.M. Eldreth (Shouns), buried in North Carolina, died: 4 Jun 1925, record (1925) #: 265.

Mason Guy HINKLE, born: 26 May 1925, parents: Earl Hinkle and Reba Nave (Carter Co. TN), cause of death: illegible, informant: Jane Hinkle (Butler), buried: Rainbolt Cem, died: 5 Jun 1925, record (1925) #: 266.

John G. WALKER, born: 29 May 1850 in North Carolina, married, parents: John Walker (NC) and Rebecca Walker (NC), cause of death: "organic leision of heart", informant: G.C. Walker (Crandull), died: 6 Jun 1925, record (1925) #: 267.

Jane BORAN, black, born: 7 Oct 1865 in North Carolina, parents: Jacob Williams and Phillis Williams (NC), cause of death: "apoplexy, informant: Charles Boran, died: 7 Jun 1925, record (1925) #: 268.

Emaline HECK, age 68 years, born in North Carolina, widow, parents: Phillip Rash (NC) and Nancy Williams (NC), cause of death: "apoplexy", informant: Wiley Heck, died: 7 Jun 1925, record (1925) #: 269.

Ethel SHOUN, born: 31 Jan 1889, married, parents: L.C. Shuffield and Sallie Renfro, cause of death: "double lobar pneumonia", informant: Andy Shoun (Mountian City), buried: Little Doe, died: 8 Jun 1925, record (1925) #: 270.

Bartin D. RASH, born: 4 Feb 1925, parents: James E. Rash and Annie Stout, cause of death: not stated, informant: John L. Stout (Neva), died: 10 Jun 1925, record (1925) #: 271.

Lucinda BURTON, born: 16 Jun 1925, parents: A. Lafayette Burton and Lucinda Isaacs, cause of death: "not known, child was born at 8 months", informant: A.L. Burton (Butler), buried: Sugar Grove Cemetery, died: 18 Jun 1925, record (1925) #: 272.

William Ralph MANUEL, born: 6 Apr 1924, parents: L.G. Manuel (NC) and B.M. Bishop, cause of death: "supposed to have died from colera", informant: L.G. Manual (Crandull), buried: Blevins Cemetery, died: 19 Jun 1925, record (1925) #: 273.

Frank ADAMS, born: 5 Jul 1923, parents: W.J. Adams and Martha Church, cause of death: "croupous laryngites", informant: W.J. Adams (Doeville), died: 30 Jun 1925, record (1925) #: 274.

David R. STOUT, born: 12 Aug 1856, married, parents: George P. Stout and Nancy Courtner, cause of death: "heart dropsy", informant: Elizabeth Arnold (Doeville), died: 3 Jul 1925, record (1925) #: 275.

W. Eugene DOUGHERTY, born: 20 Oct 1870, married, parents: Thos Dougherty (NC) and Polly M... (illegible), cause of death: "acute dilation of heart", informant: F.C. Dougherty (Butler), Sugar Grove Cem, died: 5 Jul 1925, record (1925) #: 276.

Elizabeth J. MILLER, age 86 years, widow, parents:
Franklin Morley and Hannah Razor, cause of death:
"chronic intestinal nephritis", informant: G.H. Miller
(Crandull), buried: Gentry Cemetery, died: 8 Jul 1925,
record (1925) #: 277.

Arthur GARR, born: 29 Apr 1905, single, parents: Mack
Garr (NC) and Florence Mitchell (NC), cause of death:
"affected from infancy with hemiplegia gortre, death
sudden", informant: Alfred McQueen (Mountain City),
buried: Rash Cemetery, died: 15 Jul 1925, record
(1925) #: 278.

Martha G. DUGGER, born: 5 Aug 1861, married, parents:
A.B. Greenwell (NC) and Mary Cable (not sure of last
name spelling), cause of death: "pulmonary
tuberculosis", informant: S.B. Dugger (Butler),
buried: Rainbolt Cemetery, died: 19 Jul 1925, record
(1925) #: 279.

Albert C. COLE, born: 25 Apr 1856, married, parents:
Washington Cole and Sarah A. Shoun, cause of death:
"chest crushed by automobile", informant: Walter Shoun
(Mountain City), buried: Reece Cemetery, died: 28 Jul
1925, record (1925) #: 280.

Elizabeth DAY, born: 20 May 1845, widow, parents:
William Bunton and Sarah Shuffield, cause of death:
"apoplexy", informant: Geo Day (Butler), Crosswhite
Cemetery, died: 31 Jul 1925, record (1925) #: 281.

Clinard SLUDER, born: 8 Jul 1925, male, parents: Dona
H. Sluder and Hattie S. Miller, stillborn, informant:
Dona Sluder (Crandull), buried: Gentry Cemetery, died:
8 Jul 1925, record (1925) #: 282.

Lonie WATSON, female, parents: Volney Watson (NC) and
Mamie A. Walker, stillborn, informant: Volney Watson
(Crandull), buried: Gentry Cemetery, born/died: 19 Jul
1925, record (1925) #: 283.

Alice Annie BLEVINS, born: 2 May 1869, widow, parents:
Joel Heaberline (Russell Co. VA) and Lucinda Blevins,
cause of death: "cancer liver", informant: G.R.
Blevins (Crandull), buried: Blevins Cemetery, died: 1
Aug 1925, record (1925) #: 284.

Rosa Lee COLEMAN, born: 18 Jan 1925, parents: Coy
Coleman (NC) and Mable Oliver (NC), cause of death:
"typhoid fever", informant: S.J. Heaton (Butler),
buried: Coleman Cemetery, died: 18 Aug 1925, record
(1925) #: 285.

Ellen White ROBINSON, born: 25 May 1855, married,
parents: Daniel Sweney (VA) and Nancy Estep (Carter
Co. TN), cause of death: "mitral regurgitation",
informant: W.W. Robinson (Mountain City), buried:
Robinson Cem, died: 21 Aug 1925, record (1925) #: 286.

Velma NORRIS, born: 12 Mar 1924, parents: Flenor
Norris and Lottie Robinson, cause of death: "cholera",
informant: Flenor Norris (Doeville), buried: Norris
Cemetery, died: 23 Aug 1925, record (1925) #: 287.

Dora HODGSON, born: 26 Oct 1875 in North Carolina,
married, parents: Monroe Wyatt and Susie Starns (NC),
cause of death: "pulmonary tuberculosis", informant:
W.A. Hodgson (New Castle, IN), buried: Blevins
Cemetery, died: 27 Aug 1925, record (1925) #: 288.

David H. ROARK, born: 11 Aug 1925, parents: A.L. Roark
(NC) and A.A. Lewis (NC), death death: "acute
colitis", informant: A.L. Roark (Shouns), buried in
North Carolina, died: 28 Aug 1925, record (1925) #:
289.

Anna Mae EASTRIDGE, born: 28 Sep 1923, parents:
William C. Eastridge (Ashe Co. NC) and Eula Curd,
cause of death: "thought to be flux or colitis",
informant: William C. Eastridge (Shouns), buried: Curd
Cemetery, died: 29 Aug 1925, record (1925) #: 290.

James Hamilton JORDAN, age 67 years, 7 months and 23
Days, parents: James Jordan (NC) and Sarah Crosswhite,
cause of death: "apoplexy", informant: J.W. Jordan,
died: 3 Sep 1925, record (1925) #: 291.

Paul B. RUTTER, born: 21 Jan 1923, parents: Ernest
Rutter and Ellen Rankins, cause of death: "nephritis",
informant: Ernest Rutter (Crandull), buried: Blevins
Cemetery, died: 3 Sep 1925, record (1925) #: 292.

Grady Arvil BREWER, born: 30 Aug 1904, single,
parents: A.L. Brewer and Susie Fritts, cause of death:
"typhoid fever", informant: A.L. Brewer (Doeville),
died: 4 Sep 1925, record (1925) #: 293.

Nancy JOHNSON, born: 28 Sep 1846 in North Carolina,
widow, parents: John Main (NC) and Pollie Potter,
cause of death: "broncho pneumonia", informant: A.C.
Johnson (Shouns), buried: Johnson Cemetery, died: 10
Sep 1925, record (1925) #: 294.

Celia A. SHOUN, born: 3 Jan 1854, parents: Asa Reece
(NC) and Catherine Wagner, death cause: "accidental
bruise on hand, blood poisoning", informant: Asa W.
Shoun, died: 11 Sep 1925, record (1925) #: 295.

Lestie Gertrude GENTRY, born: 22 Jul 1924, parents:
J.M. Gentry and Atha Rutherford, cause of death:
"acute indigestion from eating tomatoes which had been
sprayed", informant: J.M. Gentry (Crandull), buried:
Gentry Cem, died: 11 Sep 1925, record (1925) #: 296.

David E. GENTRY, born: 20 Jan 1868, parents: father's
name not stated and Elizabeth Gentry, cause of death:
"acute indigestion or neuralgie of heart", buried:
Gentry Cem, died: 13 Sep 1925, record (1925) #: 297.

Mrs. Bettie HEUSON, age 66 years, married, parents:
James F... (illegible) and Nancy Elliott (SC), cause
of death: "pellegra", informant: Richard Wilson, died:
20 Sep 1925, record (1925) #: 298.
Earl CROW, born: 7 Jan 1925, parents: Charlie Crow
(Carter Co. TN) and Julia Robinson, cause of death:
"spinal meningitis", informant: Charlie Crow
(Doeville), buried: Brookshire Cemetery, died: 27 Sep
1925, record (1925) #: 299.
John H. STALCUP, born: 2 Aug 1863, married, parents:
John H. Stalcup and Betsy Robinson, cause of death:
"pulmonary tuberculosis", informant: Mrs. J.H.
Stalcup, died: 2 Oct 1925, record (1925) #: 300.
Mary Velena KIRBY, born: 26 Jun 1925 at Ashe Co. NC,
parents: James Kirby (Ashe Co. NC) and Docia Shumate
(Ashe Co. NC), death cause: "flux", informant: James
Kirby (Laurel Bloomery), buried: Ashe County, North
Carolina, died: 3 Oct 1925, record (1925) #: 301.
J.W. SHEPHERD, born: 28 Jul 1915, parents: John
Shepherd and Callie Heck, cause of death: "run over by
a truck, accidental, fracture skull", informant: C.F.
Blevins (Crandull), buried: Blevins Cemetery, died: 5
Oct 1925, record (1925) #: 302.
R.G. GENTRY, born: 31 Jul 1923, parents: R.B. Gentry
and M.E. Walker (NC), cause of death: "meningitis
caused by a fall from the bed", informant: R.B. Gentry
(Crandull), died: 11 Oct 1925, record (1925) #: 303.
Hettie SHELTON, born: 17 Oct 1924, parents: C.F.
Shelton (NC) and B.M. Shepard, cause of death: "cause
unknown", informant: Kelly Arnold (Shouns), buried:
Arnold Cem, died: 14 Oct 1925, record (1925) #: 304.
Infant ARNOLD, female, parents: W.B. Arnold and Myrtle
Pleasant, cause of death: "atelectosis", informant:
W.B. Arnold (Doeville), buried: Rambo Cemetery, died:
19 Oct 1925, record (1925) #: 305.
Olivene NICHOLS, female, age 53 years, born in North
Carolina, single, parents: John Nichols (NC) and Mary
McGee (NC), cause of death: "cancer of bowels and
uterus", Blevins Cemetery, died: 25 Oct 1925, record
(1925) #: 306.
Walter B. REECE, born: 11 Apr 1901, married, parents:
John R. Reece and Victoria Reece (NC), cause of death:
"pulmonary tuberculosis", informant: John R. Reece
(Trade), died: 27 Oct 1925, record (1925) #: 307.
Ezekil G. BRADLEY, born: 16 Mar 1854, married,
parents: Irvin Kyle Bradley and Nancy Jane Smith,
cause of death: "broncho pneumonia and brights
disease", informant: L.L McQueen (Butler), buried:
Allen Cem, died: 27 Oct 1925, record (1925) #: 308.

Florence WHITE, age 46 years, born in Virginia, married, parents: John Smith (VA) and Florence Smith (VA), cause of death: "apoplexy", informant: T.G. White (Mountain City), died: 29 Oct 1925, record (1925) #: 309.

Infant SHULL, male, parents: Charles Shull and Celia Greer, stillborn, parents: Charles Shull (Neva), died: 4 Oct 1925, record (1925) #: 310.

Amanda ANDERSON, age 65 years, born in Virginia, married, parents: "unknown", cause of death: "apoplexy", informant: E.D. Anderson (Butler), buried: Dugger Cem, died: 1 Nov 1925, record (1925) #: 311.

Wiley W. LONG, born: 8 Jan 1892, married, parents: Ed E. Long (NC) and E. Ellen Heaberlin, cause of death: "pulmonary tuberculosis", informant: Ed. Long (Crandull), buried: Blevins Cemetery, died: 6 Nov 1925, record (1925) #: 312.

Wilford J. PRICE, born: 21 Oct 1925, parents: Wilford Price and Ada Denney, cause of death: "broncho pneumonia fever", informant: Wilford Price (Shouns), buried: Arnold Cemetery, died: 6 Nov 1925, record (1925) #: 313.

Elizabeth GRINDSTAFF, born: 16 Jul 1846, widow, parents: Andrew Cable and Rebecca Bradley, cause of death: "broncho pneumonia", informant: Dock Cable (Butler), buried: McEwen Cemetery, died: 11 Nov 1925, record (1925) #: 314.

Joshua TRIVETT, age about 64 years, married, parents: John Trivett (NC) and Lucy Greer (NC), cause of death: "hemipligia", informant: Lizzie Trivett (Shouns), buried: Woods Cemetery, died: 12 Nov 1925, record (1925) #: 315.

Infant GRINDSTAFF, female, parents: Stacy Grindstaff and Maggie McQueen, cause of death: "premature birth", born/died: 18 Nov 1925, record (1925) #: 316.

James Millard BLEVINS, born: 28 Mar 1862, married, parents: James Blevins and Sarah Berry, cause of death: "sarcoma of right jaw", informant: M.F. Blevins (Crandull), buried: Blevins Cemetery, died: 23 Nov 1925, record (1925) #: 317.

Hubert VAUGHT, born: 17 May 1910, parents: John H. Vaught and Joda Lineback, cause of death: "alcoholic poison, found dead, drank poison whiskey", informant: R.L. Sheffield (Butler), buried: Lineback Cemetery, died: 24 Nov 1925, record (1925) #: 318.

Connelly BISHOP, born: 12 Nov 1907, parents: R.L. Bishop (NC) and Margaret Nichols (NC), cause of death: "spinal meningitis", informant: R.L. Bishop, Blevins Cemetery, died: 4 Dec 1925, record (1925) #: 319.

Samantha Isabell GREENWELL, born: 11 May 1867, married, parents: Thomas Hamby (Carter Co. TN) and Matilda Laws, cause of death: "organic heart disease, found dead", informant: Alfred Greenwell (Butler), died: 6 Dec 1925, record (1925) #: 320.

Stacy LUNSFORD, born: 4 Apr 1909, parents: Wm H. Lunsford (Carter Co. TN) and Matilda Dugger, cause of death: "typhoid fever", informant: W. H. Luncsford (Butler), buried: Crosswhite Cemetery, died: 6 Dec 1925, record (1925) #: 321.

Mary Emeline POPE, born: 7 May 1861 in North Carolina, widow, parents: Joe Thomas (NC) and Nancy Stout (NC), cause of death: "general paralysis", informant: Alice Pope (Shouns), buried: Martin Cemetery, died: 7 Dec 1925, record (1925) #: 322.

G.H. LEE, age 62 years, born in North Carolina, parents: "don't know", cause of death: "died a natural death", informant: Baxter Roberts (Mountain City), buried: Wright Cemetery, died: 16 Dec 1925, record (1925) #: 323.

Hattie Mae SHELTON, born: 17 Oct 1924, parents: C.F. Shelton (NC) and Bessie Shepard, cause of death: "diptheria", informant: C.F. Shelton (Shouns), buried: Arnold Cem, died: 17 Dec 1925, record (1925) #: 324.

Samuel NEELY, age 56 years, married, parents: William Neely and Jane Gentry, cause of death: "cholecystisis with gall stones", informant: Sallie Butler (Lauerl Bloomery), buried: Acre Field Cemetery, died: 18 Dec 1925, record (1925) #: 325.

Katherine BAKER, black, age 72 years, born at Ashe Co. NC, widow, parents: (first name not stated) Horton (Ashe Co. NC) and mother's name not stated, cause of death: "cancer breast", informant: James Baily (Mountain City), buried: Creston, NC, died: 22 Dec 1925, record (1925) #: 326.

Amanda Caroline POTTER, age 68 years, born in North Carolina, widow, parents: Wiloby Morgan (NC) and Malissie Elliotte (NC), cause of death: "cancer of uterus", buried: Evans Cemetery, died: 28 Dec 1925, record (1925) #: 327.

Luther WILLIN, born: 18 Dec 1925, parents: Thos Willin and Jane Forrester, cause of death: "not right when born, cause unknown", buried: Dunn Cemetery, died: 29 Dec 1925. record (1925) #: 328.

Hesekat THOMAS, age 79 years, born in North Carolina, married, parents: Jack Thomas (NC) and Nancy (last name illegible), cause of death: "cancer liver", died: 17 Jan 1926, record (1926) #: 1055.

Stella G. RED, Negro, born: 25 Apr 1897, married, parents: L.K. Anderson (NC) and Nancy Wagner, cause of death: "exophtholnic goiter", informant: S.K. Anderson (Shouns), died: 20 Jan 1926, record (1926) #: 1056.

Jack Taylor FORRESTER, born: 3 Jan 1852, parents: Andy Forrester and Phoebe Proffitt, cause of death: "pneumonia fever with organic heart disease, informant: Filmore Forrester (Neva), died: 27 Jan 1926, record (1926) #: 1057.

Alfred Clinton FORRESTER, born: 22 Oct 1887, married, parents: Jackson T. Forrester and Nancy Tester, cause of death: "broncho pneumonia fever", informant: R.B. Slimp (Butler), buried: Neva, TN, died: 28 Jan 1926, record (1926) #: 1058.

Alice HEAD, born: 27 Jan 1900, single, parents: Scott Head and Oma Forrester, cause of death: "tuberculosis", informant: Scott Head (Shouns), buried: Dunn Cemetery, died: 28 Jan 1926, record (1926) #: 1060.

Carrie Lee STANTON, born: 13 Jan 1926 (?), parents: Grocon Stanton and Martha Arney, cause of death: not stated, informant: Grocon Stanton (Neva), died: 11 Jan 1926, record (1926) #: 1061.

Martha STANTON, born: 10 Jun 1889, married, parents: John Arney and Elizabeth Moody, cause of death: not stated, informant: Grace Stanton (Neva), died: 17 Jan 1926, record (1926) #: 1062.

Mary E. STALCUP, born: 11 Oct 1858, widow, parents: D.R. Howard and Elva O. Shoun, cause of death: "pneumonia", informant: Stacy Stalcup (Doeville), buried: Rambo Cemetery, died: 4 Jan 1926, record (1926) #: 1063.

Dealtha ASHLEY, age 76 years, widow, parents: father's name not stated and Mary A. Gentry, cause of death: "chronic nephritis and myocarditis", informant: J.S. Neeley (Laurel Bloomery), buried: Acre Field Cemetery, died: 18 Feb 1926, record (1926) #: 3540.

Eliza DAVIS, born: 28 Feb 1827 in Wilkes Co. NC, parents: illegible, cause of death: illegible, informant: M.L. Davis (Damascus, VA), buried: Davis Cemetery, died: 13 Feb 1926, record (1926) #: 3541.

John SALES, Negro, age 70 years, widower, parents: not known, cause of death: "chronic heart disease", died: 26 Feb 1926, record (1926) #: 3542.

Irvin R. JENKINS, age 78 years, married, parents: Roland Jenkins and Elizabeth Wilson, cause of death: "brights disease" informant: M.B. Jenkins (Mountain City), buried: Jenkins Cemetery, died: 23 Feb 1926, record (1926) #: 3543.

J.S. JENKINS, born: 7 Jun 1856, parents: Benjamin
Jenkins and Nancy Donnelly, cause of death: "brights
disease", informant: Mrs. J.S. Jenkins (Mountian
City), died: 21 Feb 1926, record (1926) #: 3544.

Harrison Rhea DONNELLY, born: 1 Jun 1899, single,
parents: Joe S. Donnelly and Mary E. Rhea, cause of
death: "lobar pneumonia", informant: R. Ross Donnelly
(Shouns), died: 12 Feb 1926, record (1926) #: 3545.

Norman OSBORN, born: 12 Feb 1926, parents: David
Osborn (NC) and Lizzie May, cause of death:
"diptheria", informant: Callie Cornett (Shouns),
buried: Arnold Cemetery, died: 26 Feb 1926, record
(1926) #: 3546.

Blaine B. HODGE, born: 25 Oct 1925, parents: Boone F.
Hodge and Anna Wilson, cause of death: "diptheria",
informant: Anna Hodge (Trade), buried: Reece Cemetery,
died: 4 Feb 1926, record (1926) #: 3547.

Francis HAGAMAN, male, age 58 years and 6 months, born
in North Carolina, parents: John Hagaman (NC) and Liza
Dougherty, cause of death: "tuberculosis of heart and
right lung", informant: Flora Miller (Butler), died:
11 Feb 1926, record (1926) #: 3548.

Anna Ruth ANDERSON, born: 5 Oct 1925, parents: J.S.
Anderson and Alice Moorley, cause of death: "broncho
pneumonia fever", informant: J.S. Anderson (Butler),
buried: Sugar Grove Cemetery, died: 19 Feb 1926,
record (1926) #: 3549.

Matncia Christina HODGE, age 46 years, single,
parents: T.C. Hodge (NC) and Penina Riner (NC), cause
of death: "ovarian cyst", informant: T.C. Hodge
(Crandull), buried: Blevins Cemetery, died: 4 Feb
1926, record (1926) #: 3550.

Penina HODGE, age 70 years, born in North Carolina,
married, parents: D. Riner (NC) and mother's name
unknown, cause of death: "pulmonary tuberculosis",
informant: T.C. Hodge (Crandull), buried: Blevins
Cemetery, died: 9 Feb 1926, record (1926) #: 3551.

Mary A. MCQUEEN, born: 10 Aug 1845, widow, parents:
William Cornett (Grayson Co. VA), and Pauline Reece
(Ashe Co. NC), cause of death: "valvular heart
disease", informant: E.C. McQueen (Mountain City),
buried: Wills Cemetery, died: 29 Mar 1926, record
(1926) #: 6556.

Duffey William MILAN, born: 7 Dec 1925, parents:
Tilden Milan (NC) and Mae Ray, cause of death:
"broncho pneumonia", informant: Emmett Wilson (Laurel
Bloomery), buried: Valley Cemetery, died: 23 Mar 1926.

Euerua Morefield JENKINS, age 70 years, widow, parents: Vincen R. Morefield and mother's name unknown, cause of death: "broncho pneumonia", informant: R.L. Jenkins, buried: Jenkins Cemetery, died: 5 Mar 1926, record (1926) #: 6558.

Elizabeth DAVENPORT, born: 14 Aug 1821 (age 104 years, 7 months and 14 days), born at Ashe Co., North Carolina, widow, parents: Jeremiah Osborn (Ashe Co. NC) and Christine Graybeal (Ashe Co. NC), informant: E. Johnson (Shouns), buried: Farmers Cemetery, died: 28 Mar 1926, record (1926) #: 6559.

Goldie Agnes DUNN, born: 30 Oct 1925, parents: Denney Dunn and Effie Reece, cause of death: "broncho pneumonia", informant: Denney Dunn (Shouns), died: 3 Mar 1926, record (1926) #: 6560.

Harret E. SLIMP, born: 11 Mar 1843, parents: Abraham Nave and Sallie Wilson, cause of death: "disease of heart", informant: J.E. Slimp (Shouns), died: 11 Mar 1925 (note: record shows year as 1925 although filed in 1926 records), record (1926) #: 6561.

John A. PRICE, born: 15 Sep 1842, married, parents: Mansfield Price and Rebecca Hawkins, death cause: "chronic intestinal nephritis", informant: R.C. Morefield, died: 11 Feb 1926, record (1926) #: 6562.

Thomas DOWELL, born: 14 Jan 1871, parents: Thomas Potter and Linza Dowell (NC), cause of death: "organic heart disease", informant: Thomas Dowell (Shouns), died: 14 Feb 1926, record (1926) #: 6563.

Stacy PHIPPS, born: 11 Apr 1904, parents: John Phipps (NC) and Alice Eggers, cause of death: "tuberculosis", died: 22 Feb 1926, record (1926) #: 6564.

Dora HUFFMAN, born: 22 Feb 1926, parents: Jessie Huffman and Jane Proffitt, cause of death: not stated, informant: John Tester (Neva), died: 24 Feb 1926, record (1926) #: 6565.

Nancy DUGGER, born: 25 Mar 1855, widow, parents: A. Bert Greenwell and Mary Cable, cause of death: "pulmonary tuberculosis" informant: Frank Dugger (Butler), buried: Wolf Cemetery, died: 25 Mar 1926, record (1926) #: 6566.

Cinda RAMBO, born: Sep 1845, age 81 years, widow, parents: Joseph Robinson and Katie Razor, cause of death: "regurgitation of heart", informant: G.A. Stout (Mountain City), buried: Brookshire Cemetery, died: 27 Mar 1926, record (1926) #: 6567.

Jack Thomas SCHWER, born: 1 Mar 1926, parents: C.L. Schwer and Willie Hawks (NC), cause of death: "premature birth, 7 months", informant: R.E. Hawks (Crandull), died: 3 Mar 1926, record (1926) #: 2568.

Frances Angel E. MILLER, born: 23 Sep 1925, parents:
F.R. Miller and Laura E. Williams, cause of death:
"flue", informant: W.F. Williams (Mountain City),
buried: Gentry Cemetery, died: 11 Mar 1926, record
(1926) #: 6569.

Elizabeth GARLAND, age 82 years, widow, parents: "not
known", cause of death: "exoplesmic goiter, old age",
informant: B.J. Blevins (Crandull), buried: Blevins
Cemetery, died: 26 Mar 1926, record (1926) #: 6560.

Virginia Louise WILSON, born: 27 Feb 1926, parents:
Kemp Wilson and Cora Miller, death cause: not stated,
informant: Kemp Wilson (Trade), buried: Zionville, NC,
died: 4 Mar 1926, record (1926) #: 6571.

William Hobart MCELYEA, born: 26 Dec 1925, parents:
Robert McElyea and Mary Proffitt, cause of death:
"broncho pneumonia", informant: L.H. McElyea (Mountain
City), buried: Shingletown Cemetery, died: 10 Apr
1926, record (1926) #: 9543.

David CRESS, age 74 years, single, parents: William
Cress and (mother's first name not stated) Elliott
(VA), cause of death: "cancer liver", informant: Jno
K. Wilson (Mountian City), buried: Mountain View
Cemetery, died: 30 Apr 1926, record (1926) #: 9544.

Emma WILCOX, born: 27 Jun 1858, married, parents:
Jonse Potter and Susie Mains, cause of death:
"cerebral hemorrhage", informant: W.M. Wilcox
(Shouns), died: 19 Apr 1926, record (1926) #: 9545.

Mrs. Nannie GENTRY, age between 68 and 70 years,
married, parents names not stated, cause of death:
"chronic brights disease", informant: Isaac Gentry
(Mountain City), buried: Phillippi Cemetery, died: 16
Apr 1926, record (1926) #: 9546.

Mrs. Rose B. WILLIAMS, age 52 years, 8 months and 27
days, born in Virginia, parents: Antonio Dopralo
(Italy) and Martha Saly (VA), cause of death: "auqina
pectoras", informant: Nellie Gray Williams (Mountain
City), buried: Bristol, VA, died: 13 Apr 1926, record
(1926) #: 9547.

Infant ASBURY, male, parents: Robert Asbury and Adrian
Owens (VA), cause of death: "premature birth", buried:
Phillippi Cemetery, born/died: 4 Apr 1926, record
(1926) #: 9548.

Emes HALL, female, born: 29 Jul 1887, married,
parents: Maurice Curd and Fanny Eastridge, cause of
death: "pneumonia fever", informant: C.H. Hall
(Shouns), buried: Hall Cemetery, died: 21 Apr 1926,
record (1926) #: 9549.

Infant HICKS, female, parents: Jos R. Hicks (VA) and Rose E. Shull, death cause: "traumitism incident to delivery, broken femur, etc", informant: Jos R. Hicks (Bakers Gap), died: 13 Mar 1926, record (1926) #: 9550.

Mary Dove (Hazlewood) GRAYBEAL, born: 6 Mar 1896 at Carter Co. TN, married, parents: Pleasant Hazlewood (Patrick Co. VA) and Nancy S. Smith, cause of death: "tumor of brain", informant: L.B. Graybeal (Mountain City), buried: Butler, TN, died: 23 Apr 1926, record (1926) #: 9551.

Elizabeth ARNOLD, born: 8 Nov 1857, married, parents: Nick Robinson and Mary Howard, cause of death: "chronic diarrhea", informant: J.H. Arnold (Butler), buried: Arnold Cemetery, died: 8 Apr 1926, record (1926) #: 9552.

Cresia PROFFITT, age about 70 years, born in North Carolina, parents: father's name unknown and Huldah Tanner (NC), cause of death: "cancer of nose", informant: Lydia Proffitt (Doeville), buried: Proffitt Cemetery, died: 22 Apr 1926, record (1926) #: 9553.

Myrtle SHUPE, born: 21 Mar 1926, parents: Tracy Shupe and mother's name illegible, cause of death: "broncho pneumonia", buried: Wilson Cemetery, died: 7 Apr 1926, record (1926) #: 9554.

Samuel TILLEY, born: 9 Oct 1838 in North Carolina, married, parents: J.H. Tilley (NC) and Cynthia Moore (NC), cause of death: "old age and fall which fractured femur", informant: Martha Tilley (Mountain City), died: 24 Apr 1926, record (1926) #: 9555.

Agnes Mae HODGE, born: 28 May 1924 in Virginia, parents: C.N. Hodge (NC) and Anna Roark (NC), cause of death: "pneumonia broncho", informant: Thos Hodge (Crandull), buried: Blevins Cemetery, died: 2 Apr 1926, record (1926) #: 9556.

Franklin L. WALLACE, born: 22 Jun 1870, married, parents: George W. Wallace and Mary Stephens (NC), cause of death: "tuberculosis, epilepsy", informant: Forest Reece (Trade), buried: Wallace Cemetery, died: 24 Apr 1926, record (1926) #: 9557.

Fay Lucile DAVIS, parents: W.E. Davis (NC) and Cora Jane Brown (NC), cause of death: "acute pulmonary congestion", informant: W.E. Davis (Shouns), buried: Davis Cemetery, born/died: 18 May 1926, record (1926) #: 12107.

Gladys M. DUNN, born: 12 May 1926, parents: J.G. Dunn and Susan Main, cause of death: "unknown", informant: J.G. Dunn (Shouns), buried: McEwen Cemetery, died: 21 May 1926, record (1926) #: 12108.

Lydia SHOUN, age about 65 years, born in North Carolina, parents: Thomas Stout and Lizzie Potter, cause of death: "brights disease", informant: J.G. Shoun (Shouns), buried: Osborn Cemetery, died: 26 Apr 1926, record (1926) #: 12109.

Thomas L. WAGNER, born: 10 Nov 1853, married, parents: Nathaniel T. Wagner and Elizabeth Baker, cause of death: "influenza", informant: J.J. Davis (Vaughtsville), died: 30 May 1926, record (1926) #: 12110.

Mary GRINDSTAFF, born: 12 Sep 1849, age 76 years, 8 months and 7 days, parents: Morgan Swift and Sallie Cable, death cause: "died a natural death, cause unknown", informant: D.V. Grindstaff, buried: Fletcher Cem, died: 19 May 1926, record (1926) #: 12111.

Eula Elizabeth SHUPE, born: 31 Mar 1926, parents: Sherman Shupe and Emma Laws, cause of death: "pneumonia", buried: Wilson Cemetery, died: 26 Apr 1926, record (1926) #: 12112.

Alexander WALLACE, born in 1840, age 86 years, parents: Drewery Wallace (VA) and Elizabeth Snyder, cause of death: not stated, informant: Roby Wallace (Trade), buried: Wallace Cemetery, died: 7 May 1926, record (1926) #: 12113.

William JOHNSON, age 60 years, born at Wilkes Co. NC, married, parents: John Johnson (Wilkes Co. NC) and Susa Shoe (Wilkes Co. NC), cause of death: "pulmonary tuberculosis", informant: Robert Johnson (Trade), buried: Potter Cemetery in North Carolina, died: 3 May 1926, record (1926) #: 12114.

Margaret DUGGER, born: 17 Aug 1854, widow, parents: William Vines and Malvina Dugger, cause of death: "erysiplas", informant: Clayton Dugger (Butler), died: 4 May 1926, record (1926) #: 12115.

Mrs. Minnie DOSS, age about 40 years, born in Virginia, married, parents: not stated, cause of death: "accidentally killed in automobile wreck", informant: W.L. Greene, buried at Damascus, VA, died: 21 Jun 1926, record (1926) #: 14524.

Marcus Clay LUTTRELL, born: 30 Oct 1852, married, parents: Richard H. Luttrell (VA) and Mary Ann Treadway, cause of death: "apoplexy", informant: Mrs. M.C. Luttrell (Mountain City), died: 29 Jun 1926, record (1926) #: 14525.

Cintha VANOVER, born: 23 Jan 1848 in Georgia, widow, parents: Samuel Martin (VA) and (mother's first name not stated) Ledford (GA), cause of death: "broncho pneumonia", informant: R.J. Dunn (Shouns), Dunn Cemetery, died: 27 Jun 1926, record (1926) #: 14526.

Mary E. WALKER, born: 16 Dec 1839, age 86 years, 5 months and 26 days, widow, parents: John Campbell (NC) and mother's name not known, cause of death: "old age, lobar pneumonia", informant: J.C. Walker (Doeville), buried: Campbell Cemetery, died: 12 Jun 1926, record (1926) #: 14527.

Joseph L. CAMPBELL, born: 11 Jun 1844, married, parents: John Campbell and mother's name not known, cause of death: "chronic bronchitis", informant: Garret Phipps (Doeville), buried: Campbell Cemetery, died: 18 Jun 1926, record (1926) #: 14528.

Louzana SIMCOX, born: 1 Aug 1854 at Ashe Co. NC, married, parents: Louis Brown (Ashe Co. NC) and Betsy Osborn (Ashe Co. NC), cause of death: "organic heart disease", informant: O.P. Simcox (Butler), died: 20 Jun 1926, record (1926) #: 14529.

Goldie Viletie BENTLEY, born: 28 Mar 1912, parents: J.M. Bentley and M.B. Rankins, cause of death: "organic heart disease", informant: J.M. Bentley (Crandull), buried: Gentry Cemetery, died: 3 Jun 1926, record (1926) #: 14530.

Hairl JONES, parents: Frank Jones (NC) and Lockie Roark (NC), cause of death: "premature birth", informant: T.D. Roark (Crandull), buried: Hawk Cemetery, born/died: 10 Jun 1926, record (1926) #: 14531 (twins record below).

Carl JONES, parents: Frank Jones (NC) and Lockie Roark (NC), cause of death: "premature birth", informant: T.D. Roark (Crandull), buried: Hawk Cemetery, born/died: 10 Jun 1926, record (1926) #: 14532 (twins record above).

Lear Ellen LEWIS, born: 27 Oct 1867, married, parents: Rufus May and Annie Norris, cause of death: "spasmodic asthma", informant: G.W. Lewis (Crandull), buried: Blevins Cemetery, died: 27 Jun 1926.

Alexander GENTRY, age 71 years, 10 months and 24 days, married, parents: Oliver Gentry and mother's name not stated, cause of death: "cardiac .... (illegible)", informant: Clide Gentry (Laurel Bloomery), buried: Valley Cemetery, died: 4 Jul 1926, record (1926) #: 17062.

Mary Lee REYNOLDS, born: 7 Jun 1926, parents: Edward Reynolds and Fannie Byars, cause of death: "cholera", buried: Donnelly Cemetery, died: 13 Jul 1926, record (1926) #: 17063.

C. Ross CAUDILL, age 62 years, born in North Carolina, parents: unknown, cause of death: "peutauetis", informant: J.A. Gilbert (Laurel Bloomery), buried: Valley Cem, died: 7 Jun 1926, record (1926) #: 17064.

Burl HAYWORTH, born: 24 Jun 1926 at Ashe Co. NC, parents: Ed Hayworth and Nora Jones (Ashe Co. NC), cause of death: "unknown", informant: Melvin Jones (Shouns), buried: West Cemetery, died: 24 Jul 1926, record (1926) #: 17065.

Margaret Marie GREER, born: 27 Dec 1920, parents: Lee Greer (NC) and Mamie Millhorn, cause of death: "spinal meningitis", informant: Lee Greer, buried: Neva, TN, died: 18 Jul 1926, record (1926) #: 17066.

Infant THOMPSON, female, parents: Jessie D. Thompson and Retta Dugger, cause of death: "premature birth", born/died: 11 Jul 1926, record (1926) #: 17067.

Delace GUY, male, born: 7 Feb 1921, parents: Henry Guy (NC) and Lona Dugger, cause of death: "spinal meningitis", informant: Henry Guy (Butler), buried: Dugger Cem, died: 17 Jul 1926, record (1926) #: 17068.

William DUNN, born: 3 Aug 1844, married, parents: Henry Dunn and Mary Mink, cause of death: "chronic heart disease", informant: C.C. Dunn (Shouns), died: 12 Aug 1926, record (1926) #: 19640.

Alice SHUPE, born: 15 Feb 1874, married, parents: William Johnson and Elizabeth Shupe, cause of death: "pulmonary tuberculosis", informant: James Shupe (Mountain City), buried: Phillippi Cemetery, died: 12 Aug 1926, record (1926) #: 19641.

Ada PROFFITT, age 46 years, married, parents: John Howard and Ida Johnson, cause of death: "chronic brights disease", informant: D.P. Proffitt (Shouns), buried: Mountain View Cemetery, died: 8 Jul 1926, record (1926) #: 19642.

Nellie Orpha DOWELL, born: 2 Aug 1904, single, parents: J.M. Dowell and Elizabeth Wilson, cause of death: "typhoid fever", informant: J.M. Dowell (Shouns), buried: Dowell Cemetery, died: 7 Aug 1926, record (1926) #: 19643.

Sarah LIPFORD, age about 50 years, married, parents: G.W. May and Martha Alford (NC), cause of death: "acute nephritis", informant: Clinton Lipford, Martin Cemetery, died: 18 Aug 1926, record (1926) #: 19644.

Hesikia PRICE, born: 6 Mar 1839 in North Carolina, widower, parents: Jessie Price (NC) and Nancy Cornett (NC), cause of death: "old age", informant: James Price (Shouns), buried: Price Cem, died: 27 Aug 1926.

William EASTRIDGE, age about 32 years, born at Ashe Co. NC, married, parents: William Wishon (Ashe Co. NC) and Mandy Eastridge (Ashe Co. NC), cause of death: "accidental by falling limb while cutting timber", informant: Eula Eastridge (Shouns), buried: Curd Cemetery, died: 27 Aug 1926, record (1926) #: 19636.

Elizabeth PROFFITT, born: 15 Feb 1855, married, parents: I.E. Wilson and Jane Crosswhite, cause of death: "tuberculosis of bowels", died: 1 Aug 1926, record (1926) #: 19647.

Mrs. Mary HEATON, age 73 years, widow, parents: Wiley Dillon (NC) and mother's name not stated, cause of death: "chronic nephritis", informant: C.F. Heaton (Mountain City), buried: Shoun Cemetery, died: 17 Aug 1926, record (1926) #: 19648.

Arley WILLIAMS, age 20 years, born in North Carolina, single, parents: T.H. Williams (NC) and Liza Henson (NC), cause of death: "automobile accident", buried in North Carolina, died: 8 Aug 1926, record (1926) #: 19649.

Everett Willard RUFARD, born: 19 May 1921, parents: Carson Rufard and Rosa Farris, cause of death: "diptheria", informant: W.R. Rufard (Laurel Bloomery), buried: Waters Cemetery, died: 24 Sep 1926, record (1926) #: 22040.

Ed ROBERTS, born: 12 Mar 1875, married, parents: John M. Roberts and Catherine Phillippi (VA), cause of death: "homrcide, shot with revolver", informant: Mary Jane Roberts (Mountain City), buried: Wright Cemetery, died: 7 Aug 1926, record (1926) #: 22041.

Benjamin F. OSBORN, age 71 years, born: 1858 in North Carolina, parents: "not known", cause of death: "cancer bladder", buried: Zionville, NC, died: 19 Sep 1926, record (1926) #: 22042.

Joseph Washington HODGE, born: 12 Jan 1849 in North Carolina, married, parents: Samuel Hodge (NC) and Freelove Mullins, cause of death: "aneurysm of right common femoral artery", informant: A.L. Hodge (Shouns), died: 2 Oct 1926, record (1926) #: 24534.

John Samick HODGE, born: 16 Dec 1878, married, parents: J.W. Hodge and Mary Main, cause of death: "broncho pneumonia", informant: W.A. Potter (Shouns), died: 7 Oct 1926, record (1926) #: 24535.

Martin NEWMAN, age 64 years, married, parents: "unknown", cause of death: "chronic nephritis", informant: Mack Phillippi (Mountain City), died: 8 Oct 1926, record (1926) #: 24536.

Christenia JOHNSON, born: 4 Mar 1858 at Ashe County, NC., married, parents: James Davenport (Ashe Co. NC) and Elizabeth Osborn (Ashe Co. NC), cause of death: "brights disease", informant: E.M. Johnson (Shouns), buried: Farmer Cemetery, died: 8 Sep 1926, record (1926) #: 24537.

Jenie ROARK, born: 26 Aug 1862 in North Carolina, married, parents: Wesley Phillips (NC) and Mary Phillips (NC), cause of death: "meningitis", informant: J.C. Roark (Trade), buried: Arnold Cemetery, died: 21 Sep 1926, record (1926) #: 24538.

Ula Ethel BLEVINS, born: 13 Sep 1898, single, parents: Andrew Johnson Blevins and Laura Alice Blevins, cause of death: "pulmonary tuberculosis", informant: Laura Alice Blevins (Crandull), buried: Blevins Cemetery, died: 26 Oct 1926, record (1926) #: 24539.

Sarah MILLER, born: Dec 1874 in North Carolina, married, parents: W.W. Isenhour (NC) and Jemima Dockery (NC), cause of death: "cerebral hemorage", informant: P.J. Miller (Trade), buried: Zionville, NC, died: 23 Oct 1926, record (1926) #: 24540.

Robert H. FARTHING, age about 85 years, widower, born in North Carolina, parents: "unknown", cause of death: "apoplexy", informant: Henry Younce (Butler), buried: Meadows Cemetery, died: 31 Oct 1926, record (1926) #: 24541.

Nancy POTTER, born: 7 May 1860, married, parents: Alex Wilson (NC) and Elizabeth Stout (NC), cause of death: "chronic intestinal nephritis", informant: C.R. Potter (Shouns), died: 18 Nov 1926, record (1926) #: 26908.

Callie Virginia PENNINGTON, born: 21 Aug 1926, parents: Claude Pennington (NC) and Callie Nichols (NC), cause of death: "lobar pneumonia", informant: Claude Pennington (Mountain City), died: 28 Aug 1926, record (1926) #: 26909.

Mrs. Callie Nichols PENNINGTON, born: 2 Apr 1882 in North Carolina, parents: Reuben Nichols and Rebecca Tribble (NC), cause of death: illegible (possibly childbirth), inforamant: Claude Pennington, died: 21 Aug 1926, record (1926) #: 26910.

Ida PROFFITT, born: 29 Jul 1877, married, parents: John Howard and Mary E. Greer, cause of death: "brights disease", informant: D.D.F. Proffitt (Shouns), died: 11 Jul 1926, record (1926) #: 26911.

Joe B. LAWS, born: 2 Oct 1880, married, parents: Isaac Laws and Jonnie Greenwell, cause of death: "heart block", informant: Silas Laws (Neva), died: 8 Nov 1926, record (1926) #: 26912.

Margaret FARMER, born: 12 Nov 1858 in North Carolina, married, parents: Wm E. Trivett and mother's name not known, cause of death: "disease of heart with dropsy", informant: L.L. Stout (Bakers Gap), buried: Neva, died: 21 Oct 1926, record (1926) #: 26913.

Delma Joe LUNSFORD, born: 19 May 1926, parents: Aud
Lunsford and Lilly Ward, cause of death: not stated,
informant: Joe Lunsford (Butler), buried: Neva, died:
20 May 1926, record (1926) #: 26914.

J.G. CHURCH, age about 48 years, married, parents:
father's name not known and Rebecca Church, cause of
death: "tuberculosis", informant: R.B. Pleasant
(Doeville), buried: Church Cemetery, died: 8 Nov 1926,
record (1926) #: 26915.

Garfield LAWS, born: 30 Jul 1926, parents: James G.
Laws and Malinda Laws, cause of death: "unknown",
informant: James G. Laws (Butler), buried: Dry Run,
died: 12 Nov 1926, record (1926) #: 26916.

Gina Kate MCELYEA, born: 6 Apr 1924, parents: John T.
McElyea and Jane Proffitt, cause of death:
"tuberculosis", informant: John T. McElyea (Butler),
buried: Dry Run, died: 14 Nov 1926, record (1926) #:
26917.

Marie WATSON, born: 19 Oct 1922 in North Carolina,
parents: Dean Watson and Doxie Reece (NC), cause of
death: "broncho pneumonia fever", buried: Dugger
Cemetery, died: 19 Nov 1926, record (1926) #: 26918.

Doxie Reece WATSON, born: 8 Apr 1899 in North
Carolina, married, parents: Jas Reece (NC) and Sis
Trivett (NC), cause of death: "broncho pnuemonia and
heart lison", died: 23 Nov 1926, record (1926) #:
26919.

Joseph Harold ISAACS, born: 19 Jan 1925, parents: Joe
Isaacs and Crete McElyea, cause of death: "pneumonia
and lock bowls", informant: Joe Isaacs (Butler), died:
25 Oct 1926, record (1926) #: 26920.

Berryman BLEVINS, born: 27 Nov 1845, married, parents:
Matthew Blevins and Eliza Berry, cause of death:
"cancer of rectum and bladder", buried: Blevins
Cemetery, died: 2 Nov 1926, record (1926) #: 26921.

William H. HEABERLIN, born: 24 Oct 1852, parents: Joel
Heaberlin (NC) and Lucinda Blevins, cause of death:
"organic heart leison", informant: Lillie Gentry
(Crandull), buried: Heaberlin Cemetery, died: 24 Nov
1926, record (1926) #: 26922.

Elbert Daniel HENDERSON, born: 14 Sep 1920, parents:
Thos Henderson (NC) and Tessy Hamm (VA), cause of
death: "burned from clothes catching fire at open
flame", informant: Maggie Henderson (Damascus, VA),
buried: Mock Cemetery, died: 23 Nov 1926, record
(1926) #: 29515.

Mollie EASTRIDGE, age about 59 years, married, parents: Alex Osborn (Ashe Co. NC) and Annah Cole (Ashe Co. NC), cause of death: "chronic myocoridal disease", informant: Nola Curd (Shouns), buried: Payne Cemetery, born: 28 Dec 1926, record (1926) #: 29516.

Amanda Emeline STOUT, born: 23 May 1848, parents: John Bailey (GA) and Polly Slimp, cause of death: "lobar pneumonia", informant: L.L. Stout (Bakers Gap), buried: Neva, died: 26 Nov 1926, record (1926) #: 29517.

James S. SMITH, age 73 years, married, parents: James Smith and mother's name not known, cause of death: "pneumonia fever", informant: Mrs. J.S. Smith (Doeville), died: 16 Dec 1926.

Mary Altine NORRIS, born: 22 Mar 1926, parents: Red Norris and T.L. Morely, cause of death: "catarehl larangitis", informant: R.A. Norris (Doeville), buried: Norris Cemetery, died: 30 Dec 1926, record (1926) #: 29519.

Alexander A. BARRY, born: 4 Nov 1849, married, parents: William Barry and Sarah Dotson, cause of death: "chronic brights disease", informant: Hugh Barry (Mountain City), buried: Wilson Cemetery, died: 15 Dec 1926, record (1926) #: 29520.

Pearl ARNETT, born: 5 May 1905, widow, parents: L.W. Pennington and Alice Johnson (NC), cause of death: "pulmonary tuberculosis", informant: C.C. Blevins (Crandull), buried: Woods Cemetery, died: 10 Dec 1926, record (1926) #: 29521.

William Clyde EGGERS, born: 16 Sep 1914, parents: James G. Eggers and Callie Main, cause of death: "rhumatic fever, chronic valvuler heart disease", informant: James G. Eggers (Trade), buried: Reece Cemetery, died: 11 Dec 1926, record (1926) #: 29522.

Ezra Oliver ANDERSON, age 71 years, widower, parents: John Anderson and Mary Dugger, cause of death: "broncho pneumonia", buried: Sugar Grove Cemetery, died: 10 Dec 1926, record (1926) #: 29523.

Grizzy Ann HARMON, born: 20 Jul 1856 at Watauga Co. NC, widow, parents: Dudley Glenn (NC) and Elizabeth Ward (NC), cause of death: "apoplexy", informant: Harry Farthing (Butler), buried: Buck Creek, NC, died: 14 Dec 1926, record (1926) #: 29524.

Robert H. FARTHING, age about 85 years, born in North Carolina, parents: "unknown", cause of death: "apoplexy", informant: Henry Younce (Butler), buried: Meadows Cemetery, died: 31 Oct 1926, record (1926) #: 29525.

Nannie BROWN, age about 80 years, a patient at the county farm, parents: "unknown", cause of death: "unknown", died: 7 Oct 1926, record (1926) #: 31185.

David Marion FRITTS, born: 10 Nov 1844, widower, parents: Reuben Fritts and Uriah Cress, cause of death: "chronic nephritis", informant: W.T. Heck (Mountain City), died: 15 Dec 1926, record (1926) #: 31186.

James R. GENTRY, born: 5 Nov 1843, married, parents: Philip Gentry (NC) and Hester Cable, cause of death: "died a natural death", informant: R.J. Allen (Butler), buried: Gentry Cemetery, died: 15 Jan 1927, record (1927) #: 1026.

Lillie Wagner LOWE, born: 20 Aug 1906, married, parents: Elbert Wagner and Alice Grindstaff, cause of death: "typhoid fever", informant: Frank Grindstaff (Butler), died: 5 Jan 1927, record (1927) #: 1027.

Juila ATWOOD, born: 21 Oct 1892, married, parents: Matison Brewer and Mary Reece (NC), cause of death: illegible, informant: Pearl Atwood (Butler), buried: Dugger Cemetery, died: 30 Jan 1927, record (1927) #: 1028.

Caleb LOWE, born: 1 Jul 1852, married, parents: Abraham Lowe and Cynthia Moore (NC), cause of death: "locomotor atascia, brights", informant: Kemp Lowe (Mountain City), buried: Lowe Cemetery, died: 4 Jan 1927, record (1927) #: 1029.

Hannah ROBINSON, age: "supposed to be about 95 years", single, parents: father's name unknown and Cate Robinson, cause of death: "died a natural death", informant: Alexander Robinson, buried: Robinson Cemetery, died: 18 Jan 1927.

Lonnie HARMON, age 4 years, parents: M.L. Harmon and Zena Ward (NC), cause of death: croup, buried: Meadows Cemetery, died: 18 Jan 1927, record (1927) #: 1031.

Infant DUNN, female, born: 22 Jan 1927, parents: father not stated and Pearl Dunn, cause of death: "broncho pneumonia", informant: L.F. Thomas (Mountain City), died: 11 Feb 1927, record (1927) #: 3274.

Eva Bernice SHOUN, born: 18 Feb 1903, parents: M.L. Shoun and Mary J. Dougherty, cause of death: "pulmonary tuberculosis", informant: M.L. Shoun (Mountain City), died: 16 Jan 1927, record (1927) #: 3275.

Irene Louise PHILLIPS, born: 3 Nov 1926, parents: Lee Phillips (NC) and Sallie South (NC), cause of death: "broncho pneumonia", informant: Lee Phillips (Mountain City), buried: Phillippi Cemetery, died: 30 Jan 1927, record (1927) #: 3276.

Martha MAINS, age about 66 years, widow, born at Wilkes Co. NC, parents: John L. Church (Wilkes Co. NC) and Nancy Walters (Wilkes Co. NC), cause of death: "long continued paralysis", informant: C.H. Hall (Shouns), buried: Mains Cemetery, died: 15 Feb 1927, record (1927) #: 3277.

D. Franklin GRINDSTAFF, born: 14 Sep 1925, parents: Hugh M. Grindstaff and Lillie Gilbert, cause of death: "charbris infantum", informant: Hugh M. Grindstaff (Butler), died: 7 Feb 1927, record (1927) #: 3278.

John Franklin GOODWIN, born: 8 Nov 1849 in Carter Co. TN, parents: Alen Goodwin (Carter Co. TN) and Raley Heaton, cause of death: "heart disease", buried: Cobbs Creek Cemetery, died: 7 Feb 1927, record (1927) #: 3279.

Iamtha Sophie LOYD, born: 17 Jan 1844, married, parents: Suirth Neeley and (mother's first name not stated) Bridges, cause of death: "chronic myocardiri", informant: T. Loyd (Mountain City), died: 15 Feb 1927, record (1927) #: 3280.

Eliza NUTTER, born: 21 May 1841 in Virginia, widow, parents: Robert Smith (VA) and Sarah Taylor (VA), cause of death: "organic heart disease", informant: Zalie Minton (Crandull), buried: Blevins Cemetery, died: 14 Feb 1927, record (1927) #: 3281.

Jane REYNOLDS, born: 16 Dec 1841, married, parents: Thomas Greer and Mary Arter (VA), cause of death: "cerebral hemorhage", informant: S.B. Greer (Laurel Bloomery), buried: Gentry Cemetery, died: 31 Mar 1927, record (1927) #: 5530.

Gladis Kathleen BURTON, born: 26 Dec 1926, parents: Martin Burton (West, VA) and (first name illegible) Gentry, cause of death: "lobar pneumonia", informant: Scott Gentry (Mountain City), buried: Gentry Cemetery, died: 9 Mar 1927, record (1927) #: 5531.

Richard Baxter GENTRY, born: 28 May 1886, married, parents: Marion Gentry and Elva Gilbert, cause of death: "chronic endocarditis", informant: Marion Gentry (Laurel Bloomery), buried: Valley Cemetery, died: 17 Mar 1927, record (1927) #: 5532.

Ray Devner JORDAN, born: 15 Mar 1927, parents: J.W. Jordan and Vadie Robinson, cause of death: "premature birth weakness", died: 28 Mar 1927, record (1927) #: 5533.

Roxie GENTRY, born: 17 Feb 1897, married, parents: Alex Barry and Naomi Harper, cause of death: "tuberculosis", informant: John Gentry (Mountain City), died: 22 Mar 1927, record (1927) #: 5534.

Infant PROFFITT, male, parents: Stacy Proffitt and Pearl South, cause of death: "premature birth", born/died: 18 Mar 1927, record (1927) #: 5535. (twin below)

Infant PROFFITT, male, parents: Stacy Proffitt and Pearl South, cause of death: "premature birth", born/died: 18 Mar 1927, record (1927) #: 5536. (twin above)

Jessie Jenkins WILSON, female, age 39 years, married, parents: Jessie Jenkins and Marilda Stout, cause of death: "apoplexy", buried: Wilson Cemetery, died: 5 Mar 1927, record (1927) #: 5537.

Orlie ESTES, age 27 years, born in Virginia, single, parents: Jeff Estes (VA) and Lydia Blevins (VA), cause of death: "pulmonary tuberculosis", buried: Gentry Cemetery, died: 7 Mar 1927, record (1927) #: 5538.

Mary GREEN, age 70 years, married, parents: David Bumgardner (NC) and Caroline Snyder, cause of death: "apoplexy", informant: Millard Bumgardner (Trade), buried: Zionville, NC, died: 13 Mar 1927, record (1927) #: 5539.

Lachanah T. JOHNSON, born: 21 Apr 1853 in North Carolina, married, parents: Camel Johnson (NC) and Katy Baker (NC), cause of death: "chronic heart disease", informant: Maggie Johnson (Ashland, NC), buried: Trade, TN, died: 26 Mar 1927, record (1927) #: 5540.

Joel EASTRIDGE, born: 30 Mar 1837 in North Carolina, widower, parents: Pleasant Eastridge (NC) and Phoeba Graybeal (NC), cause of death: "apoplexy", informant: Phoeba Graybeal Jenkins (Mountain City), died: 7 Apr 1927, record (1927) #: 7989.

Catherine M. HOWELL, born: 3 Jan 1847 in North Carolina, widow, parents: Stephen Williams (NC) and Mary Grimsley (NC), cause of death: "broncho pneumonia", informant: Joe Williams (Shouns), buried: Arnold Cemetery, died: 3 Apr 1927, record (1927) #: 7990.

Texis MARTIN, female, born: 15 Mar 1910, parents: G.W. Martin and Rebecca L. Smith, cause of death: "typhoid fever", informant: G.W. Martin (Shouns), buried: Martin Cemetery, died: 11 Apr 1927, record (1927) #: 7991.

Gurnie Edward ROARK, born: 31 Jan 1927, parents: McKinley Roark and Elsie Vanover (NC), cause of death: "broncho pneumonia", informant: McKinley Roark (Shouns), buried: Arnold Cemetery, died: 14 Apr 1927, record (1927) #: 7992.

Harriett Lucindy STEWART, born: 15 Nov 1856 in North Carolina, widow, parents: Andy Jones (NC) and Mary Andrews (NC), cause of death: "influenza, broncho pneumonia", informant: W.C. Stewart, buried: Arnold Cemetery, died: 15 Apr 1927, record (1927) #: 7993.

Jarrett A. PHILLIPS, born: 22 Oct 1858, married, parents: John Phillips and Rachel Arnold, cause of death: "pellagra", informant: John Phillips (Shouns), buried: Arnold Cemetery, died: 28 Apr 1927, record (1927) #: 7994.

Leah Norris GREER, born: 16 Sep 1846 at Watauga Co. NC, widow, parents: Jim Norris (Watauga Co. NC) and Ruth Lunceford (Watauga Co. NC), cause of death: "suposed organic heart disease", informant: Robert M. Devalut (Butler), died: 9 Mar 1927, record (1927) #: 7995.

Lairinda ALLEN, born: 27 Mar 1863, married, parents: Frank Howard and Elva Shoun, cause of death: "flue", informant: R.G. Allen (Butler), buried: Rambo Cemetery, died: 26 Apr 1927, record (1927) #: 7996.

Infant FORRESTER, male, parents: Luther Forrester and C..(illegible) Morefield, cause of death: not stated, born/died: 5 Mary 1927, record (1927) #: 10530.

Noah Williams JENKINS, born: 2 Mar 1875, married, parents: Jessie C. Jenkins and Nanlda Elizabeth Stout, cause of death: "lobar pneumonia", informant: Roy Johnson (Trade), died: 1 May 1927, record (1927) #: 10531.

James C. DONNELLY, born: 20 Oct 1839, married, parents: William Donnelly and Sallie McQueen, cause of death: "lobar pneumonia", informant: Alice Donnelly (Mountain City), died: 24 May 1927, record (1927) #: 10532.

B. Carroll HOWARD, born: 4 May 1924, parents: Dave Howard and Susan Potter, cause of death: "broncho pneumonia", informant: Dave Howard (Shouns), buried: Potter Cemetery, died: 6 Mar 1927, record (1927) #: 10533.

David Smith EASTRIDGE, born: 7 May 1875, married, parents: Barnabas Eastridge and Rebecca Payne, cause of death: "acute intestinal (rest illegible)", buried: Eastridge Cemetery, died: 19 May 1927, record (1927) #: 10534.

Sarah Fine GRINDSTAFF, born: 21 Jan 1863, married, parents: George Stout and mother not stated, cause of death: "myocardites of heart", informant: John Grindstaff (Butler), died: 11 May 1927, record (1927) #: 10535.

Ruben SWINEY, born: 20 Jun 1907, single, parents: J.C. Swiney and Mary Estep, cause of death: "tuberculosis of lungs", informant: Sam Garland (Doeville), Campbell Cem, died: 15 May 1927, record (1927) #: 10536.

Stacy BROWN, born: 10 Apr 1902, married, parents: John Brown (NC) and McKinsey Hayworth (NC), death cause: "typhoid fever", informant: Cora Brown (Butler), died: 16 May 1927, record (1927) #: 10537.

Callie ORNEAL, age about 38 years, single, parents: Joe Orneal and Rebecca Rymer, cause of death: "unknown", informant: Rebecca Flether (Butler), buried: Grindstaff Cemetery, died: 21 May 1927, record (1927) #: 10538.

Joe ORNEAL, age about 88 years, widower, parents: William Orneal (NC) and Jane Bletcher (Fletcher ?) (NC), cause of death: "unknown", informant: Matilda Fletcher (Butler), buried: Grindstaff Cemetery, died: 21 May 1927, record (1927) #: 10539.

James T. RAMBO, born: 16 Mar 1838, married, parents: Aaron Rambo and mother's name unknown, cause of death: "parcoma of stomach", informant: Mollie Rambo (Doeville), buried: Rambo Cemetery, died: 27 May 1927, record (1927) #: 10540.

Grady MAIN, born: 2 Apr 1927, parents: John Main and Lillie Wallace, cause of death: "unknown", informant: John Main (Trade), buried: Reece Cemetery, died: 26 May 1927, record (1927) #: 10541.

Martha C. BUNTON, born: 15 Jan 1871, married, parents: Smith Hately and Catherine Green, death cause: "tuberculosis", informant: S.R. Bunton, Whitehead Cem, died: 11 May 1927, record (1927) #: 10542.

Mattie WOOD, born: 7 Jun 1882 in North Carolina, married, parents: Cleveland Isaacs (NC) and Catherine Hilard (NC), cause of death: "cancer of uterus", informant: Alvin Vaught (Mountain City), died: 2 Jun 1927, record (1927) #: 12971.

William Edward BUTLER, Jr., born: 13 Jan 1894, married, parents: E.E. Butler, Sr. and Ella Baker (NC), cause of death: "acute nephritis", informant: E.E. Butler, Sr. (Mountain City), buried: Mountain View Cem, died: 21 Jun 1927, record (1927) #: 12972.

Sarah Louise EASTRIDGE, born: 29 Feb 1881 at Ashe Co. NC, married, parents: Marion Praither (Ashe Co. NC) and Mary Eastridge (Ashe Co. NC), cause of death: "chronic nephritis", informant: W.W. Eastridge (Johnson City, TN), buried: Payne Cemetery, died: 24 May 1927, record (1927) #: 12973.

Mrs. Susan A. STOUT, born: 5 Jan 1844, widow, parents: George Morley and Hannah Razor, cause of death: "chronic intestinal nephritis", informant: S.A. Stout (Mountain City), buried: Morley Cemetery, died: 17 Jun 1927, record (1927) #: 12974.

William Tyler ROBERTS, born: 10 Mar 1892, married, parents: Edward Roberts and Julia Dillon, cause of death: "gastric ulcer with tuberculosis of lungs", died: 18 Jun 1927, record (1927) #: 12975.

Daniel Washington GARLAND, born: 6 Apr 1862, parents: Samuel Garland and Elizabeth Heaton, cause of death: "mitral regurgitation of heart", informant: Rebecka Walker (Crandull), buried: Woods Cemetery, died: 21 Jun 1927, record (1927) #: 12976.

Elizabeth WRIGHT, born: 1 Jul 1857, widow, parents: Landon Crosswhite and Caroline Buckels, cause of death: "hemiplegia", informant: Robert Wright (Crandull), buried: Gentry Cemetery, died: 4 May 1927, record (1927) #: 12977.

Walter PHILLIPPI, age 25 years, single, parents: D.P. Phillippi and Alice Luttrell, cause of death: "typhoid fever", informant: Jas S. Arnold (Mountain City), buried: Phillippi Cemetery, died: 16 Jul 1927, record (1927) #: 15482.

Marice Eurh JENKINS, age 14 years, parents: father not stated and Miss. Darcia Jenkins, cause of death: not stated, informant: M.B. Jenkins (Mountain City), buried: Jenkins Cemetery, died: 22 Jul 1927, record (1927) #: 15483.

Paul Junior ROBINSON, born: 21 Oct 1926, parents: Gordia Robinson and Sallie Stout, cause of death: "cholera", informant: Gordia Robinson (Butler), buried: Rambo Cemetery, died: 30 Jun 1927, record (1927) #: 15484.

Infant TESTER, male, parents: Carl Tester (NC) and Janie Ward (NC), cause of death: "premature birth", born/died: 18 Jul 1927, record (1927) #: 15485.

William E. PARKER, born: 22 Oct 1860 in North Carolina, parents: Jonathon L. Parker (NC) and Mary Foster (NC), cause of death: "cancer of liver", informant: W.R. Parker (Mountain City), buried: Parks, NC, died: 30 Jul 1927, record (1927) #: 15486.

Eliza Jane LUTTRELL, born: 22 Oct 1856, widow, parents: William Johnson and Betsy Shupe, cause of death: "chronic brights", informant: Gus Luttrell (Mountain City), buried: Phillippi Cemetery, died: 8 Aug 1927, record (1927) #: 17916.

Henry Scott FORRESTER, born: 27 Jun 1871, married,
parents: Andrew Forrester and Phoebe Proffitt, cause
of death: "disease of heart and nephritis", informant:
A.J. Forrester (Mountain City), buried: Phillippi
Cemetery, died: 19 Aug 1927, record (1927) #: 17917.
Kelley M. MILLER, born: 15 Dec 1878 at Edison, NC,
married, parents: Lee Miller (Edison, NC) and Polly
Greer (Todd, NC), cause of death: "internal hemorhage,
automobile accident", informant: Ida B. Miller
(Creston, NC), buried: Creston, NC, died: 24 Aug 1927,
record (1927) #: 17918.
George Willard ADAMS, born: 24 Sep 1876 in North
Carolina, married, parents: Abner Adams (NC) and
Isabel Combs (NC), cause of death: "pellegra",
informant: Mrs. J.M. Barlow (Trade), buried: Riddles
Ford, NC, died: 29 Aug 1927, record (1927) #: 17919.
Lemis BRANCH, age 52 years, parents: "not known",
cause of death: "apoplexy", informant: Mack Phillippi
(Mountain City), buried: County Poor Farm, died: 4 Feb
1927, record (1927) #: 17920.
Lewis Everett ATWOOD, born: 3 Jan 1927, parents: John
V. Atwood and Julia E. Bowman (Carter Co., TN), cause
of death: "acute colitis", informant: Pearl Atwood
(Butler), buried: Dugger Cemetery, died: 28 Aug 1927,
record (1927) #: 17921.
Dennis ROBINSON, born: 30 Mar 1924, parents: W.H.
Robinson and (first name illegible) Stout, cause of
death: "cholera", died: 15 Aug 1927, record (1927) #:
17922.
Ida DUNN, born: 4 Jul 1895, married, parents: John
Rash and Margaret Wilson, cause of death: "chronic
nephritis", informant: H.C. Dunn (Trade), buried:
Wallace Cemetery, died: 14 Aug 1927, record (1927) #:
17923.
Isaac Hamilton REECE, born: 21 Aug 1853, married,
parents: Hughlie Reece (NC) and Matilda Madron (NC),
cause of death: "pulmonary tuberculosis", informant:
James Reece (KY), buried: Valley Cemetery, died: 19
Sep 1927, record (1927) #: 20206.
Columbus F. JENNINGS, born: 11 Nov 1847 in North
Carolina, married, parents: Wiley Jennings (NC) and
Rebecca Fielts (NC), cause of death: "chronic brights
disease", died: 7 Sep 1927, record (1927) #: 20207.
Elizabeth DOWELL, age 85 years, single, parents: Jno
L. Dowell (NC) and Nancy Jarvis (NC), cause of death:
"diarrhea", informant: W.A. Potter (Shouns), buried:
Potter Cemetery, died: 23 Sep 1927, record (1927) #:
20208.

Russell Wills GREER, born: 5 Oct 1872, married, parents: Joseph Greer and Mary Jane Smith, cause of death: "typhoid fever", informant: J.S. Greer (Lodi, VA), died: 3 Oct 1927, record (1927) #: 22405.

Edward ROGERS, age about 65 years, born in Virginia, married, parents: "not known", cause of death: "chronic nephritis", informant: J.M. Parsons (Mountain City), died: 5 Oct 1927, record (1927) #: 22406.

N. G. WARD, born: 14 Aug 1871, married, parents: James Ward and Nancy Stout, cause of death: "myacordial insufficiency", informant: C.R. Ward (Neva), died: 19 Oct 1927, record (1927) #: 22407.

Sallie CHURCH, born: 29 Jul 1874, widow, parents: Sam Deloach and Louise Deloach, cause of death: "abscess of right ingirinal region", informant: W.B. Pleasant (Neva), died: 17 Sep 1927, record (1927) #: 22408.

Winnie Pauline ELLER, born: 7 Feb 1927, parents: Floyd Eller (NC) and Jane Stanley (NC), cause of death: "dysentary (flux)", informant: Avery Eller (Crandull), buried: Gentry Cemetery, died: 10 Oct 1927, record (1927) #: 22409.

Stacy Edward REECE, born: 2 Nov 1926, parents: Floyd Reece and Maggie Main, cause of death: "broncho pneumonia", informant: Maggie Main (Trade), buried: Reece Cemetery, died: 7 Oct 1927, record (1927) #: 22410.

Thomas Alexander BAKER, born: 30 Jan 1851, parents: Alex Baker and Anna Baker, cause of death: "unknown, died instantly", informant: Leona Bunton (Neva), buried: Baker Cemetery, died: 20 Oct 1927, record (1927) #: 22411.

Linell BURTON, born: 13 Aug 1927, parents: Raleigh Burton and Stella Reece, cause of death: "cause unknown", informant: Raleigh Burton (Butler), buried: Cable Cemetery, died: 18 Aug 1927, record (1927) #: 22412.

Paul Wayne MOREFIELD, born: 18 Jan 1926, parents: Grant Morefield and Lona Flinchurn (Fletcher ?), cause of death: "scarlet fever", informant: Fannie Flenchurn (Laurel Bloomery), buried: Eggers Cemetery, died: 13 Nov 1927, record (1927) #: 24555.

Mrs. Vada PAYNE, born: 27 Apr 1891, married, parents: Smith Johnson and Martha Cress, cause of death: "acute endo carditis", informant: Jas S. Johnson (Mountain City), buried: Cress Cemetery, died: 9 Nov 1927, record (1927) #: 24556.

John O. T. POTTER, born: Sep 1854, married, parents: J.O.T. Potter and Susan Main (NC), cause of death: "chronic valvulor heart disease", informant: C.R. Potter (Shouns), died: 10 Nov 1927, record (1927) #: 24557.

Andrew PHILLIPS, age 82 years, born in North Carolina, married, parents: John Phillips (NC) and Nancy Osborne (NC), cause of death: "pulmonary tuberculosis", informant: Roby Phillips (Mountain City), Johnson Cemetery, died: 17 Nov 1927, record (1927) #: 24558.

Godfrey B. DUNN, born: 28 Oct 1839, widower, parents: Henry Dunn and Mary Minks, cause of death: "paralysis, old age, brights disease", informant: J.G. Dunn (Shouns), buried: McEwen Cemetery, died: 1 Nov 1927, record (1927) #: 25559.

Harrison ROARK, born: 16 Jan 1854 in North Carolina, married, parents: William Roark (NC) and Susan Dougherty (NC), cause of death: "chronic intestinal nephritis", informant: J.W. Dunn (Shouns), McEwen Cemetery, died: 5 Nov 1927, record (1927) #: 22560.

Gladys GAMBILL, born: 27 Feb 1927, parents: Smith Gambill and Charlotte Gouge (NC), cause of death: "broncho pneumonia", informant: Conley Nichols (Shouns), buried: Hammons Cemetery, died: 8 Nov 1927, record (1927) #: 22561.

Susan Virginia HALL, born: 10 Aug 1884, single, parents: J.R. Hall and Bettie Arnold, cause of death: "pulmonary tuberculosis", informant: C.H. Hall (Shouns), buried: Hall Cemetery, died: 10 Nov 1927, record (1927) #: 22562.

William Walter WILLIN, born: 25 Jul 1927, parents: Clifford Willin and Florence Hall, cause of death: "cause unknown", informant: Clifford Willin (Shouns), buried: Hall Cemetery, died: 13 Sep 1927, record (1927) #: 24563.

Infant BROOKSHIRE, female, parents: Bert Brookshire and Irene Davis, cause of death: "premature delivery", informant: W.F. Davis (Mountain City), buried: Morley Cemetery, died: 23 Nov 1927, record (1927) #: 24564.

Martha Estella Barry SHUPE, born: 11 Jun 1876, widow, parents: A.A. Barry and Rachel Reece, death cause: "lobar pneumonia", died: 23 Nov 1927, record (1927) #: 24565.

Daniel C. MANUEL, born: 13 Jul 1865 in North Carolina, married, parents: George Manuel (NC) and "don't know" mother's name, cause of death: "blood clot on brain, accidental injury, fall from moving car", informant: L.G. Manuel (Crandull), buried: Blevins Cemetery, died: 3 Nov 1927, record (1927) #: 24566.

Mary Matilda WALKER, born: 24 Feb 1848 in North Carolina, widow, parents: Daniel Woodring (NC) and Carulia Rector (NC), cause of death: "senility, endo carditis", informant: G.C. Walker (Crandull), buried: Gentry Cemetery, died: 20 Nov 1927, record (1927) #: 24567.

Amanda Caroline RUPARD, born: 1 May 1869 at Ashe Co. NC, married, parents: John P. Waters (Ashe Co. NC) and Elizabeth Mabe (Ashe Co. NC), cause of death: "cancer of uterus", informant: W.R. Rupard (Mountain City), buried: Waters Cemetery, died: 3 Dec 1927, record (1927) #: 27073.

Clifford H. HALL, born: 25 May 1886, widower, parents: James Hall and Bettie Arnold, cause of death: "bronchial pneumonia and tuberculosis", informant: J.R. Hall (Shouns), buried: Hall Cemetery, died: 16 Dec 1927, record (1927) #: 27074.

Paul MILLHOUS, born: 22 May 1918, parents: Howard Millhous and Hattie Stout, cause of death: "locked bowel, supposed", informant: Wm Millhous (Butler), died: 28 Dec 1927, record (1927) #: 27-75.

Mary Luvenia MULLINS, born: 15 Aug 1886, married, parents: David P. Phillippi and Rebecca A. Luttrell, cause of death: "para thyroid, ulcer of stomach, pneumonia", informant: John H. Mullins (Mountain City), buried: Wilson Cemetery, died: 10 Aug 1927, record (1927) #: 27076.

W.H. WADDELL, born: 1 Mar 1883, married, parents: A.G. Waddell (KY) and Martha Blevins, cause of death: "brights disease", informant: Chester Blevins (Crandull), buried: Blevins Cemetery, died: 4 Dec 1927, record (1927) #: 27077.

James Vanoy BLEVINS, born: 12 Nov 1927, parents: Luther W. Blevins and Pantha Minton (NC), cause of death: "steptococcus infection", informant: Luther W. Blevins (Crandull), buried: Blevins Cemetery, died: 9 Dec 1927, record (1927) #: 27078.

Clint BURTON, Jr., born: 11 Oct 1927, parents: Clint Burton and Louise McCloud, cause of death: "infantile paralysis", informant: Faun Burton (Butler), buried: Bunton Cemetery, died: 23 Dec 1927, record (1927) #: 27079.

William Edward BUTLER, born: 13 Jan 1894, married, parents: E.E. Butler and Ella Baker (NC), cause of death: "chronic nephritis", buried: Mountain View Cemetery, died: June 1927 (day not stated), record (1927) #: 28774.

Mary Ruth ASHLEY, born: 9 Oct 1927, parents: Edward
Ashley and Margaret Spivey, cause of death: "lobar
pneumonia", informant: Everett Ashley, buried:
Mountain View Cemetery, died: 16 Oct 1927, record
(1927) #: 28775.
Bertha FORRESTER, born: 15 Jun 1907, single, parents:
Roy Forrester and Polly Sluder, cause of death:
"pulmonary tuberculosis", informant: Roy Forrester
(Mountain City), buried: Lewis Cemetery, died: 29 Dec
1927, record (1927) #: 28776.
Esther DAUGHERTY, born: 3 Oct 1847, single, parents:
Thomas Dougherty and Hanna Daugherty, cause of death:
"disease of heart", informant: W.C. Dougherty (Bakers
Gap), buried: Neva, TN, died: 22 Aug 1927, record
(1927) #: 28989.
C.S. BROOKS, Jr., born: 13 Jul 1927, parents: C.S.
Brooks (NC) and Venia Stout, cause of death: "whooping
cough", informant: C.S. Brooks (Mountain City), died:
8 Jan 1828, record (1928) #: 1116.
Calvin RUSHIN, black, born: 3 Nov 1834, parents:
father's name unknown and Cinda Rushin, cause of
death: not stated, informant: David Mock (Mountain
City), died: 20 Jan 1928, record (1928) #: 1117.
Alexander GRINDSTAFF, born: 28 Dec 1860 in Carter Co.
TN, married, parents: David Grindstaff and Louisa
Slimp, cause of death: "organic heart disease",
informant: Roby Hodge (Doeville), died: 18 Jan 1928,
record (1928) #: 1118.
Mary E. HINKLE, born: 3 Sep 1862, married, parents:
J.M. Roberts and Lucinda Arnold, cause of death:
"lobar pneumonia", buried: Wright Cemetery, died: 2
Jan 1928, record (1928) #: 1119.
A.J. HINKLE, born: 8 Nov 1852 in Carter Co. TN,
married, parents: John Hinkle (NC) and (mother's first
name not stated) Arwood (NC), cause of death: "lobar
pneumonia", buried: Wright Cemetery, died: 2 Jan 1928,
record (1928) #: 1120.
Mary Lorette ROBERTS, born: 22 Nov 1886, single,
parents: M.F. Roberts and Julia Dillon (NC), cause of
death: "cancer of breast", buried: Wright Cemetery,
died: 13 Jan 1928, record (1928) #: 1121.
Margaret WILKENSON, age 83 years, widow, parents:
Jeremiah Cornett (NC) and Polly Lewis (NC), cause of
death: "cause not known", informant: W.R. Snyder
(Trade), buried: Snyder Cemetery, died: 26 Jan 1928,
record (1928) #: 1122.

Madison M. MCCRACKEN, born: 26 Jul 1894 at Washington Co. VA, married, parents: father not stated and Jennie McCracken (Washington Co. VA), cause of death: "hydrostatic pneumonia", informant: James N. Pierce, buried: Shingletown Cemetery, died: 20 Feb 1928, record (1928) #: 3671.

Jenette Francis MOREFIELD, born: 30 Apr 1853 in North Carolina, married, parents: J.R. Nichols (NC) and Jane Elizabeth Poston (NC), cause of death: "influenza, lobar pneumonia", informant: Arther Nichols (Mountain City), died: 4 Feb 1928, record (1928) #: 3672.

Mable T.M. ROARK, born: 4 Feb 1928, parents: McKinley Roark and Elsie Vanover (NC), cause of death: "thought to be varicilla", informant: McKinley Roark (Shouns), buried: Arnold Cemetery, died: 18 Feb 1928, record (1928) #: 3673.

Martha POE, age 80 years, widow, parents: Johnson Potter and Susan Main, cause of death: "chronic intestinal nephritis", informant: John M. Potter (Shouns), died: 19 Feb 1928, record (1928) #: 3674.

Mrs. Nellie PHILLIPS, born: 28 May 1864, married, parents: Zill Eggers (NC) and (mother's first name not stated) Isaacs (NC), cause of death: "tuberculosis of lungs", buried: Neva, TN, died: 30 Jan 1928, record (1928) #: 3675.

Infant NORRIS, male, parents: Walter Norris and Mable Crow, cause of death: "premature", informant: Walter Norris (Doeville), buried: Norris Cemetery, born/died: 17 Feb 1928, record (1928) #: 3676.

Billie DUGGER, born: 28 Feb 1928, parents: Clarence Dugger and Rose Leonard, cause of death: not stated, informant: Nell Leonard (Butler), died: 29 Feb 1928, record (1928) #: 3677.

Luvena GILLEY, born: 24 Aug 1898, married, parents: Marion Leech and Martha Jacob, cause of death: "endo myocarditis", informant: Henry Gilley (Crandull), buried: Gentry Cemetery, died: 7 Feb 1928, record (1928) #: 3678.

Roby W. GUY, born: 7 Jun 1898 in North Carolina, married, parents: Horton Guy (NC) and Eliza Cannon (NC), cause of death: "tuberculosis of intestines", informant: William Guy (Trade), buried: Green Cemetery, NC, died: 29 Feb 1928, record (1928) #: 3679.

Sarah Millie CANNON, born: 3 Jan 1890, married, parents: Jack South (NC) and Elizabeth Canter (NC), cause of death: "broncho pneumonia", informant: W.A. Cannon (Butler), buried: Zion Hill Cemetery, died: 19 Feb 1928, record (1928) #: 3680.

Rachel A. MATHERSON, age 82 years, 6 months and 14 days, widow, parents: Jack Bailey (GA) and Polly Slimp, cause of death: "long standing of neuritis", informant: W.C. Matherson (Neva), died: 16 Mar 1928, record (1828) #: 6246.

David OSBORN, born: 31 Mar 1859 in North Carolina, married, parents: Alfred Osborn (NC) and Annie Arnold, cause of death: "apoplexy", informant: D.D. Hampton (Shouns), died: 31 Mar 1928, record (1928) #: 6247.

Rufus M. BLEVINS, born: 26 Apr 1854, married, parents: James Blevins and Sarah Berry, cause of death: "dieabets coma", informant: W.A. McNeill (Crandull), buried: Blevins Cemetery, died: 4 Mar 1928, record (1928) #: 6248.

James Alfred WALKER, born: 23 Mar 1928, parents: O.C. Walker and Trula Rankins, cause of death: "premature birth", buried: Gentry Cemetery, died: 31 Mar 1928, record (1928) #: 6249.

Bettie POPE, born: 5 Jun 1866, widow, parents: Robert Sexton (VA) and Mary E. Pennington (NC), cause of death: "chronic brights disease", informant: J.E. Sexton (Mountain City), buried: Shingletown Cemetery, died: 8 Apr 1928, record (1928) #: 8938.

Martha Jane MCCRACKEN, born: 26 May 1848 at Ashe Co. NC, widow, parents: Andrew Pennington (Ashe Co. NC) and Elizabeth Pope (Ashe Co. NC), cause of death: "lobar pneumonia", buried: Shingletown Cemetery, died: 21 Apr 1928, record (1928) #: 8939.

James Earl GARR, born: 23 May 1927, parents: Clayton Garr and Mary Morefield, cause of death: "lobar pneumonia", informant: Mrs. Jack Morefield, buried: Shingletown Cemetery, record (1928) #: 8940.

David Dick KEYS, born: 20 Oct 1863, married, parents: Robert W. Keys and Susan Wills, cause of death: "broncho pneumonia, influenza", informant: Guy M. Keys (Mountain City), buried: Wills Cemetery, died: 24 Apr 1928, record (1928) #: 8941.

John Monroe MORETZ, born: 5 Mar 1886 in North Carolina, single, parents: Jeff Moretz (NC) and Nancy Isaacs (NC), cause of death: "pneumonia fever", informant: Sherman Moretz (Sugar Grove, NC), buried: Shouns, TN, died: 1 Apr 1928, record (1928) #: 8942.

Eugene Kent WILSON, colored, born: 10 Oct 1927, parents: Clint Wilson and Georgia Forrester (VA), cause of death: "lobar pneumonia", informant: Clint Wilson (Mountain City), died: 4 Apr 1928, record (1928) #: 8943.

John Franklin VALENTINE, Negro, born: 5 Aug 1887 in North Carolina, divorced, parents: "father unknown" and Malinda Goins (NC), cause of death: "influenza, lobar pneumonia", informant: L.K. Anderson (Shouns), died: 13 Apr 1928, record (1928) #: 8944.

Goldie A. MAXWELL, born: 12 Mar 1908, married, parents: Irvin Sammons and Alice Sweeney, cause of death: "spinal meningitis", informant: Irvin Sammons (Mountain City), buried: Johnson Cemetery, died: 13 Apr 1928, record (1928) #: 8945.

Nancy Jane HOLCOMB, born: 20 Mar 1850 in North Carolina, widow, parents: not stated, cause of death: "chronic brights disease", informant: M.B. Holcomb (Mountain City), buried: Mountain View Cemetery, died: 30 Mar 1928, record (1928) #: 8946.

Verna HEAD, age 25 years, 11 months and 27 days, married, parents: W.S. Head and Oma Forrester, cause of death: "pulmonary tuberculosis", buried: Dunn Cemetery, died: 25 Apr 1928, record (1928) #: 8947.

Infant SHUPE, male, born: 16 Apr 1928, parents: Frank Shupe and Alice Garland, cause of death: not stated, informant: Frank Shupe (Doeville), buried: Campbell Cemetery, died: 17 Apr 1928, record (1928) #: 8948.

Infant MULLINS, male, parents: S.C. Mullins and J.M. Lee, cause of death: "premature", buried: Brookshire Cemetery, born/died: 8 Apr 1928, record (1928) #: 8949.

Mande WYATT, born: 11 Apr 1891 in North Carolina, married, parents: Lee Parsons (NC) and Susan Adams (NC), cause of death: "pulmonary tuberculosis", informant: Bob Roberts (Carndull), buried: Blevins Cemetery, died: 4 Apr 1928, record (1928) #: 8950.

Lundy THOMAS, born: 26 Jul 1890, married, parents: James Thomas (NC) and America Brown, cause of death: "pulmonary tuberculosis, pneumonia", informant: Edd Osborn (Trade), buried: Zionville, NC, died: 8 Apr 1928, record (1928) #: 8951.

Ellen SNYDER, born: 16 Mar 1906 in North Carolina, single, parents: Adam Snyder and Callie Davis, cause of death: "convulsions after birth of child", informant: Adam Snyder (Trade), buried: Snyder Cemetery, NC, died: 16 Apr 1928, record (1928) #: 8952.

Rebecca LOMAX, colored, born: 2 Apr 1878, married, parents: father's name not stated and Mary Cresorey, cause of death: "cancer of uterus", informant: Sylvester Lomax (Mountain City), died: 5 May 1928, record (1928) #: 11649.

Daniel Boone REECE, born: 2 Nov 1865, married, parents: Asa Reece and Catherine Wagner, cause of death: "cerebral hemorhage", informant: Mrs. D.B. Reece (Mountain City), died: 1 May 1928, record (1928) #: 11650.

Tice TILLEY, colored, age 31 years, parents: Jonas Tilley and Frankie Bailey, cause of death: "pulmonary tuberculosis", informant: Rev. N.D. Smith (Mountain City), buried: Holy Hill Cemetery, died: 17 May 1928, record (1928) #: 11651.

Hugh, TURNMIRE, age 74 years, born in North Carolina, parents: William Turnmire (NC) and (mother's first name not stated) Day, cause of death: "chronic brights disease", informant: Mae Phillippi (Mountain City), buried: Phillippi Cemetery, died: 20 May 1928, record (1928) #: 11652.

Edward J. ROSE, born: 23 Apr 1842 in California, parents: "names unknown", cause of death: "asthma and general breakdown, advanced age", informant: Mrs. Jon Ritchie (Butler), buried: Cobbs Creek Cemetery, died: 14 May 1928, record (1928) #: 11653.

James CORTNER, born: 4 Mar 1862, married, parents: Andrew J. Cortner (NC) and Elizabeth Smith, cause of death: "acute dilatatation", informant: Geo Cortner, buried: Doeville, TN, died: 23 May 1928, record (1928) #: 11654.

Mary Moreland NEAR, born: 26 Feb 1851, married, parents: John Heaton and Adeline Grindstaff, cause of death: "acraisis of liver", buried: Doeville, TN, died: 24 May 1928, record (1928) #: 11655.

Carril L. REED, female, born: 10 Sep 1883, married, parents: Elbert Jordan and Rettie Blevins, cause of death: "cancer of breast", informant: John Reed (Doeville), died: 5 May 1928, record (1928) #: 11656.

Alice Lena COLE, born: 13 Oct 1905, married, parents: Warren A. Blevins and Emmes Adams, cause of death: "diabetic coma", informant: W.A. Blevins (Crandull), buried: Blevins Cemetery, died: 16 May 1928, record (1928) #: 11657.

Naomi MOODY, born: 11 Jan 1858, married, parents: Martin Greenwell and A. Dugger, cause of death: "unknown", informant: S.C. Moody (Butler), buried: Sugar Grove Cemetery, died: 7 May 1928, record (1928) #: 11658.

Monroe DAVIS, age 68 years, born in North Carolina, married, parents: Richard Davis (NC) and Rosie Hugins (NC), cause of death: "apoplexy, acute dysentary", informant: Mrs. Monroe Davis, died: 16 Jun 1920, record (1928) #: 14962.

Wm. A. NORRIS, born: 4 Jul 1876, married, parents: Buck Norris (NC) and Polly J. Cornett, cause of death: "uremia", died: 19 Jun 1928, record (1928) #: 14963.

Hamilton HICKS, age about 69 years, married, parents: John Hicks (NC) and Nancy Deloach (Carter Co. TN), cause of death: "lobar pneumonia", buried: Wright Cemetery, died: 3 Jun 1928, record (1928) #: 14964.

Alfred H. BLEVINS, born: 27 Jun 1859, married, parents: James Blevins and Sarah Berry, cause of death: "intestinal nephritis and endo cardites", informant: C.F. Blevins (Crandull), buried: Blevins Cemetery, died: 9 Jun 1928, record (1928) #: 14965.

Callie TESTER, born: 12 Nov 1864 in North Carolina, married, parents: John Phillips (NC) and Pollie Pillagton (NC), cause of death: "influenza, lobar pneumonia", informant: David Tester (Neva), died: 20 Apr 1928, record (1928) #: 14966.

Martitia BROWN, born: Mar 1852, married, parents: J.O.J. Potter and Susan Main (NC), cause of death: "myo carditis, chronic brights disease", informant: R.S. Price (Shouns), died: 17 Jul 1928, record (1928) #: 16655.

Mary Snyder HOKE, born: Mar 1876, married, parents: H. Snyder (NC) and Cora Madron (NC), death cause: "acute nephritis", informant: H. Snyder (Crandull), buried: Gentry Cem, died: 19 Jul 1928, record (1928) #: 16656.

Margaret ROUSE, born: Jul 1881, married, parents: Benjamin Ford and Fansie Wright, cause of death: "cerebral hemorhage", buried: Gentry Cemetery, died: 31 Jul 1928, record (1928) #: 16657.

Mary A. SLIMP, born: 6 Jul 1855, married, parents: Ham Ward (NC) and Martha Holman (NC) cause of death: "peritonites", informant: M.A. Slimp (Neva), died: 17 Aug 1928, record (1928) #: 19207.

Daniel ROBINSON, born: 8 Feb 1854, married, parents: Zackiner Robinson and Phoeba Stout, cause of death: "heart dropsy", informant; Julia Stout (Doeville), buried: Dugger Cemetery, died: 20 Apr 1928, record (1928) #: 19208.

Catherine C. ROBINSON, born: 9 Oct 1862, married, parents: George J, Walker (NC) and Rebeca Shoun, cause of death: "tuberculosis of lungs and stomach", buried: Walker Cemetery, died: 24 Aug 1928, record (1928) #: 19209.

Infant ROBERTS, male, parents: Edward Roberts and Clydie Church, cause of death: not stated, born/died: 29 Jul 1928, record (1928) #: 19210.

Joseph J. WAGNER, born: 18 May 1863, married, parents: Joseph Wagner and Mary Vaught, cause of death: "chronic valvular heart disease", informant: Eula Wagner (Butler), buried: Sugar Grove Cemetery, died: 4 Aug 1928, record (1928) #: 19211.

Sylvester DAVIDSON, born: 15 May 1848 in Virginia, married, parents: Wm Davidson (VA) and Melvina Moore, buried: Shingletown Cemetery, died: 1 Sep 1928, record (1928) #: 21601.

James Jordan HENSON, born: 24 May 1928, parents: H.E. Henson (NC) and Cecile Johnson, cause of death: "cholera", informant: H.E. Henson (Mountain City), buried: Wagner Cemetery, died: 28 Sep 1928, record (1928) #: 21602.

Maggie THOMAS, black, age 44 years, born in North Carolina, parents: John Thomas (NC) and Lourie Dobbins (NC), cause of death: "acute colitis", informant: John Thomas (Mountain City), buried: Holy Hill Cemetery, died: 23 Sep 1928, record (1928) #: 21603.

Martha Cress JOHNSON, age 61 years, married, parents: M.L. Cress and Clara Wilson, cause of death: "pellegra", informant: A.S. Johnson (Mountain City), buried: Phillippi Cemetery, died: 22 Sep 1928, record (1928) #: 21604.

Polly WAGNER, born: 10 Sep 1845, widow, parents: Jim Jackson and Hueldy Dunn, cause of death: "chronic intestinal nephritis", informant: John M. Potter (Shouns), died: 9 Jul 1928, record (1928) #: 21605.

Bula Viola MAY, age 16 years, 2 months and 9 days, parents: J.H. May and Anna Martin, cause of death: "typhoid fever", informant: Roy Sluder (Shouns), buried: Martin Cemetery, died: 9 Sep 1928, record (1928) #: 21606.

Ellen Clementine MCQUEEN, born: 9 Mar 1857, married, parents: Wm Wesley McQueen (NC) and Beula Hitchcock (NC), cause of death: "chronic brights disease", informant: A.H. McQueen (Mountain City), died: 16 Oct 1928, record (1928) #: 23944.

Wallace C. BERRY, born: 24 Jul 1892, widower, parents: E.E. Barry and Lillie Wilson, cause of death: "burned over half of body", informant: E.E. Barry (Mountain City), died: 4 Oct 1928, record (1928) #: 23945.

Thomas Grant CROSSWHITE, born: 12 Apr 1871, widower, parents: Thomas J. Crosswhite and Rebecca Donnelly, cause of death: "chronic brights disease", informant: A.J. Wilson (Mountain City), died: 13 Oct 1928, record (1928) #: 23946.

James Woodard WARREN, colored, age 3 years, parents: Jim Warren and Jennie Thomas (NC), cause of death: "pulmonary tuberculosis", informant: Tice Thomas (Mountain City), buried: Holy Hill Cemetery, died: 27 Sep 1928, record (1928) #: 23948.

James B. FRIDDLES, born: 29 Sep 1884, married, parents: Moses Friddles and Mollie Brown, cause of death: "gun shot wound in head, suicide", informant: W.B. Mount (Shouns), buried: Wills Cemetery, died: 1 Oct 1928, record (1928) #: 23949.

W.M. REED, age 72 years, parents: James Reed and Elizabeth Proffitt, cause of death: "obstruction of bowels", informant: Noah Fletcher (Butler), buried: Proffitt Cemetery, died: 5 Oct 1928, record (1928) #: 23950.

Hattie ARNOLD, age about 27 years, married, parents: Daton Campbell and Ella Walker, cause of death: "chronic valvulor heart disease", informant: W.S. Arnold (Doeville), buried: Campbell Cemetery, died: 15 Oct 1928, record (1928) #: 23951.

James Ralph CABLE, born: 8 Jul 1928, parents: Dewey Cable and Rilda Green (NC), cause of death: "broncho pneumonia", buried: Dugger Cemetery, died: 8 Oct 1928, record (1928) #: 23952.

Frank George CHAPPELL, born: 25 Aug 1928, parents: William Chappell and mother's name illegible, cause of death: "spinal meningitis", informant: William Chappell (Butler), buried: Laurel Bloomery, died: 23 Oct 1928, record (1928) #: 23953.

Hattie Hodge TRIPLETT, born: 19 Apr 1885 in North Carolina, married, parents: Robert Hodge (NC) and Sarah Tounson (NC), cause of death: "pulmonary tuberculosis", informant: George Triplett (Butler), buried: Cobbs Creek Cemetery, died: 30 Oct 1928, record (1928) #: 23954.

Stella BURTON, parents: Raleigh Burton and Stella Reece, cause of death: "atelectosis", informant: Ralph Burton (Butler), buried: Cable Cemetery, born/died: 24 Oct 1928, record (1928) #: 23955.

Kitty WATSON, born: 10 Jan 1925, parents: Thomas C. Watson and Leckie Gregg, cause of death: "second degree burn (clothing caught fire at open fireplace)", informant: Thomas C. Watson (Butler), buried: Dugger Cemetery, died: 26 Oct 1928, record (1928) #: 23956.

Mack GARR, age 75 years, born in North Carolina, parents: not stated, cause of death: "cerebral hemorrage", informant: A.H. McQueen, buried: Owens Cemetery, died: 22 Nov 1928, record (1928) #: 26255.

Cora Lee FURCHESS, born: 10 Oct 1928, parents: Scott Furchess and Verne Snyder, cause of death: "broncho pneumonia", informant: H. Warren (Shouns), died: 8 Nov 1928, record (1928) #: 26256.

Dan DAVIS, born: 15 Jun 1924, parents: Arthur A. Davis and Mary Ann Dunn, cause of death: "membraneous larangitis", informant: A.A. Davis (Shouns), died: 14 Nov 1928, record (1928) #: 26257.

Lindsy ELLISON, born: 26 Nov 1845 in North Carolina, single, parents: Wm Ellison and Bettie Mitchell (NC), cause of death: "broncho pneumonia", informant: Lewis Ellison (Shouns), died: 26 Nov 1828, record (1928) #: 26258.

Jones TILLEY, born: 19 Nov 1826 in North Carolina (age 101), parents: "unknown", widower, cause of death: "chronic myo cardites", informant: Mack Phillippi, died: 19 Nov 1928, record (1928) #: 26259.

Landon MAY, born: 25 Dec 1905, married, parents: J.H. May and Annie Martin, cause of death: "typhoid fever", informant: Wesley Dunn, died: 30 Nov 1928, record (1928) #: 26260.

Wilborn BROWN, born: 20 Aug 1856 in North Carolina, widower, parents: Louis Brown (NC) and Elizabeth Osborn (NC), cause of death: "chronic intestinal nephritis", informant: R.S. Price (Shouns), died: 30 Sep 1928, record (1928) #: 26261.

C.M. SNYDER, female, born: 6 Oct 1846, married, parents: David M. Stout and Sallie Shoun, cause of death: "chronic myocardites", informant: A.S. Snyder (Shouns), died: 12 Nov 1928, record (1928) #: 26262.

James SWIFT, born: 13 Oct 1919, parents: James D. Swift (NC) and Aerolina Harmon (NC), cause of death: "broncho pneumonia", informant: J.W. Vanoy (Neva), died: 24 Oct 1928, record (1928) #: 26263.

J.C. CAMPBELL, born: 29 Aug 1928 at Carter Co. TN, parents: father's name not stated and Mary Campbell (Carter Co. TN), cause of death: "broncho pneumonia", informant: John Reed (Butler), died: 21 Nov 1928, record (1928) #: 26264.

Lee CRUISE, male, age 73 years, born in North Carolina, married, parents: "don't know", cause of death: "paraphlegia", informant: John Cruise (Damascus, VA), died: 3 Nov 1928, record (1928) #: 26265.

Polly Geneva THOMAS, born: 12 Jan 1926, parents: B.R. Thomas (NC) and Anna Eggers (NC), cause of death: "clothing caught fire and child burned to death", informant: B.R. Thomas (Trade), buried: Union Cemetery, died: 21 Nov 1928, record (1928) #: 26266.

Isaac C. HAMMONS, age 69 years, born in North Carolina, married, parents: Marsh Hammons (NC) and Mahola Osborn (NC), cause of death: "chronic heart disease", informant: Rebecca Hammons (Trade), Reece Cemetery, died: 29 Oct 1928, record (1928) #: 26269.

Jane Geneva BUNTON, born: 2 Nov 1868, married, parents: Wash White and Sabra Bunton, cause of death: "typhoid fever", informant: B.I. Bunton (Butler), buried: Bunton Cemetery, died: 2 Nov 1928, record (1928) #: 26268.

Lenis Kate CAMPBELL, born: 28 Oct 1928, parents: Thomas Campbell and Esther Bunton, cause of death: "unknown", informant: Esther Campbell (Butler), buried: Bunton Cemetery, died: 7 Nov 1928, record (1928) #: 26269.

Joel SIMMONS, born: 17 Dec 1843 in North Carolina, widower, parents: John Simmons (NC) and Bettie Caudill (NC), death cause: "influenza and pneumonia", informant: C.H. McQueen (Mountain City), Shingletown Cemetery, died: 31 Dec 1928, record (1928) #: 29178.

James K. WOOD, born: 5 Dec 1862, married, parents: Barton Wood (NC) and Eveline McGee (NC), cause of death: "influenza", informant: Mollie Wood (Shouns), died: 5 Dec 1928, record (1928) #: 29179.

William Franklin WILLIAMS, born: 6 Jan 1869, married, parents: W.A. Williams and Delilah Sullivan (Sullivan Co. TN), cause of death: "spinal injuries from automobile accident", informant: Clyde Williams (Mountain City), buried: Mountain View Cemetery, died: 12 Dec 1928, record (1928) #: 29180.

Alfred Jackson WILSON, born: 31 Jul 1877, parents: William D. Wilson and Martha Hampton, cause of death: "lobar pneumonia, influenza", informant: Mack Wilson (Mountain City), died: 23 Dec 1928, record (1928) #: 29181.

Polly MOREFIELD, age 60 years, married, parents: Thomas Forrester and Pollie Proffit, cause of death: "epedemic influenza, heart disease", informant: Walter McKinney (Shouns), buried: Voughtsville, died: 26 Dec 1928, record (1928) #: 29182.

Infant STEPHENS, female, parents: Dexter Stephens and Rettie Fritts, death cause: not stated, informant: F.S. Snyder, died: 2 May 1928, record (1928) #: 29183.

Stacy Junior STOUT, born: 13 Dec 1928, parents: Stacy (Burton) Stout and Fannie Stout, cause of death: not stated, informant: Dallas Hodge (Butler), died: 28 Dec 1928, record (1928) #: 29184.

Infant LOWE, male, born: 7 Dec 1928, parents: James Lowe and Gladys Wilson, cause of death: "premature delivery", informant: Wm Wilson (Mountain City), died: 8 Dec 1928, record (1928) #: 29185.

L.C. FLETCHER, born: 19 Dec 1928, parents: Cecil H. Fletcher and Berthe B. Shuffield, cause of death: not stated, informant: Cecil H. Fletcher (Crandull), buried: Carter Co. TN, died: 21 Dec 1928, record (1928) #: 29186.

Clarence Edgar HUTCHINSON, born: 12 Aug 1928, parents: C.B. Hutchinson and A.S. Blevins, cause of death: "influenza", informant: C.B. Hutchinson (Crandull), buried: Blevins Cemetery, died: 29 Dec 1928, record (1928) #: 29187.

Marvin S. WILSON, age 43 years, married, parents: William Wilson and Nannie Potter (NC), cause of death: "chronic heart disease", informant: James M. Parks (Trade), buried: Potter Cemetery, died: 15 Dec 1928, record (1928) #: 29188.

Sarah WATSON, age about 67 years, "all her life has been insane", parents: William Watson and Susan Bunton, cod "pneumonia fever", died: 21 Dec 1928, record (1928) #: 29189.

John ADAMS, born: 28 Jun 1853, married, parents: Benjamin Adams (NC) and Rhoda Goodman, cause of death: "influenza, lobar pneumonia", informant: R.R. Brown (Mountain City), died: 23 Oct 1928, record (1928) #: 31149.

Dorothy May STONE, born: 4 Jul 1928 at Dant, VA, parents: Cal Stone (NC) and Nelia Warren, cause of death: "influenza", died: 25 Oct 1928, record (1928) #: 31150.

Kenzia STOUT, age 73 years, 8 months and 18 days, married, parents: William Howard and mother's name not known, cause of death: "chronic brights disease", died: 5 Nov 1928, record (1928) #: 31152.

Halsie SHORES, age about 73 years, born in North Carolina, widow, parents: Thomas Woods (NC) and mother's name illegible (Wilkes Co. NC), cause of death: "pneumonia", informant: Frank Jenkins (Mountain City), buried: Shingletown Cemetery, died: 2 Jan 1929, record (1929) #: 1869

Andrew Cass EASTRIDGE, born: 20 Jan 1866, married, parents: Joel Eastridge (Ashe Co. NC) and Martha Rominger (Ashe Co. NC), cause of death: "lobar pneumonia, influenza", informant: James Eastridge (Mountain City), buried: Family cemetery, died: 6 Jan 1929, record (1929) #: 1870.

Cyrus Gilbert LATHOM, born: 4 Apr 1875 in North Carolina, married, parents: D.C. Lathom (NC) and Elizabeth Graybeal (NC), cause of death: "influenza, pulmonary tuberculosis", informant: Wm Breeding (Mountain City), buried: Owens Cemetery, died: 9 Jan 1929, record (1929) #: 1871.

Malinda SHUPE, born: 8 Jan 1928, parents: Luther Shupe and Lonia Fritts, cause of death: "broncho pneumonia, influenza", informant: Chas Shupe (Mountain City), buried: Valley Cemetery, died: 13 Jan 1929, record (1929) #: 1872.

John A. LATHOM, born: 6 Jul 1925 in Virginia, parents: C.G. Lathom and Matry Michum (KY), cause of death: "influenza, broncho pneumonia", informant: Wm Breeding (Mountian City), buried: Owens Cemetery, died: 16 Jan 1929, record (1929) #: 1873.

Mary MITCHELL, born: 8 Jan 1845 in North Carolina, inmate at county home, parents: John A. Mitchell (NC) and Samantha Jones (NC), cause of death: "influenza, lobar pneumonia", informant: Pete Landers (Mountain City), buried: County Home Cemetery, died: 18 Jan 1929, record (1929) #: 1874.

George W. BROCE, born: 27 Mar 1861 in Sullivan Co. TN, married, parents: George W. Broce and Amanda Lambert (VA), cause of death: "influenza, lobar pneumonia", informant: Mande Broce (Mountain City), died: 2 Jan 1929, record (1929) #: 1875.

Billy Alexander PLESS, born: 14 May 1926, parents: Quincy Edward Pless (NC) and Evelyn Morefield McCain, cause of death: "scarlet fever", died: 11 Jan 1929, record (1929) #: 1876.

Miss Fronia WAGNER, born: 8 Aug 1846, single, parents: M.M. Wagner and Mary Fyffe (NC), cause of death: "influenza, lobar pneumonia", informant: James S. Wagner (Mountain City), buried: Wagner Cemetery, died: 1 Jan 1929, record (1929) #: 1877.

John Argile SAMMONS, born: 15 Jan 1927, parents: Irvin Sammons and Alice Sweeney, cause of death: "broncho pneumonia", informant: J.L. Sammons, buried: Phillippi Cemetery, died: 18 Jan 1929, record (1929) #: 1878.

Sarafina JENKINS, age 78 years, widow, parents: David Owens (NC) and mother's name not stated, cause of death: "influenza, lobar pneumonia", informant: Kite Thomas (Mountain City), buried: Phillippi Cemetery, died: 24 Jan 1929, record (1929) #: 1879.

Elizabeth BROGLIN, born: 26 Jan 1846, inmate at county home, parents: Andy Broglin (NC) and mother's name unknown, cause of death: "chronic brights disease", died: 26 Jan 1929, record (1929) #: 1880.

Mary Malinda WARREN, born: 11 Jun 1891 in North Carolina, single, parents: Cornelius Warren (NC) and Elizabeth Thomas (NC), cause of death: "chronic heart disease", informant: H.C. Warren (Shouns), died: 30 Jan 1929, record (1929) #: 1881.

Rebecca TAYLOR, born: 5 May 1859 in North Carolina, married, parents: Calvin Farmer (NC) and Emeline Graybeal (NC), cause of death: "influenza, lobar pneumonia", informant: Columbus Taylor (Shouns), died: 4 Jan 1929, record (1929) #: 1882.

James Hamilton MAY, born: 13 Apr 1859, married, parents: Washington May and Martha Alfred (NC), cause of death: "influenza, pneumonia fever", informant: Roy Sluder (Shouns), died: 6 Jan 1929, record (1929) #: 1883.

Clara Martitia JOHNSON, born: 7 Mar 1875, married, parents: James Martin (NC) and Nancy Stout, death cause: "influenza, pneumonia fever", informant: Roy Sluder, died: 18 Jan 1929, record (1929) #: 1884.

Robert STURGILL, born: 27 Feb 1879, married, parents: Joe Sturgill (NC) and (mother's first name not stated) French (VA), cause of death: "pneumonia, flue", informant: Wiley Mount (Shouns), buried: Damascus, VA, died: 5 Jan 1929, record (1929) #: 1885.

Rebecca Jane PROFFITT, born: 8 Jan 1847, widow, parents: Richard Tester and Rebecca Jackson, cause of death: "influenza, lobar pneumonia", informant: J.M. Tester (Neva), buried: Voughtsville, died: 13 Jan 1929, record (1929) #: 1886.

Citha Louisa PROFFITT, born: 23 Feb 1864, parents: Thomas Forrester and Polly Proffitt, cause of death: "influenza", informant: Will Proffitt (Neva), died: 15 Jan 1929, record (1929) #: 1887.

Rachel Annie KELLER, born: 13 Dec 1925, parents: Joe Keller (NC) and Lillie Laws, cause of death: not stated, informant: Lillie Keller (Butler), died: 6 Jan 1929, record (1929) #: 1888.

Mrs. Nancy PRICHARD, born: 15 Oct 1860, married, parents: James Dugger and (mother's first name not stated) Riner, cause of death: "miningitis", informant: J.E. Dugger (Butler), buried: Family cemetery, died: 14 Jan 1929, record (1929) #: 1889,

Winnie C. WILSON, born: 4 Dec 1850, widow, parents: Mike Smith and Susie Smith, cause of death: "supposed to be old age", informant: Newt Wilson (Crandull), buried: Gentry Cemetery, died: 15 Jan 1929, record (1929) #: 1890.

David MCQUEEN, born: 29 Dec 1850, married, parents: Rice McQueen and Betsy Blevins, cause of death: "lobar pneumonia, old age", informant: Marcus McQueen (Crandull), buried: McQueen Cemetery, died: 11 Jan 1929, record (1929) #: 1891.

Dellie Wilma WYATT, born: 3 Apr 1904, married, parents: Elbert W. Watson (NC) and N.V. Johnson, cause of death: "pulmonary tuberculosis", informant: Jake Wyatt (Crandull), buried: Blevins Cemetery, died: 27 Jan 1929.

Alice POTTER, age 62 years, married, parents: Jordan Heck and Eliza Snyder, cause of death: not stated, informant: Drewry Potter (Trade), buried: Potter Cemetery, died: 3 Jan 1929, record (1929) #: 1893.

William Franklin GRAYSON, born: 9 May 1853, married, parents: J.W.M. Grayson (NC) and Julia A. Williams, cause of death: "influenza, lobar pneumonia", informant: A.G. Grayson (Trade), died: 7 Jan 1929, record (1929) #: 1894.

Susan Jane CABLE, born: 9 Aug 1861, age 68 years, married, parents: W.L. Greenwell and Elizabeth Dugger, cause of death: "influenza, broncho pneumonia" informant: John Cable (Butler), buried: Cable Cemetery, died: 15 Jan 1929, record (1929) #: 1895.

Ella Pauline FARTHING, born: 10 Sep 1925, parents: Harry Farthing (Sugar Grove, NC) and Ella Eggers, cause of death: "lobar pneumonia followed by diptheria", died: 19 Jan 1929, record (1929) #: 1896.

Mary Elizabeth DAVIS, born: 10 Apr 1858 in North Carolina, married, Parents: John Lazenley (NC) and Cathern Seus (NC), cause of death:"brain tumor", informant: N.H. Davis (Damascus, VA), buried: Southerland, TN, died: 6 Feb 1929, record (1929) #: 5315.

Abraham Lincoln MAY, born: 2 Jan 1907, married, parents: Garfield May and (first name not stated) Hodge, cause of death:"struck by railway train", informant: Garfield May (Trade), died; 4 Feb 1929, record (1929) #: 5316.

Walter Fred ISAACS, born: 21 Dec 1928, parents: Jack Isaacs (NC) and Mary Swift (NC), cause of death:not stated, informant: Jack Isaacs (Mountain City), died: 13 Feb 1929, record (1929) #: 5317.

Robert E. GRANT, born: 12 Feb 1929, parents: Edgar A. Grant and Hazel Bell Bingham (NC), cause of death:"acute pulmonary odines", informant: Edgar A. Grant (Shouns), died: 16 Feb 1929, record (1929) #: 5318.

Carrie Rebecca LOMAX, colored, born: 20 Jan 1929, parents: father not stated and Hettie Belle Lomax, cause of death:not stated, informant: Sylvester Lomax, died: 21 Feb 1929, record (1929) #: 5319.

Macon Randolph WILLS, born: 7 Nov 1842, widower, parents: P.D. Wills and Sophia McGowan, cause of death: "cerebral heamorhage", informant: H.J.D. Wills (Shouns), died: 22 Feb 1929.

Ivan WILLIN, born: 11 Oct 1913, parents: Thomas Willin and Minnie Forrester, cause of death: "infection of leg, cause unknown", informant: J.M.W. Hammons (Shouns), buried: Dunn Cemetery, died: 23 Feb 1929, record (1929) #: 5321.

Villas J. PAYNE, born: 3 Mar 1905, single, parents: R.S. Payne and Maggie Osborn (Ashe Co. NC), cause of death: "Hodgkins disease", informant: R.S. Payne (Shouns), buried: Payne Cemetery, died: 27 Feb 1929, record (1929) #: 5322.

Millard Ivan FORRESTER, born: 10 Jun 1910, single, parents: Roy Forrester and Polly Sluder (NC), cause of death: "pulmonary tuberculosis", informant: Mandy Roark (Shouns), buried: Shouns Forrester Cemetery, died: 28 Feb 1929, record (1929) #: 5323.

Diana PROFFITT, born: 1 Jul 1845 in North Carolina, widow, parents: Thomas Davis (NC) and Susana Holman (NC), cause of death: "chronic heart disease", informant: Wiley Stout (Shouns), died: 8 Feb 1929, record (1929) #: 5324.

Infant STOUT, female, born: 16 Feb 1929, parents: David P. Stout and Eva Grindstaff, cause of death: not stated, informant: Geo Grindstaff (Doeville), buried: Neva, died: 17 Feb 1929, record (1929) #: 5325.

H.A. MCEWEN, born: 25 Apr 1852, married, parents: Samuel McEwen and Matilda Smithpeters, cause of death: "apoplexy", informant: J.W. McEwen (Doeville), buried: McEwen Cem, died: 3 Feb 1929, record (1929) #: 5326.

John NAVE, born: 2 Mar 1850, married, parents: Leonard Nave and Celia Colbox (note: must be Colbaugh), cause of death: "dementia paralytica", informant: Nettie Nave (Doeville), buried: Nave Cemetery, died: 16 Feb 1929, record (1929) #: 5327.

William A. MATHERLY, born: 14 Dec 1886 at Carter Co. TN, married, parents: Joseph Matherly (Carter Co. TN) and Venie Smithpeters, cause of death: "chronic rhumatism, flue", informant: Eddie Matherly (Butler), buried: Matherly Cemetery, died: 20 Jan 1929, record (1929) #: 5328.

John ARNEY, age 74 years, married, parents: Mitchell Arnry and Sarah Robinson, cause of death: not stated, buried: Rankins Cemetery, died: 1 Feb 1929, record (1929) #: 5329.

Fanny Catherine CROSSWHITE, born: 6 Aug 1873, married, parents: Alfred Stout and Susana Morley, cause of death: "flu and pneumonia, endocarditis", informant: Clyde Crosswhite (Crandull), buried: Crosswhite Cemetery, died: 11 Feb 1929, record (1929) #: 5330.

Sarah C. TAYLOR, born: 21 Apr 1865, widow, parents: Ezekiel Curd and Polly Ann Hammons, cause of death: "chronic brights disease", informant: R,H, Taylor (Mountain City), buried: Cornett Cemetery, died: 2 Mar 1929, record (1929) #: 8123.

Rufus B. BOLDIN, born: 29 Jan 1863, parents: Austin Boldin (NC) and Lucy Lawson (NC), cause of death: "brights disease", informant: Austin Boldin (Mountain City), died: 6 Mar 1929, record (1929) #: 8124.

Julia May GENTRY, born: 9 May 1916 at Washington Co. VA, parents: James F. Gentry and Kate Taylor (NC), death cause: "obstructive jaundice" informant: James F. Gentry (Laurel Bloomery), buried: Taylorsville, VA, died: 26 Mar 1929, record (1929) #: 8125.

Mary Jane THOMPSON, colored, age 79 years, born at Coldwell Co. NC, prents: not stated, cause of death: "chronic heart disease", informant: Jim Mock (Mountain City), died: 4 Mar 1929, record (1929) #: 8126.

Richard H. BUTLER, born: 25 Oct 1847, married, parents: R.R. Butler (VA) and Emeline Donnelly, cause of death: "angina pectoris", informant: A.G. Grayson, died: 19 Mar 1929, record (1929) #: 8127.

Virginia HENSLEY, born: 21 Feb 1929, parents: J.T. Hensley (NC) and Ida Fenner, cause of death: "lobar pneumonia", informant: Smith Fenner (Mountain City), died: 21 Mar 1929, record (1929) #: 8128.

Louisa An MCQUEEN, born: 3 Apr 1856, divorced, parents: Finley McQueen and (first name not stated) Shoun, cause of death: "lobar pneumonia", informant: Wade McQueen (Butler), buried: Rainbolt Cemetery, died: 15 Mar 1929, record (1929) #: 8129.

Martha GREENWELL, born: 28 Dec 1853, widow, parents: Silas Clark and Jane Morley, cause of death: "influenza, colitis", informant: R.R. Greenwell (Butler), died: 3 Mar 1929, record (1929) #: 8130.

Warren Lee WARD, born: 7 Mar 1929 (date almost illegible), parents: Joseph Warren Ward (Watauga Co. NC) and Josie Lee Perkins (Ashe Co. NC), cause of death: "supposed hives", informant: Bob Perkins, died: 10 Mar 1929, record (1929) #: 1831.

George J. ANDREWS, born: 14 Dec 1928, parents: Wheeler Andrews and Mary Finey (Carter Co. TN), cause of death: illegible, informant: Wheeler Andrews (Butler), died: 13 Mar 1929, record (1929) #: 8132.

William DELOACH, born: 12 Mar 1870 in Carter Co. TN, married, minister, parents: Sam Deloach (Carter Co. TN) and Louise Garrison (Carter Co. TN) cause of death: "tuberculosis", informant: C.H. Deloach (Doeville), died: 21 Mar 1929, record (1929) #: 8133.

Laura Kate CAMPBELL, born: 14 Jun 1928 in Sullivan Co. TN, parents: Wilder Campbell and Laurie Gregg, cause of death: "pneumonia", died: 8 Mar 1929, record (1929) #: 8134.

Rebecca CORNETT, age and date of birth not stated, born in North Carolina, married, parents: Ryley Hamby and Cynthey Hamby, cause of death: "chronic brights disease", born: 28 Mar 1929, record (1929) #: 8135.

Mary Jane CRUSE, born: 8 Jul 1848 in North Carolina, widow, parents: Jim Rice (NC) and Cela Rice (NC), cause of death: not stated, informant: C.L. Cruze (Linchburg, VA), buried: Shady, TN, died: 3 Apr 1929, record (1929) #: 10815.

William, M. ? (Surname Illegible), born: 12 Feb 1860, married, parents: William (surname illegible) (VA) and Eliza Crowel (VA), cause of death: "cardiac..(illegible)..", buried: Southerland Cemetery, died: 25 Apr 1929, record (1929) #: 10816.

Joseph SPRIGGS, age about 50 years, born at Hawkins Co. TN, married, parents: Terry Spriggs (VA) and Mary Jane Hamilton (Wythe Co. VA), cause of death: "not stated, died suddenly", informant: C.W. York (Laurel Bloomery), buried: Damascus, VA, died: 5 Mar 1929, record (1929) #: 10817.

Bula DAVIS, born: 17 Mar 1927, parents: Willie Davis and Cora D. Roark, cause of death: "supposed to be flu", informant: David Roark (Crandell), buried: Gentry Cemetery, died: 18 Apr 1929, record (1929) #: 10818.

William F. SCOTT, born: 9 Mar 1880, married, parents: James Scott and mother's name "not known", cause of death: "myrocodis", informant: R.W. Scott (Crandull), buried: Scott Cemetery, died: 23 Apr 1929, record (1929) #: 10819.

G.W. SNYDER, age 69 years, married, parents: Washington Snyder and Sarah Morefield, cause of death: "chronic intestinal nephritis", buried: Snyder Cemetery, died: 3 Apr 1929, record (1929) #: 10820.

John BUMGARDNER, born: 20 Aug 1860, married, parents: David Bumgardner (NC) and Caroline Snyder, cause of death: "chronic brights diesese", informant: Walter Bumgardner (Mountain City), buried: Arnold Cemetery, died: 6 Apr 1929, record (1929) #: 10821.

Fannie FLINCHERN, born: 8 Oct 1883, married, parents: Thomas McElyea and Margaret Nolen, cause of death: illegible, informant: Margaret McElyea (Lodi, VA), buried: Eggers Cemetery, died: 10 May 1929, record (1929) #: 13123.

William Franklin REID, born: 28 Sep 1909, single, parents: Noah Reid and Ida Fritz, cause of death: "gun shot wound above heart by accidental discharge of shotgun in his own hands", informant: Noah Reid (Laurel Bloomery), buried: Valley Cemetery, died: 24 May 1929, record (1929) #: 13124.

Lemuel GENTRY, born: 6 Apr 1905, single, parents: James Gentry and Memphis Wills, cause of death: "tuberculosis of lungs", informant: J.W. Gentry (Mountain City), buried: Phillippi Cemetery, died: 11 Apr 1929, record (1929) #: 13125.

Mollie DONNELLY, born: 5 Dec 1855, single, parents: Alex Donnelly and Matilda Sullivan, cause of death: "apoplexy", informant: Alice Donnelly (Mountain City), died: 28 Apr 1929, record (1929) #: 13126.

Mrs. Mollie RAINBOLT, born: 26 Mar 1867, married, parents: John Shupe and Fannie Shoun, cause of death: "broncho pneumonia", buried: Cobbs Creek Cemetery, died: 19 Jan 1929, record (1929) #: 13127.

Mrs. Ellen LIPFORD, born: 8 Nov 1889, parents: Criss Kite and Sarah McQueen, death cause: "broncho pneumonia", buried: Cobbs Creek Cemetery, died: 2 Feb 1929, record (1929) #: 13128.

Miss Julia LOWE, born: 10 Apr 1908, parents: father's name not stated and Matilda Campbell, cause of death: "tuberculosis and pneumonia", informant: Matilda Campbell (Butler), buried: Cobbs Creek Cemetery, died: 3 Feb 1929, record (1929) #: 13129.

Wm Billie STOUT, age about 58 years, born in North Carolina, parents: Wm E. Stout (NC) and mother's name "not known", cause of death: tuberculosis menengitis", informant: J.F. Grindstaff (Doeville), buried: Slimp Cemetery, died: 6 May 1929, record (1929) #: 13130.

Miss Mary RAINBOLT, age 79 years, 4 months and 6 days, single, parents: Dugger Rainbolt and Lucinda Venable, cause of death: "pneumonia broncho", informant: Matilda Rainbolt (Butler), buried: Cobbs Creek Cemetery, died: 21 Apr 1929, record (1929) #: 13131.

Doris Nellie SHOUN, born: 25 Apr 1929, parents: Pedro Shoun and Laura Roberts, cause of death: "illegible", informant: John Dillon (Mountain City), died: 28 May 1929, record (1929) #: 13132. (Note: see record below) Michael SHOUN, born: 23 Mar 1908, single, parents: Pedro Shoun and Laura Roberts, cause of death: "spinal menengitis", informant: John Dillon (Mountain City), died: 31 May 1929, record (1929) #: 13133.

Della Waunetia MAY, born: 20 May 1929, parents: Ray May and Theola McGlamery, cause of death: "cause unknown", informant: Ray May (Trade), buried: Reece Cemetery, died: 24 May 1929, record (1929) #: 13134.

Anderson MOODY, born: 29 Jan 1910, single, parents: Will R. Moody and Margaret Anderson, cause of death: "instant death caused by falling tree", informant: W.R. Moody (Butler), buried: Sugar Grove Cemetery, died: 12 Apr 1929, record (1929) #: 13135.

Joseph Franklin SCHMIDT, (known as Frank Smith), born: 29 Sep 1853 in Germany, married, parents: Joseph Franklin Schmidt (Germany) and mother's name not known, cause of death: "gastric cancer", informant: George Creed (Laurel Bloomery), buried: Cornett Cemetery, died: 17 Jun 1929, record (1929) #: 15349.

Margaret SHUPE, born: 17 Apr 1846, widow, parents Wilham Blevins and Catherine Berry, cause of death: "lobar pneumonia", buried: Phillippi Cemetery, died: 7 Jun 1929, record (1929) #: 15250.

Van Della WARREN, born: 8 Jun 1929, parents: Don Warren and Mae Dunn, cause of death: "umbelical infection", informant: Don Warren (Shouns), died: 20 Jun 1929, record (1929) #: 15351.

Maggie BARRETT, born: 12 Apr 1893, married, parents: J.M. Dowell and Elizabeth Wilson, cause of death: "chronic pulmonary tuberculosis", informant: S.E. Dowell (Shouns), buried: Dowell Cemetery, died: 15 Jun 1929, record (1929) #: 15352.

Sarah Elizabeth HAMMONS, born: 2 Jul 1870, married, parents: John Forrester and Ellen Snyder, cause of death: "chronic brights disease", informant: W.M. Hammons, died: 10 May 1929, record (1929) #: 15353.

Margaret D. MCKINNEY, born: 29 Mar 1855, married, parents: Allen T. Carriger and Margaret E.C. Pearce, death cause: "chronic intestinal nephritis", buried: Hunter, TN, died: 3 Jun 1929, record (1929) #: 15354.

Roby Barton BROWN, born: 4 Aug 1841 in North Carolina, parents: James Brown (NC) and Harriett Farthing (NC), cause of death: "chronic brights disease", informant: Margaret Donnelly (Shouns), died: 8 Jun 1929, record (1929) #: 15355.

Martha ELLIS, born: 15 Oct 1859 in North Carolina, age 71 years, 7 months and 20 days, married, parents: Soloman Roten (NC) and Elizabeth Younce (NC), cause of death: "apoplexy", informant: Florence Ellis (Butler), died: 5 Jun 1929, record (1929) #: 15356.

Walter HARRIS, born: 30 Mar 1924, parents: J.Q. Harris (NC) and Margaret Smythe, cause of death: "poleomyelitis, acute anterior", informant: Margaret Harris (Butler), died: 27 Jun 1929, record (1929) #: 15357.

Amanda STEWART, age 84 years, widow, parents: Jesse Snyder and Elizabeth Stout, cause of death: "chronic.. (illegible).., age", informant: M.F. Stewart (Crandull), buried: Woods Cemetery, died: 1 Jun 1929, record (1929) #: 15358.

William H. BLEVINS, born: 24 Sep 1886, single, parents: David H. Blevins and Laurie Smith, cause of death: "hemorrhage of brain, paralysis", informant: Geo Blevins (Crandull), buried: Blevins Cemetery, died: 5 Jun 1929, record (1929) #: 15359.

David Garfield DOWELL, born: 18 Jun 1929, parents: father's name "not known" and Lena Dowell, cause of death: not stated, informant: Martha J. Parks (Trade), buried: Price Cemetery, died: 19 Jun 1929, record (1929) #: 15360.

Ruth Mae FARMER, born: 8 Oct 1907, married, parents: J.E. Sexton and Dora Newland, cause of death: "puerperal septicocrina", informant: J.E. Sexton (Mountain City), buried: Shingletown Cemetery, died: 28 Jun 1929, record (1929) #: 17749.

Bessie Myrtle DOTSON, born: 30 Nov 1899, single, parents: Geo W. Dotson and Colla O. Grayson, cause of death: "chronic pulmonary tuberculosis", informant: O.D. Dotson (Shouns), buried: Trade, TN, died: 1 Jul 1929, record (1929) #: 17750.

Hanner NYE, born: 15 Jul 1841 at Jefferson, NC, widow, parents: Timothy Poe (NC) and Mary Dickerson (NC), cause of death: "chronic pulmonary tuberculosis", informant: Lee Nye (Shouns), died: 4 Jul 1929, record (1929) #: 17751.

James W. JOHNSON, Sr., born: 19 Sep 1844, married, parents: Allen Johnson and Pollie Johnson, cause of death: "apoplexy", informant: Mrs. Oscar Johnson, died: 10 Jul 1929, record (1929) #: 17752.

Andy J. OSBORN, born: 15 Sep 1861, married, parents: Isaac Osborn (NC) and Lydia Potter, cause of death: "myocordial degeneration auriculor fibilation", informant: Bettie Dunn (Shouns), buried: Bristol, died: 2 Jul 1929, record (1929) #: 17753.

Inos TRIVETT, female, age about 28, married, parents: Thomas Martin and Celia M. Dunn, cause of death: "chronic pulmonary tuberculosis", informant: J.G. Dunn (Shouns), buried: Martin Cemetery, died: 29 JUn 1929, record (1929) #: 17754.

Charlie DICKEN, born: 26 Jan 1928, parents: Thomas Dicken and Cassie O'Neil, cause of death: illegible, informant: Thomas Dicken (Neva), died: 11 Jul 1929, record (1929) #: 17755.

Joseph L. STEPHENS, born: 27 May 1873 in North Carolina, married, parents: Thomas Stephens (NC) and Mary Johnson (NC), cause of death: "chronic intestinal nephritis, pneumonia", informant: B.O. Fritts (Vaughtsville), died: 16 Jul 1929, record (1929) #: 17756.

Mary Elizabeth STOUT, born: 14 Nov 1861, married, parents: Jacob Lowe and Sarah Gambill, cause of death: "myosordial insufficiency", informant: J.M. Stout (Doeville), buried: Stout Cemetery, died: 31 Jul 1929, record (1929) #: 17757.

Walter MILSAP, born: 2 Jan 1879 in North Carolina, married, parents: Eleam Milsap (NC) and Juley Willard (NC), cause of death: "run over by an engine at.....)", died: 13 Jul 1929, record (1929) #: 17758.

Pauline BYERS, born: 3 Nov 1927, parents: Calvin Byers and Lillie Gilbert, cause of death: "cholera", informant: Clyde Byers (Butler), buried: Rainbolt Cemetery, died: 22 Jul 1929, record (1929) #: 17759.

Minnie ISAACS, parents: Charlie Isaacs (NC) and Mamie Jenkins, cause of death: "premature birth", informant: D.A. Swift (Butler), born/died: 26 Jul 1929, record (1929) #: 17760.

Winne ISAACS, born: 26 Jul 1929, parents: Charlie Isaacs (NC) and Mamie Jenkins, cause of death: "premature birth", informant: D.A. Swift (Butler), died: 27 Jul 1929, record (1929) #: 17761.

Henry LOWE, born: 5 Jul 1922, parents: Jacob Lowe and Belle Lowe, cause of death: "polionyilites", informant: Claude Stout, died: 18 Jul 1929, record (1929) #: 17762.

Mary Ivaline BARRY, born: 16 Feb 1929, parents: Hugh Barry and Alice Grindstaff, cause of death: "acute colitis", informant: Hugh Barry (Mountain City), died: 25 Jul 1929, record (1929) #: 17763.

Zachariah Taylor SCOTT, born: 25 Apr 1847, widower, parents: Geo W. Scott (VA) and Anna Cole, cause of death: "acute nephritis and acute endo carditis", informant: Edney Neal (Crandull), buried: Woods Cemetery, died: 13 Jul 1929, record (1929) #: 17764.

R.E. MAYS, born: 28 Mar 1929, parents: Raymond Mays and Loony Blevens, cause of death: "pneumonia", informant: G.R. Blevins (Crandull), buried: Blevins Cemetery, died: 25 Jul 1929, record (1929) #: 17765.

Ruth Kathryn CABLE, born: 19 Jul 1929, parents: Devey Cable and Rilda Greene (NC), cause of death: "inanition", informant: Dewey Cable (Butler), buried: Cable Cem, died: 31 Jul 1929, record (1929) #: 17766.

Ilene Faw MOREFIELD, born: 12 Jul 1928, parents: Ferd Morefield and Margaret Warren, cause of death: "intero colitis", buried: Owens Cemetery, died: 3 Aug 1929, record (1929) #: 20185.

Wilmer Louise FROST, born: 16 May 1929, parents: Fred Frost and Mary Trivett, cause of death: "jaundice and diarrhea", died: 13 Aug 1929, record (1929) #: 20186.

John Henry REEVES, colored, born: 2 Jun 1907, married, parents: George Reeves (NC) and Julia Thompson (NC), cause of death:"lobar pneumonia", died: 5 Aug 1929, record (1929) #: 20187.

Loura MAXWELL, black, age 69 years, born in North Carolina, married, parents: Andrew Dobbins (NC) and Laura Dobbins (NC), cause of death:"cancer stomach", inforant: Rhubin Maxwell, buried: Mountain View Cemetery, died: 8 Aug 1929, record (1929) #: 20188.

Eliza S. FORRESTER, born: 17 Feb 1851, widow, parents: Jarred Mansfield Price (NC) and Rebecca Hawkins (NC), cause of death:"cerebral hemorrhage", informant: Nancy Ellen Arnold (Mountain City), died: 9 Aug 1929, record (1929) #: 20189.

Mary Katherine MOORE, born: 16 Mar 1863, married, parents: Lewis Guthrie and Rhoda Moore, cause of death:"cancer stomach", died: 10 Aug 1929, record (1929) #: 20190.

Ella Nora DUNN, born: 24 Jul 1929, parents: J.G. Dunn and Susie Main, cause of death: "unknown", informant: J.W. Dunn, died: 2 Aug 1929, record (1929) #: 20191.

Mary PHILLIPS, age about 71 years, born in North Carolina, widow, parents: Andy Jones (NC) and Mary Andrews (NC), cause of death: "pellagra", informant: Clyde Arnold (Shouns), buried: Phillips Cemetery, died: 29 Jul 1929, record (1929) #: 20192.

John C. STOUT, born: 28 Jan 1927, parents: Thomas Stout and Pollie Smith, cause of death: "meningites", informant: Thomas Stout (Shouns), buried: Arnold Cemetery, died: 29 Jun 1929, record (1929) #: 20193.

Delilah Catherine REECE, born: 4 Mar 1864, widow, parents: Jas F. Ward and Nancy Stout, cause of death: "colitis", informant: H.W. Reece (Neva), died: 12 Aug 1929, record (1929) #: 20194.

Louisa Matilda SHULL, born: 9 Mar 1842 at Carter Co. TN, single, parents: John Shull (NC) and Sallie James, cause of death: "apoplexy", buried: Cobbs Creek Cemetery, died: 14 Aug 1929, record (1929) #: 20195.

Robert Earl MILLER, born: 1 Apr 1929, parents: Fred R. Miller and Laura A. Williams, cause of death: "pneumonia, double lobar", informant: J.R. Miller (Crandull), buried: Gentry Cemetery, died: 7 Apr 1929, record (1929) #: 20196.

Mrs. Rilda CABLE, born: 29 Aug 1906 in North Carolina, married, parents: George Green (NC) and Lizzie Elliott (NC), cause of death: "child birth", buried: Cable Cemetery, died: 2 Aug 1929, record (1929) #: 20197.

Junior Lindberg SMITH, born: 30 Jun 1928, parents: Walter Fred Smith and Minnie Allen, cause of death: "drowned in a tub of water in the yard", informant: W.A. Davidson (Mountain City), buried: Shingletown Cemetery, died: 29 Sep 1929, record (1929) #: 22393.

Nancy E. PHILLIPPI, born: 3 Jul 1853, married, parents: William Barry and Sarah Dotson, cause of death: "fracture of neck femur, fall", informant: Mrs. Birdie Phillippi (Mountian City), Phillippi Cemetery, died: 8 May 1929, record (1929) #: 22394.

Raymond JONES, born: 1 Jun 1924, parents: father "not known" and Blanche Jones (NC), cause of death: "died suddenly", buried: Ashe Co. NC, died: 11 Sep 1929, record (1929) #: 22395.

Mamie ARNOLD, born: 3 Aug 1916, parents: John Arnold and Martha Church, cause of death: "typhoid fever", informant: John Arnold (Doeville), died: 16 Sep 1929, record (1929) #: 22396.

Mary A. MCKEE, born: 23 Mar 1855, single, parents: Alf McKee and Elizabeth Heaton, cause of death: "hart dropsy", informant: W.S. Garland (Doeville), buried: Garland Cemetery, died: 3 Aug 1929, record (1929) #: 22397.

James C. BUCKLES, born: 12 May 1853, married, parents: Wm H. Buckles (VA) and Mary J. Davidson (VA), cause of death: "pulmonary hemorrhage, heart block", buried: Gentry Cem, died: 5 Sep 1929, record (1929) #: 22398.

Dan Artel PRESNELL, born: 13 Sep 1923 in North Carolina, parents: Wesley Presnell (NC) and Nola Trivett (NC), death cause: "asteomyilitis", buried in North Carolina, died: 13 Sep 1929, record #: 22399.

Nancy Catherine GUFFIE, age about 65 years, married, parents: Wesley Smith and Leliah Laws, cause of death: "tuberculisis liver", informant: George Guffey (Butler), buried: Allen Cemetery, died: 17 Sep 1929, record (1929) #: 23400.

Lessie HENDERSON, born: 1 Mar 1891, married, parents: Monroe Harris (VA) and Lizzy Perry (NC), cause of death: "brain tumor", informant: Chas Henderson (Damascus, VA), buried: Damascus, VA, died: 7 Oct 1929, record (1929) #: 24766.

Smith C. ADAMS, born: 27 Feb 1851, married, parents: Benjamin Adams (NC) and Rhoda Goodwin, cause of death: "appendicitis", informant: Edgar Adams (Mountain City), buried: Phillippi Cemetery, died: 11 Oct 1929, record (1929) #: 24767.

Elizabeth REEVES, colored, born: 16 Aug 1871 in North Carolina, married, parents: David Maxwell (NC) and Hannah Maxwell (NC), cause of death: "cancer of breasts", informant: G.W. Reeves (Mountain City), buried: Shouns, died: 17 Oct 1929, record (1929) #: 24768.

Garfield ARNOLD, born: 16 Jan 1904, married, parents: John Arnold and Martha Church, cause of death: "typhoid fever", informant: John Arnold (Doeville), buried: Shouns Cemetery, died: 21 Oct 1929, record (1929) #: 24769.

James B.D. ROBINSON, born: 14 Dec 1859, widower, parents: (first name illegible) Robinson and Elizabeth Howard, cause of death: "apoplexy", informant: Jas D. Robinson (Butler), buried: Doeville, died: 29 Oct 1929, record (1929) #: 24770.

Senter C. YOUNCE, born: 3 Dec 1850 in North Carolina, married, parents: Abraham Younce (NC) and mother's mame "don't know", cause of death: "moorcordial insufficiency", informant: Mrs, S.C. Younce (Butler), buried: Cobbs Creek Cemetery, died: 8 Oct 1929, record (1929) #: 24771.

Vena C. ROBERTS, born: 6 Feb 1881, married, parents: John M. Stout and Mary Lowe, cause of death: "cancer of breasts", informant: Gray Roberts, buried: Stout Cemetery, died: 14 Oct 1929, record (1929) #: 24772.

Norman Harold MAIN, born: 30 Sep 1929, parents: G. Marion Main and Viola M. Wyatt, cause of death: "premature birth, 8 months", buried: Blevins Cemetery, died: 3 Oct 1929, record (1929) #: 24773.

Jas J. WRIGHT, born: 24 Oct 1845, married, parents: Moses Wright (VA) and Lidia Cole, cause of death: "softening of brain", informant: A.J. Wright (Crandull), buried: Blevins Cemetery, died: 13 Oct 1929, record (1929) #: 24774.

Marie MOREFIELD, born: 10 Sep 1929, parents: Joe Morefield and Florence Proffitt, cause of death: "facial eripipelas", informant: Alvin Dunn, buried: Cornett Cem, died: 9 Nov 1929, record (1929) #: 27046.

Gladys ABEL, born: 2 Feb 1925, parents: Clinton Abel and Kate Gentry, cause of death: "dyptheria", informant: H.C. Abel (Laurel Bloomery), died: 3 Nov 1929, record (1929) #: 27047.

Mary ROBINSON, age 86 years, widow, parents: Lee Farris and Jane Spear, death cause: "chronic brights disease", died: 29 Aug 1929, record (1929) #: 27048.

Mary Jane GENTRY, born: 4 Aug 1928, parents: Samuel P. Gentry and Reba Arnold, cause of death: "tomaine poisoning", informant: Sam Gentry (Mountain City), died: 18 Nov 1929, record (1929) #: 27049.

Mary SNYDER, age 59 years, born in North Carolina, widow, parents: John Anderson (NC) and Mary Grines (NC), informant: G.W. Howard (Shouns), buried: Arnold Cemetery, died: 30 Nov 1929, record (1929) #: 27050.

Infant STANSBERRY, male, parents: John Stansberry (NC) and Mary Alice Fritz, death cause: "premature birth, 6 months", informant: John Fritts (Vaughtsville), died: 3 Nov 1929, record (1929) #: 27051.

Robert E. WRIGHT, born: 15 Aug 1852 in Virginia, widower, parents: Wm S. Wright (VA) and mother's name not stated, cause of death: "apoplexy", informant: C.C. Wright (Mountain City), buried: Wright Cemetery, died: 15 Nov 1929, record (1929) #: 27052.

James Lawson SMITH, born: 9 Dec 1849 at Carter Co. TN, widower, parents: Henderson Smith (Carter Co. TN) and Ellen Wilson, cause of death: "chronic brights disease", informant: John H. Smith (Mountain City), buried: Wilson Cemetery, died: 15 Oct 1929, record (1929) #: 27053.

Opel Drexie VANOVER, born: 13 May 1923, parents: Winston Vanover (NC) and Virdie Lipford, cause of death: "acute nephritis, hemorrhage", informant: Avery Lipford (Crandull), died: 15 Nov 1929, record (1929) #: 27054.

Gale MAY, male, born: 7 Jun 1916, parents: Riley May and Pearl Snyder, cause of death: "fracture of base of brain, bruises on mouth and lips and chest, supposed to be accidental", buried: Gentry Cemetery, died: 18 Nov 1929, record (1929) #: 27055.

Jerline MILLER, born: 20 Apr 1929, parents: E.E. Miller and M.C. Roark (NC), cause of death: not stated, buried: Gentry Cemetery, died: 27 Nov 1929, record (1929) #: 27056.

Nancy Emaline WALLACE, age supposed to be 58 years, born in North Carolina, married, parents: E.N. Martin (NC) and Purda Stewart (NC), cause of death: "....carditis. ..(illegible)", informant: Jordan Wallace, died: 30 Nov 1929, record (1929) #: 27057.

Delmas James POTTER, born: 23 Feb 1929, parents: John Potter and Ida Cable, cause of death: "cholera", buried: Cable Cemetery, died: 21 Aug 1929, record (1929) #: 27059.

John Calvin BROOKS, born: 7 Nov 1855 in North Carolina, married, parents: Eli Brooks (NC) and Jane Black (NC), cause of death: "apoplexy", informant: Thomas Brooks (NC), buried in North Carolina, died: 7 Nov 1929, record (1929) #: 27060.

Wiley R. RUPARD, born: 5 May 1866 in North Carolina, married, parents: Carney Rupard (NC) and Mary Dishman (NC), cause of death: "intestinal obstruction", informant: J.C. Rupard (Laurel Bloomery), died: 25 Dec 1929, record (1929) #: 29766.

Andy Clinton SLIMP, born: 8 Oct 1860, married, parents: Andy Slimp and Martha Jones, death cause: "diabetes, brights disease", informant: David Slimp, died: 4 Dec 1929, record (1929) #: 29767.

Jennie M. SHOUN, born: 5 Aug 1860 in North Carolina, married, parents: William Maxwell (NC) and Julia Parkin (NC), cause of death: "chronic brights disease", buried: Wilson Cemetery, died: 9 Dec 1929, record (1929) #: 29768.

William Riley PHILLIPS, born: 29 Dec 1865, parents: Jim Phillips and (first name not stated) Netherly, cause of death: "brights disease", died: 23 Dec 1929, record (1929) #: 29769.

Caroline JOHNSON, born: 9 Jan 1845, widow, parents: Hyder Mitchell and Sallie Slimp, cause of death: "chronic brights disease", informant: Mrs. J.K. Wilson (Mountain City), buried: Phillippi Cemetery, died: 28 Dec 1929, record (1929) #: 29770.

William Henry SHOUN, born: 31 Aug 1924, parents: Joseph M. Shoun and Della C. Richardson, cause of death: "unknown, found dead in bed", died: 10 Dec 1929, record (1929) #: 29771.

Mary Catherine STURGALL, born: 24 Mar 1879, married, parents: (first name not stated) Tipton and "don't know mother's name", cause of death: "organic heart disease, lobar pneumonia", informant: G.A. Sturgall (Crandull), buried: Washington Co. VA, died: 14 Dec 1929, record (1929) #: 29772.

R.K. REYNOLD, age 74 years, born in North Carolina, widower, parents: William Reynolds and mother's name unknown, cause of death: "chronic brights disease", buried: County Home Cemetery, died: 2 Jan 1930, record (1930) #: 1057.

Ancy E. SMITH, male, born: 13 Apr 1920, parents: Ira Smith (NC) and Sallie Turnmire (NC), cause of death: "acute endo carditis", informant: Mrs. Mat Flannigan (Mountain City), died: 27 Jan 1930, record (1930) #: 1058.

George Franklin NETHERLY, age 81 years, widower, parents: Frank Reece and Betsy Netherly, cause of death: "lobar pneumonia", informant: Elbert Davis (Shouns), buried: Neva, died: 1 Jan 1930, record (1930) #: 1059.

Elizabeth E. FARTHING, born: 8 sEp 1842, widow, parents: Eliga Daugherty and Eva Mast, cause of death: "chronic heart disease", informant: R.G. Vannoy (Neva), buried: Neva, died: 9 Jan 1930, record (1930) #: 1060.

Allie E. JOHNSON, born: July 1888 in Ashe Co. NC, married, parents: Sam P. Jones (Ashe Co. NC) and Lettie Roark (Ashe Co. NC), cause of death: "heart dropsy", informant: C.M. Johnson (butler), buried: Brown Cem, died: 13 Jan 1930, record (1930) #: 1061.

Mrs. Sallie MCELYEA, age 54 years, 1 month and 7 days, married, parents: Huston Mains and Eliza Mains, cause of death: "chronic valvulor heart disease", died: 17 Jan 1930, record (1930) #: 1062.

Ruby R. PROFFITT, born: 14 Dec 1929, parents: Sam Proffitt and Rettie Proffitt, cause of death: not stated, informant: Sam Proffitt, buried: Proffitt Cemetery, died: 15 Jan 1930, record (1930) #: 1063.

W.B. WALKER, Jr., born: 8 Aug 1924 at Carter Co. TN, parents: W.B. Walker and Loura Greer, cause of death: not stated, buried: Campbell Cemetery, died: 20 Jan 1930, record (1930) #: 1064.

Mattie Gertrude CURTIS, born: 28 Aug 1846 at Caldwell Co. NC, single, parents: Hezekiah Curtis (NC) and Celia Coffee (NC), cause of death: "apoplexy", informant: F.G. Curtis (Butler), died: 2 Jan 1930, record (1930) #: 1065.

Rosa Ival MORLEY, born: 5 Mar 1895, married, parents: Lafayet Wagner and Neome Wagner, cause of death: "pulmonary tuberculosis", died: 5 Jan 1930, record (1930) #: 1066.

Spencer CABLE, born: 14 Jan 1918, single, parents: James P. Cable and Nancy N. Stout, cause of death: "pernicious anemia", informant: James Cable (Butler), died: 27 Jan 1930, record (1930) #: 1067.

Joseph M. BUCHANAN, born: 7 Sep 1844 in North Carolina, married, parents: Arter Buchanan (NC) and Clarrissa Baker (NC), cause of death: "apoplexy", White Cem, died: 23 Jan 1930, record (1930) #: 1068.

Clyde B. HUTCHINSON, born: 11 Dec 1895, married, parents: William Hutchinson (NC) and Eliza J. Garland (KY), cause of death: "double lobar pneumonia", informant: Eliza Arnold (Crandull), buried: Blevins Cemetery, died: 9 Jan 1930, record (1930) #: 1069.

Laura DAVIDSON, born: 9 Sep 1853 at Ashe Co. NC, widow, parents: Andrew Pennington (Ashe Co. NC) and Elizabeth Pope (Ashe Co. NC), cause of death: "cerebral hemorhage, brights disease", informant: Dona Davidson (Mountain City), buried: Shingletown Cemetery, died: 15 Feb 1930, record (1930) #: 3396.

Thomas J. POTTER, born: 7 May 1844 in North Carolina, widower, parents: J.O.T. Potter and Susan Main, cause of death: "chronic myocarditis", informant: John M. Potter (Shouns), buried: Potter Cemetery, died: 9 Feb 1930, record (1930) #: 3397.

Walter David LANDERS, black, born: 2 Sep 1928, parents: Peter Landers (NC) and Lillie Preston, cause of death: "spinal meningitis", informant: Peter Landers (Mountain City), buried: Mountain View Cemetery, died: 16 Feb 1930, record (1930) #: 3398.

Jane DOUGHERTY, born: 10 Jan 1846, widow, parents: John Daurty (NC) and mother's name illegible, cause of death: "cancer womb", informant: Mack Phillippi (Mountain City), buried: County Home Cemetery, died: 20 Feb 1930, record (1930) #: 3399.

Robert Hugh JOHNSON, age 46 years, married, parents: A.S. Johnson and Martha Cress, cause of death: "acute alcoholism, myocarditis", informant: A.S. Johnson (Mountain City), buried: Phillippi Cemetery, died: 22 Feb 1930, record (1930) #: 3400.

Mary M. PAYNE, born: 16 Dec 1838 at Ashe Co. NC, single, Zebulon Payne (Ashe Co. NC) and Charity Church (Ashe Co. NC), cause of death: "old age", informant: R.S. Payne (Shouns), buried: Payne Cemetery, died: 23 Feb 1930, record (1930) #: 3401.

Infant MCELYEA, female, parents: Howard McElyea and Emma Roark (NC), cause of death: "premature delivery at 6th month", informant: Howard McElyea (Neva), died: 19 Feb 1930, record (1930) #: 3402.

Bulah Lee STOUT, born: 31 Mar 1922, parents: Walter H. Stout and Effie D. Matherly, cause of death: "endocarditis", informant: Walter H. Stout (Butler), buried: Cobbs Creek Cemetery, died: 8 Feb 1930, record (1930) #: 3403.

James Devar KELLER, born: 18 Dec 1929, parents: Geo L. Keller (NC) and Esther Grindstaff, cause of death: "bronchial pneumonia", informant George Keller (Butler), died: 18 Feb 1930, record (1930) #: 3404.

Sarah POTTER, born: 10 Jun 1863, widow, parents: John Greenwell and Caroline Wolf (NC), cause of death: "myocardial insufficiency, nephritis", died: 24 Feb 1930, record (1930) #: 3405.

David STOUT, age 73 years, 10 months and 3 days, married, parents: Godfrey Stout and Eliz Crosswhite, cause of death: "bronchial pneumonia", informant: deceased's wife (Doeville), died: 2 Feb 1930, record (1930) #: 3406.

Joseph B. CROSSWHITE, age 47 years, married, parents: Alonzo Crosswhite and Mary Robinson, cause of death: "brights disease", informant: Gene H. Mullins (Mountain City), died: 10 Feb 1930, record (1930) #: 3407.

Sarah STOUT, born: 9 Mar 1868, married, parents: Pat Wills and (first name not stated) Pafford (VA), cause of death: "carcinoma of liver", informant: g.H. Pierce (Mountain City), buried: Shoun Cemetery, died: 19 Feb 1930, record (1930) #: 3408.

Cora Catherine GREER, born: 17 Sep 1929, parents: David M. Greer (NC) and Bertha Rambo, cause of death: illegible, informant: H. Blaine Stout (Doeville), died: 28 Feb 1930, record (1930) #: 3409.

Margie LIPFORD, parents: Edmond A. Lipford and Nilia M. Martin, cause of death: "premature birth at 7 months", buried: Martin Cemetery, born/died: 28 Feb 1930, record (1930) #: 3410.

Nola V. GREER, born: 10 Oct 1917, parents: Luke H. Greer (NC) and Loretta M. Roark (NC), cause of death: "accidentally shot by little 9 year old brother", buried: Ashland, NC, died: 26 Feb 1930, record (1930) #: 3411.

Thomas DUGGER, born: 23 Jan 1890, married, parents: John Dugger and Margaret Vines, cause of death: "broncho pneumonia", informant: Carl Arney (Butler), buried: Sugar Grove Cemetery, died: 23 Feb 1930, record (1930) #: 3412.

John BROWN, age 69 years, born in North Carolina, parents: Lewis Brown (NC) and mother's name unknown, cause of death: "chronic brights disease", buried: County Home Cemetery, died: 6 Mar 1930, record (1930) #: 6011.

Arthur Tilson LEWIS, born: 2 Apr 1882 in North Carolina, parents: Henderson Lewis (NC) and Nancy Vanover (NC), cause of death: "chronic intestinal nephritis", informant: Rosie Lewis (Shouns), buried in North Carolina, died: 21 Feb 1930, record (1930) #: 6012.

Winnie Lee GARLAND, born: 14 May 1928, parents: Lipford Garland and Nina Davis, cause of death: "broncho pneumonia", informant: J.G. Garland (Doeville), buried: Garland Cemetery, died: 9 Mar 1930, record (1930) #: 6013.

Linville E.C. HOLLOWAY, born: 8 Apr 1851 in North Carolina, widower, parents: Linville Hollowey (NC) and Elizabeth Brookshire (NC), cause of death: "brights disease", informant: Don C. Walker (Butler), died: 23 Feb 1930, record (1930) #: 6014.

John Elias DUGGER, age 72 years, 11 months and 11 days, widower, parents: James Dugger and Rebecca Vines, cause of death: "broncho pneumonia fever", buried: Cobbs Creek, died: 16 Mar 1930, record (1930) #: 6015.

Isaac M. ROBERTS, born: 28 Jul 1852, married, parents: R.A. Roberts and (first name illegible) Rambo, cause of death: "apoplexy", informant: A.L. Stout (Mountain City), died: 20 Mar 1930, record (1930) #: 6016.

Abel HARBIN, born: 11 Aug 1858 at "Ardle" Co. North Carolina, married, parents: Thomas Harbin (NC) and Julia Johnson (NC), cause of death: "cancer liver", died: 26 Mar 1930, record (1930) #: 6017.

Jacob LOWE, age 30 years, married, parents, James Lowe and Sarah Roberts, cause of death: "blood poisoning, head", informant: James Lowe (Mountain City), died: 28 Feb 1930, record (1930) #: 6018.

Burl Roy PHILLIPS, born: 26 Jan 1930, parents: father's name not given and Bonnie L. Mains, cause of death: "broncho pneumonia", informant: Marion Maine (Crandull), died: 26 Mar 1930, record (1930) #: 6019.

Maggie MORETZ, born: 26 Mar 1911, married, parents: A.L. Smith and Corda Killins (NC), cause of death: "acute brights disease", buried: Shouns, died: 7 Apr 1930, record (1930) #: 8627.

Clarence Jasper LEWIS, born: 1 Feb 1928, parents: Willie Lewis (NC) and Anna Bess Gentry, cause of death: "broncho pneumonia, influenza", informant: J.N. Gentry (Mountain City), buried: Phillippi Cemetery, died: 9 Apr 1930, record (1930) #: 8628.

William Mahlon HOWARD, born: 7 Feb 1863, married, parents: William N. Howard and Rhoda Dougherty (Ashe Co. NC), cause of death: "cerebral hemorhage", informant: R.J. Howard (Mountain City), died: 20 Apr 1930, record (1930) #: 8629.

Eugene Richard WARREN, born: 8 Apr 1930, parents: Thomas Warren (NC) and Virginia Truett (NC), cause of death: "erysipelas, left leg", informant: Thomas Warren, died: 30 Apr 1930, record (1930) #: 8630.

Liddy Fine DAY, age 71 years, married, parents: William Lewis and Betsy Courtner, cause of death: "apoplexy", informant: C.F. Day (Neva), buried: Neva, died: 24 Apr 1930, record (1930) #: 8631.

William CABLE, born: 9 Nov 1869, married, parents: Benjamin Cable and Susie Simerly, cause of death: "broncho pneumonia fever", buried: Cable Cemetery, died: 3 Apr 1930, record (1930) #: 8632.

James Floyd THOMAS, born: 14 Oct 1868 at Washington Co. VA, parents: David Thomas (VA) and mother's name not stated, cause of death: "pellagra", informant: Roy D. Thomas (Abingdon, VA), buried: Acre Field Cemetery, died: 31 May 1930, record (1930) #: 11166.

Tennis HARRIS, female, born: 28 Aug 1855 in North Carolina, unmarried, parents: Henderson Harris (NC) and Feraby Fields (NC), cause of death: "influenza, broncho pneumonia", informant: Guy Keys (Mountain City), buried: Shingletown Cemetery, died: 26 Apr 1930, record (1930) #: 11167.

Tilda Victoria MOREFIELD, born: 20 Jul 1896, single, parents: Ham Morefield and Jenettne Nichols (NC), cause of death: "lobar pneumonia", died: 12 May 1930, record (1930) #: 11168.

Nellia Alice OWENS, born: 16 Sep 1899, single, parents: N.D. Owens and Sallie McConnel, cause of death: illegible, informant: N.D. Owens (Damascus, VA), buried: Damascus, VA, died: 18 May 1930, record (1930) #: 11169.

Elvira JOHNSON, born: 1 Mar 1859 in Virginia, widow, parents: Lee Roy Ray (NC) and Jane Thomas (VA), cause of death: "chronic brights disease", informant: A.L. Johnson (Mountain City), buried: Wagner Cemetery, died: 21 May 1930, record (1930) #: 11170.

Tyrle V. BAUGUESS, born: 4 Jun 1867 in North Carolina, parents: Osborne Bouguess (NC) and Fannie Roberts (NC), cause of death: "cerebral hemorhage" informant: Mrs. Lucy Wills, died: 29 May 1930, record #: 11171.

Vestel Loid PRICE, born: 14 Apr 1930, parents: W.E. Price and Ada Belle Denney, cause of death: "unknown", informant: W.V. Price (Shouns), buried: Arnold Cemetery, died: 17 May 1930, record (1930) #: 11172.

Robert Lafayette CRESS, born: 19 Jul 1869, married, parents: J.G. Wilson and Sarah Cress, death cause: "cancer", informant: J.R. Hecks, died: 29 May 1930.

Virginia Pauline ALLEN, born: 22 Jan 1922, parents: father not stated and Ruthie Allen, cause of death: "acute rheumatic fever with endo carditis", informant: J.E. Sexton (Mountain City), buried: Shingletown Cemetery, died: 5 Jun 1930, record (1930) #: 13746.

Mary Ellen GENTRY, born: 13 Jul 1855, widow, parents: John Fritz and Iffy Spear, cause of death: "cerebral hemorhage", informant: Walker Gentry (Laurel Bloomery), buried: Gentry Cemetery, died: 14 Jun 1930, record (1930) #: 13747.

Mahala Rebecca MORRISON, born: 2 Mar 1842 in Virginia, parents: Hiram Ramsey (VA) and Mary Berry (VA), cause of death: "cancer of breast", informant: Mrs. Sallie Keys (Mountain City), buried: Wills Cemetery, died: 26 Jun 1930, record (1930) #: 13748.

Jacob N. STOUT, born: 4 May 1856, widower, parents: Nicholas Stout and Polly Dunn, cause of death: "chronic brights disease", informant: J.H. Stout (Elizabethton, TN), buried: Damascus, VA, died: 4 Jun 1930, record (1930) #: 13749.

Joseph Lincoln CHAPPELL, born: 31 Mar 1873, married, parents: Francis M. Chappell (NC) and Sarah A. Grigston, cause of death: "chronic brights disease", informant: W.F. Chappell (Shouns), died: 11 Jun 1930, record (1930) #: 13750.

Lillie WAGNER, born: 26 Dec 1867, married, parents: Jacob W. Dunn and Nancy Wagner, cause of death: "acute nephritis", died: 17 Jun 1930, record (1930) #: 13751.

Ulyssis Grant ARNOLD, born: 28 Oct (year omitted), age 61 years, parents: father's name unknown and Anna Arnold, cause of death: "chronic brights disease", informant: Mrs. Ellen Arnold (Mountain City), died: 31 Mar 1930, record (1930) #: 13752.

Blanche WILLIN, born: 14 Jun 1930, parents: Clarence Willin and Florence Hall, cause of death: "unknown", informant: Clifford Willin (Shouns), buried: Hall Cemetery, died: 23 Jun 1930, record (1930) #: 13753.

Jacob I. NEATHERLY, born: 3 Jan 1875, married, parents: S.H. Neatherly and Mary Tester, cause of death: "chronic intestinal nephritis", informant: Dan Neatherly (Neva), buried: Neva, died: 10 Jun 1930, record (1930) #: 13754.

Mary Magolna LAWS, born: 21 Jun 1864, married, parents: Joe Lowe and Jennie Miller, cause of death: "chronic myocordial degeneration", informant: Jas E. Laws (Butler), buried: Neva, died: 18 Jun 1930, record (1930) #: 13755.

Laura Emily STOUT, born: 17 Nov 1877 in North Carolina, married to L.L. Stout, parents: George Sammons (NC) and Nancy Escue, cause of death: "pulmonary tuberculosis", informant: L.L. Stout (Neva), died: 24 Jun 1930, record (1930) #: 13756.

Mary Virginia ROBERTS, born: 21 Aug 1862 in Virginia, widow, parents: Fleming Mays (VA) and Deborah Denton (VA), cause of death: "pulmonary tuberculosis", informant: A.L. Stout (Mountain City), died: 5 Jun 1930, record (1930) #: 13757.

Robert L. STOUT, born: 22 Dec 1883, married, parents: Ham Stout and Callie Wills, cause of death: "acute nephritis", informant: Fuller Stout (Mountain City), died: 20 Jun 1930, record (1930) #: 13758.

J.C. STEWART, age 9 months and 5 days, parents: Marion F. Stewart and Inez Stewart (VA), cause of death: "illio colitis (flux)", informant: Jack Stewart, died: 5 Jun 1930, record (1930) #: 13759.

Beulah CROSSWHITE, born: 17 Feb 1930, parents: Stacy Crosswhite and Ethel Sluder (NC), cause of death: "lobar pneumonia", informant: C.D. Sluder (Crandull), died: 6 Jun 1930, record (1930) #: 13760. (twins record below)

Eulah CROSSWHITE, born: 17 Feb 1930, parents: Stacy Crosswhite and Ethel Sluder (NC), cause of death: "lobar pneumonia", informant: B.L. Sluder (Crandull), died: 6 Jun 1930, record (1930) #: 13761. (twin)

James Earl MABE, born: 10 Nov 1928 in Virginia, parents: Alex Mabe and Blanche Jenkins, cause of death: "colitis", informant: R.L. Jenkins (Mountain City), buried: Cornett Cemetery, died: 9 Jul 1930, record (1930) #: 16290.

Cora MCQUEEN, Negro, born: 23 Jul 1901, married, parents: Finley Preston and Rachel McQueen, cause of death: "pulmonary tuberculosis", informant: Thomas McQueen (Mountain City), died: 28 Jul 1930, record (1930) #: 16291.

Elizabeth DONNELLY, born: 16 Dec 1845 in North Carolina, parents: Nathaniel Rominger (NC) and Elizabeth Greer (NC), cause of death: "chronic intestinal nephritis", informant: Mrs. Margaret Donnelly (Shouns), died: 30 Jul, 1930, record (1930) #: 16292.

Sarah E. ONEAL, born: 15 Jul 1864, married, parents: John Fletcher (NC) and Rebecca Rymer (NC), cause of death: "carcinoma of uterus", informant: J.E. Oneal (Neva), buried: Neva, died: 5 Jul 1930, record (1930) #: 16293.

Thomas Franklin GRINDSTAFF, born: 1 Apr 1871, married, parents: Isaac Grindstaff and Mary C. Robinson, cause of death: "heart failure, rhumatism", died: 10 Jul 1930, record (1930) #: 16294.

Wm C. WILSON, born: 10 Feb 1865, married, parents: Andrew J. Wilson and Julia (last name illegible), cause of death: "cirhosis of liver", informant: Mrs. Wm C. Wilson (Butler), buried: Cobbs Creek Cemetery, died: 21 Jul 1930, record (1930) #: 16295.

Cecil GARLAND, born: 21 Mar 1927, parents: Wheeler Garland and Bessie Church, cause of death: not stated, informant: Wheeler Garland (Doeville), died: 26 Jul 1930, record (1930) #: 16296.

Virginia Lee CHURCH, born: 12 Sep 1928, parents: father's name not given and Eulah May Church, cause of death: illegible, informant: J.C. Church (Mountain City), died: 12 Jul 1930, record (1930) #: 16297.

Mary C. GENTRY, born: 1 Sep 1851, widow of Mahlon Gentry, parents: Alfred Stout and Mary Howard, cause of death: "hemiplgia", informant: J.M. Gentry, buried: Gentry Cem, died: 23 Jul 1930, record (1930) #: 16298.

Mary E. BLANKENBECKLER. born: 28 Jun 1842 in Virginia, widow, parents: Wilham Hilhard (VA) and Mary Ramsey (VA), cause of death: "chronic brights disease", informant: Mrs, Sallie Allen (Mountain City), died: 6 Aug 1930, record (1930) #: 18814.

Rebecca GENTRY, born: 17 Jun 1885, married, parents: Elbert Lewis (NC) and Parlee Crosswhite, cause of death: "cancer womb", informant: Mrs. J.A. Wison (Mountian City), died: 9 Aug 1930, record (1930) #: 18815.

Bennie SMITH, born: 26 Feb 1930, parents: A.L. Smith and Corda Killings (NC), cause of death: "whooping cough", informant: A.L. Smith (Shouns), died: 11 Aug 1930, record (1930) #: 18816.

Margaret Louis HENSLEY, born: 12 May 1930, parents: J.T. Hensley (NC) and Ida Fenner, cause of death: not stated, informant: Ethel Gentry (Mountain City), died: 16 Aug 1930, record (1930) #: 18817.

Gracie Marelita ELLIS, born: 16 Mar 1846 in North Carolina, widow, parents: Joe Ashley (NC) and Hannah Farmer (NC), cause of death: "acute brights disease and fractured hip", informant: Robert Ellis (Mountain City), died: 16 Aug 1930, record (1930) #: 18818.

Fred Elbert BURGISS, born: 5 Jul 1930, parents: McKinley Burgiss and Mary Simms, cause of death: "whooping cough", informant: McKinley Burgiss, died: 23 Jul 1930, record (1930) #: 18819.

Ora Lee WARD, born: 24 Mar 1930, parents: Chas Ward (NC) and Blanche Farthing, cause of death: "whooping cough and broncho pneumonia", informant: Chas Ward (Mountain City), buried: Mountain View Cemetery, died: 24 Jul 1930, record (1930) #: 18820.

Millard Filmore BROWN, born: 31 Jan 1857 at Ashe Co. NC, married, parents: John T. Brown (Ashe Co. NC) and Nancy Younce (Ashe Co. NC), cause of death: "chronic intestinal nephritis", informant: L.B. Morley (Mountain City), died: 18 Aug 1930, record (1930) #: 18821.

Alexander Asa MARTIN, born: 16 May 1929, parents: Nick Martin and Rettie Reece, cause of death: "thought to be broncho pneumonia", informant: Nick Martin (Shouns), buried: Martin Cemetery, died: 14 Jun 1930, record (1930) #: 18822.

Jackson M. DOUGHERTY, 7 Jul 1854, single, parents: Eliga Dougherty and Eva Mast, cause of death: "diabetes", informant: Dewey Swift (Neva), died: 21 Jul 1930, record (1930) #: 18823.

Joseph Y. DAVIS, age 53 years, 7 months and 22 days, married, parents: Eli Davis and Nancy Slimp, cause of death: "revolver wound of chest, suicidal", informant: W.T. Davis (Neva), buried: Brown Cemetery, died: 31 Jul 1930, record (1930) #: 18824.

James David SLEMP, born: 14 Feb 1860, married, parents: David Slemp and Katherine Lowe, cause of death: "hemorrhage of brain", informant: John Slemp (Butler), died: 9 Aug 1930, record (1930) #: 18825.

Anna Lee HARPER, born: 16 Jul 1908, married, parents: Taylor Johnson and Martha Jenkins, cause of death: "typhoid fever", informant: Jerry Harper (Mountain City), buried: Wilson Cemetery, died: 19 Aug 1930, record (1930) #: 18826.

Fred LONG, Jr., born: 1 Jul 1930, parents: Fred Long and Roxie A. (surname illegible), cause of death: "not properly developed", Blevins Cem, died: 13 Aug 1930.

Nancy Lucile ISAACS, age 6 years and 16 days, parents: Jack Isaacs and Mary Swift (NC) cause of death: "pellagra, infantile paralysis", informant: Jack Isaacs, died: 9 Sep 1930, record (1930) #: 20986.

Leroy MCQUEEN, colored, age 11 months, parents: William McQueen and Willie Wilson, cause of death: "acute colitis", informant: Clint Wilson (Mountain City), died: 13 Sep 1930, record (1930) #: 20987.

Samuel R. RHEA, born: 22 Mar 1868, married, parents: Robert C. Rhea (West VA) and Caroline McQueen, cause of death: "chronic myocarditis", informant: Chas C. Rhea, died: 29 Sep 1930, record (1930) #: 20988.

Callie Lora HAMMONS, born: 17 Feb 1909, married, parents: Tilmon Simcox and Cora Payne, cause of death: "acute ..(illegible).. nephritis", informant: S.B. Gambill (Shouns), buried: Payne Cemetery, died: 17 Jul 1930, record (1930) #: 20989.

Edgar MCELYEA, born: 2 Mar 1907, single, parents; Roy McElyea and Bettie Holsclaw (NC), cause of death: "apoplexy", informant: Roy McElyea (Shouns), died: 1 Sep 1930, record (1930) #: 20990.

Doran H. ROBINSON, born: 26 Apr 1904, single, parents: David R. Robinson and Sallie Pleasant, cause of death: "tuberculosis", informant: E.G. Robinson (Doeville), buried: Rambo Cemetery, died: 3 Sep 1930, record (1930) #: 20991.

Aby WHITEHEAD, female, born: 28 May 1884 in Carter Co. TN, married, parents: Pamel Campbell and Rebecca Pirce, cause of death: "myocordeal insufficiency", informant: Carson Whitehead (Butler), died: 22 Sep 1930, record (1930) #: 20992.

Catilana SLIMP, born: 28 Jun 1875, married, parents: Phillip Tiney (NC) and (first name illegible) Greenwell, cause of death: "cancer of head and tuberculosis", informant: Jeril Slimp (Butler), died: 5 Apr 1930, record (1930) #: 20993.

Reuben POTTER, born: 21 Feb 1845 in North Carolina, widower, parents: Enoch Potter and Anna Stout, cause of death: "disease of heart, brights disease", informant: Enoch Potter (Trade), buried: Potter Cemetery, died: 12 Sep 1930, record (1930) #: 20994.

Fred STANLEY, born: 2 Oct 1930, parents: Sollie Stanley (Ashe Co. NC) and Mae Winters, cause of death: not stated, informant: Wm V. Winters (Mountain City), buried: Winters Cemetery, died: 9 Oct 1930, record (1930) #: 23182.

Rena Jane MILLER, born: 5 Mar 1850 in North Carolina, widow, parents: Jonathon Perry (VA) and Rebecca Hash (NC), cause of death: "chronic myocarditis", informant: C.W. York (Laurel Bloomery), buried: Acre Field Cemetery, died: 17 Oct 1930, record (1930) #: 23183.

T.A. NEELEY, born: 28 Dec 1865, married, parents: Hugh S. Neeley and Hanner E. Hand (VA), cause of death: "hemoplegia hemorrhage", informant: Mrs. T.A. Neeley (Damascus, VA), buried: Mock Cemetery, died: 26 Oct 1930, record (1930) #: 23184.

Emma Virginia MCELYEA, born: 7 Sep 1889, married, parents: Dan Rash and Betty Ann Dennings (NC), cause of death: "acute nephritis", informant: J.E. Rash (Shouns), died: 3 Oct 1930, record (1930) #: 23185.

Rachel E. ALLEN, born: 15 Jul 1854 at Jonesboro, TN, married, parents: John Nelson and Ester Ferguson (Washington Co. TN), cause of death: "fractured hip, hyperstatic pnuma", informant: W.L. Allen (Mountain City), died: 14 Oct 1930, record (1930) #: 23186.

253

Margaret Caroline RHEA, born: 10 May 1846, widow, parents: Samuel McQueen and Rachel Wagner, cause of death: "broncho pneumonia", informant: E.B. Rhea (Shouns), died: 16 Oct 1930, record (1930) #: 23187.

Mrs. Parrie WARD, born: 21 Feb 1879 in North Carolina, married, parents: J.H. South (NC) and mother's name not stated, cause of death: "pulmonary tuberculosis", informant: James Hicks (Neva), died: & Oct 1930, record (1930) #: 23188.

Carrie May HAMMONS, born: 15 Aug 1909, married, parents: Frank McCoy and Evaline Tester, cause of death: illegible, informant: Asa Main (Shouns), died: 8 Oct 1930, record (1930) #: 23189.

Pauline GRINDSTAFF, born: 29 Aug 1930, parents: father's name not stated and Valie Proffitt, cause of death: "whooping cough", informant: Valie Grindstaff (Doeville), buried: Proffitt Cemetery, died: 27 Oct 1930, record (1930) #: 23190.

Sarah Matilda RAINBOLT, age 82 years, 5 months and 14 days, single, parents: Dugger Rainbolt and Lucinda Venable, cause of death: "influenza", informant: May Ward (Fish Springs, TN), buried: Cobbs Creek Cemetery, died: 13 Oct 1930, record (1930) #: 23191.

Calvin C. WRIGHT, born: 11 Jan 1925, parents: father's name not stated and Lillie Wright, cause of death: "croup", buried: Gentry Cemetery, died: 25 Oct 1930, record (1930) #: 23192.

Mary M. STURGALL, parents: Oscar C. Sturgall and Ola Hale, cause of death: "premature birth at 7 months", born/died: 30 Oct 1930, record (1930) #: 23193.

Jefferson Davis MORETZ, born: 19 May 1861 in North Carolina, married, parents: John Moretz (NC) and Jane Miller (NC), cause of death: "influenza, lobar pneumonia", informant: Wiley Moretz (Shouns), died: 21 Nov 1930, record (1930) #: 25486.

Joseph Parker PLESS, born: 17 Oct 1858 in North Carolina, married, parents: Eliga Pless (NC) and Margaret Smith (NC), cause of death: "cerebral hemorhage", informant: Mrs. J.P. Pless (Mountain City), died: 22 Nov 1930, record (1930) #: 25487.

Daisy VAUGHT, born: 22 Sep 1887, married, parents: Enoch Ashely (NC) and Mattie Robinson (NC), cause of death: "abscess liver, acute nephritis", informant: Alvin Vaught (Mountain City), buried: Neva, died: 9 Sep 1930, record (1930) #: 25488.

Lynnie Mae EASTRIDGE, born: 21 Apr 1925 in North Carolina, parents; R.S. Eastridge (NC) and Ruth Farmer (NC), death cause: "epileptic fits", informant: Harlie Eastridge, died: 7 Nov 1930, record (1930) #: 25489.

Rebecca STOUT, born: 26 Mar 1890, single, parents:
T.J. Stout and Margaret C. Wagner, cause of death:
"tuberculosis", informant: C.B. Matherly (Doeville),
died: 16 Nov 1930, record (1930) #: 25490.

Nancy GREER, age 1 year, 6 months and 25 days,
parents: Roby Greer and Virdie Martin, cause of death:
"broncho pneumonia", buried: Greer Cemetery, died: 28
Nov 1930, record (1930) #: 25491.

Laudrine EGGERS, male, born: 20 May 1849, widower,
parents: Brazila Eggers (NC) and Mary Isaacs (NC),
cause of death: "chronic brights disease", informant:
Garfield Eggers (Trade), buried: Reece Cemetery, died:
20 Nov 1930, record (1930) #: 25492.

Edward East BUTLER, born: 5 Fb 1864, married, parents:
R.R. Butler (VA) and Eleline Donnelly, cause of death:
"agina pectoris", informant: E.E. Butler (Mountain
City), died: 13 Dec 1930, record (1930) #: 28110.

Ruby LECHCOE, born: 5 Jun 1906, divorced, parents:
G.T. Lechcoe (NC) and Effie Thomas, cause of death:
"lobar pneumonia", died: 19 Dec 1930, record (1930) #:
28111.

Bessie M. DUNN, born: 4 Oct 1890, married, parents:
Joe Main and Amanda Dunn, cause of death:
"tuberculosis menengitis", informant: C.C. Dunn
(Shouns), died: 22 Dec 1930, record (1930) #: 28112.

Carson R. KITE, born: 6 Nov 1930, parents: Randal Kite
and Lexie Stalcup, cause of death: "atelectosis",
informant: Randal Kite (Doeville), buried: Stalcup
Cemetery, died: 14 Dec 1930, record (1930) #: 28115.

William Payton GAMBILL, age 78 years, born at Wilkes
Co. NC, married, parents: Franklin Gambill (Wilkes Co.
NC) and Frankie Caudill (Wilkes Co. NC), cause of
death: "lobar pneumonia", informant: S.B. Gambill
(Shouns), buried: Hammons Cemetery, died: 20 Nov 1930,
record (1930) #: 28113.

Sarah Fina MCQUEEN, born: 2 Feb 1858, widow, parents:
Joe Wagner and Mary Vaught, cause of death: "lobar
pneumonia", informant: T.S. McQueen (Shouns), died: 10
Dec 1930, record (1930) #: 28114.

Phes Milton HAZLEWOOD, born: 15 Apr 1849 in Virginia,
married, parents: (first name illegible) Hazlewood and
Bettie Rogers, cause of death: "double pneumonia",
informant: Mrs. Phes Hazlewood (Butler), died: 26 Dec
1930, record (1930) #: 28116.

Samuel C. LOWE, born: 23 Feb 1863, married, parents:
Jacob Lowe and Sarah Gambill, cause of death: "augina
pectoris", informant: Walter Lowe (Mountian City),
buried: Lowe Cemetery, died: 27 Dec 1930, record
(1930) #: 28117.

Charlotte LOWE, parents: Roy Lowe and Cassie Lowe, cause of death: not stated, born/died: 31 Dec 1931, record (1930) #: 28118.

Austin THOMAS, born: 19 May 1930, parents: B.R. Thomas (NC) and Annie Eggers (NC), cause of death: "pneumonia, supposed", informant: Annie Thomas (Trade), buried at Mable, NC, died: 2 Dec 1930, record (1930) #: 28119.

Martitia EGGERS, age 30 years, married, parents: father's name not known and Polly Dotson, cause of death: "fall poisoning", informant: R.R. McGlamery (Trade), buried: Zionville, NC, died: 15 Jun 1930, record (1930) #: 28120.

James A. DUGGER, born: 13 Apr 1847, widower, parents: James A. Dugger and Rhoda Cable, cause of death: "heart dropsy", informant: J.C. Dugger (Butler), died: 20 Nov 1930, record (1930) #: 28121.

Arthur CABLE, born: 1 Nov 1882, married, parents: C. Burton Cable and Katherine Guy, cause of death: "typhoid fever", informant: Trula Cable (Butler), buried: Sugar Grove Cemetery, died: 24 Oct 1930, record (1930) #: 28122.

Julia Kate COURTNER, born: 29 Mar 1930, parents: John Courtner and Mattie Ward, cause of death: "acute ..(illegible). nephritis", informant: John Courtner (Neva), died: 23 Dec 1930, record (1930) #: 29857.

William A. BROWN, born: 3 May 1854 at Ashe Co. NC, married, parents: B.S. Brown (Ashe Co. NC) and Susan Younce (Ashland, NC), cause of death: "broncho pneumonia", informant: Robt B. Brown (Mountain City), died: 23 Jan 1931, record (1931) #: 1022.

Noah Jacob WAGNER, born: 16 Apr 1844, widower, parents: M.M. Wagner and Mary Fife (NC), cause of death: "chronic brights disease", informant: C.M. Wagner (Mountain City), died: 26 Jan 1931, record (1931) #: 1023.

Quincy Roscoe BROWN, born: 2 Feb 1916, parents: John Brown and Kizzie Hayworth, cause of death: "diarrhea", informant: George Brown (Shouns), buried: Dunn Cemetery, died: 4 Jan 1931, record (1931) #: 1024.

Alzenia Reece SHOUN, born: 27 Jun 1855 in North Carolina, wife of P.H. Shoun (Butler), parents: Hiram Reece (NC) and mother's name unknown, cause of death: "pneumonia, cirrhosis and brights disease", died: 5 Jan 1931, record (1931) #: 1025.

Sarah GRINDSTAFF, age about 75 years, married, parents names not stated, cause of death: "heart dropsy", informant: Danell Grindstaff (Doeville), died: 13 Jan 1931, record (1931) #: 1026.

Infant DAVIS, born: 23 Jan 1931, parents: Claud Davis (NC) and Mattie Triplett (NC), cause of death: "premature birth", died: 24 Jan 1931, record (1931) #: 1027.

Bettie Lew ISAACS, born: 1 Oct 1930, parents: Jim Isaacs (NC) and Bell Glenn (NC), cause of death: not stated, died: 1 Jan 1931, record (1931) #: 1028.

Roderick B. GENTRY, born: 2 Jun 1891, married, parents: Mahlon Gentry and Mary C. Stout, cause of death: "cerebral heomrrhage", informant: J.M. Gentry (Crandull), died: 23 Jan 1931, record (1931) #: 1029.

Eliza C. BLEVINS, born: 4 Sep 1878, married, parents: S.D. Dugger and McNary King, cause of death: "influenza and broncho pneumonia", informant: Jake Campbell (Butler), buried: Crosswhite Cemetery, died: 29 Jan 1931, record (1931) #: 1030.

Dana Dewitt MCCLOUD, born: 8 Dec 1930, parents: "don't know father's name" and Mary McCloud, cause of death: "ictines neonatonas", died: 6 Jan 1931, record (1931) #: 3390.

Callie P. WARREN, colored, born: 28 Apr 1904, married, parents: John Wilson (VA) and Emma Flannigan (VA), cause of death: illegible, informant: John W. Wilson (Mountain City), died: 1 Feb 1931, record (1931) #: 3391.

Fannie PHILLIPS, born: 18 Feb 1840, widow, ward of county home, parents: "don't know", cause of death: "chronic brights disease", died: 18 Feb 1931, record (1931) #: 3392.

Effie Ellen Snyder ROBINSON, born: 14 Sep 1903, parents: Wiley Snyder and Callie Slimp, cause of death: "perforated stomach from ulcer", informant: J.H. Robinson (Doeville), died: 25 Jan 1931, record (1931) #: 3393.

Fannie Agnes RASH, born: 8 Mar 1911, married, parents: Austin Bolden and Minnie Mains, cause of death: "died sudden and unexpected", informant: Austin Bolden (Mountian City), buried: Shingletown Cemetery, died: 7 Feb 1931, record (1931) #: 5799.

Rosa Bell HAM, born: 20 Jan 1931 in North Carolina, parents: father not stated and Effie Ham (NC), cause of death: not stated, informant: Joe Ham (Green Co. VA), died: 11 Feb 1931, record (1931) #: 5800.

Susie HALL, born: 3 Mar 1845, widow, parents: Wm Hall (NC) and Bettie Arnold (NC), cause of death: "apoplexy", informant: S.T. Taylor (Shouns), buried: County Home, died: 3 Mar 1931, record (1931) #: 5801.

Louise Caroline SAMMONS, age 80 years and 4 months, married, parents: not known, cause of death: "influenza and lobar pneumonia", informant: J.L. Sammons, died: 10 Mar 1931, record (1931) #: 5802.

William FENNER, age 76 years, single, parents: James Fenner and Nancy Elliott (NC), cause of death: "influenza, lobar pneumonia", informant: R.J. Fenner, died: 10 Mar 1931, record (1931) #: 5803.

Alvin TILLEY, age 69 years, born in North Carolina, married, parents: (first name not known) Jones (NC) and (first name not known) Tilley (NC), cause of death: "chronic brights disease", informant: Jim Howard (Mountain City), buried: McEwen Cemetery, died: 2 Mar 1931, record (1931) #: 5804.

Infant TESTER, male, parents: Walter Tester and Mary Pardue (NC), cause of death: "premature birth", Shouns, died: 23 Feb 1931, record (1931) #: 5805.

Alice Lucil LIPFORD, parents: W.E. Lipford and Nora Turnmire (NC), cause of death: unknown, born/died: 17 Mar 1931, record (1931) #: 5806.

Nora LIPFORD, age about 44 years, married, parents: Hugh Turnmire (NC) and (first name unknown) Pope (NC), cause of death: "childbirth", informant: W.E. Lipford (Shouns), buried: Powell Cemetery, died: 22 Mar 1931, record (1931) #: 5807.

Susan WYATT, born: 25 Dec 1857 in North Carolina, married, parents: Will Storns (NC) and mother's name unknown, cause of death: "chronic diarrhea", informant: J.M. Mains (Crandull), buried: Blevins Cemetery, died: 4 Mar 1931, record (1931) #: 5808.

Thomas Odell WHITE, born: 23 Oct 1852 at Carter Co. TN, married, parents: Robert White and Finnie Wagoner, cause of death: "chronic cherosis of liver, old age", informant: A.T. White (Benham, KY), buried: Grindstaff Cemetery, died: 7 Mar 1931, record (1931) #: 5809.

Ham NEELEY, born: 20 Nov 1900, single, parents: Sam Neeley and Rebecca Morefield, cause of death: "gun shot wound through heart, self inflicted with shot gun, suicidal", informant: Sam Neeley (Laurel Bloomery), buried: Acre Field Cemetery, died: 18 Apr 1931, record (1931) #: 8374.

Maggie BURKETT, Negro, born: 16 May 1895, married, parents: Noah Anderson and Mary Goins (NC), cause of death: "cancer womb", informant: L.K. Anderson (Shouns), died: 28 Apr 1931, record (1931) #: 8375.

Mary Eveline JENNINGS, born: 24 Jan 1850, widow, parents: Thomas S. Smyth (VA) and Margaret C. Donnelly, death cause: "cancer stomach", informant: John V. Smyth, died: 30 Apr 1931, record #: 8376.

Mrs. Bell DUNN, born: 24 Mar 1897, married, parents: not stated, cause of death: "broncho pneumonia", informant: M.G. Hodge (Shouns), died: 9 Apr 1931, record (1931) #: 8377.

Lillie Belle MATHESON, age 46 years, parents: George Neatherly and Catherine Tester, cause of death: "meningitis", informant: Wm Matherson (Elizabethton, TN), buried: Elizabethton, TN, died: 21 Apr 1931, record (1931) #: 8378.

Robert D. TESTER, born: 30 Mar 1843, married, parents: Nathaniel Tester and Nancy McElyea, cause of death: "influenza and lobar pneumonia", died: 23 Mar 1931, record (1931) #: 8379.

Letha Viola LIPFORD, age 31 years, 1 month and 3 days, married, parents: Luther Osborn (NC) and Julia Greer, death cause: "cerebral hemorrhage", informant: Owen Lipford, died: 11 Apr 1931, record (1931) #: 8380.

Susannah M. JENKINS, born: 22 Sep 1841, widow, parents: David M. Stout and Sarah Stout, cause of death: "chronic intestinal nephritis", informant: Sarah Jenkins (Trade), buried: Jenkins Cemetery, died: 3 Apr 1931, record (1931) #: 8381.

Laura WAGNER, born: 7 May 1862, widow, parents: father's name not known and Louise Moore (NC), cause of death: "lobar pneumonia", informant: Bessie Wagner (Shouns), died: 7 May 1931, record (1931) #: 10801.

John Wesley PHILLIPS, born: 10 Jan 1860 at Todd, NC, parents: John Phillips (NC) and Mary Phillips (NC), cause of death: "chronic intestinal nephritis, cerebral hemorrhage", informant: S.C. Stout (Shouns), died: 18 May 1831, record (1931) #: 10802.

Luvenia LUNCEFORD, born: 17 Oct 1850, widow, parents: A.L. Goodwin and Malinda Goodwin, cause of death: "heart dropsy", informant: Dewey Cable (Butler), buried: Crosswhite Cemetery, died: 11 May 1931, record (1931) #: 10803.

Caroline ISAACS, born: 28 Aug 1862, widow, parents: Joseph Dugger and Polly Stepp (VA), cause of death: "chronic valvular heart disease", informant: Abe Isaacs (Harvey, Illinois), buried: Sugar Grove Cemetery, died: 24 May 1931, record (1931) #: 10804.

Henry B. WILLS, age 74 years, 3 months and 2 days, husband of Mrs. Sallie Wills, parents: Russel B. Wills and Rebecca Elizabeth Duff (Washington Co., VA), cause of death: "chronic brights disease", informant: Miss Francis Wills (Mountain City), buried: Wills Cemetery, died: 6 Jun 1931, record (1931) #: 13032.

Susan Rebecca KEYS, born: 12 Nov 1859, single,
parents: Robert W. Keys and Susan Wills, cause of
death: "chronic brights disease", informant: G.M. Keys
(Mountian City), buried: Wills Cemetery, died: 15 Jun
1931, record (1931) #: 13033.
James Lawson GOODWIN, born: 4 Mar 1881, married,
parents: James Goodwin and Alice Johnson, cause of
death: "gun shot wound, homicidal", buried: Phillippi
Cemetery, died: 5 Jun 1931, record (1931) #: 13034.
Mrs. Fannie THOMAS, age 56 years, born in North
Carolina, married, parents: not stated, cause of
death: "pulmonary tuberculosis", informant: R.F.
Icenhour (Mountain City), died: 17 May 1931, record
(1931) #: 13035.
Thomas LUNSFORD, age 2 years, 9 months and 12 days,
parents: Don Lunsford and Bessie Isaacs (NC), cause of
death: "menigro perlomuaum (?)", informant: Don
Lunsford (Neva), died: 12 Apr 1931, record (1931) #:
13036.
Biner PHIPPS, female, age 57 years, born in North
Carolina, parents: William Graybeal (NC) and Amanda
Rhoten (NC), cause of death: "pulmonary tuberculosis",
informant: D.S. Phipps (Mountain City), died: 1 Jun
1931, record (1931) #: 13037.
Mack WALLACE, age 70 years, married, parents: Alex
Wallace and Nancy Caronette (NC), cause of death:
"cancer liver", informant: Jordan Wallace (Trade),
died: 28 Jun 1931, record (1931) #: 13038.
Mary SHORES, age about 75 years, born in North
Carolina, widow, parents not stated, cause of death:
"hart dropsy", informant: Gar. Dugger (Butler),
buried: Dugger Cemetery, died: 1 Jun 1931, record
(1931) #: 13039.
Alex Clarence HODGE, born: 19 Oct, age 3 years, 7
months and 14 days, parents: Fate Hodge and Mamie
Dugger, cause of death: "measles and pneumonia",
informant: Fate Hodge (Butler), buried: Baker
Cemetery, died: 2 Jun 1931, record (1931) #: 13040.
Bula May STANSBERRY, born: 7 Jun 1931, parents: Henry
Stansberry and China Phillips, cause of death:
"whooping cough", informant: Henry Stansberry
(Butler), buried: Mt. Gilead Cemetery, died: 27 Jun
1931, record (1931) #: 13041.
Margaret Elizabeth GREER, born: 23 Jul 1870, married,
parents: L.L. Ray and Isabella Gentry, cause of death:
"cholera", informant: John F. Greer (Laurel Bloomery),
buried: Taylors Valley Cemetery, died: 24 Jul 1931,
record (1931) #: 15308.

Infant NEELEY, male, parents: C.W. Neeley and Francis Waters, cause of death: "congenital heart condition", informant: C.W. Neeley (Damascus, VA), died: 20 Jun 1931, record (1931) #: 15309.

Geter Stoffle DUNN, born: 17 Oct 1930, parents: Edward Dunn and Radell McCoy, cause of death: "broncho pneumonia", informant: W.N. Riddle (Shouns), died: 19 Jul 1931, record (1931) #: 15310.

Mamie Lee GENTRY, age 20 years, 8 months and 28 days, single, parents: James Gentry and Memphis Wills, cause of death: "pulmonary tuberculosis", buried: Phillippi Cemetery, died: 30 Jun 1931, record (1931) #: 15311.

Lee REEVES, Negro, born: 8 Apr 1871, married, parents: John Reeves (NC) and Rindy McMIllan (NC), cause of death: "acute brights disease", informant: L.K. Anderson (Shouns), died: 7 Apr 1931, record (1931) #: 15312.

A.J. DYSON, age 77 years, born in North Carolina, married, parents: Jackson Dyson (NC) and Martha Miller (NC), cause of death: "chronic brights disease", informant: Cute Price (Shouns), died: 23 Apr 1931, record (1931) #: 15313.

Lizzie JONES, born: 24 Dec (year not stated) in North Carolina, age about 25 years, married, parents: Roby Eastridge (NC) and Ruth Farmer (NC), cause of death: not stated (note: probably was childbirth related, twins died within a few days), informant: W.S. Jones (Neva), died: 7 Jul 1931, record (1931) #: 15314.

Early JONES, born: 30 Jun 1931, parents: W.S. Jones (NC) and Lizzie Eastridge (NC), cause of death: not stated, informant: W.S. Jones (Neva), died: 13 Jul 1931, record (1931) #: 15315. (twin's record below)

Louise Edna HODGE, born: 9 May 1931, parents: Andy Hodge and Lizzie Potter (NC), cause of death: "acute colitis", informant: Andy Hodge (Neva), died: 17 Jul 1931, record (1931) #: 15316.

Bearly JONES, born: 30 Jun 1931, parents: W.S. Jones (NC) and Lizzie Eastridge (NC), cause of death: not stated, informant: W.S. Jones (Neva), died: 20 Jul 1931, record (1931) #: 15317. (twin's record above)

Herbert WALKER, born: 7 May 1931, parents: Brownlow Walker and Malissie Arnold, cause of death: not stated, informant: Brownlow Walker (Doeville), died: 9 Jul 1931, record (1931) #: 15318.

R.J. BROOKSHIRE, born: 20 Jul 1869, married, parents: Joel Brookshire (NC) and Caroline Robinson, cause of death: "pellagra", informant: S.G. Brookshire (Mountain City), buried: Brookshire Cemetery, died: 21 Jun 1931, record (1931) #: 15319.

Martha L. STOUT, age 75 years, born in North Carolina, widow of David Stout, parents: Franklin Norris (NC) and Sallie Green (NC), cause of death: "typhoid, heart failure and brochial pneumonia", informant: J. Blaine Stout (Doeville), died: 24 Jul 1931, record (1931) #: 15320.

W. Susan CHURCH, born: 16 Aug 1882, married, parents: Hyder Smith and Malinda Hodge, cause of death: "cancer womb", informant: Jess Church (Mountain City), buried: Shoun Cem, died: 27 Jul 1931, record (1931) #: 15321.

Edward SCOTT, Jr., born: 14 Apr 1930, parents: Edward Scott and Mada Garland, cause of death: illegible, informant: F.R. Scott (Crandull), buried: Scott Cemetery, died: 14 Jul 1931, record (1931) #: 15322.

Thomas Ware ARNOLD, born: 19 Mar 1847, widower, parents: John Arnold (NC) and Nancy King (NC) cause of death: "lobar pneumonia", informant: S. Chas Arnold (Jefferson, NC), buried: Green Valley, NC, died: 3 Jul 1931, record (1931) #: 15323.

Nancy Roark ARNOLD, born: 4 May 1840 in North Carolina, married, parents: Ephram Roark (Ashe Co. NC) and Millie Graybeal (Ashe Co. NC), cause of death: "chronic brights disease", informant: T.A. Madron, buried: Mountain View Cemetery, died: 3 Jul 1931, record (1931) #: 15324.

Leander GREEN, born: 29 Jan 1861 in North Carolina, widower, parents: Tom Green (NC) and Nancy Council (NC), cause of death: "fracture skull, accidentally run down by automobile", buried: Zionville, NC, died: 16 Jul 1931, record (1931) #: 15325.

Norman WIDBY, born: 6 Aug 1911, married, parents: Sam Widby (NC) and Ollie Maxwell, cause of death: "typhoid fever", informant: George Reeves (Mountain City), died: 11 Aug 1931, record (1931) #: 17771.

William Harrison OSBORN, born: 24 Aug 1855 in North Carolina, married, parents: John Presley Osborn (NC) and Pollie Jones (NC), cause of death: "chronic brights disease", buried: Shouns, died: 24 Aug 1931, record (1931) #: 17772.

David P. GREENWELL, born: 17 Jan 1857, widower of Samantha Greenwell, parents: Burton Greenwell (NC) and Mary Cable, cause of death: "pulmonary tuberculosis", informant: Alfred Greenwell (Butler), died: 10 Aug 1931, record (1931) #: 17773.

Ida Louisa JARRETT, born: 29 Mar 1865 in Pennsylvania, wife of Wm Allen Jereatt, parents: Henry Shafer (PA) and Margaret Mason (PA), cause of death: "tuberculosis of bowls", buried: Dry Run, died; 13 Aug 1931, record (1931) #: 17774.

Teddie Ray MORLEY, age 6 months and 22 days, parents: D.J. Morley and C.D. Reece, cause of death: "illio colitis", informant: D.J. Morley (Crandull), died: 1 Aug 1931, record (1931) #: 17775.

Earl Frederick WATERS, age 3 years, 6 months and 5 days, parents: Clint Waters and Bertha Neeley, cause of death: "diptheria", informant: Robert Roberts (Crandull), died: 25 Sep 1931, record (1931) #: 19982.

Julia Kate MCELYEA, parents: W.D. McElyea and Ollie Wilson, cause of death: "congenital weakness", buried: Vaughtsville, born/died: 6 Sep 1931, record (1931) #: 19983.

John M. ARNOLD, age 58 years, 11 months and 16 days, born in North Carolina, married, parents: Thomas Wear Arnold and Astoria Mahood (VA), cause of death: "apoplexy", informant: S.C. Arnold (Jefferson, NC), buried: Shouns, died: 22 Sep 1931, record (1931) #: 19984.

Hattie JOHNSON, born: 20 Aug 1926, parents: J.W. Johnson and Lillie Reece, cause of death: "diptheria", informant: Lillie Johnson (Shouns), buried: McEwen Cemetery, died: 19 Aug 1931, record (1931) #: 19985.

Alice S. CROWDER, age 70 years, 5 months and 20 days, born in North Carolina, wife of Alex Crowder, parents: William Moretz (NC) and Sarah Cander (NC), cause of death: "cancer stomach", died: 28 Aug 1931, record (1931) #: 19986.

John T. WARD, born: 16 Apr 1854, widower, parents: John Ward and mother's name not stated (note: she was Nancy Wilson, daughter of Tapley Wilson), cause of death: "broncho pneumonia", informant: John Courtner (Neva), died: 26 Aug 1931, record (1931) #: 19987.

Mrs. Amanda LOWE, born: 16 Dec 1855, widow, parents: J.M. Roberts and Lucinda Arnold, cause of death: "dropsy", informant: Kemp Lowe (Mountain City), Lowe Cemetery, died: 7 Sep 1931, record (1931) #: 19988.

Celia J. WRIGHT, born: 11 Dec 1840, widow of J.J. Wright, parents: George W. Scott and Annie Cole, cause of death: "supposed senility", informant: C.C. Blevins (Crandull), buried: Gentry Cemetery, died: 26 Sep 1931, record (1931) #: 19989.

Virginia BURTON, parents: Raleigh Burton and Stella Reece (NC), death cause: "premature birth:", Cable Cemetery, born/died: 9 Sep 1931, record #: 19990.

Robert BARKER, born: 15 Dec 1927 in Virginia, parents: Robert Barker (VA) and Imogene Huggins, cause of death: "croup", informant: Oscar Huggins (Mountain City), buried: Damascus, VA, died: 31 Oct 1931, record (1931) #: 22147.

Dorothy Mae BRYANT, born: 1 Oct 1916, parents: Amos Bryant (NC) and Julia Ann Bryant (NC), cause of death: "facial ensipelitis", informant: Wm Dishman (Mountain City), died: 26 Oct 1931, record (1931) #: 22148.

Robert VANCE, age 63 years, married, parents: John Vance and Mary Wilcox, cause of death: "cancer bladder", died: 6 Sep 1931, record (1931) #: 22149.

Ruby Lee ATWOOD, born: 28 May 1929, parents: John V. Atwood and Eva Strickland, cause of death: illegible, informant: George Atwood (Butler), died: 16 Oct 1931, record (1931) #: 22152.

Hobert WALKER, born: 7 May 1931, parents: Brownlow Walker and Malissie Arnold, cause of death: "not stated, found dead in bed", informant: Brownlow Walker (Doeville), buried: Campbell Cemetery, died: 29 Oct 1931, record (1931) #: 22150.

Joseph W. GREEN, born: 3 Dec 1843 in North Carolina, husband of Flora Price Green, parents: Isaac Green (NC) and Mary McCandles (NC), cause of death: "apoplexy", informant: Flora Green (Butler), died: 4 Oct 1931, record (1931) #: 22151.

Annie MCELYEA, born: 9 Oct 1872, single, parents: Landon McElyea and Alzenia Tester, cause of death: "pelgia", informant: John McElyea (Butler), buried: Dry Hill Cemetery, died: 24 Oct 1931, record (1931) #: 22153.

Georgia GREER, born: 4 Jun 1909, married, parents: Will Robinson and Mollie Lowe, cause of death: "pellagra", informant: N.J. Greer (Doeville), born: 19 Oct 1931, record (1931) #: 22154.

Oscar Dean RASH, born: 27 May 1927, parents: Frank Rash and Rosa Wallace (NC), cause of death: "typhoid fever", informant: Frank Rash (Trade), died: 16 Oct 1931, record (1931) #: 22155.

Nella May WILLIN, born: 7 Oct 1931, parents: George Willin and Stella Reece, cause of death: not stated, informant: George Willin (Trade), buried: Reece Cemetery, died: 17 Oct 1931, record (1931) #: 22156.

Charlie THOMAS, born: 10 Aug 1878 at Ashe Co. NC, widower, parents: Jack Thomas (Ashe Co. NC) and Melvina Newberger (Ashe Co. NC), cause of death: "chronic brights disease", informant: Hagy Campbell (Mountain City), buried: Wills Cemetery, died: 30 Nov 1931, record (1931) #: 24422.

James R. HALL, born: 26 Jul 1847, widower, parents: Billie Hall (NC) and Betsy Arnold, cause of death: "chronic intestinal nephritis, cerebral hemorrhage", informant: May Arnold (Shouns), buried: Hall Cemetery, died: 1 Nov 1931, record (1931) #: 24423.

Selmer W. STOUT, born: 14 Jun 1930, parents: Wayne Stout and Maude Robinson, cause of death: "broncho pneumonia", informant: Wayne Stout (Doeville), buried: Rambo Cem, died: 10 Nov 1931, record (1931) #: 24424.

Massie L. GARLAND, female, born: 21 Mar 1928, parents: T.R. Garland and Sarah Robinson, cause of death: "not known", informant: T.R. Garland (Doeville), Campbell Cemetery, died: 25 Nov 1931, record (1931) #: 24425.

Thelma Blanch BISHOP, born: 2 Nov 1928, parents: Millane Bishop and Goldie E. Rambo, cause of death: "diptheria", informant: M.F. Bishop (Crandull), buried: Blevins Cemetery, died: 11 Nov 1931, record (1931) #: 24426.

Dayton Harold MOREFIELD, born: 28 Sep 1931, parents: Joe R. Morefield and Florence Proffitt, cause of death: "acute lobar pneumonia", informant: J.R. Morefield (Mountain City), buried: Cornett Cemetery, died: 12 Nov 1931, record (1931) #: 26759.

Lee ELDRITH, born: 10 Feb 1873 in North Carolina, married, parents: Wesley Eldrith (NC) and Tillie Dunn (NC), cause of death: "pellagra, chronic nephritis", informant: Joe Eldrith (Mountain City), buried: Rash Cemetery, died: 11 Jun 1931, record (1931) #: 26760.

Nathaniel Taylor WAGNER, born: 18 Nov 1856, widower, husband of Lily Wagner, parents: Nathaniel Wagner and Betsy Ann Baker, cause of death: "cerebral hemorrhage", informant: Ava Potter (Shouns), buried: Wagner Cem, died: 17 Dec 1931, record (1931) #: 26761.

Mrs. Sallie Elizabeth WILLIAMS, born: 14 Jan 1867 in Virginia, widow, parents: W.M. Crawford (VA) and Catherine Ann Shuritz (VA), cause of death: not recorded, informant: Clyde Williams (Mountain City), buried: Mountain View Cemetery, died: 6 Nov 1931, record (1931) #: 26762.

David SAMMONS, born: 9 Aug 1853, widower, parents: John Sammons (England) and Eliza Shouns, cause of death: "apoplexy", informant: T.L. Sammons (Mountain City), died: 7 Nov 1931, record (1931) #: 26763.

J. Hamilton MOREFIELD, born: 2 May 1864, married, parents: John R. Morefield and Matilda Minnick (VA), cause of death: "eryopelas, right leg", informant: Mrs. Sarah Jane Price (Mountain City), died: 28 Nov 1931, record (1931) #: 26764.

Bettie DUNN, born: 26 Oct 1841, widow, parents: Isaac Osborn and Lydia Potter, cause of death: "chronic intestinal nephritis", informant: J.G. Powell (Shouns), buried: Dunn Cemetery, died: 28 Nov 1931, record (1931) #: 26765.

Infant ARNOLD, female, parents: William Odis Arnold and Dottie Walker, cause of death: "premature birth", informant: William Arnold (Neva), died: 27 Dec 1931, record (1931) #: 26766.

David A. TESTER, age 59 years, married, husband of Ella Tester, parents: Robert D. Tester and Susanah Tester, cause of death: "apoplexy", informant: Tom Neatherly (Neva), died: 16 Oct 1931, record (1931) #: 26767.

Millard TESTER, born: 16 May 1928 at Buffalo, NY, parents: Luther M. Tester and Anna Radomski (Buffalo, NY), cause of death: "broncho pneumonia", informant: Lon Tester (Neva), buried: Maymead, died: 25 Oct 1931, record (1931) #: 26768.

James Dudley GILBERT, born: 10 Jul 1878, married, parents: James Dudley Gilbert and Rebecca Bagwell, cause of death: not stated, informant: J.W. Vannoy (Neva), died: 22 Sep 1931, record (1931) #: 26769

Francis M. MOODY, born: 8 Apr 1847 at Coldwell Co. NC, married, parents: Benjamin Moody and Rhoda Hatton (NC), cause of death: "apoplexy, informant: J.C. Lord (Blowing Rock, NC), died: 28 Dec 1931, record (1931) #: 26770.

John R. MARTIN, born: 17 Oct 1854, married, parents: Joe Martin and Annie Lowe, cause of death: "influenza, lobar pneumonia", informant: Robert Jones (Mountain City), died: 5 Dec 1931, record (1931) #: 26771.

Thomas MARTIN, age 70 years, born in North Carolina, parents: George Martin (NC) and mother's name not stated, cause of death: "said to be pneumonia", buried: Wallace Cemetery, died: 12 Dec 1931, record (1931) #: 26772.

Bettie Ann RASH, born: 10 Dec 1852, married, parents: Wiley Jennings (NC) and Rebecca Phillips (NC), cause of death: "pneumonia", informant: Monroe Rash (Trade), Greer Cem, died: 23 Dec 1931, record (1931) #: 26773.

Bettie Jane EGGERS, born: 2 Jan 1932 in Virginia, parents: Arthur Eggers and Eller Wilson, death cause: "pneumonia", informant: W.B. Eggers, buried: Taylor Valley, died: 31 Jau 1932, record (1932) #: 823.

James R. H. SMYTH, born: 21 Jun 1853, married, parents: Thomas S. Smyth (VA) and Margaret C. Donnelly, cause of death: "cancer liver", informant: T.H. Smyth, died: 8 Jan 1932, record (1932) #: 824.

Shelton PAYNE, born: 6 Oct 1918, parents: W.B. Payne and Ollie V. Potter, cause of death: "abscess liver", informant: John M. Potter (Shouns), died: 20 Jan 1932, record (1932) #: 825.

Stephen PHILLIPPI, born: 20 May 1853, married, parents: David Phillippi (VA) and Jane Fry (VA), cause of death: "cancer stomach", informant: John Phillippi (Mountain City), buried: Phillippi Cemetery, died: 27 Jan 1932, record (1932) #: 826.

Eliza Jane ADAMS, born: 22 Nov 1856, widow, parents: Richard H. Luttrell (VA) and Mary Treadway, cause of death: "apoplexy", informant: Mrs. O.M. Vermillion (Mountain City), died: 29 Jan 1932, record (1932) #: 827.

Della DUNN, born: 6 Sep 1883, single, parents: Godfrey B. Dunn and Rachel M. Wilson, cause of death: "pulmonary tuberculosis", informant: J.G. Dunn (Shouns), buried: McEwen Cemetery, died: 20 Jan 1932, record (1932) #: 828.

Loura Elizabeth ROARK, born: 29 May 1879, married, parents: Alfred Osborn (NC) and Sendy Elison (NC), cause of death: "apoplexy, died nearly sudden", informant: J.C. Roark (Shouns), buried: Arnold Cemetery, died: 22 Jan 1932, record (1932) #: 829.

Jacob N. STOUT, born: 11 Aug 1846, widower, wife was Amanda Stout, parents: Daniel Stout and Mary Vaught, cause of death: "broncho pneumonia, chronic intestinal nephritis", informant: L.L. Stout (Neva), died: 10 Jan 1932, record (1932) #: 830.

Nancy Elizabeth DAVIS, age 71 years, 5 months and 5 days, married, husband is W.T. Davis, parents: David Slimp and Eveline Mathison (NC), cause of death: "chronic pulmonary tuberculosis", informant: W.T. Davis (Neva), died: 13 Jan 1932, record (1932) #: 831.

Thomas James COPLING, born: 5 May 1848, husband of Caroline Copling, parents: father's name not stated and Caroline Copling, cause of death: "pneumonia", informant: Effie Matherly (Butler), died: 26 Jan 1932, record (1932) #: 832.

Joel Wagner DYER, age 83 years, 7 months and 29 days, born in North Carolina, widower, wife's name was Sarah Elizabeth Walker, parents: Joel Dyer (NC) and (first name not stated) Harmon (NC), cause of death: "apoplexy", informant: J.W. Dyer (Mountain City), died: 6 Jan 1932, record (1932) #: 833.

Caleb J. SHOUN, born: 1 Mar 1861, married to Sarah Fine Shoun, parents: Robert L. Shoun and Elizabeth Slimp, cause of death: "chronic nephritis", buried: Shoun Cemetery, died: 24 Jan 1932, record (1932) #: 834.

Martin Dearl PIERCE, born: 6 Oct 1930, parents: George Pierce and Vada Stout, cause of death: "lobar pneumonia", died: 25 Jan 1932, record (1932) #: 835.

Mrs. Mary Wilson DAVIS, born: 14 Jul 1854, married, parents: Elijah Wilson and Sarah Shoun, cause of death: "burn, acute nephritis", informant: James F. Davis (Mountain City), died: 25 Jan 1932, record (1932) #: 836.

Norman Russell WILLS, born: 13 Oct 1847, married to Mattie C. Wills, parents: Peter Dick Wills and Sophia McGuowen (VA), cause of death: "anjina pectoris", informant: Karl Wills (Mountain City), died: 3 Feb 1932, record (1932) #: 2861.

James Herbert WATERS, born: 29 Jan 1932, parents: William C. Waters and Birtha E. Hamby, cause of death: "not stated, found dead in bed", informant: C.W. Neeley (Damascus, VA), buried: Neeley Cemetery, died: 15 Feb 1932, record (1932) #: 2862.

Edgar ALLEN, born: 31 May 1924, parents: father's name not stated and Ruth Allen, cause of death: "typhoid fever", informant: Isaac Allen (Mountain City), buried: Shingletown Cemetery, died: 18 feb 1932, record (1932) #: 2863.

Delia RASH, born: 27 Feb 1870, married, parents: F.M. Chappell (NC) and Sarah Grigston (NC), cause of death: "supposed to be pneumonia", informant: Verna Dotson (Shouns), buried: Snyder Cemetery, died: 27 Feb 1932, record (1932) #: 2864.

Noah Henly GREER, born: 16 Feb 1884, married, parents: father's name not stated and Bettie Greer, cause of death: "pulmonary tuberculosis", informant: Noah Pennington (Mountain City), buried: Valley Cemetery, died: 6 Mar 1932, record (1932) #: 5140.

Mary POTTER, born: 3 Mar 1932, parents: W.A. Potter and Tallulah Wagner, cause of death: "premature birth", informant: W.A. Potter (Shouns), died: 4 Mar 1932, record (1932) #: 5141.

Talullah Wagner POTTER, born: 18 Sep 1896, married, parents: Nathaniel Taylor Wagner and Josephine Dugger, cause of death: "influenza, lobar pneumonia, child birth", informant: W.A. Potter (Shouns), died: 4 Mar 1932, record (1932) #: 5142.

Sarah Ellen GREEN, born: 13 Sep 1864, widow of Wm. Green, parents: Hugh Reece and Surang Miller, cause of death: "pulmonary edema", informant: James Ross Green (Shouns), died: 10 Mar 1932, record (1932) #: 5143.

James Andrew SHOUN, born: 14 Sep 1848, husband of Mag Shoun, parents: Isaac Harey Shoun and Mary Graybeal (NC), cause of death: "chronic brights disease", died: 13 Mar 1932, record (1932) #: 5144.

Margaret R. BELTZBOONE, age 73 years, widow, parents: U.T. Greenwell (NC) and Elizabeth Dugger, cause of death: "influenza, broncho pneumonia", informant: A.C. Brown (Mountain City), died: 14 Mar 1932, record (1932) #: 5145.

Dayton Crocket WAGNER, born: 3 Sep 1902, single, parents: Clyde M. Wagner and Ada Wills, cause of death: "accidental drowning, car turned off of bridge, fractured skull", informant: H.J.D. Wills (Shouns), died: 17 Mar 1932, record (1932) #: 5146.

Maurine JOHNSON, born: 12 Apr 1930, parents: J.C. Johnson and M.S. Price (NC), cause of death: "dystheria longingitis", informant: J.C. Johnson (Shouns), buried: Johnson Cemetery, died: 4 Mar 1932, record (1932) #: 5147.

Olamae VANOVER, born: 12 Mar 1932, parents: Charley Dunn and Clara Vanover (NC), cause of death: "flue", informant: Roby Vanover (Shouns), buried: Dunn Cemetery, died: 18 Mar 1932, record (1932) #: 5148.

Floyd GREEN, born: 9 Jan 1923 in North Carolina, parents: James Green (NC) and Nolia Cook (NC), cause of death: "blood poisoning from infected foot (cut on broken glass)", buried: North Carolina, died: 15 Mar 1932, record (1932) #: 5149.

George W. GRIFFITH, born: 2 Jun 1864 in North Carolina, parents: father's name unknown and Jamie Griffith (NC), cause of death: illegible, buried: Allen Cemetery, died: 31 Mar 1932, record (1932) #: 5150.

Maggie Naoma REECE, born: 4 Jul 1874 in North Carolina, married, parents: Harrison Roberts (NC) and Polly Madron (NC), cause of death: "acute lobar pneumonia", informant: H.C. Brown (Trade), Zionville Cemetery, died: 27 Mar 1932, record (1932) #: 5151.

David CANTER, age 43 years, single, born blind, parents: Enoch Canter (NC) and Sallie Miller (NC), cause of death: "supposed to be pneumonia", informant: Joe Wilson (Trade), buried: Reece Cemetery, died: 27 Mar 1932, record (1932) #: 5152.

Taylor BUNTON, born: 11 Jun 1856, married, parents: Elija Bunton and Emily Dugger, cause of death: "high blood pressure and stomach trouble", inforant: R.C. Lunceford (Butler), buried: Bunton Cemetery, died: 8 Mar 1932, record (1932) #: 5153.

Daniel Boone BAKER, born: 10 Jul 1842, married, parents: Alexander W. Baker and Naomi Bradley, cause of death: "disease of heart", informant: Alex M. Baker (Butler), buried: Mountain View Cemetery, died: 14 Mar 1932, record (1932) #: 5154.

William GUIN, born: 8 Apr 1861, married, parents: William Guin and Julia Day, cause of death: "tuberculosis", informant: Mrs. Julia Guin (Butler), buried: Baker Cemetery, died: 4 Jan 1932, record (1932) #: 5155.

Cola Agnes BOLDEN, born: 26 Jan 1828 in North Carolina, widow, parents: Beasley Mabe (NC) and Martha Lawson (NC), cause of death: "chronic myocartitis", informant: Austin Boldin (Mountain City), buried: Family Cemetery, died: 7 Apr 1932, record (1932) #: 7751.

Adam Mast DOUGHERTY, born: 1 Mar 1847, single, parents: Elijah Dougherty and Eva Mast, cause of death: "influenza, lobar pneumonia", informant: Ray Shoun (Mountain City), buried: Neva, died: 28 Feb 1932, record (1932) #: 7752.

Ethel E. Smith CARRIGER, born: 7 May 1893, single, parents: Geo Smith and Grant Carriger, cause of death: "kidney infection", informant: Geo Walker (Butler), buried: Cardens Bluff, died: 30 Apr 1932, record (1932) #: 7753.

Hamilton B. HOWARD, born: 14 Dec 1862, married, parents: William Howard and Lydia Cole, cause of death: "paralysis", informant: Wheeler Howard (Doeville), buried: Shoun Cemetery, died: 17 Apr 1932, record (1932) #: 7554.

Amanda MCGLAMERY, age 86 years, born in North Carolina, widow, parents: John Bishop (NC) and Elizabeth Smith (NC), cause of death: "diabetes", informant: W.F. McGlamery (Trade), buried: Reece Cemetery, died: 11 Apr 1932, record (1932) #: 7555.

Mary POWELL, born: 14 Dec 1846, widow, parents: Isaac Osborn (NC) and Lydia Potter, cause of death: "influenza, pneumonia", informant: Danford Powell (Shouns), buried: Powell Cemetery, died: 27 May 1932, record (1932) #: 10103.

Isabele MURRAY, age about 75 years, widow, parents: William Proffitt and Polly South, death cause, "brights disease", informant: Jake Murray, buried: Holden Cem, died: 14 May 1932, record (1932) #: 10104.

Loyd Ed. GILBERT, born: 24 Apr 1923, parents: Leonard Gilbert and Frances Cable, cause of death: "influenzy followed by pneumonia", informant: Sam Lockner (Butler), buried: Cable Cemetery, died: 24 Apr 1932, record (1932) #: 10105.

George DOWELL, born: 7 Aug 1930, parents; Sherman Dowell and Lizzie Potter, cause of death: "acute colitis", informant: Sherman Dowell (Shouns), died: 5 Jun 1932, record (1932) #: 12415.

Andrew Jackson SMITH, born: 16 Mar 1854, married, parents: Henderson Smith and (first name not stated) Wilson, cause of death: "apoplexy", informant: King Nelson (Mountain City), buried: Wilson Cemetery, Doe Valley, died: 18 Jun 1932, record (1932) #: 12416.

Andrew MCELYEA, born: 1 Jun 1879, widower, parents: Larkin McElyea and Katy Tester, cause of death: "apoplexy", informant: McKinley McElyea (Shouns), died: 3 Jun 1932, record (1932) #: 12417.

Dora SWINEY, born: 6 Feb 1931, parents: Hobert Swiney and Mary Walker, cause of death: "colitis", informant: Hobert Swiney (Doeville), buried: Campbell Cemetery, died: 28 Jun 1932, record (1932) #: 12418.

Boyd SCOTT, age 7 months and 8 days, parents: Edgar Scott and Mada Garland, cause of death: "cholera", informant: Edgar Scott (Crandull), buried: Scott Cemetery, died: 19 Jun 1932, record (1932) #: 12419.

Robert R. ARNOLD, born: 17 Jun 1839, parents: John Arnold and Nancy Arnold, cause of death: "chronic brights disease", informant: S.T. Taylor (Shouns), died: 26 Jun 1932, record (1932) #: 14691.

Lou Eller EGGERS, born: 11 Aug 1893, married, parents: David Wilson and Minnie Gilbert, cause of death: "chronic brights disease", informant: W.B. Eggers (Laurel Bloomery), buried: Eggers Cemetery, died: 6 Jun 1932, record (1932) #: 14692.

John Quncy HAYWORTH, born: 10 Apr 1858 in North Carolina, widower, parents: Nathan Hayworth (NC) and Kizzie Welch (NC), cause of death: "diabetes", died: 19 Jun 1932, record (1932) #: 14693.

James Elbert MCQUEEN, Negro, born: 28 Apr 1904, widower, parents: Mack McQueen and Emma Mock, cause of death: "pulmonary tuberculosis", informant: Mack McQueen (Shouns), died: 4 Jul 1932, record (1932) #: 14694.

Lena Suzanie HAYWORTH, age about 5 months, parents: Robert Hayworth and May Yates, cause of death: "colitis", informant: Bob Hayworth (Mountain City), buried: Dunn Cemetery, died: 12 Jul 1932, record (1932) #: 14695.

Edward M. MADRON, born: 19 Jun 1874, widower, parents: Washington Madron and Elva Arnold, cause of death: "accidental injury to head", informant: Paul Madron (Mountain City), buried: Trade, died: 21 Jul 1932, record (1932) #: 14696.

Janice JONES, born: 23 Mar 1925 in New Mexico, parents: Marvin Jones (NC) and Ora Dowell, cause of death: "scarlet fever", informant: W.C. Dowell (Shouns), died: 15 Jul 1932, record (1932) #: 14697.

William C. DOUGHERTY, age 82 years and 22 days, parents: Thomas Dougherty and Hannah McBride, cause of death: "cyslitis", buried: Neva, TN, died: 31 Jul 1932, record (1932) #: 14698.

Susan C. ROBINSON, born: 22 Dec 1859, widow, parents: Hamilton Allen and Rachel Shoun, cause of death: "tuberculosis", informant: Garda Robinson, Rambo Cemetery, died: 5 Jul 1932, record (1932) #: 14699.

Lois Phillis BUNTON, born: 18 May 1931, parents: Frank Bunton and Pearl Bunton, cause of death: "colitis", informant: Scott Bunton (Butler), buried: Sugar Grove Cemetery, died: 8 Jul 1932, record (1932) #: 14700.

Mary C. HEATON, born: 10 Sep 1847 in North Carolina, widow, parents: William Gambill (NC) and Elizabeth Razor (NC), cause of death: "brights disease", informant: Sam Heaton (Butler), died: 30 May 1932, record (1932) #: 14701.

Dr. Thomas R. DONNELLY, (dentist) born: 26 Mar 1866, married, parents: James Doran Donnelly and Francis Orr (VA), cause of death: "chronic brights disease", informant: Mrs. Margaret Donnelly (Shouns), died: 9 Aug 1932, record (1932) #: 17019.

Mary Elizabeth DUNN, born: 15 Mar 1849, widow, parents: James Hicks and Mattie Emeline Johnson (VA), cause of death: "influenza, broncho pneumonia", informant: Henry Dunn (Shouns), buried: family cemetery, died: 17 Aug 1932, record (1932) #: 17020.

Elizabeth PHILLIPPI, born: 1 Mar 1851 in Virginia, widow, parents: David Phillippi (VA) and Jane Fry (VA), cause of death: "chronic brights disease", informant: J.R. Phillippi (Mountain City), buried: Phillippi Cemetery, died: 16 Jul 1932.

Elsie Mae PHILLIPS, born: 25 Apr 1932, parents: Joe Phillips and Bell Daugherty (VA), death cause: "probably indigestion from improper feeding", informant: Joe Phillips, died: 18 Aug 1932, record (1932) #: 17022.

Hobart NICHOLS, age 35 years, 6 months and 7 days, born in North Carolina, husband of Lilia E. Nichols, parents: father's name not stated and Olivine Nichols (NC), cause of death: "collapse of lungs from pulmonary tuberculosis", informant: Leonard Nichols (Crandull), buried: Blevins Cemetery, died: 13 Aug 1932, record (1932) #: 17023.

John Andrew VAUGHT, born: 6 Oct 1875 in Virginia, widower, parents: George Vaught (VA) and Mecca Caloline Pennington (VA), cause of death: "chronic brights disease", informant: Ray Vaught (Mountain City), died: 9 Sep 1932, record (1932) #: 19039.

Cordie POE, born: 11 Apr 1894, married, parents: Jim Wheatley (Ohio) and Martha Pancake (Ohio), cause of death: "cancer of liver", informant: William Poe (Shouns), died: 15 Sep 1932, record (1932) #: 19040.

Ethel Grace HOUK, born: 10 Aug 1917, parents: Estil Houk (NC) and Ada Johnson, cause of death: "pulmonary tuberculosis", informant: Haynes Johnson (Mountain City), died: 19 Sep 1932, record (1932) #: 19041.

D.H. LUNSFORD, parents: Charlie A. Lunsford and Lillie Ward, cause of death: "premature birth", born/died: 17 Aug 1932, record (1932) #: 19042.

Armina ROBINSON, born: 6 Mar 1847, widow, parents: John Speer (VA) and Secina Clauson (VA), cause of death: "influenza, broncho pneumonia", informant: Joe Robinson (Mountain City), buried: home cemetery, died: 4 Sep 1932, record (1932) #: 19043.

Robert KELLY, born: 30 Aug 1932, parents: Spencer Kelly and Lizzie Eggers, cause of death: "bold hives", informant: Enoch Potter (Trade), buried: Potter Cemetery, died: 16 Sep 1932, record (1932) #: 19044.

David Franklin WAGNER, born: 4 Oct 1862, married, parents: Daniel Wagner and Nancy Hardin (NC), cause of death: "cerebral hemorrhage", informant: Mrs. H.C. Donnelly, died: 4 Oct 1932, record (1932) #: 21125.

Ransom L. JENKINS, born: 4 Jan 1853, married, parents: Roland Jenkins and Betsy Wilson, cause of death: "apoplexy", informant: George Jenkins (Mountain City), died: 5 Oct 1932, record (1932) #: 21126.

L.A. KING, born: 4 Aug 1849 at Ashe Co. NC, widower, parents: father's name unknown and Sarah King (Ashe Co. NC), cause of death: "chronic brights disease", informant: C.W. King (Mountain City), died: 27 Oct 1932, record (1932) #: 21127.

John F. EGGERS, born: 1 May 1867 in North Carolina, husband of Sarah Eggers, parents: Abner Eggers (NC) and Sally Younce (NC), cause of death: "chronic intestinal nephritis", informant: T.A. Eggers (Elizabethton, TN), Union Cemetery, Mable, NC, died: (day not recorded) Oct 1932, record (1932) #: 21128.

Thomas JENKINS, born: 13 Sep 1892, married, parents: William Jenkins and Fina Owens, cause of death: "apoplexy", informant: R.F. Fenner, Phillippi Cemetery, died: 4 Apr 1932, record (1932) #: 21129.

Catherine Phillippi ROBERTS, born: 24 Jan 1843 in Virginia, widow, parents: David Phillippi (VA) and Jestie Crigger (VA), cause of death: not stated, informant: Baxter Roberts (Mountain City), buried: Wright Cemetery, died 9 Oct 1932, record (1932) #: 21130.

J.C. WILSON, born: 30 Sep 1931, parents: D.W. Wilson and Eliza Wilson, cause of death: "seems to have choked to death", informant: D.W. Wilson (Mountain City), buried: Wilson Cemetery, died: 21 Oct 1932, record (1932) #: 21131.

Stacy ROARK, born: 14 Jan 1907, single, parents: David Roark (NC) and Marelda Snyder (NC), cause of death: "pulmonary tuberculosis, lobar pneumonia", informant: R.W. Scott (Crandull), died: 31 Oct 1932, record (1932) #: 21132.

J.T. WILSON, age 1 year and 17 days, parents: Dan Wilson and Liza Wilson, cause of death: "diptheria", buried: Doe Valley, died: 17 Oct 1932, record (1932) #: 21133.

Iva D. WILLS, born: 29 Apr 1891, divorced, parents: Joseph E. Elrod and Etta Donnally, cause of death: "cancer of liver", informant: W.T. Smythe, died: 5 Nov 1932, record (1932) #: 23467.

Luinda HODGE, age about 50 years, wife of John Hodge, parents: David Roark (NC) and Loulia Snyder, cause of death: "dupasal neuralgia of hart", died: 9 Oct 1932, record (1932) #: 23468.

Ruben GARLAND, born: 22 Aug 1932, parents: Wheeler Garland and Bessie Church, cause of death: not stated, informant: Wheeler Garland (Doeville), died: 30 Nov 1932, record (1932) #: 23469.

W.B. REECE, born: 1 May 1857, husband of Amanda Reece, parents: Boyd Reece (NC) and Mary Kilby (NC), cause of death: "myocartial insufficiency", died: 27 Nov 1932, record (1932) #: 23470.

Thomas MARTIN, born: 20 Jan 1900 in North Carolina, married, parents: Roy Martin (NC) and Oma Potter (NC), cause of death: "gun shot wound in abdomen", informant: Jim Martin (Damascus, VA), buried: Damascus, VA, died: 9 Dec 1932, record (1932) #: 26263.

Ellen CHAPPELL, born: 29 Jan 1877 in North Carolina, married, parents: John Osborn (NC) and Sarah Jane Shepard (NC), cause of death: "nterine carcinoma", informant: Stacy Chappell (Laurel Bloomery), buried: Southerland Cemetery, died: 12 Dec 1932, record (1932) #: 26264.

Disey D. DOWELL, born: Jun 1881, married, parents: Steven Taylor and Rebecca Farmer (NC), cause of death: "lobar pneumonia", informant: Joseph Dowell (Mountain City), buried: Shingletown Cemetery, died: 13 Nov 1932, record (1932) #: 26265.

Calvin Richard JENKINS, born: 11 Dec 1843, married, parents: Roland Jenkins and Elizabeth Wilson, cause of death: "apoplexy", informant: Mainard Jenkins (Mountain City), buried: Phillippi Cemetery, died: 11 Dec 1932, record (1932) #: 26266.

David A. DAVIS, born: 30 Oct 1866, married, parents: Eli Davis and Nancy Slimp, cause of death: "lobar pneumonia", informant: Mrs. D.A. Davis, by Paul Everett (Mountain City), died: 20 Dec 1932, record (1932) #: 26267.

Elizabeth Jane CHURCH, born: 22 Jun 1851 in North Carolina, widow, parents: John Eller and Melvina Marfield (NC), cause of death: "auto infection, pneumonia", informant: W.D. Eggers (Mountain City), buried: Wilson Cemetery, died: 29 Nov 1932, record (1932) #: 26268.

Reubin MAXWELL, black, age 85 years, born in North Carolina, parents: Barton Maxwell (NC) and mother's name unknown, cause of death: "cancer of intestines", informant: Arther McQueen (Mountain City), died: 21 Dec 1932, record (1932) #: 26269.

Ruth Ellen HERNDON, born: 9 Nov 1932, parents: D.E. Herndon (VA) and Bessie Stewart, cause of death: "lobar pneumonia", buried: Cross Cemetery, died: 31 Dec 1932, record (1932) #: 26270.

Curlee OSBORNE, born: 14 Nov 1909, married, parents: John Arnold and Maggie Hall, cause of death: "pellagra", informant: M.R. Hall (Shouns), buried: Hall Cemetery, died: 23 Jul 1932, record (1932) #: 26271.

Mrs. Ritta TRIVETT, born: 28 dec 1893 in North Carolina, widow, parents: Finley Trivett (NC) and Eliza Reece (NC), cause of death: "myocardial insufficiency", informant: Helen Trivett (Butler), buried: Beech Creek, NC, died: 6 Dec 1932, record (1932) #: 26272.

Smithpeter Napoleon SMITH, born: 30 JUn 1866, psysician, married, parents: William Lafayette Smith (Fish Springs) and Louise Smithpeter, cause of death: "lobar pneumonia", informant: Mrs. Smithpeter N. Smith (Butler), buried: home cemetery, died: 19 Dec 1932, record (1932) #: 26273.

Clarance WHITE, born: 26 Jul 1929, parents: David D. White and Addie Eggers, cause of death: "pneumonia and whooping cough", died: 22 Dec 1932, record (1932) #: 26274.

M. Jordan SLIMP, age about 64 years, widower, parents: Martin Slimp and Caroline Bailey, cause of death: "pelagra", died: 26 Dec 1932, record (1932) #: 26275.

A.D. VONCANAN, born: 8 Jul 1879, husband of Mary Voncanan, born at Carter Co, TN, parents: Louis Voncanan and Anna Kinch, cause of death: "heart lieson", died: 31 Dec 1932, record (1932) #: 26276.

O.C. WALKER, born: 22 Jan 1882 in North Carolina, married, parents: J.C. Walker (NC) and Lottie Proffitt (NC), cause of death: "hemeplegia, influenza", informant: W.G. Walker (Crandull), buried: Woods Cemetery, died: 1 Dec 1932, record (1932) #: 26277.

Mary Lois THOMAS, age 8 months and 29 days, parents: B.R. Thomas (NC) and Annie Eggers (NC), cause of death: "pneumonia fever", informant: Clyde Thomas (Trade), buried: Thomas Cemetery, died: 27 dec 1932, record (1932) #: 26278.

Carlon REECE, female, age 1 year, 6 months and 27 days, parents: Floyd Reece and Maggie Main, cause of death: "pneumonia fever", informant: Howard Reece (Trade), buried: Reece Cemetery, died: 30 Dec 1932, record (1932) #: 26279.

Dorothy Lee HARMON, born: 18 Apr 1932, parents: Marton Harmon (NC) and Louvinia Harmon (NC), cause of death: "unknown", informant: Mrs. Marton Harmon (Butler), buried: Meadows Cemetery, died: 10 dec 1932, record (1932) #: 26280.

Martitia WALKER, age 84 years, 11 months and 19 days, widow, parents: Alex Snyder and Peggy Southead, cause of death: "chronic myocarditis", informant: W.R. Walker (Neva), died: 30 Dec 1932, record (1932) #: 28333.

Bertie Phillippi REECE, born: 4 Apr 1892, married, parents: Pierce Phillippi and Alice Luttrell, cause of death: "lobar pneumonia", informant: Mack Phillippi, buried: Phillippi Cemetery, died: 24 Jan 1933, record (1933) #: 1070.

Mrs. Martia BROWN, born: 1 Jun 1864 in North Carolina, widow, parents: Will Nelson (NC) and Mary Nelson (NC), cause of death: "cancer of liver", informant: Lura Potter (Mountain City), died: 2 Jan 1933, record (1933) #: 1071.

Pollie DOUGHERTY, born: 9 Apr 1847 in North Carolina, widow, parents: Hiram McBride (NC) and Mary Farthing, cause of death: "chronic myocarditis and brights disease", informant: M.L. Shoun (Mountain City), buried: Butler, died: 21 Jan 1933, record (1933) #: 1072.

Joseph W. STOUT, born: 7 Feb 1904, married, parents: Allen M. Stout and Abbie Martin, cause of death: "angina pectoris", informant: John M. Potter (Shouns), died: 24 Jan 1933, record (1933) #: 1073.

Mary DAVIS, born: 25 Apr 1860, widow, parents: Ruben Fletcher and Betsy Moreland, cause of death: "influenza", informant: C.A. Davis (Doeville), buried: Rambo Cemetery, died: 3 Jan 1933, record (1933) #: 1074.

Lucinda MCEWEN, born: 31 Jan 1836, widow, parents: Andy Cable and Edna Bradley, cause of death: "broncho pneumonia fever", informant: J.W. McEwen (Doeville), buried: McEwen Cemetery, died: 13 Jan 1933, record (1933) #: 1075.

Mrs. Ollie VALENTINE, born: 23 Feb 1900, wife of James A. Valentine, parents: L.B. Morley and Lissie McQueen, cause of death: "post partim hemorrhage", informant: Mrs. Taylor Smith (Butler), died: 31 Jan 1933, record (1933) #: 1076.

Martha JORDAN, born: 31 May 1860, widow, parents: Wm H. Shoun and Liza Loyd, cause of death: "pulmonary tuberculosis", informant: J.W. Jordan, buried: Doe Valley, died: 26 Jan 1933, record (1933) #: 1076.

D.F. WILSON, age 1 year, 3 months and 2 days, parents: William Wilson and Maud Miller, cause of death: "pneumonia", buried: Wallace Cemetery, died: 6 Jan 1933, record (1933) #: 1078.

Juanita Joyce CANNON, born: 12 Dec 1932, parents: Henry C. Cannon (NC) and Jessie Mac Shull (NC), cause of death: "whooping cough", informant: Rogers Harmon (Butler), buried: Mount Gilead Cemetery, died: 7 Jan 1933, record (1933) #: 1079.

William Mack TESTER, born: 19 Sep 1873, husband of Mina Tester, parents: Columbus Tester and Sallie McElyea, cause of death: "asthima, heart leakage", informant: Claude Tester (Butler), buried: Sugar Grove Cemetery, died: 7 Jan 1933, record (1933) #: 1080.

John L. LOCKNER, born: 4 Dec 1932, parents: Sam Lockner and Frances Cable, cause of death: "whooping cough", informant: Susan Dugger (Butler), died: 27 Jan 1933, record (1933) #: 1081.

Cresie E. HOWARD, age 74 years, 11 months and 12 days, born in North Carolina, widow of Melen Howard, parents: Andrew Johnson (NC) and Eveline Fletcher (NC), cause of death: "influenza, lobar pneumonia", informant: R.T. Howard, buried: Mountain View Cemetery, died: 4 Feb 1933, record (1933) #: 3314.

Marion Emmett LEWIS, born: 8 Aug 1871 in North Carolina, married, parents: David W. Lewis (NC) and (first name not stated) Tilley (NC), cause of death: "lobar pneumonia", informant: J.C. Lancaster (Shouns), died: 6 Feb 1933, record (1933) #: 3315.

James P. WILLS, born: 6 Mar 1864, married, parents: David W. Wills and Mary Cress, cause of death: "cancer of stomach", informant: M.M. Robinson (Mountain City), died: 12 Feb 1933, record (1933) #: 3316.

Laura S. NORRIS, born: 9 May 1933, parents: Joe Norris (NC) and Ila Reece, cause of death: "probably broncho pneumonia", informant: Joe Norris (Shouns), died: 17 Feb 1933, record (1933) #: 3317.

Lewis SHEARS, colored, age 52 years, born in North Carolina, parents" "not known", cause of death: "influenza, broncho pneumonia", informant: George Reeves (Mountain City), died: 19 Feb 1933, record (1933) #: 3318.

Helen Marie MAXWELL, born: 3 Feb 1933, parents: John Maxwell (NC) and Bettie Smith, cause of death: "lobar pneumonia", informant: John Maxwell (Mountain City), died: 20 Feb 1933, record (1933) #: 3319.

Clara WARREN, born: 18 Apr 1895 in North Carolina, married, parents: Alexander Crowder (NC) and Alice Moretz (NC), cause of death: "lobar pneumonia", informant: Luther Crowder (Shouns), died: 22 Feb 1933, record (1933) #: 3320.

Joseph Frederick FENNER, born: 25 Oct 1872, married, parents: James Fenner and Nancy Elliott (NC), cause of death: "chronic valvulor heart disease", informant: Walter Fenner, died: 28 Feb 1933, record #: 3321.

Mary HODGE, born: 25 Oct 1847, widow, parents: John Main (NC) and Polly Potter, cause of death: "chronic intestinal nephritis", informant: A.L. Hodge (Shouns), died: 2 Feb 1933, record (1933) #: 3322.

Myrtle Katherine HODGE, born: 19 Feb 1933, parents: Edward Lafayette Hodge (NC) and Mamie Lee Dugger, cause of death: "lobar pneumonia", informant: Edward Lafayette Hodge (Neva), died: 19 Feb 1933, record (1933) #: 3323.

Daniel NEATHERLY, born: 29 Aug 1870, married, parents: Jourdan Neatherly and Mary Tester, cause of death: "broncho pneumonia", informant: Paul Neatherly (Shouns), buried: Vaughtsville, died: 22 Feb 1933, record (1933) #: 3324.

Jaye MARRY, born: 23 Feb 1933, parents: Charles W. Marry (Bristol) and Clara (last name illegible)(KS), cause of death: illegible, died: 26 Feb 1933, record (1933) #: 3325.

James Abner MCCLOUD, born: 15 Jul 1873, married to Rosie McCloud, parents: Terness McCloud and Mary Duncan, cause of death: "absesed lungs", informant: Mrs. Henry Dugger (Butler), died: 27 Feb 1933, record (1933) #: 3326.

Mary E. NORRIS, born: 30 Nov 1932, parents: Fane Norris and Pearl Miller, cause of death: not stated, informant: Elbert Norris (Doeville), buried: Wilson Cemetery, died: 6 Feb 1933, record (1933) #: 3327.

Junior B. WALKER, born: 16 Sep 1931, parents: W.M. Walker and Laira Greer, cause of death: "not known", informant: W.M. Walker (Doeville), buried: Campbell Cemetery, died: 27 Feb 1933, record (1933) #: 3328.

Infant ROBERTS, female, parents: Walter Roberts and Edna Sue Horn, cause of death: "premanture birth", informant: Walter Roberts (Mountain City), born/died: 15 Feb 1933, record (1933) #: 3329.

E.H. STOUT, born: 3 Aug 1860, widower, parents: David W. Stout and Sallie Shoun, cause of death: "apoplexia", informant: Fuller Stout (Mountain City), died: 17 Feb 1933, record (1933) #: 3330.

Martha Jane HICKS, age 68 years, married, parents: Wiley Dillon and mother's name not stated, cause of death: not recorded, informant: Wiley Dillon (Mountain City), buried: Wright Cemetery, died: 22 Feb 1933, record (1933) #: 3331.

Mack N. GENTRY, born: 23 Oct 1923, parents: James A. Gentry and Mary Morefield, cause of death: "influenza and .. (illegible).. ", buried: Laurel Bloomery, died: 26 Mar 1933, record (1933) #: 5672.

John DOWELL, born: 20 Jun 1871, married, parents: John Hawkins and Darling Dowell, cause of death: "lobar pneumonia", informant: W.A. Potter (Shouns), died: 7 Mar 1933, record (1933) #: 5673.

Jacob H. POTTER, born: 8 Aug 1879, married, parents: Enoch Potter and (first name not stated) Main, cause of death: "thought to be heart failure", informant: W.A. Dowell (Shouns), buried: Forrester Cemetery, died: 11 Mar 1933, record (1933) #: 5674.

Martitia POWELL, born: 2 dec 1855, age 78 years, 3 months and 11 days, single, parents: (first name not stated) Proffitt and Caroline Powell (Wilkes Co. NC), cause of death: not recorded, informant: Conley Powell (Shouns), died: 13 Mar 1933, record (1933) #: 5675.

Asa C. FORRESTER, born: 17 May 1891, married, parents: Calvin Farmer and Jane Forrester, cause of death: "pulmonary tuberculosis", informant: William Hammons, buried: Hammons Cemetery, died: 31 Mar 1933, record (1933) #: 5676.

James MARTIN, born: 3 Jan 1933, parents: Nick Martin and Bettie Reece, cause of death: not stated, informant: Nick Martin, buried: Martin Cemetery, died: 12 Jan 1933, record (1933) #: 5677.

Bettie MARTIN, age 32 years, married, parents: A.R. Reece and Jane Main, cause of death: "broncho pneumonia", informant: Nick Martin (Shouns), buried: Martin cemetery, died: 8 Jan 1933, record (1933) #: 5678.

Andrew Calton JOHNSON, age 62 years, born at Watauga Co. NC, widower, husband of Titia Johnson, parents: Andrew Johnson (Wilkes Co. NC) and Nancy Main (Ashe Co. NC), cause of death: "lobar pneumonia", informant: M.C. Johnson (Shouns), buried: Martin Cemetery, died: 13 Jan 1933, record (1933) #: 5679.

Elizabeth LUNSFORD, born: 23 Nov 1845 in North Carolina, widow of General Lunsford, parents: General Lunsford (NC) and Elizabeth Swift (NC), cause of death: "supposed organic heart disease", informant: Ananity Keller (Butler), died: 20 Mar 1933, record (1933) #: 5680.

Helen ATWOOD, born: 11 Mar 1933, parents: John Vernon Atwood and Eva Stricland, cause of death: illegible, informant: Rachel Atwood (Butler), died: 25 Mar 1933, buried: Dugger Cemetery, record (1933) #: 5681.

Clyd Tester DUGGER, born: 5 Sep 1929, parents; Ray Dugger and May Presnell (NC), cause of death: "pneumonia, tuberculosis", informant: Ray Dugger (Butler), died: 1 Feb 1933, record (1933) #: 5682.

John REECE, born: 3 Mar 1867, married, parents: Landon Reece and Caroline Thomas (NC), cause of death: "apoplexy", informant: Robert Thomas (Trade), died: 3 Mar 1933, record (1933) #: 5683.

Alford Alexander DOTSON, born: 26 Jan 1850, married, parents: Allen Dotson and Delila Pierce, cause of death: "chronic intestinal nephritis", informant: W.S. Wilson (Trade), buried: home cemetery, died: 21 Mar 1933, record (1933) #: 5684.

Cecil Earl DOWELL, born: 11 Dec 1931, parents: Charley C. Dunn and Lena Dowell, cause of death: not stated, informant: Lena Dowell (Shouns), died: 27 Mar 1933, record (1933) #: 5685.

Charles Willis POTTER, born: 30 Mar 1932, parents: Phillip Potter and Mary Campbell, cause of death: "cholera", informant: Phillip Potter (Butler), buried: Sugar Grove Cemetery, died: 15 Mar 1933, record (1933) #: 5686.

Leaah Elizabeth BUNTON, born: 13 Feb 1933, parents: James Bunton and Bertha Wolfe, cause of death: "unknown", informant: James Bunton (Butler), buried: Sugar Grove Cemetery, died: 13 Feb 1933, record (1933) #: 5687.

Ellen Annie WILSON, born: March 1869, married, parents: R.U. Gentry and Sallie Gilliland, cause of death: "pulmonary tuberculosis", informant: Earl Wilson (Laurel Bloomery), buried: Valley Cemetery, died: 15 Apr 1933, record (1933) #: 7874.

Virginia Louise BRYANT, born: 25 Feb 1933, parents: Sam Bryant and Beulah Michaels, cause of death: "broncho pneumonia", informant: Sam Bryant (Shouns), died: 1 Apr 1933, record (1933) #: 7875.

Ruby MARTIN, age 10 years, 10 months and 4 days, parents: Walter Martin and Dona Mains, cause of death: "lobar pneumonia", informant: Walter Martin (Shouns), buried: Martin Cemetery, died: 6 Apr 1933, record (1933) #: 7876.

Nannie Elvina KITE, born: 14 Mar 1859, widow of J.A. Kite, parents: John Baner (NC) and Elizabeth Bishefl (NC), cause of death: "brights disease", informant: Eva Atwood, died: 17 Apr 1933, record (1933) #: 7878.

Wesley DUNN, born: 5 Apr 1848, married, parents: Henry Dunn and Mary Mink, cause of death: not stated, informant: J.W. Dunn (Shouns), buried: Hammons Cemetery, died: 10 Feb 1933, record (1933) #: 7877.

Jane RHYMER, born: 22 Apr 1846, widow, parents: Benjamin Moody (NC) and Rhoda Haton (NC), cause of death: "chronic brights disease", informant: Robert Coldwell (Butler), died: 22 Apr 1933, record (1933) #: 7879.

Infant HOLDEN, male, born: 26 Apr 1933, parents: father not stated and Verda Holden, cause of death: "malformation of heart (?)" died: 30 Apr 1933, record (1933) #: 7880.

Mrs. Rachel GARLAND, born: 13 Apr 1839, widow, parents: Joe Shoun and Polly Wills, cause of death: "influenza", informant: J.W.R. Allen (Doeville), buried: Rambo Cemetery, died: 4 Apr 1933, record (1933) #: 7881.

Kermit BUNTON, born: 11 Jan 1932, parents: father not stated and Rosa Bunton, cause of death: "pneumonia fever", informant: R.L. Bunton (Butler), buried: Sugar Grove Cem, died: 17 Apr 1933, record (1933) #: 7882.

John STANTON, born: 20 Dec 1932, parents: Conley Stanton and May Barlow, cause of death: "stomach trouble", informant: Conley Stanton (Butler), buried: Mountain View Cemetery, died: 21 Feb 1933, record (1933) #: 7883.

Elizabeth ARNOLD, age 68 years, 8 months and 2 days, widow, parents: John Fritz and Isabel Spear, cause of death: "duodenal ulcer", buried: Acre Field Cemetery, died: 7 May 1933, record (1933) #: 9910.

Edward MICHAEL, born: 25 Jul 1920, parents: Millard Michael (NC) and Easter Sturgill (NC), cause of death: "apoplexy", informant: M.F. Michael (Mountain City), buried: Donnelly Cemetery, died 6 May 1933, record (1933) #: 9911.

Margaret Emaline MORLEY, born: 7 May 1860, widow, parents: father's name unknown and Lucinda Morefield, cause of death: "chronic brights disease", informant: Verna Forrester (Mountain City), buried: Donnelly Cemetery, died: 7 May 1933, record (1933) #: 9912.

Nannie LAWS, born: 6 May 1888, married, parents: R.W. Seehorn (KY) and Mollie Galloway, cause of death: "pulmonary tuberculosis", informant: John M. Seehorn (Shouns), died: 10 May 1933, record (1933) #: 9913.

Joseph B. STOUT, age 81 years, 4 months and 1 day, married, parents: Nick Stout (NC) and Pollie Dunn, cause of death: "chronic intestinal nephritis, fracture femur", informant: John M. Potter (Shouns), died: 11 May 1933, record (1933) #: 9914.

Billie Ruth MCELYEA, born: 6 Sep 1931, parents: W.D. McElyea and Ollie Wilson, cause of death: "spinal meningitis", informant: W.D. McElyea (Mountain City), buried: Vaughtsville, died: 12 May 1933, record (1933) #: 9915.

Laura WARD, born: 14 Feb 1888, wife of Wm H. Ward, parents: Henry Fletcher and Julia Bryant, cause of death: "cancer of uterus", informant: Wm H. Ward (Butler), buried: home cemetery, died: 12 May 1933, record (1933) #: 9916.

Noah Franklin BROOKSHIRE, born: 10 Jun 1867, widower of Laura Brookshire, parents: Joel Brookshire (NC) and Edna Caroline Robinson, cause of death: "influenza, broncho pneumonia", informant: J.F. Brookshire (Elizabethton, TN), buried: Doe Valley Cemetery, died: 18 Mar 1933, record (1933) #: 9917.

John Lee WALSH, born: 10 Sep 1863 in North Carolina, married, parents: Thomas Walsh (NC) and Susan Tribel (NC), cause of death: "ulcer of stomach", informant: W.A. Walsh (Mountain City), buried: Doe Valley Cemetery, died: 24 Mar 1933, record (1933) #: 9918.

Frank STANTON, born: 1 May 1863, husband of Ollie Stanton, parents: Frank Stanton, Sr. (NC) and Polly Dugger, cause of death: "heart dropsy", informant: Hobart G. Stanton (Butler), buried: Baker Cemetery, died: 6 May 1933, record (1933) #: 9919.

Nat T. WILLS, born: 15 Aug 1859, married, parents: Russell Wills and Elizabeth Duff (VA), cause of death: "cerebral hemorrhage", informant: Lucy L. Wills, died: 24 Jun 1933, record (1933) #: 12027.

Phoebe JENKINS, age 72 years, 9 months and 1 day, born in North Carolina, widow, parents: Joel Eastridge (NC) and Sarah Rominger (NC), cause of death: "chronic valvulor heart disease", informant: George W. Jenkins (Mountain City), buried: Phillippi Cemetery, died: 26 Jun 1933, record (1933) #: 12028.

Alma Lorraine SLUDER, born: 21 Oct 1932, parents: Bob Sluder (NC) and Alma Gentry, cause of death: "colitis", date of death not stated, death certificate filed 10 Jul 1933, record (1933) #: 12029.

Dicy Barry HARPER, born: 25 Mar 1870, widow, parents: Alex Barry and Rachael Reece, cause of death: "influenza", died: 10 May 1933, record (1933) #: 12030.

John ARNOLD, born: 11 Jun 1881, married, parents: William Morefield and Brina Arnold, cause of death: "chronic intestinal nephritis", informant: John Osborn (Shouns), buried: Hall Cemetery, died: 31 May 1933, record (1933) #: 12031.

Albert Wayne PROFFITT, born: 5 Feb 1930, parents: Clyde Proffitt and Conie Mae Morefield, cause of death: "broncho pneumonia", informant: J.V. Morefield (Neva), died: 17 Jun 1933, record (1933) #: 12032.

Raoner JOHNSON, female, born: 1 Feb 1856, widow of J.C. Johnson, parents: (first name not stated) Guinn (NC) and mother's name unknown, cause of death: "myocardial insufficiency, chronic nephritis", buried: Brown Cemetery, died: 22 Jun 1933, record (1933) #: 12033.

Tom STOUT, born: 7 Jul 1910, single, parents: L.L. Stout and Laura Sammons, cause of death: "pulmonary tuberculosis", informant: L.L. Stout (Neva), died: 22 May 1933, record (1933) #: 12034.

Aquilla ARNOLD, age 87 years, 2 months and 8 days, married, parents: Billie Arnold and Polly Fry (VA), cause of death: "pneumonia", informant: F.C. Dougherty (Butler), buried: Neva, died: 10 Mar 1933, record (1933) #: 12035.

Robert Grant WILLS, born: 30 Jan 1877, married, parents: Macon R. Wills and Jennie Grant (VA), cause of death: "suicide by firearm, shot with pistol through head", informant: H.F.D. Wills (Shouns), died: 17 Mar 1933, record (1933) #: 12036.

Joseph G. SIMCOX, born: 10 Nov 1879, married, parents: Aaron H. Simcox (NC) and May C. Vaught, cause of death: "carcinoma of intestines", informant: T.C. Simcox (Neva), buried: home cemetery, died: 24 Mar 1933, record (1933) #: 12037.

Sue Preston Shelly LEWIS, born: 16 Oct 1858 in West Virginia, widow, parents: Joseph Scott Grigsby (WVA) and Hannah Elizabeth Porter, cause of death: "typhoid", informant: A.G. Lewis (Shouns), died: 29 Jul 1933, record (1933) #: 14328.

Annis Head NICHOLS, born: 2 Feb 1889, married, parents: W.S. Head and Oma Forrester, cause of death: "peritonitis", informant: R.S. Nichols (Mountain City), died: 22 Jul 1933, record (1933) #: 14329.

Nancy Naome WAGNER, born: 27 Nov 1861, married to I.L. Wagner, parents: Alexander Wagner and Nancy Catherine Baker, cause of death: "tuberculosis of bowls", informant: Oscar Donnelly (Butler), died: 16 Jul 1933, record (1933) #: 14330.

Nola Catherine DAVIS, born: 4 Jul 1933, parents: Novel Davis and Stella Lowe, cause of death: "congenital obstruction of bowel", buried: Shouns Cemetery, died: 7 Jul 1933, record (1933) #: 14331.

Robert Ray PRICE, born: 1 Sep 1932, parents: C.A. Price (NC) and Maude Blevins (NC), cause of death: "illio colitis", informant: C.A. Price (Crandull), died: 13 Jul 1933, record (1933) #: 14332.

Mae POTTER, born: 13 Sep 1886, wife of Don Potter, parents: father's name not stated and Mary Ann Heck, cause of death: "leakage of heart", buried: Potter Cemetery, died: 10 Jul 1933, record (1933) #: 14333.

Jacob A. GARLAND, born: 25 Aug 1848, widower, husband of Susan Cole, parents: Jessie Garland and Susan Cole (Carter Co. TN), cause of death: "brights disease", informant: Calie Garland (Trade), died: 11 Jul 1933, record (1933) #: 14334.

William Andrew WILSON, age 72 years, 9 months and 5 days, born in North Carolina, husband of Nannie Wilson, parents: William Wilson and Martha Main, cause of death: not recorded, informant: Nannie Wilson (Trade), buried: Potter Cemetery, died: 17 Jun 1933, record (1933) #: 14335.

Daniel Charles HENDISON, born: 19 Dec 1932, parents: Charles Hendison (VA) and Shela Triffic (NC), cause of death: "illio colitis", informant: Charles Hendison (Damascus, VA), buried: Damascus, VA, died: 6 Aug 1933, record (1933) #: 16664.

Richard Henry GENTRY, age 67 years, 1 month and 16 days, married, parents: Benjamin Gentry and Mary Hawkins, cause of death: "chronic brights disease", informant: Mrs. R.H. Gentry (Laurel Bloomery), buried: Valley Cemetery, died: 21 Jul 1933, record (1933) #: 16665.

Isaac WARD, age about 61 years, married to Mattie Ward, parents: Daniel Ward and Nancy Moreland, cause of death: "colitis", informant: Mattie Ward (Butler), died: 28 Aug 1933, record (1933) #: 16666.

Hubert Ray MILLHORN, born: 8 Oct 1928, parents: Robert H. Millhorn and Hattie Stout, cause of death: "diptheria", informant: Mrs. Hattie Millhorn (Butler), died: 31 Aug 1933, record (1933) #: 16667.

Virginia Lee SMITH, born: 11 Apr 1933, parents: Martin N. Smith and Liza Jane Grindstaff, cause of death: not stated, informant: J.T. Grindstaff (Doeville), died: 11 Apr 1933, record (1933) #: 16668.

Vina Dillon SHOUN, born: 1 Jun 1850 in North Carolina, widow, parents: Absolom W. Dillon and Celia L. Boltenhammer (NC), cause of death: "chronic brights disease", informant: John W. Dillon, buried: Wrights Cemetery, died: 11 Aug 1933, record (1933) #: 16669.

Clarence Eugene GARLAND, born: 13 Jun 1898, professor, West VA State University, husband of Irene Slez Garland, parents: Thomas K. Garland and Bell Cole, cause of death: "endo and myo carditis, nephritis", informant: T.K. Garland (Crandull), died: 7 Aug 1933, record (1933) #: 16670.

America THOMAS, born: 14 Sep 1868 at Wilkes Co. NC, married, parents: Ezekiel Brown (NC) and Susa Brown (NC), cause of death: "intestinal obstruction", informant: Wesley Brown (Trade), died: 3 Sep 1933, record (1933) #: 18776.

T. Stanley SMYTHE, born: 21 Mar 1854, County Clerk and Master, Chancery Court, married to Lillian S. Smythe, parents: Thomas S. Smythe (VA) and Margaret C. Donnelly, cause of death: "valvulor heart disease", informant: John W. Smythe (Mountain City), buried: Mountain View Cemetery, died: 17 Oct 1933, record (1933) #: 21075.

Peter SHOUN, age 75 years, single, parents: Jacob Shoun and Celia Cole, cause of death: "disease heart", informant: W.H. Lowe, buried: Shouns Cemetery, died: 5 Oct 1933, record (1933) #: 21076.

Georgie Lee STOUT, born: 26 Jan 1900, married to Mill L. Stout, parents: J.C. Hutchinson and M.E. Arnold, cause of death: "acute nephritis", informant: J.C. Hutchinson (Crandull), buried: Blevins Cemetery, died: 29 Oct 1933, record (1933) #: 21077.

David Carl DUGGER, born: 31 Jan 1933, parents: Roy Dugger and Della Mae Snyder, cause of death: "membrance croup", informant: Ray Dugger (Butler), buried: Snyder Cemetery, died: 20 Oct 1933, record (1933) #: 21078.

Charles C. RHEA, born: 28 Jul 1881, single, parents: Dr. Robert C. Rhea and Caroline McQueen, cause of death: "chronic myocarditis", died: 1 Nov 1933, record (1933) #: 23447.

Mrs. Sallie ALLEN, age 56 years, 7 months and 24 days, born in Virginia, wife of W.C. Allen, parents: J. Marion Blankenbeckler (VA) and Mary E. Hillard (VA) cause of death: "cancer of liver", informant: W.C. Allen (Mountain City), died: 6 Nov 1933, record (1933) #: 23448.

James E. LAWS, age 70 years, married, parents: William Laws and Betty Coutner, cause of death: "suicide with shot gun", informant: Cora Laws (Butler), buried: Neva, died: 31 Oct 1933, record (1933) #: 23449.

Maggie L. CORUM, born: 20 Sep 1933, parents: Walter Corum (NC) and Julie France (KY), cause of death: "erysipilas of face and trunk", informant: Walter Corum, buried: Tester Cemetery, died: 31 Oct 1933, record (1933) #: 23450.

Edith P. LAWS, born: 29 Aug 1928, parents: Jasper Laws (11 Aug 1897) and Lizzie Fritts (19 Oct 1894), cause of death: "diptheria", informant: Jasper Laws (Butler), died: 26 Sep 1933, record (1933) #: 23451.

Rosa Ethel MCCOY, born: 2 Jun 1933, parents: Milton McCoy and Bell Corum (NC), cause of death: "whooping cough", informant: T.H. Corum (Neva), died: 23 Jul 1933, record (1933) #: 23452.

Ida STEVENS, born: 10 Aug 1913, single, parents: Benjamin Stevens and Sarah May, cause of death: "typhoid", informant: Benjamin Stevens (Butler), died: 10 Nov 1933, record (1933) #: 23453.

Fannie Lee ROBINSON, born: 20 Aug 1932, parents: Gorda P. Robinson and Sallie Stout, cause of death: "double pneumonia", informant: Gorda P. Robinson (Butler), buried: Rambo Cemetery, died: 15 Nov 1933, record (1933) #: 23454.

Rosa WRIGHT, born: 4 Mar 1896 in Virginia, wife of W.H. Wright, parents: George W. Hines (VA) and M.E. Pennington (NC), cause of death: "supposed to have died from heart failure", informant: M.E. Sluder (Crandull), buried: Blevins Cemetery, died: 18 Nov 1933, record (1933) #: 23455.

Dr. Walter W. WIDENER, born: 29 Jun 1871 in Virginia, married, parents: Samuel A. Widener (VA) and Elizabeth English (VA), cause of death: "aortic insufficiency, cerebral hemorrhage", died: 23 Dec 1933, record (1933) #: 26988.

Richard CURD, born: 11 Oct 1859, married, parents: Ezekiel Curd and Polly Ann Hammons, cause of death: "general brights disease", buried: Dunn Cemetery, died: 21 Dec 1933, record (1933) #: 26989.

Elsie STANTON, age about 50 years, married, parents: Calvin Farmer (NC) and Jane Forrester, cause of death: "TB of lungs" informant: Will Shepard (Shouns), buried: Forrester Cemetery, died: 22 Dec 1933, record (1933) #: 26990.

Eliza ARNOLD, age 86 years, widow, parents: Jordan Heck and Betty Neatherly, cause of death: "disease heart", informant: W.C. Arnold (Neva), died: 17 Nov 1933, record (1933) #: 26991.

Jessie Eveline STEVENS, born: 2 Oct 1915, single, parents: Benjamin Stevens (NC) and Sarah May, cause of death: "typhoid fever", informant: Benjamin Stevens (Butler), died: 9 dec 1933, record (1933) #: 26992.

John L. LUNSFORD, born: 14 Dec 1933, parents: Caud Lunsford and Lillie Ward, cause of death: "unknown", died: 18 Dec 1933, record (1933) #: 26993.

Daniel S. ROARK, born: 22 Aug 1852, widower, husband of Bettie aAnn Rash, parents: Amos Rash (NC) and Rebecca Colimon (NC), cause of death: "chronic intestinal nephritis", informant: M.A. Rash (Trade), died: 15 Dec 1933, record (1933) #: 26994.

Haydin POTTER, born: 21 Sep 1932, parents: Frank Potter and Bessie Main, cause of death: not stated, informant: Bessie Potter (Trade), buried: Reece Cemetery, died: 19 Dec 1933, record (1933) #: 26995.

Katherin MOREFIELD, born: March 1868 in North Carolina, married, parents: John Simmons and Mary Smith, cause of death: "cerebral hemorrhage", informant: Miss Ruth Morefield (Mountain City), buried: Shingletown Cemetery, died: 11 Dec 1933, record (1933) #: 27811.

William PARRISH, born: 22 Feb 1852 at Wilkes Co. NC, widower, parents: father's name unknown and Adeline Thompson (NC), cause of death: "cancer of face", informant: Clint Waters (Damascus, VA), died: 23 Dec 1933, record (1933) #: 27812.

Eliza PENNINGTON, born: 22 Oct 1856, widow, parents: Dick Gentry and Sallie Gillin, cause of death: "heart attack", buried: Valley Cemetery, died: 28 Dec 1933, record (1933) #: 27813.

Elsie STANTON, age 51 years and 2 months, wife of John Stanton, parents: Calvin Farmer and Jane Forrester, cause of death: "not stated", informant: Charley Forrester, buried: Forrester Cemetery, died: 21 Dec 1933, record (1933) #: 27814.

Mrs. John DICKENS, born: 14 May 1884, married, parents: S.Q. Dugger and Liddie Price, cause of death: "cerebral hemorrhage", informant: John Dickens (Neva), died: 2 Dec 1933, record (1933) #: 27815.

Sarah L. PROFFITT, age 66 years, born in North Carolina, widow, parents: David Whitaker (NC) and Martha Paul (NC), cause of death: "chronic brights disease", buried: Parker Cemetery, died: 12 Jun 1933, record (1933) #: 28206.

Lillie WOODARD, born: 10 Feb 1877, married, parents: Calvin Farmer and Jane Forrester, cause of death: "heart dropsy", informant: C.A. Potter (Shouns), buried: Woodard Cemetery, died: 29 Jun 1933, record (1933) #: 28342.

Robert ABLE, born: 20 May 1846, widower, parents: Lean Able and mother's name unknown, cause of death: "heart attack", informant: W.E. Able (Laurel Bloomery), buried: Taylor Valley, died: 17 Jan 1934, record (1934) #: 895.

Infant PRUITT, male, born: 13 Jan 1934, parents: Clarence A. Pruitt and Pearl Robinson, cause of death: not stated, informant: Robert Robinson (Mountain City), buried: Wilson Cemetery, died: 16 Jan 1934, record (1934) #: 896.

Nellie Jane WAGNER, born: 7 May 1930, parents: Lee Roy Wagner and Florence Potter, cause of death: "burn from open grate, clothing caught fire", informant: Lee Roy Wagner (Shouns), died: 16 Jan 1934, record (1934) #: 897.

Ruby Dian HORN, born: 11 Sep 1927, parents: Worley Horn and Bell Icenhour (NC), cause of death: "broncho pneumonia", informant: Nell Icenhour (Mountain City), buried: Vaughtsville, died: 18 Jan 1934, record (1934) #: 898.

Sarah L. SHOUN, age 86 years, 5 months and 17 days, widow of J.A. Shoun, parents: Nicholas G. Robinson and Mary Howard, cause of death: "lobar pneumonia", informant: M.E. Wilson (Mountain City), buried: Pandora Shoun Cemetery, died: 25 Jan 1934, record (1934) #: 899.

Alvin Gilham GRAYSON, age 71 years, 7 months and 1 day, husband of Ethie Butler Grayson, parents: J.W.M. Grayson (NC) and Julie Williams (NC), cause of death: "cirrhosis of liver", informant: Mrs. H.C. Donnelly (Shouns), died: 21 Jan 1934, record (1934) #: 900.

Andy GENTRY, born: 1855, widower, parents: Wash Gentry and Pollie Gentry (NC), cause of death: "chronic brights disease", buried: Wilson Cemetery, died: 3 Feb 1934, record (1934) #: 3139.

Phillip David STOUT, born: 14 Aug 1853, widower, wife
was Kinzie Stout, parents: Alfred Stout and Susannah
Lowe, cause of death: "chronic brights disease",
informant: Dana Stout (Mountain City), died: 3 Feb
1934, record (1934) #: 3140.

Sherman DUNN, age 58 years, 7 months and 20 days,
husband of Callie Dunn, parents: Joe Dunn and Nancy
Elizabeth Osborn (NC), cause of death: "acute
alcoholism", informant: Selmer Johnson (Mountain
City), buried: Cold Springs Cemetery, died: 6 Jan
1934, record (1934) #: 3141.

Edgar CROWDER, born: 10 Feb 1934, parents: W.T.
Crowder (NC) and Pearl Moretz (NC), cause of death:
"congenital weakness" informant: W.T. Crowder
(Shouns), died: 10 Feb 1934, record (1934) #: 3142.

Houston Riley ELSWICK, born: 23 Sep 1895 at Sullivan
Co. TN, husband of Nettie Nave Elswick, parents: Van
Elswick (Sullivan Co. TN) and Lidia Hatcher (Sullivan
Co. TN), cause of death: "lobar pneumonia", informant:
Mrs. Pearl Moody (Johnson City, TN) , buried: Neva,
died: 17 Feb 1934, record (1934) #: 3143.

James N. PARSONS, age 65 years, 6 months and 28 days,
husband of Alice Parsons, parents: Henry Parsons (NC)
and Sarah Forrester (NC), cause of death: "carcinoma
of liver", informant: Alice Parsons (Mountain City),
died: 26 Feb 1934, record (1934) #: 3144.

Lewis WILSON, born: 28 Oct 1901, single, parents: John
Wilson (VA) and Emma Flanagan (VA), cause of death:
"abscess of liver", informant: John Wilson (Mountain
City), died: 22 Jan 1934, record (1934) #: 3145.

Denver ANDERSON, Negro, age 16 years, 8 months and 2
days, parents: Milton Anderson and Maggie Goins, cause
of death: "broncho pneumonia", informant: Milton
Anderson, died: 29 Jan 1934, record (1934) #: 3146.

Malinda Goins ANDERSON, Negro, born: 10 May 1866 in
Ashe Co. NC, wife of L.K. Anderson, parents: W.A.
Goins (Ashe Co. NC) and Frankie Fields (Ashe Co. NC),
cause of death: "apoplexy" died: 31 Jan 1934, record
(1934) #: 3147.

Thomas H. WILLEN, age 53 years, husband of Jane
Willen, parents: Thomas Willen and Liddie Potter,
cause of death: "lobar pneumonia", informant: Cliff
Willen (Shouns), buried: Dunn Cemetery, died: 18 Feb
1934, record (1934) #: 3148.

David Webster MCEWEN, age about 62 years, divorced,
parents: William McEwen and mother's name illegible,
cause of death: "pneumonia", died: 23 Feb 1934, record
(1934) #: 3149.

Tennessee LOYD, age 91 years and 14 days, widower of Sophie Loyd, parents: John Loyd (VA) and Annie Crosswhite (VA), cause of death: "cerebral hemorrhage", buried: Doe Valley, died: 12 Feb 1934, record (1934) #: 3150.

Mary Mabel RASH, born: 6 Jun 1928 at Ashe Co. NC, parents: R.H. Rash (Ashe Co. NC) and Maggie Woodard (Ashe Co. NC), cause of death: "pneumonia", informant: R.W. Rash (Mountain City), buried: Ashland, NC., died: 18 Feb 1934, record (1934) #: 3151.

Sherman Gain BROOKSHIRE, born: 31 Aug 1888, married, parents: Noah Brookshire and Laura Sheers, cause of death: "pulmonary tuberculosis", buried: Doe Valley, died: 25 Feb 1934, record (1934) #: 3152.

Bettie OSBORN, born: 2 Mar 1861, widow of Benjamin Osborn, parents: John Musgrave and mother's name not known, cause of death: "lobar pneumonia", informant: Luther Osborn (Trade), buried: Zionville, NC, died: 6 Feb 1934, record (1934) #: 3153.

Jennie REECE, born: 7 Sep 1881 in North Carolina, wife of Robert Reece, parents: James South (NC) and Lydia Hammons, cause of death: "broncho pneumonia", informant: Maggie Reece (Trade), buried: Zionville, NC., died: 8 Jan 1934, record (1934) #: 3154.

James M. WALLACE, born: 18 Aug 1867, husband of Elmina Wallace, parents: George W. Wallace and May Stephen (NC), cause of death: "chronic valvulor heart disease", informant: Russell Wallace (Trade), buried: Wallace Cem, died: 13 Jan 1934, record (1934) #: 3155.

Mina WIDENER, born: 30 May 1864 in Virginia, widow, parents: (first name illegible) Cole (VA) and Sarah Cole (VA), cause of death: "cerebral hemorrhage", buried: Taylor Valley Cemetery, died: 16 Mar 1934, record (1934) #: 5762.

Sarrah Jean LAWS, born: 2 Feb 1865, married, parents: Jarrett Arnold and Sally Ward, cause of death: "ulcer of stomach", informant: William Laws (Butler), died: 12 Mar 1934, record (1934) #: 5763.

J.T. GARLAND, born: 28 Feb 1934, parents: Will C. Garland and Lillie Arnold, cause of death: "pneumonia fever", informant: Will C. Garland (Doeville), buried: Rambo Cemetery, died: 4 Mar 1934, record (1934) #: 5764.

John GRINDSTAFF, born: 4 Jan 1850, widower, parents: Isaac Grindstaff and Polly Heaton, cause of death: "pneumonia", informant: D.V. Grindstaff (Butler), buried: Grindstaff Cemetery, died: 23 Mar 1934, record (1934) #: 5765.

Hamilton RASH, Jr., age 3 years, born at Ashland, NC, parents: Hamilton Rash (NC) and Maggie Woodard (NC), cause of death: "pneumonia", informant: Winfred Rash (Mountain City), died: 9 Mar 1934, record (1934) #: 5766.

Mattie ARNEY, age 56 years, 3 months and 3 days, widow of John Robinson, parents: William Lowe and Titia Stalcup, cause of death: "lobar pneumonia", informant: Pauline Robinson (Doeville), died: 13 Mar 1934, record (1934) #: 5769.

Mrs. Mary Lewis HOWE, born: 2 Feb 1881 in North Carolina, married, parents: David H. Lewis (NC) and (first name not stated) Gilley (NC), cause of death: "bronchial pneumonia", informant: Emmett H. Howe (Mountain City), buried: Morley Cemetery, died: 16 Feb 1934, record (1934) #: 5768.

Polly MCGLAMERY, age about 55 years, wife of Roscoe McGlamery, parents: Jordan Dotson and Pashie Cornett (NC), cause of death: "not known, died suddenly", informant: W.F. McGlamery (Trade), buried: Zionville, NC., died: 7 Mar 1934, record (1934) #: 5769.

Bettie Seve MCELYEA, born: 29 Mar 1934, parents: W.D. McElyea and Ollie Wilson, cause of death: "lobar pneumonia", informant: W.D. McElyea (Mountain City), buried: Vaughtsville, died: 14 Apr 1934, record (1934) #: 8480.

Nancy MORETZ, born: 19 Jan 1864 in North Carolina, widow of Jefferson D. Moretz, parents: James Isaacs (NC) and Nancy Eggers, cause of death: "obstruction of bowels", informant: R.J. Moretz (Shouns), died: 14 Apr 1934, record (1934) #: 8481.

Infant NICHOLS, female, born: 22 Apr 1934, parents: W.A. Nichols (NC) and Bonnie Dickens, cause of death: "congenital weakness", buried: Mountain View Cemetery, died: 23 Apr 1934, record (1934) #: 8482.

J.R. FLETCHER, age 58 years, 8 months and 26 days, born in Virginia, parents: "unknown", cause of death: "chronic brights disease", informant: Sam Nichols (Mountain City), died: 12 Mar 1934, record (1934) #: 8483.

Barbara Anne COTTRELL, born: 10 Feb 1931 at Boone, NC, parents: J.D. Cottrell (NC) and Hazel Irene Carriger, cause of death: "measles, broncho pneumonia", buried: Boone, NC, died: 23 Mar 1934, record (1934) #: 8484.

Charlie Theodore DAVIDSON, age 29 years, 9 months and 6 days, single, parents: Silvister Davidson (VA) and Mandy (illegible) Davidson, cause of death: "lobar pneumonia", buried: Shingletown Cemetery, died: 22 Feb 1934, record (1934) #: 8485.

Emert STANSBURY, age about 46 years, married, parents: Duff Stansbury (NC) and Martha Norris (NC), cause of death: "alcoholic poison", buried: Mabel, NC, died: 9 Apr 1934, record (1934) #: 8486.

Nettie Louerita GRINDSTAFF, born: 14 Mar 1914, single, parents: James T. Grindstaff and Bessie E. Wilson (Washington Co. VA), cause of death: "pneumonia", informant: J.T. Grindstaff (Doeville), died: 19 Apr 1934, record (1934) #: 8487.

James Kent WOLF, born: 21 Mar 1931, parents: Dan C. Wolf and Rosie White, cause of death: "pneumonia", informant: Dan C. Wolf (Butler), buried: Sugar Grove Cemetery, died: 20 Feb 1934, record (1934) #: 8488.

Willie DAVIS, born: 26 Sep 1932, parents: Jack Davis and Josie Hicks, death cause: "pneumonia", informant: Lawrence Robards, died: 7 Apr 1934, record #: 8489.

Coleman Shelby PLUMMER, age 1 year, 1 month and 25 days, parents: E.L. Plummer and C.B. Gentry, cause of death: not recorded, informant: E.L. Plummer (Crandull), died: 17 Apr 1934, record (1934) #: 8490.

James Calvin WALKER, born: 14 Jul 1852 in North Carolina, married, parents: William Walker (NC) and (first name not stated) Beshears (NC), cause of death: "supposed to be carcinoma of the bladder", informant: W.T. Walker (Crandull), buried: Woods Cemetery, died: 13 Feb 1934, record (1934) #: 8491.

Infant CORUM, male, parents: father's name not stated and Naimia Jenkins, cause of death: "mother thinks child strangled to death", informant: Mrs. R.L. Jenkins (Mountain City), buried: Cornett Cemetery, born/died: 14 May 1934, record (1934) #: 10853.

Edward Glenn CORUM, born: 3 Mar 1907, married, parents: B.G. Corum, and George Ann Owens, cause of death: "bilateral pneumonia", informant: Roy Riddles (Mountain City), buried: Winters Cemetery, died: 1 Apr 1934, record (1934) #: 10854.

Robert Floyd MCELYEA, age 36 years, husband of Mary McElyea, parents: Landon Henry McElyea and Jermie L. Allen (NC), cause of death: "double pneumonia", informant: Callie McElyea (Mountain City), died: 4 Apr 1934, record (1934) #: 10855.

James Alfred TRIPLETT, born: 29 Oct 1934, parents: Glenn Triplett and Bertha Eldrith, cause of death: "lobar pneumonia", informant: Gene Eldrith (Mountain City), died: 6 Apr 1934, record (1934) #: 10856.

Infant CURD, male, parents: W.M. Curd and Lela Dunn, cause of death: "premature birth", informant: W.M. Curd (Shouns), buried: N. Wagner Cemetery, born/died: 22 May 1934, record (1934) #: 10857.

Mrs. Sarah Sirena ROBINSON, born: 27 Aug 1857, widow, parents: David Wills and Sallie Cress, cause of death: "lobar pneumonia", informant: M.M. Robinson (Mountain City), buried: Robinson Cemetery, died: 30 May 1934, record (1934) #: 10858.

Lydia DOWELL, born: 4 May 1873, widow, parents: Thomas (last name illegible) and Lydia Dowell, cause of death: "broncho pneumonia", informant: C.S. Dowell (Shouns), buried: Potter Cemetery, died: 8 May 1934, record (1934) #: 10859.

Silas A. CLARK, age 79 years, married, parents: Silas A. Clark and Jane Morley, cause of death: "bronchial pneumonia", informant: R.A. Mast (Neva), died: 2 May 1934, record (1934) #: 10860.

Stacy Edgar HODGE, age 3 years, 1 month and 22 days, parents: Edgar Hodge and Jessie Vaught, cause of death: "broncho pneumonia, menengitis", buried: Lunkin Branch, died: 19 May 1934, record (1934) #: 10861.

Louisa PROFFITT, age 96 years, born in North Carolina, widow of Pless Proffitt, parents: "unknown", cause of death: "chronic brights disease", buried: Tester Cemetery, died: 19 May 1934, record (1934) #: 10862.

William NEATHERLY, born: 5 Nov 1933, parents: Paul Neatherly and Buleah Walker, cause of death: "broncho pneumonia", informant: William Proffitt (Neva), died: 19 Apr 1934, record (1934) #: 10863.

Nomia Elizabeth BROWN, born: 27 Oct 1839 at Watauga Co. NC, single, parents: James Brown (Watauga Co. NC) and Harriett N. Farthing (Watauga Co. NC), cause of death: "broncho pneumonia", informant: J.A. Shull (Neva), died: 22 Feb 1934, record (1934) #: 10864.

Infant FRITTS, male, parents: Oscar Fritts and Nell Wagner, cause of death: not stated, born/died: 22 Jan 1934, derc 10865.

Nanie ROBINSON, born: 17 May 1888, married to Jas D. Robinson, parents: L.L. McQueen and Catherine Bradley, cause of death: "lobar pneumonia", informant: J.P. Robinson (Butler), buried: Cobbs Creek, died; 17 May 1934, record (1934) #: 10866.

Paul WARD, born: 5 Mar 1932, parents: Willard Ward (NC) and Nora Green (NC), cause of death: "possibly colitis", informant: Walter Caldwell (Butler), died: 24 May 1934, record (1934) #: 10867.

Sarah Fina SHOUN, born: 12 Apr 1863, widow, parents: Godfrey Stout and Elizabeth Crosswhite, cause of death: "chronic brights disease", informant: W.H. Shoun (Mountain City), buried: Shoun Cemetery, Doe Valley, died: 7 May 1934, record (1934) #: 10868.

Mrs. Myrtle KIRBY, born: 23 Jul 1910, married to Conley Kirby, parents: Clint Loggins and Belle Roberts, cause of death: "pulmonary tuberculosis", informant: Ed Roberts (Mountain City), buried: Morley Cemetery, Doe Valley, died: 11 May 1934, record (1934) #: 10869.

Mrs. Jennie MORLEY, age 56 years, born in North Carolina, married, parents: John (last name illegible) and Victoria Vanover (NC), cause of death: "cerebral hemorrhage", buried: Morley Cemetery, died: 16 May 1934, record (1934) #: 10870.

Ida SCOTT, born: 19 Apr 1880, wife of F.R. Scott, parents: Dock Brown and Martha Thomas, cause of death: "pneumonia", informant: R.W. Scott (Crandull), died: 31 Mar 1934, record (1934) #: 10871.

Roby WILSON, born: 2 Apr 1908, husband of Inez Eggers, parents: Marvin Wilson and Freddie Parks, cause of death: "fracture to base of skull, from block thrown by shingle saw", informant: Roby Wallace (Trade), died: 10 May 1934, record (1934) #: 10872.

Grant DUGGER, born: 25 Mar 1914, single, parents: M.A. Dugger and Emily Isaacs (NC), cause of death: "apoplexy", informant: E.A. Dugger (Butler), died: 23 May 1934, record (1934) #: 10873.

Herbert STANBERRY, born: 14 Mar 1914, single, parents: J.R. Stanberry and Etta Burton, cause of death: "supposed to be some kind of brain trouble", informant: Troy Stanberry (Butler), died: 17 Feb 1934, record (1934) #: 10874.

Nancy Jane STURGILL, born: 22 Aug 1860, widow, parents: John Howard (NC) and Mary Greer, cause of death: "chronic brights disease", informant: Edd Sturgill (Laurel Bloomery), buried: Shingletown Cemetery, died: 18 Jun 1934, record (1934) #: 13237.

Russell LEWIS, born: 22 Mar 1934, parents: Robert Lewis (NC) and Dona Phipps (NC), cause of death: "unknown", informant: W.M. Buchanan, buried: Ashe Co. NC, died: 7 May 1934, record (1934) #: 13238.

James E. GENTRY, age about 74 years, married, parents: Richard Gentry and Sallie Gilland, cause of death: "chronic nephritis", informant: Roy Gentry (Laurel Bloomery), buried: Valley Cemetery, died: 3 Mar 1934, record (1934) #: 13239.

George TAYLOR, age 41 years and 3 months, husband of Alice Taylor, parents: Columbus Taylor (NC) and Pollie Cole (NC), cause of death: "fracture skull, fell from moving truck", informant: Roy Vanover (Shouns), died: 2 Jun 1934, record (1934) #: 13240.

Marion HAMMONS, male, born: 28 Jun 1933, parents: Andy Hammons and Leah Arnold, cause of death: "lobar pneumonia", informant: Columbus Taylor (Shouns), buried: Hammons Cemetery, died: 15 May 1934, record (1934) #: 13241.

John M. STOUT, age 76 years, 8 months and 27 days, widower, parents: Godfrey Stout and Elizabeth Crosswhite, cause of death: "cancer bladder", informant: Retta Stout (Mountain City), died: 3 Jun 1934, record (1934) #: 13242.

Biner PERKINS, age 10 months, parents: Rosco Perkins (NC) and Alice Perkins, cause of death: "ilio colitis", informant: M.G. Hodge (Shouns) died: 15 Jun 1934, record (1934) #: 15783.

Soloman R. TRIBBETT, born: 18 May 1865, married, parents: father's name not stated and Bettie Tribbett, cause of death: "kidney and bowel trouble", died: 19 Jul 1934, record (1934) #: 15784.

Nada Corina SCOTT, born: 18 Jun 1911, married to Ed Scott, parents: Jessie Garland and Eliza Blevins, cause of death: "cancer of breast", informant: Eliza Garland (Crandull), buried: Scott Cemetery, died: 6 Jul 1934, record (1934) #: 15785.

Kate R. REECE, born: 24 Oct 1933, parents: Franklin Reece and Jessie Leffman, cause of death: "acute colitis", informant: Edd Gentry (Laurel Bloomery), buried: Valley Cemetery, died: 11 Jul 1934, record (1934) #: 18301.

Clery TESTER, age 76 years, 2 months and 13 days, wife of Alex Tester, parents: John McElyea and Katy (Catherine) Tester, cause of death: "cerebral hemorrhage", informant: Nute McElyea (Elizabethton, TN), died: 8 Aug 1934, record (1934) #: 18302.

Mrs. Jennie GREEN, born: 4 Oct 1867, wife of J.B. Green, parents: Samuel Foster and M... (illegible) Bailey, cause of death: "chronic myocarditis", informant: Ray Green (Shouns), buried: Green Cemetery, died: 15 Jul 1934, record (1934) #: 18303.

Ollie PIERSON, age 64 years, 4 months and 25 days, born in Virginia, husband of Sarah Church, parents: Rufus Pierson and Jane Mink, cause of death: "chronic myocarditis", informant: Walter Pierson (Neva), died: 23 Jul 1934, record (1934) #: 18304.

Teddy Ray ROBINSON, born: 4 May 1934 in McMinn Co. TN, parents: Dewy Robinson and Zara Mae Hinson (McMinn Co. TN), cause of death: not stated, informant: Wayne Stout (Doeville), buried: Sweetwater, TN, died: 25 Aug 1934, record (1934) #: 18305.

John NAVE, born: 5 Sep 1896, husband of Bettie Nave, parents: David Nave and Amelia Moore (NC), cause of death: "gunshot wound to right chest, homicide", informant: David Nave (Mountain City), died: 6 Aug 1934, record (1934) #: 18306.

Ruby Ethel LEWIS, age 6 months, parents: Willie Lewis (NC) and Nanabeth Gentry, cause of death: "colitis", informant: J.S. Shupe (Mountain City), buried: Doe Valley, died: 21 Aug 1934, record (1934) #: 18307.

David WRIGHT, born: 19 Apr 1856, married, parents: Andy Wright and Susan Wright, cause of death: "chronic brights disease", informant: James Wright (Crandull), buried; Gentry Cemetery, died: 15 Aug 1934, record (1934) #: 18308.

Louise E. JOHNSON, born: 16 May 1859, widow, parents: Bartly Wood and Evelyn Council, cause of death: "high blood pressure, heart disease", informant: Effie Jenkins (Trade), died: 24 Jul 1934, record (1934) #: 18309.

Melvin JONES, age 68 years, born in Ashe Co. NC, married, parents: Samuel Jones (Ashe Co. NC) and Katie Lewis (Ashe Co. NC), cause of death: "by being shot or murdered", informant: J.F. Jones (Shouns), buried: West Cemetery, died: 30 Sep 1934, record (1934) #: 20622.

Nick G. WAGNER, age 74 years, 9 months and 25 days, married, parents: Joe Wagner and Mary Vaught, cause of death: "chronic intestinal nephritis, lobar pnuemonia", informant: Lee Wagner (Shouns) died: 5 Sep 1934, record (1934) #: 20623.

Nannie Beth LEWIS, age 30 years, wife of Willie Lewis, parents: Jim Gentry and Memphis Wills, cause of death: "pulmonary tuberculosis", informant: J.F. Shupe (Mountain City), buried: Wilson Cemetery, died: 15 Sep 1934, record (1934) #: 20624.

Dorsie Jean ADAMS, born: 29 Apr 1934, parents: Millie Adams and Hazel Hicks, cause of death: illegible, informant: Hazel Adams, buried: Wright Cemetery, died: 10 Aug 1934, record (1934) #: 20625.

Cham Bell SHOUN, age 62 years, 11 months and 25 days, married to Peter Shoun, parents: Albert Lowe and Kinzie Robinson, cause of death: "apoplexy", informant: Peter L. Shoun (Mountain City), buried: Doe Valley, died: 30 Aug 1934, record (1934) #: 20626.

Balmer HUGGINS, age 31 years, married to Josie Huggins, parents: Oscar R. Huggins (NC) and Lillie Dotson, cause of death: "lobar pneumonia", informant: Oscar Huggins (Mountain City), died: 1 Oct 1934, record (1934) #: 22972.

Vira LIPFIRD, age 49 years and 5 months, married to
B.V. Lipfird, parents: D.M. Arnold and Alice Osborn,
cause of death: "lobar pneumonia", informant: B.V.
Lipfird (Shouns), died: 11 Oct 1934, record (1934) #:
22973.

Susah TILLEY, age 78 years and 3 days, born in North
Carolina, widow of Alvin Tilley, parents: Andy Hampton
and Pashie Hampton, cause of death: "chronic brights
disease", informant: J.J. Snyder (Shouns), died: 15
Oct 1934, record (1934) #: 22974.

Blanche Marie HAMMONS, age 5 years, 4 months and 5
days, parents: Bascom Hammons and Lourie South (NC),
cause of death: "broncho pneumonia", informant: Bascom
Hammons (Shouns), died: 18 Oct 1934, record (1934) #:
22975.

Jamia Lee SMITH, born: 26 Sep 1934, parents: father
not stated and Mary Smith, cause of death: "not
known", informant: Mary Smith (Butler), died: 4 Oct
1934, record (1934) #: 22976.

Burley Kate ROBINSON, age 32 years, 11 months and 13
days, single, parents: Samuel Robinson and Sallie
Stout, cause of death: "pulmonary tuberculosis",
informant: Samuel Robinson (Mountain City), buried:
Doe Valley, died: 22 Oct 1934, record (1934) #: 22977.

Minnie STOUT, born: 31 Jan 1899, wife of Bill Stout,
parents: J.M. Fritts and Vina Stout, cause of death:
"typhoid fever", informant: Bill Stout (Mountain
City), buried: Wright Cemetery, died: 14 Aug 1934,
record (1934) #: 22978.

S.C. PARKS, female, born: 23 May 1860, widow of W.E.
Parks, parents: Billy Brewer (NC) and Jane Nelson
(NC), cause of death: "cardiac condition", died: 11
Oct 1934, record (1934) #: 22979.

Nancy GREER, born: 4 Oct 1833 in North Carolina, age:
101 years and 11 days, widow of Alex Greer, parents:
Billie Osborn (NC) and Lydia Price (NC), cause of
death: "unknown", informant: Taft Greer (Trade),
buried: Greer Cemetery, died: 15 Oct 1934, record
(1934) #: 22980.

Nannie Rebecca MOREFIELD, age 77 years, 5 months and
20 days, born in North Carolina, widow of J.W.
Morefield, parents: Jessie Warden (NC) and Sarah
Hutchinson (NC), cause of death: "hypostatic
pneumonia", died: 10 Nov 1934, record (1934) #: 25381.

Rebecca GENTRY, born: 2 Sep 1858, widow, parents:
Elias Worley and Vinia Grace, cause of death: "chronic
myocarditis", informant: Roy Gentry (Laurel Bloomery),
buried: Southerland Cemetery, died: 22 Nov 1934,
record (1934) #: 25382.

Infant PHILLIPS, female, parents: Joe Phillips and Belle Dougherty (VA), cause of death: not stated, born/died: 23 Feb 1934, record (1934) #: 25383.

Rachel ARNOLD, age about 76 years, widow, parents: Daniel Morefield and Annie Neatherly, cause of death: "organic heart disease", informant: Lissie Grindstaff (Doeville), died: 1 Nov 1934, record (1934) #: 25384.

Celia Birbary LAWS, born: 7 Nov 1861, widow of Isaac Laws, parents: Alfred (last name illegible) and mother's name illegible, cause of death: "organic heart disease", informant: George Laws, buried: Dry Run, died: 19 Oct 1934, record (1934) #: 25385.

Mrs. Sallie OWENS, age about 75 years, born in Grayson Co. VA, married to John Owens, parents: Amous Bryant (Grayson Co. VA) and Eliza Johnson (Ashe Co. VA) (NC ?), cause of death: "pneumonia", informant: J.G. Bryant (Meadow View, NC), buried: Owens Cemetery, died: 15 Dec 1934, record (1934) #: 28082.

Robert L. MADRON, born: 6 Aug 1872, married, parents: John Madron and Celia Reece, cause of death: "automobile accident, fracture of cerviacl ver... (illegible)", informant: Mrs. Nora Madron (Laurel Bloomery), died: 10 Oct 1934, record (1934) #: 28083.

John K. WILSON, born: 5 Nov 1853, married to Phoebe Wilson, parents: Richard L. Wilson and mother's name not stated, cause of death: "chronic brights disease", informant: E.A. Wilson (Greeneville, TN), died: 11 Dec 1934, record (1934) #: 28084.

Elbert Ross FLANNERY, age 1 month and 26 days, parents: John Flannery (NC) and Rader Dugger, cause of death: not stated, informant: Fayte Hodge (Neva), died: 18 Dec 1934, record (1934) #: 28085.

Harbin Cane MOREFIELD, born: 7 Apr 1906, married to Lola Morefield, parents: R.R. Morefield and Pollie Forrester, cause of death: "pulmonary tuberculosis", informant: J.V. Morefield (Neva), buried: Maymead, died: 27 Nov 1934, record (1934) #: 28086.

John M. RILEY, born: 10 Apr 1858, widower of Emma Riley, parents: father's name not stated and Martha Hatcher, cause of death: "high blood pressure", informant: J.A. Riley (Butler), buried: Bluff City, TN, died: 19 Dec 1934, record (1934) #: 28087.

Catherine E. HOWELL, born: 26 Aug 1912 in Indiana, wife of Wm Thomas Howell, parents: W.S. Parks (Indiana) and Bertha (last name illegible) (Indiana), cause of death: "mistral regurgitation of heart", informant: Thomas Howell (Butler), died: 28 Dec 1934, record (1934) #: 28088.

Nancy Emily WOLFE, born: 25 Mar 1866, married, parents: John Anderson and Mary Dugger, cause of death: "organic heart disease", buried: Sugar Grove Cemetery, died: 4 Oct 1934, record (1934) #: 28089.

Mary Lee Francis PERKINS, born: 7 Jul 1914 in North Carolina, married, parents: Hurd Ward (NC) and Vernia (last name illegible)(NC), cause of death: "main cause, tuberculosis", informant: David Perkins (Doeville), buried: North Carolina, died: 22 Oct 1934, record (1934) #: 28090.

John MATHERLY, born: 15 Sep 1850, husband of Lillie Neatherly, parents: father's name not stated and Flerbia Haynes, cause of death: illegible, died: 13 Nov 1934, record (1934) #: 28091.

Eddie May WHITE, female, age 28 years, 11 months and 30 days, married, parents: J.W. Matherly and Lillie Wagner (Carter Co. TN), cause of death: "pulmonary tuberculosis", died: 23 Nov 1934, record (1934) #: 28092.

Henry Jones POWERS, born: 17 Oct 1934, parents: Dean Powers (NC) and Nora Lee Jones, cause of death: not stated, informant: J.C. Jones (Mountain City), buried: Roberts Cemetery, died: 28 Oct 1934, record (1934) #: 28093.

May West RUDOLPH, born: 8 Oct 1934, parents: Francis R. Rudolph and Ellen Ellora Blevins, cause of death: "broncho pneumonia", informant: Ellen Blevins (Crandull), buried: Blevins Cemetery, died: 27 Dec 1934, record (1934) #: 28094.

Martha Jane PARKS, age 84 years, born in North Carolina, married to J.M. Parks, parents: Elija Dotson and Annie Eggers (NC), cause of death: "carcinoma of face", informant: Allen M. Stout (Moutain City), buried: Parks Cemetery, died: 2 Dec 1934, record (1934) #: 28095.

Rebecca C. POTTER, born: 20 Aug 1860 in North Carolina, married, parents: Phillip Church (NC) and Ona Trivett (NC), cause of death: "paralysis", informant: G.L. Potter (Butler), buried: Sugar Grove Cemetery, died: 18 Dec 1934, record (1934) #: 28096.

Wiley GREENWELL, born: 3 Dec 1897, married, parents: J.M. Greenwell and Elmira Dugger, cause of death: "broncho pneumonia", informant: Tine Greenwell (Beech Creek, NC), died: 13 Nov 1934, record (1934) #: 28097.

Amanda CABLE, age about 78 years, married, parents: Levi Guy and Lydia May, cause of death: "parlaysis", informant: W.G. Cable (Butler), buried: Guy Cemetery, died: 29 Jul 1934, record (1934) #: 28098.

Phylis Eula ANDERSON, born: 26 Sep 1932, parents: Earl Anderson and Estle Gregg, cause of death: "inflamation of stomach caused by indigestion", informant: Earl Anderson (Butler), buried: Sugar Grove Cemetery, died: 14 Apr 1934, record (1934) #: 28099.

Sammie FUGIT, born: 19 Jun 1934, parents: Calvin Fugit and Addie Dugger, cause of death: "colitis", informant: Calvin Fugit (Butler), buried: Sugar Grove Cemetery, died: 19 Oct 1934, record (1934) #: 30614.

Martha FONDREN, born: 29 Mar 1841, widow of Thomas Fondren, parents: father's name not stated and Mary An Arnold, cause of death: "apoplexy", informant: Lark Arnold (Shouns), died: 9 Jun 1934, record (1934) #: 30679.

Leah CURD, born: 1 Mar 1905, married to W.M. Curd, parents: father's name unknown and Rosa Pennell, cause of death: illegible, informant: W.M. Curd (Shouns), Wagner Cem, died: 15 Jun 1934, record (1934) #: 30680.

Claud Melvin HORN, born: 4 Jun 1934, parents: Robert Horn and Susan Heaton, cause of death: "colitis", informant: John Heaton (Shouns), died: 22 Aug 1934, record (1934) #: 30681.

Martha MOREFIELD, born: 28 Aug 1858, widow, parents: John R. Morefield and Matilda Minick (VA), cause of death: "influenza", informant: R. Ross Morefield (Shouns), buried: Vaughtsville, died: 25 Aug 1934, record (1934) #: 30682.

Mary Virginia WILSON, parents: Shelton Wilson and Grace Dotson, death cause: "premature birth", informant: Shelton Wilson (Mountain City), died: 5 Oct 1934, record (1934) #: 30683.

Ellie RANKINS, born: 1 Jul 1867, wife of W.P. Rankins, parents: John Vance (NC) and Mary Wilcox (NC), cause of death: "apoplexy", informant: W.P. Rankins, died: 12 Oct 1934, record (1934) #: 30684.

Thomas WARREN, born: 17 Sep 1896, married to Virginia Warren, parents: Roby Warren and Celia Dotson, cause of death: "chronic brights disease", informant: John Norris, died: 19 Oct 1934, record (1934) #: 30685.

Annie Lucile PHILLIPS, age 7 months and 23 days, parents: Tyler Phillips and Annie May Dyson, cause of death: "measles and diptheria", informant: Tyler Phillips (Mountian City), buried: Donnelly Cemetery, died 10 Nov 1934, record (1934) #: 30686.

John Franklin DOTSON, born: 22 Aug 1854, married to Loretta Dotson, parents: Allen Dotson and Delila Price, cause of death: "carcinoma of stomach", informant: A.E. Dotson (Shouns), died: 18 Nov 1934, record (1934) #: 30687.

Eliza HICKS, born: 20 Mar 1871, widow of Albert Hicks, parents: Tommie Perkins and May Phillippi, cause of death: "cancer womb", informant: Robert Asbury (Mountain City), died: 19 Nov 1934, record (1934) #: 30688.

Pauline Marie PARSONS, born: 5 Nov 1934, parents: William Parsons and Perdie Phillips, cause of death: "premature birth", informant: William Parsons (Mountain City), died: 26 NOv 1934, record (1934) #: 30689.

Callie DUNN, born: 6 Jan 1887, married to Joe Dunn, parents: Joe Main and Lourena Main, cause of death: "hypostatic pulmonary congestion", informant: John M. Potter (Shouns), died: 10 Jan 1935, record (1935) #: 997.

Emma B. WILSON, Negro, born: 5 Jun 1872, wife of John Wilson, parents: David (last name illegible) and Ann Flannagan (VA), cause of death: "broncho pneumonia", died: 11 Jan 1935, record (1935) #: 998.

Verda DOWELL, born: 14 Feb 1898, wife of George Dowell, parents: Robert (last name illegible) and Harriett Jones (NC), cause of death: "lobar pneumonia", informant: George Dowell (Shouns), buried: Dowell Cemetery, died: 3 Jan 1935, record (1935) #: 999.

Infant PRICE, female, parents: Ben Price (NC) and Jane Forrester, cause of death: "premature birth", informant: Mrs. Jane F. Price, born/died: 10 Jan 1935, record (1935) #: 1000.

T.G. MILLHORN, born: 20 Jan 1902, married, parents: Wm Millhorn and Lula V. Barns, cause of death: "endocarditis of heart", died: 9 Jan 1935, record (1935) #: 1001.

Joseph Lenard DAVIS, born: 24 Sep 1904 in Virginia, parents: M.L. Davis (NC) and Callie J. Ashley (NC), cause of death: "cut on right side of neck, self inflicted, suicide", informant: M.L. Davis (Damascus, VA), buried: Davis Cemetery, died: 22 Jan 1935, record (1935) #: 1002.

Bobby Glenn GENTRY, born: 5 Feb 1935, parents: Fred Gentry and Belive Lefman, cause of death: "broncho pneumonia", informant: E.H. Gentry (Laurel Bloomery), buried: Gentry Cemetery, died: 8 Feb 1935, record (1935) #: 3447.

Edward LEAPER, Negro, born: 10 Apr 1910, married, parents: John Luper and Tuanna Leaper (NC), cause of death: "typhoid fever", informant: Mrs. Ed Luper, buried: Moutanin City Colored Cemetery, died: 9 Feb 1935, record (1935) #: 3448.

Okra WILLIAMS, born: 5 Jul 1932, parents: Cebert Widener and Ezra Mae Williams (KY), death cause: "lobar pneumonia", died: 12 Feb 1935, record #: 3449.

Alexander Thomas BERRY, born: 21 Oct 1858, widower of Louvenia Crockett Berry, parents: Robert Edmonson Berry and Rachel Ann Hicks, cause of death: "carcinoma of stomach, bladder and liver", informant: Mrs. J.C. Muse (Mountian City), died: 9 Feb 1935.

Mrs. Susan H. GENTRY, born: 27 Jan 1852 in Washington County, married, parents: George Hensley (Washington Co.) and Susan Hensley (Washington Co.), cause of death: "chronic brights disease", informant: G.T. Huskin (Elizabethton, TN), buried: Phillippi Cemetery, died: 16 Feb 1935, record (1935) #: 3451.

Mary Elizabeth WAGNER, born: 10 Jun 1866, widow of N.G. Wagner, parents: D.C. Worley and Disey Hunt, cause of death: "lobar pneumonia", informant: Lee Wagner (Shouns), buried: Vaughtsville, died: 2 Feb 1935, record (1935) #: 3452.

Martin A. SLIMP, born: 20 Feb 1852, widower of Mary Ann Slimp, parents: John Slimp and Catherine Cook, cause of death: "organic heart disease", buried: Neva, died: 13 Feb 1935, record (1935) #: 3453.

C.M. STAMPLER, born: 30 Mar 1851 in North Carolina, married, parents: Wilburn Stampler (NC) and Cyaina Wagner (NC), cause of death: "apoplexy", informant: Henry Stampler (Mountain City), buried: Wright Cemetery, died: 19 Feb 1935, record (1935) #: 3454.

Lillie Belle GARLAND, born: 16 Sep 1878, married to T.C. Garland, parents: father's name illegible and Martha Walker, cause of death: "influenza and lobar pneumonia", buried: Gentry Cemetery, died: 25 Feb 1935, record (1935) #: 3455.

Alexander BUMGARDNER, born: 15 Jan 1853, husband of Stella Bumgardner, parents: David Bumgardner (NC) and Caroline Snyder, cause of death: "said to be high blood pressure and paralysis", informant: Stella Bumgardner (Trade), buried: Arnold Cemetery, died: 14 Feb 1935, record (1935) #: 3456.

Roy EGGERS, age about 54 years, born in North Carolina, parents; James Eggers (NC) and Eliza Phillips (NC), cause of death: "chronic valvulor heart disease", informant: M.F. Keller (Butler), died: 16 Feb 1935, record (1935) #: 3457.

George Washington MAXWELL, born: 4 Nov 1861, married, parents: Henry Maxwell (NC) and Elizabeth Farris, cause of death: "uremia due to chronic nephritis", informant: Fred J. Thomas (Laurel Bloomery), died: 9 Mar 1935, record (1935) #: 6014.

B.W. GREER, born: 4 Nov 1859, husband of Martha Greer, parents: Joe Greer and Jane Smith, cause of death: "apoplexy", informant: Oliver Gentry (Laurel Bloomery), buried: Gentry Cemetery, died: 28 Mar 1935, record (1935) #: 6015.

Dorothy MCQUEEN, Negro, born: 28 Aug 1924, parents: Arthur McQueen and Susie Anderson, death cause: "lobar pneumonia", died: 8 Mar 1935, record (1935) #: 6016.

Alexander Richard PARKS, Negro, born: Jan 1872 in North Carolina, husband of Mollie Wilson Parks, parents: John Parks (NC) and (first name not stated) Edwards (NC), cause of death: "cerebral hemorrhage", informant: Mrs. A.R. Parks, buried: Holy Hill Cemetery, died: 15 Mar 1935, record (1935) #: 6017.

Bettie Lee DUNN, born: 18 Feb 1935, parents: Wesley Dunn and Susie Main, cause of death: "not known", informant: J.G. Dunn (Shouns), buried: McEwen Cemetery, died: 8 Mar 1935, record (1935) #: 6018.

Elbert HUTTON, born: 7 Sep 1863 in Virginia, widower of Elizabeth Hutton, parents: Elbert Hutton (VA) and Elizabeth Stephens (VA), cause of death: "chronic brights disease", buried in North Carolina, died: 29 Mar 1935, record (1935) #: 6019.

(Illegible) Ellen STOUT, born: 5 Jan 1872, single, parents: Alfred A. Stout and Susannah Morley, cause of death: "chronic brights disease", buried: Morley Cemetery, died: 17 Mar 1935, record (1935) #: 6020.

Maria Farthing TRIPLETT, born: 23 Jun 1861, wife of J.F. Triplett, parents: (first name illegible) Farthing (NC) and Margaret Adams (NC), death cause: "brights disease", died: 28 Mar 1935, record #: 6021.

Eliga E. MILLER, born: 15 Jun 1858, husband of Lizzie Miller, parents: John Miller and Sarah Wright, cause of death: "lobar pneumonia", informant: Austin Miller (Bristol, TN), buried: Woods Cemetery, died: 16 Mar 1935, record (1935) #: 6022.

Irdine HORN, born: 18 Apr 1935, parents: Joe Horn (Ashe Co. NC) and Sarah Calhoone (Ashe Co. NC), cause of death: "unknown", informant: Joe Horn (Green Cove, VA), died: 22 Apr 1935, record (1935) #: 8550.

Frank THOMAS, Negro, born: 3 Apr 1913 in North Carolina, parents: T.C. Thomas (NC) and Emma Red (NC), cause of death: "pneumonia lobar", died: 3 Apr 1935, record (1935) #: 8551.

Susie MCQUEEN, Negro, born: 15 Mar 1885, wife of Arthur McQueen, parents: Noah Anderson (NC) and Jane Goins (NC), cause of death: "influenza, broncho pneumonia", informant: Arthur McQueen, buried: Holy Hill Cem, died: 16 Apr 1935, record (1935) #: 8552.

Lucy ARCHER, age 54 years, 11 months and 23 days, widow of Andy Archer, parents: R.N. Blevins and Maggie Blevins, cause of death: "lobar pneumonia", buried: Crandell, died: 17 Apr 1935, record (1935) #: 8553.

James W. SMITH, age 80 years, widower, parents: Hardin Smith and Adilia Parker, cause of death: "cancer face", died: 8 Apr 1935, record (1935) #: 8554.

Leonard Ray NICHOLS, born: 30 Mar 1935, parents: Hobart Nichols and Birhta J. Lane (VA), cause of death: illegible, buried: Blevins Cemetery, died: 1 Apr 1935, record (1935) #: 8555.

Sarah Catherine FORRESTER, born: 28 Aug 1857 in Virginia, widow of Henry Scott Forrester, parents: Daniel Crigger (VA) and Matilda Lantern (VA), cause of death: "anjina pectoris", informant: Mrs. (illegible) Loyd (Mountain City), buried: Forrester Cemetery, died: 7 May 1935, record (1935) #: 10797.

Robie Milton SLUDER, born: 11 Aug 1876 in North Carolina, husband of Magnalia Sluder, parents: Harrison Sluder (NC) and (first name not stated) Tucker (NC), cause of death: "chronic brights disease", informant: Mrs. R.C. Sluder (Mountain City), buried: Webb Cemetery, died: 8 May 1935, record (1935) #: 10798.

Arthur DAVIS, age 63 years and 10 months, born at Mabel, NC, husband of Maryan Davis, parents: Arthur Davis and mother's name not stated, cause of death: "was found dead, verdict of inquiry: broken neck, struck on head with shot gun", informant: Charlie Nye (Shouns), died: 12 May 1935, record (1935) #: 10799.

Elmer D. CAMPBELL, born: 22 Apr 1935, parents: Dale Campbell and Hattie Hayworth, cause of death: "enysepelas", informant: Dale Campbell (Doeville), buried: Potter Cemetery, died: 30 May 1935, record (1935) #: 10800.

Joe Justin WILSON, colored, born: 25 May 1934, parents: Joe Lincoln Wilson and Jennie (last name illegible), cause of death: "bronchial pneumonia", died: 10 Apr 1935, record (1935) #: 10801.

Jensie Louise WAGNER, born about 1840, married to Nat Wagner, parents: John Dowell and mother's name unknown, cause of death: "chronic brights disease", buried: Potter Cemetery, died: 28 Apr 1935, record (1935) #: 10802.

Mary Lucinda GOODWIN, born: 21 Oct 1852, widow of John Franklin Goodwin, parents: Peter L. Shoun and Mary Loyd, cause of death: "yellow jaundice", informant: Abner C. Farthing (Butler), died: 25 May 1935, record (1935) #: 10803.

Sarah Fine GENTRY, born: 6 Apr 1857, widow of James R. Gentry, parents: William A. Morley and Elizabeth Blevins, cause of death: "chronic brights disease", informant: R.L. Allen (Butler), buried: Gentry Cemetery, died: 16 May 1935, record (1935) #: 10804.

Mrs. Mary Catherine LEE, born: 11 Feb 1862, widow, parents: George Brookshire and Caroline Robinson, cause of death: "chronic brights disease", informant: R.A. Lee (Mountain City), buried: Brookshire Cemetery, died: 2 May 1935, record (1935) #: 10805.

Mrs. Cora Lee SNYDER, born: 5 Jun 1871 in North Carolina, wife of Hiram Snyder, parents: Robert Vannoy (NC) and Fillis Madron (NC), cause of death: "tuberculosis", informant: Hiram Snyder (Crandull), buried: Gentry Cemetery, died: 2 May 1935, record (1935) #: 10806.

Wilham WINTERS, born: 15 Oct 1853 in North Carolina, widower of May Winters, parents: Wilham Winters (NC) and Lara Shell (NC), cause of death: "chronic brights disease", informant: Richard Wood (Mountian City), died: 2 Jun 1935, record (1935) #: 13200.

Chelsie SAMMONS, born: 4 Mar 1915, single, parents: Ervin Sammons and Alice Sweny (VA), cause of death: "pulmonary tuberculosis", informant: Ervin Sammons (Mountain City), died: 12 Jun 1935, record (1935) #: 13201.

Stella Cole ELLER, born: 19 Apr 1935, parents: Calvin Eller (NC) and Varder Hammons (NC), cause of death: "cause unknown", informant: Wilham Hammons (Shouns), buried: Hammons Cemetery, died: 19 Jun 1935, record (1935) #: 13202.

Infant KITE, male, parents: Conley Kite and Billa Lee Norris, cause of death: "premature birth", informant: Conley Kite (Doeville), buried: Mullins Cemetery, born/died: 29 Jun 1935, record (1935) #: 13203.

Minnie HODGE, born: 1 Jan 1891, wife of Steve Hodge, parents: A.J. (last name illegible) and Aley Owens (NC), cause of death: "pneumonia lobar", informant: Steve Hodge (Crandell), buried: Hodge Cemetery, died: 1 Jun 1935, record (1935) #: 13204.

John Terry FULLER, born: 26 Nov 1860 at Adkin, NC, husband of Sallie W. Fuller, Spanish-American War Veteran, parents: Joseph W. Fuller (Danville, VA) and Betty John Terry (VA), cause of death: "numerous causes including chronic bronchitis", informant: Mrs. W.L. Cook (Erwin, TN), died: 20 Jul 1935, record (1935) #: 15545.

James Miller GRAYBEAL, born: 4 Jan 1923, parents: George Graybeal and Annie Wilson, cause of death: "septicima", informant: Annie Graybeal (Mountain City), died: 4 Jul 1935, record (1935) #: 15546.

Henry Lulter SAMMONS, born: 10 Jul 1935, parents: Arthur Sammons and Magie Patridg, cause of death: illegible, died: 14 Jul 1935, record (1935) #: 15547.

Infant MURPHEY, female, parents: Frank Murphey and Lessie Tucker (NC), cause of death: "premature birth", informant: Frank Murphey (Mountain City), born/died: 29 Jul 1935, record (1935) #: 15548.

Maud NAVE, born: 20 Oct 1894, single, school teacher, parents: R.L. Nave and Nora Baker, cause of death: "pulmonary tuberculoisis", informant: Eula Nave (Shouns), died: 30 Jul 1935, record (1935) #: 15549.

Garfield GREER, born: 19 Mar 1899, single, parents: Isaac Greer (NC) and Lucinda Greer (NC), cause of death: "asthma cardiac", informant: Isaac Greer (Shouns), died: 31 Jul 1935, record (1935) #: 15550.

Pauline OWENS, born: 4 Oct 1934, parents: Glen Owens and Carrie Owens, cause of death: "inflamation of stomach, indigestion", died: 25 Jun 1935, record (1935) #: 13551.

David J. SLIMP, born: 17 Jan 1846, widower of Harriett Elizabeth Slimp, parents: John Slimp and Katie Cook, cause of death: "chronic brights disease", informant: S.S. Stout (Neva), died: 10 Jul 1935, record (1935) #: 13552.

Nathaniel Canada SHULL, born: 3 Feb 1862 in North Carolina, husband of Laura Catherine Shull, parents: father's name not known and Caroline Shull, cause of death: "cerebral hemorrhage", informant: C.R. Shull (Neva), died: 1 Jul 1935, record (1935) #: 13553.

John Keener MOUNT, born: 29 Sep 1871 at Montgomery, AL, printer, widower of Roberta Mount, parents: Thomas L. Mount (Alexandria, VA) and Sophia L. Kunn (Baltimore, MD), cause of death: "suicide by hanging", informant: Mrs. Mary Mount Jones (Radford, VA), buried: Baltimore, MD, died: 3 Jul 1935, record (1935) #: 13554.

Catherine Elizabeth WAUGH, born: 28 Jul 1920, parents: Eck Waugh (NC) and Mollie McQueen, cause of death: "lobar pneumonia", buried: Mountain View Cemetery, died: 16 Aug 1935, record (1935) #: 17919.

Alice MITCHELL, born: 7 May 1865 in Ashe Co. NC, widow, parents: Jack McMillon (NC) and Mary Mitchell (NC), cause of death: "chronic brights disease", informant: Lillie Landers, buried: Holy Hill Cemetery, died: 16 Aug 1935, record (1935) #: 17920.

Robert Blaine CROWDER, born: 5 Mar 1935, parents: Manley Crowder (NC) and Ella Warren, cause of death: "acute colitis", informant: Manley Crowder (Shouns), died: 25 Aug 1935, record (1935) #: 17921.

Barbara Janis DOWELL, born: 15 Oct 1933, parents: Fred Dowell and Nannie Simcox, cause of death: "colitis", informant: Fred Dowell, died: 15 Aug 1935, record (1935) #: 17922.

Roddy Cleveland BLEVINS, born: 13 Jul 1884, husband of Lillie Blevins, parents: David Henry Blevins and Laura Smith, cause of death: "high blood pressure, himiplegia", informant: Woodrow Blevins (Crandell), buried: Blevins Cemetery, died: 14 Aug 1935, record (1935) #: 17923.

Edith Opal WAGNER, born: date not recorded, married, parents: Robert Hamilton and Anna Reed, cause of death: "typhoid fever and poisoned kidneys", informant: Vaughan Wagner (Neva), buried: Baker Cemetery, died: 30 May 1935, record (1935) #: 17924.

John Cisco TREADWAY, born: 14 Sep 1854 in North Carolina, husband of Sallie Treadway, parents: Andy Treadway and Sallie Robinson (NC), cause of death: "hypostatic pneumonia, terminal", informant: Margaret Schneider (Shouns), died: 14 Sep 1935, record (1935) #: 20231.

Eliza Lue DUNN, age 76 years, widow, parents: Joe Dunn and Eliza Dunn, cause of death: "angina pectoris", informant: Joe Dunn (Mountain City), died: 30 Sep 1935, record (1935) #: 20232.

Loyal B. HAMPTON, born: 6 Nov 1933, parents: John W. Hampton and Ada Plummer (VA), cause of death: "colitis", informant: James W. Hampton (Shouns), died: 14 Sep 1935, record (1935) #: 20233.

John W. HAWKINS, born: 25 Jun 1860, husband of Julia Hawkins, parents: John Hawkins and Nancy Reece, cause of death: "organic heart disease", informant: Clyde C. Hawkins (Neva), died: 16 Sep 1935, record (1935) #: 20234.

Bettie Gene WATTS, born: 2 Sep 1935, parents: Bob Watts (NC) and Verda Holden, cause of death: "neighbors called it bold hives", died: 24 Sep 1935, record (1935) #: 20235.

Joseph P. CHURCH, born: 14 Jan 1871 in North Carolina, husband of Callie Church, parents: Calvin Church (Wilksboro, NC) and Mary U. Echuister (Wilkesboro, NC), cause of death: "diabetes", died: 16 Sep 1935, record (1935) #: 20236.

Rufus POPE, age about 82 years, born in North Carolina, married, parents: John Pope (NC) and Nancy Graybeal (NC) cause of death: not stated, informant: Martha Pope (Mountain City), buried: Owens Cemetery, died: 3 Oct 1935, record (1935) #: 22393.

Lena Martin NICHOLS, age 20 years, 10 months and 4 days, wife of R.S. Nichols, parents: Oliver Martin (NC) and Mary Susan Mills (West VA), cause of death: "spontaneous abortion at 4 weeks, pelvic infection and broncho pneumonia", informant: Mary Susan Fletcher, died: 29 Oct 1935, record (1935) #: 22394.

Jacob DAUGHERTY, born: 10 May 1851, husband of Dora Daugherty, parents: Elijah Daugherty and Eva Mast (Watauga Co. NC), cause of death: "valvulor heart disease", informant: Rosa Lee Daugherty (Neva), died: 8 Oct 1935, record (1935) #: 22395.

Lottie HARPER, born: 11 May 1895 in North Carolina, wife of Nelson Harper, parents: Thomas Price (NC) and Zelphia Sluder (NC), cause of death: "rupture of gastric ulcer", informant: Nelsa Harper (Mountain City), buried: Shady Valley, died: 14 Sep 1935, record (1935) #: 22396.

James OWENS, born: 30 Jul 1883, married to Jane Owens, parents: R.J. Owens and Ferby Woods (NC) cause of death: not stated, informant: Elmer Breeding (Mountain City), buried: Oak Cemetery, died: 13 Nov 1935, record (1935) #: 24731.

Clint H. ABLE, Jr., born: 16 Sep 1935, parents: Clint H. Able and Kate Gentry, cause of death: "obstruction of bowel", informant: Clint H. Abel (Laurel Bloomery), buried: Taylor Valley, died: 20 Sep 1935, record (1935) #: 24732.

R. Wilson SEEHORN, born: 9 Aug 1850 in Kentucky, married to Maggie Seehorn, parents: John Seehorn (KY) and Mary Seehorn (KY), cause of death: "chronic intestinal nephritis", informant: John Seehorn (Shouns), died: 11 Nov 1935, record (1935) #: 24733.

Isaac Lafayette GENTRY, age 81 years, 7 months and 3 days, widower of Mary Elizabeth Fenner, parents: Monroe Gentry and Pacific Shoun, cause of death: "chronic brights disease", died: 22 Oct 1935, record (1935) #: 24734.

James M. PARKS, born: 8 Nov 1855 in North Carolina, widower of Jane Parks, parents: Alfred Parks (NC) and Allie D. Gilley (NC), cause of death: "chronic brights disease", informant: Charlie Parks (Trade), died: 8 Nov 1935, record (1935) #: 24737.

Mrs. Abbie SLUDER, age 67 years, wife of A.L. Sluder, parents: Alex Greer and Nancy Osborn (Ashe Co. NC), cause of death: "aortic regurgitation", informant: D.H. Sluder (Crandell), died: 30 Nov 1935, record (1935) #: 24736.

Blanche ROARK, born: Oct 1914, single, parents: S.A. Roark and Oma Roark (NC), cause of death: "acute nephritis", informant: J.C. Roark (Shouns), buried: Arnold Cem, died: 3 Dec 1935, record (1935) #: 27699.

Wallace Brown LIPFORD, born: 6 Oct 1935, parents: Ray Lipford and Perdita Davis, cause of death: "congenital heart disease", buried: Davis Cemetery, died: 21 Dec 1935, record (1935) #: 27700.

Edward PHILLIPS, born: 3 Dec 1935, parents: Andrew Phillips (NC) and Myrtle Reece, cause of death: not stated, died: 3 Dec 1935, record (1935) #: 27701.

Lossie STANTON, male, born: 1 Mar 1911, husband of Elsie Ward, parents: Grayson Stanton and Martha Arney, cause of death: "went rabbit hunting, found dead, shot through left breast", informant: Grayson Stanton (Neva), buried: Nave Cemetery, died: 26 Dec 1935, record (1935) #: 27702.

Mrs. Ossie Olla GRINDSTAFF, born: 23 Jul 1883 in Carter Co. TN, wife of Vaught Grindstaff, parents: Thomas Smoot (NC) and Ceily Matherly, cause of death: "pellagra", informant: Vaught Grindstaff (Butler), died: 3 Nov 1935, record (1935) #: 27703.

Locie LIPFIRD, female, born: 29 Sep 1932, parents: Clint Lipfird and Hessel Green, cause of death: "diptheria", informant: Sherman Lipfird (Shouns), died: 22 Dec 1935, record (1935) #: 27704.

Delmas Clide CABLE, born: 11 Dec 1935, parents: Dewey Cable and Josie Laws, cause of death: "unknown", informant: Dewey Cable (Butler), buried: Cable Cemetery, died: 12 Dec 1935, record (1935) #: 27705.

Margaret COWANS, born: 18 Mar 1871, single, parents: T.B. Cowans and Nancy J. Anderson, cause of death: "heart dropsy", informant: Mrs. W.M. Wolfe (Butler), buried: Cowans Cemetery, died: 5 Jul 1935, record (1935) #: 27706.

John A. DUGGER, born: 2 Feb 1872, married, parents: James K. Dugger and Mollie Guy, cause of death: "heart dropsy", informant: L.R. Dugger (Butler), buried: Dugger Cem, died: 21 Mar 1935, record (1935) #: 27707.

Francis Patrick BRUMIT, born: 16 Nov 1935, parents: Harold Ryder Brumit (Elizabethton, TN) and Ida Lucille Welch (Jonesboro, TN), cause of death: "acute indigestion", buried: Grindstaff Cemetery, died: 25 Nov 1935, record (1935) #: 30217.

Lucile MUSE, born: 29 Jun 1912, school teacher, single, parents: Joe C. Muse (VA) and Margaret Berry, cause of death: "pneumonia lobar", informant: Joe C. Muse (Mountain City), buried: East Hill Cemetery, died: 4 Jan 1936, record (1936) #: 1194.

Joseph Thomas LEFLER, born: 29 Jul 1866, husband of Hanna Allen Lefler, parents: Charles Lefler (NC) and Ester V. Tulburt (NC), cause of death: "apoplexy", informant: Mrs, Joe T. Lefler (Mountain City), buried: East HIll Cemetery, died: 23 Jan 1936, record (1936) #: 1195.

Shirley Jane SEEHORN, born: 4 Jun 1935, parents: Reed Seehorn and Ruth Madron, cause of death: "lobar pneumonia", informant: Reed Seehorn (Shouns), died: 25 Jun 1936, record (1936) #: 1196.

Infant GENTRY, female, born: 22 Jan 1936, parents: Stacy Gentry and Mae Riddle, cause of death: "lobar pneumonia", died: 26 Jan 1936, record (1936) #: 1197.

Alvin Columbus ALLEN, born: 5 Apr 1852 at Ashland, NC, husband of Martitia Perkins, parents: Jesse Allen (Ashland, NC) and Elizabeth Sluder (NC), cause of death: "acute nephritis", informant: Mrs. F.K. Sexton (Abingdon, VA), buried: Price Cemetery, died: 17 Jan 1936, record (1936) #: 1198.

Juanita POTTER, born: 15 Jul 1935, parents: Delis Potter and Mannie Dunn, cause of death: "pneumonia fever", informant: Delis Potter (Shouns), buried; McEwen Cemetery, died: 31 Jan 1936, record (1936) #: 1199.

Fred S. SNYDER, born: 8 Jun 1855, husband of Susan Snyder, parents: David Snyder and Rebecca Mitchell, cause of death: "acute nephritis", informant: J.A. Shull (Neva), died: 4 Jan 1936, record (1936) #: 1200.

Florence Catherine HOPKINS, born: 26 Mov 1921 at Carter Co. TN, parents: James Hopkins (Carter Co. TN) and Mary Lunceford (Sullivan Co. TN), cause of death: "spinal meningitis", informant: James Hopkins (Doeville), died: 9 Jan 1936, record (1936) #: 1201.

Clayton EGGERS, born: 14 Oct 1882, married, parents: Will Eggers and Mary Robards, cause of death: "cancer bladder, lobar pneumonia", informant: J.R. Jones, died: 1 Jan 1936, record (1936) #: 1202.

McNary King DUGGER, born: 30 Jun 1840, widower, parents: Robert King (NC) and Susan Weaver (NC), cause of death: "broncho pneumonia", informant: R.W. Dugger (Butler), buried: Dugger Cemetery, died: 26 Jan 1936, record (1936) #: 1203.

Joe B. SNYDER, born: 3 Jul 1849, husband of Ester
Snyder, parents: Dave Snyder and Becca Mitchell, cause
of death: "acute brights disease", died: 20 Feb 1936,
record (1936) #: 3861.

John Larkin MAYS, born: 22 Mar 1869 at Coldwell Co.
NC, husband of Martha Mays, parents: John Mays (NC)
and Nancy Cozart (NC), cause of death: "lobar
pneumonia", informant: J.W. Mays (Neva), buried in
North Carolina, died: 29 Feb 1936, record (1936) #:
3862.

Charlotte V. MCEWEN, born: 6 Sep 1927, parents: Joseph
Wade McEwen and Ida Lee Lowe, cause of death: "lobar
pneumonia", buried: Rambo Cemetery, Doe Valley, died:
1 Feb 1936, record (1936) #: 3863.

Soloman S. PENNINGTON, born: 25 Sep 1862 in Ashe Co.
NC, husband of Lillie Pennington, parents: Daniel
Pennington (Ashe Co. NC) and Elizabeth Osborne, cause
of death: "sarcoma of jaw", informant: J.W. Pennington
(Crandull), buried: Woods Cemetery, died: 9 Feb 1936,
record (1936) #: 3864.

Alice EASTRIDGE, born: 7 Jan 1871 in North Carolina,
wife of William Eastridge, parents: Calvin Allen and
(mother's first name not stated) Pennington (NC),
cause of death: "heart trouble, high blood pressure",
informant: Roy Eastridge (Damascus, VA), died: 17 Feb
1936, record (1936) #: 3865.

Jamelia MCQUEEN, born: 19 Jul 1898, wife of Albert
McQueen, parents: O.B. Hanley (Syria/Turkey), and N.C.
Morley, cause of death: "carcinoma of bowels and
stomach", informant: Roby McQueen, died: 26 Feb 1936,
record (1936) #: 3866.

Shirley Francis GENTRY, born: 4 Jan 1930, parents:
James Gentry and Mary E. Morefield, cause of death:
"influenza, broncho pneumonia", informant: James
Gentry (Damascus, VA), buried: Acre Field Cemetery,
died: 8 Mar 1936, record (1936) #: 6878.

Ellen J. EGGERS, born: 9 Feb 1847 in Washington Co.
VA, widow of Land... (illegible) Eggers, parents: Andy
Reed (VA) and Martha Denkins (VA), cause of death:
"broncho pneumonia", informant: Walter Eggers (Laurel
Bloomery), buried: Eggers Cemetery, died: 12 Jan 1936,
record (1936) #: 6879.

Eveline STOUT, born: 3 Mar 1856, widow of Joe B.
Stout, parents: Wilham Arnold and Susie Snyder, cause
of death: "influenza, broncho pneumonia", informant:
W.R. Stout, died: 9 Mar 1936, record (1936) #: 6880.

Mary PIERCE, born: 7 Mar 1871, single, parents: Allen
Pierce and Betty Dotson, death cause: "influenza,
lobar pneumonia", died: 9 Mar 1936, record #: 6881.

Thomas WALSH, born: 7 Jun 1866, widower of Rose Walsh, parents: John Walsh (NC) and Bettie Tribble (NC), cause of death: "influenza, broncho pneumonia", informant: Eugene Walsh (Shouns), died: 10 Mar 1936, record (1936) #: 6882.

Susan WILHAMS, born: 4 May 1862, widow of William Wilhams, parents: John Main and Pollie Potter, cause of death: "chronic brights disease", informant: Joe Wilhams (Shouns), buried: Wilhams Cemetery, died: 24 Mar 1936, record (1936) #: 6884.

Alexander CROWDER, born: 1 Jul 1856 in North Carolina, widower of Alice Crowder, parents: Dudley Crowder (VA) and Sarah (surname not stated) (VA), cause of death: "chronic brights disease", informant: W.T. Crowder (Shouns), died: 3 Feb 1936, record (1936) #: 6885.

William H. JORDAN, born: 27 Sep 1881, husband of Hattie Jordan, parents: J.H. Jordan and Martha Shoun, cause of death: "apoplexy", informant: J.H. Jordan (Mountain City), died: 30 Jun 1936, record (1936) #: 6886.

Ellen LONG, born: 3 Jan 1861, wife of Ed Long, Parents: Joel Heaberlin (VA) and Lucinda Blevins, cause of death: "lobar pneumonia", informant: Ed Long (Crandull), buried: Blevins Cemetery, died: 3 Mar 1936, record (1936) #: 6887.

Ola WRIGHT, born: 14 Jul 1931, parents: George W. Wright and Callie Gentry, cause of death: "acute nephritis", informant George W. Wright (Crandull), buried: Gentry Cemetery, died: 9 Mar 1936, record (1936) #: 6888.

Robert R. RUTTER, born: 12 Mar 1886, husband of Alice Rutter, parents: B.N. Rutter and Margaret Heaberlin, cause of death: "influenza", informant: Silas Rutter (Crandull), buried: Blevins Cemetery, died: 14 Mar 1936, record (1936) #: 6889.

Pearl PARKS, born: 13 Aug 1929, parents: Robert W. Parks and Verda Denny, cause of death: "thought to be pneumonia", buried: Parks Cemetery, died: 10 Feb 1936, record (1936) #: 6890.

Ollie Caroline WINTERS, born: 21 Dec 1897, wife of W.V. Winters, parents: R.L. Jenkins and Annie Corum (VA), cause of death: "chronic intestinal nephritis, cerebral hemorrhage", informant: R.L. Jenkins (Mountain City), buried: Cornett Cemetery, died: 12 Apr 1936, record (1936) #: 9482.

John CHANDLER, age about 68 years, married, parents: "don't know", cause of death: "lobar pneumonia", informant: N.A. Pennington (Laurel Bloomery), buried: Valley Cem, died: 21 Apr 1936, record (1936) #: 9843.

Viller GREER, female, age 36 years, 6 months and 19 days, born in North Carolina, wife of Roby Greer, parents: Ambrose Lewis (NC) and Minnie Roten (NC), cause of death: illegible, informant: Joe Ham (Green Cove, VA), buried: Green Cove, VA, died: 16 Jan 1936, record (1936) #: 9844.

John R. DICKENS, born: 8 Dec 1858 in North Carolina, husband of Julia Dickens, parents: Daniel Dickens (NC) and Melicia Johnson, cause of death: "lobar pneumonia", informant: R.M. Dickens (Mountain City), buried: Donnelly Cemetery, died: 16 Apr 1936, record (1936) #: 9845.

L.O. KELLY, born: 4 Jul 1902 in North Carolina, husband of Florence Kelly, parents: B.V. Kelly (Crumpler, NC) and Mary Bare (Crumpler, NC), cause of death: "auto accident, chest injury", informant: Mrs. Florence Kelly (Crumpler, NC), buried: Dixon Cemetery, died: 19 Apr 1936, record (1936) #: 9846.

J.C. PROFFITT, age 2 years, 1 month and 6 days, parents: J.G. Proffitt and Faye Dugger, cause of death: "bronchial pneumonia", informant: Mrs. J.G. Proffitt (Butler), died: 1 Apr 1936, record (1936) #: 9847.

Mrs. Ruth Reynolds SHERWOOD, born: 22 Aug 1906 at Tazwell, VA, wife of James C. Sherwood, parents: Rev. J.C. Reynolds (Newport, VA) and Elizabeth Holland Shawver (Tazewell Co. VA), cause of death: "cancer of breast and liver", informant: Mrs. R.W. Wood (Humboldt, TN), died: 14 Mar 1936, record (1936) #: 9848.

Mrs. Darcus B. PROFFITT, born: Jun 1852 at Watauga Co. NC, married, parents: Benjamin Moody (NC) and Hattie Haten (NC), cause of death: "lobar pneumonia", informant: Ida Garland (Butler), died: 26 Mar 1936, record (1936) #: 9849.

J.W.R. ALLEN, born: 4 Jul 1863, married, parents: Hamilton Allen and Rachel Shoun, cause of death: "influenza and broncho pneumonia", informant: Robert Allen (Doeville), died: 14 Apr 1936, record #: 9850.

Ruby Pearl PIERCE, born: 5 Mar 1920, parents: Alex Pierce and Martha Hinkle, cause of death: "influenza and broncho pneumonia", informant: Vada Hinkle (Mountain City), buried: Pierce Cemetery, died: 4 Apr 1936, record (1936) #: 9851.

Daniel Boon SHOUN, born: 19 Oct 1871, single, parents: Samuel E. Shoun and Mary Rebecca McCowan, cause of death: "chronic brights disease", informant: Mrs. Ollie Cornett (Mountain City), died: 14 Apr 1936, record (1936) #: 9852.

J.F. ROBERTS, born: 1 Jan 1859, widower of Ellen Roberts, parents: Tom Roberts and Lizzie Roberts, cause of death: "pulmonary tuberculosis", informant: Ed Roberts (Mountain City), buried: Morley Cemetery, died: 17 Apr 1936, record (1936) #: 9853.

Wayne HICKS, born: 13 Feb 1926, parents: Bill Hicks and Eva Davis, cause of death: illegible, informant: Bill Hicks (Mountian City), buried: Wright Cemetery, died: 24 Apr 1936, record (1936) #: 9854.

Infant ROBERTS, male, parents: Walter B. Roberts and Edna Sue Horn, cause of death: "premature about 2 months", born/died: 26 Apr 1936, record (1936) #: 9855.

Hubert Wayne SLUDER, parents: Dana H. Sluder and Hattie Miller, cause of death: "premature birth", informant: Dana Sluder (Crandull), buried: Gentry Cemetery, born/died: 1 Apr 1936, record (1936) #: 9856.

Canada Mod WILLIAMS, born: 5 Oct 1916, single, parents: Rufus Williams and Nancy C. Garland, cause of death: "lobar pneumonia", informant: R.A. Cole, buried: Gentry Cemetery, died: 30 Apr 1936, record (1936) #: 9857.

Amanda Evaline DAVIDSON, born: 12 Apr 1872 in North Carolina, widow of Sylvester Davidson, parents: Edd Burchett (NC) and Pattie McElyea, cause of death: "bronchial pneumonia, chronic myocarditis", informant: O.B. Rhymer (Mountain City), buried: Shingletown Cemetery, died: 4 May 1936, record (1936) #: 12696.

Thomas Edward RITCHISON, age 24 days, born in North Carolina, parents: father not stated and Etta Ritchison, cause of death: "bronchial pneumonia, abscess left chest", died: 11 May 1936, record (1936) #: 12697.

Jacob Harrison SAMMONS, born: 18 Nov 1899, husband of Effie Sammons, parents: George Sammons and Nancy Jane Sammons, cause of death: "pulmonary tuberculosis", informant: Dayton Sammons (Mountain City), buried: Donnelly Cemetery, died: 27 Apr 1936, record (1936) #: 12698.

Ina Bell ROBINSON, born: 8 Apr 1910, wife of Allen Robinson, parents: Roby Davis (Mabel, NC) and Dona Roberts, cause of death: "influenza, bronchial pneumonia", informant: Irene Brookshire (Mountain City), buried: Morley Cemetery, died: 5 May 1936, record (1936) #: 12699.

Billie Eugene DAVIS, born: 23 Apr 1935, parents: James Davis and Lola Reece (NC), death cause: "diptheria", died: 29 Apr 1936, record (1936) #: 12700.

Edith Faye OSBORNE, born: 21 Apr 1936, parents: Noah Osborne (NC) and Bonnie Church (NC) cause of death: "congenital heart", informant: Noah Osborne (Crandull), died: 11 May 1936, record (1936) #: 12701.

Edsel Wayne CRESS, age 2 years, 3 months and 18 days, parents: Claude Cress and Hazel Johnson, cause of death: "shoulder infection, thought to be strept", informant: R.G. Johnson (Mountain City), buried: Phillippi Cemetery, died: 13 Jun 1936.

Mabel WILLIAMS, born: 16 Jun 1926, parents: Bainer Williams and Lilie Greer, cause of death: "not known", informant: Stacy Roark (Shouns), buried: Greer Cemetery, died; 16 Jun 1936, record (1936) #: 15282.

N. Jennie SNYDER, born: 6 May 1887 in North Carolina, wife of J.D. Snyder, parents: S.S. Younce (NC) and Mary Roten (NC), cause of death: "anjina pectoris", informant: J.D. Snyder (Neva), buried: Davis Cemetery, died: 13 Jun 1936, record (1936) #: 15283.

Houn L. WEAVER, born: 29 May 1866 in North Carolina, husband of Mrs. Sallie Jane Weaver, parents: John Weaver (NC) and Martha Burton (NC), cause of death: "apoplexy", informant: G.L. Weaver (Butler), buried: Pierce Cemetery, died: 9 JUn 1936, record (1936) #: 15284.

Infant HANCK, male, born: 25 Jun 1936, parents: Estel Hanck (NC) and Ada Johnson, cause of death: "premature birth, bronchial pneumonia", informant: Will Fenner, died: 5 Jul 1936, record (1936) #: 17603.

John M. PAYNE, born: 28 Apr 1845, husband of Myrtle Payne, parents: Zebulon Payne (NC) and Charity Lipps (NC), cause of death: "senility", informant: L.M. Payne (Jonesboro, TN), died: 1 Jul 1936, record (1936) #: 17604.

Martha PRICE, born: 12 Jun 1870 in North Carolina, widow of Wiley Price, parents: "unknown", cause of death: "apoplexy", buried: Fish Springs, died: 22 Jun 1936, record (1936) #: 17605.

Mary Laura COOPER, born: 25 Jul 1896 at Watauga Co. NC, wife of Jessie Cooper, parents: George Monroe Guinn (Washington Co. TN) and Martha Atwood, cause of death: "typhoid fever", informant: G.M. Guinn (Neva), died: 3 Jul 1936, record (1936) #: 17606.

John M. RAINBOLT, born: 15 Jun 1865, minister, married, parents: John H. Rainbolt and Matilda Dugger, cause of death: "chronic myocarditis", informant: Mrs. Daniel Berry (Butler), died: 2 Jul 1936, record (1936) #: 17607.

Nellie Jane STANSBERRY, born: 15 Oct 1919, parents: father not stated and Martha Stansberry, cause of death: "not known", informant: John Stansberry (Neva), died: 11 Jul 1936, record (1936) #: 17608.

Ruby Jane ARNOLD, born: 13 May 1936, parents: W.K. Arnold and Elsie Adams, cause of death: "not known", died: 15 Jun 1936, record (1936) #: 17609.

Retha Esther OSBORNE, born: 17 Jun 1934, parents: J.W. Osborne (NC) and N.J. Jones (NC), cause of death: "cholera", informant: F.W. Osborne (Crandull), Osborne Cemetery, died: 21 Jul 1936, record (1936) #: 17610.

Balely Dean BROWN, born: 20 Feb 1936, parents: Russell Brown (Ashe Co. NC) and Virginia Gentry, cause of death: "purpura hemarragicia", informant: Russell Brown (Laurel Bloomery), buried: Gentry Cemetery, died: 1 Aug 1936, record (1936) #: 20123.

Reba Mae BOWLING, born: 4 Aug 1936, parents: Austin Bowling and Purdie Morefield, cause of death: "premature birth", informant: Austin Bowling (Mountain City), buried: Shingletown Cemetery, died: 4 Aug 1936, record (1936) #: 20124.

Reba Lee BOWLING, born: 4 Aug 1936, parents: Austin Bowling and Purdie Morefield, cause of death: "premature birth", informant: Austin Bowling (Mountain City), buried: Shingletown Cemetery, died: 5 Aug 1936, record (1936) #: 20125.

Tilda Louisa BLEVINS, born: 22 Oct 1896 in North Carolina, wife of Guy Blevins, parents: father's name not known and Rebecca Mannel, cause of death: "tuberculosis of the long bones", informant: Rebecca Mannel, buried: Blevins Cemetery, died: 5 Aug 1936, record (1936) #: 20126.

John W. WOOD, born: 12 Jan 1886, single, parents: W.B. Wood and Ella Southerland (NC), cause of death: "apoplexy", informant: Mrs. H.C. Donnelly (Shouns), died: 4 Sep 1936, record (1936) #: 22685.

Maggie SEEHORN, born: 3 Jan 1867, widow of R. Wilson Seehorn, parents: F.M. Chaple (NC) and Sarah Grigston, cause of death: "entirilis", buried: Chappell Cemetery, died: 14 Sep 1936, record (1936) #: 22686.

Laura Katherine SHULL, born: 13 May 1862, widow of N.C. Shull, parents: Hamilton Ward and Martha Holden, cause of death: illegible, informant: C.R. Shull (Neva), died: 25 Sep 1936.

R.M. MCKINNEY, born: 14 Jul 1856, widower of Maggie McKinney, parents: Bill McKinney and Beckie Treadway, cause of death: "apploexia", informant: Mike McKinney (Elizabethton, TN), buried: Watauga Valley, died: 8 Aug 1936, record (1936) #: 22688.

Mrs. Minnie J. WALSH, born: 11 Mar 1885, wife of W.G. Walsh, parents: George D. Atwood (KY) and Rachel Greenwell, cause of death: "mitral regurgitation", informant: Maude Atwood (Butler), died: 7 Sep 1936, record (1936) #: 22689.

Mary Jane STOUT, born: 12 Oct 1864, widow of Dave Stout, parents: Mart Greenwell (NC) and Agga Dugger (NC) cause of death: "organic heart disease", informant: G.D. Stout, buried: Stout Cemetery, died: 11 Sep 1936, record (1936) #: 22690.

D.S. SHOEMAKER, Jr., born: 3 Aug 1936, parents: D.S. Shoemaker and Hazel Crosswhite, cause of death: "prematurely born", informant: Hazel Shoemaker (Mountain City), died: 3 Aug 1936, record (1936) #: 22691.

Dallas Olden CAMPBELL, born: 29 Oct 1914, single, invalid, parents: Dana Campbell and Ella Crosswhite, cause of death: "eplepsy", informant: Hazel Shoemaker, died: 4 Aug 1936, record (1936) #: 22692.

Herbert GENTRY, born: 12 Mar 1936, parents: "don't know father's name" and Martha E. (last name illegible), cause of death: "colitis", informant: Martha E. Gentry (Crandull), died: 26 Sep 1936, record (1936) #: 22694.

Mrs. Naomi Catherine HANEY, born: 15 Jun 1864, divorced from Ollie B. Haney, parents: "unknown", cause of death: "pulmonary tuberculosis", informant: J. Donnely Haney (Crandull), buried: Morley Cemetery, died: 28 Sep 1936, record (1936) #: 22695.

Ann WILSON, age 96 years, 4 months and 21 days, born in Virginia, widow of Andrew S. Wilson, parents: David Phillippi (VA) and Jestia Cregor, cause of death: "cancer jaw", informant: Joe. Wilson, buried: Wilson Cemetery, died: 21 Aug 1936, record (1936) #: 22693.

Tommie Carl FARMER, born: 2 Jun 1936, parents: Luther Farmer and Pearl Gentry, cause of death: "acute entero colitis", informant: Luther Farmer (Mountain City), died: 7 Oct 1936, record (1936) #: 25010.

Fred B. DAVIS, born: 20 Nov 1913, single, parents: W.L. Davis and Ida O. Warren, cause of death: "typhoid fever, hemorage of bowel", informant: W.L. Davis (Shouns), buried: Lewis Cemetery, died 21 Oct 1936, record (1936) #: 25011.

Walter H. SHUPE, born: 31 Mar 1907, husband of Polly Arnold Shupe, parents: John Shupe and Corda Shupe, cause of death: "homicide by firearm, self inflicted wound of head with rifle bullet", informant: Clarence Shupe (Mountain City), buried: Phillippi Cemetery, died: 27 Oct 1936, record (1936) #: 25012.

Hanert WOODARD, male, age 8 years, 6 months and 20 days, parents: Newton Woodard and Alice Woodard (NC), death cause: "rheumatic fever", informant: Ernest Woodard, died: 27 Oct 1936, record (1936) #: 25013.

Norma Vel DUVALL, born: 17 Dec 1935, parents: Tom M. Duvall and Lockie Arney, cause of death: "colitis", informant: Lockie Duvall (Neva), died: 27 Sep 1936, record (1936) #: 25014.

Rosco DELOACH, Jr., age: 6 months and 13 days, parents: Roscoe Deloach and Stella Grindstaff, cause of death: "unknown", died: 18 Oct 1936, record (1936) #: 25015.

Margaret RUTTER, born: 8 Oct 1855, widow of B.N. Rutter, parents: Joel Heberland and Lucinda Blevins, cause of death: "senility", informant: N.H. Heberland (Shady), died: 20 Oct 1936, record (1936) #: 25016.

Delilah MAINS, born: 10 Oct 1876, wife of L.H. Mains, parents: Alex Greer and Nancy Osborne (NC), death cause: "congestive heart", informant: J.M. Mains (Shady), died: 27 Nov 1936, record (1936) #: 27449.

Infant BAILEY, colored, male, (twin), parents: James Bailey and Viola Parks, cause of death: "premature", informant: Viola Parks Widby, born/died: 12 Nov 1936, record (1936) #: 27450.

Infant BAILEY, colored, male, (twin), parents: James Bailey and Viola Parks, cause of death: "premature", informant: Viola Parks Widby, born/died: 12 Nov 1936, record (1936) #: 27451.

Clyde Melvin JONES, born: 4 Sep 1936 in Kentucky, parents: J.M. Jones (KY) and Chloe Lewis, cause of death: "broncho pneumonia", informant: J.M. Jones (Majestic, KY), buried: Jones Cemetery, died: 3 Nov 1936, record (1936) #: 27452.

James S. LAWS, born: 9 Mar 1855, widower, parents: (first name not stated) Laws and (first name not stated) Smith, cause of death: "heart failure, myocarditis", informant: D.M. Laws (Elizabethton, TN), Stallings Cem, died: 3 Apr 1936, record #: 27353.

Maggie GARLAND, born: 24 Dec 1885, wife of L.C. Garland, parents: William Greer and Emma Thomas (Watauga Co. NC), cause of death: "carcinoma of gall bladder and liver", informant: L.C. Garland (Trade), died: 28 Sep 1936, record (1936) #: 27454.

Laura Price TAYLOR, born: Mar 1854 in Alleghany Co. NC, widow of Samuel Taylor, parents: John Price (Alleghany Co. NC) and Melinda Thompson (Ashe Co. NC), cause of death: not stated, informant: Joe Eastridge (Mountain City), buried: Cornett Cemetery, died: 4 Dec 1936, record (1936) #: 30197.

Alfred Gerald POTTER, born: 8 Sep 1936, parents: Thomas Potter and Maude M. Price (NC), cause of death: "lobar pneumonia", informant: Thomas Potter (Shouns), buried: Creston, NC, died: 8 Dec 1936, record (1936) #: 30198.

D.H. LOVE, born: 20 Nov 1936, parents: Herman Love and Georgia Snyder, cause of death: "lobar pneumonia", informant: Herman Love (Shouns), buried: Trade, died: 11 Dec 1936, record (1936) #: 30199.

William G. LOVE, born: 15 Oct 1873 in North Carolina, husband of Mrs. Rebecca Love, parents: Joe Love (NC) and Malinda Dotson, cause of death: "chronic brights disease", informant: Ira Love (Trade), died: 15 Dec 1936, record (1936) #: 30200.

Inez LOVE, born: 1 Jan 1932, parents: Herman Love and Georgia Snyder (NC), cause of death: "diptheria", informant: Herman Love (Shouns), buried: Trade, died: 22 Dec 1936, record (1936) #: 30201.

Mrs. Katherine LUNCEFORD, age 68 years, married, parents: John Lunceford and Katherine Lunceford, cause of death: "mitral insufficiency", died: 23 Dec 1936, record (1936) #: 30202.

John C. ROUSE, born: 25 Aug 1899, married, parents: C.B. Rouse and Margaret Ford, cause of death: "myo endo corditis, influenza", informant: Mrs J.C. Rouse (Shady Valley), buried: Garland Cemetery, died: 7 Dec 1936, record (1936) #: 30203.

Dale SNYDER, age 7 years and 7 months, parents: Charlie Snyder and Sarah Wilson, cause of death: "scarlet fever, bronchial pneumonia", informant: Charlie Snyder (Shouns), buried: Wallace Cemetery, died: 1 Dec 1936, record (1936) #: 30204.

Mrs. Lena WALLACE, age about 68 years, single, parents: Alexander Wallace and Nancy Cornett (NC), cause of death: "chronic brights disease", informant: M.A. Rash (Trade), buried: Wallace Cemetery, died: 28 Dec 1936, record (1936) #: 30205.

Margaret Ida WAGNER, born: 18 Nov 1862, widow of W.E. Wagner, parents: Daniel Wagner and Nancy Winston (NC), cause of death: "hypostatic pneumonia", informant: Mrs. L.M. Wagner (Kingsport, TN), died: 30 Dec 1936, record (1936) #: 32098.

Infant ARNOLD, male, parents: Herman Arnold and Dicil Forrester, death cause: "unknown", informant: Clyde Potter, died: 19 Dec 1936, record (1936) #: 32099.

Mary Bell BUNTING, born: 10 Nov 1929, parents: Dewey Bunting and Ethel Caroline Stout, cause of death: "diptheria", informant: Dewey Bunting (Neva), buried: Baker Cem, died: 26 Oct 1936, record (1936) #: 32100.

Willard BUNTING, born: 29 Aug 1936, parents: Fonnie
Bunting and Sallie Cable, death cause: "unknown",
informant: Maggie Bunting (Butler), buried: Bunting
Cemetery, died: 7 Sep 1936, record (1936) #: 32101.

Frank Clark DAUGHERTY, born: 15 Nov 1875, husband of
Lillina Smalling Daugherty, parents: Thomas J.
Daugherty and Pollie McBride, cause of death: "organic
heart disease", informant: M.L. Shoun (Mountain City),
buried: Sugar Grove Cemetery, died: 28 Sep 1936,
record (1936) #: 32102.

O. Honest WOODARD, born: 30 Mar 1928, parents: Newt
Woodard and Alice Woodard (NC), cause of death:
"rheumatci fever", informant: Noah Woodard (Shouns),
buried: Woodard Cemetery, died: 22 Oct 1936, record
(1936) #: 32693.

Lewis H. MAINS, born: 29 Nov 1859, widower, parents:
John Mains and (first name not stated) Revis (NC),
cause of death: not stated, informant: George W. Mains
(Mountain City), buried: Shady Valley, died: 8 Jan
1937, record (1937) #: 1016.

Hubert Fred MCELYEA, born: 7 Jan 1937, parents: Fred
Perdue and Anis McElyea, cause of death: not stated,
buried: Owens Cemetery, died: 20 Jan 1937, record
(1937) #: 1017.

Francis May JENKINS, born: 25 Dec 1936, parents: Tom
Jenkins and Bessie Phillips, cause of death: "lobar
pneumonia", informant: Tom Jenkins, buried: Michaels
Cemetery, died: 22 Jan 1937, record (1937) #: 1018.

Rachel Greer WILLS, born: 9 Feb 1856, wife of James L.
Wills, parents: Joesph Greer and Patten Neal (VA),
cause of death: "third degree burns over entire body
(house fire)", informant: Charlie Greer (Lodi, VA),
died: 29 Jan 1937, record (1937) #: 1019.

James L. WILLS, born: 12 Dec 1851, husband of Rachel
Wills, parent: John Wills and Jane Smith, cause of
death: "third degree burns over entire body (house
fire)", informant: Charles Greer (Lodi, VA), died: 29
Jan 1937, record (1937) #: 1020.

Edith Price WARD, born: 2 Apr 1867 in North Carolina,
wife of Frank Ward, parents: Sam Price (NC) and
Caroline Cable, cause of death: "organic hearth
disease", informant: Sam Day (Neva), buried: Baker
Cemetery, died: 4 Jan 1937, record (1937) #: 1021.

Alexander ARNOLD, born: Jun 1839, widower, parents:
Dan Arnold and Susie Snyder, cause of death:
"pneumonia lobar", informant: Horn Arnold (Neva),
buried: Arnold Cemetery, died: 16 Jan 1937, record
(1937) #: 1022.

Minnie Adlade MINKS, born: 17 Apr 1869, single,
parents: John W. Minks and Mary Vaught, cause of
death: "heart disease", informant: L.J. Minks
(Shouns), died: 26 Jan 1937, record (1937) #: 1023.

Bonita WRIGHT, born: 24 Apr 1934, parents: George W.
Wright and Carrie Gentry, cause of death: "influenza,
broncho pneumonia", informant: George W. Wright (Shady
Valley), buried: Gentry Cemetery, died: 4 Jan 1937,
record (1937) #: 1024.

Henry ROBINSON, born: 6 Nov 1862, husband of Malinda
Robinson, minister, parents: Henry M. Robinson (Ashe
Co. NC) and Margarete Swift (Watauga Co. NC), cause of
death: "lobar pneumonia", informant: Frank Robinson,
buried: Blevins Cemetery, died: 16 Jan 1937, record
(1937) #: 1022.

Eliza Jane LEFFMAN, born: 20 Jan 1846 in Wilkes Co.
NC, widow, parents: Bennie Carter (NC) and mother's
name not stated, cause of death: not stated,
informant: H.F. Leffman (Laurel Bloomery), buried:
State Line Cemetery, died: 23 Feb 1937, record (1937)
#: 3427.

Mrs. Cordelia WOOD, born: 27 Jan 1870 in Ashe Co. NC,
wife of Sam Wood, parents: Jim Holman (NC) and
Margaret Greer (NC), cause of death: "hypostatic
pneumonia", informant: S.S. Wood (Mountain City),
buried: Donnelly Cemetery, died: 26 Feb 1937, record
(1937) #: 3428.

Mary Jane KITE, born: 25 Apr 1859, married, parents:
John Rainbolt and Matilda Vendiable, cause of death:
"pulmonary tuberculosis", informant: G.W. Kite
(Butler), buried: Cobbs Creek, died: 13 Feb 1937,
record (1937) #: 3429.

Joseph Winfield KITE, born: 25 Apr 1856, widower,
parents: George W. Kite (Carter Co. TN) and Violet
Matherson, cause of death: "influenza", informant:
G.W. Kite (Butler), buried: Cobbs Creek, died: 23 Feb
1937, record (1937) #: 3430.

Catherine MCQUEEN, age 88 years, 2 months and 11 days,
married, parents: Irwin Bradley (VA) and Niama Smith,
cause of death: "apploxy", informant: L.B. Morley
(Butler), buried: Butler Cemetery, died: 27 Jan 1937,
record (1937) #: 3431.

Miss Eliza CARRIGER, born: 17 May 1860, single,
parents: Allen L. Carriger and Cerline Pierce, cause
of death: "organic heart disease", informant: George
Walker (Butler), buried: Hunter, TN, died: 11 Feb
1937, record (1937) #: 3432.

Jackie Curtis PHILLIPPI, male, parents: Justin Phillippi and Lula Barry, cause of death: "premature birth", informant: Justin Phillippi, born/died: 2 Mar 1937, record (1937) #: 6397.

Patsy Ann PHILLIPPI, born: 19 Jan 1937, parents: Emory Phillippi and Dora Blanche Bowers, cause of death: "influenza", informant: Emory Phillippi (Mountain City), died: 25 Mar 1937, record (1937) #: 6398.

Julia Eveline VAUGHT, born: 6 May 1854, widow of David H. Vaught, parents: Daniel Snyder and (first name unknown) Forrester, cause of death: "chronic valvulor heart disease", informant: J.R. Vaught (Shouns), buried: Vaught Cemetery, died: 20 Mar 1937, record (1937) #: 3399.

Ellen DAVIS, born: 28 Oct 1865, wife of Robert D. Davis, parents: John Hawkins (Wilkes Co. NC) and Nancy Reece, cause of death: "organic heart disease", informant: Mrs. Maude Ward (Neva), died: 10 Feb 1937, record (1937) #: 6400.

Andrew Hamilton MCQUEEN, born: 7 Oct 1874, husband of Rose McQueen, cause of death: "organic heart disease", informant: Mrs. John C. Gilbert (Butler), buried: Butler Cem, died: 3 Mar 1937, record (1937) #: 6401.

Shirley Jean SWIFT, born: 29 Jan 1937, parents: Stacy Swift and Verna Ethel Harbin, cause of death: "inter cranial hemorrhage", informant: Stacy Swift (Mountain City), buried: Wilson Cemetery, died: 1 Feb 1937, record (1937) #: 6402.

Wiley E. TAYLOR, born: 9 Jun 1885, husband of Tilarime Taylor, parents: Andy Taylor and Sarah Reed, cause of death: "acute intestinal obstruction caused by abdominal injury of 14 years ago", informant: Mrs. W.E. Taylor, died: 20 Apr 1937, record (1937) #: 9160.

Mrs. Nora MADRON, born 1877 in North Carolina, widow, parents: Joe Tyree (NC) and (first name not stated) Roark (NC), cause of death: "influenza", informant: R.R. Madron (Roanoke Rapids, MI), buried: Family Cemetery, died: 11 Mar 1937, record (1937) #: 9161.

Ada HOUCK, age about 36 years, wife of Estle Houck, parents: Smith Johnson and Martha Cress, cause of death: "pulmonary tuberculosis", informant: Estel Houck (Mountain City), buried: Iron Mountain, died: 20 Apr 1937, record (1937) #: 9162.

Arthor EASTRIDGE, age 40 years, born in Ashe Co. NC, husband of Alice Woodard Eastridge, parents: Will Eastridge (NC) and mother's name not known, cause of death: "influenza, broncho pneumonia", informant: D.G. Woodard (Shouns), buried: Forge Creek, died: 26 Apr 1937, record (1937) #: 9163.

Robert A. TESTER, born: 10 Dec 1850, widower, parents: William Tester and Jane Proffitt, cause of death: "cancer on face", informant: T.S. Tester (Butler), buried: Sugar Grove Cemetery, died: 3 Apr 1937, record (1937) #: 9164.

Mrs. Eliza WATSON, born: 29 Apr 1868, widow of Thomas R. Watson, parents: Thomas Gregg and Harriett Pierce, cause of death: "cancer on breast", informant: Mrs. Hattie Brown (Butler), buried: Dugger Cemetery, died: 5 Mar 1937, record (1937) #: 9165.

Nolan Bruce HODGE, born: 5 Mar 1935, parents: Lester Paul Hodge and Jane Dunn, cause of death: "broncho pneumonia", informant: A.L. Hodge (Shouns), buried: Stout Cemetery, died: 2 May 1937, record (1937) #: 11664.

Pauline JENNINGS, born: 21 Jun 1920, parents: Tom Jennings and Archie Dishman (Wilkesboro, NC), cause of death: "apoplexy", informant: Tom Jennings (Shouns), buried: Jennings Cemetery, died: 4 May 1937, record (1937) #: 11665.

David Pearson PHILLIPPI, born: 22 Feb 1856 in Wythe Co. VA, husband of Alice Phillippi, parents: David Phillippi (Wythe Co. VA) and Jane Frye (Wythe Co. VA), cause of death: "lobar pneumonia", informant: Mack Phillippi, buried: Phillippi Cemetery, died: 11 May 1937, record (1937) #: 11666.

John Wesley GENTRY, born: 10 Oct 1865, married, parents: Wash Gentry and Frankie Gentry, cause of death: "broncho pneumonia", buried: Wilson Cemetery, died: 22 May 1937, record (1937) #: 11667.

John W. SMYTHE, III, born: 29 Mar 1937, parents: John W. Smythe, Jr. and Buist Demint (Murfreesboro, TN), cause of death: illegible, died: 24 May 1937, record (1937) #: 11668.

Alice Grigston OSBORNE, born: 24 Sep 1862, widow of William H. Osborne, parents: James M. Grigston and Clara Jenkins, cause of death: "chronic intestinal nephritis", informant: C.C. Canter, buried: Chappell Cemetery, died: 26 May 1937, record (1937) #: 11669.

Mrs. Eliza Catherine CRESS, age 76 years, widow of James A. Cress, parents: William Blevins and Catherine Berry, cause of death: "chronic brights disease, acute colitis", informant: S.F. Gentry, buried: Phillippi Cemetery, died: 27 May 1937, record (1937) #: 11670.

Nancy Ellen ARNOLD, born: 18 Aug 1870, widow of Grant Arnold, parents: (first name not stated) Gilbert and Eliza Price, cause of death: "carcinoma of rectum", informant: E.G. Arnold, buried: Phillippi Cemetery, died: 13 Apr 1937, record (1937) #: 11671.

Mrs. Louise ROARK, born: 5 Oct 1855, widow of W.T. Roark, parents: J.C. Main and Polly Potter, cause of death: "influenza", informant: J.C. Roark (Shouns), buried: Arnold Cemetery, died: 2 Mar 1937, record (1937) #: 11672.

Janet Sue BROOKSHIRE, born: 26 Mar 1934, parents: Sam Brookshire and Bonnie Carver, cause of death: "congenital malformation of bile duct", died: 7 May 1937, record (1937) #: 11673.

James Billie WILSON, parents: W.M. Wilson and Maude Miller, cause of death: "premature", informant: Mrs. Ed Wilson (Shouns), buried: Trade, born/died: 3 May 1937, record (1937) #: 11674.

Loneviney C. BROCE, born: 22 Apr 1849 in Iredell Co. NC, widow of George W. Broce, parents: John Millsaps (NC) and Sallie Clanton (NC), cause of death: "chronic brights disease", informant: Miss Maude Broce, buried: Mountain View Cemetery, died: 1 Jun 1937, record (1937) #: 13958.

William F. PARDUE, born: 10 May 1856 in Wilkes Co. NC, widower of Catherine Pardue, parents: John Pardue (NC) and Freelove Mullins, cause of death: "chronic brights disease", informant: John Pardue (Shouns), Brookshire Cemetery, died: 11 Jun 1937, record (1937) #: 13959.

N.W. SNYDER, age 66 years, parents: Alexander Snyder and Amanda Stout, cause of death: "chronic valvulor heart disease, cerebral hemorrhage, informant: A.M. Snyder (Vaughtsville), buried: Stone Dam Cemetery, died: 23 Jun 1937, record (1937) #: 13960.

David Garfield SHUPE, born: 28 Mar 1881, married, parents: Daniel Shupe and Cordelia Smith, cause of death: "chronic intestinal nephritis, cerebral hemorrhage", informant: Emma Shupe, buried: Wilson Cemetery, died: 25 Jun 1937, record (1937) #: 13961.

John MILLER, age 72 years, husband of Callie Miller, parents: father's name not recorded and Sallie Wright, cause of death: "pulmonary tuberculosis", informant: Callie Miller (Shady Valley), buried: Wood Cemetery, died: 20 Jun 1937, record (1937) #: 13962.

Farney D. REEVES, age 38 years and 8 months, wife of S.S. Reeves, parents: A.H. Blevins and Malinda Scott, cause of death: illegible, informant: S.S. Reeves (Shady Valley), buried; Blevins Cemetery, died: 30 Jun 1937, record (1937) #: 13963.

David H. GROGAN, born: 23 Feb 1874, married, parents: Elijah Grogan (NC) and Rhoda Younce (NC), cause of death: "heat exhaustion, acute myocadital failure", informant: Claud Grogan (Trade), buried: Zionville Cemetery, died: 2 Jun 1937, record (1937) #: 13964.

Sarah Lucky Barry LOYD, born: 4 Jul 1864, widow of Joe L. Loyd, parents: Richard Hamilton Barry and May Caroline Price, cause of death: "chronic myocarditis", buried: Mountain View Cemetery, died: 12 Jul 1937, record (1937) #: 16411.

Mrs. Annie MAY, age 68 years, 2 months and 10 days, widow of Ham May, parents: James Martin (NC) and Nancy Stout (NC), cause of death: "chronic intestinal nephritis", informant: D.M. Martin (Shouns), buried: Martin Cemetery, died: 4 Jul 1937, record (1937) #: 16412.

Earl ROARK, born: 6 Jul 1935, parents: McKinley Roark and Elsie Vanover (NC), cause of death: "lobar pneumonia fever", informant: J.C. Roark (Shouns), buried: Arnold Cemetery, died: 21 Jul 1937, record (1937) #: 16413.

Mrs. Dillie Elizabeth MULLINS, born: 17 Jul 1847, widow, parents: Joseph Robinson and Katie Rasor, cause of death: "acute colitis", informants: J.M. Lowe and R.F. Mullins, buried: Robinson Cemetery, died: 4 Jul 1937, record (1937) #: 16414.

Samuel Edgar ROBINSON, born: 30 Jun 1868, husband of Mrs. Sallie Robinson, parents: James Robinson (VA) and Mary Reece, cause of death: "pulmonary tuberculosis", informant: F.E. Robinson, died: 9 Jun 1937, record (1937) #: 16415.

John Wesley DILLON, born: 27 Apr 1868, married, parents: John Dillon (NC) and Loretta Botehammer (NC), cause of death: "gastro-entera colitis caused by over eating cherries", informant: Wiley Dillon (Mountain City), buried: Wilson Cemetery, died: 11 Jul 1937, record (1937) #: 16416.

Joseph Macon SHOUN, born: 14 May 1866, divorced from Dillie Richinsin, parents: Caleb Shoun and Rachel Southerland, cause of death: "lobar pneumonia", informant: J.C. Shoun, buried: Doe Valley, died: 16 Jul 1937, record (1937) #: 16417.

Mrs. Sarah CANTER, born: 7 Apr 1876 at Meat Camp, NC, wife of John Canter, parents: E.N. Miller (NC) and Elizabeth Miller (before marriage)(NC), cause of death: "unknown", informant: W.R. Miller (Trade), buried: Arnold Cemetery, died: 20 Jul 1937, record (1937) #: 16418.

Wilma E. ANDERSON, born: 23 Feb 1936, parents: Rush Anderson (VA) and May Gentry, cause of death: "whooping cough", buried: Southerland Cemetry, died: 2 Aug 1937, record (1937) #: 18870.

Elsie Mae GILBERT, born: 14 Mar 1937, parents: D.E. Gilbert and Louise East (West VA), cause of death: illegible, informant: J.H. Gilbert (Laurel Bloomery), buried: Southerland Cemetery, died: 8 Aug 1937, record (1937) #: 18871.

Danford DOWELL, female, age 32 years, wife of Link Dowell, parents: Charlie Dunn and Rebecca Head, cause of death: "chronic brights disease", informant: Link Dowell (Mountain City), died: 17 Aug 1937, record (1937) #: 18872.

Infant FORRESTER, male (twins), parents: Charles F. Forrester and Eva Lewis (NC), cause of death: "premature", born/died: 9 Aug 1937, record (1937) #: 18873.

David Ensley CORNETT, born: 12 Nov 1847 at Green Valley, NC, husband of Mrs. Jennie V. Cornett, Civil War soldier, parents: Wesley Cornett (Ashe Co. NC) and Sallie Mahola (Ashe Co. NC), cause of death: "brights disease", informant: Ham Cornett (Deep Gap, NC) buried: Mountain View Cemetery, died: 24 Aug 1937, record (1937) #: 18874.

Mrs. Lydia Caroline PAYNE, born: 24 Jul 1854 in Ashe Co. NC, widow of F.M. Payne, parents: David Farmer (NC) and Elizabeth Graybeal (NC), cause of death: "chronic intestinal nephritis", informant: Mrs. T.E. Simcox, buried: Farmer Cemetery, died: 31 Aug 1937, record (1937) #: 18875.

David L. PHIPPS, born: 1 Aug 1882 in Carter Co., TN, husband of Tittia Phipps, parents: Peter Phipps and Betsy Blevens, cause of death: "cerebral hemorrhage", informant: Peter Phipps (Doeville), buried: Phipps Cemetery, died: 14 Aug 1937, record (1937) #: 18876.

Rosa Wanda GARLAND, born: 26 Mar 1937, parents: Sam W. Garland and Julia Cassie Campbell, death cause: "joundice", died: 27 Apr 1937, record (1937) #: 18877.

Autry Keys MORELEY, born: 23 May 1937, parents: D.J. Morely and C.D. Pierce, cause of death: "colitis", informant D.J. Morely (Doeville), died: 8 Aug 1937, record (1937) #: 18878.

Wilder CAMPBELL, born: 28 Aug 1904, husband of Martha Campbell, parents: Major Campbell and Lania Garland, cause of death: "pulmonary tuberculosis", informant: James Campbell (Shady Valley), died: 9 Aug 1937, record (1937) #: 18879.

Albert Lewis WATSON, born: 20 Feb 1932, parents: Albert Wilson and Bonnie Mains, cause of death: "purpura hemorragia", informant: Albert Watson (Mountain City), buried: Shady Valley, died: 7 Sep 1937, record (1937) #: 21022.

William T. GREER, born: 11 Mar 1862, widower of Mrs.
Elizabeth Ray Greer, parents: Joseph Greer and Mary
Jane Smith, cause of death: "apoplexy, sudden death",
informant: John F. Greer (Laurel Bloomery), buried:
Taylors Valley Cemetery, died: 25 Sep 1937, record
(1937) #: 21023.
Sam NICHOLS, Jr., born: 6 Aug 1934, parents: Sam
Nichols and Lena Martin, cause of death: "diptheria",
buried: Wilson Cemetery, died: 5 Sep 1937, record
(1937) #: 21024.
Mrs. Lou Ellen HALL, born: 22 Sep 1875 at Boone, NC,
widow of John Hall, parents: Jeff Dyson (NC) and Mary
Jane Winscott (NC), cause of death: "chronic brights
disease", informant: Green Dyson (Mountain City),
buried: Donnelly Cemetery, died: 24 Sep 1937, record
(1937) #: 21025.
Harm Warner KITE, born: 15 Nov 1861, married, parents:
Washington Kite and Violet Matherson, cause of death:
"cirrhosis of liver", informant: Bertie Kite (Butler),
buried: Cobbs Creek Cemetery, died: 17 Sep 1937,
record (1937) # 21026.
Sarah FLETCHER, age 71 years, married, parents: Feeb
Fletcher and Rebecca Jane Forrester, cause of death:
not stated, informant: D.S. McQueen (Butler) died: 30
Sep 1937, record (1937) #: 21027.
Mrs. Cora Elizabeth GENTRY, born: 17 Aug 1883, wife of
W.L. Gentry, parents: Jim Berry and Callie Pierce,
cause of death: "sugar diabetes", informant: W.L.
Berry (Butler), buried: Gentry Cemetery, died: 3 Apr
1937.
Annie GENTRY, born: 14 Aug 1928, parents: Jim Gentry
and Rossie Cornett, cause of death: "diptheria",
informant: Jim Gentry (Mountain City), buried: Wilson
Cemetery, died: 19 Sep 1937, record (1937) #: 21029.
Ruby Joe CANTER, born: 7 Feb 1929 at Toms Creek, VA,
parents: William Canter and Ella Wilson, cause of
death: "ilio colitis", informant: William Wilson
(Trade), buried: Arnold Cemetery, died: 1 Sep 1937,
record (1937) #: 21030.
Infant ALLEN, born: 17 Oct 1937, parents: Bruce Eller
and Grace Allen, cause of death: not stated,
informant: Bruce Eller (Mountain City), buried:
Shingletown Cemetery, died: 20 Oct 1937, record (1937)
#: 23146.
Joseph B. SWIFT, born: 20 Sep 1856 in North Carolina,
widower, parents: Wilburn Swift (NC) and mother's name
unknown, cause of death: "chronic brights disease",
informant: James Swift (Damascus, VA), died: 3 Oct
1937, record (1937) #: 23147.

Samuel Richard Alexander TURNER, born: 12 Jul 1881, husband of Ada Turner, parents: Murphey Turner (NC) and Marria (surname unknown), cause of death: "cancer prostate", informant: Ada Turner (Mountain City), buried: Holy Hill Cemetery, died: 12 Oct 1937, record (1937) #: 23148.

Mrs. Mary ISAACS, born: Sep 1888 at Mabel, NC, wife of Jack Isaacs, parents: Jack Swift (NC) and Rhoda Younce (NC), cause of death: "chronic brights disease", informant: Jack Isaacs (Mountain City), buried: Union Cemetery, buried: Mabel, NC, died: 22 Oct 1937, record (1937) #: 23149.

Rosa Lee WARREN, born: 19 Sep 1937, parents: Edgar Warren and Ruth Mandeline Tester, cause of death: "child had severe cold", informant: Edgar Warren (Shouns), buried: Lewis Cemetery, died: 25 Oct 1937, record (1937) #: 23150.

Gurney F. WAGNER, colored, born: 29 Sep 1918, single, parents: Charlie Hardin (NC) and Annie Wagner, cause of death: "burned to death in building", informant: Tild Wagner (Shouns), buried: Wagner Cemetery, died: 29 Oct 1937, record (1937) #: 23151.

L.D. MCQUEEN, born: 25 Sep 1854, married, parents: William McQueen and Rachel Slimp, cause of death: "lobar pneumonia", informant: Mrs. Mattie Waugh (Mountain City), buried: Butler Cemetery, died: 3 Oct 1937, record (1937) #: 23152.

Clarence Mitchell ARNOLD, born: 15 Oct 1914, single, parents: James B. Arnold and Elizabeth Swift, cause of death: "cancer stomach", informant: James B. Arnold (Mountain City), buried: Wilson Cemetery, died: 13 Oct 1937, record (1937) #: 23153.

Floyd MCQUEEN, born: 26 Jan 1869, husband of Fannie Vance, parents: Alex McQueen and Mary Brown, cause of death: "gastric carcinoma", buried: Garland Cemetery, died: 2 Oct 1937, record (1937) #: 23154.

Mrs. Nancy WALLACE, born: 3 Apr 1841 in Creston, NC, widow of Alex Wallace, parents: Jerry Cornett (NC) and Jane Lewis (NC), cause of death: "cerebral hemorrhage", informant: Walter Johnson (Trade), buried: Wallace Cemetery, died: 23 Oct 1937, record (1937) #: 23155.

Robert JOHNSON, Negro, born: 1880, husband of Sarah Johnson, parents: Ross Johnson and Susie Wilson, cause of death: "chronic brights disease", informant: Mandy Jones, buried: Holy Hill Cemetery, died: 13 Nov 1937, record (1937) #: 25426.

John W. ARNOLD, born: 16 Mar 1865 in Lee Co., VA, widower of Mrs. Ollie Arnold, parents: Merritt Arnold (VA) and Elizabeth Davis (VA), cause of death: "chronic brights disease", informant: John R. Winters (Laurel Bloomery), buried: Michaels Cemetery, died: 7 Sep 1937, record (1937) #: 25427.

Sarah Virginia COLE, born: 4 Apr 1857 in Virginia, wife of J.E. Cole, parents: William Byress (VA) and Susan Ow... (illegible)(VA), cause of death: "blood clot on brain", buried: Gentry Cemetery, died: 25 Nov 1937, record (1937) #: 25428.

Mrs. Mary TRIPLETT, born: 1851 at Holston Valley, TN, widow of Thomas Toliver Triplett, parents: "unknown", cause of death: "chronic brights disease", informant: J.F. Triplett (Shouns), buried: Wills Cemetery, died: 18 Dec 1937, record (1937) #: 28050.

Charles BROWN, born: 17 Nov 1937, parents: Marvin Brown and Ida Simcox, cause of death: "unknown", informant: C.L. Brown (Shouns), buried: Payne Cemetery, died: 21 Nov 1937, record (1937) #: 28051.

Asa Alexander STOUT, born: 25 Dec 1871, husband of Annie Stout, parents: Daniel Stout and Mary Holman, cause of death: "chronic valvulor heart disease, carcinoma of stomach", informant: Sam Stout (Hartsville, Ohio), buried: Stout Cemetery, died: 11 Dec 1937, record (1937) #: 28052.

Maggie POOLE, born: 3 Jun 1882 in North Carolina, single, parents: Dr. Henry Poole and Gillie White, cause of death: "chronic heart disease", informant: Conley Poole (Doeville), buried: Stalling Cemetery, died: 21 Dec 1937, record (1937) #: 28053.

Elizabeth Hester FARTHING, age 76 years, 1 month and 29 days, born in Watauga Co., NC, widow of Dora Harmon Farthing, parents: Elijah Farthing (NC) and Amanda Oliver (NC), cause of death: "cardio nephritis", informant: Myrtle Farthing, buried: Pinola, NC, died: 23 Nov 1937, record (1937) #: 28054.

Mrs. E.S. BOWMAN, born: 15 Sep 1849, widow, parents: Ben Hyder and Mrs. Hughes, death cause: "pneumonia", died: 27 Nov 1937, record (1937) #: 28055.

Richard A. NORRIS, born: 28 Aug 1848 in Boone, NC, wife: Mrs. Polly L. Norris, parents: Franklin Norris (NC) and Lou Green (NC), cause of death: "apoplexy", Ray Norris, died: 17 Dec 1937, record (1937) #: 28056.

Isaac M. SHOUN, born: 6 Apr 1862, husband of Alice Shoun, parents: Harvey Shoun and Mary Graybeal (Ashe Co. NC), cause of death: "blood poison", informant: Mrs. Maude S. Miller, buried: Wilson Cemetery, died: 18 Apr 1937, record (1937) #: 28057.

Florence ROBERTS, born: 19 May 1892 in Virginia, wife of Jake Roberts, parents: Elcany Blevins and (first name not stated) Fleener (VA), death cause: "endo carditis", died: 7 Dec 1937, record #: 28058.

William J. CROSSWHITE, born: 11 Dec 1865, husband of Sallie Crosswhite, parents: Landon Crosswhite and Caroline Buckles, cause of death: "paraplegia", informant: C.C. Crosswhite (Shady Valley), died: 28 Dec 1937, record (1937) #: 28059.

William W.G. HAMBY, born: 2 Feb 1869 in North Carolina, husband of Gertie V. Hamby, parents: "unknown", cause of death: "lobar pneumonia", informant: Mrs. Gertie V. Hamby (Damascus, VA), buried: Sutherland, TN, died: 24 Jan 1938, record (1938) #: 946.

Sam CROWLEY, age: "guess at 56 to 63 years", divorced, parents: "unknown", cause of death: "acute brights disease", died: 13 Jan 1938, record (1938) #: 947.

Marry M. DOTSON, born: 6 Jan 1864, wife of A.E. Dotson, parents: Franklin Chapel (NC) and Sarah Grigston, cause of death: "chronic myocarditis", informant: Mrs. Dean Dotson (Shouns), died: 27 Jan 1938, record (1938) #: 948.

Mrs. Martha WAGNER, born: 9 May 1906, wife of R.M. Wagner, parents: Jim Smith and Martha Fritts, cause of death: "enciphalitis", informant: R.M. Wagner (Shouns), buried: Wagner Cemetery, died: 29 Jan 1938, record (1938) #: 949.

Andy DUVALL, born: 24 Mar 1872 at Jefferson, NC, husband of Mrs. Mary Duvall, parents: Thomas Duvall (Bina, NC) and Caroline Treadway (NC), cause of death: "carcinoma of (illegible)", informant: Winford Duvall (Neva), buried: Cool Springs Cemetery, died: 8 Jan 1938, record (1938) #: 950.

David M. MAINS, born: 24 Feb 1882, husband of Mrs. Maggie Mains, parents: Joe Mains and Mandy Dunn, cause of death: "pulmonary tuberculosis, broncho pneumonia", informant: Dick Mains (Shouns), buried: Stout Cemetery, died: 23 Jan 1938, record (1938) #: 951.

Nancy DAY, born: 5 Mar 1873 at Sugar Grove, NC, wife of S.E. Day, parents: Sam Price (NC) and Caroline Cable (NC), cause of death: "chronic intestinal nephritis", informant: S.E. Day (Neva), buried: Cove Creek Cem, died: 24 Jan 1938, record (1938) #: 952.

Willard Ray STOUT, born: 12 Apr 1923, parents: J. Blaine Stout and Etoila B. Hicks (Hampton, TN), cause of death: "miningitis and tonsilitis", informant: J. Blaine Stout (Doeville), buried: Stout Cemetery, died: 12 Jan 1938, record (1938) #: 953.

George Millard LOVE, born: 26 Apr 1877 in Vilas, NC, husband of Mrs. Lizzie Love, parents: Joseph Love (NC) and Malinda Dotson, cause of death: "chronic brights disease", informant: Rodger R. Love (Trade), buried: Dotson Cemetery, died: 15 Jan 1938, record (1938) #: 954.

James M. MCQUEEN, born: 14 Nov 1863, husband of Mary A. McQueen, parents: William McQueen and Rachel Slimp, cause of death: "chronic heart diesese", informant: David L. McQueen (Elizabethton, TN), buried: Butler, died: 5 Jan 1938, record (1938) #: 955.

Mary M. HORN, born: 26 Dec 1937, parents: Robert Horn (Bristol, TN) and Susa Heaton, cause of death: "whooping cough, broncho pneumonia", informant: Robert Horn (Mountain City), buried: Shoun Cemetery, died: 22 Feb 1938, record (1938) #: 3178.

Maude Price POTTER, born: 10 Feb 1906 at Ashland, NC, wife of Thomas Potter, parents: H.J. Price (Ashland, NC) and Malissa Ford, cause of death: "bronchial pneumonia", informant: O.T. Price (Ashland, NC), buried: Price Cemetery, Ashland, NC, died: 11 Feb 1938, record (1938) #: 3179.

William Franklin ROARK, born: 23 Jun 1881, divorced from Mrs. Polly Roark, parents: William T. Roark (Ashe Co. NC) and Luza Main (Ashe Co. NC), cause of death: "gun shot wound of chest, homicidal", informant: J.C. Roark (Shouns), buried: Arnold Cemetery, died: 13 Feb 1938, record (1938) #: 3180.

Mrs. Eula EASTRIDGE, born: 11 Nov 1898, widow of Will Eastridge, parents: Alvin Curd and Susan Eastridge, cause of death: "broncho pneumonia", informant: R.S. Payne (Shouns) buried: Curd Cemetery, died: 17 Feb 1938, record (1938) #: 3181.

Linda F. DISHMAN, born: 10 Oct 1892, single, parents: Adolphus Dishman (NC) and Dora Gambill (NC), cause of death: "lobar pneumonia", informant: Clyde H. Stout (Shouns), died: 25 Feb 1938, record (1938) #: 3182.

Dora DISHMAN, born: 20 Apr 1866 in North Carolina, wife of Adolphus Dishman, parents: Frank Gambill (NC) and (first name not stated) Cardell (NC), cause of death: "cerebral hemorrhage, broncho pneumonia", informant: Otto Stout (Shouns), buried: Payne Gap, NC, died: 24 Jan 1938, record (1938) #: 3183.

Mrs. Sarah M. CHURCH, born: 16 Nov 1880, wife of A.G. Church, parents: Larkin M. McElyea and Caroline Pardue (NC), cause of death: "myocarditis, pulmonary edima", informant: A.G. Church (Butler), buried: Davis Cemetery, died: 21 Feb 1938, record (1938) #: 3184.

Mary Susan SAMMONS, born: 16 Nov 1889, wife of J.L. Sammons, parents: Taylor Johnson and Caroline Cress, cause of death: "lobar pneumonia", informant: R.G. Johnson (Mountain City), buried: Johnson Cemetery, died: 16 Mar 1938, record (1938) #: 5502.

Clinton B. CURD, born: 21 Aug 1937, parents: Alfred E. Curd and Ira Dunn, cause of death: "lobar pneumonia", Dunn Cemetery, died: Mar 1938, record (1938) #: 5504.

Robert Daniel TRIVETT, born: 12 Mar 1938, parents: John R. Trivett and Roana Johnson, cause of death: "influenza", informant: John F. Trivett, buried: Woods Cemetery, died: 15 Mar 1938, record (1938) #: 5504.

Mrs. Amanda Sammons POTTER, born: 18 Dec 1858, widow of William Potter, parents: David Sammons and Eliza Shores, cause of death: "lobar pneumonia", informant: Mrs. Lee R. Wagner (Vaughtsville), buried: Pleasant View Cemetery, died: 14 Mar 1938, record (1938) #: 5505.

Leonard C. HARBIN, born: 15 Aug 1885 at Watauga Co. NC, husband of Mattie Harbin, parents: Abe Harbin (NC) and Martha Eggers (NC), cause of death: "heart disease", informant: S.L. Harbin, buried: Wilson Cemetery, died: 9 Feb 1938, record (1938) #: 5506.

Frank DOWELL, born: 15 Feb 1938, parents: Sherman Dowell and Lizzie Potter, cause of death: "premature birth", buried: Potter Cemetery, died: 16 Feb 1938, record (1938) #: 5507.

Mrs. Grace OSTER, born: 21 Nov 1865 at Meadeville, PA, wife of George A. Oster, parents: James D. Devers (Warren, PA) and Orinda Worland (Covington, KY), cause of death: "influenza, broncho pneumonia", informant: George D. Oster (Richland, VA), buried: Mountain View Cemetery, died: 2 Apr 1938, record (1938) #: 7714.

Oscar Bert WILSON, born: 27 Dec 1902, single, parents: Abraham Wilson and Martha M. Cress, cause of death: "influenza, broncho pneumonia", informant: Mrs. D.E. Stalcup (Doeville), died: 14 Apr 1938, record (1938) #: 7915.

Mrs. Ollie MCELYEA, born: 16 Apr 1892 at Silverstone, NC, wife of W.D. McElyea, parents: W.L. Wilson (NC) and Elmiraa Reece (NC), cause of death: "influenza, broncho pneumonia", buried: Mountain View Cemetery, died: 18 Apr 1938, record (1938) #: 7916.

Infant ARNOLD, male, born: 10 Mar 1938, parents: William H. Arnold (VA) and Grace Walker, cause of death: "premature birth", informant: William Arnold (Neva), born/died: 11 Mar 1938, record (1938) #: 7917.

Mrs. Nancy STOUT, born: 1858, wife of Joe Stout, parents: George Grindstaff and Elizabeth Courtner, cause of death: not recorded, buried: Grindstaff Cemetery, died: 3 Apr 1938, record (1938) #: 7918.

Eliza Jane STOUT, age 87 years, 7 months and 5 days, widow of Columbus Stout, parents: Henry Powell and Rebecca Elliott, cause of death: "acute indigestion", informant: Hazel Crosswhite, buried: Walker Cemetery, died: 16 Apr 1938, record (1938) #: 7919.

Elia Wills SHOUN, born: 21 Jan 1862, widow of J.W. Shoun, parents: Russell B. Wills (VA) and Elizabeth R. Duff (VA), cause of death: "appoplexy", informant: Nat Shoun (Johnson City, TN), buried: Wilson Cemetery, died: 22 Apr 1938, record (1938) #: 7920.

Mary Love MILLER, born: 24 Apr 1938, parents: Charles M. Miller and Sylvia Walker, cause of death: "premature birth", died: 25 Apr 1938, record (1938) #: 7921.

Laurinda BUCKLES, born: 20 Jun 1864, widow of Frank Buckles, parents: W.M. Scott and Margaret Blevens, cause of death: "cerebral hemorrhage", buried: Gentry Cemetery, died 8 Feb 1938, record (1938) #: 7922.

Hannah Cornelia Alice WARREN, born: 27 May 1885 in Watauga Co., NC, divorced from Roby Warren, parents: Isaac Reece (NC) and Cornelia Camel (NC), cause of death: "tuberculosis", informant: Ruby Warren (Trade), buried: Zionville, NC, died: 5 Apr 1938, record (1938) #: 7923.

Ethel COLVIN, born: 2 Feb 1903 in Virginia, resident of Fort Knox, KY, married to William M. Colvin, parents: Thomas E. Worley (VA) and Edmon Ison (VA), cause of death: "circulation collapse", informant: Mrs. Thomas E. Worley (Damascus, VA), buried: Roe Cemetery, died: 10 May 1938, record (1938) #: 10172.

Infant MAY, male, parents: Adell May (Ashe Co. NC) and Maggie Jones (Ashe Co. NC), cause of death: "7 month, very weak", informant: Luther Jones (Shouns), buried: Warren Cemetery, born/died: 29 Apr 1938, record (1938) #: 10173.

Alice Osborne SNYDER, born: 4 Sep 1879 at Suterland, NC, wife of Jacob Snyder, parents: Frank Osborne (NC) and Emma Wilson (NC), cause of death: "carcinoma of uterus and liver", informant: Jacob Snyder (Shouns), buried: Snyder Cemetery, died: 21 Apr 1938, record (1938) #: 10174.

Stella Alice GUY, born: 27 Jan 1938, parents: Holland Guy (Sullivan Co. TN) and Hester Campbell, cause of death: "not known", died: 29 Jan 1938, record (1938) #: 10175.

Infant SWIFT, male, parents: John Swift and Kate Harper, cause of death: "premature infant", buried: Wilson Cemetery, born/died: 16 May 1938, record (1938) #: 10176.

Mrs. Dora ROBERTS, born: 11 May 1897 at Zionville, NC, wife of James Roberts, parents: William Reece (Zionville, NC) and Elizabeth Davis (Zionville, NC), cause of death: "severe burns from neck to knees from catching fire from kitchen stove", informant: Mas. Elizabeth Davis, buried: Morley Cemetery, died: 19 May 1938, record (1938) #: 10177.

Rebecca MILLSAPS, born: 21 Jul 1881, widow of Elem Millsaps, parents: Daniel S. Rash and Betty Ann Jennings (NC), cause of death: "carcinoma of stomach, fractured hip", informant: M.A. Rash (Trade), buried: Greer Cemetery, died: 21 May 1938, record (1938) #: 10178.

Jane MCCLINE, born: 19 Apr 1933, parents: John McCline (NC) and Julia Trivette, cause of death: "spinal meningitis", informant: W.R. Waters (Damascus, VA), buried: Sutherland Cemetery, died: 19 Jun 1938, record (1938) #: 12621.

Eli HAMM, born: 8 Aug 1862 in North Carolina, husband of Jensie Hamm, parents: Enoch Hamm (NC) and Della Woods (NC), cause of death: "sudden death, no doctor", informant: Mrs. Eli Hamm (Damascus, VA), buried: Damascus, VA, died: 18 Jun 1938, record (1938) #: 12622.

Betty GENTRY, born: 11 Oct 1937, parents: M.J. Gentry and Chessie Severt (West Jefferson, NC), cause of death: "gastro-entro-colitis", buried: Gentry Cemetery, died: 23 May 1938, record (1938) #: 12623.

Francis Wills GRANT, born: 9 Nov 1855, widow of H.T. Grant, parents: Peter Dick Wills and Sophia McCown, cause of death: "chronic nephritis", informant: Miss Fannie Keene (Shouns), buried: Shouns Cemetery, died: 1 Jun 1938, record (1938) #: 12624.

Callie EASTRIDGE, born: 19 Jul 1873, widow of Dave Eastridge, parents: W.R. Davis (Grayson, VA) and Seny Stone, cause of death: "chronic brights disease, informant: R.A. Davis (Shouns), buried: Payne Cemetery, died: 20 Jun 1938, record (1938) #: 12625.

Pollie Marie ROARK, born: 31 Dec 1937 at Tazwell, VA, parents: Burl Roark and Maggie Lunceford, cause of death: "pertussis", informant: Burl Roark (butler), buried: Brown Cemetery, died: 20 Jun 1938, record (1938) #: 12626.

Vonna Lee ARNOLD, age 1 year and 13 days, parents: W.K. Arnold and Elsie Adams, cause of death: "pneumonia", buried: Adams Cemetery, died: 23 Jun 1938, record (1938) #: 12627.

Lucinda ANDERSON, born: 2 Mar 1869, single, parents: John Anderson and Mildred Dugger, cause of death: "tuberculosis", informant: Clyde Anderson (Butler), died: 17 Jan 1938, record (1938) #: 12628.

Mrs. Eliza NEELY, born: 23 Feb 1880, widow, parents: Tom McQueen and (first name not stated) Cornett, cause of death: "bronchial pneumonia, cardiac, asthma", informant: Mrs. Crike Mooser (Laurel Bloomery), died: 6 Jul 1938, record (1938) #: 15021.

Tiny Catherine ROARK, born: 1866 in Virginia, wife of Wilson T. Roark, parents: Bill Widner (VA) and (first name not stated) Buskell (VA), cause of death: "chronic myocarditis, hypertension", informant: Charlie Roark (Mountain City), buried: Shingletown Cemetery, died: 27 Jul 1938, record (1938) #: 15022.

Infant SLUDER, male, parents: Forrest Sluder and Ancil Lewis, cause of death: "premature", informant: Ray Sluder (Shouns), buried: Lewis Cemetery, born/died: 8 Jul 1938, record (1938) #: 15023.

Nancy M. MORETZ, born: 4 Apr 1873 in North Carolina, wife of Smith Moretz, parents: (first name not stated) Nelson (NC) and (first name not stated) Simmons (NC), cause of death: "hypertension", informant: Mrs. Joe Denton (Shouns), buried: Shipley Cemetery, died: 20 Jul 1938, record (1938) #: 15024.

Evelyn STOUT, born: 3 Jul 1938 (record marked "twins"), parents: R.F. Stout and Maude Smith, cause of death: "premature", informant: R.F. Stout (Shouns), buried: Stout Cemetery, died: 4 Jul 1938, record (1938) #: 15025.

J.L. BISHOP, born: 12 May 1861 in North Carolina, husband of Ottie Bishop, parents: Elbert Bishop (NC) and (first name not stated) Mottern (NC), cause of death: "died suddenly", informant: Hillery Bishop (Shady), died: 1 Jul 1938, record (1938) #: 15026.

Francis BUCKLES, born: 1 Oct 1937, parents: Glenn Buckles and Ruth Roark, cause of death: "pernicious (illegible)", buried: Garland Cemetery, died: 2 Jul 1938, record (1938) #: 15027.

J.E. MILLER, born: 22 Mar 1877 at Watauga Co., NC, husband of Mrs. Nannie Miller, parents: J.P. Miller (Millers Gap, NC) and Tempie Potter (Meat Camp, NC), cod "chronic heart disease", informant: Charles Miller (Trade), buried: Reece Cemetery, died: 2 Jul 1938, record (1938) #: 15028.

Rosecrance GENTRY, born: 28 Nov 1860, married, parents: General R. Gentry and Eliza Rambo, cod "acute pulmonary congestion", informant: Ham Swift (Mountain City), buried: Wilson Cemetery, died: 13 Aug 1938, drec 17444.

Cassie M. BROCE, born: 1874, wife of Jake E. Broce, parents: Robert P. Walsh (NC) and Polly Roberts, cause of death: "lobar pneumonia", informant: W.A. Walsh (Mountain City), buried: Eggers Cemetery, died: 10 Aug 1938, record (1938) #: 17445.

Jane SPEARS, born: 15 Sep 1865 in North Carolina, widow of John Spears, parents: names unknown, cause of death: "apoplexy", buried: Shady Valley, died: 2 Aug 1938, record (1938) #: 19677.

Noah M. LUNCEFORD, age 70 years, widower of Catherine Lunceford, parents: General Lunceford (NC) and Bettie Swift (NC), cause of death: "spinal syphilis", informant: James Hopkins (Doeville), buried: Dugger Cemetery, died: 3 Sep 1938, record (1938) #: 19678.

William L. GENTRY, born: 17 Mar 1878, widower of Cora E. Gentry, parents: J.R. Gentry and Sarafina Morley, cause of death: "influenza, pulmonary tuberculosis", informant: J.M. Gentry (Butler), buried: Gentry Cemetery, died: 10 Sep 1938, record (1938) #: 19679.

Mrs. Hartilna Caldona COPLEY, born: 18 Jun 1861, widow, parents: John Rainbolt and Tilda Veniable, cause of death: "cardio nephritis", informant: D.S. McQueen (Butler), buried: Cobbs Creek, died: 16 Jul 1938, record (1938) #: 19680.

Benjamin F. HASH, age 82 years, 5 months and 28 days, born in Virginia, widower, parents: Joe Hash (VA) and (first name not stated) Hacker, cause of death: "old age", informant: Mrs. Eli Ham (Damascus), died: 24 Sep 1938, record (1938) #: 21963.

May MacDonald WAGNER, born: 1 Sep 1935, parents: Till Wagner and Goldie Tilley, cause of death: "scarlet fever, bronchial pneumonia", informant: Till Wagner (Shouns), buried: Wagner Cemetery, died: 12 Oct 1938, record (1938) #: 21964.

Alice Elizabeth STARNES, born: 14 Jun 1864, widow of Fred Starnes, parents: Hamilton Ward and Martha Holman (NC), cause of death: "brights disease", informant: Mrs. J.M. Lunceford (Butler), buried: Brown Cemetery, died: 18 Oct 1938, record (1938) #: 21965.

Joseph Thomas BRIGGS, born: 4 Nov 1882 at Ore Knob, NC, husband of Mrs. Dora L. Briggs, parents: Samuel Briggs (NC) and Martha Wilson (NC), cause of death: "lobar pneumonia", informant: Dora Briggs, buried: Davis Cem, died: 21 Oct 1938, record (1938) #: 21966.

Dean Marshall HAWKINS, born: 5 May 1912, single, parents: E.T. Hawkins and Lottie Vaught, cause of death: "died suddenly, cause unknown", informant: E.T. Hawkins (Shouns), died: 25 Oct 1938, record (1938) #: 21967.

Walter W. WORLEY, born: 22 Mar 1876 at Bluff City, TN, husband of Tullah Worley, parents: E.H. Worley (Bluff City, TN) and Martha Ella Faw (Boones Creek, TN), cause of death: "coronary disease, myocarditis", informant: Tom P. Worley (Bluff City, TN), buried: Capt Brown Cemetery, died: 26 Oct 1938.

J.B.F. BLEVINS, born: 8 May 1856, husband of Amanda Blevins, parents: William Blevins and Nancy Graybeal (NC), cause of death: "broncho pneumonia", informant: Bible record, died: 29 Oct 1938, record (1938) #: 21969.

Ray Scott GREER, born: 17 Oct 1938, parents: Roby Lee Greer (NC) and Pauline Horn (NC), cause of death: not stated, informant: Roby Lee Greer (Green Cove, VA), buried: Green Cove, died: 30 Oct 1938, record (1938) #:: 24369.

Mrs. Mollie Snyder SCOTT, age 86 years, widow of Billie Scott, parents: David Snyder and Rebecca Mitchell, cause of death: "myocarditis, bronchial pneumonia", informant: J.D. Snyder (Neva), buried: Davis Cemetery, died: 23 Nov 1938, record (1938) #: 24370.

Lynie Maxie WALKER, born: 6 Feb 1907 at Silver Hill, KY, wife of C.H. Walker, parents: B.M. Wright (VA) and Ollie Salyers, cause of death: "child birth", informant: C.H. Walker (Neva), buried: Walker Cemetery, died: 27 Nov 1938, record (1938) #: 24371.

Bobbie Ray WRIGHT, born: 13 Feb 1935, parents: Robert Wright (Elizabethton, TN) and Cora May Harper, cause of death: "lobar pneumonia", informant: Robert Wright (Shady Valley), buried: Garland Cemetery, died: 22 Nov 1938, record (1938) #: 24372.

Mrs. Margaret MAIN, born: 14 Apr 1847, widow of Calvin Main, parents: Jefferson May and Mary Arnold, cause of death: "chronic valvulor heart disease, fractured hip", informant: Vina Southerland (Trade), died: 7 Nov 1938, record (1938) #: 24373.

Mrs. Laura Elizabeth HOLCOMB, born: 26 Jul 1860 at Creston, NC, wife of M.B. Holcomb, parents: William Maxwell (Fig, NC) and Julia Parker (Creston, NC) cause of death: "chronic brights disease", informant; M.B. Holcomb (Mountain City), buried: Mountain View Cemetery, died: 12 Dec 1938, record (1938) #: 27057.

John Henry CRESS, born: 3 Feb 1870, husband of Callie Cress, parents: S.D. Cress and Eliza Pafford (Marion, VA), cause of death: "cerebral hemorrhage, hypertension", informant: J.C. Cress (Mountain City), buried: Phillippi Cemetery, died: 18 dec 1938, record (1938) #: 27058.

Jacob Smith VAUGHT, born; 12 Sep 1857, husband of Calliona Vaught, parents: Joseph L. Vaught and Louisa Mast, cause of death: "chronic myocarditis", buried: Vaught Cemetery, died: 29 Dec 1938, record (1938) #: 27059.

Landon Henry MCELYEA, born: 22 Apr 1861, husband of Janette McElyea, parents: George W. McElyea and (first name not stated) Morefield, cause of death: "hit by car, fractured skull", informant: Mrs. Janette McElyea (Mountain City), buried: Shingletown Cemetery, died: 27 Dec 1938, record (1938) #: 28811.

Matilda FLETCHER, born: 5 May 1871, wife of William Fletcher, parents: William O'Neil and mother's name unknown, cause of death: "chronic nephritis", informant: Dillie Fletcher (Johnson City, TN), died: 10 Jul 1938, record (1938) #: 28812.

Sarah Catherine BUNTING, born: 8 Jun 1869, wife of U.S. Bunting, parents: Martin Greenwell (Wilkes Co. NC) and Rebecca Vines (Watauga Co. NC) cause of death: "carcinoma of stomach", informant: Spencer Bunting (Butler), buried: Elk River, died: 10 Jul 1938, record (1938) #: 28813.

Ottie Creed GREGG, born: 6 Dec 1922, parents: J. Clyde Gregg and Ethel Lewis (NC), cause of death: "accidentally shot with double barrel gun by another boy", buried: Dugger Cemetery, died: 8 Sep 1938, record (1938) #: 29387.

Mary L. GREER, age 80 years, born in North Carolina, wife of Wilburn Greer, parents: Maion Prather (NC) and mother's name not stated, cause of death: "chronic brights disease", died: 6 Jan 1939, record (1939) #: 950.

Hattie Ruth GREER, born: 5 Jan 1923, parents: father's name not known and Nettie Greer, cause of death: "chronic valvulor heart disease", informant: John F. Greer (Laurel Bloomery), buried: Taylor Valley, died: 13 Jan 1939, record (1939) #: 951.

Mrs. Nancy Anna Ingram BUTLER, born: 28 Dec 1848 at Todd, NC, widow of R.H. Butler, parents: John Ingram (Sands, NC) and Martha Ray (Todd, NC), cause of death: "hypostatic pneumonia, fractured hip", informant: Dr. J.C. Butler, died: 4 Jan 1939, record (1939) #: 952.

Wayne Ripley GENTRY, born: 10 Dec 1938, parents: J.M. Gentry and Aitha Ruterford, cause of death: "lobar pneumonia", informant: J.M. Gentry (Shady Valley), buried: Gentry Cemetery, died: 26 Jan 1939, record (1939) #: 953.

John LEWIS, born: 22 Jan 1875 at Hamilton, VA, husband of Clyda Mae Lewis, Spanish American War veteran, parents: Sam Lewis (Leesburg, VA) and Sarah Bell (Leesburg, VA), cause of death: "heart dropsy", buried: Hall Cemetery, died: 13 Jan 1939, record (1939) #: 954.

Hazel Florence LOWE, born: 7 May 1935, parents: Dewey Lowe and Annie Crosswhite, cause of death: "measles, broncho pneumonia", died: 30 Jan 1939, record (1939) #: 955.

William Martin WARREN, born: 14 Sep 1866, husband of Mrs. Martha Warren, parents: Cornelius Warren (Taylorsville, NC) and Elizabeth Thomas, cause of death: "apoplexy", informant: Martha Warren (Trade), buried: Zionville Cemetery, died: 4 Jan 1939, record (1939) #: 956.

William GREER, born: 1862 in North Carolina, widower of Mary Greer, parents: Andrew Greer (NC) and (first name not stated) Lorance (NC), cause of death: "cardiac hypertrophy", informant: John Greer (Mountain City), died: 16 Feb 1939, record (1939) #: 3063.

Sarah M. FRITTS, born: 22 Jun 1863, widow, parents: John Pierce and (first name not stated) Greer, cause of death: "encephatitis", informant: Ted Fritts (Laurel), died: 24 Jan 1939, record (1939) #: 3064.

Jemima Reece WARREN, born: 17 Mar 1865, wife of H.K. Warren, parents: Jacob Reece and Eliza Oliver (NC), cause of death: "influenza, broncho pneumonia", informant: H.K. Warren (Shouns), buried: Lewis Cemetery, died: 5 Feb 1939, record (1939) #: 3065.

Holly TUCKER, born: 8 Apr 1903, wife of James Tucker, parents: Alex Woodard and (first name not stated) Fluks, cause of death: "tuberculosis", informant: James Tucker (Meadow View, NC), buried: Wright Cemetery, died: 8 Feb 1939, record (1939) #: 3066.

Robert Mason GENTRY, born: 16 Dec 1938, parents: Col Lillard Gentry and Etoila Lowe, cause of death: "influenza, bronchial pneumonia", informant: Col Lillard Gentry, buried: Jack Brookshire Cemetery, died: 3 Feb 1939, record (1939) #: 3067.

Phylis Gean HARPER, born: 17 Dec 1938, parents: John Harper and Viola Gentry, cause of death: "acute colitis", buried: Wilson Cemetery, died: 9 Feb 1939, record (1939) #: 3068.

Cynthia Caroline JOHNSON, born: 13 Sep 1857 at
Toliver, NC, widow of William Dixon Johnson, parents:
Marshall Galloway (NC) and Sallie Cook (Boone, NC),
cause of death: "paralysis, apoplexy", informant: W.M.
Johnson, buried: Phillippi Cemetery, died: 14 Mar
1939, record (1939) #: 5521.
Triphanie MILLS, born: 6 Jul 1837 at Floyd Co, VA,
(age 101), widow of Anderson Mills, parents: John
Eggers (West VA), and Lucy Duncan, cause of death:
"myocarditis", informant: Mary Susan Miller, buried:
Wilson Cemetery, died: 27 Mar 1939, record (1939) #:
5522.
Hobert Eugene MCCOY, born: 2 Jul 1935, parents: Hobert
McCoy (Knox Co., TN) and Crittie May Kear (Sevier Co,
TN), cause of death: "measles, bronchial pneumonia",
informant: Crittie May Wishon, buried: Mountain View
Cemetery, died: 24 Feb 1939, record (1939) #: 5523.
Bessie ROBERTS, age: approximately 55 years, widow of
W.H. Roberts, parents: George Manuel (NC) and (first
name not stated) Hamby (NC), cause of death:
"carcinoma right breast", informant: R.E. Roberts
(Shady Valley), buried: Kenney Blevins Cemetery, died:
8 Mar 1939, record (1939) #: 5524.
John Norman HUTCHINSON, born: 11 Sep 1930, parents:
Fred Hutchinson and (first name not stated) Watson,
cause of death: "lobar pneumonia", informant: Fred
Hutchinson (Shady Valley), buried: Kenney Blevins
Cemetery, died: 14 Mar 1939, record (1939) #: 5525.
Maggie Bell STOUT, born: 14 Feb 1873, wife of Elbert
E. Stout, parents: Alexander Ward and Caroline Shull
(NC), cause of death: "paralysis caused by apoplexia",
informant: E.E. Stout (Neva), buried: Wards Cemetery,
died: 27 Mar 1939, record (1939) #: 5526.
Lucinda GARLAND, born: 20 Nov 1870, widow of William
Hector Garland, parents: John Walker and Polly
Campbell, cause of death: "cancer of liver",
informant: John Garland (Doeville), buried: Rankin
Cemetery, died: 4 Mar 1939, record (1939) #: 5527.
Jonathan Riley NORRIS, born: 1 Feb 1855 in North
Carolina, husband of Susan Robinson, parents: Franklin
Norris (NC) and Mrs. Green, cause of death: "acute
nephritis", informant: H.H. Norris (Doeville), died:
24 Mar 1939, record (1939) #: 5528.
Filmore MORELAND, born: Apr 1861, widower of Nancy
Moreland, parents: John MOreland and mother's name not
stated, cause of death: "unknown", buried: Moreland
Cemetery, Doeville, died: 3 Feb 1939, record (1939) #:
5529.

J.D. MORELAND, Jr., born: 17 Oct 1938, parents: Danford Moreland and Tiny Fritts, cause of death: not stated, died: Jan ? 1939, buried: 4 Feb 1939, record (1939) #: 5530.

Eugene Lindsey BLEVINS, born: 18 Aug 1918, single, parents: George Blevins and Maggie L. Handy (NC), cause of death: "lobar pneumonia", informant: George Blevins (Crandell), buried: Blevins Cemetery, died: 25 Mar 1939, record (1939) #: 5531.

Mrs. Lossie KING, born: 2 Apr 1890, wife of Jim King, parents: John South (NC) and mother's name unknown, cause of death: "chronic valvulor heart disease", informant: C.W. King (Mountain City), buried: Thomas Cemetery, died: 4 Apr 1939, record (1939) #: 8123.

David GREER, born: 20 Oct 1861, husband of Sarah Greer, parents: Alex Greer (NC) and Nannie Osborne (NC), cause of death: "chronic myocarditis, broncho pneumonia", informant: J.R. Williams (Shouns), buried: Potter Cemetery, died: 24 Apr 1939, record (1939) #: 8124.

John Grant LEWIS, born: 7 May 1937, parents: Dave C. Lewis and (first name not stated) Blevins, cause of death: not stated, informant: D.C. Lewis (Shady Valley), buried: Kenney Blevins Cemetery, died: 24 Apr 1939, record (1939) #: 8125.

Jettie FORRESTER, born: 5 Mar 1916, single, parents: Asa Forrester and Mary Hammons, cause of death: "pulmonary tuberculosis, influenza, broncho pneumonia", buried: Hammons Cemetery, died: 24 Mar 1939, record (1939) #: 8126.

Cora WOODARD, born about 1888 at Hemlock, NC, wife of Isaac Woodard, parents: Sam Jones (Hemlock, NC) and (first name unknown) Roark (Hemlock, NC), cause of death: "chronic brights disease", informant: Isaac Woodard (Shouns), buried: Woodard Cemetery, died: 29 Jun 1939, record (1939) #: 8127.

Bobbie Harold Butler JOHNSON, born: 4 Feb 1938, parents: Denver Johnson and Ruth Dunn, cause of death: "flue followed by broncho pneumonia", informant: Denver Johnson (Shouns), buried: Dunn Cemetery, died: 30 Jan 1939, record (1939) #: 8128,

Mrs. Mary A. ROBINSON, born: 14 Jun 1886, wife of W.H. Robinson, parents: Thomas J. Stout and Callie Wagner, cause of death: "acute nephritis, myocarditis, influenza", informant: W.H. Robinson (Doeville), buried: Rambo Cemetery, died: 25 Mar 1939, record (1939) #: 8129.

Janette Dean MCELYEA, born: 10 Jul 1872, widow of L.H. McElyea, parents: Alvin Eastridge and (first name not stated) Eastridge, cause of death: "influenza, bronchial pneumonia", informant: Mrs. Elizabeth McElyea (Mountain City), buried: Shingletown Cemetery, died: 28 Mar 1939, record (1939) #: 10554.

Calvin ELLER, born: 18 Jul 1875 at Ashe Co. NC, husband of Myrtle Eller, parents: John Eller (Ashe Co. NC) and Caty Eldrith (NC), cause of death: "chronic brights disease", informant: Myrtle Eller (Mountain City), died: 12 May 1939, record (1939) #: 10555.

Mrs. Nellie Bryan Adams MILLER, born: 14 Mar 1909, wife of J.A. Miller, parents: R.S. Adams and Lillie Jenkins, cause of death: "acute nephritis, circulatory collapse", informant: J.A. Miller (Mountain City), buried: Mountain View Cemetery, died: 16 May 1939, record (1939) #: 10556.

Barbara Sue TESTER, born: 26 Apr 1939, parents: Clyde Tester and Opal Garland, cause of death: illegible, informant: Clyde Tester (Neva), buried: Tester Cemetery, died: 16 May 1939, record (1939) #: 10557.

Billy Odell BRINKLEY, parents: Odell Brinkley and Artie Rosetta Lewis (NC), buried: Shady Valley, born/died: 6 May 1939, record (1939) #: 10558.

Joe A. GENTRY, born: 18 Oct 1865, husband of Martha Gentry, parents: David Gentry and Elizabeth Greer, cause of death: "cerebral hemorrhage, lobar pneumonia", informant: Miss Mary Gentry (Laurel Bloomery), buried: Acre Field Cemetery, died: 3 May 1939, record (1939) #: 12772.

Infant TRIVETT, male, parents: John Trivett and Roanna Johnson, cause of death: "enlarged liver", informant: John Trivett (Shouns), buried: Trivett Cemetery, born/died: 11 Jun 1939, record (1939) #: 12773.

Billie ADAMS, born: 26 Jun 1862, married, parents: Billie Adams and Susie Anne Crosswhite, cause of death: "bronchial pneumonia, chronic myocardits", informant: Martha Adams (Doeville), died: 25 May 1939, record (1939) #: 12774.

Edward Glenn OWENS, born: 23 Sep 1937, parents: Edward Owens and Eula Church, cause of death: "influenza, bronchial pneumonia", buried: Shoun Cemetery, died: 25 Apr 1939, record (1939) #: 12775.

Lizzie J. EGGERS, born: 17 May 1859 at Wilkes Co. NC, widow of James Eggers, parents: Jonathan Phillips (Wilkes Co. NC) and Margaret Brookshire (Wilkes Co. NC), cause of death: "influenza, broncho pneumonia", informant: Mrs. Laura Potter (Trade), buried: Potter Cemetery, died: 19 Mar 1939, record (1939) #: 12776.

James CARDWELL, born: 16 Apr 1868, husband of Mary Cardwell, parents: Harrison Cardwell and (first name not stated) Minton, cause of death: "organic heart disease", informant: Mary Cardwell (Butler), buried: Midway Cemetery, died: 9 May 1939, record (1939) #: 12777.

Arvil PROFFITT, Jr., born: 15 Jan 1939, parents: Arvil Proffitt and Virgia Smith (VA), cause of death: "not stated, found dead in bed", buried: Proffitt Cemetery, died: 29 Jan 1939, record (1939) #: 12778.

Idoma HAGAMAN, female, born: 2 Feb 1939, parents: Stansberry Hagaman and Flora Hagaman, cause of death: "spinal bifida", informant: Flora Hagaman (Butler), died: 25 May 1939, record (1939) #: 12779.

Phyllis Gene MOORE, born: 22 Sep 1938, parents: Walter Moore and Edith Miller, cause of death: "circulatory failure", informant: Walter Moore (Shady Valley), buried: Wood Cemetery, died: 8 Jan 1939, record (1939) #: 12780.

Evalee PARSONS, born: 12 May 1938, parents: Bill K. Parsons and Prudia Phillips, cause of death: "acute gastr entiro colitis", informant: Bill K. Parsons (Mountain City), buried: Donnelly Cemetery, died: 17 Jul 1939, record (1939) #: 15083.

Donald Eugene NORRIS, parents: David Smith Norris and Gladys Pauline Maxwell, cause of death: not stated, buried: Acre Field Cemetery, born/died: 27 Jul 1939, record (1939) #: 15084.

Mrs. Annie DURHAM, born: 14 Feb 1878 in North Carolina, resident of Johnson City, TN, widow of James Durham, parents: don't know father's name and Margaret Goines (NC), cause of death: "apoplexy", informant: Robert Goines (Bristol, TN), buried: Citizens Cemetery, died: 4 Jul 1939, record (1939) #: 15085.

Hattie Thomas CALLOWAY, age 54 years, born at Creston, NC, widow of Shade Calloway, parents: "don't know", cause of death: "acute colitis", died: 30 Jun, 1939, record (1939) #: 15086.

Miss Martha DINKEN, age: estimated 99 years, born in North Carolina, parents: unknown, cause of death: "chronic brights disease", county home resident, buried: Lefler Cemetery, died: 14 Jul 1939, record (1939) #: 15087.

Chalmer MAY, born: 7 Jul 1939, parents: Stacy May and Carrie Woodard, cause of death: "atalectosis of lungs", informant: Mrs. (Will) Bonnie May (Shouns), buried: May Cemetery, died: 8 Jul 1939, record (1939) #: 15088.

Margaret MCQUEEN, born: 29 Apr 1939, parents: Earl McQueen and Edrie Blevins, cause of death: "acute colitis", informant: Earl McQueen (Shady Valley), buried: Garland Cemetery, died: 24 Jul 1939, record (1939) #: 15089.

Robert H. BLANKENBECKLER, born: 17 Oct 1864, husband of Mrs. Ollie Blankenbeckler, parents: Marion Blankenbeckler (Smythe Co, VA) and Margaret Robinson (Smythe Co, VA), cause of death: "valvulor heart disease", buried: Phillippi Cemetery, died: 5 Aug 1939, record (1939) #: 17417.

Jordan WALLACE, born: 6 Jan 1865, husband of Mrs. Lola Wallace, parents: Alex Wallace and Nancy Cornett, cause of death: "intestinal influenza, broncho pneumonia", informant: Mrs. Lola Wallace (Trade), buried: Wallace Cemetery, died: 6 Aug 1939, record (1939) #: 17418.

Casper C. STANTON, born: 7 Sep 1866, married, parents: Franklin B. Stanton (NC) and Polly Dugger, cause of death: "apoplexy", informant: wife, buried: Stanton Cemetery Butler, died: 21 Aug 1939, record (1939) #: 17419.

George W. LEWIS, born: 30 Aug 1870 in Carter Co. TN, married, parents: Lawson Lewis (Carter Co, TN) and Isabell Campbell (Carter Co, TN), cause of death: "poison kidneys, chronic nephritis", informant: Emma Lewis (Butler), died: 24 Jun 1939, record (1939) #: 17420.

Betty Lu SHELTON, born: 14 Apr 1937, parents: father unknown and Bessie Shelton, cause of death: not stated, informant: Bessie Shelton (Shouns), buried: Hampton, died: 12 Sep 1939, record (1939) #: 19635.

Bynum E. NICHOLS, born: 31 Dec 1898, husband of Frankie Brown Nichols, parents: W.A. Nichols (Hemlock, NC) and Lula Winebarger (Ashland, NC), cause of death: "found dead on his farm with wultiple cut wounds", informant: Francis Nichols (Mountain City), buried: Phillippi Cemetery, died: 24 Sep 1939, record (1939) #: 19636.

Mary L. WAGNER, Negro, parents: Till Wagner and Goldia Mock, cause of death: "premature", informant: Till Wagner (Shouns), buried: Wagner Cemetery, born/died: 24 Aug 1939, record (1939) #: 19637.

Wilma Chestialee GILLEY, born: 19 May 1939, parents: Elmer Haggia Gilley and Viola Campbell, cause of death: not stated, informant: Elmer Haggia Gilley (Mountain City), buried: Buck Wright Cemetery, died: 28 May 1939, record (1939) #: 19638.

Elva Catherine BLACKBURN, born: 7 Feb 1881, wife of
H.J. Blackburn, parents: Ambrose Garland and Lucinda
Blevins, cause of death: "carcinoma of left breast,
liver and lungs", informant: E.E. Garland (Mountain
City), buried: Gentry Cemetery, died: 9 Aug 1939,
record (1939) #: 19639.

Louise MULLINS, born: 14 Apr 1939, parents: Ronda
Mullins and Madora Kite, cause of death: "unknown",
informant: Ronda Mullins (Doeville), buried: Mullins
Cemetery, died: 14 Apr 1939, record (1939) #: 21824.

Mrs. Sarah Jane PRICE, born: 8 Feb 1859, widow of John
Price, parents: John R. Morefield and Matilda Minnick
(Washington Co. VA), cause of death: "myocarditis,
chronic pulmonary congestion", informant: Mrs. Ada
Gentry (Mountain City), buried: Morefield Cemetery,
died: 22 Nov 1939, record (1939) #: 24090.

John Wesley WILSON, Negro, born: 5 Aug 1870 at
Washington Co. VA, widower of Emma Carrigan, parents:
Isaac Lethcoe (Washington Co. VA) and Linda Wilson
(Washington Co, VA), cause of death: "lobar
pneumonia", informant: A.A. Lethcoe (Glace Springs,
VA), buried: Holy Hill Cemetery, died: 25 Nov 1939,
record (1939) #: 24091.

Robert HOWARD, born: Nov 1879, husband of Mrs. Susan
Smith Howard, parents: George W. Howard and Martitia
Payne, cause of death: "cerebral hemorrhage,
hypertension", informant: Luther Howard (Shouns),
buried: Martin Cemetery, died: 10 Nov 1939, record
(1939) #: 24092.

Mrs. Mollie May OSBORNE, born: 17 Apr 1884, widow of
Gaston Osborne, parents: Tobe May and Mahalia Jackson,
cause of death: "chronic myocarditis, bronchial
pneumonia", informant: Firman Osborne (Shouns),
buried: McEwen Cemetery, died: 14 Nov 1939, record
(1939) #: 24093.

Christopher Columbus TESTER, born: 10 Jul 1869,
husband of Mrs. Martha Jackson Tester, parents: James
Tester and mother's name not recorded, cause of death:
"apoplexia, organic heart disease", informant: Jake
Tester (Shouns), buried: Tester Cemetery, died: 17 Nov
1939, record (1939) #: 24094.

Jessie Calvin CHURCH, born: 18 Aug 1886, widower of
Susie Smith Church, parents: Jessie C. Church (Wilkes
Co, NC) and Martha Watson (Wilkes Co. NC), cause of
death: "organic heart disease", informant: Eula Mae
Owens (daughter), buried: Shouns Cemetery, died: 31
Oct 1939, record (1939) #: 24095.

John Buckman HICKS, born: about 1851, widower of Martha Jane Hicks, parents: John Hicks and mother's name unknown, cause of death: "chronic brights disease", informant: Bill Hicks, buried: Buck Wright Cemetery, died: 30 Oct 1939, record (1939) #: 24096.

Joe Alexander GILBERT, born: 28 Apr 1878, husband of Mrs. Laura Fritts Gilbert, parents: Ranson L. Gilbert and Sarah McQueen, cause of death: "pulmonary congestion, associated asthma", informant: N.A. Pennington (Laurel Bloomery), buried: Taylors Valley, died: 1 Dec 1939, record (1939) #: 26579.

Mrs. Margaret Shoun DONNELLY, born: 19 Dec 1848, widow of Harrison C. Donnelly, parents: Henderson Shoun and Sarah Baker, cause of death: "angina pectoris", informant: Mrs. Vic Wills (Shouns), buried: Shouns Church Cem, died: 3 Dec 1939, record (1939) #: 26580.

Hattie FORRESTER, born: 2 Oct 1913, single, parents: Asa Forrester and May Hammons, cause of death: "tuberculosis pulmonary", informant: B.C. Hammons (Shouns), buried: Shouns Cemetery, died: 16 Dec 1939, record (1939) #: 26581.

Shirley Luna MCQUEEN, born: 21 Sep 1939, parents: T.K. McQueen and Mary Ann Cook (Mitchell, NC), cause of death: "pyloric stenosis", informant: T.K. McQueen (Butler), buried: McQueen Cemetery, died: 31 Oct 1939, record (1939) #: 26582.

Bert Elmer BROOKSHIRE, born: 3 Apr 1903, husband of Irene Davis, parents: Noah Brookshire and Laura Spear, cause of death: "pulmonary tuberculosis", informant: Mrs. Irene Brookshire, buried: Morley Cemetery, died: 29 Nov 1939, record (1939) #: 26583.

Mrs. Sallie CROSSWHITE, born: 22 Aug 1872 at Ashe Co. NC, widow of William T. Crosswhite, parents: John Jones (NC) and (first name not stated) Ashland (NC), cause of death: "pulmonary edima", informant: Clyde Crosswhite (Shady Valley), buried: Gentry Cemetery, died: 7 Dec 1939, record (1939) #: 26584.

Regiema PHILLIPS, born: 14 Dec 1939, parents: Arthur James Phillips and Viola Mae Phillips (before marriage), cause of death: "not stated, found dead in bed", informant: Arthur J. Phillips (Shady Valley), buried: Gentry Cemetery, died: 16 Dec 1939, record (1939) #: 26585.

George Wesley BROWN, born: 26 May 1860 at Wilkes Co, NC, husband of Mrs. Mary Mae Brown, parents: Ezekiel Brown (KY) and Susie Brown (Wilkes Co. NC), cause of death: "chronic brights disease", informant: A.N. Brown (Zionville, NC) buried: Zionville, NC, died: 5 Dec 1939, record (1939) #: 26586.

Rose Nell BUNTON, born: 14 Feb 1935, parents: Fawn Bunton and Sallie Cable, cause of death: "probably pneumonia", informant: Fawn Bunton (Butler), buried: Bunton Cemetery, died: 15 Feb 1939, record (1939) #: 26587.

Joseph Daniel GRINDSTAFF, born: 20 Jun 1864, husband of Nancy C. Grindstaff, parents: Jacob F. Grindstaff and Lucrissa E. Reece, cause of death: "organic heart disease", informant: Mrs. J.D. Grindstaff (Butler), buried: Grindstaff Cemetery, died: 21 Feb 1939, record (1939) #: 26588.

Martha Lorana Stout GRINDSTAFF, born: 14 Aug 1872, wife of I.S. Grindstaff, parents: T.J. Stout and Susan Grindstaff, cause of death: "lobar pneumonia", informant: C.M. Grindstaff (Butler), buried: Cable Cemetery, died: 29 Nov 1939, record (1939) #: 28255.

Bruce Lee PAYNE, born: 28 Mar 1921, single, parents: M.V. Payne and Sallie Payne, cause of death: "drowned swimming", informant: Glen Snyder (Butler), buried: Payne Cemetery, died: 10 Sep 1939, record (1939) #: 28256.

Rosevelt WALLACE, Jr., born: 7 Dec 1939, parents: Rosevelt Wallace, Sr., and Elizabeth B. Robinson, cause of death: "premature birth", informant: Rosevelt Wallace (Shady Valley), buried: Wallace Cemetery, died: 9 Dec 1939, record (1939) #: 28568.

Nelson GREGG, born: 18 May 1860 in Carter Co. TN, husband of Sarah Ellen Gregg, parents: James Gregg (Carter Co. TN) and Loginie Gregg (NC), cause of death: not stated, informant: Sarah Ellen Gregg (Butler), buried: Crosswhite Cemetery, died: 15 Nov 1939, record (1939) #: 28569.

Selma Florentine CURTIS, born: 2 Nov 1861 at Greene Co. TN, widow, parents: Paul G. Roseblott (Germany) and Emma Malone (Greene Co. TN), cause of death: "probably gastric carcinoma", informant: Mrs. D.R. Shearer (Johnson City, TN), buried: Pierce Cemetery, died: 12 Dec 1939, record (1939) #: 28570.

Coonrod Burt CABLE, born: 22 Jan 1852, widower, parents: Coonrod Burt Cable and Jane Whitehead (Carter Co. TN), cause of death: "bronchial pneumonia", informant: T.L. Cable (Butler), buried: Dugger Cemetery, died: 16 Nov 1939, record (1939) #: 28571.

Enoch PILK, born: 17 Jul 1864 in North Carolina, husband of Clemantine Pilk, parents: Samuel Pilk (NC) and Lena Lunsford, cause of death: "cardio nephritis", informant: Gurnie Turbiefield (Butler), buried: Whitehead Cemetery, died: 30 Jan 1940, record (1940) #: 1156.

Sarah Bell BAKER, born: 28 Aug 1878, single, parents: Thomas Alexander Baker and Lorie Bunton, cause of death: "lobar pneumonia", informant: V.K. Wagner (Johnson City, TN), buried: Baker Cemetery, died: 28 Jan 1940, record (1940) #: 1157.

James Oscar REECE, born: 15 Jan 1940, parents: John Kermit REECE and Myrtle Eldrith, cause of death: "broncho pneumonia", informant: Kermit Reece (Shouns), buried: Reece Cemetery, died: 3 Feb 1940, record (1940) #: 3721.

Mrs. Julia Alice DICKENS, born: 19 Mar 1869 at Washington Co., TN, widow of John Dickens, parents: father's name unknown and Sarah Huskins, cause of death: "circulatory collapse", informant: Mrs. Cora Snyder, buried: Wills Cemetery, died: 22 Feb 1940, record (1940) #: 3722.

Marcus Edward MILLER, born: 23 May 1932, parents: James Austin Miller (Sullivan Co., TN) and Nellie Bryan Adams, cause of death: "rheumatic fever, valvulor heart disease", buried: Mountain View Cemetery, died: 25 Feb 1940, record (1940) #: 3723.

Mary R. SNYDER, born: 14 May 1861, widow of Alexander M. Snyder, parents: Amos Rash (Watauga Co. NC) and Rebecca Coleman (Watauga Co. NC), cause of death: "influenza, broncho pneumonia", informant: Mrs. T.H. Cayles, buried: Mountain View Cemetery, died: 14 Jan 1940, record (1940) #: 3724.

James Wade HAMPTON, born: 8 May 1896, husband of Mrs. Ada Hampton, parents: Jim Hampton and Victoria Atkins (NC), cause of death: "flue followed by broncho pneumonia fever", informant: Mrs. Ada Hampton (Shouns), buried: Jones Cemetery, died: 23 Feb 1940, record (1940) #: 3725.

Benjamin Franklin LEFFMAN, born: 15 Nov 1872 at Wilkes Co. NC, husband of Titia Gentry, parents: John Leffman (Wilkes Co. NC) and Eliza Carter (Wilkes Co. NC), cause of death: "chronic myocarditis, valvulor heart disease", informant: Ferd Gentry (Laurel Bloomery), buried: Taylor Valley Cemetery, died: 8 Jan 1940, record (1940) #: 1149.

John Allen SEVERT, born: 25 Aug 1889 at Ashe Co., NC, husband of Minnie M. Severt, parents: Edmond Severt (NC) and (first name not stated) Mast (NC), cause of death: "chest cold, arterio sclerosis, angina pectoris", informant: Mrs. John Severt (Damascus, VA), buried: Sutherland Cemetery, died: 19 Jan 1940, record (1940) #: 1150.

William Stacy WILSON, born: 31 Dec 1871, husband of
Mrs. Emma Wilson, parents: Joseph Wilson and Elizabeth
Jones (Watauga Co. NC), cause of death: "myocarditis,
pneumonia", informant: O.H. Wilson (Mountain City),
buried: Dotson Cemetery, died: 1 Jan 1940, record
(1940) #: 1151.

Mrs. Bettie Virginia KENT, born: 16 Oct 1868 at Emory
Henry College, VA, wife of J.C. Kent, parents: James
R. Lloyd (Washington Co. VA) and Charlotte Johnson
(Johnson City, TN), cause of death: "angina pectoris",
informant: J.C. Kent (Glade Springs, VA), died: 8 Jan
1940, record (1940) #: 1152.

Mrs. Sarah Fritts HECK, born: 28 Dec 1869, wife of
Wiley Thomas Heck, parents: David Marion Fritts and
Martha Wooten (Washington Co, VA), cause of death:
"chronic brights disease", informant: W.T. Heck,
buried: Mountain View Cemetery, died: 8 Jan 1940,
record (1940) #: 1153.

Lillie Mabra GENTRY, born: 4 Aug 1880, wife of Charles
S. Gentry, parents: W.T. Heaberlin and Elizabeth
Ritter (Mississippi), cause of death: "acute cardiac
....(illegible)", informant: Mrs. Marcus McQueen
(Shady Valley), buried: McQueen Cemetery, died: 29 Jan
1940, record (1940) #: 1154.

Ronda CABLE, female, born: 11 Jan 1858, widow,
parents: Hash Bowman and Martha Osborn (NC), cause of
death: not recorded, informant: James P. Cable (son),
buried: Cable Cemetery, died: 23 Jan 1940, record
(1940) #: 1155.

Walter Preston PIERSON, born: 19 Nov 1902 in
Washington Co., VA, husband of Ellen Church, parents:
Ollie Pierson (Washington Co. VA) and Mollie Jane
Mitchell (NC), cause of death: "lobar pneumonia",
informant: Earl Perkins (Shouns), buried: Tester
Cemetery, died: 1 Feb 1940, record (1940) #: 3726.

Tommie George BROWN, born: 24 Sep 1939, parents: Dewey
Brown and Addie Moore (Sullivan Co. TN), cause of
death: "broncho pneumonia", informant: Dewey Brown
(Neva), buried: Chatman, Bristol, died: 8 Feb 1940,
record (1940) #: 3727.

Sarafina TESTER, born: 7 Nov 1861, widow of Andrew J.
Tester, parents: Andy John Forrester and Phoebe
Proffitt, cause of death: "lagrippe", informant: R.S.
Tester (Shouns), buried: Green Cemetery, died: 21 Feb
1940, record (1940) #: 3728.

William Loyd DUGGER, born: 18 Aug 1939, parents:
father's name unknown and Rader Dugger, cause of
death: illegible, informant: Rader Dugger, buried:
Baker Cem, died: 11 Jan 1940, record (1940) #: 3729.

Doris Marie SHEPHERD, born: 26 Jan 1940, parents: Wiley Shepherd and Ocie Gentry, cause of death: "congenital circulatory condition", buried: Heaberlin Cemetery, Shady Valley, died: 11 Feb 1940, record (1940) #: 3730.

Sallie Manda BLEVINS, born: 6 Oct 1858, widow of J.B.F. Blevins, parents: unknown, cause of death: "congestive heart disease, myocarditis", informant: Roy Blevins (Shady Valley), buried: Blevins Cemetery, died: 24 Jan 1940, record (1940) #: 3731.

Etta STANBERRY, born: 7 Mar 1883, widow, parents: John Burton and Celia Cable, cause of death: "tumor of the stomach", informant: R.C. Stanberry (Butler), buried: Bunton Cemetery, died: 17 Mar 1940, record (1940) #: 6733.

Elizabeth SHUMATE, age approximately 73 years, widow of Lee Shumate, parents: unknown, cause of death: "influenza, bronchial pneumonia, myocarditis", informant: Scott Rupard (Laurel Bloomery), buried: family cemetery, died: 23 Apr 1940, record (1940) #: 9449.

Sophonia WARD, born: 30 Oct 1855, widow of Reeves Ward, parents: William A. Williams and Delilah Sullivan, cause of death: "carcinoma of stomach", informant: Clyde Williams (Mountain City), buried: Mountain View Cemetery, died: 4 Apr 1940, record (1940) #: 9450.

Mrs. Elizabeth Norris LOWE, born: 25 Oct 1852 at Watauga Co. NC, widow of Abram R. Lowe, parents: Franklin Norris (Watauga Co. NC) and Sallie Green (Watauga Co. NC), cause of death: "cold, lagrippe", informant: R.S. Lowe (Mountain City), buried: Lowe-Campbell Cemetery, died: 16 Apr 1940, record (1940) #: 9451.

James PRICE, born: 13 Mar 1859, reared by Price family, husband of Rosa Price, parents: Taylor Hall and Martha Arnold, cause of death: "apoplexy", buried: Price Cem, died: 12 Mar 1940, record (1940) #: 9452.

Mrs. Alice Wagner WARD, born: 7 May 1856, wife of John F. Ward, parent: Dan Wagner and Nancy Hardin (Ashe Co. NC), cause of death: "chronic myocarditis", informant: Mrs. Roby Wills (Shouns), buried: Wagner Cemetery, died: 15 Mar 1940, record (1940) #: 9453.

David E. HENSON, born: 8 Jan 1859 at Watauga Co. NC, widower of Elizabeth Fenner Henson, parents: Jordan Henson (Watauga Co. NC) and Katie Emaline Stout, cause of death: "chronic myocarditis, terminal pulmonary congestion", buried: Wilson Cemetery, died: 31 Jan 1940, record (1940) #: 9454.

Carrie May WILLIAMS, born: 24 May 1903, divorced from
Clyde Williams, parents: Jake L. May and Della
Cornett, cause of death: "cancer womb", informant:
Lizzie Lipfird (Shouns), buried: Hampton Cemetery,
Shouns, died: 23 Apr 1940, record (1940) #: 9455.

Tilman F. BROWN, born: 16 Nov 1877, husband of Flossie
A. Brown, parents: M.F. Brown (NC) and (first name not
stated) Hodge, cause of death: "chronic valvulor heart
disease", informant: Dana Simcox (Shouns), buried:
Brown Cemetery, died: 2 Mar 1940, record (1940) #:
9456.

Haskel Clay CURD, born: 9 Jul 1939, parents: Dan Curd
and Lula Howard, cause of death: "broncho pneumonia,
respiratory infection", informant: Dan Curd (Shouns),
died: 10 Mar 1940, record (1940) #: 9457.

Margaret Janice MARTIN, born: 5 Mar 1940, parents:
Russell Martin (McDowell, W. VA) and Mary M. Martin
cause of death: "pneumonia", informant: Russell T.
Martin (Shouns), buried: Martin Cemetery, died: 17 Mar
1940, record (1940) #: 9458.

Rosa MAUK, born: 21 Mar 1871, wife of John K. Mauk,
parents: Joe Snyder and Catherine Cress, cause of
death: "lobar pneumonia", informant: Mrs. Nannie Crowe
(205 Wilson Ave, Johnson City, TN), died: 16 Mar 1940,
record (1940) #: 9459.

Steve LOWE, born: 27 Sep 1899, single, parents: Will
Lowe (Carter Co. TN) and Minerva Holder, cause of
death: "tuberculosis", informant: Ruby Lowe (Butler),
buried: Lowe Cemetery, died: 20 Apr 1940, record
(1940) #: 9460.

Roy FRITTS, born: 15 May 1883, husband of Mrs. Stella
Fritts, parents: Fred Fritts and mother's name
unknown, cause of death: "probably coronary
thrombosis", informant: R.D. Fritts (Doeville),
buried: Fletcher Cemetery, died: 10 Mar 1940, record
(1940) #: 9461.

Malissie Cathrene ROBINSON, born: 12 Sep 1886 at
Carter Co. TN, wife of Elbert Robinson, parents: John
Elliott and Pollie Blevins (Carter Co. TN), cause of
death: "lobar pneumonia", informant: Mrs. Lottie
Norris (Doeville), buried: family cemetery, died: 14
Mar 1940, record (1940) #: 9462.

Mrs. Rebecca Wilson WALLACE, born: 22 Jun 1854 at
Watauga Co. NC, wife of J.H. Wallace, parents: William
Wilson and Martha Main (Watauga Co. NC), cause of
death: "influenza, broncho pneumonia", informant: D.M.
Wilson (brother), buried: Wallace Cemetery (Trade),
died: 12 Apr 1940, record (1940) #: 9463.

Clarice Louisie SNYDER, born: 13 Jul 1866 at Watauga
Co. NC, wife of W.R. Snyder, parents: William Simpson
Wallace and Susan Cornett (Watauga Co. NC), cause of
death: "cerebral hemorrhage", buried: Snyder Cemetery
(Trade), died: 29 Apr 1940, record (1940) #: 9464.

William H. JENKINS, born: 30 Oct 1857 at Nashville,
TN, husband of Victoria Jenkins, parents: Ben Jenkins
and Amanda Moreland, cause of death: "disease
unknown", informant: Lon Jenkins, Moreland Cemetery,
Doeville, died: 16 Apr 1940, record (1940) #: 9465.

John H. VAUGHT, born: 8 Sep 1861, widower, parents:
J.H. Vaught, Sr. and Sarah Bailey, cause of death:
"high blood pressure and pulmonary ....(illegible)",
informant: Joe Vaught (Butler), died: 16 May 1940,
record (1940) #: 9466.

Charles Loyd GREGG, born: 13 Sep 1926, parents: Leason
Gregg (Coldwell, NC) and Myrtle Warren (Watauga Co.
NC), cause of death: "brights disease", informant:
Leason Gregg (Butler), buried: Dugger Cemetery, died:
20 Apr 1940, record (1940) #: 9467.

Mrs. Callie Thomas CRAWFORD, born: 11 May 1873, widow
of D.H. Crawford, parents: Sidney Thomas and Amanda
Jenkins, cause of death: "diabetes, myocarditis,
terminal pulmonary congestion", informant: Mande
Crawford (Mountain City), buried: Mountain View
Cemetery, died: 3 Apr 1940, record (1940) #: 9468.

Sarah H. FARRIS, born: 6 May 1881 at Watauga Co., NC,
widow, parents: Bill Shores (Coldwell, NC) and Ella
Smith (Watauga Co. NC), cause of death: "lobar
pneumonia, myocarditis", informant: Mary Jones Farris
(Mountain City), buried: Shingletown Cemetery, died:
11 May 1940, record (1940) #: 11937.

Columbus L. LEFFMAN, age estimated at 65 years, born
at Wilkes Co., NC, husband of Mrs. Fannie Dunn
Leffman, parents: John Leffman (Wilkes Co. NC) and
Elizie Carter (Wilkes Co. NC), cause of death:
"pulmonary tuberculosis", informant: Carl W. Leffman
(Laurel Bloomery), buried: Sutherland Cemetery, died:
18 May 1940, record (1940) #: 11938.

Barbara Louise RAY, born: 24 Sep 1884, wife of Jesse
H. Ray, parents: Hamilton Gregg and Laura Gilbert,
cause of death: "heart failure", informant: Jesse F.
Ray (Laurel Bloomery), buried: Taylors Valley
Cemetery, died: 24 May 1940, record (1940) #: 11939.

Winnie S. Dunn WAGNER, born: 8 Feb 1858, wife of A.B.
Wagner, parents: Jacob Dunn and Nancy Wagner, cause of
death: "injured in fall, acute congestion of kidneys",
informant: J.D. Wagner (Shouns), buried: Wagner-Ward
Cemetery, died: 4 May 1940, record (1940) #: 11940.

Adam Bynum WAGNER, born: 14 may 1859, widower of Winnie Wagner, parents: Daniel Wagner and Nancy Hardin (Ashe Co. NC), cause of death: "broncho pneumonia", informant: J.D. Wagner (Shouns), buried: Wagner Cemetery, died: 9 May 1940, record (1940) # 11941.

Lucy HAMPTON, age estimated at 58 years, county home resident, parents: unknown, cause of death: "chronic brights disease", died: 17 May 1940, record (1940) #: 11942.

Smith M. MCQUEEN, born: 22 Feb 1885, husband of Vadie McQueen, parents: L.L. McQueen and Laurinda McQueen (maiden name), cause of death: "influenza, broncho pneumonia", informant: Mrs. S.M. McQueen (Mountain City), buried: McQueen Cemetery, died: 23 May 1940, record (1940) #: 11943.

Mrs. Susan L. CURD, born: 22 Dec 1874, widow of Alvin Curd, parents: Joel Eastridge and Sarah Rominger, cause of death: "chronic nephritis, broncho pneumonia", informant: Mrs. John NcNutt (Detroit, MI), buried: Curd Cemetery, died: 26 May 1940, record (1940) #: 11944.

Infant TESTER, female, parents: Vonnie L. Tester and Pearl Hicks, cause of death: "unknown", informant: Vonnie L. Tester (Neva), buried: Tester Cemetery, born/died: 24 May 1940, record (1940) #: 11945.

Thomas J. WHITE, age about 80 years, born at Carter Co., TN, husband of Roena Shoemaker, parents: Dick White and Sarah Ann Bunton, cause of death: "organic heart disease", informant: D.E. Goodwin (Butler), buried: White Cemetery, died: 25 Feb 1940, record (1940) #: 11946.

William Alfred ROBINSON, born: 9 Sep 1939, parents: Dana L. Robinson and (first name not stated) Reed (Dayton, TN), cause of death: "lobar pneumonia", informant: Dana L. Robinson (Shady Valley), buried: Kenney Blevins Cemetery, died: 25 May 1940, record (1940) #: 11947.

Thomas PROFFITT, born: 31 Dec 1851, widower of Darcus Moody, parents: John Proffitt (NC) and Liddy Robinson (NC), cause of death: "lagrippe", informant; Mrs. Eddie Hinkle (Elizabethton, TN), died: 6 May 1940, record (1940) #: 11948.

Lovie Lucinda BAKER, born: 9 Jun 1859, widow of Thomas A. Baker, parents: (first name not stated) Bunton and Jane Whitehead, cause of death: "lagrippe and paralysis", informant: V.K. Wagner (Butler), buried: Baker Cemetery, died: 24 Mar 1940, record (1940) #: 11949.

Mrs. Rebekah E. DONNELLY, born: 17 Nov 1880 at
Bradford, Pennsylvania, wife of Hugh H. Donnelly,
parents: Elmer Viall (PA) and Adaline Tome (PA), cause
of death: "cancer liver", informant: H.S. Donnelly
(Mountian City), buried: Mountain View Cemetery, died:
9 Jun 1940, record (1940) #: 14246.

Max Browne COLE, born: 9 Feb 1928, parents: Richard
Cole (SC) and Margaret Brown (Cocke Co. TN), cause of
death: "influenza and broncho pneumonia", informant:
Mrs. A.E. Brown (Mountian City), buried: Mountain View
Cemetery, died: 9 Jun 1940, record (1940) #: 14247.

William Andrew DOWELL, born: 13 Apr 1864, husband of
Annis Cordelia Dowell, parents: James E. Dowell
(Wilkes, Co. NC) and Malinda Dunn, cause of death:
"tuberculosis of kidneys", informant: Fred Dowell
(Shouns), buried: Dunn Cemetery, died: 14 Jun 1940,
record (1940) #: 14248.

Winnie Sarafine DAVIS, born: 4 Aug 1868, wife of Will
H. Davis, parents: Peter Shoun and (first name not
stated) Moore (NC), cause of death: "apoplexy",
informant: J.R. Davis (Mountain City), buried: Shoun
Cemetery, died: 19 Jun 1940, record (1940) #: 14249.

Mrs. Susie BREWER, born: 6 Oct 1865, wife of A.L.
Brewer, parents: A.J. Fritts and Lou Porch, cause of
death: "cancer of the tongue", informant: James Brewer
(Butler), buried: Slimp Cemetery, died: 24 Jun 1940,
record (1940) #: 14250.

Mrs. Lelia Kiser BUTLER, born: 27 Jan 1862, wife of
S.D.G. Butler, parents: John Lewis Kiser and Alice
Moore, cause of death: "anjina pectoris", informant:
S.D.G. Butler (Mountain City), buried: Mountain View
Cemetery, died: 1 Jun 1940, record (1940) #: 16492.

Mrs. Kate Murphey SMYTHE, born: 17 Jul 1888, wife of
John W. Smythe, parents: Kemp Murphey and Susan Wills,
cause of death: "chronic myocarditis, nephritis",
informant: John W. Smythe (Mountain City), buried:
Mountain View Cemetry, died: 12 Jul 1940, record
(1940) #: 16493.

Carl Edgar ARNOLD, born: 17 Jan 1931 at Jenkins,
Kentucky, parents: Buice Arnold and Mae Eldreth, cause
of death: "drowned", buried: Phillippi Cemetery, died:
26 Jul 1940, record (1940) #: 16494.

Mrs. Mary Pearl WALSH, born: 14 Oct 1915, wife of Will
Walsh, parents: John Triplett and Bertha Rambo, cause
of death: "hemorrhage from intestinal tract",
informant: Will Walsh (Shouns), buried: Shoun
Cemetery, Doeville, died: 26 May 1940, record (1940)
#: 16495.

William Alexander STALCUP, born: 9 Feb 1865, husband of Mrs. Callie Stalcup, parents: John H. Stalcup (VA) and Elizabeth Robinson, cause of death: "chronic brights disease", informant: Mrs. Jake Lowe (Butler), buried: Stalcup Cemetery, died: 1 Jul 1940, record (1940) #: 16496.

John Harrison REED, born: 6 Sep 1865, husband of Mrs. Mollie Lowe, parents: James Reed (NC) and Elizabeth Proffitt, cause of death: "apoplexy", informant: Mrs. J.E. Reed (Butler), buried: Smith Cemetery, Carter Co. TN, died: 7 Jul 1940, record (1940) #: 16497.

Luzins BLEVINS, born: 17 Aug 1864, widow of George Blevins, parents: Wash Bowman and Martha Osborne (NC), cause of death: "hypostatic pneumonia, chronic myocarditis", buried: Cable Cemetery, died: 28 Jun 1940, record (1940) #: 16498.

Kyle POTTER, born: 1930 at Carter County, TN, parents: Millard Potter (Carter Co. TN) and Pearl Bunton (Carter Co. TN), cause of death: "organic heart disease and articular rhumatism", informant: Millard Potter (Butler), buried: Bunton Cemetery, died: 21 Jan 1940, record (1940) #: 16499.

William M. KIRBY, born: 6 Oct 1863 at Avery County, NC, widower of Bertha Roberts, parents: Avery Kirby (NC) and Margaret Kirby (NC), cause of death: "chronic valvulor heart disease and broncho pneumonia", informant: Mrs. Virgie Moretz (Shouns), buried: Moretz Cemetery, Watauga Co., NC, died: 21 Oct 1940, record (1940) #: 23244.

Priscilla LAWS, born: 24 Mar 1892, wife of Robert S. Laws, parents: George Neatherly and Catherine Tester, cause of death: "diptheria and myocarditis", informant: Miss Agnes Laws (Neva), died: 10 Oct 1940, record (1940) #: 23245.

Ethel Rosa CROSSWHITE, born: 25 Aug 1892 in North Carolina, wife of Stacy Crosswhite, parents: Melvin Crosswhite (NC) and Ethel Sluder, cause of death: "pulmonary tuberculosis", informant: Stacy Crosswhite (Shady Valley), buried: family cemetery, died: 14 Oct 1940, record (1940) #: 23246.

Edgar Lewis MAIN, born: 29 Jul 1938, parents: George Main and Bessie Watson, cause of death: "acute colitis", buried: Owens Cemetery, died: 17 Sep 1940, record (1940) #: 21049.

Rosa Ellen PRICE, born: 14 Feb 1877, widow of James Price, parents: Enoch Potter and Martha Brown, cause of death: "circulatory failure", informant: W.L. Snyder (Shouns), buried: Price Cemetery, died: 3 Sep 1940, record (1940) #: 21050.

Vernie Allen SPURGEON, Negro, female, born: 20 Jun
1940, parents: James Howard Spurgeon (Washington Co.,
TN) and Clara Earl Woodby, cause of death: not stated,
buried: Holy Hill Cemetery, died: 4 Sep 1940, record
(1940) #: 21051.

John Willie DENKINS, born: 19 Nov 1876, husband of
Mrs, Millie Denkins, parents: father's name unknown
and Martha Denkins (Yadkin Co., NC), cause of death:
"heart failure", buried: Leffler Cemetery, died: 9 Sep
1940, record (1940) #: 21052.

William Thomas SMYTHE, born: 27 May 1859, husband of
Mrs. Etta Donnelly Smythe, parents: Thomas S. Smythe
(Smythe Co., VA) and Margaret C. Donnelly, cause of
death: "chronic brights disease", buried: Mountain
View Cemetery, died: 19 Sep 1940, record (1940) #:
21053.

Mrs. Lura Callie SALMONS, born: 13 Feb 1893 at Watauga
Co., NC, wife of W.S. Salmons, parents: D.N. Shaw
(Forsyth, NC) and Isabella Robinson (Ashe Co., NC)
cause of death: "cerebral hemorrhage and bronchial
penumonia", informant: William S. Salmon, buried:
Brown Cemetery, died: 31 Aug 1940, record (1940) #:
21054.

Carl Edward TAYLOR, born: 23 Jun 1939, parents:
Bradley Taylor and Pearl Howard, cause of death:
"broncho pneumonia", informant: Pearl Taylor (Shouns),
buried: McEwen Cemetery, died: 27 Aug 1940, record
(1940) #: 21055.

Eugene Loyd TESTER, born: 11 Sep 1897, husband of Mrs.
Nelia Forrester Tester, parents: C. Columbus Tester
and Martha Ann Jackson, (Watauga Co., NC), cause of
death: "valvulor heart disease, pneumonia", informant:
U.G. Tester (Leona Mines, VA), buried: Tester
Cemetery, died: 9 Aug 1940, record (1940) #: 21056.

Ralph Haynes WALSH, born: 4 Apr 1923, parents:
Roderick Butler Walsh and Vada Ethel Shoun, cause of
death: "septic heart disease" died: 4 Sep 1940, record
(1940) #: 21057.

William Bethel DAVIS, born: 15 May 1850, husband of
Mrs. Elizabeth Davis, parents: Tom Davis (Wilkes Co.,
NC) and Martha Church (Wilkes Co., NC), cause of
death: "chronic brights disease", died: 21 Aug 1940,
record (1940) #: 21058.

E.D. WAGNER, born: 12 May 1881, widower, parents: D.B.
Wagner and Alice Smith, cause of death: "chronic
nephritis, uremia", buried: Wagner Cemetery, died: 6
Jul 1940, record (1940) #: 21059.

Vadia J. CORNETT, born: 3 Mar 1890, wife of William Oscar Cornett, parents: Eugene C. Johnson and (first name not stated) Ray, cause of death: "bronchial pneumonia, gastric ulcer", buried: Cornett Cemetery, died: 18 Sep 1940, record (1940) #: 25485.

Jerry DOWELL, born: 26 Sep 1940, parents: Lester S. Dowell and Vuna M. Dunn, cause of death: "acute pulmonary congestion", buried: McEwen Cemetery, died: 28 Sep 1940, record (1940) #: 25486.

Richard Thomas POTTER, born: 17 Sep 1940, parents: Thomas G. Potter and Thelma Phillips, cause of death: "cerebral hemorrhage", buried: Tester Cemtery, died: 18 Sep 1940, record (1940) #: 27766.

Charles Kemp SHOUN, born: 7 Jan 1939, parents: Frank C. Shoun and Charlotte Bingham (Watauga Co., NC), cause of death: "lobar pneumonia", buried: Shoun Cemetery, died: 12 Aug 1940, record (1940) #: 27767.

Elizabeth PARKER, born: 7 Aug 1860 in North Carolina, wife of James H. Parker, parents: Joshua Cox (NC) and (first name not stated) Perry (NC), cause of death: "congestive heart failure, broncho pneumonia, asthma", informant: Anna Anderson (Kingsport, TN), buried: Aire Cemetery, died: 20 Nov 1940, record (1940) #: 29479.

Susan Elizabeth BAUGUESS, born: 25 Mar 1872 at Carter County, TN, widow, parents: John Wesley Smith and Delila Laws, cause of death: "chronic brights disease", informant: Mrs. Nat Wills, died: 15 Dec 1940, record (1940) #: 29480.

John THOMAS, Negro, born: 25 Dec 1862 at North Wilksboro, NC, husband of Ancie Thomas, parents: Sam K. Thomas (Ashe Co., NC) and Reainer Thomas (maiden name), cause of death: "chronic brights disease", buried; Holy Hill Cemetery, died: 30 Dec 1940, record (1940) #: 29481.

Fannie H. MALONE, born: 18 Mar 1885, wife of Thomas James Malone, parents: William Bledsoe (Ashe Co., NC) and Louise Vaught, cause of death: "high blood pressure", buried: Primative Baptist Church cemetery, died: 12 Nov 1940, record (1940) #: 29482.

John Redford HAMMONS, born: 22 Apr 1859, husband of Bessie C. Hammons, parents: Henry W. Hammons and Sarah Willen, cause of death: "chronic valvulor heart disease", informant: Bessie Hammons, buried: Hammons Cem, died: 11 Nov 1940, record (1940) #: 29483.

John Emmitt GRINDSTAFF, born: 31 Oct 1859, widower of Sarah Grindstaff, parents: Nicholas Grindstaff and Sarah Wagner, cause of death: "cerebral hemorrhage, pneumonia", informant: Sherman Grindstaff (Eliz., TN), died: 25 Dec 1940, record (1940) #: 29484.

James BENTLY, born: 4 Sep 1919, single, parents: George Bently and Mary Bowling, cause of death: "neoplastic colhexia, carcinoma forearm", informant: George Bently (Shady Valley), buried: Gentry Cemetery, died: 28 Nov 1940, record (1940) #: 29485.

George Edward COLSTON, born: 6 Oct 1921, resident of Grundy County, TN, parents: "unknown", death cause: "carbon monoxide poisoning from automobile exhaust", died: 14 Nov 1940, record (1940) #: 29791.

Joseph Dayton ARNOLD, born: 26 Dec 1919, husband of Nova Reed Arnold, parents: W.K. Arnold and Hattie Campbell, cause of death: "carbon monoxide poisoning from automobile exhaust, accidental", died: 14 Nov 1940, record (1940) #: 29792.

Alex SNYDER, born: 1874 at Ashe County, NC, husband of Mollie Snyder, parents: Landon Snyder and Clara Martin (Ashe Co., NC), cause of death: "cancer right arm", informant: Joe Snyder (Trade), buried: Snyder Cemetery, died: 13 Nov 1940, record (1940) #: 29793.

Longoe Lafayette JENKINS, born: 21 May 1905, husband of Thelma Jenkins, parents: William H. Jenkins and Victoria Lunsford, cause of death: "ulcer of stomach", informant: Mrs. Victoria Jenkins (Butler), buried: Moreland Cemetery, died: 12 Nov 1940, record (1940) #: 29794.

Peter Hilton SHOUN, born: 7 Aug 1850, widower, parents: Harvey Shoun and Arlene Reece, cause of death: "organic heart disease", informant: Mary Dishman (daughter), buried: Rainbolt Cemetery, died: 27 Jun 1940, record (1940) #: 29795.

Evelyn Marie HATLEY, born: 21 Sep 1940, parents: L.R. Hatley (NC) and Eula Arbell Potter, cause of death: : "don't know", informant: L.R. Hatley (Butler), buried: Sugar Grove Cemetery, died: 5 Oct 1940, record (1940) #: 29796.

Caroline NORRIS, born: 16 Jun 1844 at Watauga Co., NC, single, parents: not stated, cause of death: "senility", informant: W.H. Norris (Butler), buried: Buntontown, died: 13 Mar 1940, record (1940) #: 29974.

Ora Willard FLETCHER, born: 15 May 1896, husband of Beckie Fletcher, parents: William C. Fletcher and Tilda O'Neil, cause of death: "unknown", informant: William C. Fletcher (father), buried: Cable Cemetery, died: 15 Apr 1940, record (1940) #: 30014.

Dayton Parker WILLS, born: 8 Feb 1887, widower, parents: Baxter Gannaway Wills and Mary Elizabeth Wilson, cause of death: "angina pectoris", informant: Oscar Wills (Mountain City), buried: Wills Cemetery, died: 1 Jan 1941, record (1941) #: 1150.

James Hamilton PARKER, born: 7 Feb 1861, husband of Elizabeth Parker, parents: Calvin Parker and (first name not stated) Worley, cause of death: "chronic myocarditis", informant: Mrs. W.P. Parker (Laurel Bloomery), buried: Acre Cemetery, died: 3 Jan 1941, record (1941) #: 1151.

Florence A. ABLE, born: 10 Mar 1856, widow, parents: James Able and (first name not stated) Gentry, cause of death: "influenza, bronchial pneumonia", informant: Joe Pennington (Laurel Bloomery), buried: Acre Field Cemetery, died: 22 Jan 1941, record (1941) #: 1152.

Verna Eldrith VANOVER, born: 18 Jan 1906, wife of Ira Vanover, parents: James Roby Eldrith (Ashe Co., NC) and Flossie Willen, cause of death: "cancer womb", buried: Willen Cemetery, died: 15 Jan 1940, record (1941) #: 1153.

Elbert Hamilton HICKS, born: 4 Nov 1872 at Sullivan Co., TN, divorced, Baptist minister, parents: William Henry Hicks (Sullivan Co., TN) and Mary Ann Frazier (Sullivan Co., TN), cause of death: "heart attack, chronic myocarditis, automobile accident", informant: Mrs. J. Blaine Stout, buried: Mountain View Cemetery, died: 14 Jan 1940.

Bettie Lou RIDDLE, born: 11 Jan 1941, parents: Roy Riddle (Ashe Co., NC) and Mary Belle Winters, cause of death: "premature", died: 11 Jan 1941, record (1941) #: 3721.

Mattie Lou GENTRY, born: 19 Jan 1872 at Ashe County, NC, widow, parents: David Ashley (NC) and (first name not stated) Graybeal (NC), cause of death: "crebral thrombosis, arterio sclerosis", informant: Mary Gentry (Laurel Bloomery), buried: Acre Field Cemetery, died: 31 Jan 1941, record (1941) #: 3722.

Hattie Belle LOMAX, Negro, born: 14 Sep 1908, single, parents: Robert S. Lomax (Wilkes Co., NC) and Rebecca Cresson, cause of death: "suicide due to shotgun wound", informant: R.S. Lomax (Shouns), buried: Holy Hill Cem, died: 16 Feb 1941, record (1941) #: 3723.

Mrs. Martha C. ROARK, born: 13 Apr 1865 in North Carolina, widow of Harrison Roark, parents: Frank Main (NC) and Jennie Bailey (NC), cause of death: "general bright and flue", informant: J.W. Dunn, buried: McEwen Cemetery, died: 6 Feb 1941, record (1941) #: 3724.

Wash W. HAMPTON, born: March 1852 at Ashe County, NC, husband of Mrs. Pauline Osborne Hampton, parents: Andrew Hampton and Pashia Lewis (Ashe Co., NC), cause of death: "influenza, broncho pneumonia", informant: D.D. Hampton (Shouns), buried: Arnold Cemetery, died: 25 Jan 1941, record (1941) #: 3725.

Bertha DAY, born: March 1907, parents: father's name unknown and Martha Day, cause of death: "lagrippe", informant: W.D. Day (Neva), buried: Baker's Gap, died: 1 Feb 1941, record (1941) #: 3726.

Beulah Mae HODGE, born: 27 Jan 1941, parents: Arthur Burt Hodge and Mary Ruby Barnes (Watauga Co., NC), cause of death: "unknown", buried: Baker Cemetery, died: 9 Feb 1941, record (1941) #: 3727.

Andy MILLER, age 60 years, born at Sullivan Co., TN, husband of Mrs. Bessie Miller, parents: "unknown", death cause: "dropsy", informant: Fain Norris, Norris Cemetery, died: 5 Feb 1941, record (1941) #: 3728.

Callie Campbell NEATHERLY, born: 31 Mar 1875, widow of Joseph D. Neatherly, parents: L.C. Campbell and Candas Rainbolt, cause of death: "pneumonia", informant: F.M. Matherly (Butler), buried: Butler Cemetery, died: 26 Jan 1941, record (1941) #: 3729.

Constance Doloris ROBINSON, born: 10 Nov 1940 at Banner Elk, NC, parents: Thidore K. Robinson and Carline Younce (Mabel, NC), cause of death: "influenza, broncho pneumonia", informant: Mrs. T.K. Robinson, buried: Shoun Cemetery, died: 11 Jan 1941, record (1941) #: 3730.

Mrs. Elizabeth M. MCFADDEN, born: 3 Jan 1860 in North Carolina, widow of George M. McFadden, parents: David Miller and Elmira Moffett (NC), cause of death: "broncho pneumonia", informant: Wiley McFadden (Trade), buried: Arnold Cemetery, died: 17 Feb 1941, record (1941) #: 3731.

Martin L. HOLLOWAY, born: 25 Jun 1876 at Tazwell, VA, husband of Mrs. Lillie Profitt Holloway, parents: Felix Holloway and Susie Laws, cause of death: "influenza, bronchial pneumonia", informant: Lillie Holloway (Butler), buried: Cable Cemetery, died: 15 Feb 1941, record (1941) #: 3732.

Betty Jean COWAN, born: 5 Jan 1941, parents: Wiley Thomas Cowan and Julia (illegible), cause of death: "pneumonia", died: 16 Jan 1941, record (1941) #: 3733.

Mrs. Sallie Wills FULLER, born: 22 Jun 1860, widow of John T. Fuller, parents: James H. Wills and Eliza Ann Orr (Rockbridge, VA), cause of death: "carcinoma stomach", informant: Mamie Fuller Cook (Mrs. W.L. Cook, Erwin, TN), buried: Mountain View Cemetery, died: 23 Mar 1941, record (1941) #: 6366.

Olive C. SCOTT, born: 2 Oct 1856, divorced, parents: Samuel Shoun and (first name not stated) McCowan, cause of death: "chronic myocarditis, hyperstatic pneumonia", informant: Mrs. Mack J. Cornett, buried: Cornett Cem, died: 25 Feb 1941, record (1941) #: 6367.

Infant SAMMONS, female, born: 24 Feb 1941, parents:
Robert Sammons and Gretrude Humpford (West VA), cause
of death: "premature", informant: Ewing Sammons,
buried: Johnson Cemetery, died: 26 Feb 1941, record
(1941) #: 6368.

George Wells GUY, born: 8 Jan 1941, parents: George
Samuel Guy (Watauga Co., NC) and Winnie Eller
Icenhour, cause of death: "unknown", informant: Roy
Icenhour, buried: Liberty Cemetery, died: 5 Mar 1941,
record (1941) #: 6359.

Myrtle Victory ICENHOUR, born: 8 Apr 1901 at Watauga
Co., NC, wife of Roy Icenhour, parents: B.F. Stevens
(Watauga Co., NC) and Sarah May (Watauga Co., NC),
cause of death: "influenza and broncho pneumonia",
informant: Roy Icenhour, buried: Phillippi Cemetery,
died: 12 Mar 1941, record (1941) #: 6370.

John M. TESTER, born: 5 Mar 1869, husband of Vergie
Tester, parents: Henry Tester and Elizabeth Tester
(maiden name), cause of death: "infulenza, broncho
pneumonia", informant: Clay Tester (Neva), buried:
Tester Cemetery, died: 15 Mar 1941, record (1941) #:
6371.

David Ray STALCUP, born: 5 Mar 1887, husband of Mrs.
Virgie Mae Stalcup, parents: Aron Joseph Stalcup and
Mary Howard, cause of death: "lobar pneumonia,
pellagra", informant: Mae Stalcup (Doeville), buried:
Stalcup Cemetery, died: 3 Mar 1941, record (1941) #:
6372.

Mrs. Mary Ann Hopkins THOMAS, born: 31 Mar 1863 at
Ashe Co., NC, widow of James W. Thomas, parents:
George Hopkins (Ashe Co., NC) and Ellen Setzer (Ashe
Co., NC), cause of death: "carcinoma of pancreas,
terminal pulmonary congestion", informant: Mrs. John
W. Dyer, buried: St. Johns Cemetery, Watauga Co., NC,
died: 19 Mar 1941, record (1941) #: 6373.

Mrs. Ina BLEVINS, born: 28 Feb 1864 in North Carolina,
widow of Millard Blevins, parents: Cleve Hutchinson
(NC) and Jane Sparks (NC), cause of death: "chronic
heart disease", informant: Arthur Blevins, buried:
Kenney Blevens Cemetery, died: 28 Mar 1941, record
(1941) #: 6374.

Joseph Harrison LOVE, born: 16 Oct 1850 at Watauga
Co., NC, widower, parents: Thomas Love (Watauga Co.,
NC) and Malinda Dotson, cause of death: "chronic
brights disease", informant: Roger Love (Trade),
buried: Dotson Cemetery, died: 7 Mar 1941, record
(1941) #: 6375.

Mrs. Margaret Wilson RASH, born: 16 Nov 1865 at
Watauga Co., NC, parents: father's name unknown and
Rebecca Wilson (Watauga Co., NC), cause of death:
"cerebral heomorrhage", informant: Ernest Rash
(Trade), buried: Wallace Cemetery, died: 8 Mar 1941,
record (1941) #: 6376.

Archie WILSON, born: 6 Mar 1941, parents: W.M. Wilson
(Ashe Co., NC) and Mande Miller, cause of death:
"jaundice", informant: W.M. Wilson (Shouns), buried:
Wallace Cemetery, died: 17 Mar 1941, record (1941) #:
6377.

Mrs. Amanda Dugger REECE, born: 10 Dec 1854, widow,
parents: Joseph Dugger and Mary Stepp, cause of death:
"probably died of heart failure", informant: Miss Inez
Reece (Butler), buried: Sugar Grove Cemetery, died: 2
Mar 1941, record (1941) #: 6378.

Hollace ANDERSON, born: 21 Aug 1926, parents: Don
Anderson and Flossie Stanton, cause of death: "locked
bowels", buried: Sugar Grove Cemetery, died: 23 Feb
1941, record (1941) #: 6379.

Mary E. MOREFIELD, born: 12 Apr 1862 at Ashe Co., NC,
widow, parents: David Ashley (NC) and Nancy Graybeal
(NC), cause of death: "myocarditis, terminal
hypostatic pneumonia", informant: A.J. Bolden, buried:
Acre Field Cemetery, died: 13 Apr 1941, record (1941)
#: 8875.

Mrs. Carrie Cole JENKINS, born: 25 Dec 1862, widow,
parents: Washington Cole and Sarah Shoun, cause of
death: "chronic brights disease", informant: Winnie
Cole Adams, buried: Mountain View Cemetery, died: 6
Apr 1941, record (1941) #: 8876.

Samuel I. WOOD, born: 24 Dec 1859 at Russell Co., VA,
widower, parents: Henry Wood and Vinia Worley (Ashe
Co., NC), cause of death: "influenza, bronchial
pneumonia", informant: S.S. Wood, buried: Donnelly
Cemetery, died: 13 Apr 1941, record (1941) #: 8877.

Richard Andy WOOD, born: 14 Sep 1940, parents: R. Earl
Wood and Ruby Dyson, cause of death: "influenza,
bronchial pneumonia", informant: Earl Wood, Donnelly
Cemetery, died: 18 Apr 1941, record (1941) #: 8878.

Hazel M. MORETZ, born: 4 Sep 1940, parents: Raleigh
Moretz (Watauga Co., NC) and Mae Moody, cause of
death: "influenza, bronchial pneumonia", informant:
Raleigh Moretz, buried: Brookshire Cemetery, died: 23
Apr 1941, record (1941) #: 8879.

Richard J. ARNOLD, born: 28 Aug 1858, single, parents:
Melvin Arnold and Elizabeth Elliott, cause of death:
"chronic brights disease", informant: C.F. McGlamery
(Trade), died: 27 Apr 1941, record (1941) #: 8880.

Elsie Vanover ROARK, born: 29 Dec 1903 at Ashe Co.,
NC, wife of Mckinley Roark, parents: Grant Vanover
(Ashe Co., NC) and Laura Osborne (Ashe Co., NC), cause
of death: "influenza, pneumonia, child birth",
informant: J.C. Roark (Shouns), buried: Arnold
Cemetery, died: 2 Apr 1941, record (1941) #: 8881.

Robert Alex TESTER, born: 26 Apr 1875, widower,
parents: James Tester and Sarah Jane Wilson, cause of
death: "chronic heart disease", informant: Milburn
Tester (Neva), buried: Green Cemetery, died: 18 Apr
1941, record (1941) #: 8882.

Charles Delbert MCELYEA, born: 21 Feb 1941, parents:
Edward McElyea and Ivalee Roark (Ashe Co., NC), cause
of death: "congenital hives", buried: Snyder Cemetery,
died: 1 Mar 1941, record (1941) #: 8883.

Julia Wagner HAWKINS, born: 10 Dec 1875, widow of John
Hawkins, parents: Noah Wagner and (first name not
stated) Jackson, cause of death: "brights disease",
informant: A.C. Hawkins (Shouns), buried: family
cemetery, died: 24 Mar 1941, record (1941) #: 8884.

Mollie JENKINS, born: 9 May 1887 at Carter Co., TN,
wife of David Jenkins, parents: Pleas Pierce (Carter
Co., TN) and Sallie Bowers (Carter Co., TN), cause of
death: "cardio nephritis", informant: David Jenkins,
buried: Pierce or Matherly Cemetery, died: 3 Apr 1941,
record (1941) #: 8885.

John H. ARNOLD, born: 12 Mar 1855, widower, parents:
Joe Robinson and Clara Arnold, cause of death:
"paralysis", informant: G.G. Arnold (Doeville), Arnold
Cemetery, died: 9 Jan 1941, record (1941) #: 8886.

Mrs. Mamie Mae ROBINSON, born: 16 Apr 1913, wife of
Frank Robinson, parents: Floyd Reece and Maggie Mains,
cause of death: "carcinoma of (illegible) gland",
informant: Frank Robinson (Trade), buried: Reece
Cemetery, died: 5 Apr 1941, record (1941) #: 8887.

Reuben Edward HAWKS, born: 22 Mar 1858 at Carroll Co.,
VA, widower of Matilda Hawks, parents: "unknown",
death cause: "probably senility", informant: Clyde
Hawks, died: 14 Apr 1941, record (1941) #: 8888.

Mollie Leonard PAYNE, born: 1864 at Sullivan Co., TN,
widow of James Payne, parents: Leonard Delaney and
Rachel Cole, cause of death: "unknown", informant:
Mrs. Laura Ward (Piney Flats, TN), died: 8 Apr 1941,
record (1941) #: 8889.

Mrs. Sarah Ann Nancy BAKER, born: 17 May 1846, widow,
parents: John S. Vaught and Rebecca Shoun, cause of
death: "paralysis", informant: A.M. Baker (Butler),
buried: Baker Gap Baptist Cemetery, died: 13 Mar 1941,
record (1941) #: 8890.

James Paul STANSBERRY, born: 5 Mar 1933, parents: R.C. Stansberry and Callie Cannon (Avery Co., NC), cause of death: "abscess of brain", buried: Burton Cemetery, died: 15 Mar 1941, record (1941) #: 8891.

Mary Johnson GRANT, born: 4 Oct 1857, widow of Parker S. Grant, parents: Harvey Johnson (Ashe Co., NC), and Catherine Johnson, cause of death: "myocarditis, nephritis", informant: Edgar A. Grant (Shouns), died: 2 May 1941, record (1941) #: 11249.

George Alexander HOPKINS, born: 20 Apr 1876 at Ashe Co., NC, husband of Fannie Colvard, parents: George W. Hopkins (Ashe Co., NC) and Elenor Setzer (Ashe Co., NC), cause of death: "chronic brights disease", informant: J.S. Hopkins (High Point, NC) buried: Happy Valley Cemetery, Carter Co., TN, died: 5 May 1941, record (1941) #: 11250.

Mrs. Bonnie Lee Sheets RAMSEY, born: 23 Nov 1893 at Ashe Co., NC, widow of Joe Ramsey, parents: Eugene Sheets (Ashe Co., NC) and Sarah Ann Roten (Ashe Co., NC), cause of death: chronic myocarditis", informant: Walter Sheets (Neva), buried: Pottsville, PA, died: 1 May 1941, record (1941) #: 11251.

Tommie Hall DICKENS, born: 8 May 1940, parents: Dan Dickens and Pearl Smith, cause of death: "acute indigestion", buried: Wilson Cemetery, died: 26 May 1941, record (1941) #: 13619.

Loyd Roger CORNETT, born: 21 Apr 1941, parents: Robert Cornett (Watauga Co., NC) and Vernia Johnson, cause of death: "whooping cough", informant: M.C. Johnson (Shouns), buried: Johnson Cemetery, died: 17 May 1941, record (1941) #: 13620.

Wanda Lou VANNOY, born: 14 Apr 1941, parents: John W. Vannoy (Watauga Co., NC) and Etta Harmon (NC), cause of death: "bullous rash of entire body", buried: Brown Cemetery, died: 15 Apr 1941, record (1941) #: 13621.

Mrs. Mary Ann MUNDAY, born: 9 Feb 1852 at Watauga Co., NC, widow of Joe Munday, parents: Mark Holsclaw (NC) and Eliza Munday (NC), cause of death: "hypostatic pneumonia", informant: Mrs. B.D. Clark, Suterland Cemetery, died: 6 Jun 1941, record (1941) #: 13622.

William Eli FLETCHER, born: 15 Nov 1869 at Sullivan Co., TN, widow of Matilda Fletcher, parents: John Fletcher and mother's name unknown, cause of death: "cardio reval", informant: Debbie Fletcher (Johnson City, TN), died: 4 Jun 1941, record (1941) #: 13623.

Margaret Anna B. HARMON, born: 8 Aug 1925, parents: John Harmon (NC) and Claudia Harmon (NC), cause of death: "organic heart trouble", buried: Butler Cemetery, died: 14 Feb 1941, record (1941) #: 13624.

Billie Lee SNYDER, born: 28 Jan 1941, parents: Lee Snyder (Ashe Co., NC) and Josephine Snyder (maiden name)(Ashe Co., NC), cause of death: "pertussis, bronchial pneumonia", informant: Mrs. H.A. Potter (Shouns), buried: Snyder Cemetery, died: 20 Jun 1941, record (1941) #: 13617.

David M. GREER, born: 11 Mar 1887 at Watauga Co., NC, widower, parents: Reuben Greer (Watauga Co., NC) and Mary Seats (Watauga Co., NC), cause of death: "chronic brights disease", buried: Mountain View Cemetery, died: 21 May 1941, record (1941) #: 13618.

Charles Edward ARNOLD, age estimated at 66 years, husband of Christina Arnold, parents: Calvin Arnold and Callie Phillippi, cause of death: "abscess of lung", buried: Phillippi Cemetery, died: 23 Aug 1941, record (1941) #: 18279.

Mrs. Jane CURD, age estimated at 78 years, wife of Dave Curd (age 78), parents: Jerry Woodard (Forsyth Co. TN) and Nancy West, cause of death: "cancer womb", informant: D.G. Woodard (Shouns), buried: Woodard Cemetery, died: 20 Aug 1941, record (1941) #: 18280.

William JOINS, born: 31 Dec 1940, parents: Cleve Joins and Bertie Rash (Ashe Co. NC), cause of death: "chronic brights disease", informant: Ham Rash, buried: Owens Cemetery, died: 29 Aug 1941, record (1941) #: 18281.

Smith ARNOLD, born: 9 Apr 1877 in Ashe County, NC, divorced from Bertha Arnold, parents: William Arnold (Ashe Co. NC) and Katherine Ashley (Ashe Co. NC), cause of death: "unknown, light stroke 8 months ago", informant: Jess Eller, buried: Phillippi Cemetery, died: 14 May 1941, record (1941) #: 20438.

Jack A. MILLER, age about 73 years, husband of Mrs. Susan Miller, parents: father's name unknown and Kattie Miller, cause of death: "cerebral hemorrhage, bronchial pneumonia", informant: Mrs. Susan Miller, buried: Wilson Cemetery, died: 12 Sep 1941, record (1941) #: 20439.

Mrs. Sallie ALLEN, born: 13 Jun 1880, wife of Carter Allen, parents: Daniel Stout and Mary Ann Arnold, cause of death: "bronchial pneumonia", buried: Arnold Cemetery, died: 12 Sep 1941, record (1941) #: 20440.

Maggie M. PRICE, born: 8 Sep 1901, wife of Alva C. Price (age 50), parents: Robert M. Davis and Prudia South (Watauga Co. NC), cause of death: "gastro entiro colitis, bronchial pneumonia", informant: Alva C. Price (Shouns), buried: Davis Cemetery, died: 30 Aug 1941, record (1941) #: 20441.

Gerlian FORSTER, born: 6 May 1915 at Lee County, VA, single, parents: Joe Forester and Clyde Poteet (Lee Co., VA), cause of death: "bronchial pneumonia", informant: Clyde Forster (Neva), buried: Tester Cemetery, died: 30 Aug 1941, record (1941) #: 20442.

Otis Levi DUGGER, Jr., born: 11 Apr 1941, parents: Otis Levi Dugger, Sr. and Parlie Dugger (maiden name), cause of death: "asphyxia", informant: Otis Levi Dugger (Neva), buried: Bakers Cemetery, died: 24 Jul 1941, record (1941) #: 20443.

Bell Lowe PLEASANT, born: 2 Jul 1902, wife of Ben Pleasant (age 57), parents: Charlie Lowe and Molly Miller, cause of death: "pulmonary tuberculosis, acute brights disease", informant: Mrs. Doran Lowe (Mountain City), buried: Roberts Cemetery, died: 9 Aug 1941, record (1941) #: 20444.

William McKinley BUMGARDNER, born: 15 Feb 1895, single, parents: George Washington Bumgardner and Nancy Elizabeth Dotson, cause of death: "anjina pectoris", informant: Mrs. Ora Snyder (Trade), Dotson Cemetery, died: 29 Sep 1941, record (1941) #: 20445.

Mrs. Etta M. BUTLER, born: 29 May 1868 at Ashe County, NC, widow of Edward E. Butler, parents: John Baker (Ashe Co. NC) and Deliah Eller (Ashe Co. NC), cause of death: "chronic brights disease", informant: Margaret Butler Brown (Mountain City), buried: Mountain View Cemetery, died: 31 Aug 1941, record (1941) #: 20446.

Mrs. Martha Gentry GREER, born: 21 Sep 1869, widow of Ben W. Greer, parents: Andrew Gentry and Margaret Worley, cause of death: "chronic brights disease", informant: Mrs. K.K. Widener (Glade Springs, VA), buried: Gentry Cemetery, died: 23 Oct 1941, record (1941) #: 22557.

Mary Alice Elizabeth REEVES, colored, born: 1 Jun 1876, widow of Lee Reeves, parents: Calvin Rustin and Louisa Thomas (Ashe Co. NC), cause of death: "cancer stomach", informant: Cynthia Mock (Mountain City), Wagner Cem, died: 5 Oct 1941, record (1941) #: 22558.

Mrs. Ollie Jones WILLEN, born: 7 Nov 1910 at Ashe County, NC, wife of Ray Willen, parents: Frank Jones (Ashe Co. NC) and Rose Eastridge, cause of death: "suicide, shot herself with a shot gun, died in 5 to 10 minutes", informant: Ray Willen (Shouns), West Cemetery, died: 3 Oct 1941, record (1941) #: 22559.

Betsy Lou ELDRETH, born: 15 Aug 1941, parents: Ambrose Eldreth (Ashe Co. NC) and Elzina Coldron (Ashe Co. NC), cause of death: "colitis", informant: Ambrose Eldreth and Leshia Rash, buried: Eldreth Cemetery, died: 7 Oct 1941, record (1941) #: 22560.

Irene ROARK, born: 27 Mar 1941, parents: William McKinley Roark and Elsie Vanover (Ashe Co. NC), cause of death: "marasmus", informant: McKinley Roark (Shouns), buried: Arnold Cemetery, died: 16 Jul 1941, record (1941) #: 22561.

John F. WARD, born: 27 Jan 1861, widower, parents: James Ward and Nancy Stout, cause of death: "chronic brights disease", informant: Gladys Ward Wills (Shouns), buried: Wagner Cemetery, died: 15 Nov 1941, record (1941) #: 24815.

John L. STOUT, born: 30 Dec 1868, husband of Mrs. Alice Wilson Stout (age 75), parents: Daniel Stout and Mary Holman, cause of death: "chronic brights disease", informant: Mrs. Hattie Stout (Johnson City, TN), buried: Wilson Cemetery (Neva), died: 24 Nov 1941, record (1941) #: 24816.

Victoria W. REEVES, Negro, born: 27 Mar 1906, single, parents: George W. Reeves (Ashe Co. NC) and Julie Thompson (Watauga Co. NC), cause of death: "influenza, broncho pneumonia", informant: George W. Reeves (Mountain City), buried: Reeves Cemetery, died: 25 Nov 1941, record (1941) #: 24817.

Calvin J. BYERS, born: 17 Aug 1873, husband of Mrs Lillie Gilbert (age 45), parents: David Byers and Mary E. Lipford, cause of death: "unknown", informant: Mrs. Lillie Byers (Butler), buried: Rainbolt Cemetery, died: 27 Nov 1941, record (1941) #: 24818.

Charles Elbert LOWE, born: 23 Dec 1872, husband of Mrs. Mollie Ann Lowe (age 72), parents: William Harrison Lowe and Sarah Pleasant (NC), cause of death: "hypostatic pneumonia", informant: James W. Lowe (Mountain City), buried: Alex Roberts Cemetery, died: 21 Nov 1941, record (1941) #: 24819.

Hardin Samuel REEVES, born: 18 Feb 1867 at Wilkes County, NC, husband of Mrs. Virgie M. Reeves, parents: John F. Reeves (Wilkes Co. NC) and Julaan Hutchison (NC), cause of death: "influenza, bronch pneumonia", informant: Lucas Reeves (Shady Valley), Blevins Cemetery, died: 19 Nov 1941, record (1941) #: 24820.

Selma BUNTON, born: 8 Sep 1937, parents: Fawn Bunton and Sallie Cable, cause of death: "unknown", informant: Mrs. Delia Cable (Butler), Buntontown Cemetery, died: 13 Nov 1941, record (1941) #: 24821.

William Ulyssis Grant CABLE, born: 7 Jun 1880, husband of Mrs. Will Cable (age 47), parents: Conrad Burton Cable and Amanda Katherine GUY, cause of death: "broncho pneumonia", informant: Kermit Cable (Butler), buried: Cable Cemetery, died: 17 Nov 1941, record (1941) #: 24822.

Mrs. Emma Virginia ADAMS, born: 14 Feb 1861, widow of John Adams, parents: Samuel Northington (Raleigh, NC) and Sarah Needham (Ashe Co. NC), cause of death: "acute colitis, nephritis, broncho pneumonia", informant: B.M. Adams (Mountain City), buried: Mountain View Cemetery, died: 14 Jul 1941, record (1941) #: 15995.

Margaret Bell RHEA, born: 4 Aug 1873, single, parents: Robert Campbell Rhea (Clarksburg, W. VA) and Caroline McQueen, cause of death: "coronary acclusion", informant: E. Bruce Rhea (Shouns), buried: Shouns Church Cemetery, died: 26 Jul 1941, record (1941) #: 15996.

Eugene ROARK, born: 27 Mar 1941, parents: William McKinley Roark and Elsie Vanover (Ashe Co. NC), cause of death: "marasmus, premature birth", buried: Arnold Cemetery, died: 6 Jul 1941, record (1941) #: 15997.

Howard Elvin OSBORNE, born: 5 Jan 1941, parents: Firman Osborne and Mae Roark, cause of death: "bronchial pneumonia". informant: Firman Osborne (Shouns), buried: Powell Cemetery, died: 10 Jul 1941, record (1941) #: 15998.

Helen Marie DICKENS, born: 28 Jan 1941, parents: Arthur Wayne Dickens (Ashe Co. NC) and Edna Hammons, cause of death: "acute colitis", buried: Tester Cemetery, died: 14 Jul 1941, record (1941) #: 15999.

Myrtle Wandalee RASH, born: 24 Nov 1939, parents: Walter Dewey Rash (Ashe Co. NC) and Cleo Farris, cause of death: "cholera", informant: Dewey Rash (Shady Valley), buried: Shingletown Cemetery, died: 1 Jul 1941, record (1941) #: 16000.

David Henry BARRY, born: 8 Jun 1885, husband of Jettie Barry, parents: Melvin Barry and (first name not stated) Scott, cause of death: "recurrent lung abscess of old chest injury", informant: Mrs. D.H. Barry (Shady Valley), buried: Gentry Cemetery, died: 3 Jul 1941, record (1941) #: 16001.

Ray Burl LEWIS, born: 1 Jul 1940, parents: James C. Lewis (Watauga Co. NC) and Gertrude Miller (Watauga Co. NC) cause of death: "acute colitis", informant: James C. Lewis (Trade), buried: Zionville Church, NC, died: 5 Jul 1941, record (1941) #: 16002.

Alexander Hamilton FRITTS, born: 17 Jul 1863, husband of Mrs. Millie South Fritts, parents: Reuben Fritts (Davidson Co. NC) and Kiziah Cress (Washington Co. VA), cause of death: "chronic brights disease", informant: R.D. Fritts (Mountain City), buried: Phillippi Cemetery, died: 2 Dec 1941, record (1941) #: 27112.

John Manuel POTTER, born: 29 Oct 1871, husband of Mrs. Terie Wagner Potter (age 67), parents: Thomas Jefferson Potter and Margaret Dunn, cause of death: "cerebral hemorrhage, broncho pneumonia", informant: Mrs. Roy Price (Shouns), buried: Potter Cemetery, died: 12 Dec 1941, record (1941) #: 27113.

Albert B. PHILLIPPI, born: 1 Aug 1870, husband of Rettie Cress Phillippi (age 70), parents: David Phillippi and Jane Frye, cause of death: "illegible, nephritis", informant: Roxie Arnold, (West VA), buried: Phillippi Cemetery, died: 17 Dec 1941, record (1941) #: 27114.

John H. JOHNSON, born: 1 Dec 1941, parents: Booker B. Johnson and Lura May, cause of death: "inter cranial hemorrhage", informant: Booker Johnson (Shouns), buried: McEwen Cemetery, died: 3 Dec 1941, record (1941) #: 27115.

Emma Jean DOWELL, born: 6 Dec 1941, parents: Lester Dowell and Verna Dunn, cause of death: "blue baby", buried: McEwen Cemetery, died: 6 Dec 1941, record (1941) #: 27716.

Roy Butler WILLIAMS, born: 18 Dec 1941, parents: father's name not stated and Ethel Williams, cause of death: "influenza and broncho pneumonia", informant: Runer Williams (Shouns), buried: Greer Cemetery, died: 23 Dec 1941, record (1941) #: 27117.

William McKinley LAWS, born: 14 Aug 1874, widower of Sallie Arnold Laws, parents: William Laws and Elizabeth Courtner, cause of death: "la grippe", informant: Mollie Laws (Butler), buried: Laws Cemetery, died: 18 Dec 1941, record (1941) #: 27118.

Lillie Catherine ROBINSON, born: 20 Apr 1874, divorced, parents: James Robinson and Mary Reece, cause of death: "lobar pneumonia", informant: Mrs Sallie Robinson (Mountain City), buried: Reece Cemetery, died: 28 Dec 1941, record (1941) #: 27119.

George Washington REEVES, colored, born: 27 Mar 1871, widower, parents: John Reeves (Ashe Co. NC) and Rinda McMillian (NC), cause of death: "influenza, broncho pneumonia", informant: Dexter Reeves (West VA), buried: Berea Baptist Church Cemetery, died: 28 Dec 1941, record (1941) #: 28792.

369

Abel, Bertha	46	Adams, Mae Wills	107
Abel, Bessie	80	Adams, Margaret	302
Abel, Clinton	241	Adams, Martha	341
Abel, Curt	80	Adams, Millie	295
Abel, Curtis	113,115	Adams, Minerva	63
Abel, Ed.	46	Adams, Nellie Bryan	347
Abel, Gladys	241	Adams, Roda	59
Abel, Henry Clayton	80	Adams, R.S.	341
Abel, H.C.	241	Adams, Sarah	152
Abel, Infant	115	Adams, Smith C.	240
Abel, Lillie Victoria	113	Adams, Sudie	129
Abel, Molvinie E.	113	Adams, Susan	220
Abel, Robert	46,113	Adams, Susanah	152
Abel, Sarah Ann	116	Adams, Wilbur	55
Able, Clint H.	307	Adams, Wilburn	113
Able, Clint H., Jr.	307	Adams, William James	37
Able, Florence A.	358	Adams, Winnie Cole	361
Able, James	138,358	Adams, Worley	155
Able, Launia M.	138	Adams, W.J.	152,155,189
Able, Lean	287	Adams. Billie	341
Able, Lucy Ellen	134	Adkins, Lucy	151
Able, Luther M.	138	Agers, Infant	68
Able, Robert	287	Agers, W.D.	68
Able, W.E.	287	Alfred, Martha	202,229
Absher, Mary	90	Allen, Alvin Columbus	309
Absher, Sarah	71	Allen, A.L.	82
Abshire, Caris Valie	106	Allen, Bertha	167
Acre, Lucy	89	Allen, Calvin	310
Adams, Abner	213	Allen, Carter	38,70,91
Adams, Adline	118	111,364	<
Adams, B.M.	107,367	Allen, Carter Stanley	70
Adams, Benjamin	50,227	Allen, Dealia	109
240	<	Allen, Edgar	267
Adams, Caroline	73,170	Allen, Grace	326
Adams, Dorsie Jean	295	Allen, Hamilton	271,312
Adams, Easter	182	Allen, Hattie	23
Adams, Edgar	240	Allen, Infant	326
Adams, Eliza Jane	266	Allen, Isaac	267
Adams, Elsie	315,334	Allen, James R.	164
Adams, Emma Virginia	367	Allen, James W.	91
Adams, Emmes	221	Allen, Jermie, L.	291
Adams, Frank	189	Allen, Jessie	309
Adams, George Willard	213	Allen, J.W.R.	280,312
Adams, Hazel	295	Allen, Lairinda	210
Adams, Infant	37	Allen, Mary Elizabeth	16
Adams, John	227,367	Allen, Minnie	239
Adams, Joseph	88	Allen, Ogden	82
Adams, Lena Kate	107	Allen, Rachel E.	252

Allen, Rankins 111
Allen, Robert 312
Allen, Ruth 267
Allen, Ruthie 247
Allen, R.G. 210
Allen, R.J. 207
Allen, R.L. 304
Allen, Sallie 250,285
364 <
Allen, Thomas 38
Allen, Vancy 109
Allen, Virginia P. 247
Allen, W.C. 285
Allen, W.L. 164, 252
Anderson, Amanda 193
Anderson, Anna 356
Anderson, Anna Ruth 196
Anderson, Arthur 99,184
Anderson, Asbell 180
Anderson, Bettie 155
Anderson, Caroline 187
Anderson, Clyde 334
Anderson, Cora 123
Anderson, Denver 288
Anderson, Don 361
Anderson, Earl 299
Anderson, Eugene Wyatt 57
Anderson, Ezra Oliver 206
Anderson, E.D. 193
Anderson, Hollace 361
Anderson, John 206,241
298,334 <
Anderson, John S. 120
Anderson, Jule 177
Anderson, J.C. 115
Anderson, J.R. 120,155
Anderson, J.S. 163,196
Anderson, Lucinda 334
Anderson, L.K. 173,195
220,257,260,288 <
Anderson, Malinda G. 288
Anderson, Mamie L. 173
Anderson, Margaret 50,104
163,173,188,235 <
Anderson, Mary 136
Anderson, Milton 136,288
Anderson, Nancy 33,174
Anderson, Nancy J. 308

Anderson, Noah 2,257,302
Anderson, Phylis Eula 299
Anderson, Rush 324
Anderson, Susia 99
Anderson, Susie 187,188
302 <
Anderson, Susie B. 120
Anderson, Tamalchus E.120
Anderson, Vicy 125
Anderson, William H. 57
Anderson, Wilma E. 324
Andrews, George J. 233
Andrews, Mary 238
Andrews, Mary 210
Andrews, Wheeler 233
Andrews, William 171
Archer, Andy 303
Archer, Lucy 303
Arker, Bertha 42
Arnett, Pearl 206
Arnette, William 155
Arney, Bessie 120
Arney, Carl 245
Arney, C.F. 127
Arney, Docia 127
Arney, D.J. 118
Arney, Ellen 130
Arney, Epsy 125
Arney, Franklin 173
Arney, Godfrey 120
Arney, Honey Danner 67
Arney, Honey L. 67
Arney, Isaac 118,120,177
Arney, Isaac (Mrs) 177
Arney, Joe 27
Arney, John 52,120,173
195,232 <
Arney, Joseph 177
Arney, Joseph D. 118
Arney, J.A. 67
Arney, J.D. 123
Arney, Lucey 104
Arney, Martha 171,195,308
Arney, Mary 131
Arney, Mattie 290
Arney, Mitchell 232
Arnie, Ettie 91
Arnie, Lockie 317

Arnie, Martha	158	Arnold, G.G.	362
Arnie, Ordie	136	Arnold, Hattie	224
Arnold, Alexander	319	Arnold, Hattie Millon	68
Arnold, Alfred	84	Arnold, Herman	318
Arnold, Alice	43	Arnold, Horn	319
Arnold, Andrew J.	95	Arnold, Infant	102,117
Arnold, Anna	37,248	192,265,318,331	<
Arnold, Annie	219	Arnold, James	80
Arnold, Aquilla	282	Arnold, James B.	68,327
Arnold, Baxter Grant	88	Arnold, James S.	144,212
Arnold, Bertha	364	Arnold, Jane	133
Arnold, Betsy	263	Arnold, Jarett	37
Arnold, Bettie	215,216	Arnold, Jarrett	289
256	<	Arnold, Jennie	178
Arnold, Billie	282	Arnold, Jesse	28
Arnold, Brina	282	Arnold, Jessie	120
Arnold, Bruce	353	Arnold, Jim	71
Arnold, Callie	37	Arnold, John	64,76,96
Arnold, Calvin	364	111,187,239,240,261<
Arnold, Carl Edgar	353	270,274,282	<
Arnold, Cassie	161	Arnold, John Henry	88
Arnold, Charles E.	364	Arnold, John H.	362
Arnold, Christina	364	Arnold, John M.	262
Arnold, Clara	362	Arnold, John W.	328
Arnold, Clarence	84	Arnold, Joseph	104
Arnold, Clarence M.	327	Arnold, Joseph P.	80
Arnold, Clayton	8	Arnold, Jospeh D.	357
Arnold, Clyde	171,180,238	Arnold, J.B.	68
Arnold, C.M.	91	Arnold, J.H.	64
Arnold, Dan	319	Arnold, J.M.	6
Arnold, Dayton Hunter	61	Arnold, J.S.	91
Arnold, Delilah O.	111	Arnold, Kelly	192
Arnold, D.M.	296	Arnold, Kinnie	61
Arnold, Ed	100	Arnold, Lark	299
Arnold, Eddie	22	Arnold, Leah	294
Arnold, Eliga	81	Arnold, Leva	136
Arnold, Eligah	63	Arnold, Lilian M.	182
Arnold, Eliza	244,286	Arnold, Lillie	289
Arnold, Elizabeth	24,180	Arnold, Louisie	110
189,199,280	<	Arnold, Lucinda	126,217
Arnold, Ellen	96,248	262	<
Arnold, Elva	270	Arnold, Mabel	84
Arnold, Emanuel	136	Arnold, Mack	127,144
Arnold, Eula	144	Arnold, Malissie	260,263
Arnold, E.G.	322	Arnold, Mamie	239
Arnold, Garfield	240	Arnold, Marion	63
Arnold, Garfield	83	Arnold, Martha	137,349
Arnold, Grant	322	Arnold, Mary	59,336

Arnold, Mary Ann   299,364
Arnold, Mary E.   95
Arnold, May   263
Arnold, Melvin   34,361
Arnold, Merida   43
Arnold, Merritt   328
Arnold, Milton   102
Arnold, Mollie   117
Arnold, Mollie V.   84
Arnold, M.E.   284
Arnold, M.W.   179
Arnold, M...   80
Arnold, Nancy   4,81,149
   270   <
Arnold, Nancy Ellen   322
   238   <
Arnold, Nancy Roark   261
Arnold, Nettie   64
Arnold, Nettie Belle   100
Arnold, Nova Reed   357
Arnold, Ollie   328
Arnold, Onnie   168
Arnold, Pollie   63
Arnold, Rachel   210,297
Arnold, Reba   241
Arnold, Richard J.   361
Arnold, Robert M.   71
Arnold, Robert R.   270
Arnold, Roxie   368
Arnold, Ruby Fay   171
Arnold, Ruby Jane   315
Arnold, Sallie   179
Arnold, Sarah E.   84
Arnold, Smith   364
Arnold, Susan   185
Arnold, Susie   73,174
Arnold, S. Charles   261
Arnold, S.C.   262
Arnold, Thelma Pauline   71
Arnold, Thomas Ware   261
   262   <
Arnold, Ulyssis Grant   248
Arnold, Vonna Lee   334
Arnold, Wilham   310
Arnold, William   265,331
   364   <
Arnold, William H.   331
Arnold, William Odis   265

Arnold, W.B.   169,182,192
Arnold, W.C.   286
Arnold, W.K.   161,315,334
   357   <
Arnold, W.L.   164
Arnold, W.S.   224
Arnold, Zallie   13
Arnold, ...   64
Aron, Thomas   18
Arrendell, Polly   150
Arter, Mary   208
Arwood, ...   217
Asbery, Reba   98
Asbury, Infant   198
Asbury, Ray   19
Asbury, Robert   198,300
Asham, John   120
Ashely, Everett   217
Ashland, ...   345
Ashley, Callie J.   300
Ashley, Catherine   67
Ashley, David   358,361
Ashley, Dealtha   195
Ashley, Edward   217
Ashley, Ellen   104
Ashley, Enoch   158,253
Ashley, Joe   250
Ashley, Mary Ruth   217
Ashley, Mattie   158
Ashley, Mollie   138
Ashley, Patsey   89
Ashley, Ruth   2
Ashley, W.M.   77
Atkins, Margaret   114
Atkins, Victoria   347
Atkins, ...   187
Atwood, Eva   280
Atwood, George   263
Atwood, George D.   316
Atwood, Helen   279
Atwood, Joe Vernon   279
Atwood, John V.   213,263
Atwood, Juila   207
Atwood, Lewis E.   213
Atwood, Martha   93,314
Atwood, Maude   316
Atwood, Pearl   207,213
Atwood, Rachel   279

Atwood, Ruby Lee	263	
Ausborn, Annie	157	
Ausbury, Betty	1	
Ausbury, Della	1	
Bagwell, Rebecca	265	
Bailey, Caroline	274	
Bailey, Frank	88,137,177	
Bailey, Frankie	221	
Bailey, Infant	317	
Bailey, Jack	219	
Bailey, Jackson	116	
Bailey, James	88,183,194	
317	<	
Bailey, Jennie	358	
Bailey, Jess	88	
Bailey, John	9,206	
Bailey, Lee	19	
Bailey, Lorette	109	
Bailey, Lucy	95	
Bailey, Mary	129	
Bailey, M...	294	
Bailey, Sarah	351	
Bailey, Thomas	177	
Bailey, William	45	
Baird, Temperance	117	
Baker, Alex	214	
Baker, Alex M.	268	
Baker, Alexander W.	268	
Baker, Anna	214	
Baker, A.M.	173,362	
Baker, Betsy Ann	264	
Baker, Bud	105	
Baker, Clarrissa	243	
Baker, Daniel Boone	268	
Baker, Eliza	105	
Baker, Elizabeth	200	
Baker, Ella	211,216	
Baker, Ellen	142	
Baker, Frank	105	
Baker, John	365	
Baker, Katherine	194	
Baker, Katy	209	
Baker, Laura A.	20	
Baker, Lovie Lucinda	352	
Baker, Lyndia	87	
Baker, Nancy Catherine	283	
Baker, Nora	305	
Baker, Sarah	345	
Baker, Sarah Ann N.	362	
Baker, Sarah Bell	347	
Baker, Thomas Alex	214	
Baker, Thomas A.	347,352	
Baker, Tom	88	
Baker, ...	23,54	
Baldwin, Massie O.	111	
Baldwin, William W.	111	
Balur, Augusta	19	
Baly, Amamda	94	
Baner, John	280	
Ban..., Earl	21	
Bare, Mary	312	
Bare, Meacy	53	
Barker, Robert	262	
Barlow, Alma R.	184	
Barlow, James D.	68	
Barlow, James J.	49,68	
Barlow, J.M.	213	
Barlow, May	280	
Barlow, Rosabell	175	
Barlow, Vivian Eller	49	
Barnes, Mary Ruby	359	
Barnett, Maggie	235	
Barns, Lula V.	300	
Barry, Alex	175,208,282	
Barry, Alexander A.	206	
Barry, A.A.	215	
Barry, David Henry	367	
Barry, David Isaac	53	
Barry, Dicie	110	
Barry, Dora Marie	182	
Barry, D.H. (Mrs)	367	
Barry, D.K.	161	
Barry, Estellie	165	
Barry, E.E.	223	
Barry, Hugh	53,122,175	
206,237	<	
Barry, Jettie	367	
Barry, Joel	28	
Barry, John Clarence	122	
Barry, Laura	121	
Barry, Lula	321	
Barry, Mary Ivaline	237	
Barry, Melvin	367	
Barry, Stacy	161,182	
Barry, Stacy E.	175	
Barry, T.J.	3	

Barry, Virginia Ruth 161
Barry, William 206,239
Barry, William H. 324
Bashel, James 127
Bass, Jane 88
Bauguess, Susan E. 356
Bauguess, Tyrle V. 247
Bear, Ellen 179
Bear, Isaac 80
Bear, Mollie 80
Beard, Akly 97
Beeler, A.B. 89
Beeler, Martha Lucy 89
Bell, Hazel 230
Bell, Sarah 338
Beltzboone, Margaret 268
Benfield, Cora 151
Bentley, Eveline 143
Bentley, George D. 143
Bentley, Goldie V. 201
Bentley, John 102,132
Bentley, J.M. 201
Bently, Birtha 100
Bently, Charlie 25
Bently, George 100,357
Bently, Henry Monroe 24
Bently, Herald W. 102
Bently, James 357
Benton, Ora 138
Berry , Laura 88
Berry, Alexander A. 62
Berry, Alexander T. 301
Berry, Catherine 181,235
    322 <
Berry, Catherine M. 40
Berry, Charles 188
Berry, Daniel (Mrs) 314
Berry, D. Hugh 54
Berry, D.H. 188
Berry, Eliza 205
Berry, Eliza J. 176
Berry, Elizabeth 131
Berry, E.W. 68
Berry, Infant 68
Berry, Isaac Daniel 54
Berry, Jennia C. 175
Berry, Louvenia C. 301
Berry, Margaret 309

Berry, Mary 248
Berry, Robert E. 301
Berry, Sarah 193,219,222
Berry, Wallace C. 223
Berry, William Melvin 188
Berry, W.L. 326
Beshears, ... 291
Biar, Patton 164
Billings, Alice 71
Bingham, Charlotte 356
Bishefl, Elizabeth 280
Bishop, B.M. 189
Bishop, Charles, E. 20
Bishop, Connelly 193
Bishop, Elbert 25,71,73
    334 <
Bishop, Eli 71
Bishop, Helen 183
Bishop, Hillery 334
Bishop, John 73,269
Bishop, J.C. 73
Bishop, J.L. 334
Bishop, Margaret L. 112
Bishop, Millane 264
Bishop, M.F. 264
Bishop, Nancy E. 112
Bishop, N.N. 46,60
Bishop, Ottie 334
Bishop, Reece 183
Bishop, Robert L. 60
Bishop, R.L. 71,112,193
Bishop, S.J. 183
Bishop, Thelma Blanch 264
Black, Jane 242
Blackburn, Andrew 173
Blackburn, Blonde 21
Blackburn, Callie 27
Blackburn, Eva C. 344
Blackburn, Florence 1
Blackburn, Gladys 186
Blackburn, H.J. 344
Blackburn, J.B. 83
Blackburn, Lacy 11
Blackburn, Melvania 152
Blackburn, Nancy 150
Blackburn, Noah 80
Blackburn, N.J. 43
Blackburn, Pearl 152,186

Blackburn, Phineous H.173
Blackburn, Richard W. 80
Blackburn, Rosa   128
Blackburn, R.O.   39,80
Blackburn, Soloman   173
Blackburn, Tan Rew   43
Blackburn, Verdie   100
Blackburn, William M. 39
Blackburn, W.B.   128
Blackburn, Zella May 152
Blackburn, Zon   10
Blanches, Mary   57
Blankenbeckler, C.T. 140
Blankenbeckler, Due V.140
Blankenbeckler, J.M. 285
Blankenbeckler, Marion343
Blankenbeckler, Mary 250
Blankenbeckler, Nanie 116
Blankenbeckler, Ollie 343
Blankenbeckler, Oscar 74
  116   <
Blankenbeckler, Robt. 343
Blankenbeckler, Wm.   74
Bledsoe, William   356
Blevins, Alfred H.156,222
Blevins, Alice Annie 190
Blevins, Amanda   336
Blevins, Andrew J.   204
Blevins, Arthur   360
Blevins, A.H.   323
Blevins, A.S.   227
Blevins, Berryman   205
Blevins, Bessie B.   172
Blevins, Betsy   230,325
Blevins, Blanch   133
Blevins, B.J.   198
Blevins, Chester   216
Blevins, Chester C. 131
Blevins, C.C.   206,262
Blevins, C.F.   192,222
Blevins, C.R.   190,238
Blevins, David Henry 306
Blevins, David H. 181,236
Blevins, Dennis O.   163
Blevins, Dorcus B.   156
Blevins, Dual   161
Blevins, D.H.   160
Blevins, Edith B.   154

Blevins, Edney   138
Blevins, Edrie   343
Blevins, Elcany   329
Blevins, Eliza   168,294
Blevins, Eliza C.   256
Blevins, Elizabeth   160
  164,304   <
Blevins, Ellen   298
Blevins, Ellen Ellora 298
Blevins, Eugene L.   340
Blevins, E.A.   72
Blevins, E.G.   171
Blevins, George   168,236
  340,354   <
Blevins, George S.   40
Blevins, Grover D.   155
Blevins, Guy   315
Blevins, G.S.   181
Blevins, Herman   133
Blevins, Hiram B.   12
Blevins, Ina   360
Blevins, Infant   154
Blevins, Ira   154
Blevins, James   53,193
  219,222   <
Blevins, James M.   193
Blevins, James S.   168
Blevins, James Vanoy 216
Blevins, Jessie W.   110
  154   <
Blevins, J.B.F.   336,349
Blevins, J.W.   56
Blevins, Laura Alice 204
Blevins, Lillie   306
Blevins, Loony   238
Blevins, Lucinda 190,205
  311,317,344   <
Blevins, Luta M.   178
Blevins, Luther W.   216
Blevins, Luzins   354
Blevins, Lydia   125,209
Blevins, Maggie   303
Blevins, Margaret 96,145
  185,332   <
Blevins, Marice E.   212
Blevins, Martha Ellen 50
Blevins, Martin E.   38
Blevins, Mathus   176

Blevins, Matthew   205
Blevins, Maude   283
Blevins, Millard   360
Blevins, Mina Grace   133
Blevins, Myrtle P.   56
Blevins, M.F.   193
Blevins, Nancy   60
Blevins, Nathaniel   20
Blevins, Orval Gray   110
Blevins, O.M.   50
Blevins, Pollie   350
Blevins, Ralph Eugene   171
Blevins, Rettie   221
Blevins, Roddy C.   306
Blevins, Rouena   134
Blevins, Roy   349
Blevins, Roy P.   152
Blevins, Rufus M.   219
Blevins, Russell H.   163
Blevins, R.N.   303
Blevins, Sallie Manda   349
Blevins, Sarah E.   38,40
Blevins, Stella   183
Blevins, Susannah   123
Blevins, Tilda Louisa   315
Blevins, T.E.   161
Blevins, Ula Ethel   204
Blevins, Vinnie E.   60
Blevins, Virgie   107
Blevins, Warren A.   221
Blevins, Washington   123
Blevins, Wesley   133,134
Blevins, Wesley J.   155
Blevins, Wilham   235
Blevins, William   40,181
         322,336   <
Blevins, William M.   176
         236   <
Blevins, Woodrow   306
Blevins, W.J.   155
Blevins, W.T. (Mrs)   158
Blevins, W.W.   38
Blevins, ...   113,340
Bolden, Austin   256
Bolden, A.J.   361
Bolden, Cola Agnes   269
Boldin, Austin   232,269
Boldin, Rufus B.   232

Boltenhammer, Celia L.284
Boman, Christopher   44
Boman, William M.   44
Boran, Charles   189
Boran, Jane   189
Bor..., Ora   77
Botehammer, Loretta   324
Bougess, Osborne   247
Bowers, Dora Blanche   321
Bowers, Millie Ida   97
Bowers, Sallie   362
Bowling, Alice   100
Bowling, Austin   315
Bowling, Mary   357
Bowling, Mary Alice   143
Bowling, Reba Lee   315
Bowling, Reba Mae   315
Bowling, S.H.   100
Bowman, David   177
Bowman, D...   41
Bowman, Eva   49
Bowman, E.S. (Mrs)   328
bowman, Hash   348
Bowman, Julia E.   213
Bowman, Lucy   49
Bowman, Mannie Louise   177
Bowman, Martha Osborn   104
Bowman, R.L.   104
Bowman, Sallie   104
Bowman, Thomas   41
Bowman, Wash   354
Bowman, William   49
Bowman, W.B.   104
Brace, G.W.   150
Brace, J.W.   150
Bradley, Catherine   292
Bradley, Edna   276
Bradley, Erven   106
Bradley, Eva   106
Bradley, Ezekil G.   192
Bradley, Infant   141
Bradley, Irvin Kyle   192
Bradley, Irwin   320
Bradley, J.K.   59
Bradley, Lila   145
Bradley, Mary E.   78
Bradley, Mary Jane   75
Bradley, Nancy C.   152

Bradley, Naomi 268
Bradley, Neta 141
Bradley, Peter Kyle 78
106 <
Bradley, Rebecca 193
Bradley, Richard 152
Branch, Lemis 213
Breeding, Elmer 307
Breeding, William 228
Brewer, Annie 83
Brewer, A.G. 83
Brewer, A.J. 84
Brewer, A.L. 191,353
Brewer, Billie 296
Brewer, Grady Arvil 191
Brewer, James 353
Brewer, Joseph 84
Brewer, Lola 18
Brewer, Matison 207
Brewer, Miles F. 84
Brewer, Susie 353
Brewer, Winey 67
Bridges, Jane 181
Bridges, ... 208
Briggs, Dora L. 335
Briggs, Joseph Thomas 335
Briggs, Samuel 335
Brinkley, Billy Odell 341
Brinkley, Odell 341
Brinkley, Wile 88
Broce, Cassie M. 335
Broce, George W. 228,323
Broce, Jake E. 335
Broce, Loneviney C. 323
Broce, Maude 228,323
Broglin, Andy 228
Broglin, Elizabeth 228
Brooks, A.C. 36
Brooks, A.J. 124
Brooks, Benie Mae 99
Brooks, Billie 99
Brooks, Carrie 68
Brooks, C.S. 217
Brooks, C.S., Jr. 217
Brooks, Edgar Dave 92
Brooks, Eli 242
Brooks, John Calvin 242
Brooks, J.C. 110
Brooks, Kemp 92
Brooks, Mary 147
Brooks, Rebecca 81
Brooks, Robin 110
Brooks, R.K. 92
Brooks, R.R. 81
Brooks, Thomas 242
Brooks, Virgie Myrtle 25
Brooks, Walter 99
Brookshire, Bert E. 345
Brookshire, Cassie 51
Brookshire, Eliizabeth246
Brookshire, George 304
Brookshire, Infant 215
Brookshire, Irene 313,345
Brookshire, Jenet Sue 323
Brookshire, Joel 92,184
215,260,281 <
Brookshire, J.F. 281
Brookshire, Laura 281
Brookshire, Lila Mae 139
Brookshire, Margaret 341
Brookshire, Noah 289,345
Brookshire, Noah F. 281
Brookshire, Reuette 69,92
Brookshire, R.J. 260
Brookshire, Sam 323
Brookshire, Sherman G.289
Brookshire, S.G. 260
Brookshire, Venie 80,83
Brookshire, W.D. 51,139
184 <
Brown, America 220
Brown, Arthur Ray 124
Brown, Augusta 99
Brown, A.C. 268
Brown, A.E. (Mrs) 353
Brown, A.N. 345
Brown, Balely Dean 315
Brown, B.S. 255
Brown, Celia 54
Brown, Charles 328
Brown, Charlie 121
Brown, Cora 211
Brown, Cora Jane 199
Brown, C.L. 328
Brown, Dewey 348
Brown, Dock 293

Brown, Emory   58
Brown, Ethel   84,97,99
Brown, Ezekiel   284,345
Brown, E.L.   84,99,180
Brown, E.S.   129,180
Brown, Flossie A.   350
Brown, George   255
Brown, George Wesley 345
Brown, Harve E.   58
Brown, Hattie   322
Brown, Hirbert Wade   84
Brown, H.C.   268
Brown, Infant   99
Brown, Jackson   121
Brown, James   235,292
Brown, John   211,245,255
Brown, John T.   251
Brown, J.H.   97
Brown, J.M.   117
Brown, Kizzie   117
Brown, Lewis   245
Brown, Lillie   51
Brown, Lizina   173
Brown, Louis   201,225
Brown, Margaret   353
Brown, Margaret B.   365
Brown, Martha   130,354
Brown, Martha C.   173
Brown, Martia   275
Brown, Martitia   222
Brown, Marvin   328
Brown, Mary   327
Brown, Mary Mae   345
Brown, Millard F.   251
Brown, Mollie   224
Brown, M.F.   51,184,350
Brown, Nannie   207
Brown, Nomia E.   292
Brown, Patsey   121
Brown, Quincy Roscoe 255
Brown, Robert B.   255
Brown, Roby   177
Brown, Roby Barton   235
Brown, Ruby G.   129
Brown, Russell   315
Brown, R.B.   102,107
Brown, R.R.   173,227
Brown, Sarah L.   51

Brown, Snoull Lee   180
Brown, Stacy   211
Brown, Susa   284
Brown, Susie   345
Brown, Tilman F.   350
Brown, Tommie George 348
Brown, T.F.   97
Brown, Wesley   284
Brown, Wilborn   225
Brown, William   58,177
Brown, William A. 124,255
Brown, W.A.   148
Browqn, James W.   3
Bruer, Will   149
Bruer, William E.   149
Brumit, Francis P.   308
Brumit, Harold Ryder 308
Bruon, Retta   174
Bryand, Maggie   141
Bryand, Sam   141
Bryant, Amos   168,263
Bryant, Amous   297
Bryant, Dorothy Mae 263
Bryant, Edith   168
Bryant, Fannie   38
Bryant, George   168
Bryant, Julia   281
Bryant, Julia Ann   263
Bryant, J.G.   297
Bryant, Lorene Grace 141
Bryant, Rebecca   124
Bryant, Sam   280
Bryant, Samuel   141
Bryant, Virginia L. 280
Buce, J.F.   7
Buchanan, Arter   243
Buchanan, Bessie   80
Buchanan, J,M.   80
Buchanan, Joseph M. 243
Buchanan, J.B.   80
Buchanan, J.M.   83
Buchanan, Mary Essa 83
Buchanan, W.M.   293
Buckles, Caroline 212,329
Buckles, E.J.   77
Buckles, Francis   334
Buckles, Frank   332
Buckles, Glenn   334

Buckles, James C.   239
Buckles, Laura   185
Buckles, Laurinda   332
Buckles, William   185
Buckles, William F.   185
Buckles, William H.   239
Buckner, Sarah   38
Bumgardner, Alexander   301
Bumgardner, Clarence   33
Bumgardner, David   43,209
    234,301   <
Bumgardner, George W.   365
Bumgardner, G.W.   43
Bumgardner, Hattie L.   76
Bumgardner, Jimmie   33
Bumgardner, John   43,234
Bumgardner, Mary   115
Bumgardner, Millard   209
Bumgardner, M.F.   76
Bumgardner, Stella   301
Bumgardner, Walter   234
Bumgardner, William M.365
Bunting, Dewey   166,318
Bunting, Elizabeth   122
Bunting, Fonnie   319
Bunting, Harrison   153
Bunting, Maggie   319
Bunting, Mary Bell   318
Bunting, Millard   319
Bunting, N.   179
Bunting, Sarah C.   337
Bunting, Spencer   337
Bunting, U.S.   337
Bunting, Walter   166
Bunting, W.H.   166
Bunton, Anna Francis   182
Bunton, B.I.   226
Bunton, Dana Linell   167
Bunton, Elija   268
Bunton, Ellie   93
Bunton, Esther   226
Bunton, Faun   216
Bunton, Fawn   346,366
Bunton, Frank   271
Bunton, George   82
Bunton, James   279
Bunton, Jane Geneva   226
Bunton, Jannie   88

Bunton, Kermit   280
Bunton, Leaah E.   279
Bunton, Leona   214
Bunton, Lois Phillis   271
Bunton, Lorie   347
Bunton, Luther S.   161
Bunton, Martha C.   211
Bunton, Mary   113
Bunton, Nancy Jane   40
Bunton, Nannie   95
Bunton, Ot   133
Bunton, Pearl   271,354
Bunton, Rebecca   167
Bunton, Rosa   280
Bunton, Rose Nell   346
Bunton, R.L.   280
Bunton, Sabra   226
Bunton, Samuel   161
Bunton, Sarah   172
Bunton, Sarah Ann   352
Bunton, Saran   36
Bunton, Scott   167,271
Bunton, Selma   366
Bunton, Susan   227
Bunton, Susuan   43,44
Bunton, S.R.   211
Bunton, Taylor   82,268
Bunton, William   190
Bunton, William G.   182
Bunton, ...   352
Burchett, Edd   313
Burgess, Laura   61
Burgess, Mattie Pearl   163
Burgess, Sally   82
Burgis, Infant   121
Burgis, McKinley   121
Burgis, Wiley   121
Burgiss, Fred Elbert   250
Burgiss, McKinley   250
Burkett, Maggie   257
Burnette, Franklin   156
Burnette, Infant   156
Burtin, John L.   115
Burtin, Virginia   262
Burton, Alfred Taylor   115
Burton, Alma L.   117
Burton, A. Lafayette   189
Burton, A.L.   182,189

Burton, A.L., Jr. 182
Burton, Celia 155
Burton, Clint 216
Burton, Clint, Jr. 216
Burton, Conrad 366
Burton, Coy M. 19
Burton, Dora 150
Burton, Etta 293
Burton, Gladis K. 208
Burton, Hiram 125
Burton, Joe 55
Burton, John 349
Burton, John Q. 125
Burton, Joseph Bride 55
Burton, Linell 214
Burton, Lucinda 189
Burton, Martha 33,314
Burton, Martin 208
Burton, Nat Romulus 135
Burton, Raleigh 146,214
  224,262 <
Burton, Ralph 224
Burton, Ray 146
Burton, Riley 117
Burton, Stella 224
Burton, Tom 110
Burton, Troy E. 33
Buskell, ... 334
Bussell, Poisley 39
Bussell, Sarah A. 39
Bussell, William F. 39
Butler, Edward East 254
Butler, Edward E. 365
Butler, Etta M. 365
Butler, E.E. 216,254
Butler, E.E., Sr. 211
Butler, Flora 53
Butler, Infant 139
Butler, James D. 139
Butler, James G. 140
Butler, James R. 59
Butler, J.C. (Dr) 337
Butler, J.S. 94
Butler, Lelia Kiser 353
Butler, Mattie 91
Butler, Nancy Anna I. 337
Butler, Richard H. 232
Butler, R.H. 337

Butler, R.H. (Mrs) 141
Butler, R.R. 140,232,254
Butler, Sallie 194
Butler, S.G.D. 353
Butler, William E. 211
  216 <
Buton, Emla 13
Byars, Alenzo 108
Byars, David 108
Byars, Fannie 201
Byers, Calvin 237
Byers, Calvin J. 366
Byers, Clyde 237
Byers, David 366
Byers, Lynda 96
Byers, Pauline 237
Byrd, Eliza 102
Byress, William 328
Cable, Amanda 165,298
Cable, Andrew 193
Cable, Andy 276
Cable, Arthur 255
Cable, Ben 155
Cable, Benjamin 86,247
Cable, Benjamin D. 86
Cable, B.D. 145
Cable, Caroline 319,329
Cable, Carrol 18
Cable, Celia 115,349
Cable, Conrad Burt 346
Cable, Cora 13
Cable, C. Burton 255
Cable, Delia 366
Cable, Delmas Clide 308
Cable, Dewey 224,238,258
  308 <
Cable, Dock 193
Cable, Elizabeth 119,154
  166 <
Cable, Elmine 69
Cable, Frances 269
Cable, Francis 276
Cable, Gladys A. 54
Cable, Hazle 137
Cable, Hester 207
Cable, Ida 242
Cable, James 243
Cable, James P. 243,348

Cable, James Ralph 224
Cable, Jane 114
Cable, John 230
Cable, John A. 18
Cable, Kermit 366
Cable, Mary 190,197,261
Cable, Rhoda 255
Cable, Rilda 239
Cable, Rodie 65
Cable, Rody 43
Cable, Ronda 348
Cable, Ruth Kathryn 238
Cable, Sallie 200,319
346,366 <
Cable, Spencer 243
Cable, Susan Jane 230
Cable, Susanna 111
Cable, Tempa 50
Cable, Thomas 122
Cable, Thomas W. 54
Cable, Trula 255
Cable, T.J. 346
Cable, U.G. 137
Cable, Will 366
Cable, William 86,111
247 <
Cable, William U.G. 366
Cable, W.F. 146
Cable, W.G. 298
Calahan, James 52
Calahan, Maggie 52
Caldwell, Walter 292
Calhoon, Sarah 302
Calloway, Hattie T. 342
Calloway, Joe 150
Calloway, Shade 342
Camel, Cornelia 332
Cammel, Louisa 97
Campbell, Ada 172
Campbell, Alice 179
Campbell, Callie 152
Campbell, Cordelia 78
Campbell, Dale 303
Campbell, Dallas O. 316
Campbell, Dana 316
Campbell, Daton 224
Campbell, David L. 178
Campbell, Dayton 61

Campbell, D.A. 159,176
Campbell, Easter 138
Campbell, Ellen 147
Campbell, Elmer 50
Campbell, Elmer D. 303
Campbell, Esther 226
Campbell, Finnie 155
Campbell, George W. 83
Campbell, Hagy 263
Campbell, Hattie 61,357
Campbell, Hester 332
Campbell, H.A. 137
Campbell, Infant 58,159
176 <
Campbell, Isaac 46
Campbell, Isaac H. 50
Campbell, Isabell 343
Campbell, Jake 256
Campbell, James 138,325
Campbell, John 51,123
168,201 <
Campbell, Joseph L. 201
Campbell, Jula N. 148
Campbell, Julia C. 325
Campbell, J.C. 225
Campbell, J.J. 58
Campbell, Latitia 110
Campbell, Laura Kate 233
Campbell, Lenis Kate 226
Campbell, Lillie May 132
Campbell, Lizzie 17
Campbell, Loura B. 119
Campbell, L.C. 359
Campbell, Major 325
Campbell, Martha 325
Campbell, Martha Ann 182
Campbell, Mary 130,225
Campbell, Mary L. 27
Campbell, Matilda 234
Campbell, N.D. 27,119
152,155 <
Campbell, Pemel 252
Campbell, Polly 181,339
Campbell, Powell 83
Campbell, Rasa L. 174
Campbell, Richard L. 92
Campbell, Robert 174
Campbell, R.D. 175

Campbell, R.L.	132		Cardwell, J.G.	69
Campbell, Sabra	131		Cardwell, J.R.	146
Campbell, Sallie	73		Cardwell, Mary	342
Campbell, Sam	152		Cardwell, Nora	69
Campbell, Samuel	58,105		Cardwell, Rosco	160
161	<		Carico, Samuel M.	24
Campbell, Sarah	27,59		Carier, Alva	42
67,175	<		Carier, Sallie S.	42
Campbell, Sarah E.	55		Carpenter, Annie	150
Campbell, Selmer	46		Carrigan, Emma	344
Campbell, Thomas	226		Carriger, Allen L.	320
Campbell, Vicie	67		Carriger, Allen T.	235
Campbell, Viola	343		Carriger, Betsy	110
Campbell, Wilborn	138		Carriger, Eliza	320
Campbell, Wilder	233,325		Carriger, Ethel E.	269
Campbell, Worley	105		Carriger, Grant	269
Campbell, W.D.	147,161		Carriger, Hazel Irene	290
Campbell, Zacharia	67		Carrol, Julia A.	45
Campbell, Zelda Pearl	92		Carroll, Betty	143
Campbell, ...	75		Carrtner, Nancy	158
Campbil, Lemiel	26		Carter, Bennie	320
Cander, Sarah	262		Carter, Eliza	347
Cannon, Callie	363		Carter, Elizie	351
Cannon, Eliza	218		Carter, Maryon	34
Cannon, Henry C.	276		Carthur, Julia Ann	187
Cannon, Juanita Joyce	276		Carver, Bonnie	323
CAnnon, Sarah Millie	218		Catron, Sidury	178
Cannon, W.A.	218		Caudell, Moses	53
Canter, C.C.	322		Caudell, Nancy Jane	53
Canter, David	268		Caudill, Bettie	226
Canter, Elizabeth	173,218		Caudill, C. Ross	201
Canter, Enoch	114,268		Caudill, Frankie	254
Canter, John	324		Caudill, Moses	129
Canter, J.H.	173		Caudill, Stephen	129
Canter, Louisa E.	173		Caudill, Willard	129
Canter, Nancy	114		Cawood, Celil Carl	166
Canter, Ruby Joe	326		Cawood, Lillian Ruth	165
Canter, Sarah	324		Cawood, W.J.	166
Canter, Will	78		Cawood, W.P.	165
Canter, William	326		Cayles, C.H. (Mrs)	347
Capmbell, R.D.	152		Chandler, John	311
Carby, Susa	48		Chapel, Franklin	329
Cardell, ...	330		Chapel, F.M.	3
Cardue, Clara	87		Chaple, F.M.	315
Cardwell, Boyd R.	146		Chappell, Ellen	273
Cardwell, Harrison	342		Chappell, Francis M.	248
Cardwell, James	342		Chappell, Frank G.	224
Cardwell, John	160		Chappell, F.M.	267

Chappell, Joseph L.   248
Chappell, Stacy   273
Chappell, William   224
Chappell, W.F.   248
Chester, Clifford L.   68
Christie, Vera   94
Church, Ainer   95
Church, Alexander   64
Church, Amos   71
Church, A.G.   330
Church, Bessie 83,250,273
Church, Bonnie   314
Church, Callie   306
Church, Calvin   306
Church, Calvin J.   27
Church, Charity   244
Church, Charley   71
Church, Charlie   161
Church, Clydie   222
Church, Elizabeth Jane   274
Church, Elizabeth J.   113
Church, Eula   341
Church, Eulah May   250
Church, Garfield   98
Church, Hugh M.   71
Church, Infant   127
Church, Irvin   98
Church, James   104
Church, Jeff   64
Church, Jess   261
Church, Jesse C.   41
Church, Jessie Calvin   344
Church, Jessie C.   118,344
Church, John Linville   41
Church, John L.   208
Church, Joseph P.   306
Church, J.C.   127,250
Church, J.G.   205
Church, J.L.   41,49
Church, Lena   142
Church, Marry   71
Church, Martha   96,155
            189,239,240,355 <
Church, Martha Louise   37
Church, Mary Ann   55
Church, Mollie   97
Church, Phillip   298
Church, Rebecca   205

Church, Sallie   214
Church, Sanna   49
Church, Sarah   294
Church, Sarah Arnold   104
Church, Sarah M.   330
Church, Susan   55,113
Church, Susie Smith   344
Church, T.J.   47
Church, Virginia Lee   250
Church, W. Susan   261
Claimans, Infant   72
Claimans, Worley   72
Clanton, Sallie   323
Clark, B.D. (Mrs)   363
Clark, Lafayette   13
Clark, Mary   72
Clark, Silas   232
Clark, Silas A.   292
Clauson, Sedna   272
Clawson, Nancy   179
Clock, Eller   81
Coalman, Venia   46
Coffee, Celia   150,243
Coffee, McCaleb   153
Coffee, Sarah   125
Coffee, S.W.   67
Coffee, Thomas   67
Coffie, Jerrie   153
Coinstner, Lida   42
Colbaugh, Celia   231
Colbaugh, Susie   152
Colbert, Betsy   153
Colbolt, Celia   180
Colbox, Celia   231
Coldron, Elzina   365
Coldwell, Robert   280
Cole, Albert C.   190
Cole, Alice   50
Cole, Alice Lena   221
Cole, Anna   68,206,237
Cole, Annie   131,158,262
Cole, Bell   284
Cole, Bishop J.   116
Cole, Callie   116
Cole, Celia   284
Cole, Della   133,134
Cole, D.N.   56
Cole, Earl   35

Cole, Elan	26		Cook, Sallie	339	
Cole, Isaac E.	73		Cook, Walsey	163	
Cole, Jessie	54		Cook, W.L. (Mrs)	304,359	
Cole, Joseph Alexander	116		Cooper, Jessie	314	
Cole, J.A.	75		Cooper, Mary Laura	314	
Cole, J.A. (Mrs)	133,134		Copey, Hartilna C.	335	
Cole, J.B.	328		Copling, Caroline	266	
Cole, Lidia	240		Copling, Thomas James	266	
Cole, Lydia	269		Corentt, Jeremiah	217	
Cole, Max Browne	353		Cornett, Callie	196	
Cole, M.E.	21		Cornett, David Ensley	325	
Cole, Pollie	293		Cornett, Della	39,350	
Cole, Rachel	362		Cornett, Filmore	180,183	
Cole, Richard	353		Cornett, Ham	325	
Cole, R.A.	88,105,162,313		Cornett, Infant	160	
Cole, Sallie R.	73		Cornett, Jennie V.	325	
Cole, Sara	98		Cornett, Jerry	327	
Cole, Sarah	289		Cornett, Loyd Roger	363	
Cole, Sarah A.	26		Cornett, Mack J. (Mrs)	359	
Cole, Sarah Virginia	328		Cornett, Mary	186	
Cole, Susan	106,283		Cornett, Maud	30	
Cole, Susie	80,168		Cornett, Milborn	31	
Cole, Washington	190,361		Cornett, M.C.	186	
Cole, ...	289		Cornett, Nancy	202,318	
Coleman, Coy	118,190		343	<	
Coleman, Mary	118		Cornett, Newt	160	
Coleman, Rebecca	286,347		Cornett, N.V.	39	
Coleman, Rosa Lee	190		Cornett, Ollie	312	
Colston, George E.	357		Cornett, Ora	176	
Colton, Lucy	89		Cornett, Oscar	160	
Colvard, Fannie	363		Cornett, Pashie	290	
Colvin, Ethel	332		Cornett, Polly J.	222	
Colvin, William M.	332		Cornett, Ray Blaine	148	
Combs, Andrew	94		Cornett, Rebecca	233	
Combs, Byron G.	21		Cornett, Relee	183	
Combs, Infant	184		Cornett, Reuben	148	
Combs, Isabel	213		Cornett, Robert	363	
Combs, Manley	184		Cornett, Rosa	187	
Comer, Polly	29		Cornett, Rossie	326	
Congden, Rebecca	109		Cornett, Roy	186	
Cook, Catherine	301		Cornett, Susan	351	
Cook, Elbert	163		Cornett, Sylvester	121	
Cook, Elizabeth	119		Cornett, Sylvester Jr.	121	
Cook, Jacob	119		Cornett, Trillie	180	
Cook, Katie	305		Cornett, Vadia J.	356	
Cook, Mamie Fuller	359		Cornett, Wesley	325	
Cook, Mary Ann	345		Cornett, William	196	
Cook, Nolia	268		Cornett, William O.	356	

Cornett, ...   85,334
Correll, Hiley   24
Cortner, Andrew J.   221
Cortner, James   221
Corum, Annie   42,311
Corum, Bell   285
Corum, Belle   170,181
Corum, Bernic C.   159
Corum, Bessie   58,174
Corum, B.G.   291
Corum, Ed   174
Corum, Edward Glenn   291
Corum, Infant 31,100,181
    291   <
Corum, Maggie L.   285
Corum, Martha   79
Corum, Ray   157
Corum, Robert Galen   79
Corum, Roy   100,170
Corum, R.G.   31
Corum, T.H.   285
Corum, Walter   285
Cottrell, Barbara Anne290
Cottrell, J.D.   290
Council, Evelyn   295
Council, Nancy   81,261
Courtner, Betsy   247
Courtner, Betty   285
Courtner, Elizabeth   332
    368   <
Courtner, George   221
Courtner, Infant   188
Courtner, John   255,262
Courtner, Julia Kate   255
Courtner, Nancy   189
Courtner, R. Allen   188
Cowan, Beatris   55
Cowan, Betty Jean   359
Cowan, Floy   55
Cowan, Julia   359
Cowan, Nancy Jane   61
Cowan, Wiley Thomas   359
Cowans, Flossie   158
Cowans, Margaret   308
Cowans, T.B.   308
Cox, Joshua   356
Cozart, Nancy   310
Cozart, William   50

Cramer, William   30
Crawford, Blanch   118
Crawford, Callie T.   351
Crawford, Diskey Hagn 147
Crawford, D.H.   351
Crawford, Infant   24
Crawford, Mande   351
Crawford, William   147
Crawford, W.M.   264
Creed, George   235
Creed, George F.   178
Cregor, Jestia   316
Cresorey, Mary   220
Cress, Alvon Ray   91
Cress, Anna   173
Cress, A.M.   91,160
Cress, Callie   337
Cress, Caroline   331
Cress, Catherine   350
Cress, Claude   314
Cress, Daniel   164
Cress, Daniel H.   152
Cress, David   198
Cress, Edsel Wayne   314
Cress, Eliza C.   322
Cress, Georgia Mae   45
Cress, John Henry   337
Cress, John M.   148
Cress, J.C.   337
Cress, Kiziah   367
Cress, Martha   65,91,214
    321,244   <
Cress, Martha M.   331
Cress, Mary   277
Cress, Michael   42
Cress, Minnie   174
Cress, Mollie   154
Cress, Myrtle   160
Cress, M.L.   223
Cress, Nealey   105
Cress, Nicholas   152
Cress, Reeves   175
Cress, Robert L.   247
Cress, Rufus   140
Cress, R.L.   173,174
Cress, Sallie   292
Cress, Sarah   247
Cress, S.D.   337

Cress, Uriah 207
Cress, Vina 9
Cress, William 198
Cress, Willie Lucile 173
Cress, W.A. 91
Cress, W.L. 160
Cresson, Rebecca 358
Crigger, Daniel 303
Crigger, Jestie 272
Crissinger, Oliver 63
Cross, Jacob 22
Cross, Jeanette O. 63
Crosswhite, Alonzo 11
Crosswhite, Alonzo 245
Crosswhite, Anna 124
Crosswhite, Annie 289,338
Crosswhite, Annie 177
Crosswhite, Beulah 249
Crosswhite, Clyde 232,345
Crosswhite, Cora 74
Crosswhite, C.C. 329
Crosswhite, C.M. 87
Crosswhite, Eliz 245
Crosswhite, Elizabeth 292
294 <
Crosswhite, Ella 316
Crosswhite, Ellen 29
Crosswhite, Elvine 42
Crosswhite, Ethel R. 354
Crosswhite, Eulah 249
Crosswhite, Fanny C. 232
Crosswhite, George 28
Crosswhite, Hazel 316,332
Crosswhite, Jane 203
Crosswhite, Jessie 152
Crosswhite, John 40,56
Crosswhite, Joseph B. 245
Crosswhite, Landon 212
329 <
Crosswhite, Mary E. 80
Crosswhite, Melvin 354
Crosswhite, Mollie 132
Crosswhite, Nannie 24
Crosswhite, Parlee 250
Crosswhite, Rebecca J. 19
Crosswhite, Sallie 329
345 <
Crosswhite, Sarah 191

Crosswhite, Soloman 56
Crosswhite, Stacy 249,354
Crosswhite, Susie A. 341
Crosswhite, Thomas G. 223
Crosswhite, Thomas J. 223
Crosswhite, William 40
Crosswhite, William J. 329
Crosswhite, William T. 345
Crosswhite, ... 68
Crosswhite. Ben 75
Crouse, Mary A. 59
Crow, Arvil C. 92
Crow, Charles 45
Crow, Charlie 45,90,165
192 <
Crow, Clyde 45
Crow, Earl 192
Crow, Grace 90
Crow, Jack 54
Crow, Myrtle 25
Crow, Nauel 165
Crow, Sallie 92
Crow, Tyler 54
Crow, ... 77
Crowder, Alex 262
Crowder, Alexander 277
311 <
Crowder, Alice 311
Crowder, Alice S. 262
Crowder, Clarence 114
Crowder, Dudley 311
Crowder, Eadeth P. 71
Crowder, Edgar 288
Crowder, Ida May 114
Crowder, Luther 277
Crowder, Manley 114,306
Crowder, Manley M. 71
Crowder, Robert B. 306
Crowder, Sarah 311
Crowder, Wiley 114
Crowder, W.S. 172
Crowder, W.T. 288,311
Crowder. E.C. 114
Crowe, Nannie 350
Crowel, Eliza 233
Crowley, Sam 329
Cruise, John 225
Cruise, Lee 225

Crumley, Eva	87	Danly, Nancy	51
Cruse, James	57	Danner, Eldeed	22
Cruse, Mary Jane	233	Danner, Infant	117
Cruze, C.L.	233	Danner, Runa	117
Cuddy, Lake	95	Danner, R.L.	67
Cuddy, Ollie	1	Danner, ...	67
Culbert, James	165	Darnell, ...	7
Curd, Alfred E.	331	Daugherty, Bell	271
Curd, Alvin	86,330,352	Daugherty, Dora	307
Curd, Arthur Cecil	186	Daugherty, Eliga	243
Curd, Clinton, B.	331	Daugherty, Elijah	307
Curd, Conley	44	Daugherty, Esther	217
Curd, Dan	350	Daugherty, Frank C.	319
Curd, Dave	364	Daugherty, Hanna	217
Curd, Ella Lee	86	Daugherty, Jacob	307
Curd, Eula	191	Daugherty, Lillina S.	319
Curd, Ezekiel	86,232,286	Daugherty, Rosa Lee	307
Curd, Fonia May Belle	178	Daugherty, Thomas J.	319
Curd, Fronice	175	Daurty, John	244
Curd, Haskel Clay	350	Davenport, Charles	98
Curd, Hester	54	Davenport, Elizabeth	197
Curd, Infant	132,175,291	Davenport, James	203
Curd, Jane	364	Davidson, Amanda E.	313
Curd, Leah	299	Davidson, Charlie T.	290
Curd, Lida	105	Davidson, Creed F.	142
Curd, Margaret	52	Davidson, Dona	244
Curd, Martha	45	Davidson, Laura	244
Curd, Mary	44	Davidson, Mandy	290
Curd, Maurice	198	Davidson, Mary	185
Curd, Nola	206	Davidson, Mary J.	239
Curd, O.E.	125	Davidson, Silvister	290
Curd, Richard	286	Davidson, Spencer	14
Curd, Susan	86	Davidson, Sylvester	223
Curd, Susan L.	352	313	<
Curd, T.J.	86	Davidson, William	223
Curd, Webster	20	Davidson, William A.	142
Curd, Will	132	Davidson, W.A.	239
Curd, William	186	Davis, Airo	106
Curd, W.M.	291,299	Davis, Arthur	303
Curry, Elizabeth	56	Davis, Arthur A.	225
Curtis, Finley P.	150	Davis, A.A.	225
Curtis, F.G.	243	Davis, Billie Eugene	313
Curtis, Hezekiah	150,243	Davis, Bonnie	10
Curtis, Mattie G.	243	Davis, Bula	233
Curtis, Selma F.	346	Davis, Callie	220
Curtis, W.B.	150	Davis, Carbin D.	87
C..., Della	155	Davis, Claud	256
Dancy, Rachel	102	Davis, Clay	118,169

Davis, C.A.	276	
Davis, Dan	225	
Davis, David A.	274	
Davis, David C.	151	
Davis, Deborah	76	
Davis, Debra	52	
Davis, D.A. (Mrs)	274	
Davis, Elbert	243	
Davis, Eli	251,274	
Davis, Elija	159	
Davis, Eliza	195	
Davis, Elizabeth	328,333	
355	<	
Davis, Ellen	321	
Davis, Eva	120,313	
Davis, E.J.	87	
Davis, Fay Lucile	199	
Davis, Fred B.	316	
Davis, Hannah	183	
Davis, Infant	118,256	
Davis, Irene	215,345	
Davis, Jack	91,291	
Davis, James	38,46,151	
313	<	
Davis, James F.	78,267	
Davis, John B.	38	
Davis, John P.	91	
Davis, Joseph	69	
Davis, Joseph Lenard	300	
Davis, Joseph Y.	251	
Davis, J.B.	103	
Davis, J.F.	141	
Davis, J.J.	200	
Davis, J.M.	67	
Davis, J.R.	353	
Davis, J.V.	169	
Davis, Lacira	6	
Davis, Lizzie	38,76	
Davis, Mack	151	
Davis, Martha A.	78	
Davis, Mary	276	
Davis, Mary Elizabeth	230	
Davis, Mary Wilson	267	
Davis, Maryan	303	
Davis, Monroe	80,221	
Davis, Monroe (Mrs)	221	
Davis, M.L.	195,300	
Davis, Nancy E.	266	

Davis, Nathaniel Cole	80	
Davis, Nina	246	
Davis, Nola Catherine	283	
Davis, Novel	283	
Davis, N.H.	230	
Davis, Perdita	308	
Davis, Reta	184	
Davis, Richard	221	
Davis, Robert D.	321	
Davis, Robert M.	364	
Davis, Roby	34,313	
Davis, R.A.	333	
Davis, Sarah E.	186	
Davis, S.C.	118,184	
Davis, Thomas	89,183,231	
Davis, Tom	355	
Davis, Will S.	353	
Davis, William Bethel	355	
Davis, Willie	28,233,291	
Davis, Winnie	36	
Davis, W.E.	199	
Davis, W.F.	215	
Davis, W.H.	36,118	
Davis, W.L.	316	
Davis, W.R.	20,333	
Davis, W.T.	251,266	
Davison, Fannie	87	
Davis. Winnie S.	353	
Day, Bertha	359	
Day, C.F.	247	
Day, David	57	
Day, Debora	51	
Day, Delia	79	
Day, Elizabeth	144,190	
Day, George	190	
Day, Julia	269	
Day, Liddy Fine	247	
Day, Martha	359	
Day, Nancy	329	
Day, Ray	57	
Day, Sam	319	
Day, S.E.	329	
Day, W.D.	359	
Day, ...	221	
Deal, John	87	
Dean, Hobart	158	
Dean, Ross, D.	158	
Debush, Dorcas	58	

Deen, Loura   44
Delaney, Leonard   362
Dellinger, Blair B.   145
Dellinger, Jane   156
Dellinger, L.B.   174
Dellinger, Thomas   142,145
Dellinger, T.B.   156,158
Deloach, Celia   36
Deloach, C.H.   233
Deloach, J.A.   151
Deloach, J.M.   114
Deloach, Louise   151,214
Deloach, Nancy   222
Deloach, Nathan   114
Deloach, Rosco   317
Deloach, Rosco, Jr.   317
Deloach, Sam   214,233
Deloach, Samuel   53
Deloach, S.C.   114
Deloach, William   233
Demint, Buist   322
Denkins, Jane   188
Denkins, John Willie   355
Denkins, Martha   310,355
Denkins, Millie   355
Denney, Ada   193
Denney, Ada Belle   247
Denney, B.M.   79
Denney, J.E.   79
Denney, ... M.   79
Dennings, Betty Ann   252
Dennis, William   18
Denny, Ada   153
Denny, J.A.   75
Denny, Verda   311
Denton, Deborah   249
Denton, Joe (Mrs)   334
Devault, Robert M.   210
Devers, James D.   331
Dewey, ...   170
Dicken, Charlie   237
Dicken, Thomas   237
Dickens, Arthur Wayne   367
Dickens, Bonnie   290
Dickens, Cora   121
Dickens, Dan   363
Dickens, Daniel   312
Dickens, Dowell   163

Dickens, Edward   77
Dickens, Frank   165
Dickens, Helen Marie   367
Dickens, James Charles153
Dickens, James Edgar   163
Dickens, John   77,157
    165,185,287,347   <
Dickens, John R.   312
Dickens, John (Mrs)   287
Dickens, Julia   312
Dickens, Julia Alice   347
Dickens, Mary   130
Dickens, R.M.   312
Dickens, Thomas   153
Dickens, Tommie Hall   363
Dickerson, Mary   236
Dickson, James Roby   120
Dickson, Roy   120
Dillon, Absolom W.   284
Dillon, John   235,324
Dillon, John Wesley   324
Dillon, John W.   284
Dillon, Julia   57,212,217
Dillon, J.W.   48
Dillon, Wiley   203,278,324
Dinken, Martha   342
Dinkens, Infant   160
Dinkens, John   160
Dinkens, Millie   160
Dinkins, J.W.   146
Dishman, Archie   106,322
Dishman, Linda F.   330
Dishman, Mary   242
Dishman, Mary   357
Dishman, William   263
Dishmen, Adolphus   330
Dish..., Sarah Mabel   139
Dixon, Anie   157
Dixon, Pauline   143
Dixon, Wiley   140,157
Dixon, W.M.   140,143
Dobbins, Andrew   238
Dobbins, Hannah   184
Dobbins, Laura   238
Dobbins. Lourie   223
Dollar, Cora   91
Dollar, Cora Elizabeth 85
Dollar, C.C.   90

Dollar, Deffealsa 86
Dollar, Julia 90
Dollar, J.C. 85
Dollar, Maggie 15
Dollar, Monroe 18
Dollar, Roy Denson 85
Donally, R.E. 97
Donnelley, Eliza 2
Donnelly, Alex 234
Donnelly, Alice 210,234
Donnelly, Clifford F. 6
Donnelly, Daniel T. 119
Donnelly, Eleline 254
Donnelly, Elizabeth 249
Donnelly, Emeline 232
Donnelly, Etta 273
Donnelly, Harrison C. 345
Donnelly, Harrison R. 196
Donnelly, Hellen J. 146
Donnelly, Hugh H. 353
Donnelly, H.A. 133
Donnelly, H.C. (Mrs) 272
287,315 <
Donnelly, H.S. 353
Donnelly, James C. 210
Donnelly, James Doran 271
Donnelly, Joe S. 196
Donnelly, J.C. 146
Donnelly, Margaret 235
249,271 <
Donnelly, Margaret C. 355
257,265,284 <
Donnelly, Margaret S. 345
Donnelly, Mary E. 176
Donnelly, Mary Kate 10
Donnelly, Mollie 234
Donnelly, Nancy 196
Donnelly, Oscar 283
Donnelly, Pauline 183
Donnelly, Rebecca 223
Donnelly, Rebekah E. 353
Donnelly, R. Ross 119,141
Donnelly, Sallie 107
Donnelly, Thomas R. 271
Donnelly, William 133,210
Donnelly, William K. 133
Dopralo, Antonio 198
Doss, Minnie 200

Dotson, Alford A. 279
Dotson, Allen 50,186,279
299 <
Dotson, A.E. 299,329
Dotson, Bessie Myrtle 236
Dotson, Betty 310
Dotson, Bill 135
Dotson, Celia 299
Dotson, Dean (Mrs) 329
Dotson, D.S. 186
Dotson, Elija 298
Dotson, George W. 236
Dotson, Grace 299
Dotson, John 135
Dotson, John Franklin 299
Dotson, Jordan 290
Dotson, Laurrie 48
Dotson, Lillie 295
Dotson, Lonnie 66
Dotson, Loretta 299
Dotson, Malinda 318,330
360 <
Dotson, Marry M. 329
Dotson, Nancy E. 365
Dotson, O.D. 236
Dotson, Polly 255
Dotson, R... 135
Dotson, Sarah 206,239
Dotson, Verna 267
Dotson. Prescilla 2
Dougherty, Adam Mast 269
Dougherty, Allen 85
Dougherty, Belle 297
Dougherty, Eliga 251
Dougherty, Elijah 269
Dougherty, F.C. 121,189
282 <
Dougherty, Hannah 102
Dougherty, Jackson, M.251
Dougherty, Jane 244
Dougherty, John H. 85
Dougherty, Liza 196
Dougherty, Mahlon 105
Dougherty, Pollie 275
Dougherty, Rhoda 246
Dougherty, Susan 215
Dougherty, Susie 121
Dougherty, Thomas 217,271

Dougherty, Thomas 189
Dougherty, William C. 271
Dougherty, W. Eugene 189
Dougherty, W.C. 217
Doughtery, Thomas 121
Dowell, Annis C. 353
Dowell, Barbara Janis 306
Dowell, Callie 47,75,94
Dowell, Cassie 71
Dowell, Cecil Earl 279
Dowell, C.S. 292
Dowell, Danford 325
Dowell, Darling 278
Dowell, David G. 236
Dowell, Dewey 94
Dowell, Dewey L. 170
Dowell, Disey D. 273
Dowell, Elizabeth 213
Dowell, Emma Jean 368
Dowell, Frank 331
Dowell, Fred 306,353
Dowell, George 269,300
Dowell, James E. 141,353
Dowell, Jerry 356
Dowell, John 141,278,303
Dowell, John H. 47
Dowell, John L. 213
Dowell, Joseph 94,273
Dowell, J.A. 139
Dowell, J.M. 126,202,235
Dowell, J.S. 94
Dowell, Lena 279
Dowell, Lens 236
Dowell, Lester 368
Dowell, Lester S. 356
Dowell, Lewany 165
Dowell, Link 325
Dowell, Linza 197
Dowell, Lonnie E. 15
Dowell, Lula 143
Dowell, Lydia 292
Dowell, Malinda C. 98
Dowell, Minnie 170
Dowell, Nellie Orpha 202
Dowell, Noah 82
Dowell, Nora 104,105
Dowell, Ora 270
Dowell, Ruby Ruth 126

Dowell, Sarah Affie 143
Dowell, Sherman 47,269
  331 <
Dowell, S.E. 235
Dowell, Thomas 170,197
Dowell, Verda 300
Dowell, Wiley 82
Dowell, William 126
Dowell, William A. 353
Dowell, W.A. 278
Dowell, W.C. 270
Duball, Elizabeth 61
Duball, Haggy 61
Duff, Elizabeth 281
Duff, Elizabeth R. 332
Duff, Rebecca E. 258
Duffield, Landon 28
Dugger, Adalade 182
Dugger, Addie 150,299
Dugger, Agga 316
Dugger, Audie 66
Dugger, A. 221
Dugger, A.M. 46
Dugger, Billie 218
Dugger, Cefford 159
Dugger, Charlotte 61
Dugger, Clarence 218
Dugger, Clayton 200
Dugger, Clyd Tester 279
Dugger, Crawford 151
Dugger, Daton 18
Dugger, David Carl 284
Dugger, Delia 127
Dugger, Dow 114
Dugger, D.B. 151
Dugger, Eliza 113
Dugger, Elizabeth 230,268
Dugger, Elmira 298
Dugger, Emily 268
Dugger, Ernest Clayton 82
Dugger, Ettie 114
Dugger, E.A. 293
Dugger, Faye 312
Dugger, Frank 67,197
Dugger, Gar. 259
Dugger, Gerry 173
Dugger, Grant 293
Dugger, Henry (Mrs) 277

Dugger, Infant	59,67,136	
	147	<
Dugger, James	154,229,246	
Dugger, James A.	255	
Dugger, James C.	115	
Dugger, James K.	65,308	
Dugger, James L.	136	
Dugger, John	43,65,245	
Dugger, John A.	308	
Dugger, John A., Sr.	123	
Dugger, John Elias	246	
Dugger, John E.	65	
Dugger, Joseph	258,361	
Dugger, Joseph H.	106	
Dugger, Josephine	267	
Dugger, J.A.	108	
Dugger, J.C.	136,144,255	
Dugger, J.E.	229	
Dugger, Linda	77,165	
Dugger, Lona	202	
Dugger, Louise	125	
Dugger, Lydea	185	
Dugger, L.C.	115	
Dugger, L.R.	308	
Dugger, Mae	57	
Dugger, Malvina	200	
Dugger, Mamie	259	
Dugger, Mamie Lee	277	
Dugger, Margaret	200	
Dugger, Martha G.	190	
Dugger, Mary	206,298	
Dugger, Matilda	194,314	
Dugger, McNary	159	
Dugger, McNary King	309	
Dugger, Mildred	334	
Dugger, Myra Powers	97	
Dugger, M.A.	13,293	
Dugger, Nancy	197	
Dugger, Odnes	33	
Dugger, Otis Levi	365	
Dugger, Otis Levi, Jr.	365	
Dugger, Parlie	365	
Dugger, Peter	154,173	
Dugger, Polly	79,281,343	
Dugger, Quince	157,159	
Dugger, Rader	297,348	
Dugger, Raleigh	82	
Dugger, Ray	279,284	

Dugger, Rebecca	145
Dugger, Retta	202
Dugger, Roby	113
Dugger, Roby J.	159
Dugger, Rody	151
Dugger, Roy	284
Dugger, Roy B.	31
Dugger, R.H.	114
Dugger, R.J.	115
Dugger, R.W.	309
Dugger, Sallie	65
Dugger, Samuel	83,117
Dugger, Sandy B.	147
Dugger, Susan	276
Dugger, S.	31
Dugger, S.B.	147,190
Dugger, S.D.	256
Dugger, S.Q.	287
Dugger, Thomas	245
Dugger, T.F.	19
Dugger, William	44,106
Dugger, William Loyd	348
Dugger, Youreethy I.	44
Duncan, John A.	150
Duncan, Lucy	339
Duncan, Mary	277
Dungan, J.P.	86
Dunn, Agnes Bessie	187
Dunn, Alvin	240
Dunn, Amanda	254
Dunn, Becka	32
Dunn, Bell	164,258
Dunn, Bertha Elvira	164
Dunn, Bessie M.	254
Dunn, Bettie	236,264
Dunn, Bettie A.	127
Dunn, Bettie Lee	302
Dunn, Betty	162
Dunn, Booker	109
Dunn, Callie	57,110,171
288,300	<
Dunn, Celia M.	237
Dunn, Charles C.	166,279
Dunn, Charlie	268,325
Dunn, Cilia	85
Dunn, Cora	140
Dunn, Cora Lee	111
Dunn, C.C.	166,202,254

Dunn, Danny   111
Dunn, David   16
Dunn, Della   172,266
Dunn, Denny   149,197
Dunn, Donnie   8
Dunn, Edith   138
Dunn, Edward   260
Dunn, Elbert J.   39
Dunn, Eliza   306
Dunn, Eliza Lue   306
Dunn, Elizabeth A.   147
Dunn, Ella Nora   238
Dunn, Emanuel   136,162
Dunn, Emmer   126
Dunn, Flossie   129
Dunn, Fred   22
Dunn, F.A.   180
Dunn, George   138,187
Dunn, Geter Stoffie   260
Dunn, Gladys M.   199
Dunn, Godfrey   158
Dunn, Godfrey B.   39,162
    215,266   <
Dunn, Goldie Adams   197
Dunn, Hazel Fay   146
Dunn, Henry   138,202,215
    271,280   <
Dunn, Hueldy   223
Dunn, Hugh   166
Dunn, Huston   65
Dunn, H.C.   127,213
Dunn, Ida   213
Dunn, Infant 58,65,87,207
Dunn, Ira   331
Dunn, Jacob   351
Dunn, Jacob Willace   109
Dunn, Jacob W.   248
Dunn, Jane   322
Dunn, Jellada   95
Dunn, Joe   288,300,306
Dunn, John L.   146
Dunn, Joseph Henry   166
Dunn, Joseph N.   147
Dunn, Joseph W.   158
Dunn, Josephine   172
Dunn, Josie   56
Dunn, J.B.   39,266
Dunn, J.C.   137

Dunn, J.G. 37,199,215,215
    237,238,302   <
Dunn, J.H.   95
Dunn, J.L.   131
Dunn, J.M.   58
Dunn, J.W.   146,215, 280
    238,358   <
Dunn, Larkin   56,98,155
Dunn, Lavinia   65
Dunn, Lela   291
Dunn, Lelah   186
Dunn, Lelia   132
Dunn, Liza N.   44
Dunn, Mae   235
Dunn, Malary   166
Dunn, Malinda   353
Dunn, Mandy   329
Dunn, Mannie   309
Dunn, Margaret   368
Dunn, Mary   62,149
Dunn, Mary Ann   225
Dunn, Mary E.   138,271
Dunn, McKinley   143
Dunn, M.B.   155
Dunn, M.M.   81
Dunn, Nancy Lorettie   107
Dunn, Nellie   131
Dunn, Nora   64
Dunn, P ...   94
Dunn, Pauline   187
Dunn, Pearl   207
Dunn, Pollie   78,281
Dunn, Polly   248
Dunn, Rachel Matilda   137
Dunn, Rebecca   59
Dunn, Richard   149
Dunn, Ruth   340
Dunn, R.J.   200
Dunn, Sherman   158,288
Dunn, Tillie   264
Dunn, Umbershon   56
Dunn, Vada   146
Dunn, Verna   15,368
Dunn, Virda C.T.   131
Dunn, Vuna M.   356
Dunn, Walter McDaniel   15
Dunn, Wesley   225,280,302
Dunn, Will   166

Dunn, William	202	Eastridge, Alvin	341
Dunn, Winnie	111	Eastridge, Andrew C.	227
Dunn, W.G.	187	Eastridge, Anna Mae	191
Dunn, W.M.	87,131	Eastridge, Arthor	321
Dunn, Yarborough	166	Eastridge, A.C.	45
Durham, Annie	342	Eastridge, Barnabas	210
Durham, James	342	Eastridge, Callie	333
Duvall, Andy	329	Eastridge, Charles	72
Duvall, Fred Albert	82	Eastridge, Darnell	45
Duvall, Henry	82	Eastridge, Dave	333
Duvall, Lizzie	61	Eastridge, David Smith	210
Duvall, Lockie	317	Eastridge, Eula	202,330
Duvall, Mary	329	Eastridge, Fanny	198
Duvall, Norma Vel	317	Eastridge, Florence	16
Duvall, Thomas	329	Eastridge, Harlie	253
Duvall, Tom M.	317	Eastridge, Henry	54
Duvall, Willard	1	Eastridge, James	227
Duvall, Winford	329	Eastridge, Joe	317
Dyer, Benjamin	127	Eastridge, Joel	209,227
Dyer, Calvin V.	140	282,352	<
Dyer, Hershell C.V.	140	Eastridge, Lizzie	260
Dyer, Joel	266	Eastridge, Lynnie Mae	253
Dyer, Joel Wagner	266	Eastridge, Mandy	202
Dyer, John	62	Eastridge, Mary	53,127
Dyer, John W.	125	211	<
Dyer, John W. (Mrs)	360	Eastridge, Mollie	206
Dyer, J.W.	266	Eastridge, Nancy	87
Dyer, Sarah	125	Eastridge, Pleasant	209
Dyson, Andy	124,169,170	Eastridge, Rener	16
Dyson, Annie May	299	Eastridge, Roby	260
Dyson, A.J.	260	Eastridge, Rose	365
Dyson, Carl	169	Eastridge, Roy	310
Dyson, Eva Maud	73	Eastridge, R.S.	253
Dyson, Green	326	Eastridge, Sallie S.	138
Dyson, Infant	73,120	Eastridge, Sarah L.	211
137,170,124	<	Eastridge, Susan	330
Dyson, Jackson	260	Eastridge, Will	330
Dyson, Jeff	326	Eastridge, William	202
Dyson, Matilda	120	310	<
Dyson, Mattie	21	Eastridge, William C.	191
Dyson, Ruby	361	Eastridge, W.W.	72,211
Dyson, Rum	73	Echuister, Mary U.	306
Dyson, R.F.	120	Edison, Earl	16
Dyson, Worley	124	Edmison, M.G.	21
Dyson, W.C.	137	Edmonds, Fannie	8
Ease, Louise	325	Edwards, Bessie	118
Eastridge, Alice	310	Edwards, James	36
Eastridge, Alice W.	321	Eggers, Abner	272

Eggers, Addie 274
Eggers, Agnes 30
Eggers, Alexander C. 80
Eggers, Alice 197
Eggers, Anna 152,225
Eggers, Annie 255,275,298
Eggers, Arthur 265
Eggers, A.C. 80
Eggers, Bettie Jane 265
Eggers, Brazila 63,254
Eggers, Charles 35
Eggers, Clayton 309
Eggers, Ella 230
Eggers, Ellen J. 310
Eggers, Frank 35
Eggers, Garfield 254
Eggers, Grant 39
Eggers, Hannah 117
Eggers, Hiram 63,156
Eggers, Inez 293
Eggers, Infant 145,161
Eggers, James 301,341
Eggers, James G. 206
Eggers, John 339
Eggers, John F. 272
Eggers, Landrine 117
Eggers, Land.. 310
Eggers, Laudrine 254
Eggers, Lizzie 272
Eggers, Lizzie J. 341
Eggers, Lou Eller 270
Eggers, L.G. 80
Eggers, Mable 122
Eggers, Martha 331
Eggers, Martitia 255
Eggers, Mary 39,121,136
Eggers, Myrtle 161,185
Eggers, Nancy 290
Eggers, Nelle 157
Eggers, Rettie 136
Eggers, Roby 156
Eggers, Roy 63,156,301
Eggers, Sarah 272
Eggers, T.A. 272
Eggers, Venia E. 131
Eggers, Waller 145
Eggers, Walter 310
Eggers, Will 309

Eggers, William Clyde 206
Eggers, William D. 122
Eggers, W.B. 265,270
Eggers, W.D. 274
Eggers, Zill 218
Eggese, Johnie 28
Eisenhour, Katie 117
Eldreth, Ambrose 365
Eldreth, Betsy Lou 365
Eldreth, John Wesley 188
Eldreth, Levi 188
Eldreth, Mae 353
Eldreth, W.M. 188
Eldridge, Bell 184
Eldrith, Bertha 291
Eldrith, Caty 341
Eldrith, Gene 291
Eldrith, Infant 181
Eldrith, James Roby 358
Eldrith, Joe 264
Eldrith, J.R. 100
Eldrith, Lee 264
Eldrith, Lettie 181
Eldrith, Myrtle 347
Eldrith, Roby 181
Eldrith, Ruby Jane 100
Eldrith, Wesley 264
Elison, Abbie 135
Elison, Alphns E. 135
Elison, Betsy 135
Elison, Jerry 135
Elison, Perl 16
Elison, Sendy 266
Eller, Avery 214
Eller, Bruce 326
Eller, Calvin 304,341
Eller, Charles 177
Eller, Cora 175
Eller, Deliah 365
Eller, Floyd 214
Eller, Harrison H. 130
Eller, Housford 135
Eller, Infant 177
Eller, James 144
Eller, Jess 77,364
Eller, Jesse 52
Eller, John 274,341
Eller, Joseph Franklin 52

Eller, Mary 69
Eller, Mary D. 148
Eller, Melviania 129
Eller, Myrtle 341
Eller, Stella Cole 304
Eller, S.J. 135
Eller, S.P. 73
Eller, Winnie Pauline 214
Ellie, Lettie 146
Ellie, Rebecca P. 100
Elliott, Bishop M. 86
Elliott, Bro.. 37
Elliott, B.M. 37
Elliott, Elizabeth 361
Elliott, Infant 28,86
Elliott, John 350
Elliott, John D. 10
Elliott, Lizzie 239
Elliott, Malissie 194
Elliott, Nancy 129,192
257,277 <
Elliott, Nancy E. 66
Elliott, Peter 169
Elliott, P.B. 171
Elliott, Raymond H. 117
Elliott, Rebecca 332
Elliott, Susan 104,115
Elliott, Susie 136
Elliott, Thomas 37
Elliott, Walter 66,117
Elliott, ... 198
Ellis, Florence 236
Ellis, Gracie Marelita 250
Ellis, Lizzie 103
Ellis, Martha 236
Ellis, Robert 100,250
Ellison, Charlie C. 149
Ellison, Clyde 188
Ellison, C.C. 188
Ellison, D.H. 149
Ellison, Elmira 36
Ellison, Emmett 177
Ellison, Infant 177
Ellison, Jacob 149
Ellison, Lewis 225
Ellison, Lindsy 225
Ellison, Sarah 188
Ellison, William 225

Elrod, Calloway 62
Elrod, Joseph E. 273
Elrod, Polly 173
Elswick, Houston R. 288
Elswick, Nettie Nave 288
Elswick, Van 288
Emmett, Felty 105
Emmett, Tilda 105
English, A.B. 147
English, Elizabeth 285
Escue, Nancy 248
Estep, Colonel 103
Estep, Infant 55
Estep, John 59,78
Estep, John R. 55
Estep, Mary 66,211
Estep, Mary E. 55
Estep, Minnie Jane 65
Estep, Nancy 190
Estep, Ode 169
Estep, Walter 78
Estes, Fostenia 26
Estes, Jeff 209
Estes, J.D. 125
Estes, Mannie 26
Estes, Orlie 209
Evans, Brison 140
Evans, Gertrude 179
Evans, Josie 76
Everett, Paul 274
E..., William Wallace 2
Farland, Samuel 80
Farmer, Ada 75
Farmer, Calvin 229,278
286,287 <
Farmer, Claud 165
Farmer, David 8,53,325
Farmer, Donsie 143
Farmer, Dora 125
Farmer, Fielder 125
Farmer, George 139
Farmer, Hannah 250
Farmer, Hattie Mcbell 17
Farmer, Hubert 53
Farmer, Infant 103
Farmer, J.P. 159,165
Farmer, Luther 316
Farmer, Lydia C. 120

Farmer, Margaret 204
Farmer, Nancy Lacira 159
Farmer, Neva 61
Farmer, Rebecca 273
Farmer, Robert 103
Farmer, Robert S. 176
Farmer, Ruth 253,260
Farmer, Ruth Mae 236
Farmer, Spencer 161
Farmer, Tommie Carl 316
Farmer, William 139,161
Farmer, William H. 74
Farmer, Willie 176
Farmer, ... 74
Farnsworth, S.K. (Mrs)182
Farris, Cleo 367
Farris, Elizabeth 301
Farris, Lee 241
Farris, Mary Jones 351
Farris, Rosa 203
Farris, Sarah H. 351
Farthing, Abner 98
Farthing, Abner C. 303
Farthing, Annie 60
Farthing, Bessie 128
Farthing, Blanche 250
Farthing, Brown 84
Farthing, Calvin 128
Farthing, Caroline F. 153
Farthing, C. Clapton 168
Farthing, David Jessie 84
Farthing, D.J. 82
Farthing, D.J. (Mrs) 84
Farthing, Eliazbeth E.243
Farthing, Elijah 328
Farthing, Elizabeth H.328
Farthing, Ella P. 230
Farthing, Eugene 5
Farthing, Harriett 235
Farthing, Harriett N. 292
Farthing, Harry 206,230
Farthing, Hattie 82
Farthing, Infant 168
Farthing, John S. 60
Farthing, J.C. 128
Farthing, Louisa 128
Farthing, Mary 275
Farthing, Myrtle 328

Farthing, Norma R. 98
Farthing, Rachel 168
Farthing, Raleigh R. 78
Farthing, Robert H. 204
206 <
Farthing, Walter H. 78
Farthing, William Y. 60
Farthing, ... 302
Faw, Martha Ella 336
Felts, Rebecca 178
Fenis, Melvice 148
Fenner, Alexander 69
Fenner, Berna 9
Fenner, Bettie 9
Fenner, Charles 74
Fenner, Clyde 9
Fenner, Eliza 1
Fenner, Elizabeth 143
Fenner, Glenn Hobart 74
Fenner, Ida 232
Fenner, Ida 250
Fenner, Jake 41
Fenner, James 41,129,257
277 <
Fenner, James Richard 69
Fenner, Jane 69
Fenner, Joseph 74
Fenner, Joseph F. 277
Fenner, Lem 69
Fenner, Mary E. 307
Fenner, Nancy 37
Fenner, Pearl 140
Fenner, Rachel 129
Fenner, R.F. 272
Fenner, R.J. 257
Fenner, Smith 105,232
Fenner, Walter 277
Fenner, Will 314
Fenner, William 257
Fenner, ... 98
Ferguson, Ester 252
Fields, Feraby 247
Fields, Frankie 288
Fields, Rebecca 213
Fife, Mary 255
Filler, John F. 102
Finey, Mary 233
Finey, Phillip 179

Fipps, Sarah 36
Fittts, Delcenia 152
Flanagan, Emma 288
Flanery, Joe 158
Flanery, John Joseph 158
Flannagan, Ann 300
Flannery, Elbert Ross 297
Flannery, Joe 143
Flannery, John 297
Flannery, R.A. 143
Flannery, Tilda 143
Flannigan, Emma 256
Flannigan, Mat (Mrs) 243
Fleener, ... 329
Fletcher, Beckie 60,357
Fletcher, Bertha 99
Fletcher, Bettie 86
Fletcher, Cecil H. 227
Fletcher, Daniel 164,186
Fletcher, David 179,183
Fletcher, Debbie 363
Fletcher, Dillie 337
Fletcher, Eveline 276
Fletcher, Feeb 326
Fletcher, Henry 281
Fletcher, James 98,186
Fletcher, Jane 211
Fletcher, John 186,249
263 <
Fletcher, Julia 98
Fletcher, Juliatte 124
Fletcher, J.R. 290
Fletcher, Leta Hazel 98
Fletcher, Lisey 59
Fletcher, Lizy 156
Fletcher, L.C. 227
Fletcher, Martha E. 164
Fletcher, Martin 34,73
118 <
Fletcher, Matilda 337,363
Fletcher, Myrtle 98,146
160 <
Fletcher, Noah 224
Fletcher, Ora 98
Fletcher, Ora Willard 357
Fletcher, Rebecca 29,46
211 <
Fletcher, Ruben 45,276

Fletcher, Samuel 32
Fletcher, Sarah 326
Fletcher, Silas 66
Fletcher, Stacy 66,73
Fletcher, Susan 66,307
Fletcher, William 337
Fletcher, William C. 357
Fletcher, William E. 363
Flinchern, Fannie 214,234
Flinchurn, Lona 214
Fluks, ... 338
Foltz, Rebecca 133
Fondren, Martha 299
Fondren, Thomas 299
Ford, Annie 169
Ford, Benjamin 222
Ford, John R. 56
Ford, John Wesley 56
Ford, Malissa 330
Ford, Margaret 318
Ford, M.A. 138
Ford, Smith 182
Fore, Cecil 34
Forester, Joe 365
Forrester, Albert 56
Forrester, Alfred C. 195
Forrester, Andrew 213
Forrester, Andy 195
Forrester, Andy John 348
Forrester, Anna 66
Forrester, Asa 340,345
Forrester, Asa C. 278
Forrester, Atha 111
Forrester, Attry 148
Forrester, A.J. 95,97
182,187,213 <
Forrester, Bertha 217
Forrester, Betie Ann 107
Forrester, Betsy 52
Forrester, Bettie 132
Forrester, Blanche 31
Forrester, Bud 170
Forrester, Bulah 49,65
Forrester, B.B. 47
Forrester, Charles 168
Forrester, Charles F. 325
Forrester, Charlie 286
Forrester, Coni 170

Forrester, Cora 169
Forrester, Danford 8
Forrester, Dicil 318
Forrester, Dortha Ree 160
Forrester, Eliza S. 238
Forrester, Filmore 195
Forrester, Floyd 56
Forrester, Francis 47
Forrester, Georgia 219
Forrester, Hattie 345
Forrester, Henry S. 213
303 <
Forrester, Inez Dora 146
Forrester, Infant 101,171
184,210,325 <
Forrester, Jack T. 195
Forrester, Jackson T. 195
Forrester, Jane 194,278
286,287,300 <
Forrester, Jettie 340
Forrester, John 235
Forrester, J.M.R. 108
Forrester, J.R. 116,146
Forrester, Lilie 144
Forrester, Lottie 117
Forrester, Luther 210
Forrester, Luther 160,171
Forrester, Mannie 157
Forrester, Millard F. 80
Forrester, Millard I. 231
Forrester, Minnie 231
Forrester, Monroe 107
Forrester, Nancy 129
Forrester, Nancy Jane 168
Forrester, Nora 62
Forrester, Oda 184
Forrester, Oma 171,195
184,220,283 <
Forrester, Oma J. 108
Forrester, Patty 8
Forrester, Petibue 5
Forrester, Pollie 297
Forrester, Polly 180
Forrester, Rebecca 180
Forrester, Rebecca J. 326
Forrester, Robert S. 170
Forrester, Rosevelt 116
Forrester, Roy 217,231

Forrester, Ruby Cake 54
Forrester, Sam 63
Forrester, Sarah 42,45
135,288 <
Forrester, Sarah C. 303
Forrester, Scott 54,101
Forrester, Thomas 132,226
229 <
Forrester, Thomas P. 21
Forrester, Verna 281
Forrester, William 52,90
168,186 <
Forrester, ... 149,321
Forster, Clyde 365
Forster, Gerlian 365
Foster, Mary 212
Foster, Nancy 88
Foster, Samuel 294
Foster, W.M. 88
Fraker, Mary 41
France, Julie 285
Frayson, Lessie F. 108
Frazier, Mary Ann 358
French, ... 229
Friddles, James B. 224
Friddles, Moses 224
Fritts, Agnes 14
Fritts, Alexander H. 367
Fritts, Andy 34
Fritts, A.J. 48,134,353
Fritts, Braidy 163
Fritts, Brown 134
Fritts, B.O. 182,237
Fritts, Christian 108,175
Fritts, David Marion 207
348 <
Fritts, Eula Maud 12
Fritts, Ezekial 45
Fritts, Fred 175,350
Fritts, Infant 17,292
Fritts, John 241
Fritts, J.M. 296
Fritts, Laura 50
Fritts, Lizzie 285
Fritts, Lomia 228
Fritts, Louisa 48
Fritts, Lutitia 97,131
Fritts, Martha 329

Fritts, McKinley 130
Fritts, Mollie South 367
Fritts, Nancy 29
Fritts, Oscar 292
Fritts, Polly 166
Fritts, Rettie 226
Fritts, Reuben 207,367
Fritts, Roy 350
Fritts, R.D. 350,367
Fritts, Sarah M. 338
Fritts, Scott 113
Fritts, Selvie 102
Fritts, Silvy 130
Fritts, Stella 350
Fritts, Susie 191
Fritts, Ted 338
Fritts, Tiny 340
Fritts, Winnie F. 86
Fritts, Winnie M, 89
Fritz, Allen 89,115,125
Fritz, Fronia 58
Fritz, Gladys Lucil 89
Fritz, Ida 234
Fritz, Infant 115,125
Fritz, Isaac Allen 115
Fritz, James 71
Fritz, Joesph M. 187
Fritz, John 187,248,280
Fritz, J.A. 187
Fritz, Mary Alice 241
Fritz, Mary Saphronia 72
Fritz, Ruby 142
Frost, Fred 238
Frost, Mary Lee 55
Frost, Wilmer Louise 238
Fry, Polly 282
Frye, Jane 266,268,271
        322 <
Fuggetta, Calvin 182
Fuggetta, William F. 182
Fugit, Calvin 299
Fugit, Sammie 299
Fulkes, J.C. 137,151
Fulkes, Pauline 137
Fulks, Lillie 57
Fulks, Odell 3
Fullbright, Nancy 151
Fuller, Annie P. 6

Fuller, John Terry 304
Fuller, John T. 359
Fuller, Joseph W. 304
Fuller, Maggie 36
Fuller, Sallie Wills 359
Fuller, Sallie W. 304
Fuller, S.A. 77
Furchess, Cora Lee 225
Furchess, Millard 61
Furchess, N.Y. 86
Furchess, Ray 61
Furchess, Scott 225
Furgerson, Andrew 23
Fyffe, Mary 228
F..., James 192
Galahar, Earl 172
Gallaine, Safronia 106
Galloway, Marshall 339
Galloway, Mollie 281
Gambill, Billie 164
Gambill, Dora 330
Gambill, Frank 330
Gambill, Franklin 254
Gambill, Gladys 215
Gambill, Jessey M. 164
Gambill, Lillie 161,181
Gambill, Sarah 237,254
Gambill, Smith 215
Gambill, S.B. 173,215,254
Gambill, William 271
Gambill, William B. 33
Gambill, William P. 254
Garfield, Sallie B. 98
Garland, Alice 220
Garland, Allan 60
Garland, Ambrose 168,344
Garland, Auston W. 107
Garland, Bessie 26
Garland, Callie 83,283
Garland, Cecil 250
Garland, Charlie D. 107
Garland, Clarence E. 284
Garland, Daniel W. 212
Garland, Delmar 81
Garland, Donley 83
Garland, Edgar 169
Garland, Eliza 294
Garland, Eliza J. 244

Garland, Elizabeth 198
Garland, Ethel 37
Garland, E.C. 43
Garland, E.E. 344
Garland, Glen 20
Garland, Ida 312
Garland, Infant 144,169
    178 <
Garland, Irene Slez 284
Garland, Jacob A. 283
Garland, James 168
Garland, Jesse H. Sr. 106
Garland, Jessie 283,294
Garland, Jessie H. 81
Garland, John 339
Garland, J.C. 60
Garland, J.G. 246
Garland, J.L. 46,61
Garland, J.R. 289
Garland, Lania 325
Garland, Laura 163
Garland, Laura A. 29,50
Garland, Laura S. 46
Garland, Lewis 27,80,106
Garland, Lillie Belle 301
Garland, Lipford 246
Garland, Lucinda 339
Garland, Lulu 50
Garland, L.C. 317
Garland, Mada 261,270
Garland, Maggie 317
Garland, Maggie E. 107
Garland, Malinda 60
Garland, Massie L. 264
Garland, M.G. 107
Garland, Nancy C. 313
Garland, Opal 341
Garland, Rachel 280
Garland, Robert M. 178
Garland, Rosa Wanda 325
Garland, Ruben 273
Garland, Rushia 186
Garland, R.F. 91
Garland, R.T. 100
Garland, Sam 211
Garland, Sam W. 325
Garland, Samuel 178,212
Garland, Sanford 100

Garland, S. Florence 186
Garland, S.F. 36
Garland, Thomas K. 284
Garland, T.C. 301
Garland, T.F. 98,100
Garland, T.K. 284
Garland, T.R. 264
Garland, Vady 27
Garland, Wheeler 64,83
    250,273 <
Garland, William H. 339
Garland, Winnie Lee 246
Garland, Worley C. 60
Garland, Worley G. 60
Garland, W.M. 144,178
Garland, W.S. 239
Garonette, Nancy 259
Garr, Arthur 190
Garr, Clayton 219
Garr, James Earl 219
Garr, Mack 190,224
Garrison, John 151
Garrison, Louisa 53
Garrison, Louise 233
Gelnn, Alonzo P. 145
Genrty, Pearl 101
Gentry, Ada 344
Gentry, Alex 2
Gentry, Alexander 201
Gentry, Alexander L. 180
Gentry, Alma 282
Gentry, Andrew 365
Gentry, Andrew N. 102
Gentry, Andy 287
Gentry, Anna Bess 246
Gentry, Annie 326
Gentry, Asa 144
Gentry, A.S. 26
Gentry, Barthal 3
Gentry, Bartholemew 113
Gentry, Baxter R. 98
Gentry, Benjamin 52,283
Gentry, Benjamin J. 105
Gentry, Bessie C. 111
Gentry, Betty 333
Gentry, Bobby Glenn 300
Gentry, Callie 311
Gentry, Carrie 320

Gentry, Charles S.	348	Gentry, James F.		232
Gentry, Charlie	17	Gentry, James R.		207,304
Gentry, Claude	133	Gentry, Jane	67,138,194	
Gentry, Clide	201	Gentry, Jim		295,326
Gentry, Col Lilliard	338	Gentry, Joe A.		341
Gentry, Con..	161	Gentry, John		72,208
Gentry, Cora E.	326,335	Gentry, John A.		101
Gentry, Cornelia	37	Gentry, John J.		102
Gentry, C.B.	291	Gentry, John Wesley		322
Gentry, C.L.	101	Gentry, Julia May		232
Gentry, Dalisa	14	Gentry, J. Oliver		58
Gentry, David	38,341	Gentry, J.L.		179
Gentry, David E.	191	Gentry, J.M.	191,256,338	
Gentry, Dick	180,286	Gentry, J.N.		246
Gentry, Dora	170,171	Gentry, J.R.		335
Gentry, Ed	90,133	Gentry, J.W.		121,234
Gentry, Edd	294	Gentry, Kate	80,241,307	
Gentry, Eliga	63	Gentry, Kisey		53
Gentry, Elizabeth	191	Gentry, Lafayette		98
Gentry, Elsie Belle	9	Gentry, Leach		121
Gentry, Ethel	250	Gentry, Lemuel		234
Gentry, E.H.	300	Gentry, Lestie G.		191
Gentry, Faye	74	Gentry, Liddia		120
Gentry, Ferd	111,347	Gentry, Lillie		205
Gentry, Frankie	322	Gentry, Lillie Mabra		348
Gentry, Fred	102,300	Gentry, Liza		90
Gentry, Frederick	101	Gentry, Louisa		171
Gentry, F.C.	171	Gentry, Mack N.		278
Gentry, General	37,90	Gentry, Maggie		63
102,186	<	Gentry, Mahlon	250,256	
Gentry, General R.	335	Gentry, Mahlon	144,186	
Gentry, G.G.	141	Gentry, Mamie Lee		260
Gentry, G.G. Jr.	141	Gentry, Margaret		113
Gentry, Harve	121	Gentry, Margaret E.		6
Gentry, Herbert	316	Gentry, Marion		208
Gentry, Hobart	162	Gentry, Martha		341
Gentry, Hugh Rosecrans	52	Gentry, Martha E.	111,179	
Gentry, H.C.	1,37	316		<
Gentry, Ida Melissa	72	Gentry, Mary	21,144,341	
Gentry, Infant	121,309	358		<
Gentry, Isaac	74,198	Gentry, Mary A.		195
Gentry, Isaac L.	307	Gentry, Mary C.		250
Gentry, Isabella	259	Gentry, Mary Ellen		248
Gentry, James	187,234,260	Gentry, Mary E.		102
310	<	Gentry, Mary Jane		241
Gentry, James A.	278	Gentry, Mary S.		71
Gentry, James D.	102	Gentry, Mattie Lou		358
Gentry, James E.	293	Gentry, May		324

Gentry, Melvin	63,113,115	
Gentry, Memphis M.	97	
Gentry, Mildred D.	92	
Gentry, Millard	29	
Gentry, Mollie	40	
Gentry, Monise	179	
Gentry, Montoe	307	
Gentry, M.J.	333	
Gentry, Nanabeth	295	
Gentry, Nannie	198	
Gentry, Nelie	182	
Gentry, Noah	111	
Gentry, Ocie	349	
Gentry, Oliver	201,302	
Gentry, Oni	29	
Gentry, Onie	180	
Gentry, O.R.	179	
Gentry, Parnaissie	90	
Gentry, Pearl	29,316	
Gentry, Phillip	207	
Gentry, Pollie	287	
Gentry, Polly C.	26	
Gentry, Rebecca	250,296	
Gentry, Richard	46,104 293	<
Gentry, Richard B.	208	
Gentry, Richard Henry	283	
Gentry, Robert Martin	46	
Gentry, Robert Mason	338	
Gentry, Robert Worley	58	
Gentry, Roderick B.	256	
Gentry, Rosecrance	335	
Gentry, Roxie	208	
Gentry, Roy	293,296	
Gentry, Roy W.	53	
Gentry, R.B.	192	
Gentry, R.G.	192	
Gentry, R.H.	53	
Gentry, R.H. (Mrs)	283	
Gentry, R.U.	280	
Gentry, Sallie	90	
Gentry, Sallie Liona	187	
Gentry, Sam	241	
Gentry, Samuel P.	241	
Gentry, Sara Fine	304	
Gentry, Scott	208	
Gentry, Sherman Howard	53	
Gentry, Shirely F.	310	

Gentry, Stacy	309	
Gentry, Susan H.	301	
Gentry, S.F.	322	
Gentry, Titia	347	
Gentry, Vernia Rebecca	63	
Gentry, Victoria	115	
Gentry, Viola	338	
Gentry, Virginia	315	
Gentry, Walker	101,248	
Gentry, Wash	287,322	
Gentry, Wayne Ripley	338	
Gentry, William	46,105	
Gentry, William L.	335	
Gentry, William Oliver	72	
Gentry, W. Oliver	58	
Gentry, W. Scott	92	
Gentry, W.L.	49	
Gentry, W.O.	58,71	
Gentry, ...	208,358	
Gilbert, Carie	133	
Gilbert, Cellie	5	
Gilbert, Denly	164	
Gilbert, Dudley	133	
Gilbert, D.E.	325	
Gilbert, Elsie Mae	325	
Gilbert, Elva	208	
Gilbert, James Dudley	265	
Gilbert, Joe Alex.	345	
Gilbert, John (Mrs)	321	
Gilbert, J.A.	201	
Gilbert, J.H.	325	
Gilbert, Laura	351	
Gilbert, Laura Fritts	345	
Gilbert, Leonard	269	
Gilbert, Lillie	208,237 366	<
Gilbert, Loyd Ed.	269	
Gilbert, Lula Bell	132	
Gilbert, Luther R.	17	
Gilbert, Minnie	270	
Gilbert, Othor O.	18	
gilbert, Ranson L.	345	
Gilbert, Rebecca	39	
Gilbert, Samuel	39	
Gilbert, ...	322	
Gilland, Sallie	293	
Gilland, Sarah	104	
Gilland, Sarah Jane	6	

Gilley, Annie D.	307	Grace, John		44
Gilley, Elmer Haggia	343	Grace, Mariah		166
Gilley, Henry	218	Grace, Vinia		296
Gilley, Luvena	218	Graland, Will C.		289
Gilley, Wilma C.	343	Grant, Archibold	44,176
Gilley, ...	290	Grant, Edgar A.		363
Gilliland, Infant	44	Grant, Edgar A.		230
Gilliland, Sallie	280	Grant, Francis Wills	333
Gilliland, Sarah	46,180	Grant, H.T.	44,333
Gilliland, Will B.	44	Grant, Jennie		282
Gillin, Sallie	286	Grant, Mary Johnson	363
Gillon, Roy	18	Grant, Parker S.		363
Glenn, Bell	256	Grant, Robert E.		230
Glenn, Curtis	173	Grant, T.S.		4
Glenn, Dudley	206	Gray, Caroline	138,158
Glenn, Mary E.	87	Graybeal, Annie		305
Glenn, Newel	156	Graybeal, Bascomb		51
Glenn, Newell	145	Graybeal, Christine	197
Glenn, W.D.	87	Graybeal, Elizabeth	160
Glover, John	65,154	228,325		<
Glover, Robert E.	65	Graybeal, Emeline		229
Goines, Margaret	342	Graybeal, George		305
Goins, Gregin	108	Graybeal, Hazie		51
Goins, Infant	180	Graybeal, Inez		144
Goins, Jane	302	Graybeal, James M.		305
Goins, Maggie	288	Graybeal, John		60
Goins, Malinda	220	Graybeal, Joseph		103
Goins, Mary	257	Graybeal, J.F.		60
Goins, Robert	180	Graybeal, L.B.		199
Goins, W.A.	136,288	Graybeal, Martha		83
Goodman, Rhoda	227	Graybeal, Mary	188,267
Goodman, S.M.	40	328		<
Goodurn, Ronder H.	178	Graybeal, Mary H.		199
Goodurn, R.N., Jr.	178	Graybeal, Millie		261
Goodwin, Albert	55	Graybeal, Nancy	120,307
Goodwin, Allen	208	336,361		<
Goodwin, A.L.	258	Graybeal, Oscar		51
Goodwin, Catherine	74	Graybeal, Phoebe		209
Goodwin, D.E.	352	Graybeal, Will		54
Goodwin, James	259	Graybeal, William		259
Goodwin, James Lawson	259	Graybeal, W.H.		132
Goodwin, John F.	208,303	Graybeal, ...		358
Goodwin, Malinda	55,258	Grayson, Alvin Gilham	287
Goodwin, Mary Lucinda	303	Grayson, A.G.	230,232
Goodwin, Rhoda	50,240	Grayson, Ben		84
Goodwin, Samuel H.	55	Grayson, Colla O.		236
Goodwin, S.A.	74	Grayson, Elmer		84
Gouge, Charlotte	215	Grayson, Ethie Butler	287

405

Grayson, Gilliam B.	108	Greene, W.L.	200
Grayson, G.B.	108	Greenwell, Alfred	194,261
Grayson, J.W.M.	287,230	Greenwell, A. Bert	197
Grayson, Sarah Jane	48	Greenwell, A.B.	30,190
Grayson, William F.	230	Greenwell, Burton	261
Green, Alice	164	Greenwell, Catherine	179
Green, Catherine	211	Greenwell, David P.	261
Green, David	134	Greenwell, Eliza J.	31
Green, Dorra	5	Greenwell, Elysa	113
Green, Flora Price	263	Greenwell, Jane	150
Green, Floyd	268	Greenwell, Jennia	184
Green, George	239	Greenwell, John	245
Green, Hessel	308	Greenwell, Jonnie	204
Green, Isaac	263	Greenwell, J.M.	298
Green, James	268	Greenwell, Mart	316
Green, James A.	81	Greenwell, Martha	232
Green, James Ross	267	Greenwell, Martin	221,337
Green, Jennie	294	Greenwell, Nancy	114
Green, Joseph	43	Greenwell, Rachel	316
Green, Joseph W.	263	Greenwell, Rader	54
Green, J.B.	294	Greenwell, R.R.	232
Green, Laura	87	Greenwell, Samantha	261
Green, Leander	261	Greenwell, Samantha I.	194
Green, Lottie	171	Greenwell, Tine	298
Green, Lou	328	Greenwell, U.T.	268
Green, Louise	53	Greenwell, Wiley	298
Green, Mary	209	Greenwell, ...	34,252
Green, Nettie	84	Greer, Adelade	80
Green, Nora	292	Greer, Alex	296,317,308
Green, Ray	294	340	<
Green, Rilda	224	Greer, Alexander	47,105
Green, Salina	160	Greer, Amanda	62
Green, Sallie	261,349	Greer, Andrew	338
Green, Samuel B.	7	Greer, Anne	142
Green, Sarah	5	Greer, Ben	80
Green, Sarah Ellen	267	Greer, Ben W.	365
Green, Stella	89	Greer, Betsy	186
Green, Thomas	81	Greer, Bettie	75,267
Green, Tom	261	Greer, Blanch	80
Green, William	89,267	Greer, B.W.	302
Green, William A.	81	Greer, Caroline	45
Green, ...	339	Greer, Celia	193
Greene, George	115	Greer, Charles	319
Greene, G. Wiseman	170	Greer, Charlie	319
Greene, Lee	115	Greer, Clarence R.	54
Greene, Litha Estes	170	Greer, Cora Catherine	245
Greene, M.H.	170	Greer, David	75,340
Greene, Rilda	238	Greer, David M.	245,364

Greer, Dicie 102
Greer, Dollie Annis 17
Greer, Edd 136
Greer, Elizabeth 49,249
    341 <
Greer, Elizabeth Ray 326
Greer, Ellis 136
Greer, Ethel 128
Greer, Garfield 305
Greer, Georgia 263
Greer, Grady O. 158
Greer, Hattie Ruth 337
Greer, Infant 38,54,180
Greer, Ira 6
Greer, Isaac 122,305
Greer, James 45,62,84
    105,158 <
Greer, Joe 302
Greer, John 338
Greer, John F. 259,326
    337 <
Greer, Joseph 214,319
    326 <
Greer, Julia 258
Greer, June 122
Greer, J.S. 186,214
Greer, Laira 278
Greer, Leah Norris 210
Greer, Lee 202
Greer, Lelar 180
Greer, Lilie 314
Greer, Loura 243
Greer, Lucinda 305
Greer, Lucy 193
Greer, Lucy Anna 122
Greer, Luke H. 245
Greer, Mae 103
Greer, Margaret 51,98,320
Greer, Margaret E. 259
Greer, Margaret Marie 202
Greer, Martha 302
Greer, Martha Gentry 365
Greer, Martilda 62
Greer, Martitia 134
Greer, Mary 293,338
Greer, Mary E. 204
Greer, Mary Jane 186
Greer, Mary L. 337

Greer, Myrtle 54
Greer, Naley 34
Greer, Nancy 52,90,168
    254,296 <
Greer, Nettie 52,337
Greer, Noah Henly 267
Greer, Nola V. 245
Greer, N.J. 263
Greer, Ora 158
Greer, Polly 105,213
Greer, Rachel 97
Greer, Ray Scott 336
Greer, Reuben 364
Greer, Roby 254,312
Greer, Roby Lee 336
Greer, Russell Wills 214
Greer, R.W. 169
Greer, Samuel 116
Greer, Samuel B. 38
Greer, Sarah 340
Greer, S.B. 208
Greer, Taft 296
Greer, Thomas 208
Greer, Thomas Hawkins 169
Greer, Thomas M. 45
Greer, Tom 180
Greer, Viller 312
Greer, Wilburn 337
Greer, William 317,338
Greer, William J. 67
Greer, William T. 326
Greer, ... 177
Greg, Elizabeth J. 65
Gregg, Charles Loyd 351
Gregg, Clarence 113
Gregg, Clyde 75
Gregg, Craton 75
Gregg, Ella 187
Gregg, Estle 299
Gregg, Ettie 161
Gregg, Hamilton 351
Gregg, Hannah 156
Gregg, James 346
Gregg, Joseph H. 44
Gregg, Juanita Jane 44
Gregg, J. Clyde 337
Gregg, J.C. 86
Gregg, J.H. 156

Gregg, Laurie   233
Gregg, Leason   351
Gregg, Leckie   224
Gregg, Loginie   346
Gregg, Lou   75
Gregg, Mary F.   113
Gregg, Nelson   346
Gregg, Ottie Creed   337
Gregg, Sarah Ellen   346
Gregg, Thomas   322
Gregg, William H.   22
Gregg, Willie Gray   86
Gregg, ...   122
Grenwell, W.L.   230
Grewville, Selva   102
Griffey, Cleveland   35
Griffith, George W.   268
Griffith, Jamie   268
Grigsby, Joseph Scott   283
Grigston, James M.   322
Grigston, Sarah   267,315
   329   <
Grigston, Sarah A.   248
Grimsley, Mary   162,209
Grindstaff, Adeline   221
Grindstaff, Alex   19
Grindstaff, Alexander   217
Grindstaff, Alice   53,181
   122,207,237   <
Grindstaff, Annie Mae   138
Grindstaff, Catherine   169
Grindstaff, Danell   255
Grindstaff, David   217
Grindstaff, D.B.   183
Grindstaff, D.V.   200,289
Grindstaff, Earl   23
Grindstaff, Elizabeth   193
Grindstaff, Esther   244
Grindstaff, Eva   231
Grindstaff, Frank   207
Grindstaff, Franklin   208
Grindstaff, General W.   183
Grindstaff, George 89,231
   332   <
Grindstaff, George   332
Grindstaff, G.M.   346
Grindstaff, Hugh M.   208
Grindstaff, H.R.   26

Grindstaff, Infant   143
   193   <
Grindstaff, Isaac   249,289
Grindstaff, I.A.   163
Grindstaff, I.S.   346
Grindstaff, Jacob F.   170
   346   <
Grindstaff, Jake   89
Grindstaff, James T.   170
   291   <
Grindstaff, Jessie   138
Grindstaff, John   210,289
Grindstaff, John E.   356
Grindstaff, Johnson   175
Grindstaff, Joseph D.   169
   346   <
Grindstaff, Juanita M.   169
Grindstaff, J.D. (Mrs)   346
Grindstaff, J.F.   146,234
Grindstaff, J.T.   284,291
Grindstaff, Lessie   187
   297   <
Grindstaff, Liza Jane   284
Grindstaff, Martha L.   346
Grindstaff, Mary   200
Grindstaff, Mary Alice   54
Grindstaff, Nancy   48
Grindstaff, Nancy C.   346
Grindstaff, Nettie L.   291
Grindstaff, Nicholas   170
   183,356   <
Grindstaff, Ossie O.   308
Grindstaff, Panford   163
Grindstaff, Pauline   253
Grindstaff, Pollie   73
Grindstaff, Polly   108,175
Grindstaff, Roby   143
Grindstaff, Samuel   30
Grindstaff, Sara Fine   210
Grindstaff, Sarah   255,356
Grindstaff, Sherman   356
Grindstaff, Stacy   193
Grindstaff, Stella   317
Grindstaff, Susan   92,346
Grindstaff, Thomas   77
Grindstaff, Thomas F.   249
Grindstaff, Valie   253
Grindstaff, Vaught   308

Grindstaff, Waulfaurn 110
Grindstaff, Wilburn   48
Grindstaff, William   175
Grindstaff, W.H.   175
Grindstaff, ...   64,153
     177   <
Grines, Mary   241
Grogan, Claud   323
Grogan, David H.   323
Grogan, Elijah   323
Grosswhite, Nancy   29
Guffey, Catherine   57
Guffey, George   57,239
Guffey, Hobart   57
Gufie, Nancy C.   239
Guin, Aberham   104
Guin, Ada   23
Guin, Camel T.   93
Guin, Julia   269
Guin, Monroe   93
Guin, William   269
Guinn, George Monroe 314
Guinn, G.M.   314
Guinn, Mary   141
Guinn, ...   282
Guthrie, Lewis   238
Guy, Amanda Katherine 366
Guy, Delace   202
Guy, George Samuel   360
Guy, George Wells   360
Guy, Henry   202
Guy, Holland   332
Guy, Horton   218
Guy, H.A.   150
Guy, Katherine   255
Guy, Levi   298
Guy, Liddie   59
Guy, Mina   173
Guy, Mollie   308
Guy, Onnie   161
Guy, Roby W.   218
Guy, Stella Alice   332
Guy, Vesta   107
Guy, Vestie   108
Guy, William   218
Hacker, ...   335
Hackney, D.C.   35
Hackney, Sally   97

Hackney, Tom   97
Haddon, Vina   68
Hagaman, Flora   342
Hagaman, Francis   196
Hagaman, Idoma   342
Hagaman, John   196
Hagaman, Stansberry   342
Hagan, Calie   80
Hale, Ola   253
Hall, Betty   59
Hall, Billie   263
Hall, Clifford H.   216
Hall, C.H.   59,198,208
Hall, C.R.   215
Hall, Emes   198
Hall, Florence   140,215
     248   <
Hall, James   216
Hall, James R.   263
Hall, John   326
Hall, J.R.   215,216
Hall, Lou Ellen   326
Hall, Maggie   274
Hall, M.R.   274
Hall, Ruth   16
Hall, Susan Virginia   215
Hall, Susie   256
Hall, Taylor   349
Hall, William   256
Ham, Effie   256
Ham, Eli (Mrs)   335
Ham, Ida   72
Ham, Joe   256,312
Ham, Rosa Bell   256
Hamba, Annie   47
Hamby, Bertha E.   267
Hamby, Charles   103
Hamby, Charlie   93
Hamby, Cynthey   233
Hamby, Gertie V.   329
Hamby, Maggie   168
Hamby, Nanie   122
Hamby, Riley   233
Hamby, Thomas   194
Hamby, William W.G.   329
Hamby, Zena   103
Hamby, ...   339
Hamilton, Mary Jane   233

5

Hamilton, Robert 306
Hamm, Eli 333
Hamm, Eli (Mrs) 333
Hamm, Enoch 333
Hamm, Jensie 333
Hamm, Tessy 205
Hammons, Andy 294
Hammons, Bascom 296
Hammons, Bessie 356
Hammons, Bessie C. 356
Hammons, Blanche M. 296
Hammons, B.C. 345
Hammons, B... 78
Hammons, Callie F. 164
Hammons, Callie Lora 251
Hammons, Carrie May 253
Hammons, Catherine 32
Hammons, Clytie 181
Hammons, Edgar 162
Hammons, Edna 367
Hammons, Emes O. 162
Hammons, Everett S. 161
Hammons, Fanoie 17
Hammons, Henry W. 122,356
Hammons, Infant 42,125
Hammons, Isaac C. 226
Hammons, John Redford 356
Hammons, John R. 136
Hammons, Jonathon T. 45
Hammons, J.M.W. 168,231
Hammons, J.T. 162
Hammons, Lida 114
Hammons, Lillie 161
Hammons, Lydia 289
Hammons, Mandie B. 162
Hammons, Marion 294
Hammons, Marsh 226
Hammons, Mary 340
Hammons, Maryon 86
Hammons, Mattison L. 122
Hammons, May 345
Hammons, M.J. 176
Hammons, Pearl 136
Hammons, Polly Ann 232
286 <
Hammons, Rebecca 226
Hammons, Roy B. 162
Hammons, Sarah E. 235

Hammons, Stella Inez 162
Hammons, Sue 96,161
Hammons, S.T. 125
Hammons, Varder 304
Hammons, Wilham 304
Hammons, William 45,131
278 <
Hammons, Wise 161,181
Hammons, W.E. 164
Hammons, W.M. 42
Hamons, Cathern 5
Hamptin, Wash W. 358
Hampton, Ada 347
Hampton, Andrew 358
Hampton, Andy 296
Hampton, Callie 93,133
Hampton, D.D. 219,358
Hampton, Enola 89
Hampton, James Wade 347
Hampton, Jany 182
Hampton, Jim 347
Hampton, John W. 306
Hampton, Joseph R. 162
Hampton, Lillard 89,153
162 <
Hampton, Loyal B. 306
Hampton, Lucy 352
Hampton, Martha 226
Hampton, Nancy 162
Hampton, Pashie 296
Hampton, Pauline O. 358
Hanck, Estel 314
Hanck, Infant 314
Hand, Hannah 122
Hand, Hanner E. 252
Handy, Maggie L. 340
Haney, J. Donnelly 316
Haney, Mary 114
Haney, Naomi C. 316
Haney, O.B. 41
Hankins, Earl 88
Hankins, Martha 88
Hanley, O.B. 310
Harbin, Abe 331
Harbin, Abel 246
Harbin, Fay, 160
Harbin, John 152
Harbin, Leonard C. 331

Harbin, Mattie	331	Harper, Naomi	208
Harbin, Ray	152	Harper, Nelson	109,307
Harbin, S.L.	41,331	Harper, Omah	175
Harbin, Thomas	246	Harper, Opal	109
Harbin, Verna Ethel	321	Harper, Phylis Gean	338
Harbins, S.L.	97	Harper, William	29,37,110
Hardin, Charlie	327	Harris, Henderson	247
Hardin, Emley	161	Harris, Joel	127
Hardin, H.F.	173	Harris, J.Q.	236
Hardin, Mariah	184	Harris, Manda	107
Hardin, Mary	349	Harris, Margaret	236
Hardin, Nancy	272,352	Harris, Monroe	240
Harison, Caroline	156	Harris, Tennis	247
Harmon, Arola	93	Harris, Walter	236
Harmon, Betty	173	Hartschel, Mary J.	43
Harmon, Claude C.	176	Hasgue, Bonner	1
Harmon, Claudia	363	Hash, Benjamin F.	335
Harmon, Dora	328	Hash, Flora	84
Harmon, Dorothy Lee	275	Hash, Joe	335
Harmon, Etta	363	Hash, Rebecca	252
Harmon, Garnet M.	176	Hatcher, Lidia	288
Harmon, Grizzy Ann	206	Hatcher, Martha	297
Harmon, Joe	363	Haten, Hattie	312
Harmon, Lonnie	207	Hatley, Ceily	151
Harmon, Louvinia	275	Hatley, Evelyn Marie	357
Harmon, Margaret Anna	363	Hatley, L.R.	357
Harmon, Martin	275	Hatley, Smith	211
Harmon, Martin (Mrs)	275	Haton, Rhoda	280
Harmon, Mary	38	Hatton, Rhoda	265
Harmon, M.L.	173,207	Hawkins, A.C.	362
Harmon, Raleigh	173	Hawkins, Bess	44
Harmon, Rogers	276	Hawkins, Claud	32
Harmon, Venia	167	Hawkins, Clyde C.	306
Harmon, Walter	38	Hawkins, David S.	7
Harmon, W.R.	173	Hawkins, Dean M.	336
Harmon, ...	266	Hawkins, Eunice Louise	158
Harper, Anna Lee	251	Hawkins, E.C.	186
Harper, Arthur	28	Hawkins, E.T.	336
Harper, Cora May	336	Hawkins, Infant	40
Harper, Dicy Barry	282	Hawkins, John	306,321,362
Harper, Eli	37,106	Hawkins, John W.	306
Harper, Horton F.	110	Hawkins, Julia	306
Harper, Jerry	251	Hawkins, Julia Wagner	362
Harper, John	338	Hawkins, Landon H.	49
Harper, Kate	333	Hawkins, Martha	6,165
Harper, Laura	62	Hawkins, Mary	283
Harper, Lottie	307	Hawkins, May	169
Harper, Martha	40	Hawkins, Myrtle B.	102

Hawkins, M.F.   40
Hawkins, Nancy   90
Hawkins, Rebecca   197,238
Hawkins, Robt Alfred   186
Hawkins, Rosa   37
Hawkins, Susan Jane   44
Hawkins, Washington   49
   186   <
Hawkins, W.W.   49,158
Hawks, Clyde   362
Hawks, Edward S.   149
Hawks, Elbert   25
Hawks, Jane M.   177
Hawks, Matilda   362
Hawks, Reuben Edward   362
Hawks, R.C.   149
Hawks, R.E.   197
Hawks, Thomas   177
Hawks, Willie   197
Hayes, ...   36
Haynes, Flerbia   298
Haynes, Nancy   79
Haynes, Nelie   50
Hayworth, Andrew   154
Hayworth, Bob   270
Hayworth, Burl   202
Hayworth, Callie   43
Hayworth, Ed   202
Hayworth, Hattie   303
Hayworth, John Quncy   270
Hayworth, J.G.   104
Hayworth, J.O.   154
Hayworth, Kizzie   255
Hayworth, Lena Suzanie270
Hayworth, Lilley   ·173
Hayworth, Lura E.C.   104
Hayworth, Mary   43
Hayworth, McKinsey   211
Hayworth, Nathan   270
Hayworth, Nathan J.   104
Hayworth, Robert   270
Hayworth, Sarah Jane   147
Hayworth, Walter   43
Hayworth, ...   117
Hazlewood, Ana May   139
Hazlewood, Phes Milton254
Hazlewood, Phes (Mrs) 254
Hazlewood, Pleasant   199

Heaberlin, Elizabeth   25
Heaberlin, E. Ellen   193
Heaberlin, Infant   52
Heaberlin, James W.   97
Heaberlin, Joel   205,311
Heaberlin, Lillie L.   97
Heaberlin, Margaret   311
Heaberlin, Noah   52
Heaberlin, William H. 205
Heaberlin, W.T.   348
Heaberline, Joel   190
Head, Alice   116,195
Head, Dana Daniel   171
Head, Daniel   147
Head, Earl   116
Head, Pearl   116
Head, Rebecca   325
Head, Rosa   115,130
Head, Scott   195
Head, Verna   220
Head, W.S.   171,220,283
Heaton, Alice   39
Heaton, Andy   35
Heaton, Arlena   100
Heaton, Ben   100
Heaton, Blaine   96
Heaton, Carl G.   113
Heaton, Charles H.   59
Heaton, Columbus   134
Heaton, Cora   58,105
Heaton, C.F.   94,134,203
Heaton, Delia   94,123
Heaton, Docia   51
Heaton, Doshie   168
Heaton, Elizabeth 212,239
Heaton, Ellen   55,93,119
   132   <
Heaton, Ellen White   35
Heaton, Esther   39
Heaton, E.S.   113
Heaton, Fred   134
Heaton, George   39
Heaton, Glen   113
Heaton, Godfrey   88
Heaton, Hannah   43,63
Heaton, Henry Clay   36
Heaton, John   110,221,299
Heaton, John D.   90

Heaton, John W. 59
Heaton, Johnnie 36
Heaton, Joseph H. 53
Heaton, Julia 110,139
Heaton, J.A. 36
Heaton, Martha A. 61
Heaton, Martha E. 72
Heaton, Mary 203
Heaton, Mary C. 271
Heaton, Myrtle B. 57
Heaton, Nora Etta 57
Heaton, N.E. 57
Heaton, Polly 289
Heaton, Raley 208
Heaton, Richard L. 88
Heaton, Sam 90,96,170,271
Heaton, Susa 330
Heaton, Susan 299
Heaton, S.J. 190
Heaton, Ulah 27
Heberland, Joel 317
Heberland, N.H. 317
Heck, Arthur 7
Heck, Callie 192
Heck, Emaline 189
Heck, Gar 151
Heck, Jemima 4
Heck, Jordan 136,230,286
Heck, Jorden, Jr. 136
Heck, Mary Ann 283
Heck, Sarah Fritts 348
Heck, Wiley 189
Heck, Wiley Ross 151
Heck, Wiley Thomas 348
Heck, W.T. 207,348
Hecks, J.R. 247
Hedgepath, Atlas 174
Hedgepath, Richard 174
Hegaman, Eliza 4
Hegpath, Ellen 3
Hegpath, Infant 3
Helton, Pearl C. 6
Henderson, Charles 240
Henderson, Earl 176
Henderson, Elbert D. 205
Henderson, Hattie 112
Henderson, John 79
Henderson, Landon 62
Henderson, Lessie 240
Henderson, Maggie 205
Henderson, Pearl 176
Henderson, Thomas 205
Henderson, William 62
Hendison, Charles 283
Hendison, Daniel C. 283
Hendrix, Wilson 103
Hensley, George 301
Hensley, J.T. 232,250
Hensley, Margaret L. 250
Hensley, Susan 301
Hensley, Virginia 232
Henson, Daniel 29
Henson, David E. 349
Henson, David Ray 90
Henson, Elizabeth F. 349
Henson, H.E. 223
Henson, Infant 90
Henson, James Jordan 223
Henson, Jordan 349
Henson, J.L. 53
Henson, Liza 203
Herndon, D.E. 274
Herndon, Ruth Ellen 274
Hess, Pearl 74
Heuson, Bettie 192
Hicks, Albert 97,300
Hicks, Bill 313,345
Hicks, Elbert H. 358
Hicks, Eliza 300
Hicks, Etoila B. 329
Hicks, Hamilton 222
Hicks, Hazel 295
Hicks, Hiram 83
Hicks, Infant 22,199
Hicks, James 253,271
Hicks, John 222,345
Hicks, John Buckman 345
Hicks, Joseph R. 199
Hicks, Josie 87,91,291
Hicks, Martha Jane 278
345 <
Hicks, Mary 127,145
Hicks, Mollie 98
Hicks, Myrtle 54
Hicks, Pearl 352
Hicks, Rachel Ann 301

413

Hicks, Sallie	154	Hodge, Fate	259,297
Hicks, Wayne	313	Hodge, F. Love	67
Hicks, William Henry	358	Hodge, Ida Belle	69
Hilard, Catherine	211	Hodge, Infant	57,139
Hilhard, Wilham	250	Hodge, Jack Samick	203
Hillard, Mary E.	285	Hodge, John	273
Hilliard, Alfred	147	Hodge, John H.	153
Hilliard, Hany	147	Hodge, Joseph J.D.	146
Hilton, ...	101	Hodge, Joseph W.	203
Hines, Dock	86	Hodge, Joseph W.	183
Hines, George W.	25,86	Hodge, J.F.	102
285	<	Hodge, J.W.	203
Hines, G.W.	90	Hodge, Lester Paul	322
Hines, James E.	90	Hodge, Louise Edna	260
Hinkle, A.J.	217	Hodge, Luinda	273
Hinkle, Earl	189	Hodge, Maggie	164
Hinkle, Eddie (Mrs)	352	Hodge, Malinda	102,261
Hinkle, Jane	189	Hodge, Mary	170,277
Hinkle, John	217	Hodge, Matncia C.	196
Hinkle, Mary, E.	217	Hodge, Mayr	118
Hinkle, Mason Guy	189	Hodge, Minnie	304
Hinkle, Myrtle	167	Hodge, Minnie Malinda	153
Hinkle, Vada	312	Hodge, Myrtle K.	277
Hinson, Zara Mae	294	Hodge, M.G.	258,294
Hitchcock, Beula	223	Hodge, Nancy	8
Hobway, J.G.	154	Hodge, Nellie	42
Hobway, Mary Jane	154	Hodge, Nolan Bruce	322
Hockaday, Blanch	48	Hodge, Peggy	141
Hockaday, George	48	Hodge, Penian	196
Hockaday, Ham	72	Hodge, Robert	224
Hockey, George	48	Hodge, Roby	14,217
Hockey, Ralph E.	48	Hodge, Sam	139,167
Hoclow, Lizzie	106	Hodge, Samuel	57,203,203
Hodge, Agnes Mae	199	Hodge, Sarah	184
Hodge, Alex Clarence	259	Hodge, Stacy Edgar	292
Hodge, Andy	260	Hodge, Steve	304
Hodge, Anna	196	Hodge, Thomas	199
Hodge, Arthur Burt	359	Hodge, T.C.	196
Hodge, A.L.	203,277,322	Hodge, William R.	51
Hodge, Beulah Mae	359	Hodge, ...	230,350
Hodge, Boone F.	183,196	Hodges, Bessie	123
Hodge, B.F.	40	Hodges, James	123
Hodge, C.N.	199	Hodges, John William	123
Hodge, Dallas	146,226	Hodgson, Dora	191
Hodge, Edgar	292	Hodgson, W.A.	191
Hodge, Edward L.	277	Hoke, Mary Snyder	222
Hodge, Elaine B.	196	Holcomb, Laura E.	336
Hodge, Elizabeth	59	Holcomb, M.B.	220,336

Holcomb, Nancy Jane 220
Holden, Catherine 169
Holden, Infant 280
Holden, James J. 127
Holden, J.J. 23
Holden, Martha 315
Holden, Mary 127,171
Holden, Roby F. 127
Holden, Verda 280,306
Holden, Willis 23
Holder, Alice E. 50
Holder, Clara 144
Holder, C.E. 178
Holder, David 63,72
Holder, Davie 63
Holder, Isaac Thomas 50
Holder, Minerva 350
Holder, Nancy 144
Holder, Pattie 63
Holder, Thomas 72
Holloway, Blanche 155
Holloway, Felix 359
Holloway, Fern 132
Holloway, Kisiah 110
Holloway, Lillie 155
Holloway, Lillie P. 359
Holloway, Linville 246
Holloway, Linville E. 246
Holloway, Marry J. 8
Holloway, Martin L. 359
Holloway, R.A. 132
Holloway, Wilson 12
Holman, Dealice 141
Holman, Jim 320
Holman, Martha 222,335
Holman, Mary 328,366
Holman, Susan 231
Holsclaw, Bettie 252
Holsclaw, Mark 363
Hoover, John Beltz 174
Hoover, John B. (Mrs) 174
Hopkins, Florence C. 309
Hopkins, George 360
Hopkins, George A. 363
Hopkins, George W. 363
Hopkins, James 309,335
Hopkins, J.S. 363
Hoppers, Franklin J. 82

Horn, Ada 121
Horn, Claud Melvin 299
Horn, David 94
Horn, Edna Sue 278,313
Horn, Edron 94
Horn, Edward 94
Horn, Hubert 94
Horn, Infant 106
Horn, Irdine 302
Horn, Joe 302
Horn, Martha 94
Horn, Mary M. 330
Horn, Millard L. 149
Horn, Pauline 336
Horn, Robert 106,299,330
Horn, Ruby Dian 287
Horn, Ruth Glades 161
Horn, Thomas D. 102
Horn, Vivian Rose 102
Horn, Worley 149,161,287
Horton, Baxter 148
Horton, Gaston 148
Horton, ... 194
Houck, Ada 321
Houck, Barbara 43
Houck, Estle 321
Houk, Estil 272
Houk, Ethel Grace 272
Howard, Blanche E. 62
Howard, Burket 149
Howard, B. Carroll 210
Howard, Caldonia 131
Howard, Cresie E. 276
Howard, C.M. 16
Howard, Dave 210
Howard, David 100
Howard, D.R. 195
Howard, Elizabeth 240
Howard, Ethel 64
Howard, Frank 210
Howard, George W. 62,344
Howard, G.W. 62,136,241
Howard, Hamilton B. 269
Howard, H.B. 168
Howard, James H. 149,151
Howard, Jim 257
Howard, John 17,204,204

<

Howard, Lillie   135,168
Howard, Lula   350
Howard, Luther   344
Howard, Martha   185
Howard, Mary   57,150,199
          250,287,360   <
Howard, Melen   276
Howard, Pearl   355
Howard, Rachel   142
Howard, Rhoda   105
Howard, robert   344
Howard, R.T.   276
Howard, Susan Smith   344
Howard, Von E.   151
Howard, Wheeler   269
Howard, William   227,269
Howard, William H.   84
Howard, William M.   246
Howard, William N.   246
Howe, Emmett H.   290
Howe, Mary Lewis   290
Howell, Calvin   162
Howell, Catherine E.   297
Howell, Catherine M.   209
Howell, Sabra Alice   107
Howell, Thomas   297
Howell, William T.   297
Hudgin, Sarah   131
Huffman, Charlie   184
Huffman, Dora   197
Huffman, Jessie   197
Huggins, Balmer   295
Huggins, Imogene   262
Huggins, Josie   295
Huggins, Oscar   262
Huggins, Oscar R.   295
Hughes, ...   328
Hugins, Rosie   221
Humpford, Gretrude   360
Hunt, Julia   90
Hurley, Sudie   129
Huskins, Emory   179
Huskins, G.T.   301
Huskins, Sarah   347
Huskins, Thomas   179
Hutchinson, Clarence   227
Hutchinson, Cleve   360
Hutchinson, Clyde B.   244

Hutchinson, C.B.   227
Hutchinson, Fred   339
Hutchinson, Jane   110
Hutchinson, John N.   339
Hutchinson, Julaan   366
Hutchinson, J.C.   110,284
Hutchinson, Sarah   296
Hutchinson, William   244
Hutton, Elbert   302
Hutton, Elizabeth   302
Hyder, A.J.F.   13
Hyder, Ben   328
Hyder, B.L.   175
Hyder, Josephine   76
Hyder, Nat K.   175
Hynes, Elva   175
Hynes, Elvie   139
Hy..., Elva S.   49
H..., Clay   12
Icenhour, Alafair   188
Icenhour, Bell   287
Icenhour, Myrtle V.   360
Icenhour, Nell   287
Icenhour, Roy   360
Icenhour, Russell   188
Icenhour, R.F.   180,259
Icenhour, Winnie E.   360
Ingram, John   337
Isaacs, Adam P.   87
Isaacs, Andrew Dewey   98
Isaacs, Babe   160
Isaacs, Bessie   259
Isaacs, Bettie Lew   256
Isaacs, Carl   69,98
Isaacs, Caroline   258
Isaacs, Carrol   175
Isaacs, Charlie   237
Isaacs, Cleveland   211
Isaacs, Elias   148,160
Isaacs, Emily   293
Isaacs, Infant   69
Isaacs, Jack   123,230,251
       327   <
Isaacs, James   49,290
Isaacs, Jim   256
Isaacs, Joe   205
Isaacs, Joseph Harold   205
Isaacs, Lucinda   182,189

416

Isaacs, Martha		49
Isaacs, Mary	46,118,254	
327		<
Isaacs, Mary E.		92
Isaacs, Mary Ivalee		175
Isaacs, Minnie	123,237	
Isaacs, Nancy		219
Isaacs, Nancy Lucile		251
Isaacs, Ray		148
Isaacs, Rosa Belle		98
Isaacs, Sallie		63
Isaacs, Thomas		148
Isaacs, Walter Fred		230
Isaacs, Winne		237
Isaacs, ...	67,218	
Isenhour, Bell		161
Isenhour, Bill		149
Isenhour, John		137
Isenhour, Lear		137
Isenhour, W.W.		204
Ison, Edmon		332
Issacs, Abe		258
Is..., Elizabeth		59
Jackson, Archibald		130
Jackson, Emma		154
Jackson, James Wiley		118
Jackson, Jim		223
Jackson, Katie		56
Jackson, Katy	98,155	
Jackson, Mahalia	130,344	
Jackson, Malinda		78
Jackson, Martha Ann		355
Jackson, Mollie		53
Jackson, Rebecca		229
Jackson, Rebecca	38,118	
Jackson, R.W.		118
Jackson, Susan		103
Jackson, Thomas Russ		118
Jackson, ...		362
Jacob, Marion		218
James, Sallie		239
Jarrett. Ida Louisa		261
Jarvis, Nancy	141,213	
Jenkins, Ada		88
Jenkins, Alice		48
Jenkins, Amanda		351
Jenkins, Annie		1
Jenkins, Ben		351

Jenkins, Benjamin		196
Jenkins, Blanche		249
Jenkins, B.		76
Jenkins, Calvin R.		274
Jenkins, Carrie Cole		361
Jenkins, Catherine		65
Jenkins, Clara		322
Jenkins, Darcia		212
Jenkins, David		362
Jenkins, Effie		295
Jenkins, Eliza J.		81
Jenkins, Euerua M.		197
Jenkins, Flora Lee		42
Jenkins, Francis May		319
Jenkins, Frank		227
Jenkins, George		272
Jenkins, George W.		282
Jenkins, Hattie		92
Jenkins, Herbert W.		109
Jenkins, Hugh		71
Jenkins, Hugh A.		92
Jenkins, Hughie		92
Jenkins, Huston		120
Jenkins, Infant	23,71	
109		<
Jenkins, Irvin R.		195
Jenkins, Isaac H.		109
Jenkins, Jessie		209
Jenkins, Jessie C.		210
Jenkins, J.S.		196
Jenkins, J.S. (Mrs)		196
Jenkins, Lillie		341
Jenkins, Lon		351
Jenkins, Longoe L.		357
Jenkins, L.L.		58
Jenkins, Mainard		274
Jenkins, Mamie		237
Jenkins, Martha		251
Jenkins, Mary Belle		157
Jenkins, Mary C.		109
Jenkins, Mollie		362
Jenkins, M.B.	109,195,212	
Jenkins, Naimia		291
Jenkins, Nancy		3
Jenkins, Nat T.		157
Jenkins, Nettie		85
Jenkins, Noah Williams		210
Jenkins, N...		100

Jenkins, Ollie	47		Johnson, Andrew	56,276
Jenkins, Ollie C.	55		279	<
Jenkins, Olliv	65		Johnson, Andrew C.	47,70
Jenkins, Phoeba G.	209		279	<
Jenkins, Phoebe	282		Johnson, Asie Miner	20
Jenkins, Ransom L.	42,272		Johnson, A.C.	47,191
Jenkins, Reland	120		Johnson, A.L.	247
Jenkins, Roland	46,72		Johnson, A.S.	160,223,244
195,272,274	<		Johnson, Beatrice	101
Jenkins, Roy	210		Johnson, Betie	176
Jenkins, R.L.	42,47,53		Johnson, Bobbie H.B.	340
100,127,197,210,249,311			Johnson, Booker B.	368
Jenkins, R.L. (Mrs)	55		Johnson, Bruce	74
291	<		Johnson, Callie	105
Jenkins, Sarafina	228		Johnson, Camel	209
Jenkins, Sarah	258		Johnson, Caroline	55,242
Jenkins, Thelma	357		Johnson, Cecile	223
Jenkins, Thomas	76,272		Johnson, Charles	160
Jenkins, Tom	319		Johnson, Charlotte	348
Jenkins, Victoria	110,351		Johnson, Christenia	203
Jenkins, William	76,161		Johnson, Clara M.	229
272	<		Johnson, Clay	1
Jenkins, William H.	351		Johnson, Cynthia C.	339
357	<		Johnson, C.M.	243
Jenning, Wiley	213		Johnson, Della	77
Jennings, Betty Ann	174		Johnson, Dellie	111
333	<		Johnson, Denver	340
Jennings, Columbus F.	213		Johnson, Dorothy	159
Jennings, L.R.	178		Johnson, Elba	43
Jennings, Mary E.	257		Johnson, Eliza	297
Jennings, Pauline	322		Johnson, Ella	97
Jennings, Rebecca	64		Johnson, Elvira	247
Jennings, Stilly	182		Johnson, Emaly	90
Jennings, Susannah M.	258		Johnson, Essie	107
Jennings, Thomas	106		Johnson, Ethel	21
Jennings, Thomas J.	133		Johnson, Eugene C.	356
182	<		Johnson, E.C.	2
Jennings, Tom	322		Johnson, E.M.	203
Jennings, T.J.	64		Johnson, Glenn	101
Jennings, Wiley	133,178		Johnson, Gus	65
265	<		Johnson, Harvey	363
Jennings, William	178		Johnson, Hattie	262
Jennings, William R.	106		Johnson, Haynes	272
Jereatt, William Allen	261		Johnson, Hazel	314
Johnson, Ada	272,314		Johnson, Henry	114
Johnson, Alice	206,259		Johnson, Hugh	107,160
Johnson, Allen	236		Johnson, Ida	202
Johnson, Allie E.	243		Johnson, James	159

Johnson, James S.   214
Johnson, James W.   160
Johnson, James W.,Sr.   236
Johnson, John   56,200
Johnson, John G.   63
Johnson, John H.   368
Johnson, Julia   246
Johnson, J.C.   268,282
Johnson, J.S.   77
Johnson, J.W.   41,262
Johnson, Lachanah T.   209
Johnson, Lemon   74
Johnson, Lillie   262
Johnson, Louise E.   295
Johnson, Maggie   209
Johnson, Manda E.   51
Johnson, Marion J.   70
Johnson, Martha Cress   223
Johnson, Mary   41,237
Johnson, Mattie E.   271
Johnson, Maurine   268
Johnson, Melicia   312
Johnson, Mollie   40
Johnson, M.C.   279,363
Johnson, M.K.   339
Johnson, Nancy   191
Johnson, Nellie   91
Johnson, N.V.   230
Johnson, Ollaf Bell   47
Johnson, Oma   75
Johnson, Oscar (Mrs)   236
Johnson, Pattie   67
Johnson, Pedia   81
Johnson, Polly   236
Johnson, Raoner   282
Johnson, Rebecca   54,62
Johnson, Ret   52
Johnson, Roana   331
Johnson, Roanna   341
Johnson, Robert   200,327
Johnson, Robert Hugh   244
Johnson, Robert J.   90
Johnson, Ross   327
Johnson, R.G.   69,314,331
Johnson, Sarafinal   44
Johnson, Sarah   327
Johnson, Selmer   288
Johnson, Smith 65,214,321

Johnson, Taylor   251,331
Johnson, Thomas   53
Johnson, Thomas W.   78
Johnson, Titia   279
Johnson, T.A.   41
Johnson, Vernia   363
Johnson, Virtie   8
Johnson, Walter   327
Johnson, William   100,105
         200,202,212   <
Johnson, William D.   339
Johnson, William E.   134
Johnson, W.D.   41
Johs, Robert   141
Joins, Cleve   364
Joins, William   364
Jones, Amanda   163
Jones, Andy   163,210,238
Jones, Arthor Glen   143
Jones, Bearly   260
Jones, Bessie   78
Jones, Blanche   239
Jones, Carl   201
Jones, Celia Jane   83
Jones, Clyde Melvin   317
Jones, Dona   149
Jones, Early   260
Jones, Elizabeth   348
Jones, Fannie   62
Jones, Frank   127,201,365
Jones, Hairl   201
Jones, Harriett   300
Jones, Harrison   151
Jones, Henry Lee   180
Jones, Ida P.   43
Jones, Infant   61,76,112
Jones, James   61,76,170
Jones, James M.   112,147
Jones, Jane   144
Jones, Janice   270
Jones, John   48,89,345
Jones, John Henry   170
Jones, Josiah   89
Jones, J.C.   298
Jones, J.F.   295
Jones, J.M.   317
Jones, J.R.   309
Jones, Lester   26

Jones, Lizzie	260	Jordan, J.W. 191,208,276
Jones, Lizzie Pearl	146	Jordan, Mamie Bess 84
Jones, Luther	332	Jordan, Martha 276
Jones, Maggie	165,332	Jordan, Ray Denver 208
Jones, Mandy	327	Jordan, R.C. 167
Jones, Martha	156	Jordan, William H. 311
Jones, Marvin	270	Justice, Dicey 38
Jones, Mary Mount	305	Kear, Crittie May 339
Jones, Melvin	202,295	Keaton, F.F. 39
Jones, Mollie Emmett	105	Keaton, Ida 114
Jones, M.E.	143	Keaton, Lillie Aretta 39
Jones, Nellie E.	147	Keene, Fannie 333
Jones, Nora	202	Keller, Ananity 279
Jones, Nora Lee	298	Keller, George L. 244
Jones, N.J.	315	Keller, James Devar 244
Jones, Pollie	261	Keller, Joe 229
Jones, Raymond	239	Keller, John 89
Jones, Retha Jane	144	Keller, Lillie 229
Jones, Robert	265	Keller, M.F. 301
Jones, Roby A.	43	Keller, Phoebe 89
Jones, Ruby Selvia	92	Keller, Rachel Annie 229
Jones, R.E.	92	Kelly, B.V. 312
Jones, Sam	144,340	Kelly, Florence 312
Jones, Sam P.	243	Kelly, L.O. 312
Jones, Samantha	228	Kelly, Robert 272
Jones, Samuel	180,295	Kelly, Spencer 272
Jones, Sarah	60	Kensley, Albert 6
Jones, Sydid Jane	148	Kent, Bettie Virginia 348
Jones, Vira	127	Kent, C. 182
Jones, Walter F.	127,146	Kent, J.B. 182
Jones, Walter S.	143	Kent, J.C. 348
Jones, Will	180	Keys, David Dick 219
Jones, Willie	127	Keys, Guy 247
Jones, W.S.	260	Keys, Guy M. 219
Jones, ...	257	Keys, G.M. 259
Jons, Thomas Everett	141	Keys, John 109
Jordan, Bettie	27	Keys, John W, 178
Jordan, Callie	101	Keys, J.W. 61
Jordan, Elbert	101,221	Keys, Marcus 178
Jordan, E.S.	82	Keys, Marcus A. 17
Jordan, Hattie	311	Keys, Robert M. 259
Jordan, Hendrick	117	Keys, Robert W. 219
Jordan, Infant	117,167	Keys, Sallie 248
Jordan, James	191	Keys, Susan Rebecca 259
Jordan, James H.	191	Keys, William 158
Jordan, James W.	82	Kid, Elizabeth 163
Jordan, John	101	Kilby, Charity 72
Jordan, J.H.	86,113,311	Kilby, Infant 108

Kilby, Mary   273
Kilby, William L.   108
Killans, Corda   162
Killings, Corda   250
Killins, Corda   246
Kinch, Anna   275
Kindrel, Annie   84
King, Charles   135
King, Charles L.   139
King, C.W.   64,272,340
King, Infant   64
King, James S.   64
King, Jim   340
King, Lizzie   36
King, Lossie   340
King, L.A.   272
King, Malindy   3
King, McNary   256
King, Nancy   261
King, Robert   309
King, Sarah   272
King, ...   60
Kirby, Avery   354
Kirby, Conley   293
Kirby, Grace   89
Kirby, James   192
Kirby, Margaret   354
Kirby, Mary Velena   192
Kirby, Myrtle   293
Kirby, William M.   354
Kiser, John Lewis   353
Kite, Bertie   326
Kite, Carson   254
Kite, Conley   304
Kite, Criss   234
Kite, George W.   320
Kite, Grace   52
Kite, G.W.   320
Kite, Harm Warner   326
Kite, Infant   180,304
Kite, Joseph Winfield   320
Kite, J.A.   280
Kite, Madora   344
Kite, Margaret   154
Kite, Mary Jane   320
Kite, Nannie Elvina   280
Kite, Randal   254
Kite, Washington   326

Kite, W.M.   180
Kizer, Mary   88
Kunn, Sophia L.   305
Lamberson, John   188
Lamberson, Robert, Jr   188
Lamberson, Robert L.   188
Lambert, Amanda   150,228
Lancaster, J.C.   276
Landers, Lillie   305
Landers, Pete   92,228
Landers, Peter   244
Landers, Walter David   244
Lane, Birtha J.   303
Langston, Eveline   106
Lantern, Matilda   303
Latham, Annie   160
Latham, David   160
Latham, Emmett A.   160
Lathom, Cyrus Gilbert   228
Lathom, C.G.   228
Lathom, D.C.   228
Lathom, John A.   228
Lathom, Lydia   48
Lawrence, James B.   112
Lawrence, Sallie E.   112
Laws, Ada   12
Laws, Agnes   354
Laws, Celia Birbary   297
Laws, Cora   285
Laws, Delila   356
Laws, D.M.   317
Laws, Edith P.   285
Laws, Elizabeth R.   169
Laws, Emma   129,148,200
Laws, Garfield   205
Laws, George   297
Laws, Infant   150
Laws, Isaac   184,204,297
Laws, James E.   248,285
Laws, James G.   205
Laws, James S.   317
Laws, Jasper   285
Laws, Jerry   42,73
Laws, Joe   150
Laws, Joe B.   204
Laws, Josie   308
Laws, Lelia   239
Laws, Lillie   229

Laws, Malinda 205
Laws, Mary Magolna 248
Laws, Matilda 12,194
Laws, Mollie 368
Laws, Nannie 281
Laws, Priscilla 354
Laws, Rebecca 103
Laws, Robert S. 354
Laws, Sallie Arnold 368
Laws, Sarrah Jean 289
Laws, Silas 204
Laws, Susie 359
Laws, William 42,285,289
  368 <
Laws, William M. 368
Lawson, Laura 96
Lawson, Lucy 232
Lawson, Martha 269
Law..., Ira 32
Lazenley, John 230
Leaper, Edward 300
Leaper, Tuanna 300
Lechcoe, Isaac 344
Lehcoe, A.A. 344
Lechoe, G.T. 254
Lechoe, Ruby 254
Ledford, ... 200
Lee, Bessie 91
Lee, Edna E. 10
Lee, G.H. 194
Lee, Harrison 120
Lee, Infant 127
Lee, Jina B. 174
Lee, J.M. 220
Lee, Mary Catherine 304
Lee, Robert E. 108
Lee, Robert H. 108
Lee, R.A. 127,304
Lee, Sarah 120
Lee, Walter 174
Leech, Marion 218
Leffman, Benjamin F. 347
Leffman, Carl W. 351
Leffman, Columbus L. 351
Leffman, Eliza Jane 320
Leffman, Fannie Dunn 351
Leffman, H.F. 320
Leffman, Jessie 294

Leffman, John 347
Lefler, Charles 309
Lefler, Hanna Allen 309
Lefler, James 19
Lefler, Joe T. (Mrs) 309
Lefler, Joseph Thomas 309
Lefman, Belive 300
Lenderman, Nancy 85
Leonard, Nell 218
Leonard, Rose 218
Leonard, Tabitha 93
Lewis, Ambrose 312
Lewis, Ancil 334
Lewis, Arthur Tilson 245
Lewis, Artie Rosetta 341
Lewis, Attria 176
Lewis, A.A. 129,191
Lewis, A.G. 283
Lewis, Bertha 171
Lewis, Bettie 137
Lewis, Blanche Delina 96
Lewis, Carl 100
Lewis, Carley 123
Lewis, Charles 74
Lewis, Chelsie Lee 96
Lewis, Clarence J. 246
Lewis, Clyda Mae 338
Lewis, C.E. 133
Lewis, Dave C. 340
Lewis, David 51
Lewis, David C. 96
Lewis, David H. 290
Lewis, David W. 276
Lewis, Delila J. 184
Lewis, Drucy 85
Lewis, D.C. 340
Lewis, Earl Bruce 184
Lewis, Earl B. 184
Lewis, Elbert 250
Lewis, Emma 343
Lewis, Ethel 337
Lewis, Ethel 75,86
Lewis, Eva 325
Lewis, E... 153
Lewis, Francis 100
Lewis, Geneva 123
Lewis, George W. 343
Lewis, Gidden 85

Lewis, G.F.	38,84,85,139	
Lewis, G.W.	201	
Lewis, Henderson	245	
Lewis, Infant	38,75	
Lewis, Isaac Leander	85	
Lewis, Ivan	87	
Lewis, James	87,133	
Lewis, James C.	367	
Lewis, Jane	327	
Lewis, John	338	
Lewis, John C.	93,133	
Lewis, John Grant	340	
Lewis, J.C.	39	
Lewis, Katie	295	
Lewis, Katy	180	
Lewis, Lawson	343	
Lewis, Lear Ellen	201	
Lewis, Marion Emmett	276	
Lewis, Mary J.	84	
Lewis, Millard	15	
Lewis, Myrtle E.	100	
Lewis, Nannie Beth	295	
Lewis, N.M.	131	
Lewis, Otis	93	
Lewis, Parlee	1	
Lewis, Pashia	358	
Lewis, Pearl	74	
Lewis, Peggy	39	
Lewis, Polly	217	
Lewis, Ray Burl	367	
Lewis, Robert	293	
Lewis, Roby	75,82	
Lewis, Rosie	245	
Lewis, Ruby Ethel	295	
Lewis, Russell	293	
Lewis, Sam	338	
Lewis, Sue Preston S.	283	
Lewis, Thurman	131	
Lewis, Vernia	134	
Lewis, William	247	
Lewis, Willie	246,295	
Lewis, W.M.	131	
Lewis,. Chloe	317	
Lincaster, Claude	168	
Lincaster, Edith M.	168	
Lineback, Henry	41,172	
Lineback, Joda	193	
Lineback, Joda M.	40	
Lineback, Joseph	172	
Lineback, W.W.	172	
Linzz, Nancy	40	
Lipfird, B.V.	296	
Lipfird, Clint	308	
Lipfird, Lizzie	350	
Lipfird, Locie	308	
Lipfird, R.G.	126	
Lipfird, Sherman	308	
Lipfird, Vira	296	
Lipford, Alice Lucil	257	
Lipford, Anthony	187	
Lipford, Arch	167	
Lipford, Avery	241	
Lipford, A.A.	38	
Lipford, B.A.	187	
Lipford, Clinton	202	
Lipford, Edmond, A.	245	
Lipford, Ellen	234	
Lipford, Letha Viola	258	
Lipford, Margie	245	
Lipford, Mary E.	366	
Lipford, Nora	257	
Lipford, Owen	258	
Lipford, Ray	308	
Lipford, Rosie	167	
Lipford, R.A.	187	
Lipford, Sarah	38,202	
Lipford, Virdie	241	
Lipford, Wallace B.	308	
Lipford, W.E.	257	
Lipps, Charity	314	
Lock, Bettie	92	
Lock, Betty	63	
Lock, Caroline	69	
Lock, Jack	69	
Lock, Walter	69	
Lockner, John L.	276	
Lockner, Sam	269,276	
Logan, Kerne W.	6	
Loggins, Clint	293	
Loggins, Clinton	21	
Lomax, America	109	
Lomax, Carrie Rebecca	231	
Lomax, Hattie Belle	231	
358	<	
Lomax, Laura	162	
Lomax, Peter	185	

Lomax, Rebecca	220
Lomax, Robert S.	358
Lomax, Sylvester	220
Lomax, Sylvester	231
Long, Calvin	43
Long, Cathena Sizemore	44
Long, C.R.	43
Long, Ed	311
Long, Ed E.	193
Long, Ellen	311
Long, Fred	251
Long, Fred, Jr.	251
Long, Hugh	25
Long, H.R.	131
Long, Infant	138
Long, Jasper S.	131
Long, Jefferson	43
Long, Jefferson L.	172
Long, Lawrence J.	138
Long, Roxie A.	251
Long, Walter Andrew	172
Long, Wiley W.	193
Lorance, ...	338
Lord, J.C.	265
Love, D.H.	318
Love, George Millard	330
Love, G.M.	47
Love, Herman	318
Love, Inez	318
Love, Ira	318
Love, Joe	318
Love, Joseph	330
Love, Joseph Harrison	360
Love, J.M.	114
Love, J.M., Jr.	114
Love, Lizzie	330
Love, Rebecca	318
Love, Rodger R.	330
Love, Roger	360
Love, Thomas	360
Love, William G.	318
Lovell, Pansie	26
Loving, Disey	151
Lowe, Abraham	207
Lowe, Abram	68
Lowe, Abram R.	349
Lowe, Albert	295
Lowe, Amanda	262

Lowe, Annie	265
Lowe, Bell	120
Lowe, Belle	237
Lowe, Caleb	207
Lowe, Cassie	255
Lowe, Charles Elbert	366
Lowe, Charlie	365
Lowe, Charlotte	255
Lowe, C.H.	159
Lowe, Dewey	338
Lowe, Doran (Mrs)	365
Lowe, Duey	177
Lowe, Effie	29
Lowe, Eliza L.	49
Lowe, Elizabeth N.	349
Lowe, Etoila	338
Lowe, F.S.	49
Lowe, Hazel Florence	338
Lowe, Henry	237
Lowe, Ida	109
Lowe, Ida Lee	310
Lowe, Infant	82,92,177
227	<
Lowe, Jacob	120,237,246
254	<
Lowe, Jacob M.	82
Lowe, Jake (Mrs)	354
Lowe, James	227,246
Lowe, James W.	366
Lowe, Joe	248
Lowe, John A.	142
Lowe, John E.	68
Lowe, Joseph	68,70
Lowe, Julia	234
Lowe, J.H.	50
Lowe, J.M.	324
Lowe, Katherine	251
Lowe, Kemp	207,262
Lowe, Kinney	12
Lowe, Lillie Wagner	207
Lowe, Luttitia	70
Lowe, Malinda	50
Lowe, Mary	240
Lowe, Minirve	63
Lowe, Minnie	106
Lowe, Mollie	263,354
Lowe, Mollie Ann	366
Lowe, Robert Dale	172

Lowe, Roby   141
Lowe, Roby Jr.   141
Lowe, Roy   120,255
Lowe, Ruby   350
Lowe, R.S.   92,172,349
Lowe, Samuel C.   254
Lowe, Stella   283
Lowe, Steve   350
Lowe, Susannah   288
Lowe, U.R.   49
Lowe, Verna Golden   142
Lowe, Walter   254
Lowe, Will   63,350
Lowe, William   290
Lowe, William E.   68
Lowe, William H.   366
Lowe, Willis Roscoe   120
Lowe, W.H.   284
Lowel, Bonnie   26
Loyd, Anna   113
Loyd, Bessie   56
Loyd, Henderson   142
Loyd, Iamtha Sophie   208
Loyd, James R.   348
Loyd, Joe L.   324
Loyd, John   113,124,289
Loyd, Joseph Landon   142
Loyd, Landen   124
Loyd, Liza   276
Loyd, L.C.   123
Loyd, Mary   303
Loyd, Mary Isabella   123
Loyd, Rachel   27
Loyd, Sarah Lucky B.   324
Loyd, Sophie   289
Loyd, Tennessee   289
Loyd, T.   208
Loyd, W.W.   124
Loyd, ...   303
Lunceford, Amanda   46
Lunceford, Catherine   335
Lunceford, Enoch   50
Lunceford, General   279
  335   <
Lunceford, John   318
Lunceford, John F.   50
Lunceford, J.M. (Mrs)   335
Lunceford, Katherine   318

Lunceford, Luvenia   258
Lunceford, Maggie   333
Lunceford, Martha   165
Lunceford, Mary   144,309
Lunceford, Maud May   118
Lunceford, Noah M.   335
Lunceford, Retta   39
Lunceford, Ruth   210
Lunceford, R.C.   268
Lunceford, Zollie   144
Lunceford, Z.C.   118
Lunceford, Z.D.   46,144
Luncsford, W.H.   194
Lunsford, Aud   205
Lunsford, Betsy   66
Lunsford, Caud   286
Lunsford, Charlie A.   272
Lunsford, C.A.   163
Lunsford, Delma Joe   205
Lunsford, Don   259
Lunsford, D.H.   272
Lunsford, Elias   145
Lunsford, Elizabeth   279
Lunsford, Emaline   145
Lunsford, Enoch   14
Lunsford, Joe   177,205
Lunsford, John L.   286
Lunsford, Joseph   112
Lunsford, Lena   346
Lunsford, Rebecca   182
Lunsford, Ronda C.   177
Lunsford, Stacy   194
Lunsford, Thomas   259
Lunsford, Victoria   357
Lunsford, Vinta   163
Lunsford, William H.   194
Luper, Ed (Mrs)   300
Luper, John   300
Lusk, Polly   84
Lutrell, Richard   116
Luttrell, Alice   212
Luttrell, Alice   212,275
Luttrell, Eliza Jane   212
Luttrell, Gus   212
Luttrell, Marcus Clay   200
Luttrell, Margaret   69
Luttrell, Maud   169
Luttrell, Myrtle   54

Luttrell, M.C. (Mrs)	200	Main, Asa	108,253
Luttrell, Rebecca A.	216	Main, Bessie	134,166,286
Luttrell, Richard H.	200	Main, Callie	206
266	<	Main, Calvin	53,174,336
Lynville, Valoma	146	Main, Carl	36
Lyons, Jane	177	Main, Charles	75
L..., Mattie	124	Main, Daniel M.	146
Mabe, Alex	249	Main, David S.	164
Mabe, Beasley	269	Main, D.M.	155
Mabe, Elizabeth	216	Main, Edgar Lewis	354
Mabe, James Earl	249	Main, Emma	182
Mabe, Rebecca	177	Main, Empire	79
Machamer, Infant	183	Main, Frank	101,358
Machamer, Roy	183	Main, George	354
Madron, Celia A.	169	Main, Grady	211
Madron, Cora	222	Main, G. Marion	240
Madron, Edward M.	270	Main, Hiram E.	76
Madron, Elvie	24	Main, Houston	59
Madron, Fillis	304	Main, Infant	78,108
Madron, George W.	42	Main, James L.	92
Madron, George W., Jr.	42	Main, Jane	279
Madron, H.E.	169	Main, Joe	254,300
Madron, Jack	42	Main, John	53,75,78,102
Madron, John	297	154,166,191,211,277,311	
Madron, Martha J.	71	Main, John S.	46,174
Madron, Mary	94	Main, Joseph	78
Madron, Matilda	213	Main, Joseph Stoffer	164
Madron, Nancy L.	46	Main, Joseph W.	102
Madron, Nora	297,321	Main, Josie	133
Madron, Paul	270	Main, J.C.	323
Madron, Polly	268	Main, Lela	92
Madron, Robert L.	297	Main, Louisa	118
Madron, Ruth	309	Main, Lourena	300
Madron, R.R.	321	Main, Luza	330
Madron, T.A.	261	Main, Maggie	214,275
Madron, Washington	270	Main, Mandy Rebecca	146
Mahaffey, J.	50	Main, Margaret	53,336
Mahaffey, Rhoda F.	108	Main, Martha	283,350
Mahala, Caroline	47	Main, Martha C.	126
Mahala, David D.	45	Main, Martha E.	90
Mahala, David T.	47	Main, Mary	203
Mahala, Fred	45	Main, Mary Jane	154
Mahe, Rebecca	58	Main, Nancy	279
Mahola, Sallie	325	Main, Nellie	40
Mahood, Astoria	262	Main, Norman Harold	240
Main, Alice	33	Main, N.H.	156
Main, Argus S.	174	Main, Oscar Carl	30
Main, Arthur Blaine	156	Main, Rachel	155

Main, Rebecca	58	Marlow, Roy Fred	142
Main, Russell E.	76	Marlow, W. Newt	179
Main, Sidney	78	Marlow, W.N.	142
Main, Susan	199,215,218	Marmon, Garnet M.	176
	222,244 <	Marry, Charles W.	277
Main, Susie	238,302	Marry, Clara	277
Main, ...	278	Marry, Jaye	277
Maine, Marion	246	Marston, Annie	67
Mains, Bonnie	325	Martin, Abbie	275
Mains, Bonnie L.	246	Martin, Alexander Asa	251
Mains, David M.	329	Martin, Anna	223
Mains, Delilah	317	Martin, Annie	225
Mains, Dick	329	Martin, Bettie	279
Mains, Dora	280	Martin, Clara	357
Mains, Eliza	243	Martin, Clara M.	47,70
Mains, George W.	319	Martin, D.M.	324
Mains, Huston	243	Martin, Elias H.	51
Mains, Joe	329	Martin, Ellis N.	116
Mains, John	319	Martin, E.N.	241
Mains, J.M.	257,317	Martin, George	265
Mains, Lewis	177	Martin, G.W.	122,209
Mains, Lewis H.	319	Martin, Inez	184
Mains, L.H.	317	Martin, Infant	133
Mains, Maggie	329,362	Martin, James	229,278,324
Mains, Martha	208	Martin, Jim	273
Mains, Minnie	256	Martin, Joe	265
Mains, Susie	198	Martin, John R.	265
Mallen, Millie	111	Martin, J.W.	133
Malone, Emma	346	Martin, Lena	326
Malone, Fannie H.	356	Martin, Lona	20
Malone, Paul E.	4	Martin, Margaret J.	350
Malone, Thomas James	356	Martin, Mary M.	350
Mammons, W.M.	235	Martin, Meda M.	151
Mannel, Rebecca	68,315	Martin, Melda M.	149
Manuel, Coy	93	Martin, Nancy	122
Manuel, Daniel C.	215	Martin, Nancy J.	131
Manuel, D.C.	42	Martin, Nick	251,278,279
Manuel, Eliza	171	Martin, Nillia M.	245
Manuel, George	215,339	Martin, Oliver	307
Manuel, L.G.	189,215	Martin, Polley	39
Manuel, Mary	93	Martin, Roy	273
Manuel, Rachel	52	Martin, Ruby	280
Manuel, Samantha L.	42	Martin, Russell T.	350
Manuel, William Ralph	189	Martin, Samuel	200
Marfield, Melvina	274	Martin, Texis	209
Marhias, Mary Adaline	83	Martin, Thomas	237,265
Marlow, Henry Lee	179	273 <
Marlow, Lucrecia	102	Martin, Titia	56

Martin, Virdie	254
Martin, Walter	280
Martin, W.M.	116
Marton, Mary	111
Mason, Margaret	261
Mast, Eliza B.	70
Mast, Eva	243,251,269,307
Mast, J.M.	63
Mast, Louisa	337
Mast, Maud	176
Mast, M.L.	184
Mast, N.J.	66
Mast, R.A.	292
Mast, ...	347
Matherly, Ceily	308
Matherly, C.B.	254
Matherly, David S.	48
Matherly, D.G.	79
Matherly, Eddie	231
Matherly, Edward	45
Matherly, Effie	266
Matherly, Effie D.	244
Matherly, Fred	48
Matherly, F.M.	359
Matherly, Garfield	163
Matherly, Infant	45,163
Matherly, John	48,298
Matherly, Joseph	231
Matherly, Joseph D.	174
Matherly, J.B.	45
Matherly, J.W.	298
Matherly, Paribe R.	79
Matherly, William A.	231
Matherson, Hugh	4
Matherson, Paul	4
Matherson, Rachel A.	219
Matherson, Rettie	115
Matherson, Violet	320,326
Matherson, William	258
Matherson, W.C.	116,219
Matheson, Evaline	89
Matheson, Lillie B.	258
Mathison, Eveline	266
Mathison, Mattie	160
Matney, Argus Gaines	107
Matney, W.W.	107
Matton, Arthor	74
Matton, Mary Elizabeth	74
Mauk, John K.	350
Mauk, Rosa	350
Maxwell, Barton	274
Maxwell, David	163,240
Maxwell, Dora	23
Maxwell, Elizabeth J.	129
Maxwell, Estell	144
Maxwell, George W.	144
	301 <
Maxwell, Gladys P.	342
Maxwell, Goldie A.	220
Maxwell, Hannah	240
Maxwell, Helen Marie	277
Maxwell, Henry	301
Maxwell, John	277
Maxwell, Larkin	129
Maxwell, Loura	238
Maxwell, Martha	101
Maxwell, Marvin T.	11
Maxwell, Mary	89,125
Maxwell, Mary Ellen	115
Maxwell, Ollie	106,144
	145,159,261 <
Maxwell, Reuben	238,274
Maxwell, William	242,336
May, Abraham Lincoln	230
May, Adell	332
May, Annie	324
May, Blanche	75
May, Bonnie	342
May, Bula Viola	223
May, Carl	114
May, Chalmer	342
May, Corda	162
May, Della Waunetia	235
May, Gale	241
May, Garfield	230
May, Glen Butler	60
May, G.W.	202
May, Ham	324
May, Infant	114,332
May, Jake	33
May, Jake L.	350
May, James Hamilton	229
May, James K.	150
May, Jefferson	150,336
May, J.H.	223,225
May, J.M.	146

May, Landon   225
May, Lizzie   186,187,196
May, Lura   368
May, Lydia   15,298
May, Margaret   174
May, Mary   24
May, Nancy Jane   151
May, Nettie   41
May, Norah   64
May, Polly   130
May, Ray   235
May, Rhoda   157
May, Riley   60,241
May, Roof   135
May, Rufus   201
May, Sarah   285,360
May, Stacy   342
May, Tobe   344
May, Washington   229
May, Will (Mrs)   342
Mays, A.D.   161
Mays, A.F.   45
Mays, Clyde   176
Mays, Fleming   249
Mays, John   310
Mays, John Larkin   310
Mays, J.W.   310
Mays, Martha   310
Mays, Mary A.   52
Mays, Raymond   238
Mays, Robert Logan   98
Mays, R.E.   238
Mays, Sarah L.   48
Mays, Tom   98
Mays, W.A.   48
Mays, ...   126
Mcaren, Eddie   113
McBride, Andrew   102
McBride, Hannah   271
McBride, Hiram   275
McBride, Pollie   319
McBride, Polly   121
McCain, Evelyn M.   228
McCall, John   79
McCandles, Mary   263
McCline, Jane   333
McCline, John   333
McCloud, Dana Dewitt   256

McCloud, Elizabeth   169
McCloud, James Abner   277
McCloud, Louise   216
McCloud, Mary   256
McCloud, Rosie   277
McCloud, Terness   277
McColoch, Mattie   87
McConnel, Sallie   247
McCowan, Rebecca   312
McCowan, ...   359
McCown, Sophia   333
McCoy, Frank   253
McCoy, Hobert   339
McCoy, Hobert Eugene   339
McCoy, Infant   170
McCoy, Millard   170
McCoy, Milton   285
McCoy, Radell   260
McCoy, Rosa Ethel   285
McCoy, Wiley Adolphus   15
McCracken, Jennie   218
McCracken, Madison M.   218
McCracken, Martha J.   219
McCulloch, Infant   77
McCullough, J. Ray   77
McCuloch, Ollie   45
McDade, E.L.   66,77
McDade, Robert   66
McDade, Robert Swain   66
McDulle, E.M.   40
McElyea, Alex   79
McElyea, Alice   44
McElyea, Amanda   80
McElyea, Andrew   270
McElyea, Anis   319
McElyea, Annie   263
McElyea, Bertha   31
McElyea, Bettie Seve   290
McElyea, Billie Ruth   281
McElyea, Bug   109
McElyea, Callie   291
McElyea, Caroline   152
McElyea, Catherine   38
McElyea, Cau   174
McElyea, Charles D.   362
McElyea, Cleary   76
McElyea, Clyde   74
McElyea, Cornelia   163

McElyea, Crete 205
McElyea, David 12
McElyea, Edgar 252
McElyea, Edward 33,362
McElyea, Elizabeth 341
McElyea, Emma V. 252
McElyea, Ethel Mae 32
McElyea, Floy Ella 31
McElyea, Floy L. 89
McElyea, George W. 337
McElyea, Gina Kate 205
McElyea, Gladys M. 155
McElyea, Hattie 158
McElyea, Howard 244
McElyea, Hubert Fred 319
McElyea, Infant 49,57,74
94,134,150,171,244 <
McElyea, Jacob 62,149
McElyea, James 134,163
167 <
McElyea, James M. 149
McElyea, James W. 46
McElyea, Jane 149
McElyea, Janette 337
McElyea, Janette Dean 341
McElyea, Jasper N. 101
McElyea, Jim 94
McElyea, Joe 110
McElyea, John 150,263,294
McElyea, John Joseph 101
McElyea, John J. 101
McElyea, John T. 205
McElyea, Julia Kate 262
McElyea, Julie 139
McElyea, J.N. 76
McElyea, Landon 263
McElyea, Landon Henry 291
337 <
McElyea, Larkin 151,270
McElyea, Larkin M. 330
McElyea, L.H. 198,341
McElyea, Mac 171,179
McElyea, Mack 110
McElyea, Mack M. 57
McElyea, Maggie 104,161
McElyea, Manel 180
McElyea, Margaret 23
McElyea, Margaret L. 150

McElyea, Mary 291
McElyea, Maud 121,183
McElyea, McKinley 270
McElyea, Millard 49
McElyea, Millard F. 89
McElyea, Myrtle 151
McElyea, Nancy 45,50,72
258 <
McElyea, Nancy C. 183
McElyea, Nute 294
McElyea, Ollie 46,331
McElyea, Pattie 313
McElyea, Pearl 46
McElyea, Rachel 151
McElyea, Richard (Mrs)165
McElyea, Robert 62,198
McElyea, Robert Floyd 291
McElyea, Roy 252
McElyea, Sabra 82
McElyea, Sallie 243,276
McElyea, Stacy 48,109
McElyea, Thomas 234
McElyea, Thomas J. 183
McElyea, Wiley 167
McElyea, William C. 22
McElyea, William H. 198
McElyea, William M. 155
McElyea, W.D. 262,281,290
331 <
McEwen, Baxter 185
McEwen, Charles 51
McEwen, Charlotte V. 310
McEwen, David Webster 288
McEwen, E.C.R. 51
McEwen, Fred 135
McEwen, H.A. 231
McEwen, Joseph Wade 310
McEwen, J.D. 185
McEwen, J.W. 231,276
McEwen, Lucinda 276
McEwen, Sam 185
McEwen, Samuel 135,231
McEwen, S.R. 168
McEwen, William 288
McFaddin, Elizabeth M.359
McFaddin, George M. 359
McFaddin, George W. 64
McFaddin, John 47,64,85

McFaddin, John M.	45,70
McFaddin, Lizzie	93
McFaddin, Mamie F.	148
McFaddin, Margaret	151
McFaddin, Vada M.	85
McFaddin, Vennie L.	45
McFaddin, Wiley	148,359
McGee, Eveline	226
McGee, Mary	192
McGinnis, Infant	138
McGinnis, James	138
McGlamery, Amanda	269
McGlamery, C.F.	361
McGlamery, George F.	143
McGlamery, Polly	290
McGlamery, Roscoe	290
McGlamery, R.R.	255
McGlamery, Snooky	143
McGlamery, theola	235
McGlamery, W.F.	143,269
290	<
McGowan, Sophia	231
McGuire, Mattie Lee	71
McGuowen, Sophie	267
McKee, Alf	239
McKee, Mary A.	239
McKinney, Bill	315
McKinney, Maggie	315
McKinney, Margaret D.	235
McKinney, Mary	65
McKinney, Mike	315
McKinney, Ollie	175
McKinney, R.M.	110,315
McKinney, Walter	226
McMillan, Rinda	260,368
McMillon, Jack	305
McNeill, Ethel R.	163
McNeill, Infant	73
McNeill, Sara Jinnith	135
McNeill, Sarah J.	130
McNeill, W.A.	73,130,135
219	<
McNiel, M.A.	41
McNutt, John (Mrs)	352
McQueen, Albert	310
McQueen, Alex	327
McQueen, Alexander	75
McQueen, Alfred	190

McQueen, Andrew H.	321
McQueen, Arther	187,188
274	<
McQueen, Arthur	99,302
McQueen, Augusta A.	174
McQueen, A.H.	223,224
McQueen, Caroline	176,251
285,367	<
McQueen, Catherine	320
McQueen, Civ	88
McQueen, Civil	25
McQueen, Clyde F.	88
McQueen, Connie	169
McQueen, Cora	249
McQueen, C.H.	226
McQueen, C.W.	103
McQueen, David	230
McQueen, David L.	330
McQueen, Dorothy	302
McQueen, D.S.	326,335
McQueen, Earl	343
McQueen, Ellen C.	223
McQueen, E.C.	146,148,181
196	<
McQueen, Finley	232
McQueen, Floyd	327
McQueen, Gertie Wanda	103
McQueen, Guy	144
McQueen, Guy E.	130
McQueen, Infant	92,99,144
187,188	<
McQueen, Jamelia	310
McQueen, James Elbert	270
McQueen, James M.	330
McQueen, Jim	63,92,93
McQueen, John B.	146
McQueen, John C.	172
McQueen, John D.	93
McQueen, J.W.	109
McQueen, Laurinda	352
McQueen, Leroy	251
McQueen, Lissie	276
McQueen, Louisa A.	232
McQueen, Luther	82
McQueen, L.D.	327
McQueen, L.L.	192,292,352
McQueen, Mack	172,270
McQueen, Maggie	193

McQueen, Marcus	230	
McQueen, Marcus (Mrs)	348	
McQueen, Margaret	343	
McQueen, Mary A.	196,330	
McQueen, Mollie	305	
McQueen, Nannie	62	
McQueen, Orevil E.	130	
McQueen, Rachel	249	
McQueen, Rice	164,230	
McQueen, Roby	310	
McQueen, Roe	75	
McQueen, Rose	321	
McQueen, Ruth	158	
McQueen, Sallie	210	
McQueen, Sally	133	
McQueen, Samuel	253	
McQueen, Samuel E.P.	146	
McQueen, Sarah	234,345	
McQueen, Sarah Fina	254	
McQueen, Sarah M.	159	
McQueen, Sherman	82	
McQueen, Shirley Luna	345	
McQueen, Smith M.	352	
McQueen, Stella	63	
McQueen, Susie	302	
McQueen, S.M. (Mrs)	352	
McQueen, Thomas	159,249	
McQueen, Tom	334	
McQueen, T.K.	345	
McQueen, T.S.	254	
McQueen, Vadie	352	
McQueen, Wade	232	
McQueen, William	109,330	
McQueen, William W.	223	
McQueen, Willis	103	
McQueen Isaac Finley	75	
McQuen, William	251	
Melvin, George W.	93	
Melvin, Loretta	93	
Merlott, Matilda	145	
Michael, Edward	281	
Michael, James	111	
Michael, Millard	281	
Michael, M.F.	281	
Michael, Susan	47	
Michaels, Beulah	280	
Michaels, Cora	18	
Michaels, Kitte Lee	128	

Michaels, Mattie	18
Michaels, Milton	18
Michaels, Mollie	157
Michaels, M.F.	128
Michaels, Sarah	92
Michaels, Telilah O.	88
Michalls, Julia	42
Michum, Matry	228
Mikeals, James H.	14
Milan, Duffey William	196
Milan, Tilden	196
Mileals, Anner	14
Miller, Abraham	130
Miller, Alfred E.	102
Miller, Almira	102
Miller, Andrew Jackson	130
Miller, Andy	359
Miller, Austin	302
Miller, A.J.	83
Miller, Bessie	359
Miller, Callie	323
Miller, Catherine	46
Miller, Charles	334
Miller, Charles M.	332
Miller, Clyde	153
Miller, Cora	198
Miller, C.M.	190
Miller, David	359
Miller, David R.	118
Miller, Delilah	37
Miller, D.F.	38
Miller, E.N.	93
Miller, Edith	342
Miller, Eliga E.	302
Miller, Elizabeth	324
Miller, Elizabeth J.	190
Miller, Enlo Grace	60
Miller, Enoch	165
Miller, Ephram	46,118
Miller, E.E.	241
Miller, E.N.	324
Miller, Flora	196
Miller, Francs A.E.	198
Miller, Fred R.	239
Miller, F.R.	198
Miller, Girtrude	367
Miller, Hattie	313
Miller, Hattie S.	190

Miller, H.H.   37,40
Miller, Ida   25
Miller, Ida B.   213
Miller, Ida Jane   24
Miller, Jack A.   364
Miller, James Austin   347
Miller, Jane   253
Miller, Jennie   248
Miller, Jerline   241
Miller, John   40,302,323
Miller, John C.   46
Miller, John M.   153
Miller, Julia M.   6
Miller, J.A.   341
Miller, J.C.   118,134
Miller, J.E.   334
Miller, J.P.   334
Miller, J.R.   102,239
Miller, Kattie   364
Miller, Kelley M.   213
Miller, Lee   213
Miller, Lilian R.   166
Miller, Lizzie   302
Miller, Luther   46,60,183
Miller, Malinda   50
Miller, Mande   361
Miller, Marcus Edward 347
Miller, Martha   260
Miller, Mary Love   332
Miller, Mary Susan   339
Miller, Mattie   118
Miller, Maud   276
Miller, Maude   323
Miller, Maude S.   328
Miller, Mollie   365
Miller, Mona   33
Miller, Nancy Jane   59
Miller, Nannie   334
Miller, Nellie B.A.   341
Miller, Nick   50
Miller, Odith   21
Miller, Pearl   278
Miller, P.J.   204
Miller, Rena Jane   252
Miller, Robert Earl   239
Miller, R.J. (Mrs)   130
Miller, Sallie   268
Miller, Sarah   204

Miller, Sarang   267
Miller, Simon   10
Miller, Susan   364
Miller, Vec   83
Miller, Victoria   50
Miller, Wayne   102
Miller, Wiley   114
Miller, W.R.   102,324
Millhorn, Hattie   284
Millhorn, Hubert Ray   284
Millhorn, Mamie   202
Millhorn, Robert H.   284
Millhorn, T.G.   300
Millhorn, William   300
Millhorn, W.M.   45
Millhous, Howard   216
Millhous, Paul   216
Millhous, William   216
Millr, Wayne   173
Mills, Anderson   339
Mills, Mary Susan   307
Mills, Triphanie   339
Millsaps, Elem   333
Millsaps, John   323
Millsaps, Lacira   159
Millsaps, Rebecca   333
Milsap, Eleam   237
MIlsap, Walter   237
Minick, Matilda   299
Mink, D.W.   42
Mink, Jane   294
Mink, Loviza   179
Mink, Mary   202,280
Mink, Russell   122
Minks, Della   135
Minks, E.J.   132
Minks, John W.   320
Minks, J.O.   65
Minks, L.J.   320
Minks, Mary   132,215
Minks, Minnie   152
Minks, Minnie Adlade   320
Minks, M.L.   42
Minks, Russell   122
Minnick, Matilda   264,344
Minton, Allen   58,81,126
    164   <
Minton, Benie Bernice 153

Minton, Cynthia E.   81,153
Minton, Enoch   126
Minton, Enoch Finley   126
Minton, Hobart Henry   58
Minton, Isaac   111
Minton, James   81
Minton, Lana R.   57
Minton, Lizzie   164
Minton, Mary   153
Minton, Pantha   216
Minton, Rebecca   93
Minton, Saddie O.   164
Minton, William Lee   111
Minton, Zalie   208
Minton, ...   342
Mitchell, Alice   305
Mitchell, Becca   310
Mitchell, Bettie   225
Mitchell, Florence   190
Mitchell, Hyder   242
Mitchell, John   53
Mitchell, John A.   228
Mitchell, Mary   228,305
Mitchell, Mollie Jane   348
Mitchell, Rebecca   309,336
Mock, Alvin   63
Mock, A.F.   170
Mock, Cynthia   365
Mock, David   217
Mock, David W.   170
Mock, Emma   172,270
Mock, E.H.   2
Mock, Gilbert   63
Mock, Goldia   343
Mock, Jim   232
Mock, Lewis   170
Mock, Margaret   18
Mock, Ruth   3
Mock, Sarah   98
Mock, Will   98,109
Moffatt, William   102
Moffett, Elmira   359
Monley, Millie   41
Montgomery, Annie J.   88
Montgomery, Annie S.   103
Moody, Alice   120
Moody, Anderson   235
Moody, Benjamin   8,265,280

Moody, Benjamin   312
Moody, Devona   123
Moody, Dorcus   352
Moody, Earnest   104
Moody, Edward   37
Moody, Elcie   50
Moody, Elizabeth   195
Moody, Francis M.   265
Moody, George   144
Moody, Jim   123
Moody, John   172
Moody, Loni   173
Moody, Mae   361
Moody, Naomi   221
Moody, Pearl   288
Moody, Roy   160
Moody, S.C.   221
Moody, Tenie   163
Moody, Thomas   188
Moody, Tilda   143,158
Moody, T.L.   37
Moody, Will   155,188
Moody, Will R.   163,235
Moody, William   50,104
Moody, William D.   173
Moody, William Kyle   37
Moody, W.R.   158,173
Moore, Addie   348
Moore, Alice   353
Moore, Amelia   295
Moore, Amy   69
Moore, Cynthia   199,207
Moore, Jane   157
Moore, Louise   258
Moore, Margaret   48
Moore, Mary   66,84
Moore, Mary Jane   179
Moore, Mary Katherine   238
Moore, Mary M.   48
Moore, Matilda   171
Moore, Melvina   223
Moore, Millie   142
Moore, Nancy   142
Moore, Phllis, Gene   342
Moore, Rhoda   238
Moore, Thomas   48
Moore, Walter   342
Moore, William   171

Moore, W.M.	171	
Moore, ...	353	
Moorley, Alice	196	
Moorr, Nannie	63	
Mooser, Crike (Mrs)	334	
More, Lucinda	83	
Morefield, Adam	55,69	
Morefield, Alexander	156	
Morefield, Benjamin	3	
Morefield, Bertha	46	
Morefield, Bill Hill	70	
Morefield, Billie	30	
Morefield, Catherine	10	
Morefield, Charlie	49	
Morefield, Claudie	160	
Morefield, Conie Mae	282	
Morefield, Cora May	138	
Morefield, C...	210	
Morefield, Daniel	156,297	
Morefield, Dayton H.	264	
Morefield, Delilah	47	
Morefield, Edith R.	22	
Morefield, Eliza	177	
Morefield, Elizabeth	108	
Morefield, Ellen	104	
Morefield, Elmer	46,134	
Morefield, Emma	51	
Morefield,. Ethel	32	
Morefield, Eugene	124	
Morefield, E.C.	117	
Morefield, Ferd	238	
Morefield, Floid	156	
Morefield, Gabrial	69	
Morefield, George	55	
Morefield, Gill T.	108	
Morefield, Glen	14	
Morefield, Grant	214	
Morefield, Ham	247	
Morefield, Harbin C.	297	
Morefield, Ilene Faw	238	
Morefield, Infant	117	
Morefield, Jack	61	
Morefield, Jack (Mrs)	219	
Morefield, James	51,98 108 <	
Morefield, Jenette F.	218	
Morefield, Joe	70,240	
Morefield, Joe R.	264	

Morefield, John	49,51,104	
Morefield, John R.	299 344 <	
Morefield, J. Hamilton	264	
Morefield, J.E.	51	
Morefield, J.H.	108	
Morefield, J.V.	282,297	
Morefield, J.W.	296	
Morefield, Katherin	286	
Morefield, Landon	60	
Morefield, Lee Cindy	70	
Morefield, Lelor	32	
Morefield, Lucinda	281	
Morefield, Luna	142	
Morefield, Maggie	6	
Morefield, Margaret	124	
Morefield, Marie	240	
Morefield, Martha	299	
Morefield, Mary	82,219 278 <	
Morefield, Mary Ann	48	
Morefield, Mary E.	310 361 <	
Morefield, Mary L.	71	
Morefield, May	60	
Morefield, Melvina	274	
Morefield, Minnie	1	
Morefield, Nannie R.	296	
Morefield, Onie	186	
Morefield, Paul Wayne	214	
Morefield, Pauline	119	
Morefield, Polly	226	
Morefield, Purdie	315	
Morefield, Rachel	187	
Morefield, Ramon	96	
Morefield, Rebecca	66 177,257 <	
Morefield, Ruth	286	
Morefield, R. Ross	299	
Morefield, R.C.	197	
Morefield, R.R.	297	
Morefield, Sallie	91,100	
Morefield, Sarah	233	
Morefield, Stacy O.	134	
Morefield, Susan	111	
Morefield, Taylor	30	
Morefield, Thelma	46	
Morefield, Tilda V.	247	

Morefield, Tildy	73,103		Morley, Franklin	190
Morefield, Vincen	127		Morley, George	159,212
Morefield, Vincen R.	197		Morley, G.S.	65
Morefield, Vincent G.	178		Morley, Infant	87
Morefield, Wiley	96		Morley, Jane	232,292
Morefield, William	282		Morley, Jennie	293
Morefield, William R.	51		Morley, L.B.	251,276,320
Morefield, Zola	37		Morley, Margaret E.	281
Morefield, ...	47,337		Morley, Mellie M.	76
Moreland, Amanda	351		Morley, N.C.	310
Moreland, Betsy	45,276		Morley, Rosa Ival	243
Moreland, Danford	340		Morley, Sarafina	335
Moreland, Filmore	339		Morley, Susana	232
Moreland, John	339		Morley, Susannah	302
Moreland, J.D., Jr.	340		Morley, Teddy Ray	262
Moreland, Margaret	53		Morley, Thomas	68
Moreland, Mary	88		Morley, Thomas Butler	159
Moreland, M.F.	53		Morley, T.B. (Mrs)	68
Moreland, Nancy	284,339		Morley, T.L.	206
Moreley, Autry Keys	325		Morley, William A.	304
Morely, D.J.	325		Morley, Winnie E.	87
Moretz, Alice	277		Morley, W.D.	87
Moretz, Hazel M.	361		Morley, ...	61
Moretz, Jeff	219		Morrell, Fina	118
Moretz, Jefferson D.	253		Morrison, Mahala R.	248
	290 <		Moser, Isaac N.	75
Moretz, John Monroe	219		Moser, T.N.	75
Moretz, K.S.	59		Moser, Wesley	75
Moretz, Maggie	246		Mostey, George	41
Moretz, Nancy	290		Mostey, James J.	41
Moretz, Nancy M.	334		Mosure, John Burton	31
Moretz, Pearl	288		Mottern, ...	334
Moretz, Raleigh	361		Mount, John Keener	305
Moretz, R.J.	290		Mount, Roberta	305
Moretz, Sherman	219		Mount, Thomas L.	305
Moretz, Smith	334		Mount, Wiley	229
Moretz, Virgie	354		Mount, W.B.	224
Moretz, Wiley	253		Mullens, Joseph	67
Moretz, William	262		Mullins, Alice	51,114
Morgan, Berthie Lee	104		Mullins, Catherine	157
Morgan, John	101		Mullins, Dillie E.	324
Morgan, J.F.	140		Mullins, Freelove	203,323
Morgan, Nathaniel	76		Mullins, Gene H.	245
Morgan, William	76		Mullins, Hiley	157
Morgan, Wiloby	194		Mullins, Infant	68,220
Moorley, Alice	196		Mullins, James	131
Morley, Charles	152		Mullins, John H.	216
Morley, D.J.	262,325		Mullins, Joseph	157

Mullins, Julia C.	137	Nave, M.C.	86
Mullins, Louise	344	Nave, Nettie	231
Mullins, L.M.	68	Nave, Patsy	111
Mullins, Mary L.	216	Nave, Reba	189
Mullins, Ronda	344	Nave, R.L.	116,305
Mullins, R.F.	324	Nave, Sarah	127
Mullins, Sabra Ann	51	Nave, Sarah C.	116
Mullins, S.C.	174,220	Nave, William H.	180
Mullins, Trulove	167	Neal, Edney	237
Mullins, Viola Grace	174	Neal, Margaret	186
Munday, Eliza	363	Neal, Patten	319
Munday, Joe	363	Neal, Polly	67
Munday, Mary Ann	363	Neal, ...	119
Mundy, Geneva	6	Near, Mary Moreland	221
Murphey, Abraham	61	Neatherly, Anna	156
Murphey, Frank	305	Neatherly, Annie	297
Murphey, H.E.	61	Neatherly, Betty	40,286
Murphey, Infant	305	Neatherly, Bruce	161
Murphey, Kemp	61,353	Neatherly, Callie	5
Murray, Isabele	269	Neatherly, Callie C.	359
Murray, Jake	269	Neatherly, Catherine	14
Murry, James	27	Neatherly, Dan	248
Muse, Joe C.	309	Neatherly, Daniel	40,277
Muse, J.C.	301	Neatherly, David L.	4
Muse, Lucile	309	Neatherly, Ernest	81
Musgrave, Danford	116	Neatherly, Ernestine	81
Musgrave, John	289	Neatherly, George	258,354
Myers, Bessie	123	Neatherly, Jacob	161
M..., Francis	177	Neatherly, Jacob C.	4
M..., Polly	189	Neatherly, Jacob I.	248
M..., William	233	Neatherly, Jospeh D.	359
Nading, Mary	145	Neatherly, Jourdan	277
Nading, Mary	156	Neatherly, J.I.	161
Nance, Emiline	171	Neatherly, Lieland	54
Nave, Abigail	146	Neatherly, Lillie	298
Nave, Abraham	127,197	Neatherly, May	188
Nave, Bettie	295	Neatherly, Paul	277,292
Nave, C.M.	135	Neatherly, Ruth	54
Nave, David	151,295	Neatherly, Sallie	42
Nave, D.H.	180	Neatherly, Sally	122
Nave, D.K.	117	Neatherly, S.H.	248
Nave, Eula	305	Neatherly, Tom	265
Nave, James	65	Neatherly, Walter	81
Nave, John	231,295	Neatherly, William	42,292
Nave, Leonard	180,231	Neatherly, ...	242
Nave, Margaret Lillie	7	Needham, Sarah	367
Nave, Mary	117	Neeley, Bertha	262
Nave, Maud	305	Neeley, C.W.	260

Neeley, Ham	257	Nichels, Bettie	35
Neeley, Hugh S.	252	Nichols, Andrew	112
Neeley, Infant	260	Nichols, Annis Head	283
Neeley, J.S.	195	Nichols, Arther	218
Neeley, Margaret	13	Nichols, Byrum E.	343
Neeley, Sam	257	Nichols, Callie	204
Neeley, Suirth	208	Nichols, Conley	215
Neeley, T.A.	252	Nichols, Etta	165
Neeley, T.A. (Mrs)	252	Nichols, Francis	343
Neely, Bertha May	91	Nichols, Frankie Brown	343
Neely, Charles W.	107	Nichols, Hobart	271,303
Neely, Clinton W.	107	Nichols, Infant	19,290
Neely, C.W.	181	Nichols, Jenettne	247
Neely, Eliza	334	Nichols, John	192
Neely, Hugh Smith	181	Nichols, J.R.	218
Neely, Infant	30	Nichols, Lena Martin	307
Neely, Joseph H.	181	Nichols, Leonard	271
Neely, J. Oliver	67	Nichols, Leonard Ray	303
Neely, J.O.	38	Nichols, Lila E.	271
Neely, J.S.	67	Nichols, Lula	181
Neely, Sam	47	Nichols, Margaret	60,193
Neely, Samuel	30,194	Nichols, Olivene	192,271
Neely, Sarah Jane	38	Nichols, Rebecca	19
Neely, Smith	122	Nichols, Reuben	204
Neely, William	67,194	Nichols, R.S.	175,283,307
Neely, William Smith	91	Nichols, Sam	290,326
Neley, C.W.	267	Nichols, Sam, Jr.	326
Nelson, Andrew	48	Nichols, W.A.	181,290,343
Nelson, I.	38	Nithols, Smith	19
Nelson, Jane	58,296	Nolan, Margaret	183
Nelson, John	56,252	Noland, George W.	87
Nelson, John F.	36	Nolen, A.W.	69
Nelson, Julia	36	Nolen, Infant	69
Nelson, King	270	Nolen, Margaret	234
Nelson, Mary	275	Norman, Sallie	127
Nelson, Matilda	48	Norris, Abrsy	137
Nelson, Myrtle	9	Norris, Annie	135,201
Nelson, M.J.	56	Norris, Bessie	123
Nelson, Will	275	Norris, Betty	49
Nelson, William	56	Norris, Billa Lee	304
Nelson, ...	334	Norris, Buck	222
Netherly, Betsy	243	Norris, Caroline	357
Netherly, George F.	243	Norris, Donald Eugene	342
Netherly, Jacob	104	Norris, Elbert	278
Netherly, William B.	104	Norris, Eldridge Mack	40
Newberger, Melvina	263	Norris, Emma	35
Newland, Dora	236	Norris, Estel	12
Newman, Martin	203	Norris, E.M.	40

Norris, Fain   359,278
Norris, Flenor   191
Norris, Franklin   171,261
        328,339,349   <
Norris, H.H.   145,339
Norris, Infant 40,137,218
Norris, Jim   210
Norris, Joe   277
Norris, Johathan R.   339
Norris, John   299
Norris, Laura S.   277
Norris, Lottie   350
Norris, Lula   82
Norris, Mable   218
Norris, Mack   95,179
Norris, Mamie   188
Norris, Martha   291
Norris, Mary   69,127
Norris, Mary Altine   206
Norris, Mary E.   278
Norris, Okie Ann   95
Norris, Pollie L.   328
Norris, Ray   328
Norris, Red   206
Norris, Richard   181
Norris, Richard A.   328
Norris, Roby   169
Norris, R.A.   206
Norris, Sallie   82
Norris, Velma   191
Norris, Walter   69,218
Norris, William A.   222
Norris, W.H.   357
Northington, Samuel   367
Nutter, Eliza   208
Nye, Birthy   27
Nye, Charlie   303
Nye, Hanner   236
Nye, Lee   236
N..., Elizabeth   125
Oliver, Amanda   328
Oliver, Eliza   175,338
Oliver, Ella M.   20
Oliver, Emmet, Jr.   165
Oliver, Emmt   165
Oliver, Mable   190
Oliver, Millie   98
Oneal, J.E.   249

Oneal, Sarah E.   249
Orneal, Callie   211
Orneal, Joe   211
Orneal, Joseph   107
Orneal, Rebecca   107
Orneal, William   211
Orr, Elizabeth Ann   359
Orr, Francis   271
Orr, Margaret   44,176
Orr, Sarah   77
Osborn, Abner   104
Osborn, Alex   154,206
Osborn, Alfred   219,266
Osborn, Alice   296
Osborn, Andy J.   236
Osborn, Anlee   24
Osborn, Benjamin   289
Osborn, Benjamin F.   203
Osborn, Betsy   201
Osborn, Bettie   289
Osborn, Billie   296
Osborn, David 186,187,196
    219   <
Osborn, Edd   220
Osborn, Elijah   122
Osborn, Elizabeth 203,225
Osborn, Enoch   112
Osborn, Ephron   112
Osborn, Harrison   178
Osborn, Ida Thelmar   187
Osborn, Infant   104,115
    136   <
Osborn, Isaac 236,264,269
Osborn, Jacob   52
Osborn, Jeremiah   197
Osborn, Jerry   83
Osborn, Jessee   178
Osborn, John   104,115,122
    136,273,282   <
Osborn, John Presley   261
Osborn, Lillie B.   44
Osborn, Luther   258,289
Osborn, Lydia   112,144
Osborn, Lydia E.   130
Osborn, Maggie   231
Osborn, Mahola   226
Osborn, Martha   348
Osborn, Mollie   130

Osborn, Nancy	47,85,117	
136,154,308	<	
Osborn, Nancy E.	288	
Osborn, Nannie	340	
Osborn, Norman	196	
Osborn, R.S.	126	
Osborn, Stacy	36	
Osborn, Susan Elmas	186	
Osborn, Vada	187	
Osborn, William	122	
Osborn, William H.	261	
Osborne, Curlee	274	
Osborne, Edith Faye	314	
Osborne, Elizabeth	310	
Osborne, Ephran	17	
Osborne, Firman	244,367	
Osborne, Frank	332	
Osborne, F.W.	315	
Osborne, Gaston	344	
Osborne, Howard Elvin	367	
Osborne, James Henry	36	
Osborne, J.W.	315	
Osborne, Laura	362	
Osborne, Martha	354	
Osborne, Mollie May	344	
Osborne, Myrtle	52	
Osborne, Nancy	215,317	
Osborne, Noah	314	
Osborne, Retha Esther	315	
Osborne, Roby	81	
Osborne, Spencer	81	
Osborne, St...	36	
Osborne, William	52	
Osborne, William H.	322	
Osborne, W.L.	36	
Osborns, E.G.	53	
Osborns, Viola	53	
Oster, George A.	331	
Oster, George D.	331	
Oster, Grace	331	
Owen, David	53	
Owen, Ida Mae	53	
Owens, Adrian	198	
Owens, Aley	304	
Owens, Ann	61,76	
Owens, Annie	112,147,170	
Owens, Boone	79	
Owens, Carrie	305	

Owens, Connelly	127
Owens, Dan	65
Owens, Daniel B.	127
Owens, David	228
Owens, Della Ann	47
Owens, Edward	341
Owens, Edward Glenn	341
Owens, Eula Mae	344
Owens, Everett Hughes	65
Owens, Fina	161
Owens, Fina	272
Owens, George Ann	291
Owens, Glen	305
Owens, Infant	112
Owens, James	307
Owens, Jane	307
Owens, Jasper	61
Owens, John	297
Owens, John B.	47
Owens, Mary	55
Owens, Mary E.	54
Owens, Mattie Stone	66
Owens, Millard	49,65
Owens, Nellia Alice	247
Owens, N.D.	84,88,247
Owens, Pauline	49,305
Owens, Phache	75
Owens, Roby	112,177
Owens, R.L.	307
Owens, Sallie	297
Owens, Susan	76,112
Owens, William	39,61
Owens, William Lacy	39
Owens, ...	113
Ow..., Susan	328
O'Neal, Cassie	153
O'Neal, Jacob	5
O'Neil, Cassie	237
O'Neil, Tilda	357
O'Neil, William	337
O..., William	94
Pafford, Eliza	337
Pafford, ...	245
Palmer, Polly Ann	159
Pancake, Martha	272
Pardue, Caroline	330
Pardue, Catherine	323
Pardue, John	323

Pardue, Mary	257		Parsons, Bill K.	342
Pardue, Mary Ruth	167		Parsons, Clate	113
Pardue, William	167		Parsons, Evalee	342
Pardue, William F.	323		Parsons, Eve	119
Pardue, ...	150		Parsons, Garnet G.	182
Parker, Adilia	303		Parsons, George	119
Parker, Calvin	358		Parsons, Henry	288
Parker, Clay	25		Parsons, H.W.	182
Parker, Elizabeth	356,358		Parsons, Land	119
Parker, Hanna	12		Parsons, Lee	220
Parker, James H.	356,358		Parsons, L.A.	55
Parker, Jonathon L.	212		Parsons, Mary Ann	119
Parker, William E.	212		Parsons, Pauline M.	300
Parker, W.P. (Mrs)	358		Parsons, Rilda	69
Parker, W.R.	212		Parsons, William	300
Parkins, Hattie	86		Patrick, Bloom	67
Parks, Alexander A.	302		Patrick, Catherine M.	77
Parks, Alfred	307		Patrick, Charles	95
Parks, A.R.	302		Patrick, Eliza	52
Parks, Bertha	297		Patrick, Willis	95
Parks, Charlie	307		Patridg, Magie	305
Parks, Freddie	293		Patton, Elizabeth Ann	147
Parks, Fredie M.	101		Patton, Infant	44
Parks, James M.	227,307		Patton, J.R.	147
Parks, Jane	307		Patton, Mary	147
Parks, John	302		Patton, Thomas R.	44,147
Parks, J.M.	298		162	<
Parks, Martha Jane	298		Paul, Martha	287
Parks, Martha J.	236		Payne, Arizona	95
Parks, Myrtle Grace	79		Payne, Bernie	111
Parks, Pearl	311		Payne, Bonnie	77
Parks, Robert	101		Payne, Bruce Lee	346
Parks, Robert W.	79,311		Payne, Cbarles	111
Parks, S.C.	296		Payne, Charley	77
Parks, Viola	317		Payne, Conley	44
Parks, W.E.	296		Payne, Cora	251
Parks, W.S.	297		Payne, Dana	137
Parrish, William	286		Payne, David M.	149
Parry, Alfred C.	41		Payne, Edward Smith	149
Parry, Angeline	36		Payne, Frances M.	120
Parry, Franie	10		Payne, Francis Irene	176
Parry, G.W.D.	41		Payne, F.M.	325
Parson, Flora	184		Payne, George	65
Parson, James N.	288		Payne, Ida	107
Parson, J.M.	214		Payne, Infant	127
Parson, Landon	69,184		Payne, I.L.	164
Parsons, Alice	288		Payne, James	362
Parsons, Baxter	139		Payne, James C.	65

Payne, Joe   127,145,174
Payne, Joe Jr.   145
Payne, John M.   314
Payne, John P.   120
Payne, Lydia Caroline   325
Payne, L.M.   314
Payne, Mac   176
Payne, Maggie   17
Payne, Maggie B.   136
Payne, Martitia   344
Payne, Mary   15
Payne, Mary M.   244
Payne, Millie Leonard   362
Payne, Myrtle   314
Payne, M.V.   346
Payne, Oma   101
Payne, Rebecca   210
Payne, Revinnie P.   136
Payne, Roy Dewey   136
Payne, R.S.   83,231,244
       330   <
Payne, Sallie   346
Payne, Sarah   137
Payne, Shelton   265
Payne, Susan M.   75
Payne, U.B.   122,136
Payne, Vada   214
Payne, Villas J.   231
Payne, W.B.   265
Payne, Zebulon   244,314
Pearce, Belle W.   144
Pearce, Margaret E.C.   235
Pearce, Martha   75
Pearson, Commelia   10
Peece, Bertie P.   275
Pennell, Dillard   117
Pennell, Infant   117
Pennell, Rosa   299
Pennington, Abraham   113
Pennington, Andrew   56,219
       244   <
Pennington, Callie N.   204
Pennington, Callie V.   204
Pennington, Catherine   53
Pennington, Claude   204
Pennington, Daniel   310
Pennington, Eliza   286
Pennington, Elizabeth   154

Pennington, H.   172
Pennington, Infant   75,142
Pennington, I...   100
Pennington, Joe   358
Pennington, Joseph C.   142
Pennington, J.W.   310
Pennington, Lillie   310
Pennington, Lillie V.   50
Pennington, L.W.   206
Pennington, Malisa E.   86
Pennington, Malninie   113
Pennington, Marshall   188
Pennington, Martha   46
Pennington, Mary Ann   103
Pennington, Mary E.   219
Pennington, Mecca C.   271
Pennington, M.E.   90,285
Pennington, M.F.   75
Pennington, Nick   50
Pennington, Noah   35,267
Pennington, N.A.   311,345
Pennington, Oscar   14
Pennington, Roby   103
Pennington, Soloman S.310
Pennington, S.S.   175
Pennington, Victoria   83
Pennington, William   154
Penn..., Cora   104
Perdue, Fred   319
Perdue, John   152
Perdue, Melvina   78
Perdue, Sarah   188
Perdue, William   67
Perkins, Alice   294
Perkins, Biner   294
Perkins, Bob   232
Perkins, Celia   173
Perkins, Clinton   182
Perkins, David   298
Perkins, Earl   348
Perkins, Edna   64,147
Perkins, Franklin   65
Perkins, Jason P.   182
Perkins, Josie Lee   232
Perkins, Martitia   309
Perkins, Mary Lee F.   298
Perkins, Nancie Nye   150
Perkins, Robert   182

Perkins, Rosco	294	Phillippi, S.D.	101
Perkins, Satitia	181	Phillippi, Virgia O.S.	96
Perkins, Smiley	150	Phillippi, Walter	212
Perkins, Tommie	300	Phillips, Ada	137
Perry, Jonathon	252	Phillips, Andrew	215,308
Perry, Lizzie	240	Phillips, Annie L.	299
Perry, Rena	83	Phillips, Arthur J.	345
Perry, ...	356	Phillips, Bessie	319
Philips, Elsa	16	Phillips, Burl Roy	246
Phillippe, Jane	20	Phillips, China	259
Phillippe, Stephen	66	Phillips, Claud C.	157
Phillippi, Albert B.	368	Phillips, Coy	60
Phillippi, Alice	322	Phillips, Edward	308
Phillippi, Annie Grace	1	Phillips, Eli	132,137
Phillippi, Belle	2	Phillips, Eliza	301
Phillippi, Birdie	126,239	Phillips, Elsie Mae	271
Phillippi, Callie	364	Phillips, Fannie	256
Phillippi, Catherine	203	Phillips, Infant	296
Phillippi, David	266,271	Phillips, Ira G.	64
272,316,322,368	<	Phillips, Irene L.	207
Phillippi, David P.	216	Phillips, Jarrett A.	210
322	<	Phillips, Jim	242
Phillippi, D.P.	100,212	Phillips, Joe	271,297
Phillippi, Edward	66	Phillips, John	210,215
Phillippi, Edward T.	66	222,258	<
Phillippi, Elizabeth	271	Phillips, John Wesley	258
Phillippi, Emory	321	Phillips, John W.	157
Phillippi, Fred	135	Phillips, Jonathan	341
Phillippi, Jackie C.	321	Phillips, J.M.	56
Phillippi, John	36,96,266	Phillips, Lee	207
Phillippi, John S.	135	Phillips, Liza L.	97
Phillippi, Jossie	54,101	Phillips, Martha	137
Phillippi, Justin	321	Phillips, Mary	132,238
Phillippi, J.R.	271	258	<
Phillippi, Mack	203,213	Phillips, Matilda	124
225,244,275,322	<	Phillips, Nellie	218
Phillippi, Mae	221	Phillips, Ogn	35
Phillippi, Martha	66	Phillips, Perdie	300
Phillippi, M.C.	179	Phillips, Prudia	342
Phillippi, Nancy E.	239	Phillips, Rebecca	265
Phillippi, Patsy Ann	321	Phillips, Regiema	345
Phillippi, Pierce	275	Phillips, Roby	215
Phillippi, Rettie C.	368	Phillips, S.F.	64
Phillippi, Robert	54	Phillips, Thelma	356
Phillippi, Sallie	95	Phillips, Tyler	299
Phillippi, Samuel	101	Phillips, Viola Mae	345
Phillippi, Sarah	91	Phillips, Wesley	124,204
Phillippi, Stephen	266	Phillips, William	35

Phillips, William R.   242
Phillips, Willie   10
Phipps, Abram   170
Phipps, Biner   259
Phipps, Carmon   188
Phipps, Casey   117
Phipps, Catherine   39
Phipps, David   117,188
Phipps, David L.   325
Phipps, David S.   36
Phipps, Dona   293
Phipps, D.S.   259
Phipps, Eli   184
Phipps, Floyd   184
Phipps, Garret   181,188
          201   <
Phipps, John   170,197
Phipps, J.H.   178
Phipps, Mamie   181
Phipps, Nancy   56
Phipps, Peter   170,178
          325   <
Phipps, Polly   184
Phipps, Sarah   36
Phipps, Stacy   197
Phipps, Tittia   325
Phipps, Villas   149
Pierce, Alex   312
Pierce, Alex Stanley   125
Pierce, Allen   310
Pierce, Annie   57,139
Pierce, Cerline   320
Pierce, C.D.   325
Pierce, Deliah   186
Pierce, Delila   50,279
Pierce, D.C.   77,125
Pierce, D.P.   75
Pierce, Frankie   37
Pierce, George   75,152,266
Pierce, G.H.   245
Pierce, Harriett   322
Pierce, Infant   96
Pierce, Isaac   77,125
Pierce, James   96
Pierce, James N.   218
Pierce, John   338
Pierce, Martha   116
Pierce, Martin Dearl   266

Pierce, Mary   310
Pierce, Mary A.   152
Pierce, May   149
Pierce, Minnie   11
Pierce, Nelson   11
Pierce, Pleas   362
Pierce, Ruby Pearl   312
Pierce, R. Becky   83
Pierce, Sarah   71
Pierce, W.J.   152
Pierce, ...   51
Pierson, Ollie   294
Pierson, Rufus   294
Pierson, Walter   294
Pierson, Walter P.   348
Pilk, Clemantine   346
Pilk, Enoch   346
Pilk, Samuel   346
Pillagton, Polly   222
Pirce, Rebecca   252
Pleasant, Bell Lowe   365
Pleasant, Ben   61,365
Pleasant, Benjamin   106
Pleasant, Bessie   91
Pleasant, B.W.   131
Pleasant, Ella C.   87
Pleasant, Ethel   11
Pleasant, Eva   168
Pleasant, Garfield   185
Pleasant, Garfield A.   41
Pleasant, G.A.   87
Pleasant, Infant   49
Pleasant, Isaac   129
Pleasant, James   91
Pleasant, James Danie   131
Pleasant, John Thomas   91
Pleasant, Lora Lee   41
Pleasant, Martha   100
Pleasant, Mary   127
Pleasant, Myrtle   182,192
Pleasant, Nealie   154
Pleasant, Robert   168
Pleasant, Ruby   13
Pleasant, R.B.   129,185
          205   <
Pleasant, Sallie   252
Pleasant, Sarah   366
Pleasant, Walter B.   49

Pleasant, William G.   106
Pleasant, William H.   129
Pleasant, W.B.   214
Pleasant, W.H.   100,185
Pless, Billy A.   228
Pless, Eliga   253
Pless, Joseph Parker   253
Pless, J.P. (Mrs)   253
Pless, Quincy Edward   228
Plummer, Ada   306
Plummer, Coleman S.   291
Plummer, E.L.   291
Plummer, Landon   88
Plummer, Ruby   88
Poarch, Louis   48
Poe, Cordie   272
Poe, Elizabeth   130
Poe, Martha   218
Poe, Timothy   236
Poe, William   272
Pomaway, Mary   108
Poole, Conley   328
Poole, Henry (Dr)   328
Poole, Maggie   328
Pope, Alice   194
Pope, Bettie   96,219
Pope, Biner   37
Pope, Calvin   15
Pope, Elizabeth   219,244
Pope, John   307
Pope, Martha   307
Pope, Mary   56
Pope, Mary Emeline   194
Pope, Rebecca   100
Pope, Rufus   307
Pope, ...   257
Porch, Lou   353
Porch, Louise   134
Porter, Hannah E.   283
Poston, Jane Eliz.   218
Poteet, Clyde   365
Potter, Abraham   139,175
Potter, Aileen   158
Potter, Alfred Gerald   318
Potter, Alice   40,230
Potter, Amanda C.   194
Potter, Amanda S.   331
Potter, Amos   115

Potter, Andrew   134
Potter, Arthur   48
Potter, Ava   264
Potter, Bessie   286
Potter, Bova   149
Potter, Carl H.   62
Potter, Charles W.   279
Potter, Clarence   130
Potter, Clyde   55,318
Potter, Corela   133
Potter, C.A.   287
Potter, C.L.   298
Potter, C.R.   70,204,215
Potter, Dane   48
Potter, Daniel Boone   55
Potter, David C.   158
Potter, Delis   309
Potter, Delmas James   242
Potter, Dollie   145,156
Potter, Don   283
Potter, Drewry   230
Potter, D.C.   173
Potter, Eliza   163
Potter, Elizabeth   125,134
Potter, Ellen   24
Potter, Enoch 136,252,272
    278,354   <
Potter, Eula Arbell   357
Potter, Evert Hillery   40
Potter, E.F.   101
Potter, Florence   287
Potter, Frank   134,286
Potter, Glennie   103
Potter, Hannah   83,117
Potter, Haydin   286
Potter, Hazel   134
Potter, Holla   66
Potter, H.A.   364
Potter, Jacob   115
Potter, Jacob H.   130,278
Potter, James   62,63,134
Potter, John   242
Potter, John Manuel   368
Potter, John M.   111,139
    155,218,223,244,265,275
    281,300   <
Potter, John O.T.   215
Potter, Johnson   218

Potter, Jonse	198	Potter, Thomas 318,330
Potter, Juanita	309	Potter, Thomas G. 356
Potter, J.M.	185	Potter, Thomas J. 244,368
Potter, J.O.T.	222,244	Potter, T.J. 52
Potter, J.S.	101	Potter, T.S. 139
Potter, Kyle	354	Potter, Vina 171
Potter, Laura	341	Potter, William 5,331
Potter, Liddie	288	Potter, W.A. 66,203,213
Potter, Lizzie	122,200	267,278 <
260,269,331	<	Potter, W.J. 145
Potter, Lura	275	Pottr, Rebecca C. 298
Potter, Lydia	52,236,264	Potts, Elizabeth 97
269	<	Powel, Elizabeth 80
Potter, Mae	283	Powell, Caroline 85,278
Potter, Margaret C.	155	Powell, Conley 138,278
Potter, Martha D.	55	Powell, Danford 269
Potter, Martitia	134	Powell, Danford E. 150
Potter, Mary	101,267	Powell, Della 39
Potter, Maude Price	330	Powell, Elizie 97
Potter, Millard	354	Powell, Henry 332
Potter, Nancy	112,204	Powell, James 85,95
Potter, Nannie	227	Powell, J.G. 85,264
Potter, Noah Nathaniel	63	Powell, Marion 88
Potter, Ollie V.	265	Powell, Martha F. 88
Potter, Oma	273	Powell, Martitia 278
Potter, Otha	66	Powell, Mary 269
Potter, Phillip	279	Powell, Matilda 75
Potter, Pollie	191,311	Powell, Sarah 75
Potter, Polly	53,166,277	Powers, Dean 298
323	<	Powers, Henry Jones 298
Potter, Rachel	163,167	Powers, ... 46
Potter, Raina	177	Praither, Marion 211
Potter, Ray	130	Prather, Lilla 131
Potter, Reuben	15,163,252	Prather, Maion 337
Potter, Richard T.	356	Prather, S.L. 72
Potter, Rilda	173	Presnell, Ben 114
Potter, Rosa	115	Presnell, Dan Artel 239
Potter, R.L.	38	Presnell, James W. 114
Potter, Salva	105	Presnell, May 279
Potter, Sarah	8,156,245	Presnell, Pearl 114
Potter, Shade	132	Presnell, Wesley 239
Potter, Simon P.	142	Presnell, William H. 114
Potter, Susan	210	Preston, C.H. 102
Potter, Sus;y	101	Preston, Finley 249
Potter, Talullah W.	267	Preston, Lillie 244
Potter, Tempie	334	Preston, Wiley Elbert 102
Potter, Terie Wagner	368	Price, Alva C. 364
Potter, Thomas	165,197	Price, Annie 97

Price, Ben 300
Price, Cute 8,260
Price, C.A. 283
Price, Daniel 7
Price, Delila 299
Price, Diteltha 178
Price, Edith Mae 39
Price, Eliza 322
Price, Filmore 89
Price, Glen A. 86
Price, Hesikia 202
Price, H.J. 330
Price, Infant 300
Price, James 120,202,349
  354 <
Price, Jane F. 300
Price, Jarred M. 238
Price, Jessie 202
Price, John 317,344
Price, John A. 197
Price, Julia 159
Price, J.M. 86
Price, Liddie 287
Price, Liley 40
Price, Lottie 109
Price, Lydia 296
Price, Maggie M. 364
Price, Mansfield 197
Price, Martha 120,314
Price, Maude M. 318
Price, May Caroline 324
Price, Minnie 139
Price, M.S. 268
Price, Nancy 8
Price, Nancy 89
Price, Odell 87
Price, Ople 153
Price, O.T. 330
Price, Robert Ray 283
Price, Rosa 349
Price, Rosa Ellen 354
Price, Roy (Mrs) 368
Price, R.S. 222,225
Price, Sam 319,329
Price, Sarah Jane 264,344
Price, Thomas 138,307
Price, Thomas C. 87
Price, Vestel Loid 247

Price, Wiley 314
Price, Wilford 39,153,193
Price, Wilford J. 193
Price, W.E. 247
Price, W.V. 247
Price, ... 176
Prichard, Nancy 229
Profett, John Harrison 42
Profett, John H. 42
Proffitt, Ada 202
Proffitt, Albert W. 282
Proffitt, Alex 105
Proffitt, Arvil 342
Proffitt, Arvil, Jr. 342
Proffitt, Citha Louisa 229
Proffitt, Clyde 282
Proffitt, Cresia 199
Proffitt, Crissie L. 162
Proffitt, Daniel 168
Proffitt, Darcus B. 312
Proffitt, David 76,148
  183 <
Proffitt, Diana 231
Proffitt, Dilra 183
Proffitt, Dottie 170
Proffitt, D.D.F. 204
Proffitt, D.F. 137
Proffitt, D.P. 202
Proffitt, Effie 111
Proffitt, Elamay 117
Proffitt, Eliza 11
Proffitt, Eliza 110
Proffitt, Elizabeth 166
  203,224,354 <
Proffitt, Ellamay 59
Proffitt, Ellen 168
Proffitt, Eula 118
Proffitt, Florence 240
  264 re
Proffitt, F.S. 49
Proffitt, George 35
Proffitt, G.D. 28
Proffitt, Hannah 123
Proffitt, Harrison 148
Proffitt, Ida 204
Proffitt, Infant 59,76
  138,209 <
Proffitt, Jane 137,197

Proffitt, Jane	205,322	
Proffitt, Jody C.	162	
Proffitt, John	38,49,118	
123,148,352	<	
Proffitt, Julia	72	
Proffitt, J.C.	132,312	
Proffitt, J.G.	312	
Proffitt, J.G. (Mrs)	312	
Proffitt, J.L.	130	
Proffitt, Lottie	275	
Proffitt, Louisa	292	
Proffitt, Lydia	199	
Proffitt, Maggie	15	
Proffitt, Margrate L.	130	
Proffitt, Mary	198	
Proffitt, Monroe	35	
Proffitt, Olley	76	
Proffitt, Ollie J.	148	
Proffitt, Phoebe	195,213	
348	<	
Proffitt, Pless	292	
Proffitt, Pollie C.	15	
Proffitt, Polly	226,229	
Proffitt, Rebecca J.	229	
Proffitt, Retta	69	
Proffitt, Rettie	243	
Proffitt, Rowena	47	
Proffitt, Rowie	119	
Proffitt, Ruby R.	243	
Proffitt, Sam	243	
Proffitt, Sarah L.	287	
Proffitt, Stacy	59,209	
Proffitt, Thomas	352	
Proffitt, Thomas James	105	
Proffitt, Thornton	166	
Proffitt, Totie	9	
Proffitt, Valie	253	
Proffitt, Vanie	56	
Proffitt, Verda Mae	187	
Proffitt, Will	229	
Proffitt, William	49,111	
148,269,292	<	
Proffitt, William C.	138	
Proffitt, ...	278	
Pruitt, Clarence A.	287	
Pruitt, Infant	287	
Rab..., Martha E.	20	
Radomski, Anna	265	

Ragan, Gordon	47	
Ragan, Gordon H.	123	
Ragan, Lan R.	70	
Ragan, Muncy	47	
Ragan, Nelle	123	
Ragen, Gorden E.	70	
Rainbolt, A.M.	174	
Rainbolt, Candas	359	
Rainbolt, Dugger	143,234	
253	<	
Rainbolt, Infant	167	
Rainbolt, Janie	147	
Rainbolt, John	174,320	
335	<	
Rainbolt, John H.	314	
Rainbolt, John M.	314	
Rainbolt, Lucinda	145	
Rainbolt, Martha Ellen	143	
Rainbolt, Mary	143,145	
234	<	
Rainbolt, Matilda	7,234	
Rainbolt, McKinley	167	
Rainbolt, Mollie	234	
Rainbolt, Sarah M.	253	
Rambe, Elvy	7	
Rambo, Aaron	155,211	
Rambo, Atlantic	9	
Rambo, Bertha	245,353	
Rambo, Beulah E.	178	
Rambo, Callie	155	
Rambo, Cinda	197	
Rambo, Eliza	102,335	
Rambo, Goldie E.	264	
Rambo, Ham	72	
Rambo, Hamilton	155	
Rambo, Isaac Stacy	162	
Rambo, James T.	162,211	
Rambo, J.C.	162	
Rambo, J.W.	43	
Rambo, Lizzie	186	
Rambo, Louisa	37	
Rambo, Martha	110	
Rambo, Martha A.	59	
Rambo, Mollie	211	
Rambo, M.H. (Rev)	56	
Rambo, William	152	
Rambo, ...	246	
Ramsey, Bonnie Sheets	363	

Ramsey, Hiram	248	Rash, R.W.		289
Ramsey, Joe	363	Rash, Sarah	132,134,150	
Ramsey, Mary	250	Rash, Ulysis Grant		123
Rankins, Donald	95	Rash, Walter Dewey		367
Rankins, Ed	95	Rash, Wiley Glen		165
Rankins, Eliza	97	Rash, Winfred		290
Rankins, Ellen	191	Rasor, Katie		324
Rankins, Ellie	299	Ray, Annie Mae	123,139	
Rankins, M.B.	201	Ray, Barbara Louise		351
Rankins, Trula	219	Ray, Isabel		58
Rankins, W.P.	299	Ray, Jessie F.		351
Rankins, ...	124	Ray, Jessie H.		351
Raork, Andria A.	129	Ray, J.R.		88
Rash, Alexander A.	139	Ray, Lee Roy		247
Rash, Amos	286,347	Ray, L.L.		58,259
Rash, Arnie	174	Ray, Mae		196
Rash, Arthur Donnelly	139	Ray, Martha		337
Rash, Arthur D.	123	Ray, Mary		88
Rash, A.P.	165	Ray, Mary R.		126
Rash, Bartin D.	189	Ray, ...		356
Rash, Bertie	364	Razar, Betsy		164
Rash, Bettie Ann	265,286	Razar, ...		159
Rash, Dan	252	Razor, Abbie		188
Rash, Daniel S.	333	Razor, Elizabeth		271
Rash, Delia	267	Razor, Hannah	41,190,212	
Rash, Dewey	367	Razor, Katie		197
Rash, Ernest	361	Rece, Lydia		136
Rash, Etta	165	Rece, W.L.		187
Rash, Fannie Agnes	256	Rector, Carulia		216
Rash, Frank	263	Rector, Mary		147
Rash, Ham	364	Red, Emma		302
Rash, Hamilton	290	Red, Infant		109
Rash, Hamilton, Jr.	290	Red, Stella G.		195
Rash, James E.	189	Red, Thomas		109
Rash, John	213	Reece, Albert		103
Rash, J.	50	Reece, Alza Ellen		154
Rash, J.E.	252	Reece, Amanda		273
Rash, Leshia	365	Reece, Amanda Dugger		361
Rash, Maggie	174	Reece, Arlene		357
Rash, Margaret Wilson	361	Reece, Arther		154
Rash, Mary Mabel	289	Reece, Asa	159,221	
Rash, Monroe	265	Reece, A.C.		117
Rash, Myrtle Wandalee	367	Reece, A.R.		279
Rash, M.A.	150,286,318	Reece, Bettie		278
333	<	Reece, Boyd		273
Rash, Oscar Dean	263	Reece, Carlon		275
Rash, Phillip	189	Reece, Caroline		159
Rash, R.H.	289	Reece, Caswell T.		169

Reece, Celia 297
Reece, Charles 116
Reece, Cora 103
Reece, C.D. 262
Reece, Daniel Boone 221
Reece, Dave 126
Reece, Delilah C. 238
Reece, Doxie 205
Reece, D.B. (Mrs) 221
Reece, D.H. 114
Reece, D.L. 97
Reece, Edna May 126
Reece, Effie 149,197
Reece, Eliza 148,160,274
Reece, Elmira 331
Reece, Elvie Dunn 111
Reece, Emanuel 17
Reece, Florence 50
Reece, Floyd 214,275,362
Reece, Francis E. 140
Reece, Frank 243
Reece, Franklin 294
Reece, Harve 105
Reece, Henry Muncey 2
Reece, Hiram 255
Reece, Howard 275
Reece, Hugh 117,169,267
Reece, Hughlie 213
Reece, H.W. 238
Reece, Ila 277
Reece, Inez 361
Reece, Isaac 332
Reece, Isaac Hamilton 213
Reece, Jacob 338
Reece, James 65,104,140
163,165,167,205,213
Reece, James Kermit 347
Reece, James Oscar 347
Reece, Janie 135
Reece, Jennie 115,289
Reece, Jim 110
Reece, Joannah 169
Reece, John 279
Reece, John R. 192
Reece, Kate R. 294
Reece, Kermit 347
Reece, Lacrissa E. 346
Reece, Ladise 37

Reece, Landon 10,279
Reece, Laura 47
Reece, Lavina J. 70
Reece, Lella 24
Reece, Lillie 262
Reece, Lola 313
Reece, Lula 123
Reece, Mae Bell 104
Reece, Maggie 289
Reece, Maggie Naoma 268
Reece, Mary 79,108,117
207,324,368 <
Reece, Maud Lilian 105
Reece, Mina 137
Reece, Myrtle 308
Reece, Nancy 306,321
Reece, Nora 45,64,85
Reece, Pauline 196
Reece, Rachel 62,215,282
Reece, Rebecca 76
Reece, Rettie 251
Reece, Robert 289
Reece, Rosa 114
Reece, Rosa V. 46
Reece, Sallie 131
Reece, Sallie M. 54
Reece, Stacy Edward 214
Reece, Stella 117,135,146
214,224,262,263 <
Reece, Thad 116
Reece, Thadius 111,149
Reece, Tin 69
Reece, Victoria 192
Reece, V.B. 46
Reece, Walter, B. 192
Reece, Ward B. 131
Reece, William 333
Reece, W.B. 273
Reed, Andy 310
Reed, Anna 306
Reed, Carril L. 221
Reed, C.R. (Mrs) 188
Reed, James 224,354
Reed, Jody C. 155
Reed, John 221,225
Reed, John Harrison 354
Reed, Joseph 155
Reed, J.E. (Mrs) 354

Reed, Sarah 321
Reed, W.M. 155,224
Reed, ... 352
Reeer, Adaline 27
Reese, Asa 191
Reese, Francis 7
Reeves, Dexter 368
Reeves, Elizabeth 240
Reeves, Fanney D. 323
Reeves, George 136,238
   261,277, <
Reeves, George W. 366,368
Reeves, G.W. 240
Reeves, Hardin Samuel 366
Reeves, H.S. 121
Reeves, John 260,368
Reeves, John F. 121,366
Reeves, John Henry 238
Reeves, Lee 161,260,365
Reeves, Lucas 366
Reeves, Lula 136
Reeves, Mary Alice 365
Reeves, Mary A. 161
Reeves, S.S. 323
Reeves, Victoria W. 366
Reeves, Virgie M. 366
Reeves, Winford 25
Reid, Andrew 188
Reid, Caleb R. 188
Reid, Noah 234
Reid, William Franklin 234
Renfro, Sallie 189
Retherford, L.C. 26
Revis, ... 319
Reynolds, Edward 201
Reynolds, Jane 208
Reynolds, J.C. (Rev) 312
Reynolds, Lizzie 2
Reynolds, Mary Lee 201
Reynolds, Polly 135
Reynolds, R.K. 242
Reynolds, William 242
Rhea, Charles C. 251,285
Rhea, E. Bruce 176,367
Rhea, E.B. 253
Rhea, Margaret C. 253
Rhea, Mary E. 196
Rhea, Robert Campbell 367

Rhea, Robert C. 176,251
Rhea, Robert C. (Dr) 285
Rhea, Samuel R. 251
Rhes, Margaret Bell 367
Rhoten, Amanda 259
Rhudy, Jane 90
Rhudy, ... 47
Rhymer, Daniel 107
Rhymer, Jane 280
Rhymer, O.B. 313
Rice, Cela 233
Rice, Jim 233
Richardson, Della C. 242
Richardson, Mary 148
Richinsin, Dillie 324
Riddle, Bettie Lou 358
Riddle, Elizabeth 162
Riddle, Frank 51
Riddle, Mae 309
Riddle, Roy 358
Riddle, Stella 187
Riddle, W.M. 187
Riddle, W.N. 260
Riddles, Roy 291
Riddles, Stella 138
Riley, Emma 297
Riley, John M. 297
Riley, J.A. 297
Riner, D. 196
Riner, Penina 196
Riner, Rebecca 186
Riner, ... 229
Ritchie, Jon (Mrs) 221
Ritchie, Millie 56
Ritchie, Millie B. 110
Ritchie, Murl 64
Ritchie, Robert 64
Ritchison, Etta 313
Ritchison, Thomas E. 313
Rithcie, Millie 154
Ritter, Elizabeth 348
Roard, Stacy 314
Roark, Aaron 176
Roark, Abbie 105
Roark, Adella 132
Roark, Agness L. 131
Roark, Anna 199
Roark, Avery 95

Roark, A.L.	129,191	Roark, Maud		87
Roark, Bertha	76	Roark, McKinley	209,218
Roark, Bethel	74,123	324,362,366	<
Roark, Blanche	308	Roark, M.C.	241
Roark, Burl	333	Roark, M.E. (Mrs)	6
Roark, Charlie	334	Roark, Nora	104
Roark, Cora D.	233	Roark, N.L.	126
Roark, Daniel	86	Roark, Oma	308
Roark, Daniel S.	286	Roark, Ora	94
Roark, David	98,99,233	Roark, Pearl	171,180
273	<	Roark, Pollie Marie	333
Roark, David H.	191	Roark, Polly	330
Roark, Donnelly	104,105	Roark, Renora	105
Roark, Earl	324	Roark, Rildey	40
Roark, Edward	176	Roark, Ruth	334
Roark, Effie Mae	7	Roark, Stacy	273
Roark, Elsie Vanover	362	Roark, Suzania	153
Roark, Emma	244	Roark, S.A.	308
Roark, Ephram	261	Roark, Timothy	109
Roark, Eugene	367	Roark, Tiny Catherine	334
Roark, Eveline	51	Roark, T.D.	146,201
Roark, Glen E.	131	Roark, Walter Retze	86
Roark, Gurnie Edward	209	Roark, William	215
Roark, Harrison	8,16,215	Roark, William F.	330
358	<	Roark, William M.	366,367
Roark, H.L.	126	Roark, Wilson T.	334
Roark, Infant	109	Roark, W.F.	131
Roark, Irene	366	Roark, W.L.	98,127,131
Roark, Isaac	85	Roark, W.T.	323
Roark, Ivalee	362	Roark, ...	321,340
Roark, Jenie	204	Roark William T.	330
Roark, Jennie	175	Roarks, Emaline	10
Roark, J.C.	204,266,308	Robards, Lawrence	291
323,324,330,362	<	Robards, Mary	309
Roark, Lettie	243	Robbins, John Henry	74
Roark, Locke J.	127	Robbins, Roby	87
Roark, Lockie	201	Robbins, R.D.	74,87
Roark, Lorence	51	Robert, Edward	222
Roark, Loretta M.	245	Robert, J.M.	217
Roark, Lottie Otto	146	Roberts, Alexander	136
Roark, Louise	323	Roberts, Baxter	51,194
Roark, Loura Elizabeth	266	272	<
Roark, L.D.	126	Roberts, Belle	293
Roark, Mable T.M.	218	Roberts, Bertha	354
roark, Mae	367	Roberts, Bessie	339
Roark, Mandy	231	Roberts, Betty	11
Roark, Martha C.	358	Roberts, Bob	142
Roark, Mary An	16	Roberts, Bob	220

Roberts, Callie   71
Roberts, Catherine P.   272
Roberts, Cephas Stacy   24
Roberts, Clyde   51
Roberts, Daniel M.   52
Roberts, David A.   95
Roberts, Denver   71
Roberts, Dona   313
Roberts, Dora   333
Roberts, Doran Donally   96
Roberts, Ed   90,95,96,203
        293,313   <
Roberts, Edward   212
Roberts, Edward Jr.   90
Roberts, Elizabeth   35
Roberts, Ellen   313
Roberts, Ethel   95,96
Roberts, E.D.   71
Roberts, E.G.   94
Roberts, Fannie   247
Roberts, Felist Stout   95
Roberts, Florence   329
Roberts, Graham   125
Roberts, Gray   95,125,240
Roberts, Harrison   268
Roberts, Hester   11
Roberts, H.C.   34
Roberts, Infant   222,278
        313   <
Roberts, Isaac M.   246
Roberts, Jacob   71,139
Roberts, Jake   329
Roberts, James   333
Roberts, John   61
Roberts, John M.   203
Roberts, J.F.   313
Roberts, J.J.   110
Roberts, J.M.   28,126,262
Roberts, Laura   130,235
Roberts, Laura E.   96
Roberts, Lizzie   313
Roberts, Lonnie H.   94
Roberts, Louisa   139
Roberts, L.F.   71
Roberts, Mary   136
Roberts, Mary Jane   203
Roberts, Mary J.   90
Roberts, Mary Lorette   217

Roberts, Mary V.   249
Roberts, Millard F.   126
Roberts, M.F.   217
Roberts, Polly   141,335
Roberts, Richman   151
Roberts, Robert   262
Roberts, Rufus   142
Roberts, R.A.   29,246
Roberts, R.E.   339
Roberts, Sarah   246
Roberts, Shelton G.   125
Roberts, Sybitha   34
Roberts, Thomas   8,39,61
Roberts, Thomas S.   110
Roberts, Tom   313
Roberts, Tyler   126
Roberts, Vena C.   240
Roberts, Vernia   28
Roberts, Victoria J.   161
Roberts, Walter   278
Roberts, Walter B.   313
Roberts, William   57
Roberts, William H.   52
        142   <
Roberts, William T.   212
Roberts, W.H.   339
Robertson, Chelcie   2
Robertson, James   79
Robinson, Alexander   207
Robinson, Allen   313
Robinson, Armina   272
Robinson, Bessie   65,123
Robinson, Betsy   70,192
Robinson, Burley Kate   296
Robinson, Caroline   260
        304   <
Robinson, Cate   207
Robinson, Catherine   81
        169   <
Robinson, Catherine C.   222
Robinson, Chelcy Mary   42
Robinson, Cindy   27
Robinson, Constance D.   359
Robinson, Dana L.   352
Robinson, Daniel   59,77
        159,222   <
Robinson, Daniel S.C.   43
Robinson, David   48,187

453

Robinson, David K.	79		Robinson, Julia Ellen	45
Robinson, David R.	252		Robinson, J.D.	141
Robinson, Dennis	213		Robinson, J.G.	57
Robinson, Dewy	294		Robinson, J.H.	256
Robinson, Doran H.	252		Robinson, J.M.	138,158
Robinson, D.R.	59,150		Robinson, J.P.	164,292
Robinson, Edna C.	281		Robinson, J.R.	131
Robinson, Effie Ellen	256		Robinson, Kizzie	295
Robinson, Elbert	350		Robinson, Liddy	352
Robinson, Elizabeth	49,64		Robinson, Lila	38
138,354	<		Robinson, Lillie C.	368
Robinson, Elizabeth B.	346		Robinson, Lola	36
Robinson, Ella	118,184		Robinson, Lottie	191
Robinson, Ellen White	190		Robinson, Lucinda	72
Robinson, Eva	39		Robinson, Lura	114
Robinson, E.G.	252		Robinson, Lyda	159
Robinson, Fannie Lee	285		Robinson, Lyde	42
Robinson, Frank	320,362		Robinson, Lydia	49
Robinson, F.E.	324		Robinson, Malinda	320
Robinson, Garda	271		Robinson, Malissa	45
Robinson, Garda F.	91		Robinson, Malissie C.	350
Robinson, George H.	103		Robinson, Mamie Mae	362
166	<		Robinson, Margaret	343
Robinson, Gorda P.	285		Robinson, Martha	131
Robinson, Gordia	212		Robinson, Mary	241,245
Robinson, Grant	59		Robinson, Mary A.	340
Robinson, G.F.	91		Robinson, Mary C.	249
Robinson, Hannah	207		Robinson, Mattie	253
Robinson, Henry	24,320		Robinson, Maude	264
Robinson, Henry M.	320		Robinson, Mildridge U.	89
Robinson, Ina Bell	313		Robinson, Mollie	162
Robinson, Infant	31,43		Robinson, Moore	187
Robinson, Isabella	355		Robinson, Mo..	81
Robinson, James	81		Robinson, M.M.	277,292
Robinson, James	81,324		Robinson, Nancy	43,115
368	<		Robinson, Nanie	292
Robinson, James B.D.	240		Robinson, Nannie Fay	91
Robinson, James D.	62,103		Robinson, Nicholas	57
113,135,169,240,292<			Robinson, Nicholas G.	287
Robinson, James H.	57		Robinson, Nick	199
Robinson, James J.	103		Robinson, N.D.	150
Robinson, Joe	35,272,362		Robinson, Paul J.	212
Robinson, John	11,29,290		Robinson, Pauline	290
Robinson, John J.	166		Robinson, Pearl	287
Robinson, Joseph	197		Robinson, Ranford E.	19
Robinson, Joseph	324		Robinson, Robert	287
Robinson, Joseph H.	45		Robinson, Sallie	69,306
Robinson, Julia	165,192		324,368	<

Robinson, Samuel 296
Robinson, Samuel E. 324
Robinson, Sarah 103,138
    232,264 <
Robinson, Sarah S. 292
Robinson, Susan 339
Robinson, Susan C. 271
Robinson, Teddy Ray 294
Robinson, Thidore K. 359
Robinson, T.K. (Mrs) 359
Robinson, Ula 62
Robinson, Vada 28
Robinson, Vadie 208
Robinson, Vinnie Ruth 35
Robinson, Wade 187
Robinson, Will 263
Robinson, Will S. 89,91
Robinson, William A. 352
Robinson, Willis 31
Robinson, W.H. 213,340
Robinson, W.J. 79,81,89
Robinson, W.W. 190
Robinson, Zackiner 222
Robinson, ... 71,139
Rogers, Bettie 254
Rogers, Edward 214
Rogers, Margaret J. 53
Rominger, Martha 227
Rominger, Nathaniel 249
Rominger, Sarah 282,352
Rorak, Cora 85
Rorak, John 95
Rorak, Ldyda M. 18
Rorake, Maud 12
Roreak, Bertha 76
Rose, Edward J. 221
Rose, Janie 147
Rose, Sarah 164
Roseblott, Paul G. 346
Ross, Nanie Margaret 118
Roten, Mary 314
Roten, Minnie 312
Roten, Polly 77
Roten, Rachel 162
Roten, Sallie 167
Roten, Sarah Ann 363
Roten, Soloman 236
Roues, Venie J. 134

Rouse, C.B. 138,318
Rouse, John C. 318
Rouse, J.C. (Mrs) 318
Rouse, Lena Pearl 138
Rouse, Margaret 222
Rudolph, Francis R. 298
Rudolph, May West 298
Rudy, Jane 68
Rufard, Everett W. 203
Rufard, W.R. 203
Ruford, Carson 203
Rupard, Amanda C. 216
Rupard, Carney 242
Rupard, Emerson 72
Rupard, Emerson E. 124
Rupard, J.C. 242
Rupard, Scott 349
Rupard, Wiley 46,78
Rupard, Wiley R. 124,242
Rupard, W.R. 216
Rushin, Calvin 217
Rushin, Cinda 217
Russean, Caroline 177
Russell, George 129
Russell, Infant 129
Rustin, Calvin 124,365
Rustin, Laura 124
Rustin, Mary 161
Rutherford, Aitha 338
Rutherford, Atha 191
Rutter, Alice 311
Rutter, B.N. 311,317
Rutter, Ernest 191
Rutter, Margaret 317
Rutter, Paul B. 191
Rutter, Robert R. 311
Rutter, Silas 311
Rvans, Bertha 98
Rymer, Rebecca 211,249
Sahley, Katherine 364
Sales, John 109,195
Sales, Margaret 185
Salmon, William S. 355
Salmons, Lura Callie 355
Salmons, Nancy 9
Salmons, W.S. 355
Saly, Martha 198
Salyers, Ollie 336

Sammons, Alice 70
Sammons, Arthur 305
Sammons, Chelsie 304
Sammons, David 264,331
Sammons, Dayton 313
Sammons, Effie 313
Sammons, Ervin 304
Sammons, Ewing 360
Sammons, George 248,313
Sammons, Henry Lulter 305
Sammons, Inez 2
Sammons, Infant 360
Sammons, Irvin 220,228
Sammons, Jacob H. 313
Sammons, James Burlin 70
Sammons, James Irwin 126
Sammons, Jess 70
Sammons, John 264
Sammons, John Argile 228
Sammons, J.A. 228
Sammons, J.A. (Mrs) 63
Sammons, J.L. 257,331
Sammons, Laura 282
Sammons, Louise C. 257
Sammons, Mary Susan 331
Sammons, Nancy Jane 313
Sammons, Robert 360
Sammons, S.S. 126
Sammons, T.L. 264
Sanders, Mary 84
Sanders, Minnie O. 111
Sapp, Mary D. 39
Saunders, David 175
Saunders, Mary 175
Saylor, Infant 41
Saylor, John 41
Saylor, Sarah 41
Schmidt, Joseph F. 235
Schneider, Margaret 306
Schwer, C.L. 197
Schwer, Jack Thomas 197
Scott, Belva 152
Scott, Billie 336
Scott, Boyd 270
Scott, Ed 294
Scott, Edgar 270
Scott, Edward 261
Scott, Edward, Jr. 261

Scott, F.R. 261,293
Scott, George W. 131,158
    237,262 <
Scott, Ida 293
Scott, James 233
Scott, Malinda 323
Scott, Margarette M. 164
Scott, Matilda 156
Scott, Mollie Snyder 336
Scott, Nada Corina 294
Scott, Olive C. 359
Scott, R.W. 75,152,233
    273,293 <
Scott, William F. 233
Scott, William M. 158
Scott, W.M. 332
Scott, Zachariah T. 237
Scott, Z.A. 164
Scott, ... 367
Seats, Mary 364
Seehorn, John 307
Seehorn, John M. 281
Seehorn, Maggie 307,315
Seehorn, Mary 307
Seehorn, Reed 309
Seehorn, R. Wilson 307
    315 <
Seehorn, R.W. 281
Seehorn, Shirley Jane 309
Serber, James 5
Setzer, Elenor 363
Setzer, Ellen 360
Seus, Cathern 230
Severe, Clinton 26
Severt, Chessie 333
Severt, Edmond 347
Severt, John Allen 347
Severt, John (Mrs) 347
Severt, Minnie M, 347
Sexton, F.K. (Mrs) 309
Sexton, J.E. 52,67,82,87
    219,236,247 <
Sexton, Mary E. 56
Sexton, Robert 219
Sexton, Susie 127
Shafer, Henry 261
Shaver, Eliza 107
Shaw, Andrew 79

Shaw, Burless	52		Shoe, Susa	200
Shaw, D.N.	355		Shoemake, Walter Dewey	6
Shaw, Isabelle	101		Shoemaker, Buck	119
Shaw, Lizzie	101		Shoemaker, Christopher	58
Shaw, Melvin	79		119	<
Shaw, Melvin R.	101		Shoemaker, C.C.	47
Shaw, Roescrans, Jr.	95		Shoemaker, C.C. (Mrs)	119
Shaw, Rosecrans	95		Shoemaker, D.S.	316
Shawver, Elizabeth H.	312		Shoemaker, D.S., Jr.	316
Shearer, D.R. (Mrs)	346		Shoemaker, Frank	58
Shears, Lewis	277		Shoemaker, Hazel	316
Sheers, Laura	289		Shoemaker, Roena	352
Sheets, Eugene	363		Shoemaker, Sophia	47
Sheets, Luveny	43		Shores, Bill	351
Sheets, Walter	363		Shores, Callie	86
Sheffield, R.L.	193		Shores, Calvin	188
Shell, Lara	304		Shores, Carl	72
Shell, W.F.	14		Shores, Carl B.	39
Shell.., Maud	116		Shores, Charity	39
Shelton, Bessie	343		Shores, Elbert Glenn	72
Shelton, Betty Lu	343		Shores, Eliza	331
Shelton, C.F.	192,194		Shores, Enoch	61
Shelton, Frank	119		Shores, Everett Lee	61
Shelton, Girtie	119		Shores, Halsie	227
Shelton, Hattie Mae	194		Shores, Homer	86
Shelton, Hettie	192		Shores, Martha	139
Shepard, Bessie	50,194		Shores, Mary	259
Shepard, Biner	63,66		Shores, William	39
Shepard, B.M.	192		Shors, Callie	103
Shepard, Infant	50		Shors, Ernest	103
Shepard, Lizzie	92		Short, B.D.	139
Shepard, Martin	66		Short, Willie Lee	139
Shepard, Sarah Jane	273		Shoun, Alice	328
Shepard, Virgie	63		Shoun, Alzenia Reece	255
Shepard, Will	286		Shoun, Andrew	80
Shephard, Radnill	37		Shoun, Andy	189
Shepherd, Alfred	60		Shoun, Arthur	52
Shepherd, Doris Marie	349		Shoun, Asa W.	191
Shepherd, John	192		Shoun, A.J.	54
Shepherd, J.W.	192		Shoun, A.W.	79
Shepherd, R.M.	37		Shoun, Caleb	11,324
Shepherd, Wiley	349		Shoun, Caleb J.	266
Sheppard, Christine	100		Shoun, Callie	122
Sheppard, Florence	8		Shoun, Carl R.	89
Sheppard, John	55		Shoun, Cassie	172
Sheppard, M.D.	55		Shoun, Celia A.	191
Sherwood, James C.	312		Shoun, Cham Bell	295
Sherwood, Ruth R.	312		Shoun, Charles Kemp	356

Shoun, Cilia   54
Shoun, Cleo   130
Shoun, C.G.   74
Shoun, C.L.   68
Shoun, Daniel Boon   312
Shoun, Doris Nellie   235
Shoun, D.B.   54
Shoun, Elia Wills   332
Shoun, Eliza   113
Shoun, Elva   162,210
Shoun, Elva O.   195
Shoun, El.. Alexander   41
Shoun, Ethel   99,189
Shoun, Eva   100
Shoun, Eva Bernice   207
Shoun, E. Max   29
Shoun, Fannie   234
Shoun, Frank C.   356
Shoun, Harold Lane   89
Shoun, Harvey   328,357
Shoun, Henderson   345
Shoun, Herbert   34
Shoun, Infant   52,65,96
Shoun, Isaac   41
Shoun, Isaac   74
Shoun, Isaac Harvey   267
Shoun, Isaac M.   328
Shoun, Jacob   284
Shoun, James Andrew   267
Shoun, Jennie M.   242
Shoun, Joe   280
Shoun, John H.   35
Shoun, John S.   54
Shoun, Joseph H.   242
Shoun, Joseph Macon   324
Shoun, J.A.   287
Shoun, J.C.   324
Shoun, J.G.   200
Shoun, J.H.   65
Shoun, J.M.   123
Shoun, J.W.   332
Shoun, J.W. (Mrs)   98
Shoun, Lydia   200
Shoun, L.P.   96,130
Shoun, Mable   3
Shoun, Mag   267
Shoun, Marcellis   123
Shoun, Mariah   48

Shoun, Martha   86,311
Shoun, Mary   70,94
Shoun, Mary E.   43
Shoun, Michael   235
Shoun, M.L.   275,319
Shoun, Nat   332
Shoun, Ora   52
Shoun, Ora N.   165
Shoun, Pacific   307
Shoun, Pedro   235
Shoun, Peter   284,295,353
Shoun, Peter Hilton   357
Shoun, Peter L.   295,303
Shoun, Polly Catherine 77
Shoun, P.H.   255
Shoun, Rachel   183,271,312
Shoun, Ray   269
Shoun, Rebecca   143,222
     362   <
Shoun, Robert L.   266
Shoun, Sallie   108,225,278
Shoun, Samuel   359
Shoun, Samuel E.   54,312
Shoun, Sarah   267,361
Shoun, Sarah A.   190
Shoun, Sarah Fina   292,266
Shoun, Sarah L.   287
Shoun, Susana   77
Shoun, Thomas B.   21
Shoun, Thomas J.   165
Shoun, T.J.   165
Shoun, Vada Ethel   355
Shoun, Verna May   123
Shoun, Vina Dillon   284
Shoun, Walter   190
Shoun, William Henry   242
Shoun, William H.   276
Shoun, Winnie   118
Shoun, W.H.   292
Shouns, Eliza   264
Shuffield, Berthe B.   227
Shuffield, John   78
Shuffield, L.C.   189
Shuffield, Sarah   190
Shuffield, ...   63
Shull, A.J.   292
Shull, Caroline   135,305
     339   <

458

Name	Page
Shull, Celia	65
Shull, Charles	193
Shull, C.R.	305,315
Shull, Edward S.	52
Shull, Eva	179
Shull, Infant	193
Shull, Jessie Mae	276
Shull, John	239
Shull, J.A.	309
Shull, Laura C.	305
Shull, Laura K.	315
Shull, Louisa Matilda	239
Shull, Nathanel C.	305
Shull, Nathaniel C.	52
Shull, N.C.	315
Shull, Phillip	117
Shull, Roby	147
Shull, Rose E.	199
Shumate, Docia	192
Shumate, Elizabeth	349
Shumate, Lee	349
Shupe, Alice	202
Shupe, Ascy	97
Shupe, Betsy	212
Shupe, Charles	228
Shupe, Clarence	316
Shupe, Corda	316
Shupe, C.E.	132
Shupe, Daniel	323
Shupe, Daniel D.	165
Shupe, David Garfield	323
Shupe, Delmer Ray	153
Shupe, D.G.	153
Shupe, Elizabeth	202
Shupe, Emma	323
Shupe, Ernest	37
Shupe, Eula	12
Shupe, Eula Elizabeth	200
Shupe, Frank	220
Shupe, Henry Shelton	66
Shupe, Inez	36
Shupe, Infant	220
Shupe, James	66,202
Shupe, James W.	145,185
Shupe, Jim	66
Shupe, John	234,316
Shupe, John E.	145
Shupe, J.F.	295

Name	Page
Shupe, J.S.	295
Shupe, Laura	141
Shupe, Luther	228
Shupe, Margaret	235
Shupe, Martha	57,228
Shupe, Martha E.	215
Shupe, Mary Alice	66
Shupe, Mary C.	132
Shupe, Myrtle	199
Shupe, Okie	1
Shupe, Polly Arnold	316
Shupe, Sherman	153,200
Shupe, Thomas	19
Shupe, Thompson	185
Shupe, Tracy	199
Shupe, Troy	37
Shupe, Virginia	66
Shupe, Walter H.	316
Shupe, William	90,165
Shupe, W.T.	96,145
Shuritz, Catherine A.	264
Simcox, Aaron H.	282
Simcox, Chalarlee	52
Simcox, Dana	350
Simcox, Hugh T.	5
Simcox, Ida	328
Simcox, Infant	84,160
Simcox, James	160
Simcox, John T.	84
Simcox, Joseph G.	282
Simcox, Lenna Kate	75
Simcox, Louzana	201
Simcox, Nannie	306
Simcox, O.A.	173,180
Simcox, O.P.	201
Simcox, Thomas	52
Simcox, Tilmon	251
Simcox, T.C.	282
Simcox, T.E. (Mrs)	325
Simcox, William S.	5
Simerly, Jacob	111
Simerly, Susan	145
Simerly, Susie	155,247
Simmons, Joel	127,226
Simmons, John	226,286
Simmons, Mary	61
Simmons, T... (Mrs)	127
Simmons, ...	79,334

Name	Page
Simms, Mary	250
Simpson, Alice	171,175
Simpson, Celia	171
Simpson, Henry	171
Simpson, Luke	89
Simpson, Stella	113
Sims, Bessie	179
Sizemore, ...	44
Slemp, David	251
Slemp, James David	251
Slemp, John	251
Slimp, Andy	242
Slimp, Andy Clinton	242
Slimp, Callie	256
Slimp, Caroline	5
Slimp, Catilana	252
Slimp, Charlie	125
Slimp, David	89,242,266
Slimp, David J.	305
Slimp, D.E.	161
Slimp, D.L.	73
Slimp, Edgar Boyd	40
Slimp, Edna Mae	54
Slimp, Edward	154
Slimp, Elizabeth	266
Slimp, Ethel	30
Slimp, Frederick	40
Slimp, George	54
Slimp, Harret E.	197
Slimp, Harriett E.	305
Slimp, Jeril	252
Slimp, John	301,305
Slimp, Joseph	22
Slimp, Joseph	22,154
Slimp, J.E.	197
Slimp, Louisa	217
Slimp, Martin	274
Slimp, Martin A.	160,301
Slimp, Mary Ann	301
Slimp, Mary A.	222
Slimp, Mary M.	13
Slimp, Maud	30
Slimp, Millard	89
Slimp, Mollie	60
Slimp, M. Jordan	274
Slimp, M.A.	222
Slimp, Nancy	251,274
Slimp, Polly	116,206,219
Slimp, Rachel	327,330
Slimp, R.B.	177,195
Slimp, Sallie	242
Slimp, Samuel Carter	122
Slimp, Tiney	78
Slimp, Vennie	37
Slimp, William M.	160
Sluder, Abbie	308
Sluder, Alma Lorraine	282
Sluder, Alma Theala	113
Sluder, Ardia Blanche	119
Sluder, A.L.	308
Sluder, Bob	282
Sluder, B.L.	249
Sluder, Clinard	190
Sluder, C.D.	249
Sluder, C.E.	87
Sluder, Dana H.	313
Sluder, Dona H.	190
Sluder, D.H.	308
Sluder, Elizabeth	309
Sluder, Ethel	249,354
Sluder, Evert	87
Sluder, E.E.	60, 138
Sluder, Forrest	334
Sluder, Fred Lee	151
Sluder, Harrison	303
Sluder, Hubert Wayne	313
Sluder, Infant	60,334
Sluder, Lutitia	167
Sluder, Magnalia	303
Sluder, Magnatia	119
Sluder, M.E.	86,285
Sluder, Nora N.	60
Sluder, Polly	116,146
217,231	<
Sluder, Ray	334
Sluder, Robie Milton	303
Sluder, Roby	119
Sluder, Roy	151,229
Sluder, R.C. (Mrs)	303
Sluder, R.L.	60
Sluder, Zelphia	307
Small, William E.	148
Small, William Henry	148
Smiath, ...	317
Smith, Abner	129
Smith, Alfred	186

Smith, Alice	355	
Smith, Ancy E.	243	
Smith, Andrew Jackson	270	
Smith, A.L.	162,246,250	
Smith, Bell	141	
Smith, Bennie	250	
Smith, Bessie	92	
Smith, Bettie	73,277	
Smith, Bunnie	117	
Smith, Cora	184	
Smith, Cordelia	323	
Smith, Eliza Ann	51	
Smith, Eliza A.	182	
Smith, Elizabeth	83,89	
221,269	<	
Smith, Everett	13	
Smith, Florence	157,193	
Smith, Frank	235	
Smith, George	269	
Smith, Hardin	303	
Smith, Hayes	171,174,177	
Smith, Henderson	132,241	
270	<	
Smith, Hyder	261	
Smith, Infant	147	
Smith, Ira	243	
Smith, James	206	
Smith, James C.	147	
Smith, James Franklin	129	
Smith, James Lawson	241	
Smith, James L.	51	
Smith, James S.	206	
Smith, James W.	303	
Smith, Jamia Lee	296	
Smith, Jane	106,302,319	
Smith, Jim	329	
Smith, Joe	147	
Smith, Joe R.	90	
Smith, John	16,193	
Smith, John H.	241	
Smith, Junior L.	239	
Smith, J.G.	129	
Smith, J.M.	52	
Smith, J.S. (Mrs)	206	
Smith, Laura	306	
Smith, Laurie	236	
Smith, Louisa	157	
Smith, Lula	64	

Smith, Mamie Ruth	44
Smith, Margaret	253
Smith, Martha	134
Smith, Martha E.	166
Smith, Martin N.	284
Smith, Mary	124,286,296
Smith, Mary E.	178
Smith, Mary Jane	214,326
Smith, Matilda	73
Smith, Maude	151,334
Smith, Mike	229
Smith, Nancy Jane	152,192
Smith, Nancy S.	199
Smith, Niama	320
Smith, N.D. (Rev)	221
Smith, Pearl	363
Smith, Polly	115,238
Smith, Rebecca	52
Smith, Rebecca L.	209
Smith, Robert	160,208
Smith, Rody	162
Smith, Rolie	34
Smith, Ruby	176
Smith, Rufus	174
Smith, Ruth	18,146
Smith, Sarafina E.	43
Smith, Sarah E.	156
Smith, Smithpeter N.	274
Smith, Stella	176
Smith, Susie	229
Smith, S.J.	90
Smith, S.N.	157
Smith, S.W.	127
Smith, Taylor (Mrs)	276
Smith, Thomas Wesley	356
Smith, Virgia	342
Smith, Virginia Lee	284
Smith, Walter	146,157
Smith, Walter Fred	239
Smith, Wesley	239
Smith, Wiley	64,176
Smith, William H.	44
Smith, William L.	274
Smith, ...	59
Smithpeter, Louise	274
Smithpeter, Mary	157
Smithpeter, Matilda	185
Smithpeter, Michael	157

Smithpeters, Lanthena	174	
Smithpeters, Matilda	231	
Smithpeters, Venia	231	
Smoot, Thomas	308	
Smyth, James R.H.	265	
Smyth, John V.	257	
Smyth, Thomas R.	265	
Smyth, Thomas S.	257	
Smyth, T.H.	265	
Smythe, Etta Donnelly	355	
Smythe, John W.	284,353	
Smythe, John W., III	322	
Smythe, John W., Jr.	322	
Smythe, Kate Murphey	353	
Smythe, Lillian S.	284	
Smythe, Margaret	236	
Smythe, Thomas S.	284,355	
Smythe, T. Stanley	284	
Smythe, William T.	355	
Smythe, W.T.	273	
Snider, Anna	116	
Snider, Donna	16	
Snider, Vina	149	
Snodgrass, E...	126	
Snyder, Adam	220	
Snyder, Alex	275,357	
Snyder, Alexander	323	
Snyder, Alexander M.	347	
Snyder, Alice	84,129,130	
Snyder, Alice Osborn	332	
Snyder, Amanda	174	
Snyder, A.J.	36	
Snyder, A.M.	323	
Snyder, A.S.	225	
Snyder, Betsy Ann	62	
Snyder, Bettie	168	
Snyder, Billie Lee	364	
Snyder, Callie	92	
Snyder, Caroline	209,234	
Snyder, Catherine	21	
Snyder, Charlie	318	
Snyder, Clarice L.	351	
Snyder, Clera	51	
Snyder, Clyde Franklin	128	
Snyder, Cora	347	
Snyder, Cora Lee	304	
Snyder, C.M.	225	
Snyder, Dale	318	
Snyder, Daniel	180,321	
Snyder, Dave	310	
Snyder, David	309,336	
Snyder, Della Mae	284	
Snyder, Eliza	230	
Snyder, Elizabeth	44	
Snyder, Elizabeth	44,47	
	81,163,200	<
Snyder, Ellen	220,235	
Snyder, Ester	310	
Snyder, Etta	109	
Snyder, Evaline	94	
Snyder, Fred	164	
Snyder, Fred S.	309	
Snyder, F.S.	226	
Snyder, Georgia	318	
Snyder, Glen	346	
Snyder, G.W.	168,233	
Snyder, Hamilton	39	
Snyder, Henry	18	
Snyder, Hiram	60,304	
Snyder, H.	222	
Snyder, Ida S.	52	
Snyder, Infant	183	
Snyder, Jacob	44,332	
Snyder, James H.	39	
Snyder, Jesse	236	
Snyder, Jessie	140	
Snyder, Joe	350,357	
Snyder, Joe B.	310	
Snyder, John	78	
Snyder, Josephine	164,364	
Snyder, J.D.	314,336	
Snyder, J.J.	296	
Snyder, J.W.	165,180	
Snyder, Kate	72	
Snyder, Landon	40,357	
Snyder, Lee	364	
Snyder, Lem	156	
Snyder, Lisia	136	
Snyder, Lizzie	62	
Snyder, Loulia	273	
Snyder, Mabel	121	
Snyder, Marelda	273	
Snyder, Margaret	42	
Snyder, Martha E.	165	
Snyder, Mary	241	
Snyder, Mary R.	347	

Snyder, Matilda 99
Snyder, Matitie 56
Snyder, Mollie 357
Snyder, M.G. 84
Snyder, Nancy E. 62
Snyder, N. Jennie 314
Snyder, N.W. 323
Snyder, Ora 365
Snyder, Pearl 241
Snyder, Pearlie 60
Snyder, Rachall 156
Snyder, Rachel 136
Snyder, Rebecca 7
Snyder, R.H. 71
Snyder, Salie 42
Snyder, Samantha 183
Snyder, Stanley 121
Snyder, Susan 309
Snyder, Susie 310,319
Snyder, Thomas Howard 72
Snyder, Verne 225
Snyder, Walter Glenn 36
Snyder, Washington 233
Snyder, Wiley 256
Snyder, William R. 128
Snyder, W.L. 354
Snyder, W.M. 3
Snyder, W.R. 217,351
Snyder, ... 183
Soser, Charlie 17
South, Britain 47
South, Cassie 92
South, Jack 218
South, James 289
South, James M. 114
South, John 340
South, John H. 47
South, Josie 126
South, J.H. 253
South, Lassie 64
South, Lourie 296
South, Pearl 209
South, Polly 148,269
South, Pruda 364
South, Sallie 207
Southead, Peggy 275
Southerland, Ella 315
Southerland, Rachel 324

Southerland, Vina 336
Southerland. Fred 62
Sparks, David 110
Sparks, Jane 360
Spars, Callie 66
Spear, Iffy 248
Spear, Isabel 280
Spear, Jane 241
Spear, Laura 345
Spears, Jane 335
Spears, John 335
Speer, Barbara 75
Speer, E.G. 178
Speer, Isabella 187
Speer, John 178,272
Speer, John C. 178
Speer, Sallie 188
Spivey, Margaret 217
Spi..., Malinda 105
Spriggs, Joseph 233
Spriggs, Terry 233
Spurgeon, James H. 355
Spurgeon, Vernie A. 355
Stalcup, Aeron 64
Stalcup, Alfred Taylor 49
Stalcup, Aron Joseph 360
Stalcup, Callie 354
Stalcup, David Ray 360
Stalcup, D.E. 331
Stalcup, Elizabeth 27
Stalcup, Jackson 70
Stalcup, John H. 34,64
192,354 <
Stalcup, J.H. (Mrs) 192
Stalcup, Latitia 117
Stalcup, Lexie 254
Stalcup, Mae 360
Stalcup, Maggie 180
Stalcup, Mary E. 195
Stalcup, Stacy 195
Stalcup, Titia 290
Stalcup, Virgie Mae 360
Stalcup, William A. 354
Stalcup, W.H. 64
Stal..., Lillie 145
Stamper, ... 44
Stampler, C.M. 301
Stampler, Henry 301

Stampler, Wilburn	301	Stanton, Lossie	308
Stanberry, Etta	349	Stanton, Lottie	172
Stanberry, Herbert	293	Stanton, Martha	195
Stanberry, J.R.	293	Stanton, Mary	43
Stanberry, R.C.	349	Stanton, Ollie	281
Stanberry, Troy	293	Stanton, Roy	61
Stanbery, Dora	45	Stanton, Sarah E.	79
Stanbery, J.S.	41	Stanton, Thomas	76
Stanbury, Callie	31	Starnes, Alice E.	335
Stanbury, Eliza	13	Starnes, Cora	71
Stanley, Fred	252	Starnes, Fred	335
Stanley, Jane	214	Starnes, Paul	34
Stanley, Sollie	252	Starns, Susie	191
Stansberry, Bula May	259	Stephen, May	289
Stansberry, Center	73,110	Stephens, Dexter	226
Stansberry, Dora	74	Stephens, Elizabeth	302
Stansberry, Everett	125	Stephens, Infant	226
Stansberry, Henry	259	Stephens, Joseph L.	237
Stansberry, Infant	241	Stephens, Mary	199
Stansberry, James P.	363	Stephens, Thomas	237
Stansberry, John	93,110	Stepp, Mary	361
241,315	<	Stepp. Polly	258
Stansberry, Martha	315	Stevens, Benjamin	285,286
Stansberry, Mary	73,110	Stevens, B.F.	360
Stansberry, Nellie J.	315	Stevens, E.E.	46
Stansberry, Rebecca	73	Stevens, Ida	285
Stansberry, R.C.	363	Stevens, Infant	46
Stansberry, Sarah	137,154	Stevens, Jessie E.	286
Stansberry, Willard	93	Stevens, T.A.	40
Stansbery, Duff	291	Steward, Henry	181
Stansbery, Emert	291	Steward, Infant	181
Stanton, Carrie Lee	195	Steward, R.S.	59
Stanton, Casper C.	343	Stewart, Amanda	236
Stanton, Cleo	158	Stewart, Bessie	274
Stanton, Conley	280	Stewart, Britain	172
Stanton, Elsie	286	Stewart, Harriett L.	210
Stanton, Flossie	361	Stewart, Inez	249
Stanton, Frank	281	Stewart, Jack	249
Stanton, Frank, Sr.	281	Stewart, J.C.	249
Stanton, Franklin	79	Stewart, Marion F.	249
Stanton, Franklin B.	343	Stewart, M.F.	236
Stanton, Grace	195	Stewart, Purda	241
Stanton, Grayson	158,308	Stewart, Robert S.	172
Stanton, Grocon	195	Stewart, Rosa	10
Stanton, Hobart G.	281	Stewart, S.A.	172
Stanton, Infant	23,171	Stewart, W.C.	210
Stanton, James L.	171	Stone, Cal	227
Stanton, John	280,286	Stone, Dorothy May	227

Stone, Martha 66
Stone, Seny 333
Stone, William 66
Stornes, Alice 163
Stornes, H. 163
Storns, Frederick 163
Storns, Will 257
Stout, Ada 110
Stout, Albertte 106
Stout, Alfred 232,250,288
Stout, Alfred A. 302
Stout, Alfred H. 116
Stout, Alice 121,142
Stout, Alice Wilson 366
Stout, Allen 71
Stout, Allen M. 116,275
  298 <
Stout, Amanda 266,323
Stout, Andrew 91
Stout, Anna 252
Stout, Annie 189,328
Stout, Annie D.A. 161
Stout, Asa Alexander 328
Stout, Aubre Donja 62
Stout, A.J. 91
Stout, A.L. 246,249
Stout, A.M. 97
Stout, Bill 296
Stout, Billie 151
Stout, Bula 135
Stout, Bulah Lee 244
Stout, Carmon 9
Stout, Catherine 88
Stout, Catherine A. 147
Stout, Claude 237
Stout, Clyde H. 330
Stout, Columbus 332
Stout, C.E. 153
Stout, Dana 288
Stout, Daniel 4,8,150
  266,328,364,366 <
Stout, Daniel L. 130
Stout, Daniel M. 108
Stout, Dave 316
Stout, David 23,148,158
  245,261 <
Stout, David Edmond 76
Stout, David M. 225,258

Stout, David P. 231
Stout, David R. 153,189
Stout, David V. 4,39
Stout, David W. 278
Stout, David (Mrs) 245
Stout, Donald G. 176
Stout, Dora 64
Stout, Dorothy 12
Stout, Easter 35
Stout, Elbert E. 339
Stout, Eliza Jane 332
Stout, Elizabeth 10
Stout, Elizabeth 10,82
  146,204,236 <
Stout, Elizy 95
Stout, Ellen 152
Stout, Eller 96
Stout, Ethel Caroline 318
Stout, Etta 95
Stout, Eveline 310
Stout, Evelyn 334
Stout, E.E. 339
Stout, E.H. 76,278
Stout, Fannie 226
Stout, Fuller 249,278
Stout, Gary Lee 142
Stout, George 210
Stout, George P. 189
Stout, George W. 107
Stout, Georgie Lee 284
Stout, Godfrey 245,292
  294 <
Stout, Godfrey D. 90
Stout, Grace 13
Stout, Gre 76
Stout, G.A. 197
Stout, G.D. 316
Stout, Ham 249
Stout, Hanah 143
Stout, Hattie 216,284,366
Stout, Hubert 109
Stout, H. Blaine 245
Stout, Infant 4,37,71,231
Stout, Jackson 144
Stout, Jacob N. 248,266
Stout, Joe 332
Stout, Joe Blaine 107
Stout, Joe B. 310

Stout, John A. 161
Stout, John C. 238
Stout, John F. 22
Stout, John H. 39,96,134
Stout, John L.109,189,366
Stout, John M. 240,294
Stout, Joolian 110
Stout, Joseph 115
Stout, Joseph B. 281
Stout, Joseph W. 275
Stout, Julia 222
Stout, Julia M. 80
Stout, J. Blaine 261,329
Stout, J. Blaine (Mrs)358
Stout, J. Brown 62
Stout, J.B. 39,62
Stout, J.D. 161
Stout, J.E. 37
Stout, J.G. 103
Stout, J.H. 135,248
Stout, J.M. 42,94,97,149
  154,237 <
Stout, J.N. 115
Stout, J.P. 158
Stout, Kate 156
Stout, Katie 59,136,159
Stout, Katie Emaline 349
Stout, Katy 77
Stout, Kenzia 227
Stout, Kinzie 288
Stout, Lacuitia 23
Stout, Lantie V. 42
Stout, Laura Emily 248
Stout, Lawson E. 90
Stout, Lillie Fay 115
Stout, Lucie 97
Stout, L.L. 78,80,90,135
  204,206,248,266,282
Stout, Maggie Bell 339
Stout, Margaret 59,148
Stout, Margaret L. 150
Stout, Marilda 209
Stout, Martha 40,125
Stout, Martha A. 261
Stout, Mary 144
Stout, Mary Ann 91
Stout, Mary C. 256
Stout, Mary Elizabeth 237

Stout, Mary Jane 71,94,95
  96,316 <
Stout, Mattie 50
Stout, Mill L. 284
Stout, Minnie 296
Stout, Minnie Belle 141
Stout, Minnie B. 76
Stout, Minnie C. 68
Stout, Mollie 82
Stout, Nancy 140,194,214
  229,238,324,332,366
Stout, Nancy A. 158
Stout, Nancy N. 243
Stout, Nanlda Eliz 210
Stout, Naoma L. 176
Stout, Nettie H. 22
Stout, Nicholas 44,70
  144,248, <
Stout, Nick 281
Stout, Noah 94
Stout, Otto 330
Stout, Parker 75
Stout, Parkey 116
Stout, Phillip David 288
Stout, Phoeba 222
Stout, P. Glenn 76
Stout, Rebecca 159,254
Stout, Retta 294
Stout, Robert E. 115
Stout, Robert L. 249
Stout, Roby 151
Stout, Roy 164
Stout, Russmann W. 107
Stout, R.F. 334
Stout, R.L. 28
Stout, R.W. 106
Stout, Salina 23
Stout, Salina Edith 164
Stout, Sallie 28,38,70,72
  91,111,212,285,296 <
Stout, Sam 328
Stout, Samuel 37
Stout, Sarah 245
Stout, Selmer W. 264
Stout, Stacy 37
Stout, Stacy Junior 226
Stout, Stacy (Burton) 226
Stout, Stanley S. 37

Stout, Susan A.   212
Stout, Susannah   93
Stout, Susin   26
Stout, S.A.   116,155,212
Stout, S.C.   258
Stout, S.S.   305
Stout, Thomas   70,115,122
    125,134,200,238   <
Stout, Thomas J.   64,153
    340   <
Stout, Tom   282
Stout, T.G.   141
Stout, T.J.   254,346
Stout, Vada   266
Stout, Venia   217
Stout, Venie C.   125
Stout, Vina   296
Stout, Wain   64
Stout, Walter H.   244
Stout, Wayne   264,294
Stout, Wiley   231
Stout, Willard Ray   329
Stout, William   140,142
Stout, William A.   64
Stout, William Billie 234
Stout, William E.   234
Stout, Willie   7,22,28
Stout, W.H.   55,67,80,,81
    82,110   <
Stout, W.K.   176
Stout, W.R.   310
Stout, W.W.   60
Stout, ... Ellen   302
Street, Alfonzo   144
Street, A.J. Stuffle   73
Street, C. Stuffle   73
Street, M. Stuffle   73
Street, Silva   144
Strickland, Eva   263
Stricland, Eva   279
Strictland, Eva   279
Stuart, Paudy   51
Sturgall, Mary C.   242
Sturgall, Mary M.   253
Sturgall, Oscar C.   253
Sturgill, Benjamin   91
Sturgill, Biner   71
Sturgill, Easter   281

Sturgill, Edd   293
Sturgill, Esther   128
Sturgill, Eva Virginia 91
Sturgill, George H.   181
Sturgill, G.A.   242
Sturgill, Joe   229
Sturgill, Magnatia   119
Sturgill, Mary Lee   71
Sturgill, Nancy Jane   293
Sturgill, Robert   229
Sturgill, William   181
Stward, Britain   59
St..., Callie   48
Sulder, Ray   113
Sullivan, Delilah 226,349
Sullivan, Matilda   234
Suncox, Joseph G.   75
Surber, Walter   31
Sutherland, Joseph   183
Sutherland, Ruben   181
Sweeney, Alice   220,228
Sweeney, Baker   124
Sweeney, David   124
Sweeney, H.A.   124
Sweeney, Infant   55
Sweeney, J.C.   55
Sweiney, G.H.   118
Sweiney, Sarah   118
Sweinly, J.C.   73
Sweinly, Thomas   73
Sweney, Daniel   190
Sweney, Garrett   65
Sweney, Thomas Baty   65
Sweny, Alice   304
Swift, Bettie   335
Swift, David Hamilton   43
Swift, Dewey   93,251
Swift, D.A.   237
Swift, Elizabeth   279,327
Swift, Ethel Roberts   95
Swift, Ham   93,335
Swift, Infant   95,96,167
    333   <
Swift, Jack   327
Swift, James   225,326
Swift, James D.   225
Swift, John   333
Swift, Joseph B.   326

Swift, Lennie 93
Swift, Margarete 320
Swift, Mary 123,230,251
Swift, Mary Elizabeth 68
Swift, Morgan 200
Swift, Myrtle Ruth 43
Swift, Polly 132
Swift, Richard 95,96
Swift, Robert 93
Swift, Shirley Jean 321
Swift, Stacy 321
Swift, Susie 74
Swift, Tyler G. 93
Swift, Wilburn 326
Swift, Wiley 167
Swiney, Dora 270
Swiney, Hobert 270
Swiney, Infant 66
Swiney, Jessie 66
Swiney, J.C. 211
Swiney, Ruben 211
S..., Margaret Edna 9
Taliner, Rosa E. 38
Tanner, Huldah 199
Taylor, Abbie 172
Taylor, Abigail 59
Taylor, Alice 61,293
Taylor, Andrew 105
Taylor, Andy 321
Taylor, Bradley 355
Taylor, Bruce 105,181
Taylor, Carl Edward 355
Taylor, Columbus 229,293
  294 <
Taylor, Dicy 94
Taylor, Eli 105
Taylor, George 293
Taylor, Kate 232
Taylor, Laura Price 317
Taylor, Margaret 100
Taylor, Myrtle 161,176
Taylor, N.J. 100
Taylor, Pearl 355
Taylor, Rebecca 229
Taylor, R.H. 147,232
Taylor, Samuel 317
Taylor, Sarah 160,208
Taylor, Sarah C. 232

Taylor, Steven 273
Taylor, Sylvany 9
Taylor, S.T. 256,270
Taylor, Tilarime 321
Taylor, Wiley E. 321
Taylor, W.E. (Mrs) 321
Teals, Francis 136
Terry, Betty J. 304
Testament, Norma 2
Tester, Alex 38,294
Tester, Alzenia 263
Tester, Amanda 7
Tester, Andrew J. 348
Tester, Callie 222
Tester, Carl 212
Tester, Catherine 151,258
  294,354 <
Tester, Christopher C.344
  355 <
Tester, Claude 276
Tester, Clay 360
Tester, Clery 294
Tester, Clyde 341
Tester, Columbus 276
Tester, Connie 74
Tester, C.E. 145,156,180
Tester, Daty 270
Tester, David 222
Tester, David A. 265
Tester, David Harson 170
Tester, Duff 153
Tester, Duffie 122,135
Tester, Eada 50
Tester, Elbert 64
Tester, Elizabeth 118,360
Tester, Ella 265
Tester, Ellen 81
Tester, Eugene Loyd 355
Tester, Evaline 253
Tester, Fonzo 170
Tester, Henry 360
Tester, Henry W. 72
Tester, Infant 212,257
  352 <
Tester, Jake 344
Tester, James 344,362
Tester, John 197
Tester, John M. 72,360

Tester, Joseph D. 64
Tester, J.L. 129
Tester, J.M. 118,229
Tester, Lon 265
Tester, Lottie 111
Tester, Louies 132
Tester, Luther M. 265
Tester, Mandie 95
Tester, Martha J. 344
Tester, Marthie 96
Tester, Martin 95
Tester, Mary 32,65,248
277 <
Tester, Mathie 90
Tester, Milburn 362
Tester, Millard 265
Tester, Millard F. 180
Tester, Mina 276
Tester, Myrtle 54
Tester, Nancy 129,195
Tester, Nathaniel 45
Tester, Nathaniel 45,50
72,129,258 <
Tester, Nelia F. 355
Tester, N.C. 37,94,170
Tester, N.T. 45
Tester, Pearl 44
Tester, Polly 132
Tester, Richard 118,229
Tester, Richard R. 38
Tester, Robert 135
Tester, Robert Alex 362
Tester, Robert A. 322
Tester, Robert C. 52
Tester, Robert D. 52,258
265 <
Tester, Robin 170
Tester, Roby 135
Tester, Roy 72
Tester, Ruth M. 327
Tester, R. (Mrs) 145
Tester, R.S. 348
Tester, Sallie 45
Tester, Sarafina 49,348
Tester, Sarah F. 89
Tester, Sarah J. 132
Tester, Stacy 78
Tester, Stephen M. 72

Tester, Susan 5,172
Tester, Susanah 265
Tester, Susanna 52
Tester, Susie 137
Tester, S.M. 50,52
Tester, Tennessee 59,74
78 <
Tester, T.N. 102
Tester, T.S. 322
Tester, T.T. 149
Tester, U.G. 355
Tester, Valter F. 170
Tester, Vergie 360
Tester, Virtie 134,149
Tester, Vonnie L. 352
Tester, Walter 257
Tester, William 78,322
Tester, William Mack 276
Tester, William M. 180
Tester, W.J. 94
Tester, ... 83
Testerman, Linda 103
Thomas, Alfred 145,157
Thomas, Amanda 51
Thomas, Amanda R. 72
Thomas, America 284
Thomas, Ancie 356
Thomas, Annie 255
Thomas, Austin 255
Thomas, A.A. 72,115
Thomas, A.B. 152
Thomas, Belle 157
Thomas, B.R. 225,255,275
Thomas, Caroline 279
Thomas, Charlie 263
Thomas, Clyde 275
Thomas, David 247
Thomas, Effie 254
Thomas, Elizabeth 229,338
Thomas, Emma 317
Thomas, Ezekiel 51,79
Thomas, Fannie 259
Thomas, Frank 24,103
Thomas, Fred J. 301
Thomas, George 157,165
Thomas, Henry 136
Thomas, Hesekat 194
Thomas, Howard 165

Thomas, Jack	194,263	Tilley, Jones	225
Thomas, James	220	Tilley, J.C.	83
Thomas, James Edgar	103	Tilley, J.H.	199
Thomas, James Floyd	247	Tilley, Martha	199
Thomas, James W.	360	Tilley, Roscoe	6
Thomas, Jane	247	Tilley, Samuel	199
Thomas, Jennie	224	Tilley, Susah	296
Thomas, Joe	194	Tilley, Tice	221
Thomas, John	223,356	Tilley, Verna Kate	6
Thomas, Joseph	159	Tilley, William C.	83
Thomas, Kite	228	Tilley, ...	276
Thomas, Lanners	124	Tiney, Phillip	252
Thomas, Louisa	365	Tipton, ...	242
Thomas, Lundy	220	Toliver, Fred	45
Thomas, L.F.	207	Toliver, Infant	74
Thomas, Maggie	112,223	Toliver, Martin A.	74
Thomas, Martha	293	Toliver, M.A.	45
Thomas, Martha C.	2	Tome, Adaline	353
Thomas, Mary Ann	360	Tounson, Sarah	224
Thomas, Mary Lois	275	Townsend, Alison	67
Thomas, Nancy	194	Townsend, J.B.	67
Thomas, Polly Geneva	225	Treadway, Andy	306
Thomas, Reainer	356	Treadway, Becky	315
Thomas, Richard	105	Treadway, Caroline	329
Thomas, Robert	152,279	Treadway, Elbert	87
Thomas, Roy D.	247	Treadway, Ella	41
Thomas, Sallie	34	Treadway, John	63
Thomas, Sam K.	356	Treadway, John Cisco	306
Thomas, Sidney	351	Treadway, Mary	116,266
Thomas, Sidney J.	51	Treadway, Mary Ann	200
Thomas, Tice	224	Treadway, Sallie	306
Thomas, T.C.	302	Tribbett, Bettie	294
Thomas, Virginia B.	152	Tribbett, Soloman R.	294
Thompson, Adeline	286	Tribble, Bettie	311
Thompson, Infant	202	Tribble, Rebecca	204
Thompson, Jessie D.	202	Tribel, Susan	281
Thompson, Julie	238,366	Tribett, Ida	146
Thompson, Laura	165	Triffic, Shela	283
Thompson, Mary Jane	232	Triplet, John	38
Thompson, Melinda	317	Triplet, Nancy	51
Thompson, Zilpha	78	Triplett, Addie	61
Thomsa, Frank	302	Triplett, Birthia	26
Tiebel, Rebecca	26	Triplett, Eva	58
Tilley, Alvin	257,296	Triplett, George	116,224
Tilley, Barbie	27	Triplett, Glenn	291
Tilley, Goldie	335	Triplett, Hattie H.	224
Tilley, Hamilton	83	Triplett, James A.	291
Tilley, Jonas	221	Triplett, James Millen	38

Triplett, Jasper 58
Triplett, John 76,79,121
353 <
Triplett, John, Jr. 154
Triplett, John L. 79,119
Triplett, John Reuben 92
Triplett, John T. 154
Triplett, J.F. 302,328
Triplett, J.L. 119
Triplett, Lizzie M. 76
Triplett, Maria F. 302
Triplett, Martha S. 103
Triplett, Mary 116,328
Triplett, Mary Jane 1
Triplett, Mattie 256
Triplett, Maud 119
Triplett, Oma 121
Triplett, Oscar 58
Triplett, Thomas T. 328
Triplett, Tol 61
Triplett, Toliver 115
Triplett, William 115
Trivett, Alice 49
Trivett, Bruce 185
Trivett, Charles 185
Trivett, Elizabeth 114
Trivett, Finley 274
Trivett, Helen 274
Trivett, Infant 341
Trivett, Inos 237
Trivett, John 184,193 341
Trivett, John F. 331
Trivett, John R. 331
Trivett, Joshua 193
Trivett, Lizzie 193
Trivett, Maggie Anna 184
Trivett, Mary 114,238
Trivett, Nola 239
Trivett, Ona 298
Trivett, Ritta 274
Trivett, Robert D. 331
Trivett, Sarah E. 114
Trivett, Sis 205
Trivett, Soloman 114
Trivett, William E. 204
Trivette, Julia 333
Truett, Virginia 246
Tster, Barbara Sue 341

Tucker, Harrison 303
Tucker, Holly 338
Tucker, James 338
Tucker, Lessie 305
Tucker, L.L. 51
Tucker, ... 303
Tulburt, Ester V. 309
Turbiefield, Gurnie 346
Turley, Mattie Peck 119
Turner, Ada 327
Turner, Marria 327
Turner, Murphey 327
Turner, Samuel R.A. 327
Turnmire, Hugh 221,257
Turnmire, Nora 257
Turnmire, Sallie 243
Turnmire, William 221
Tyree, Joe 321
Underwood, Sarah Jane 77
Underwood, Thomas 77
Valentine, Clyde 108
Valentine, Frank 108
Valentine, James A. 276
Valentine, John F. 220
Valentine, Ollie 276
Vance, Fannie 327
Vance, John 263,299
Vance, Robert 263
Vandike, Infant 22
Vannoy, John 93
Vannoy, John W. 363
Vannoy, J.W. 87,265
Vannoy, Robert 304
Vannoy, R.D. 122
Vannoy, R.G. 60,160,243
Vannoy, Wanda Lou 363
Vanover, Cintha 200
Vanover, Clara 268
Vanover, Elsie 209
Vanover, Elsie 218,324
366,367 <
Vanover, Grant 362
Vanover, Ira 358
Vanover, Nancy 245
Vanover, Olamae 268
Vanover, Opel Drexie 241
Vanover, Richard 62
Vanover, Roby 268

Vanover, Roy 293
Vanover, Verna E. 358
Vanover, Victoria 84,293
Vanoy, Celia 133
Vanoy, Ida 57
Vanoy, J.W. 225
Vaughan, Victoria M. 101
Vaught, Alvin 211,253
Vaught, Callie 23
Vaught, Calliona 337
Vaught, Christina 173
Vaught, Daisy 253
Vaught, David 31
Vaught, David H. 94,321
Vaught, David S. 49,125
Vaught, George 271
Vaught, Hattie 125
Vaught, Infant 90
Vaught, Jacob Smith 337
Vaught, Jessie 292
Vaught, Joda M. 41
Vaught, Joe 351
Vaught, John Andrew 271
Vaught, John B. 143
Vaught, John H. 40,41,132
    193,351 <
Vaught, John S. 70
Vaught, John S. 70,143
    362 <
Vaught, Joseph L. 337
Vaught, Julia Eveline 321
Vaught, J.A. 188
Vaught, J.B. 49
Vaught, J.H. 40,351
Vaught, J.M. 32
Vaught, J.R. 321
Vaught, J.W. (Dr) 58
Vaught, Lottie 336
Vaught, Louise 356
Vaught, Mary 90,185,223
    254,266,295,320 <
Vaught, May C. 282
Vaught, Mertell C. 188
Vaught, Poly 149
Vaught, Rachel 78
Vaught, Ray 271
Vaught, Robert 193
Vaught, Rosco 90

Vaught, Roscoe 94
Vaught, Sallie A. 44
Vaught, Sarah 132
Vaught, Walter B. 40
Vaught, W.W. 125,143
Venable, Joseph 145
Venable, Lucinda 143,234
    253 <
Venable, Sarah E. 104
Venable, ... 63
Vendiable, Matilda 320
Venerable, Polly 137
Venerable, Ruthie R. 17
Venerable, Sara 137
Venerable, William 137
Veney, Charles Robert 106
Veney, Robert 106
Veniable, Tilda 335
Vermillion, O.M. (Mrs)266
Vestal, Clyde 44
Vestal, Wade 44
Viall, Elmer 353
Vincel, Mary 186
Vines, Grover C. 179
Vines, Margaret 245
Vines, Randal E. 179
Vines, Rebecca 246,337
Vines, William 200
Vines, ... 115
Viney, R.B. 35
VonCannan, A.D. 275
VonCannan, Louis 275
VonCannan, Mary 275
V..., Rebecca 154
Waddell, A.G. 216
Waddell, W.H. 216
Waddle, S.C. 25
Wade, America 185
Wagner, Adam Bynum 352
Wagner, Alexander 283
Wagner, Annie 327
Wagner, Arthur 187
Wagner, A.B. 111,187,351
Wagner, Becky 109
Wagner, Bessie 258
Wagner, Callie 340
Wagner, Catherine 30,71
    144,191,221 <

Wagner, Celia 174
Wagner, Charles M. 139
Wagner, Clyde M. 268
Wagner, Crumley H. 108
Wagner, Cyaina 301
Wagner, C.M. 255
Wagner, Dan 349
Wagner, Daniel 272,318
   318,352 <
Wagner, David F. 272
Wagner, Dayton C. 268
Wagner, D.B. 355
Wagner, D.E. 134
Wagner, D.M. 1
Wagner, Edith Opal 306
Wagner, Elbert 207
Wagner, Elizabeth 183
Wagner, Elizabeth V. 134
Wagner, Eula 223
Wagner, E.D. 181,355
Wagner, Fronia 228
Wagner, Gurney F. 327
Wagner, Infant 99
Wagner, I.L. 283
Wagner, James S. 228
Wagner, Jensie Louise 303
Wagner, Joe 254,295
Wagner, John 173
Wagner, Joseph 152,223
Wagner, Joseph Arthur 187
Wagner, Joseph J. 223
Wagner, J.D. 109,351,352
Wagner, J.H. 3
Wagner, J.M. 44
Wagner, Katy 44
Wagner, Lafayet 243
Wagner, Laura 258
Wagner, Lee 295,301
Wagner, Lee Roy 287
Wagner, Lee R. 331
Wagner, Lillie 48,248,298
Wagner, Lily 264
Wagner, Lutitia 182
Wagner, L.M. (Mrs) 318
Wagner, Maggie 38,77
Wagner, Margaret 254
Wagner, Margaret Ida 318
Wagner, Martha 63,170,329

Wagner, Mary 23
Wagner, Mary E. 301
Wagner, Mary L. 343
Wagner, Mary Vaught 107
Wagner, Mathias 107
Wagner, May MacDonald 335
Wagner, Myrtle 35
Wagner, M.M. 228,255
Wagner, M.R. 99
Wagner, Nancy 111,152,173
   195,248,351 <
Wagner, Nancy Naome 283
Wagner, Naoma 108
Wagner, Nat 303
Wagner, Nathaniel 264
Wagner, Nathaniel T. 200
   264,267 <
Wagner, Nell 292
Wagner, Nellie Jane 287
Wagner, Nellie King 139
Wagner, Neome 243
Wagner, Nick G. 295
Wagner, Noah 87,185,362
Wagner, Noah Jacob 255
Wagner, Polly 183,223
Wagner, Rachel 49,253
Wagner, Rebecca 155
Wagner, R.M. 329
Wagner, Sabra 146
Wagner, Sarah 356
Wagner, Tallulah 267
Wagner, Tedia 181
Wagner, Thomas L. 200
Wagner, Tice 185
Wagner, Tild 327
Wagner, Till 335,343
Wagner, Vaughan 306
Wagner, V.K. 347,352
Wagner, Walter 87
Wagner, Winnie 352
Wagner, Winnie Dunn 351
Wagner, W.E. 318
Wagner, ... 108
Wagoner, Finnie 257
Walen, Elizabeth 46
Walker, Albert 147
Walker, Annis 183
Walker, Brownlow 260,263

473

Walker, Buleah	292	Walker, Sarah J.	49,68
Walker, Calvin	166	Walker, Sylvia	332
Walker, Charlotte	166	Walker, William	291
Walker, Colonel T.	119	Walker, William H.	56
Walker, Cora	56	Walker, William R.	72
Walker, C.C.	219	Walker, W.B.	243
Walker, C.H.	336	Walker, W.B., Jr.	243
Walker, Dana M.	25	Walker, W.F. (Mrs)	186
Walker, Don C.	246	Walker, W.G.	275
Walker, Dottie	265	Walker, W.M.	278
Walker, Earl	72	Walker, W.R.	275
Walker, Ella	224	Walker, W.T.	182,291
Walker, Ellen	120	Walker, Yonce	166
Walker, George	269,320	Wall, Wilson	121
Walker, George J.	222	Wallace, Abraham L.	36
Walker, Grace	331	Wallace, Alex 259,327,343
Walker, G.C.	189,216	Wallace, Alexander	200
Walker, Herbert	260	318	<
Walker, Hobert	263	Wallace, Asa	33
Walker, Infant	38	Wallace, Bruce C.	150
Walker, James Alfred	219	Wallace, Carl Forrest 121
Walker, James Calvin	291	Wallace, Caroline	36
Walker, John 125,130,132	Wallace, C.L.	128
166,189,339	<	Wallace, Dora	130
Walker, John C.	93,119	Wallace, Drewery	200
Walker, John G.	189	Wallace, Drewry	81,163
Walker, John Smith	55	Wallace, D.	47
Walker, John Yancy C.	35	Wallace, Elmina	289
Walker, Judge	35	Wallace, Emmit	35
Walker, Julious	38	Wallace, Engleton	40
Walker, Junior B.	278	Wallace, Franklin L.	199
Walker, J.C. 55,166,201	Wallace, George W. 81,199
275	<	289	<
Walker, Lora May	93	Wallace, Grace	133
Walker, Lynie Maxie	336	Wallace, Gracie	33
Walker, L.V.	56	Wallace, Holly	33
Walker, Maggie	132	Wallace, James	88
Walker, Mamie A.	182,190	Wallace, James H.	36
Walker, Martha	73,301	Wallace, James I.	88
Walker, Martitia	275	Wallace, James M.	289
Walker, Mary	61,270	Wallace, Jane	10,133
Walker, Mary E.	201	Wallace, John H.	47
Walker, Mary Matilda	216	Wallace, John I.	141
Walker, O.C.	275	Wallace, Jordan	129,130
Walker, Rebecca	189,212	241,259,343	<
Walker, Sabra	92,132	Wallace, Joseph	48
Walker, Sarah	157	Wallace, J.H.	350
Walker, Sarah E.	266	Wallace, J.M.	36

Wallace, Lena   318
Wallace, Lillie   78
Wallace, Lillie   78,102
       154,211   <
Wallace, Lola   343
Wallace, Lon   33
Wallace, Luther Blan   33
Wallace, Mack   259
Wallace, Marion   141
Wallace, Nancy   327
Wallace, Nancy Emaline241
Wallace, Nettie   162
Wallace, Nora   129
Wallace, Ora M.   48
Wallace, Polly   132,145
Wallace, Ray   132
Wallace, Rebecca W.   350
Wallace, Roby   48,145,200
        293   <
Wallace, Roby A.   132,134
Wallace, Rosa   263
Wallace, Rosevelt   346
Wallace, Rosevelt, Jr.346
Wallace, Russell   289
Wallace, Stacy   121,142
Wallace, Thelma   133
Wallace, Verna M.   134
Wallace, Wade   88
Wallace, Walter   133
Wallace, William Dana 142
Wallace, William H.   133
Wallace, William S.   351
Wallace, W.W.   81
Waller. M.E.   192
Walser, Ralph   14
Walsh, Andrew   57
Walsh, Annei Chelcy   15
Walsh, Bettie   9
Walsh, Cevla   137
Walsh, Dennis   11
Walsh, Eugene   311
Walsh, Frank   34
Walsh, F.M.   57
Walsh, George   33
Walsh, G.J.   40
Walsh, H.A.   8
Walsh, Inez   15
Walsh, James K.   62

Walsh, John   311
Walsh, John Lee   281
Walsh, J.N.O.   57
Walsh, Kizzie   104
Walsh, Luanie   16
Walsh, Mary Pearl   353
Walsh, Minnie J.   316
Walsh, N. Gladys   62
Walsh, Ralph Haynes   355
Walsh, Ray Odell   54
Walsh, Robert   141
Walsh, Robert P.   335
Walsh, Roby F.   42,54
Walsh, Roderick   141
Walsh, Roderick B.   355
Walsh, Rose   311
Walsh, R.P.   34
Walsh, Thomas   281,311
Walsh, Thomas J.   42,141
Walsh, T.J.   80
Walsh, Will   353
Walsh, W.A.   139,281,335
Walsh, W.G.   316
Walten, ...   95
Walters, Nancy   75,208
Waltyer, Donnie   135
Ward, Alex   135
Ward, Alexander   145
Ward, Alice Wagner   349
Ward, Asa   82
Ward, Audie   5
Ward, Charles   250
Ward, Charles F.   175
Ward, Cordelia   94
Ward, C.R.   214
Ward, Daniel   284
Ward, Dolf   145
Ward, D.A.   145
Ward, D.C.   97
Ward, Edith Price   319
Ward, Elizabeth   206
Ward, Ellen   120,140,143
Ward, Elsie   308
Ward, Floid T.   86
Ward, Frank   319
Ward, Ham   222
Ward, Hamilton   315,335
Ward, Hurd   298

Ward, Infant	48,56,82		Ward, Willard	292
Ward, Isaac	284		Ward, William H.	281
Ward, Ivory Hugh	148		Ward, Zena	207
Ward, James	37,56,214,366		Warden, Jessie	296
Ward, James Asa	48		Waren, Callie P.	256
Ward, James Edward	78		Warler, W.R.	42
Ward, James F.	238		Warnn, Ella	114
Ward, Janie	212		Warren, Clara	277
Ward, Joe	127		Warren, Cornelius	229,338
Ward, John	112,262		Warren, Don	235
Ward, John F.	349,366		Warren, Edgar	327
Ward, John I.	107		Warren, Ella	306
Ward, John T.	262		Warren, Eugene Richard	246
Ward, Joseph Warren	232		Warren, Hannah C.A.	332
Ward, J.L.	125,154		Warren, H.	225
Ward, Laney	145		Warren, H.C.	229
Ward, Laura	281,362		Warren, H.K.	338
Ward, Laura C.	52		Warren, Ida O.	316
Ward, Liane Victoria	37		Warren, James Woodard	224
Ward, Lillie	163,205,272		Warren, Jamima Reece	338
286	<		Warren, Jim	224
Ward, Maggie	141		Warren, Joseph	162
Ward, Margaret	44		Warren, Landon	162
Ward, Mary A.	160		Warren, Lizzie	159
Ward, Mattie	255,284		Warren, Margaret	238
Ward, Maude	321		Warren, Martha	338
Ward, May	253		Warren, Mary Malinda	229
Ward, Milton P.	135		Warren, Myrtle	351
Ward, Missouri	112		Warren, Nelia	227
Ward, Nancy	70,188		Warren, Roby	299,332
Ward, Nannie	135		Warren, Rosa Lee	327
Ward, Noah	86		Warren, Ruby	332
Ward, N.G.	86,214		Warren, Sarah	67
Ward, Ora Lee	250		Warren, Thomas	246,299
Ward, Parrie	253		Warren, Van Della	235
Ward, Paul	292		Warren, Virginia	299
Ward, Rebecca	7,125		Warren, William M.	338
Ward, Reeves	349		Waters, Amanda	124
Ward, Roby	78		Waters, Avery	30
Ward, Sally	289		Waters, Clint	122,262,286
Ward, Selmar	175		Waters, Earl F.	262
Ward, Sophonia	349		Waters, Francis	260
Ward, Tapley	148		Waters, Francis E.	107
Ward, Thomas	145		Waters, James Hubert	267
Ward, T.P.	54		Waters, John Phillip	78
Ward, T.W.	176		Waters, John P.	216
Ward, Vernia	298		Waters, William	78
Ward, Warren Lee	232		Waters, William C.	267

Waters, W.R.	333	Welch, Kizzie	270
Watkins, Lillie	32	Wells, Isabelle	121
Watson, Albert	325	Wells, Oma	119
Watson, Albert Lewis	325	Wells, Robert	121
Watson, Bessie	182,354	West, Betsy	54
Watson, Cynthia	126	West, Deliah	127
Watson, Dean	205	West, Dililah	178
Watson, Doxie Reece	205	West, Margaret	105
Watson, Elbert W.	92,230	West, Nancy	364
Watson, Eliza	322	West, Peggy	103
Watson, Fannie A.	19	West, Riley	54,100
Watson, Flo..	29	West, ...	47
Watson, Horton	12	Whaley, Abraham	38
Watson, John	36	Wheatley, Jim	272
Watson, Kitty	224	Whitaker, David	287
Watson, Lonie	190	White, A.T.	257
Watson, Marie	205	White, Ben	75
Watson, Marth	118	White, Clarence	274
Watson, Martha	344	White, Clate	169
Watson, Mary A.	58	White, David O.	274
Watson, N.V.	92	White, Dick	352
Watson, Pink	92	White, Eddie May	298
Watson, Russell	20	White, Elizabeth	169
Watson, Sarah	227	White, Florence	193
Watson, Susan E.	45	White, Gillie	328
Watson, Thomas	122	White, Janis	82
Watson, Thomas G.	224	White, Jessie R.	35
Watson, Thomas R.	322	White, Martha C.	44
Watson, T.S.	25	White, Robert	257
Watson, Vanley	182	White, Rosie	291
Watson, Vilva Ruth	122	White, Ruby	55
Watson, Volney	190	White, Thomas J.	352
Watson, William	36,43,44	White, Thomas Odell	257
227	<	White, Tom (Mrs)	65
Watson, ...	44,339	White, T.	13
Watts, Bettie Gene	306	White, T.G.	193
Watts, Bob	306	White, Wash	226
Waugh, Catherine E.	305	Whitehead, Aby	252
Waugh, Eck	305	Whitehead, Carson	172,252
Waugh, H.	4	Whitehead, Hubert L.	172
Waugh, Mattie	327	Whitehead, James	156
Wayman, Carrie L.	3	Whitehead, Jane	122,346
Weaver, C.L.	314	Whitehead, Thomas	88
Weaver, Houn L.	314	Whitehead, Zena	164
Weaver, John	314	Widby, Anna	46
Weaver, Sallie Jane	314	Widby, Annie	72
Weaver, Susan	309	Widby, Infant	159
Welch, Ida Lucille	308	Widby, Mary	115

Widby, Norman	261	
Widby, Olie	163	
Widby, Sam	161,163	
Widby, Samuel	144,145,159	
Widby, Viola Lee May	144	
Widby, Viola Parks	317	
Widener, Bernice	103	
Widener, Bill	334	
Widener, Cebert	301	
Widener, K.K. (Mrs)	365	
Widener, Mina	289	
Widener, Samuel A.	285	
Widener, Silas T.	103	
Widener, Walter W.	285	
Widley, S.W.	79	
Widly, S.W.	185	
Widner, Sarah M.	127	
Widner, William Lester	14	
Widner, W.W.	44	
Wilcox, Alvin	68	
Wilcox, C.C.	118	
Wilcox, Edna May	118	
Wilcox, Emma	198	
Wilcox, James	69	
Wilcox, John D.	57	
Wilcox, J.D.	69	
Wilcox, Mark	49	
Wilcox, Mary	69,263,299	
Wilcox, Ramin L.	49	
Wilcox, Rebecca	69,110	
Wilcox, William	68,110	
Wilcox, W.M.	57,198	
Wiley, Ellen Stout	81	
Wiley, Stanel	81	
Wilhams, Joe	311	
Wilhams, Susan	311	
Wilhams, William	311	
Wilkerson, James Elic	142	
Wilkerson, Margaret	217	
Wilkerson, Mark	142	
Wilkins, Amanda	178	
Willard, Juley	237	
Willen, Cliff	288	
Willen, Flossie	100,358	
Willen, Irine May	147	
Willen, Jacob	16	
Willen, Jane	288	
Willen, Mary	147	
Willen, Minnie	144	
Willen, Ollie Jones	365	
Willen, Ray	365	
Willen, Sarah	356	
Willen, Sarah A.	122	
Willen, Thomas	16,288	
Willen, Thomas H.	288	
Willen, T.H.	144	
Willen, W.A.	147	
Williams, Arley	203	
Williams, Bainer	314	
Williams, Betty	177	
Williams, Canada Mod	313	
Williams, Carrie May	350	
Williams, Clyde	226,264	
349,350	<	
Williams, Ethel	368	
Williams, Ezra Mae	301	
Williams, Jacob	189	
Williams, James	126	
Williams, Joe	209	
Williams, Joseph	19	
Williams, Julia A.	230	
Williams, Julie	287	
Williams, J.R.	340	
Williams, Laura A.	239	
Williams, Laura E.	198	
Williams, Lillie	79	
Williams, Mabel	314	
Williams, Maxwell D.	126	
Williams, M.D. (Mrs)	126	
Williams, Nancy	189	
Williams, Nellie Gray	198	
Williams, Okra	301	
Williams, Phillis	189	
Williams, Pollie	139	
Williams, Rose B.	198	
Williams, Roy Butler	368	
Williams, Rufus	313	
Williams, Runer	368	
Williams, Sallie E.	264	
Williams, Stephen	162,209	
Williams, Susan	162,166	
Williams, T.H.	203	
Williams, William A.	349	
Williams, William F.	226	
Williams, W.A.	226	
Williams, W.F.	35,121,198	

Williams, W.H.   162
Willian, William   131
Willin, Blanche   248
Willin, Clarence   248
Willin, Clifford   215,248
Willin, C.O.   175
Willin, Emes O.   162
Willin, Emmes   162
Willin, Geeter   64
Willin, George   263
Willin, Ivan   231
Willin, Luther   194
Willin, Lyda Ann   175
Willin, Nella May   263
Willin, Sarah   168
Willin, Thomas   194,231
Willin, William   168
Willin, William W.   215
Willin, W.A.   64
Willis, Rachel   147
Wills, Ada   268
Wills, Baxter G.   357
Wills, Bertha Ganaway   77
Wills, Callie   249
Wills, David   292
Wills, David W.   115,277
Wills, Dayton Parker   357
Wills, Francis,   258
Wills, Gladys Ward   366
Wills, Henry B.   258
Wills, H.B.   157
Wills, H.J.D.   176,231,268
   282   <
Wills, Iva D.   273
Wills, James   97
Wills, James H.   359
Wills, James L.   319
Wills, James Newton   106
Wills, James P.   277
Wills, Jennie McGuin   176
Wills, John   67,319
Wills, John H.   115
Wills, J.P.   115
Wills, Karl   169,170,267
Wills, Lizzie Genette   9
Wills, Lucy L.   281
Wills, Macon Randolph   231
Wills, Macon R.   282

Wills, Martha   94
Wills, Mary   41,62,74
Wills, Mattie C.   267
Wills, Memphis   234,260
   295   <
Wills, M.E.   91,126
Wills, M.R.   118
Wills, Nat T.   281
Wills, Nat (Mrs)   356
Wills, Norman Russell   267
Wills, Pat   245
Wills, Peter Dick   106,267
   333   <
Wills, Peter W.   77
Wills, Polly   63,280
Wills, P.D.   231
Wills, Rachel Greer   319
Wills, Robert Grant   282
Wills, Roby   349
Wills, Russel B.   258
Wills, Russell   281
Wills, Russell B.   332
Wills, Sallie   69,258
Wills, Samuel P.   67
Wills, Sophie S.   106
Wills, Susan   158,219,259
   353   <
Wills, S. Roretta   142
Wills, T.A.   69
Wills, Vic (Mrs)   345
Wilosn, Alex   204
Wilson, Abraham   111,331
Wilson, Albert   325
Wilson, Alexander   119,172
Wilson, Alford   37
Wilson, Alfred J.   226
Wilson, Alic   109
Wilson, America   137
Wilson, Andrew J.   250
Wilson, Andrew S.   316
Wilson, Ann   316
Wilson, Anna   121,196
Wilson, Annie   183,305
Wilson, Annie Maud   31
Wilson, Archie   361
Wilson, A.J.   223
Wilson, Bessie E.   291
Wilson, Betsy   272

Wilson, Bettie A.	140
Wilson, Blain Evert	94
Wilson, Charles E.	13
Wilson, Clara	160,223
Wilson, Clint	219,251
Wilson, Crawford	149
Wilson, C.C.	36,118
Wilson, Dan	273
Wilson, Daniel	85
Wilson, Dany	90
Wilson, David	270
Wilson, D.F.	276
Wilson, D.M.	350
Wilson, D.W.	273
Wilson, Earl	129,280
Wilson, Ed	143
Wilson, Ed C.	143
Wilson, Ed (Mrs)	323
Wilson, Edgar	129,148
Wilson, Edward G.	172
Wilson, Elijah	267
Wilson, Eliza	273
Wilson, Elizabeth	37
Wilson, Elizabeth	37,108
138,195,202,235,274<	
Wilson, Ella	326
Wilson, Ellen	88,141,165
241	<
Wilson, Ellen Annie	280
Wilson, Eller	265
Wilson, Elsie Mae	3
Wilson, Elvy Grace	101
Wilson, Emma	332,348
Wilson, Emma B.	300
Wilson, Emmett	31,196
Wilson, Eugene Kent	219
Wilson, E.A.	297
Wilson, E...	132
Wilson, Fannie M.	3
Wilson, Gladys	227
Wilson, Hattie	181
Wilson, Hesekiah	177,183
Wilson, Hezakiah	47,100
Wilson, Hezekiah	90,174
Wilson, Hilda	158
Wilson, Hytie Bell	97
Wilson, H.C.	162
Wilson, Ida May	143

Wilson, Ida Wills	169
Wilson, Infant	28,31,85
121,148,157,184	<
Wilson, Isacarah	68
Wilson, I.E.	203
Wilson, Jacob	76,168
Wilson, James	151,157,168
Wilson, James Billie	323
Wilson, James G.	143
Wilson, James J.	181
Wilson, Jane	47
Wilson, Jasper Parked	97
Wilson, Jennie	303
Wilson, Jessie J.	209
Wilson, Joe	143,268,316
Wilson, Joe Justin	303
Wilson, Joe Lincoln	303
Wilson, John	152,288,300
Wilson, John A.	68,179
Wilson, John Hardy	20
Wilson, John K.	198,297
Wilson, John Wesley	344
Wilson, John W.	256
Wilson, Joseph	2,63,348
Wilson, Josie	154
Wilson, Julia	250
Wilson, Justin Greer	43
Wilson, J.C.	273
Wilson, J.G.	247
Wilson, J.K.	139
Wilson, J.K. (Mrs)	242
Wilson, J.S.	68
Wilson, J.T.	273
Wilson, J.W.	174
Wilson, Kelly	184
Wilson, Kemp	198
Wilson, Latta	41
Wilson, Lemuel	76
Wilson, Lewis	288
Wilson, Lillie	223
Wilson, Linda	344
Wilson, Liza	273
Wilson, Louis	151
Wilson, Mack	226
Wilson, Maggie	56,133
Wilson, Malinda	145
Wilson, Malissie	11
Wilson, Margaret	213

Wilson, Margie 102
Wilson, Martha 41,335
Wilson, Marvin 293
Wilson, Marvin S. 101,227
Wilson, Mary E. 20,357
Wilson, Mary Virginia 299
Wilson, Ma... 148
Wilson, Mollie 302
Wilson, M.E. 96
Wilson, M.E. 287
Wilson, Nancy 80,112,262
Wilson, Nannie 283
Wilson, Newt 229
Wilson, Nora 106
Wilson, N.M. 48
Wilson, Ollie 136,262
281,290 <
Wilson, Oscar Burt 331
Wilson, Oskar A. 59
Wilson, O.H. 348
Wilson, Pearl C. 2
Wilson, Peggy 159
Wilson, Phoebe 297
Wilson, Rachel 39
Wilson, Ray S. 149
Wilson, Rebecca 60,63
110,361 <
Wilson, Rhubin 183
Wilson, Richard 192
Wilson, Richard L. 77,143
297 <
Wilson, Rit 44
Wilson, Robert 97
Wilson, Robert D. 77,131
Wilson, Roby 293
Wilson, Roy D. 108
Wilson, R.S. 149
Wilson, Sallie 197
Wilson, Sam 157
Wilson, Samuel 151
Wilson, Sarah 59,318
Wilson, Sarah Jane 362
Wilson, Sarah J. 21
Wilson, Shelton 131,299
Wilson, Susie 327
Wilson, Tyler 121
Wilson, Victor V. 13
Wilson, Virginia L. 198

Wilson, Wheeler 169
Wilson, Will 123
Wilson, William 59,60
76,94,110,111,137 <
172,227,276,283,326<
350 <
Wilson, William A. 283
Wilson, William C. 250
Wilson, William D. 226
Wilson, William Stacy 348
Wilson, Willie 251
Wilson, Winnie C. 229
Wilson, W.L. 331
Wilson, W.M. 67,323,361
Wilson, W.S. 279
Wilson, Zederic 43,97
Wilson, ... 134,179,270
Winebarger, Clara 181
Winebarger, Lula 343
Winscott, Mary Jane 326
Winston, Nancy 318
Winter, Infant 55
Winter, John R. 84
Winters, Bonnie L. 47
Winters, Edd 174
Winters, Edward M. 58
Winters, George W. 48
Winters, Henry Evert 73
Winters, Infant 58,159
174,185 <
Winters, John 47,73,174
Winters, John Paul 84
Winters, John R. 185,328
Winters, Lanie Bruce 174
Winters, Laura M. 155
Winters, Mae 252
Winters, Martin 157
Winters, Martin Edd 159
Winters, Mary Alice 178
Winters, Mary Belle 358
Winters, Mary M. 48
Winters, May 304
Winters, Ollie C. 311
Winters, Wilham 304
Winters, William 157
Winters, William H. 48
Winters, William V. 47,55
252 <

481

Winters, W.M.	48	Woodard, Isaac	340
Winters, W.V.	311	Woodard, Jane	168
Wishon, Crittie May	339	Woodard, Jeremiah	15
Wishon, William	202	Woodard, Jerry	364
Wison, J.A. (Mrs)	250	Woodard, Lillie	287
Wold, Melvin E.	83	Woodard, Lucil	148
Wolf, Caroline	245	Woodard, Maggie	289,290
Wolf, Dan C.	291	Woodard, McKinley	148
Wolf, James Kent	291	Woodard, Newt	319
Wolf, Lola	156	Woodard, Newton	317
Wolf, Lorane	156	Woodard, Noah	319
Wolf, T.	83	Woodard, O. Honest	319
Wolf, Willey	5	Woodby, Clara Earl	355
Wolfe, Bertha	279	Woodley, Infant	106
Wolfe, Nancy Emily	298	Woodley, Sam	106
Wolfe, W.M.	308	Woodring, Daniel	216
Wood, Bartly	295	Woodring, Nancy	93
Wood, Barton	226	Woodruff, Mary	146
Wood, Cordelia	320	Woods, Aisie	39
Wood, Earl	361	Woods, Della	333
Wood, Henry	361	Woods, Ferbe	307
Wood, James K.	226	Woods, Jennie	152
Wood, John W.	315	Woods, Thomas	227
Wood, Mattie	211	Woodsay, Fannie	165
Wood, Mollie	226	Woody, Nancy	43
Wood, Richard	157,304	Worland, Orinda	331
Wood, Richard Andy	361	Worley, Elias	296
Wood, R. Earl	361	Worley, E.H.	336
Wood, R.W. (Mrs)	312	Worley, Infant	22
Wood, Sam	141,320	Worley, Margaret	365
Wood, Samuel I.	361	Worley, Thomas E.	332
Wood, S.S.	320,361	Worley, Thomas (Mrs)	332
Wood, William	4	Worley, Tom P.	336
Wood, W.B.	315	Worley, Tullah	336
Woodard, Alex	338	Worley, Vinia	361
Woodard, Alexander	57	Worley, Walter W.	336
Woodard, Alice	317,319	Worley, ...	358
321	<	Wright, Alex	12
Woodard, Bessie M.	126	Wright, Andrew	56
Woodard, Carrie	342	Wright, Andy	295
Woodard, Clyde	15	Wright, A.J.	240
Woodard, Cora	340	Wright, Bobbie Ray	336
Woodard, David	150	Wright, Bonita	320
Woodard, Deliar	126	Wright, B.M.	336
Woodard, D.G.	321,364	Wright, Calvin C.	253
Woodard, Ernest	317	Wright, Celia J.	262
Woodard, Hanert	317	Wright, C.C.	241
Woodard, Infant	57,150	Wright, David	56,77,295

Wright, Elizabeth	212
Wright, Elva L.	156
Wright, Fansie	222
Wright, George	311
Wright, George W.	311,320
Wright, James	295
Wright, James J.	240
Wright, John	56
Wright, J.J.	262
Wright, Liley	107
Wright, Lillie	253
Wright, Moses	240
Wright, Nancy	77
Wright, Ola	311
Wright, Ray	107
Wright, Robert	212,336
Wright, Robert E.	241
Wright, Rosa	285
Wright, Sallie	323
Wright, Sarah	302
Wright, Susan	56,295
Wright, William S.	241
Wright, W.H.	285
Wyatt, Dellie Wilma	230
Wyatt, Jake	230
Wyatt, Mande	220
Wyatt, Monroe	191
Wyatt, Susan	257
Wyatt, Viola M.	240
Yates, May	270
York, Adam	146
York, C.W.	252
York, Delilah	38
York, Enoch H.	146
York, Infant	38
York, Polly E.	169
York. C.W.	233
Younce, Abraham	240
Younce, Carline	359
Younce, Elizabeth	236
Younce, George	167
Younce, Henry	204,206
Younce, Lilla	171
Younce, Nancy	251
Younce, Rhoda	323,327
Younce, Sallie	272
Younce, Senter C.	240
Younce, Soloman	167
Younce, Susan	255
Younce, S.C. (Mrs)	240
Younce, S.S.	167,314